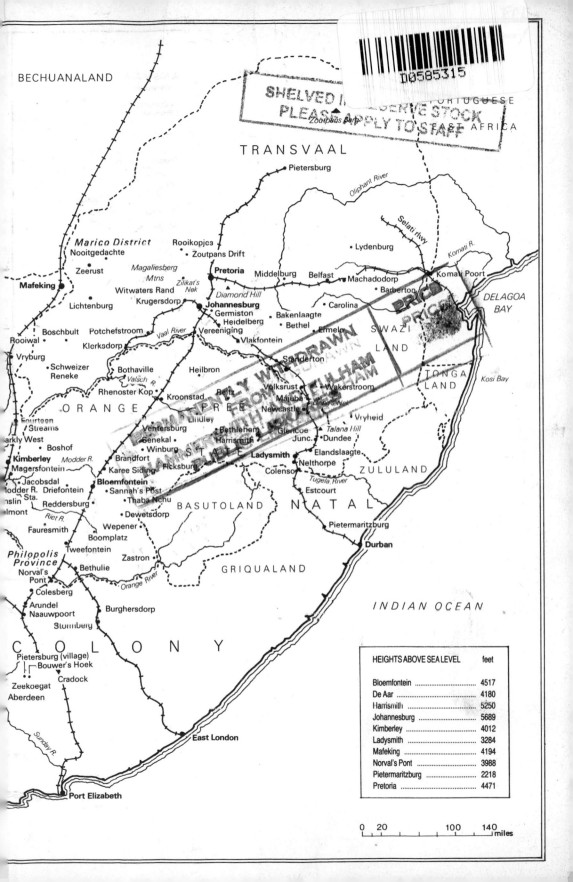

A HISTORY OF THE
BRITISH CAVALRY

1816 to 1919

by

THE MARQUESS OF ANGLESEY

F.S.A., F.R.HIST S.

VOLUME IV
1899 to 1913

A LEO COOPER BOOK

SECKER & WARBURG · LONDON

First published in Great Britain, 1986, by
Leo Cooper in association with
Martin Secker & Warburg Limited
54 Poland Street, London W 1 V 3DF
Copyright © The Marquess of Anglesey 1986
ISBN 0 436 27321 7

Typeset by Gloucester Typesetting Services
Printed in Great Britain by
Butler & Tanner Ltd., London and Frome

DEDICATED TO THE MEMORY OF
MY FRIEND AND MENTOR
THE LATE SIR ROGER FULFORD, CVO

CONTENTS

Contents

Contents

Contents

Contents

ILLUSTRATIONS

Illustrations

Illustrations

Illustrations

TEXT ILLUSTRATIONS

Text Illustrations

MAPS

ACKNOWLEDGMENTS

There are six living authors whose published works have been especially helpful to me in preparing this volume. Without the comprehensive histories of the Boer War by Byron Farwell and, particularly, Thomas Pakenham my undertaking would have been infinitely more laborious and certainly less complete. I have relied much upon their historical judgment and even more on the results of their wide-ranging original research. My gratitude to them knows no bounds. The same is true of Brian Bond and Edmund Spiers. The British military history of the period between the South African and the First World Wars has been extensively studied by both of them to the benefit of everyone who is interested in that fascinating era. Richard Holmes's masterly biography of French and David Dilks's *Curzon in India* have also proved of immeasurable assistance to me. The work of these six historians has spared me a very considerable amount of time-consuming effort. In numerous instances I have found it unnecessary to inspect important unpublished sources in person, for the job had already been done for me. I have eaten unashamedly and most thankfully of the fruits of their scholarly labours.

This volume, like its predecessors, has literally depended for its making upon the full and active cooperation of the Ministry of Defence's Chief Librarian (first, the late Mr King and then Mr Andrews, his successor) and the Library's staff. Books, papers, facts and counsel of every sort and a very great deal of time have all been unstintingly and patiently dispensed. I can never hope to pay the debt I owe for this splendid service. Of the other institutions with which I have had the pleasure of dealing and without the prompt and expert assistance of which my task would have been virtually impossible, the National Army Museum heads the list. Mr Reid, its Director, and members of his staff have always gone out of their way to provide accurate and detailed information, often of a recondite nature, whenever I have importuned them. The National Library of Scotland, the India Office Library and the London Library have, as ever, been considerate and constant in the help which they have afforded me.

Acknowledgments

Of the many individuals who have responded to my requests for unpublished letters, diaries and illustrations or advice and information, over the years of this volume's gestation, I should like to thank very specially Sir John Gilmour, Bt, DSO, Earl Haig of Bemersyde, the late Robert Poore-Saurin-Watts, F. E. G. Renshawe, Esq., Mrs Robins, Squadron-Leader J. A. H. Russell and Miss Isolde Wigram.

The painstaking researches of the late Mrs H. St G. Saunders were of inestimable benefit to my work, and the exactness of Mrs Pat Brayne's expeditious typing never ceases to astonish me.

As was the case with the first three volumes of this history, I am greatly beholden to Tom Hartman for the care and attention to detail which he, on behalf of my truly patient publishers, has devoted to the business of preparing the present one for publication.

The admirable maps owe a great deal more to the skill in interpretation of Patrick Leeson than to the rough draughts for them with which I provided him.

Finally, the forbearance of my wife and her general encouragement warrant my warmest thanks and appreciation.

'War is very interesting and exciting when you are going to it, and perhaps when you are talking about it afterwards, but not when you are there.'

TROOPER THE HON. SIDNEY PEEL,
40th (Oxfordshire) Company,
10th Battalion, Imperial Yeomanry

When you've shouted 'Rule Britannia', when
    you've sung 'God Save the Queen',
Will you kindly drop a shilling in my little
    tambourine
For a gentleman in Khaki ordered South?

RUDYARD KIPLING
in 1899 (*Daily Mail*, 31 October)

'Poor soldiers! Neglected *always*, *systematically*, and now England, frightened out of its long sleep, gets up and begins to be angry because its soldiers are not more efficient. Ah! Whose fault? *Yours*, *yours*, people of England — You have let things slide, and now you have to pay for it . . . You have been idle and have systematically refused to look after your own affairs. Right from the top — House of Lords, Commons, rich men, poor men, town and country. And now you must pay with your life's blood and you must lavish gold where expenditure in moderation, if made in time, would have been sufficient.'

LIEUTENANT-COLONEL THE EARL OF AIRLIE,
commanding the 12th Lancers,
10 February, 1900, on the Modder

'I admire the Duke of Norfolk. He came out here and insisted on doing the work of an ordinary subaltern in Tab Brassey's Company of Yeomanry.'

DOUGLAS HAIG
in 1900

PREFACE

It is a characteristic of the mounted arm that the nearer it came to extinction the more complex and in many ways the more interesting the study of it becomes. The third volume of this five-volume work covered twenty-seven years. During the thirteen years with which this penultimate volume is concerned, the scale of mounted operations undertaken by the British army, as well as the quantity of evidence about the arm generally, increased enormously. In the final volume, which is designed to encompass only six years, this growth will be seen to have intensified even more.

The present volume is dominated by the Great Boer War of 1899 to 1902. For most of its two-and-a-half years mounted operations prevailed. Without the horse in ever increasing numbers it could never have been carried on, let alone won. Yet what was known at the time as the 'Horse Question' has been largely neglected by the numerous historians who have written about the war. More important, its significance has been invariably misunderstood. For these reasons, a detailed inquiry into its many ramifications forms an important part of my account of the conflict.

It was clear from the start of my researches that the account could not be restricted to the part played by the regular cavalry. An even larger part was taken by irregular, especially colonial, units, the Imperial Yeomanry, and by the mounted infantry. Moreover the employment of these troops contributed more in the end than did that of the regulars. In consequence I have dwelt at length upon the role they played.

The other main subject with which this volume deals is the 'Great Cavalry Debate' which followed the war. This was concerned with the place of the military horseman in an age which saw the inexorable improvement and expansion of long-range breech-loading rifles, machine guns and quick-firing artillery. The controversy, which was only one ingredient in the post-war reassessment of the army's future role and character, revolved chiefly around the question of the relative merits of mounted action with the *arme blanche* and dismounted action with the rifle.

This in its most basic form resolved itself into the question: did automatic long-range fire relegate the horse to a purely transporting role or could cavalry still be employed (to use a modern term) as part of an army's 'weapons system'? It was asked too: were the days of the integrated fighting tool which was made up of man, horse and cold steel completely over? Attendant upon this question was another: which of the cavalry's services other than the delivery of the *coup de grace* so as to 'crown victory' were still essential aids to commanders in the winning of battles? Were not perhaps its strategic, reconnaissance and protection duties even more vital than hitherto? Concomitant problems such as which patterns of weapon should be carried by mounted troops and how the supposedly unique 'Cavalry Spirit' could be preserved under modern conditions also much exercised military thinkers.

All these deeply felt questionings took place against a background of increasing professionalism throughout the army. There was, of course, much discussion, too, as to what lessons ought to be adduced from the experiences of both the Boer and the Russo-Japanese Wars. All that seemed certain in this respect was the need to encourage personal initiative in the training of all ranks and for greatly improved instruction in the use of small arms. Both were in fact largely effected in spite of the continuing low class of man who could be induced to enlist in the regular army and the rather too tardy increase in the number of officers who, particularly in the cavalry, were prepared to take their profession seriously.

However much the lessons drawn from the campaigns in South Africa and the Far East may have been irrelevant to the supreme challenge which was to be posed in 1914, it is an incontrovertible fact that the army which formed the British Expeditionary Force that crossed to France in August of that year was a highly effective fighting machine. Nor can it be denied that it thus had the edge on those of its continental enemies and allies chiefly because it was the only one, with the exception of Russia, that had taken part in a modern war fought with modern weapons. The fact that the BEF was miniscule compared to the armies of France and the Central Powers in no way detracts from a remarkable achievement.

One of the most fascinating aspects of the way in which the mounted arm was made ready for the awful test ahead was the gradual transformation of the views of the old, reactionary cavalry school as represented by such men as French and Haig. It was certainly not spectacular but in view of the entrenched positions which they took up in the years immediately succeeding the Boer War, it is astonishing that it went as far as it did. Without the trials which they and numerous more junior officers underwent in that struggle I doubt whether there would have been any amelioration of their outlook at all.

I have hardly dealt at all with the reforms and conditions of the Indian Army nor have I added very considerably to what I wrote in the previous volume about the social life of officers and men at home during the period. The latter did not alter significantly and the former will be considered more fully when I examine the part played by the Indian cavalry in the First World War.

A HISTORY OF THE
BRITISH CAVALRY

1816–1919

VOLUME IV

1899–1913

'The colonizing process and particularly the Kaffir Wars, had produced a nation in arms with a commando system that enabled the country to "... put every male of fighting age into the field." '

D. H. COLE and E. C. PRIESTLEY in *An Outline of British Military History*, 1936

'Of the mounted troops we employed the regular cavalry were the least useful, probably because of their fantastic Crusader training – sticking men with lances and hacking them out of their saddles with swords.'

LIEUTENANT J. F. C. FULLER in *The Last of the Gentlemen's Wars: A Subaltern's Journal of the War in South Africa 1899–1902*, 1937, 267

'It is notorious that cavalry has performed its greatest exploits rather in virtue of its moral influence than of its capacity for inflicting grievous loss.'

COLONEL C. E. CALLWELL in *Small Wars*, 1906, 402

'[In 1961] the wildest, most improbable political dreams of Kruger's and Steyn's Boers – to be free of British interference and to make all South Africa a Boer republic – became reality for their children and grandchildren.'

BYRON FARWELL in *The Great Boer War*, 1977, 454

'The modern horseman cannot serve two masters so different as the rifle and the steel weapon. He must serve one faithfully or fail towards both. To secure "thorough efficiency" in both is an unattainable ideal.'

ERSKINE CHILDERS in *War and the Arme Blanche*, 1910, 242–3

1

'The Army is more efficient than at any time since Waterloo.'

GEORGE WYNDHAM, Parliamentary
Under-Secretary of State for War,
6 October, 1899

'We are going to fight an enemy more formidable than any whom we have encountered for many years past, and we should see to it that we meet him under conditions giving us incontestable superiority in the field.'

Memorandum to the Cabinet, THE EARL OF
LANSDOWNE, Secretary of State for War,
3 October, 1899

'We were not sufficiently prepared even for the equipment of the comparatively small force which we had always contemplated might be employed beyond the limits of this country in the initial stages of a campaign.'

THE EARL OF LANSDOWNE, Secretary of
State for War, 21 May, 1900

'The Boers have the best characteristics of the English race .... Is it against such a nation that we are to be called upon to exercise the dread arbitrament of arms?'

JOSEPH CHAMBERLAIN, defending the
Pretoria Convention of 1881

'If this thing goes on, it will be a long affair.'

GEORGE WYNDHAM, 11 September, 1899

'The Boers, 18,000 strong with fourteen guns, crossed the frontier of Natal at daybreak in three widely separated columns, while the remaining columns set themselves in movement against Kimberley, Mafeking and Cape Colony.'

Official German Great General Staff
account of the Great Boer War.[1]

(i)

Boer War, 1899–1902: causes—military unpreparedness

*   *   *

With the causes of the Second or Great Boer War of 1899–1902, this work is not greatly concerned. Here, in the certainty of flagrant oversimplification, it is enough perhaps to say that since 1877 when the British annexed the Transvaal Republic which the trekking Boers had set up in 1848, its 'Dutch' inhabitants had been restive under the restraints of British rule. (See Vol III, p. 204.) However, by the amended Pretoria Convention which ended the First Boer War of 1881 (see Vol III, p. 208), the Transvaal had regained a considerable measure of independence, 'subject to the suzerainty of Her Majesty'. The chief new factor now was the immense wealth which in the 1890s poured forth from the recently discovered gold and diamond mines. There can be no doubt that the British – not so much the Government as the Rand millionaires and their friends at home – wanted to gain control of these assets. At the same time, there were those, chief of whom was Sir Alfred (later Lord) Milner, High Commissioner in South Africa since 1897, who genuinely believed that the good of the peoples, black as well as white, of the southern part of the continent required complete annexation by the Empire. Nevertheless the morality of this approach was somewhat tarnished by the active partnership between Milner and the 'gold bugs' Wernher and Beit.

The immediate *casus belli* was the franchise grievances of the non-Dutch colonials – the Uitlanders. The number of these, because of the great mineral finds, had increased enormously in recent years, and the Transvaal Government under President Paul Kruger undoubtedly withheld from them many rights which were not denied to their Boer compatriots. Some of the more reckless of the Uitlanders had tried to precipitate a rebellion in 1895–6 when Dr (later Sir) Leander Starr Jameson led his famous, grossly incompetent 'Raid' without overt backing from the British Government. Since that farcically unsuccessful episode, which ended in Jameson's men being rounded up by the Transvaalers, the idealism and intransigence of both Milner and Kruger had pointed to a confrontation sooner or later. Although Kruger appeared, at the very latest possible moment, to climb down, the Milnerites, not without the acquiescence of Joseph Chamberlain, Secretary for the Colonies since 1895, were determined upon war. On 9 October, 1899, the Transvaal Government presented an ultimatum. On 11 October, no reply having been made to it, war was declared.

In spite of the enormous disparity between the size and wealth of the British Empire and the two Dutch Republics,* readers of the earlier volumes of this work will not be surprised to learn that the British were less well prepared for the conflict than the Boers.

As so often before in the army's history all was improvization. Among the immediate steps taken to provide the basic manpower requirements for the campaign ahead was the stopping of the normal flow of drafts of 'young soldiers attaining the age of twenty' for India. This was effected by 'asking men in India whose minimum time of service with the Colours was completed to extend their service to twelve years, offering them a bounty of £10 and two months' furlough'. 16,000 men accepted this offer. Five months after the war had started, when it was already clear that it would not be short and sharp, a personal appeal was made in the Queen's name to some 24,000 retired officers and men, 'who had already served, to re-enter upon Army service for one year at home in place of those absent in South Africa. They were formed into battalions designated "Royal Reserve Battalions". A special bounty of £12 was given to these men on re-enlistment, with a further bounty of £10 on discharge.'[2] Even this, as the war progressed, absorbing more and more men, left home defence forces far from adequate.†

* The other republic was the Orange Free State which had been founded by Boers from Cape Colony in 1836. In 1848 the British proclaimed authority over the territory, but declared it independent in the Bloemfontein Convention six years later. A defensive treaty with the Transvaal was ratified in 1889; yet in 1899 there was no certainty that the Free Staters would throw in their lot with the Transvaalers. In the event President Marthinus Theunis Steyn's forces did join with those of Kruger, but refused to go south of the Tugela River.

†During 1899 and 1900 no man of the regular cavalry was regarded as available for service overseas who had less than 12 months' service or was under twenty years of age.

After details had been left at base, each cavalry regiment of the line had a war establishment of 492 rank and file. It was found that each regiment at home with the higher peace establishment of 609 and which gave no drafts to overseas regiments, embarked for South Africa an average of about 150 reservists and that a lower establishment at home (560) which provided drafts, embarked an average of about 235 reservists. (How many of these were actually required for purely cavalry duty it is difficult to verify). (WO20/Cav/82, 30 Oct., 1903)

'Surely the men who trace their lineage back to the Brave Batavians who gave the legions of the Caesars so much trouble might have been appraised at higher worth?'

LIEUTENANT-COLONEL E. S. MAY in
A Retrospect on the South African War, 1901

'We were few in numbers and had hordes of enemies; we could not afford to waste the life of a single white man. It was too valuable.'

GENERAL DE LA REY

'[The Boer] would quit a dangerous position without damage to his moral strength, and, instead of holding out to the last, he would occupy a new one.'

From the official account of the war
prepared by the Great General Staff, Berlin.

'With the Boers, the numbers actually present in the fighting line were not, as with European troops, the measure of their effective force.'

The British Official Historian[1]

(ii)

*Boer War: Boer preparations – military organization – the fighting
burgher*

Between 1896 and the outbreak of war, Kruger had re-equipped the Transvaal armed forces at a cost of over £1,000,000. As well as building up a first-class artillery,* a second, up-to-date firearm was provided for each burgher: 37,000 Mauser .276 rifles and carbines were ordered from Krupp's in Germany. By September, 1899, there were in store at least 2,000 rounds of ammunition per firearm. Numbers of Maxim 'quick firers', known as 'pom-poms' (see p. 144), were part of Kruger's order from British manufacturers.[2]

In the Transvaal alone there were more than 25,000 fighting men; in the Orange Free State another 15,000. This combined fighting force outnumbered the British garrison about four times. The Boers' military organization was unique. By law every burgher had to possess a rifle and ammunition. Equally by law he was only liable

* The Staats Artillerie, the South African Republic Police (the 'Zarps') and the Swaziland Police were the only organizations which were constituted more or less according to European standards of military law and discipline.

to military service and not to unconditional obedience. However, most burghers were deeply religious and often felt that in being obedient they were 'finding favour in the eyes of Providence'.[3] No officer possessed the legal power to retain in the field any man who was tired of fighting.

The Commandant-General (equivalent to Commander-in-Chief) and his five Assistant Commandant-Generals were elected for a ten-year period by a ballot of all the burghers. Each electoral district nominated the commandant of its district commando, the size of which varied from less than 300 to well over 3,000 men. He usually served for five years (only three in the Free State), while the field cornets and corporals under him served as a rule for three years. In theory, and often too in practice, there was no class distinction between burghers or between leaders and led. It is said that a Cambridge graduate's boon companion for over five months was a farmer who believed the earth to be square and that the United States was 'a political division of Australia'. There was a rather smug current saying: 'Every burgher is a general and no general is greater than a burgher.'[4] No officer, whether vecht-general (fighting general), commandant (equivalent, roughly, to lieutenant-colonel), field cornet (major) or corporal (lieutenant, in charge of a squad of about twenty-five men) wore any distinguishing uniform. The corporals were elected by the burghers after the start of hostilities. They, like the field cornets, could be impeached by their men, who would then elect others to fill the vacancies. Saluting did not exist, but hand-shaking was habitual (even, to their astonishment, with British prisoners!). Drill and roll-calls were unknown to the Boer. 'You must call us burghers or farmers,' a Boer from the Wakkerstroom district told a foreign sympathizer; 'only the English have soldiers.' To be called a soldier implied in the eyes of many a Boer that he was hired to fight.[5] In theory, a *krijgsraad*, or council of war, was required before any considerable military movement could take place. 'It was possible and legal for the opinion of sixteen corporals to be adopted although fifteen generals and commandants opposed the plan with all their might.'[6]

The nearest thing in the Transvaal to a War Office was a civilian section in Pretoria manned by ten clerks. There was, though, an extremely active intelligence department. In the year before the war, the Transvaal was spending £3,250 a month on its secret service agents both in Britain and South Africa. This was about twenty times as much as British intelligence was spending in South Africa.[7]

In numerous ways the fighting burgher was superior to even the best that Britain could pit against him. First and foremost, riding a pony was his ordinary, day-to-day means of locomotion from early childhood. His horsemanship was therefore so completely natural as to be virtually a thing of instinct. Every burgher's horse was trained to stand still when its rider dismounted. 'This fact alone,' according to Amery's *Times History*, 'meant a direct increase of 33% to the effective strength of a Boer force compared with the same number of British mounted infantry in which one man in every four has to stay behind to hold the horses.' As often as not, a burgher used in the field one horse for himself, another for his camp utensils and extra clothes, and a third or even fourth for his native servant who cooked his meals and tended the horses while they grazed. On occasions British prisoners were perforce taken by their captors on trek. The experience filled them with amazement and explained the disappearance of whole commandos when every avenue of escape had apparently been closed. Having little or no transport (in the war's later stages), when they dismounted

'they tied their horses in long strings, head to tail, with an old stager in front. The animals then clambered up the almost per-pendicular rocks by a dizzy track, which the Englishman would have thought twice about attempting on foot. The Boers clam-bered after them, sometimes having to use their hands as well as their feet. And so the summit was reached and the mystery of the *cul de sac* explained.'

The Boer's solicitude for his mounts was only equalled by the care he lavished on his firearms. 'He who kept clean no other possession,' as the official historian put it, perhaps rather unkindly, 'allowed no speck of dirt on barrel or stock.'[8]

His almost intuitive sense of direction and eye for topographical features, gained chiefly from perpetual game hunting, made him an almost perfect scout. The exceptional clarity of the South African atmosphere and, in so many places, an absence of cover except from the shape of the ground itself, concentrated the burghers' powers of observation wonderfully. With its sighting accuracy and smokeless-ness the Mauser, against which the British until later in the war could set no rival weapon, enabled the burgher to strike at the extreme limit of his vision. While the British soldier, both horse and foot, was taught to believe that all training, every manoeuvre and all use of firearms were merely means to an end, and simply designed to

lead to hand-to-hand combat between men armed with cold steel –
sword, lance or bayonet – the Boer was constitutionally antipathetic
to close combat, except in the very last resort. 'He studied only safe
methods of being dangerous.' On religious and social grounds he
believed that the defensive was the better part of valour. 'He saw no
more glory in dying at an enemy's hand than in being eaten by a
lion.'[9]

It was said that, given two or three hours' start, Boer oxen could
always get away from British cavalry. As the reader progresses
through the succeeding chapters he will come to realize that this was
not quite such an exaggeration as it at first might seem. The burgher
as transport officer was time and again to be marvelled at by his
enemy. Somehow he invariably got out of his oxen, his mules, his
Cape carts, his wagons, his light, four-wheeled carriages, known
locally as spiders, and his Kaffir drivers, organization and speed quite
beyond the capacities of his British counterparts.

Above all, the Boer on commando was the very model of a pro-
vident, tough partisan guerrilla. He could subsist for a week or more
on a pocketful of *biltong* (strips of beef or venison dried in the sun),
a small bag of Boer rusks and some coffee beans tied up in a bit of
cloth.

2

'All our men had their swords sharpened
yesterday.'

MAJOR PERCIVAL MARLING, VC,
18th Hussars, writing on 12 October 1899

'Before the 18th Hussars sailed ... they bet
another regiment £500 that they would be in
Pretoria first. ... They got to Pretoria first ...
but people wished to know if they had won their
bet or not!'

Anecdotes of Soldiers[1]

(i)

Boer War: Natal: battle of Talana Hill, 20 October, 1899

In 1875 young Bernhard Drysdale Möller joined the 18th Hussars
in India. He was the first sub-lieutenant to join since the rank of cornet had been abolished. Two years later, on his regiment's return to
England, he became its junior lieutenant. By 1881 when the 18th
started a six-year stint in Ireland he had been promoted to senior
subaltern. Next year he was promoted to be junior captain. On
returning to England he achieved his majority and command of a
squadron. For a time he acted as Adjutant to the Suffolk Yeomanry
Cavalry.[2]

Möller remained a major for the next eleven years, eight of which
were spent in India. Just before his regiment left for Durban in South
Africa, where it landed in October, 1898, he at last gained the rank
of lieutenant-colonel, and with it command of his regiment. He had
served in it for just over a quarter of a century. In all that time he had
seen no active service whatever. This is not surprising since the 18th
had last been in action at Waterloo eighty-three years before.* This
uninspiring record of both Möller and his regiment is typical of the
post-Waterloo regular cavalry of Britain. Now, in the very last
months of the nineteenth-century, to the surprise of the 18th Hussars and its commanding officer, they were to be flung into a crucible
the heat of which they can never have bargained for. The same in

---

* The regiment was disbanded in 1821 and not raised again till 1858. (See
Vol II, p. 282.)

varying degrees applied to nearly the whole of the mounted arm, but Möller and the 18th were the first to feel the heat.

The 18th (which later in the war one senior general spoke of as 'the best mounted infantry in the country'), was one of the only two regular cavalry regiments in South Africa when the war broke out on 11 October, 1899.* For eleven months the regiment had been sitting in Ladysmith, North Natal, a town, according to one officer's account, 'created for the damned'.[3] With 275 mounted infantrymen and a troop of Natal Carbineers, the regiment, about 490 strong, formed the mounted part of what was now called the Glencoe Division, under the command of Major-General Sir William Penn Symons. This force, about 3,700 strong, included an infantry brigade and eighteen 15-pounder field guns. For political reasons, much pressed from home, and because Symons was keen on the idea, Lieutenant-General Sir George White, VC, who had recently arrived to supersede Symons in command in Natal, decided to hold Dundee, some miles north of Ladysmith. The position is one which it is peculiarly difficult to defend as it is overlooked by hills on all sides. A French observer likened the position to being in 'un pot de chambre'.[4]

It was here on 20 October, a dark, misty day, that the first considerable action of the war took place. By daybreak part of one of the three Boer columns which had started the invasion of Natal nine days earlier had occupied Talana Hill two miles east of Dundee. There were nearly 4,000 Boers under General Lucas Meyer, known as 'the Lion of Vreiheid', with four field guns and two Vickers Maxims. They caught Symons napping. When at about 5.30 a.m.[5] the Boer shells began to fall into the camp, the 18th's horses were ready saddled after the early morning stand-to. The three squadrons promptly retired to the north-west of the camp where they found cover in rocky ground and awaited orders. At about 6 a.m.[6] these came. The regiment, taking with it the mounted infantry and a Maxim gun, was to make a wide flanking movement to the north of Talana Hill and take up position to the west of it: 'To wait under cover, it may be for one or two hours'. Symons told Möller that he would 'send him word when to advance', but that he himself might do so if he saw 'a good opportunity'[7] to cut off the enemy's retreat from Talana Hill. This was expected to occur as soon as the British

---

* The other was the 9th Lancers which had arrived from India just before the war. It returned to India in March, 1902. (Stirling, 440.)

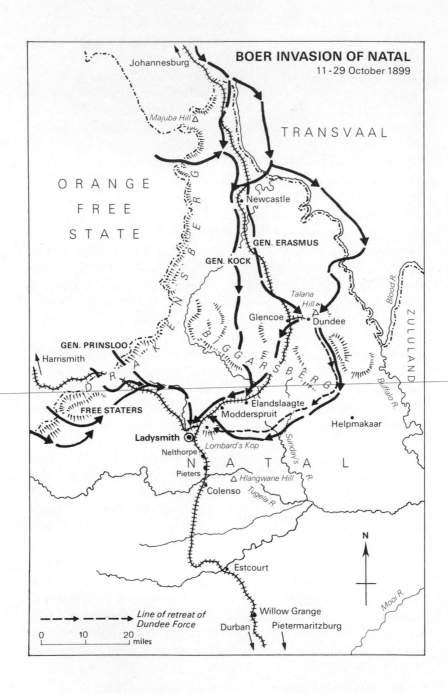

BOER INVASION OF NATAL
11 - 29 October 1899

Johannesburg

Majuba Hill

TRANSVAAL

ORANGE
FREE
STATE

Newcastle

GEN. ERASMUS

GEN. KOCK

*Talana
Hill*

Glencoe · Dundee

GEN. PRINSLOO

Harrismith

ZULULAND

Blood R.

Buffalo R.

FREE STATERS

Elandslaagte
Modderspruit

Helpmakaar

Ladysmith

Lombard's Kop

Sunday's R.

Nelthorpe

NATAL

Pieters

△ *Hlangwane Hill*

Colenso

Tugela R.

N

Estcourt

Mooi R.

Line of retreat of
Dundee Force

0   10   20
miles

Willow Grange

Durban   Pietermaritzburg

Map 1

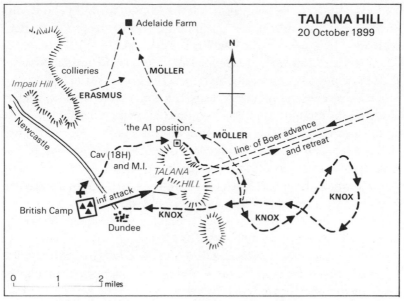

Map 2

infantry's frontal attack, following a pasting of the hill-top Boers by the 15 pounders, had succeeded.

The mounted troops now took up what Major Percival Marling, one of Möller's squadron leaders, called 'an A1 position' from where could be seen some 700 of the Boers' led horses as well as men passing ammunition up the hill by hand, about 1,200 yards off.

> 'I begged [Möller] to let us open fire on the Boer led horses with the [Maxim] machine gun, and our men dismounted, and the M.I., but he wouldn't hear of it, and told me when he wanted my advice he would ask for it . . . . Möller then took the regiment, the M.I. and our machine gun right away from the enemy in a northerly direction, leaving a perfect position under cover and completely commanding the enemy's rear.'

They soon came upon some twenty armed Boers. 'Two troops B squadron charged these men, killed two, wounded three and captured others.' This can be claimed as the very first cavalry charge of the war.

Möller had gone some way when the 18th's senior major, Eustace Chaloner Knox (known for some reason as 'Stealer Knox'), begged Möller to go back towards the enemy. 'But he wouldn't. At last, Möller sent my squadron,' wrote Marling, 'supported by Laming's,' and told Knox to go with us while he himself stayed behind with two troops B squadron, the machine gun and 1 section K.R.R.C. M.I. and 1 company Royal Dublin Fusiliers M.I.'s[8] What became of Marling's and Laming's squadrons led by Knox will appear shortly.*

Meanwhile, after bitter fighting – the Boers on Talana Hill having stood to receive the infantry's attack, a thing they were seldom to do again throughout the war – Symons, who was mortally wounded in the action, forced the enemy into retreat. As the Boers streamed down to their led horses, jumped on them and fled eastwards (the way they had come during the previous night), there was only Knox's small mounted force, no longer in its original excellent position, to confront them. Knox wisely decided to escape the annihilation which threatened him by taking avoiding action southwards. The Boers were able therefore to escape unmolested.

Möller meanwhile was proceeding northwards. 'How this handful of men', wrote Deneys Reitz, a young Boer witness,† 'came to be right in the rear of the whole Boer Army I never heard, but they were on a desperate errand, for between them and their main body lay nearly 15,000 horsemen.'‡[9]

An officer of 'B' Squadron of the 18th describes Möller's progress:

'There is no doubt we were greatly out-numbered . . . . Our Maxim gun got stuck in the muddy bottom [of a spruit] . . . . In their endeavour to extricate the gun . . . all the detachment

---

* Marling had fought in the 1881 Boer War, in Egypt, 1882, and the Sudan campaign of 1884. There, as a mounted infantryman, he had gained the Victoria Cross. He also served in the Nile Expedition of 1884–5. (See Vol III, 91, 105–6, 311.)

Major Knox had served in the Nile Expedition of 1884–5 with the Light Camel Regiment.

Major Henry Thornton Laming was soon to take command of the 24th Battalion, Imperial Yeomanry.

† Reitz was the son of Francis William Reitz, who from 1889 to 1896 was President of the Orange Free State and from 1898 to the end of the war State Secretary of the South African Republic. From 1911 to 1918 he presided over the Senate of the Union of South Africa. He died, aged ninety, in 1934, only ten years before his sixty-two year old son, Deneys, who for the last year of his life was High Commissioner for the Union in London. Deneys, an attorney by profession, held four Ministerial posts between 1933 and his death, ending up from 1939 to 1943 as Deputy Prime Minister. During the First World War he served in the British army, assuming command of the 1st Royal Scots Fusiliers in October, 1918.

‡ Almost certainly an exaggeration.

were either killed or wounded. . . . A portion of the Mounted
Infantry had been told off as escort to the Maxim, but, for some
unaccountable reason, had been removed, by order of the
commanding officer, before the gun got into difficulties.'

After a time the enemy was shaken off.

'The Colonel trusted in getting safely back round by the
Navigation Collieries . . . . Our luck, however, was dead out. . . .
My advanced scout reported the presence of Boers . . . and I
soon myself observed parties of them descending the slopes of
Impati. It was now clear to push on further in the direction we
were taking was but to court disaster. We were heading for a
new commando, which had taken no part in the battle. . . .
Thereupon the Colonel decided on taking up as strong a position as could be found handy and holding out till nightfall in
the hope of slipping away in the dark.'[10]

The new Boer forces into whose clutches Möller had gratuitously
put himself were commanded by General S. P. Erasmus* and had
recently arrived in the area of Impati Hill. From there 'they shep-
herded the soldiers', to use young Reitz's words, 'still further from
their own people' into a small farmstead known as Adelaide's Farm,
some eight miles due north of Dundee.

'We were just in time,' wrote Reitz, 'to see the soldiers jumping
from their horses, and running for cover . . . . Other burghers
were flocking in, and soon the troops were completely surrounded . . . . We were soon blazing away our first shots of the
war.
    The troops replied vigorously, but they were able to devote
comparatively little attention to us, for by now the country-
side was buzzing like an angry hive. . . . After a few minutes a
Creusot gun of the Transvaal Staats Artillery unlimbered and
opened fire [at about 1.45 p.m.].[11] The very first shell stampeded
all the troop horses. The poor maddened brutes came tearing
past us, and we leaped on our horses to head them off.'[12]

At about 3.45 p.m. a couple of Krupp guns opened fire on the farmstead at a range of only about 2,000 yards. 'At length,' wrote an

---

* Erasmus was captured over a year later, on 31 December, 1901, by 'A'
Squadron of the 18th Hussars, 'which,' as Marling put it, 'was rather interesting'.
(Marling, 293.)

officer of mounted infantry, 'our ammunition began to run short.'[13] At about 4.30 p.m. Möller very sensibly decided that no good purpose would be served by continuing the fight. 'A sheet which someone had fetched from the house,' wrote an officer of 'B' Squadron, 'was attached to a pole and raised over the wall. Above, on the hill where many of the mounted infantry were, the bugler was sounding the "cease fire". . . . We had given in!'[14]

By the time Deneys Reitz reached the farm buildings 'the soldiers had thrown down their arms and were falling in under their officers. Their leader, Colonel Möller, stood on the stoep looking pretty crestfallen.'[15] Nine officers and nearly 240 men were in the bag.[16]* Eight non-commissioned officers and men were killed; three officers and fifteen non-commissioned officers and men were wounded.[17] 'We were very well treated,' wrote an officer of mounted infantry, 'and were allowed to visit the wounded.'[18]

Major Knox, meanwhile, using considerable skill, was zig-zagging up and down all afternoon, avoiding for the most part further collision with the masses of retreating Boers. Eventually he retraced his steps. It was 7 p.m. before he regained the camp at Dundee. He lost one man killed and three wounded.[19]

It will probably never be known what induced Möller to sheer off northwards. One theory is that, in the mist, he lost his way and thought that he was retracing his steps. When the mistake was discovered he decided that his best hope would be to try to get round the north side of Impati Hill and eventually return to camp on the Newcastle road.[20] When, as has been shown, he was thwarted in that by Erasmus's fresh commandos, he hoped to be able to hold out in Adelaide's Farm till dusk when he could slip back to Dundee.

A court of inquiry held seven months later in Pretoria exonerated all concerned, but Lord Roberts, by then Commander-in-Chief in South Africa, added a report which stated that

'although no neglect or misconduct is imputed,' he was 'inclined to think that Lieut-Colonel Möller has, from the evidence produced, shown himself but little capable of exercising command, and unless his previous records are exceptionally good [which they were not], I cannot recommend that he be permitted to resume command of his regiment.'

* These figures are for the whole day's actions. It seems likely that those actually captured with Möller numbered less, perhaps not more than 150 to 200, of which about eighty-five were from the 18th. (Burnett, 24.)

Poor Möller was deprived of his command and succeeded by Knox. In August, 1900, Möller was placed on half-pay.[21]

Total casualties at Talana Hill numbered about 500, while the Boers lost only about 140 men.[22] This comparatively small-scale action has been gone into in some detail because it was the first of the war, involved the surrendering of regular cavalry and because it well illustrates what is apt to happen when a plodding regimental officer like Möller finds himself, without any previous fighting experience, faced with the awful realities of war. It seems that the poor man was too proud to take the advice of his two majors, both of whom had had earlier war experience. Had he been less determined

The Unkindest Cut of All.

The first of a number of incidents which cast a cloud over British success was the capture by the Boers of a whole squadron of the 18th Hussars at Glencoe, who were surprised when too eagerly following up the enemy. They and many subsequent prisoners were conveyed to the capital of the Transvaal.

to go his own ignorant way, Talana Hill might have been a real morale-boosting victory, though it could never have been more than a Pyrrhic one in purely military terms.

There is a story that one of the captured 18th Hussar officers asked his captors the name of the regiment which had captured him. Pulling his leg, a Boer replied that there were no regiments, only three brigades: the Afrikanders, the Boers and the Takhaars.* Between these three words there is in fact little to choose in describing the burgher. The man went on to explain: 'The Afrikander brigade is fighting now. They fight like demons. When they are killed, then the Boers take the field. The Boers fight about twice as well and hard as the Afrikanders. As soon as all the Boers are killed, then come the takhaars, and they would rather fight than eat.' The Hussar officer's comment was: 'Well if that is correct, then our job is bigger than I thought it was.'[23] So, indeed, it was to turn out to be.

* Town-bred Boers called their country cousins Takhaars, meaning men with grizzly beards and unkempt hair.

3

'*Elandslaagte*. Cavalry scouting.
> Artillery duel.
> Infantry advance.
> Infantry assault.
> Cavalry charge and pursuit.
> Lost myself and spent night on the veldt.
> Probably the prettiest day's fighting I shall ever see.'
>> Extract from the diary of LIEUTENANT JOHN NORWOOD, 5th Dragoon Guards, October, 1899

'The time had come for us to do our work, and we did it. We don't carry our lances for show.'
> Extract from a letter of
> 4861 PRIVATE W. TUXFORD, 5th Lancers

'Men on horses carrying sticks with spikes on top, came galloping at us as we were running to our horses. They pushed us up on the spikes like bundles of hay.'
> A Boer prisoner, after Elandslaagte

'[The 5th Lancers and 5th Dragoon Guards] were ready and waiting for them and as they retired across the open plain they dashed out from their place of hiding and charged well home doing great execution with their lances. But it was too dark to carry out a regular pursuit and many Dutchmen got away who would not otherwise have done so.'
> LIEUTENANT-COLONEL SIR HENRY RAWLINSON,
> Deputy Assistant Adjutant General,
> 21 November, 1899[1]

Boer War: Natal: raising of Imperial Light Horse — arrival of French and Haig — battle of Elandslaagte

In Pietermaritzburg, the capital of the British Colony of Natal, more than a month before the war began, horses were being bought and men recruited for an irregular mounted regiment, financed by big business. The chief mover in this enterprise was Aubrey Woolls-Sampson, the most fiery, eccentric of uitlanders, ex-gold-miner, wealthy financier and estate agent (see p. 252). He and Major Walter 'Karri' Davies* were the only two who after the failure of the Jameson Raid refused to petition for their release (part of the conditions imposed). Consequently they spent thirteen months in prison. During the last eighteen months of the war Woolls-Sampson became the most skilful of all the intelligence officers on the British side. Lieutenant-Colonel Sir Henry Rawlinson thought him 'a ripper'. On 21 September, 1899, the Natal but not the Cape authorities officially recognized the existence of the unit which he had raised in secret as the Imperial Light Horse. It was stipulated that a British regular officer should always command the regiment and it so happened that Lieutenant-Colonel John James Scott ('Jabber') Chisholme was available.[2] He had recently completed his five years in command of the 5th Lancers, one of the two regular regiments stationed in South Africa at the time. As a major, Chisholme had served with the 9th Lancers in the Second Afghan War during which he was severely wounded. In 1889 he had transferred to the 5th Lancers. Now, aged forty-eight, he was given the task of forming a new regiment of colonials from absolute scratch. There were to be six squadrons of eighty-six men, each formed into three troops, with four officers per squadron. 5,000 men applied. At first only 500 were accepted. Nearly half were South African born, mostly descendants of the 1820 settlers. Others were Australasians, Canadians and even Americans. Some were famous shots; others were well-known big game hunters. There were farmers, prospectors, engineers, lawyers, medical men, mine managers and officials and a sprinkling of 'old cavalry soldiers'. All were uitlanders who felt a grievance against the Transvaal government and some of them had taken part in the Jameson Raid. To virtually all of them riding and shooting were second nature. Under training at the butts, Chisholme exclaimed to Regimental Sergeant-Major Dryden (who had come with him from the 5th Lancers): 'Surely this is remarkable shooting!' To which Dryden replied: 'Yes, sir, we never saw shooting like that in the 5th!' Yet two years earlier the 5th had held all the prizes for regimental shooting in India! As time went on, the standard of recruits deteriorated, the regiment acquiring the sobriquet of the 'Imperial Light Looters'.[3]

Among the regiment's typical actions during the latter part of the war was one in which part of a squadron helped to capture three of

---

* A wealthy importer of the Western Australian jarrah and kerri timbers used in the gold mines and for railway sleepers. (Wallace, 40.)

General Christiaan De Wet's guns and 102 burghers. It took place at Slyp Steen in Cape Colony on 23 February, 1901, the forty-seventh anniversary of the founding of the Orange Free State. A fortnight before that, near Bothwell in the Transvaal, three officers and eleven men 'made a dash at the head' of a convoy, killing two burghers and capturing twenty-one, together with much plunder. These minor successes were eclipsed by the ambush at Cyferfontein on 5 January (see p. 258) and by the disaster at Lake Chrissie on 6 February, 1901 (see p. 508).[4]

During most of 1901 and up to the war's end, the 1st Regiment of the I.L.H. was commanded by Major Charles James Briggs, who had joined the King's Dragoon Guards in 1886 and who later, as a lieutenant-general, was to command the British forces at Salonika in the First World War. At Geduld farm, near Hartebeestfontein in the Western Transvaal, on 22 March, 1901, 175 of Briggs's men, with one Maxim, were on reconnaissance when some 400 of General Jacobus De la Rey's burghers charged down upon them. This was the second occasion in the war on which the Boers employed their new tactic of charging in close formation. They looked, according to an eye-witness, as they galloped over open ground, like 'a cavalry brigade in mass'. The I.L.H. were all dismounted in a thin, extended line, but most of them speedily regained their horses. 'We were all ordered to retire,' wrote Captain Patrick Hill Normand, 'squadron by squadron, covering one another.' Thus, slowly but skilfully, pressed hard for over four miles, Briggs, whose horse was shot under him, 'armed with a cigarette and a knobkerrie,' fought his way back to the security of his mountain camp. From there the enemy was forced to retreat by heavy shelling.

Two officers and five men were killed and three officers and thirteen men wounded. The Boers are thought to have lost some two dozen killed and wounded. General Jan Smuts, whose commando was part of De la Rey's force, said later that 'the rear guard action fought by the I.L.H. . . . was the most brilliant one he had seen fought by either side during the whole campaign.' In the course of the next two days, the column of which Briggs's men were a part, commanded by Major-General James Melville Babington, who had joined the 16th Lancers in 1873 and was to command with distinction a Corps in the First World War, gained a considerable victory over De la Rey at Wildefontein.* One of the last actions of any

* Lieutenant-Colonel Sir Henry Rawlinson wrote in his diary on 25 March,

consequence in which the I.L.H. was engaged took place at Tiger Kloof Spruit in Orange River Colony on 18 December, 1901, where, untypically, an ambush planned by De Wet met with complete failure.[5] (See p. 259.)

To return to October, 1899, on the 19th of that month the Imperial Light Horse arrived in Ladysmith. On that same day – the day before the action at Talana Hill – there arrived by ship at Durban two British officers, both of whom before two decades had passed were to become field-marshals and earls. Acting Major-General John Denton Pinkstone French, aged forty-seven, and Major Douglas Haig, ten years younger, had left Southampton on 23 September. French, who was the only officer proposed by Buller to have been accepted by the War Office, was being rushed out to command the cavalry in Natal under Sir George White. Haig was to act as his Brigade-Major as he had been doing for some time at Aldershot with the 1st Cavalry Brigade.* Both men had seen action in recent years. French had made his name in the 1880s with the 19th Hussars in Egypt and the Sudan (see Vol III, p. 332). Haig had distinguished himself as 'Chief Staff Officer of Cavalry' at the Atbara and at Omdurman in 1898 (see Vol III, pp. 368, 374). Both men now arrived at Ladysmith off the night train at 5.40 a.m. on 20 October. Soon after 11 a.m. Haig joined a small reconnoitring force which included 'C' Squadron of the 5th Lancers. This force confirmed what had already been suspected, namely that less than twenty-four hours earlier part of one of the three Boer invasion columns had cut the railway line at Elandslaagte, thirteen miles from Ladysmith. It turned out to consist of a weak commando of about 700 men with two guns[6] under the ancient General J. H. M. Kock who as a young man had fought at Boomplaatz in 1848 (see Vol III, p. 170).

At 9 p.m. that evening White ordered French 'to move out by road at 4 a.m. with five squadrons of Imperial Light Horse [338 men[7]] and the Natal Field Battery, followed at 6 a.m.' by half a

---

1901, that he had heard from Babington 'that he had got well into Delarey, had captured 2 15-pdrs, a pom-pom and 6 Maxims and 170 prisoners. . . . This,' he added, 'is a good business, the more so as it saves Babington from being stellen-bosched.' (Rawlinson, 25 Mar., 1901).

In February, 1900, Roberts had ordered French to replace Babington by Colonel Porter (see p. 108) as commander of the 1st Cavalry Brigade. (Cav. Div. Orders, 9 Feb., 1900, NAM 6807/159.)

* Later on, as soon as French took command of a mixed force, Haig became his 'Chief Staff Officer'.

battalion of infantry with railway and telegraph construction companies by rail. French's orders were 'to clear the neighbourhood of Elandslaagte of the enemy, and to cover' the repair of the railway and telegraph lines, thus restoring communication with the troops left at Dundee.

After shelling the enemy out of the station buildings, French withdrew in pouring rain to the Modder Spruit, out of range of the Boer 12½-pounders which replied from a nearby hill. The Natal battery's 2.5″ 7-pounders were, of course, greatly outranged.*[8] The enemy then took up a strong position with a line of entrenchments about a mile south-east of the station and French sent a telephone message (at about 8.30 a.m.) to Ladysmith 'explaining situation', as Haig put it, 'and requesting reinforcements as it was hoped enemy would attack.'[9]

The reinforcements which were quickly dispatched by train and by road brought the total of French's force up to nearly 3,500 men in all. It consisted of an infantry brigade commanded by Colonel Ian Standish Monteith Hamilton,† two batteries of 15-pounders and 'D' Squadron of the 5th Dragoon Guards. These last, 175 strong, had arrived at Ladysmith nine days earlier.‡ Their full establishment of horses, all walers averaging about 15.3 hands, 'with a lot of bone and plenty of quality', had endured a severe storm on passage from Bombay, as well as the journey in three trains from Durban. This last was by far the more trying part. One who was on it describes the ordeal:

* French would have retired anyway, as his mounted men and their horses, who had been out since early morning, 'were much fatigued' and needed rest, food and above all, water, which was only available at Modder Spruit. (Haig, 151.)

† Hamilton, who ended the war with the rank of Lieutenant-General, had served in numerous campaigns, including the Second Afghan War (see Vol III, 227) and the 1881 Boer War. In the First World War he commanded at Gallipoli. He died in 1947 at the age of ninety-four.

‡ To bring the regiment up to establishment before it sailed from India, it had been necessary to attach two officers from the 4th Dragoon Guards and another from the 11th Hussars. Also attached was a lieutenant of the Calcutta Light Horse. Those other ranks who failed to pass as fit for active service were replaced by fit men from the 4th and the 11th. Eighty-six time-expired other ranks voluntarily extended their service so as to go to South Africa. The regiment's total strength on sailing was: 18 officers, 476 other ranks, 466 squadron horses and 36 mules. Each officer was allowed three chargers. One of these he rode himself, one was ridden by his first servant, who led the third on which was carried his baggage. His second servant rode in the ranks and was mounted

'The line is a narrow-gauge one, with very steep gradients, and, in order to keep the loads down to a minimum, the horses had to be packed in open trucks, so close together that some of their heads had to be facing away from the platform. This was bad enough, as it made watering and feeding so much more difficult; but what made things very much worse was that the weather was almost continuously wet, and the floors, being of iron, became so slippery that the horses had very great difficulty in keeping their legs. Directly one got down, the others closed in on top of it, and the whole truck had to be unpacked in order to get it up again. Several horses were injured before they could be got out, and had to be left behind at various places en route.'[10] (See also p. 325.)

The commanding officer of the 5th Dragoon Guards at this time was Lieutenant-Colonel Robert Baden-Powell,* but he had been for some time on special service in South Africa and was, as we shall see, otherwise engaged. His second-in-command, Major St John Gore, had arrived from home leave on 13 October. He now took command of the three squadrons of the two 5ths. Readers of the third volume of this work will remember Captain Gore, as he then was, successfully defending at a court-martial Private Craven of the 5th Dragoon Guards who had been framed by his fellows (see Vol III, pp. 80–3). In the view of Lieutenant-Colonel Sir Henry Rawlinson (see p. 209), Gore was 'a long-nosed jabbering ass', with none of 'the qualities for a cavalry leader'. Now he was to have, as French told him afterwards, 'the honour of commanding the first real cavalry

Major St John Gore

in the troop to which his officer was attached. There were four spare horses in each squadron and the machine-gun horses formed a separate unit, though included in the total of squadron horses.

Two other squadrons were delayed in India because there had been cases of anthrax amongst their horses. They had arrived in Ladysmith by 26 October. The regiment returned to India, at the urgent request of the Indian Government, in March, 1902. (Pomeroy, I, 234–5, 261.)

The regiment had last seen action in the Crimea (see Vol II, pp. 67–8, 70–1, 76, 94).

*(See Vol III, pp. 106, 140, 160, 326, 396). Baden-Powell, who died aged eighty-four in 1941, joined the 13th Hussars in 1876 and commanded the 5th Dragoon Guards, 1897–99. From 1887 onwards he had, on and off, held staff appoint-

charge since the Crimea'. As the trainloads of infantry approached Elandslaagte in succession the two 'D' Squadrons of the two 5ths joined up with four of the squadrons of the Imperial Light Horse to clear, as Haig reported,

'the ridges on the S. side of the railway for several miles, driving considerable numbers of Boers in front of them.* The infantry were thus enabled to remain in the trains until they had reached a point closer to the enemy's position. They were then detrained in security, marched direct on to the ridge and formed at once for the attack on the enemy's position.'[11]

The infantry's attack which French, since time was pressing, launched at 1.20 p.m.,[12] before all his reinforcements had detrained, was supported by accurate artillery fire. The hill on which the Boers had entrenched themselves was only 300 feet high – half the height

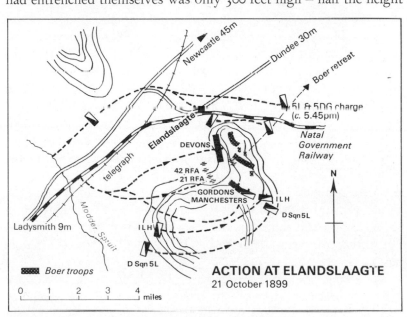

Map 3

ments as well as command of an irregular regiment of horse in South Africa. In 1903 he became Inspector-General of Cavalry. He founded the Boy Scout and Girl Guide movement in 1908. He was an amateur sculptor and draughtsman. He published twenty-eight books, including *Pig-sticking or Hog-hunting*, 1889; *Reconnaisance and Scouting*, 1890; *Vedette*, 1890; *Cavalry Instruction*, 1895.

* It was during this time that the cavalry had its 'first taste of Mauser; we now for the first time heard the screech and thud of the shell!' (Sgt G. Taylor's (5 D.G.) account, Gore, 23.)

of Talana Hill. The infantry's mode of advance differed from any hitherto practiced in action in that Hamilton ordered his men to keep exceptionally open order. The Devons on the left for instance advanced with three yards between each man. Against the Boers' magazine rifles this was wise indeed – and revolutionary. Up till now shoulder-to-shoulder had been the order of the day. On the right of the Devons were the Gordons and the Manchesters, while on their right, facing north, came the Imperial Light Horse. To their commanding officer French said: 'Well, Chisholme, what do you want to do?' 'I want,' came the answer, 'to take that hill!' 'Very well,' he was told, 'take it!'[13] Together with the regular infantry, this is just what the regiment did. According to Hamilton, the squadrons then 'rode straight in on the right ... as if they were going to gallop at the left centre of the rear of the Boer position. But soon the rise of the hill became too steep and the enemy fire too hot, so they there and then dismounted and began to climb on foot.' It was a bloody and bitter fight, but the enemy was much out-numbered, and in due course the Boers were forced to retreat north-eastwards, but not before they had fought with 'an enthusiasm of fury and utter contempt of death' such as Hamilton 'never saw them equal again'.[14] In the course of the battle the Imperial Light Horse had lost its colonel and thirteen others killed as well as thirty-four wounded.[15]* The infantry lost over 200 killed and wounded.

The enemy had been driven off a strong position of their own choosing by a well coordinated attack. Could their retreat now be converted into a rout? Where was the cavalry? Would it be in the right place at the right time, or would it be, as at Talana Hill and in so many past and future battles, out of touch or too exhausted to effect what many considered to be the mounted arm's most impor-tant battle task?

By the time the first Boers began to trickle down the hillside the light was already beginning to fade, but the two 'C' Squadrons† of the 5th Dragoon Guards (Captain Percy Henry Darbyshire) and the 5th Lancers (Captain Montague Percy Rowland) were standing to their horses in a good concealed position. This was about 1,700 yards from the enemy's right rear, within a fold of the veld near a colliery pithead not far from the station. Major Gore was alert and ready. He had just received from Haig the order to 'pursue *with*

* Two captains of the I.L.H. gained Victoria Crosses.

† 'D' Squadron, 5th Lancers, on the right flank, was too distant to take any part in the pursuit.

vigour when you see Boers beginning to fall back. . . . Press the enemy *with the lance* if you can.'[16]

'At last', he wrote, '[at about 5.20 p.m.] I saw Boers apparently coming down . . . by twos and threes: great uncertainty in the bad light as to what they were doing. Then "They're off!" "No, they're not!" "Yes, they ARE!" Sent back word to my two squadrons to "advance in line at extended files" [i.e. four yards' intervals between each horse].[17] After half a mile, our heads rose over a fold in the ground, and showed us a long stream of Boers going leisurely away from the position at right-angles to my line of advance, and about 300 yards off.

'I gave the word "gallop". When they saw us, the Boers broke in every direction, and galloped away. The ground was very stony in most parts, but there were some good grassy bits along which I was able to pick my way (being one single man), while most of the men had to go over the bad places as they happened to come to them in their line.'

Sergeant Savage was a Troop Sergeant in the 5th Dragoon Guards which charged on the right. He remembered listening to the battle

'dismounted in line at open files. . . . Such a rattle of musketry, such a booming of guns, and after a while such a downpour of rain. . . . It saturated us. The rain ceased – "Stand to your horses!" – "Mount!" and we took up a position commanding the Boers' line of retreat, and waited, mounted still in extended line. After a while the firing slackened and a few straggling horsemen were seen making off northwards. Each man said, "Why don't we go for 'em", but the time was not for a few moments. Then more came, and now was our chance; we got the order to advance. . . . I saw [Lieutenant Philip Guy] Reynolds draw his sword and endeavoured to follow him, keeping the troop together, taking pace from the centre.

'The pace increased, on and on, until we could see and pick out our man. After this I no longer tried to follow my troop leader, but rode as hard as I could for that one man. As I approached him, he dropped off his pony (a grey) and fired at someone to the right. I overtook him, and rode on for another who was some little distance in front. This fellow, by the time I got up to him, was laid on his back, and looked so helpless and so much like a civilian, that I took his arms and ammunition, and as by this time the troops were rallying, I marched him up a prisoner and handed him over to Corporal Howard, who was taking over the prisoners. This man, whilst I had my lance to his breast, asked for no mercy, but handed over his arms as a soldier who could do no more. I took the precaution to make him hand me the butt first. There was nothing of the coward about him.'[18]

Lieutenant Guy Hartley Watson, a troop commander in the 5th Dragoon Guards, remembered while waiting for his big moment, seeing

'the white smoke of the shrapnel showing plainly against the background of black thunder-clouds. It was very cold; I had on a "British warm coat", my cloak, and a mackintosh over-all, and looked for all the world like a pilot in a north-easter. . . . [Once his troop had started off] a nasty donga threw us out of line for a moment. . . . We scrambled through somehow. . . .

'A faint shout above the din! We took it to be "Charge!" and howled it with all the strength of our lungs. Till then the men had been quiet except for deep curses at the donga. A few Boers galloping now for all they were worth crossed my front about thirty yards away. I fired and gave a "Tally-ho!" and the men gave tongue like a pack of hounds. The Boers, as we passed, flung themselves off their ponies and fired over the saddles at us.

'I got one with my pistol who did this; four shots altogether I fired as we passed through them. I could not fire more, as my men pressed round me and got in the way.'[19]

Lieutenant Reynolds of the 5th Dragoon Guards

'overtook one man and gave him a point with my sword. It probably hit his bandolier, as he only fell off. A man behind me said, "All right, sir!"

'Men were dismounted by twos and threes to make single Boers prisoner, and our ranks were soon thinned out. At last we came to a spruit, and the whole line halted. A few Boers here were dismounted, and fired a few shots without doing any damage. I took a few men, and we surrounded them and made prisoners of them.[20]

Private Thomas Doolan of the 5th Lancers wrote to his mother at St Helen's a week after the fight: 'As soon as they saw the lances they threw up their rifles and ammo in the air and cried "Friends", but it was no go. . . .' Another trooper of the regiment, a native of Brighton, wrote home: 'They threw up their arms and fell on their knees for mercy; but we were told not to give them any, and I can assure you they got none. We went along sticking our lances through them – it was a terrible thing: but you have to do it in a case like this.'[21]

Ben Viljoen, later to become a Boer general, was one of the pursued:

'The British lancers were shouting "Stop, stop, you —— Boers!" . . . Revolvers were being promiscuously fired at us. . . . We could plainly hear them shouting "Stop, or I'll shoot you", or "Halt, you damned Boer, or I'll run my lance through your blessed body". . . . Looking round furtively once more I could distinguish my pursuers; I could see their long assegais; I could hear the snorting of their unwieldy horses, the clattering of their swords. These unpleasant combinations were enough to strike terror into the heart of any ordinary man.'[22]

'They were dressed,' remarked one trooper, 'in black frock coats and looked like a lot of rather seedy businessmen. It seemed like murder to kill them.'[23] There is evidence that Lance-Corporal Kelly of the 5th Lancers speared two of the fleeing Boers riding on one pony with one thrust of his lance.[24] Another Boer saved his life by holding his rifle above his head, thus deflecting a cut made at him with a sword (probably by an officer). This man later showed his rifle 'cut through the wood and partly into the barrel' to a corporal of the 18th Hussars who had been captured near Dundee.[25]

Once the cavalry had left behind them the criss-crossing dongas, the plain over which they charged was relatively flat and free of major obstacles. Their gallop had taken them one and a half miles or more from their starting point. Gore found himself about 400 yards ahead of his line. So he

'turned back to where they were being rallied. Went "files about" and galloped back over the same ground: it was now very dark, and one could see the flashes of rifles and revolvers going off. . . . Where a man threw down his arms and gave in, standing on the ground, his life was spared. . . . I took my sword going back instead of revolver, which I had used before, and found it most difficult to use.'[26]

Lieutenant Reynolds found it 'too dark to see much. When we

passed close to the Boer Hospital,' he reported, 'someone shouted "Don't fire; this is a hospital." We pulled up, and several Boers rushed out. One thrust his Mauser almost into my face – the smell of the powder almost choked me – and how he missed I can't think. I shot him through the back.'[27] Lieutenant Watson at about this moment, just as the men were finding their way back to the railway station, had a nasty experience:

'A man with a lance . . . saw me, thought I was *his* man, or would do as well. I saw his lance come down, and it suddenly dawned on me that he was riding at *me*! It all happened so quickly I had no time to think. I just managed to blurt out that "I was all right". I couldn't think of anything else to say. He called out cheerfully, "Oh, beg pardon, sir!" And well he might.'[28]

Those who had not got too far ahead in the chase now received 'a short address' from Major Gore, who called upon the 'two fifths' for three cheers.

'I heard the cheer of millions all along the route of the Jubilee procession,' wrote Sergeant Savage, 'but I never heard such a cheer as came from the 200 or so, and I am sure the Boers never heard anything like it before.

'We now with some difficulty made our way to the station; guides had to be sent ahead with lanterns to show the road; the darkness could be felt, and those who a few moments before were trying to let the Boers at Dundee know we'd won, dare not speak above a whisper, and smoking was out of the question. [Behind him Savage] distinctly heard voices. [A little later] with some hestitation, six of the enemy slowly came forward, giving themselves up. . . . Two of them were held up by the others, who said they were wounded. One of them told me his two brothers had both been killed that day; another was an Irishman. I took their arms and ammunition (one only had a "Mauser"; the others had thrown them away, to get away). I had belts of ammunition slung on my sword-hilt, and over the butt of my carbine; and round my neck were three Mausers, a pair of field-glasses, and a satchel of ammunition, whilst the pockets of my warm coat were full as they could hold of loose ammunition.'[29]

Lieutenant John Norwood of the 5th Dragoon Guards (see

p. 63) was one of those who were caught by the speed of the South African nightfall. On turning round after chasing a Boer into the darkness, he saw his squadron on the sky-line a mile or more away.

'By the time that I got back it was quite dark, and they had gone, so I wandered round to see if I could find or help any of the wounded. There were a lot of Boers lying about, but no English. To one Boer I offered brandy, but he refused it, murmuring something about "poison". Then I met Lieutenant Panchaud, Calcutta Light Horse, with Sergeant M'Kormick, six men, and about a dozen prisoners, and we tried to make our way back. However, it was such a pitch-dark night that it was impossible to move, so we took off the horses' bits to stop them champing, tied up the prisoners in a lump, and "stood to" in a donga all night. . . . It was a beastly night, cold, damp, and no rations, and I was rather surprised to see the men give up coats and blankets to the prisoners – some of whom were wounded.'[30]

The prisoners, numbering about 180,[31] were of all kinds. 'Boers, Germans, Hollanders, American-Irish, British Naturalised Boers, etc. etc. All the leaders were either shot down or taken prisoners; none escaped.' Writing home five days after the battle, Haig reported that the Boers were 'wild at the way the fugitives were killed with the lance! They say it is butchery not war.'[32] It was said that one young Boer, still alive, was found to have sixteen lance wounds. Other Boers were believed to have vowed that they would kill any lancer who in future fell into their hands.[33]*

About sixty Boers were killed at Elandslaagte and just over 100 wounded.[34] The British casualties were fifty killed and 213 wounded. The 5th Dragoon Guards suffered no casualties, while the 5th Lancers had one trooper killed and two wounded.[35] There is no question that it was a complete victory for French's force. It was to be many weeks before another occurred, and it proved, as will soon be shown, of no lasting value.

The luxury of describing it in considerable detail from the point

---

* 'Whilst going around camps this morning,' wrote Lieutenant-Colonel Rawlinson in May, 1900, 'we found the 17th Lancers with their lances all head downwards stuck in the ground – Shews how little they know of the necessity of having lances really sharp for execution.' (Rawlinson, 19 May, 1900.)

Some of the Scottish Horse used shortened lances as 'pig spears' in the guerrilla period of the war (see p. 229).

of view of the mounted arm has been indulged in because it is a very rare example of the successful co-ordination of the three arms, and an even rarer example of cavalry being skilfully employed both in screening and in pursuit. The charge of the 'two fifths' became a famous affair overnight, being blown up into a great triumph for the mounted arm. It was, indeed, the solitary genuine example of a profitable charge with the *arme blanche* in the whole war. Yet it is impossible to say that it had much effect upon the fortunes of the day. It was, after all, the dismounted men of the Imperial Light Horse and the infantry, aided by the artillery, who stormed the ridge and compelled the enemy to retreat. The charge's renown was to help in bolstering old cavalrymen's morale for years to come. Further, the foundations of the massive future reputations of the two cavalrymen, French and Haig, were laid at Elandslaagte. So, incidentally, was that of the infantryman Ian Hamilton.

4

'Natal was at the mercy of any surplus of Boers
who remained over from the investing circle.'
COLONEL CHARLES À COURT REPINGTON[1]

*Boer War: retreat to Ladysmith – failure of 'forward policy' –
battle of Ladysmith – French and Haig leave Ladysmith – Willow
Grange – Buller arrives in Cape Town – siege of Ladysmith*

The dubious victory of Talana Hill and the greater one of Elandslaagte were almost immediately shown to have failed to realize
White's hopes of keeping the Transvaal and Free State forces apart.
His plan had been to strike decisively at each in turn. It had mis-
carried. The Transvaalers and the Free Staters, it was now clear,
had united in numbers considerably superior to White's. The 'forward' policy was in ruins. White therefore ordered all troops from
Dundee and from Elandslaagte to Ladysmith, with the abandonment of all stores and even of the wounded. Commandant-General
Piet Joubert's cautious generalship was all that saved them from a
bad mauling in the course of the retreat.

If Dundee was a position peculiarly difficult to defend, Ladysmith
(the largest town in Northern Natal) was, as has been shown, even
more so, 'nestling', as it does, 'in one of the dips of the vast rolling
hills', looked down upon from all sides.[2] General Sir Redvers Buller,
who was being sent from home to take over command in South
Africa, with his past experience of the Boers and their country (see
Vol III, pp. 187, 188–90, 191–2, 198, 200, 324), had long ago
realized this. In opposition to the politicians he had made it clear
that White ought on no account to have found himself to the north
of the Tugela (pronounced Tew-gée-le) river. 'If the Boers are
bold,' he had written as early as 9 September, 'they have now the
chance of inflicting a serious reverse upon us in Natal.'[3]

Only a very morally strong, self-confident general could have
faced taking what some have since seen as the only logical step
which the situation now demanded. White was certainly not that
general. With hindsight it is easy to blame him for not at once
making a fighting retreat to the south of the Tugela, relinquishing
all the copious supplies which were still pouring into Ladysmith,
and thus escaping from the trap into which the 'forward' policy had

forced him. But surely the blow to the Empire's morale would have been far too great. Beyond this, White could have argued that he did not possess a large enough force to hold an entrenched line along the river. Yet again, as it happened, a considerable part of the Boer's strength was, in fact, to be detained for a long time north of the Tugela by the need for it to prevent White breaking out of Ladysmith. There is something, if not much, to be said for the argument that this provided a vital breathing space, that it gave time for the troops to arrive from home. Further it is almost certain that White was thinking in terms of the superiority of British regulars over 'natives' in small colonial wars and that this is why he had it in mind to smash the more numerous enemy with one 'knock-down blow', thereby avoiding a siege altogether.

On 30 October, which came to be known as 'Mournful Monday', he attempted to deliver it. His vague, complicated and ambitious three-pronged attack failed at all points. As was to prove so often the case throughout the war, the Boers were not where they were thought to be, or where a short time before the cavalry patrols had reported them to be. Consequently, the slow-moving infantry found themselves shot at from unexpected and invisible positions. These, because of the superior mobility of the enemy, changed with bewildering rapidity. Total British casualties numbered 1,272, of which 954 men were made prisoner. French's cavalry, consisting of parts of the 5th Dragoon Guards, 5th Lancers, 18th and 19th Hussars and the Natal Carbineers, suffered very few casualties in spite of being under heavy fire. 'We were all jammed in a small nullah 1½ miles long and about 10 to 20 yards wide,' wrote Major Marling of the 18th in his diary. 'I never saw such a mess. We could not get out and had to dismount. . . . All this under a pretty smart fire.'[4] Lieutenant-Colonel Gore, commanding the 5th Dragoon Guards, discovered for the first time what was to be a dominant characteristic of Boer fighting. 'One heard shots and heard bullets pass, but could see,' he wrote in his diary, 'no signs of any men who were firing: the smokeless powder makes it a very difficult job to estimate either the position or numbers of an enemy.'[5]

After the battle the inevitable retirement into Ladysmith was far from orderly. Only the covering action of the artillery and the reluctance of Joubert to allow his men to pursue prevented a rout.

'For reasons which it is difficult to understand,' says the *Times History*, 'the cavalry were allowed to save themselves by their speed alone. No attempt was made at a judicious withdrawal by regiments. Troop officers were not even given the time to form their troops. A seething mass of clubbed and broken cavalry charged down and streamed ... into the open plain, where, after a short interval, it collected and reformed itself.'

An infantry captain called the cavalry's retreat 'very nearly a stampede'.[6]*

Thus ended the battle of Ladysmith (or Lombard's Kop), a 'scrambling, inconsequential, unsatisfactory action' as Conan Doyle called it.[7] It was the first on a large scale 'in which the two military systems were fairly matched against each other'.[8]†

Three days later Buller, who had arrived at Cape Town on 31 October, asked that French and Haig should be sent to him to take immediate command of the cavalry division then on its way out.

'We left [Ladysmith] at 1 o'clock,' wrote Haig in his diary. 'The train consisted of an engine, two trucks and the guard's van, at the end of which there was a first class compartment. The General, self and two A.D.C.s travelled in first class compartment. Seven servants and the guard in the guard's van. 9 horses in one of the trucks and our baggage in the other.'

* Second-Lieutenant John Norwood and Private William Sibthorpe, 5th Dragoon Guards, gained the Victoria Cross and the Distinguished Conduct Medal respectively for galloping back 300 yards for a wounded man. Norwood picked him up, carried him on his back 'and began to walk in with him. Private Sibthorpe hereupon returned to [Norwood's] assistance and assisted in carrying the man,' all under heavy and incessant fire. Norwood reported Sibthorpe's action to his squadron commander. Sibthorpe said: 'I only followed my officer's example,' thus revealing Norwood's part. 'It is against the expressed wish of [Norwood] that I reported his share in this act of gallantry,' wrote his squadron commander. (Gore, 40–42; Stirling, 411; Pomeroy, 242.)

† Early that morning Colonel John Fielden Brocklehurst of the Royal Horse Guards had arrived to command the cavalry in Natal, relieving French for his proper task of commanding all the cavalry in South Africa. Brocklehurst (mockingly known to the troops as 'Pogglehurst' and as 'Big Brock' to his friends), according to Sir Henry Rawlinson possessed neither 'the dash nor the brains' necessary for a good cavalry commander. George Wyndham, however, thought him 'the most perfect gentleman in the British army, the kindest and nicest and most chivalrous'. He had served in the 1882 Egyptian campaign and had been in charge of remounts in the Nile expedition of 1884–85. (*Army List*, 1901, 38; 19 Dec., 1899, Papers of Lt-Col Sir H. Rawlinson, NAM 5201/33; 6 Oct., 1899, Wyndham, Guy, *Letters of George Wyndham, 1877–1913*, I, Privately Printed, 1915, 452.)

Writing next day to his wife, Haig said:

> 'The Railway Manager did not think we could get past the Boers as they had fired on the morning passenger train. [After twenty minutes] a regular volley rattled along the sides of the vehicles, and we heard several shells explode. We did not see anything for we had the wooden shutters up and we all four lay on the seats and floor of our carriage, not a very dignified position for the Cavalry Division Staff to assume – but discretion is some times the better part of valour! Three miles beyond Pieter's Station (a British post) there was a very loud report and other shots. When we got to Colenso we examined our train and found a 2½ or 3 inch shell had gone thro' the second truck! . . . If this shell had hit a wheel, not to mention the engine boiler, we would certainly have been now on our way to Pretoria. . . . I was sorry to leave them all in Ladysmith; but . . . we were *ordered* away.'[9]

As soon as this special, which was the last train out of Ladysmith, had gone by, the Boers cut the line. The siege of Ladysmith had started in earnest, and Southern Natal, defended by only two infantry battalions, seemed – but only seemed – ripe for invasion. How relieved both politicians and soldiers would have been had they realized that the strategy of the two republican governments was at this time chiefly defensive. As Thomas Pakenham, a leading modern historian of the war, has put it, 'Kruger's main political objective was a new settlement, with Britain giving the Transvaal unqualified independence.' The Boers' 'defensive-offensive' strategy which arose out of this political object and was doubtless founded on the outcome of the 1881 Boer War (see Vol III, p. 208) entailed primarily the blocking of the expected British attacks and inevitable counter-invasion. Nevertheless, Joubert made a daring raid into South Natal, gaining a tactical victory over Major-General Henry John Horoton Hildyard (see Vol III, p. 112) at Willow Grange on 23 November. But the reinforcements which were now arriving at Durban and being rushed up the line to Pietermaritzburg, combined with an accidental injury to Joubert, led the burghers to retire to the north bank of the Tugela River. There Louis Botha, aged only thirty-seven, took over command. Botha, who, in spite of a limited education, was soon to evince an innate gift for both the strategy and tactics of war, at once started fortifying the line of the river.

The 'defensive-offensive' reasoning of the Boers also seems to explain the leisurely, unadventurous nature of the Boer invasion of Cape Colony, against which the British could at first oppose virtually nothing.[10] As was not unexpected, both Mafeking, where Colonel Baden-Powell's force was a mere handful, and Kimberley, where Lieutenant-Colonel Robert Kekewich's troops were equally minimal,* were soon cut off and gradually surrounded.

Part of the Boer strategy was to secure Durban as a link to the outside world; but, in retrospect, it seems that to have made such an effort in Natal for that end, and to spend so much time and effort in besieging Ladysmith and Kimberley, constitutes a major strategic mistake. Had the commandos been sent direct to Cape Colony (four times the size of the two republics), it is not unlikely that such an invasion would have augmented their numbers by 25,000 or 30,000 mounted men. For these they had rifles and ammunition in plenty.

*   *   *

Buller on his arrival at Cape Town was just in time to learn of White's awful failure the day before. To his dismay he also learned that more than half of all the troops in South Africa, including the best of the infantry and all the regular cavalry, were now locked up in Ladysmith, Kimberley and Mafeking. The plan which had been agreed in London before he left would now have to be postponed, if not abandoned. It was no longer practicable to concentrate the Army Corps of 45,000 men, which was due to begin arriving from the second week of November, for a concerted march on Bloemfontein and Pretoria. This strategy had entirely depended, of course, upon the troops already in the theatre of war being able to contain the Boer invasion in the meantime. Especially did the whole plan of campaign rely upon White holding his own in Natal for at least two or three months. Now, as soon as the units arrived piecemeal from home, they must be rushed, irrespective of their brigading, to the various 'fronts'.

*   *   *

The part played by the cavalry brigade during the 120-day siege of Ladysmith was a small one. Like all other units, the four regular and five Colonial regiments, which to start with numbered 2,800 of the

* To hold a thirteen and a half mile perimeter, Kimberley possessed a garrison of 4,600, of which only 596 were regulars.

13,700 garrison, lost more men from disease than from enemy action.

The feeding of the horses depended to a considerable degree upon the grazing grounds within the defended perimeter. On 2 November there was only thirty-two days' forage on hand, and this did not include more than a smattering of hay and chaff. It is an astonishing fact, none the less, that for a considerable part of the siege many of the cavalry and artillery horses received a larger forage ration than was at the same time being allowed to the horses in Cape Colony during the hardest work they could possibly be called upon to do. Those in Ladysmith had, of course, to be exercised (during the darkness hours) to keep them in minimal condition. After mid-December hard forage for the horses, of which at the start there were 5,800,* was virtually exhausted.[11] Nevertheless it was not till the end of January, 1900, that the slaughter for food of the regular cavalry's horses was begun.† 'We cannot feed our men,' wrote one officer of the 5th Lancers in his diary, 'we cannot feed our horses so the horses must suffer to feed the men.'[12] Only 300 of the regular cavalry horses

Some of the horses in Ladysmith are looking a bit Poor! — B.

(seventy-five for each regiment) were retained. All other horses were turned out to graze, the idea being that if possible they should be driven into kraals at night.[13]

'In about a quarter of an hour [of first being turned out],' wrote an officer of the 5th Dragoon Guards, 'they were seized with a

---

* At the end 2,907 were still alive. (Lines, G. W. *The Ladysmith Siege*, quoted in Smith, 46.)

† Towards the end of November all sick animals not pretty well certain to recover were ordered to be destroyed. (Smith, 44.)

panic and stampeded, and galloped back towards camp, regardless of rocks, nullahs and barbed-wire. All day long they were galloping up and down the streets, so that it was hardly safe to walk there. Many were fearfully injured from falls over barbed-wire and other obstacles. Many came back to their old places in the line and stood there, whinnying, waiting for their nosebags to be put on.'

'The Man of Straw: another little joke of the 5th Lancers at Observation Hill, Ladysmith.'

These distressing scenes were repeated over a number of days. 'It was almost a relief when a number of them were requisitioned for slaughter and turned into chevril – a really excellent soup.'[14]*

Surprisingly enough it was not till a month from the siege's end that the cavalry were first used as infantry. On that day they handed in lances, swords, carbines and saddles and drew out rifles and bayonets instead.[15] It seems very strange that White did not send at least the majority of his cavalry away before the siege started, and it seems even stranger that for a very considerable period the horses were actually fed mealies. These were the chief source of foodstuff for the garrison!

* 'Beef tea', 'chevril' paste and sausages were also manufactured. A 'special potted meat' made from horse tongues was made for hospital use. (*R.C.*, IV, 254.)

5

'My great want at present is mounted men. I am
raising as many as I can.'
> BULLER to Lansdowne, 11 November, 1899

'As regards mobility we were nowhere.'
> LORD DUNDONALD

'Natal is no place for Cavalry.'
> GEORGE WYNDHAM, Parliamentary Under-
> Secretary of State for War, 12 April, 1900

'We have been much humbled – I am sure for our
good. Please God help us now to victory and
peace, all in great humility. . . . Oh! The strange
awakening to find that there is an enemy who
dares to stand and stand long in our path! I never
could have realised the feeling before. Strange
awakening! Where does love of country cease
and pride and arrogance begin?'
> THE EARL OF AIRLIE, commanding the
> 12th Lancers, 19 January, 1900[1]

*Boer War: Natal: Ladysmith Relief Force: arrival of Royals and
13th Hussars – Thorneycroft's and Bethune's Mounted Infantry –
South African Light Horse – Lord Dundonald – battle of Colenso*

Among the troops diverted from Cape Town to South Natal were
the 1st Royal Dragoons, who had been designated as part of the
Army Corps' 2nd Cavalry Brigade. Warned for service as long ago
as 18 August, the regiment embarked at Tilbury in a converted cattle
boat on 30 October. It eventually reached Durban on 26 November.
In common with all troops leaving home every man under twenty
was left in the depot. When these, the unfit and the partially trained
recruits had been deducted, the Royals needed 116 men from the
Reserve and thirty-three horses to make up to full establishment. The
training of these and the issue of khaki drill (later replaced by serge)
had to be rushed through in the short time available. The Commanding officer, Lieutenant-Colonel John Francis Burn-Murdoch, aged
forty, was almost the only member of the regiment who had ever
before seen active service. He had fought at Abu Klea and, under
Kitchener, he had commanded the Egyptian cavalry in 1896. Now he

was about to take his regiment into action for the first time. It consisted, after leaving a depot at Pietermaritzburg, of about 530 of all ranks with some 500 horses.[2]

The only other cavalry regiment sent to join the Ladysmith Relief Force was the 13th Hussars, under Lieutenant-Colonel Henry John Blagrove, at forty-five a veteran of the 2nd Afghan War and the 1882 Egyptian campaign. The regiment had been originally intended to act as Corps troops. About 590 strong* with over 500 horses, it began to arrive at Durban on 5 December, having left Liverpool in two hired transports twenty-four days before. Twenty-two horses were lost on the voyage and it is interesting to note that on a ship carrying over 300 horses there was no veterinary surgeon.[3]

The rest of the mounted troops in the force, now building up into the largest British field army since the Crimea, consisted entirely of irregulars. As early as 16 October White had authorized the formation of two mounted units. The most famous of these was Thorneycroft's Mounted Infantry. Major Alexander ('Alec') Whitelaw Thorneycroft, born in 1859, was an infantry officer who had served in the Zulu War and in the First Boer War of 1881. Twenty stone in weight and enormously energetic, Thorneycroft had recruited originally from a register which had been recently compiled by the Uitlander Committee in Pietermaritzburg containing the names of men 'desirous of serving at the front'. Fluent in Dutch and the native languages, most of them had 'travelled extensively in the interior in search of big game, prospecting expeditions, etc., and were experienced rifle shots.' Numbers had previous campaigning experience in South Africa and elsewhere. Some were bad horsemasters to begin with because they 'were accustomed to have horses of their own, and could afford Kaffirs to look after them.' Initially all the battalion's horses were cobs and ponies of 'a fair class' of South African Colonial breed, and though small for the heavy men and weights they were called upon to carry, extremely tough. Most lasted for over a year of hard work and some went right through the war. Thorneycroft's officers, all personally selected by him, were partly serving or ex-regulars and partly civilians with war experience. Others were Yeomanry officers ('who had come out from England to seek employment') and officers of the Indian Staff Corps (see Vol III, pp. 89, 97) who had brought out horses and syces on ships from

---

* Out of 184 Reservists required to make the regiment complete, only three failed to turn up.

India and were detained in South Africa. There were a few Australasians and other colonials 'who came out directly war was declared on the chance of employment'. As vacancies occurred, many commissions went to men from the ranks for distinguished service in the field. Thorneycroft's men, according to an Imperial yeoman, swore by him. 'In action he never makes mistakes, they say. . . . If there is food and forage in the land, he will get it for his men, or know the reason why.'

Nearly all the battalion's saddles and bridles had to be bought locally and were 'of an inferior quality, made of bad leather, saddles with weak trees, etc.'. The rifles were Martini-Enfields, Lee-Metfords and Lee-Enfields. In nearly every important respect Thorneycroft found none of these measured up to the Mauser. As for machine guns, Thorneycroft's 'relations in England sent out two .303 Maxim guns on tripods, with pack saddles and ammunition complete.' Later on he borrowed from the Colt Gun Company three .303 Colts. These were mounted on carriages invented by Lord Dundonald (see below). Telescopes and field glasses, so essential for successful scouting, were virtually unobtainable, so Thorneycroft had eighteen telescopes 'as used for deer-stalking' and twenty-four pairs of 'Zeiss glasses' sent out by his brother. In the Field Service Manual for Mounted Infantry there was no provision for signalling equipment. Thorneycroft eventually procured 'two Helios (Cooke & Son, London) and two lamps (Begbie & Son)'. As he pointed out, such equipment was 'a great saving in horses, which otherwise have to carry the messages'.[4] All this detail has been gone into because much of it was common to all the numerous irregular units formed during the war and because it shows how large a part private enterprise and personal expenditure played in their formation.

The other unit raised by White's order was Bethune's Mounted Infantry, known irreverently as 'Bethune's Buccaneers'. With an establishment of 500, the battalion was raised, chiefly in the Durban area, by the forty-four year old Major (later Lieutenant-General Sir) Edward Cecil Bethune* of the 16th Lancers, who had served in the

* 'An Officer of Bethune's Mounted Infantry came to me,' wrote Lord Dundonald, 'to complain that he really could not stand Colonel Bethune's language, and stated that the Colonel had called him a damned fool. I therefore had the two officers concerned before me to investigate the matter, and inquired of Colonel Bethune whether he had used the words complained of. The Colonel's reply was, "Certainly not. I would never have used those words about him." Then I asked, "What did you say to him?" "I said that he was worthless and the damnedest fool that I had ever come across!" ' (Dundonald, 100.)

Second Afghan and the First Boer Wars. Among its officers and men were a number of Australians who had come over to Natal at their own expense, so as not to miss whatever fighting was going on.

Also in the mounted brigade which was assembling at Frere in early December were a newly-formed squadron of the Imperial Light Horse and the South African Light Horse. This regiment was raised at the Cape on 8 November by Buller's Deputy Assistant Adjutant-General, Lieutenant-Colonel Charles à Court, who, adding Repington to his name, became in 1904 the famous Military Correspondent of *The Times*. The regiment had an establishment of eight squadrons, 600 strong. It was commanded by Lieutenant-Colonel Julian Hedworth George Byng (later Field-Marshal Viscount Byng of Vimy) of the 10th Hussars, whose battle experience included El Teb and Tamai (see Vol III, pp. 312, 317). A second and third regiment which were raised a little later became in January, 1900, Roberts' Horse and Kitchener's Horse.* On the first regiment's slouch hat were worn the long black tail-feathers of the Sakabulu bird (*Diatropura Procne*). Consequently the members of the regiment came to be known as 'the Sakabulus'. The regimental motto in the Zulu language was 'Feathers at the front'.†5

The men were 'mostly South Africans, with a high proportion of hard-bitten adventurers from all quarters of the world, including a Confederate trooper from the American Civil War'. 'We took,' wrote à Court, 'fine young fellows from every mail boat that arrived, and we took Texas cowboys who turned up with mules from New Orleans. The scorn in the look of the cowboys when I asked them if they could ride was worth seeing.' An entire squadron was composed of Texas cowboys and muleteers.6 The regular officers included three who became Army Commanders (Byng, Birdwood and Hubert Gough‡) and at least four who commanded divisions in the First World War. In the guerrilla stage of the war the regiment was

* In May, 1901, the men of these two units were 'allowed to take their discharge'. Only some 200 volunteered to continue serving. (Rawlinson, 29 May, 1901.)

† Winston Churchill, wearing a moustache and retaining his status as a war correspondent, served as a supernumerary lieutenant with the regiment from 2 January to 23 March, 1900. (Churchill: *Companion*, 1141). A month later, Lieutenant-Colonel Peter Legh Clowes, commanding the 8th Hussars, wrote in his diary: 'Winston Churchill with [4th Cavalry] Brigade all day – seemed to boss the show, a young ass'. (29 Apr., 1900, Clowes.)

‡ Captain William Riddell Birdwood (later Field-Marshal Lord Birdwood of Anzac and Totnes), who lived to be eighty-six, was almost immediately trans-

seldom engaged, but on 14 May, 1901, near Fauresmith, two squadrons forming part of Lieutenant-Colonel William Hugh Williams's column caught seventeen burghers, making fourteen of them prisoner, including a notable field-cornet. Nearly nine months later, on 2 February, 1902, the regiment under Byng, together with the New Zealanders and Queensland Bushmen under Colonel Francis Sudlow Garratt of the 6th Dragoon Guards, was engaged at Fanny's Home, near Harrismith, with two of De Wet's commandos. After a close combat, three of the guns lost at Tweefontein (see p. 103) were recaptured and, for only three British casualties, thirty-nine were inflicted upon the Boers.[7]

Early in 1900 certain other horsed units were raised in the Eastern Province of Cape Colony. Chief of these was Brabant's Horse, nicknamed by Haig the 'Brabantetti', from the men's undisciplined behaviour. The regiment was composed of Afrikaners, a few English farmers and, later on, volunteers who had hurried to South Africa from all parts of the Empire, as well as 'adventurers from every quarter of the globe – Poles, Jews, Texan cowboys, Mexicans, Norwegians and Swedes'. Two hundred of the regiment did useful work in Major-General William Forbes Gatacre's force south of Stormberg only a fortnight after enlistment. De Wet told the Imperial Yeomanry prisoners taken at Lindley (see p. 178) that the best marksmen he had come across were those of Brabant's Horse. At the same time they were unsurpassed in the art of foraging. Captain (later Major-General) Edward Yewd Brabant, who formed the unit, a Member of the Legislative Assembly, a veteran of the Kaffir Wars and said by Captain Frank Mussenden of the 8th Hussars, to be 'a charming old gentleman', was later placed in command of the independent Colonial Division (see p. 113).

Bayly's, Nesbitt's and Orpen's Horse* were other units raised chiefly among the Eastern Province farmers. Taking the war as a

---

ferred to the brigade staff and later became Dundonald's Brigade Major. Later, as Kitchener's Deputy Assistant Adjutant General and then Military Secretary, he dealt with all cavalry matters, the appointment of officers to irregular corps and the collection of dismounted details and their remounting and redistribution. Captain Hubert de la Poer Gough (later General Sir Hubert) (see p. 264) who came from the 16th Lancers, and who died aged ninety-three, became Brigade Intelligence Officer.

* Colonel Z. S. Bayly, who earlier commanded the Cape Mounted Rifles, Lieutenant-Colonel Richard Atholl Nesbitt, who also came from the C.M.R., and Major Redmond Newenham Morris Orpen, who for a time commanded

whole nearly two-fifths of all mounted troops (and about one-sixth of the whole force) were contributed by colonial units, the majority being South African. Most of these latter and some of the others suffered from an average enlistment period of only six months. They were, therefore, in a state of chronic change most of the time, which inevitably detracted from their efficiency. When Brabant's Horse and 'several other corps of Colonial fame' came under Haig's command in July, 1901, he dubbed them, with characteristic contempt for irregulars, 'rascally bandits. All they enlist for,' he wrote home, 'is 5/– a day and they are much annoyed if one makes them *go out and fight.* Few of them really fight! They are expensive luxuries too to keep up.' De Wet thought that, as Afrikaners, they ought 'to have been ashamed to fight against us. The English, we admitted, had a perfect right to hire such sweepings, and to use them against us, but we utterly despised them for allowing themselves to be hired.... There was not a man amongst us who would have asked better than to make prisoners of Brabant's Horse.' On 13 December, 1900, in an ambuscade at Koesberg, near Zastron, De Wet's lieutenant, Kritzinger (see p. 230), had the satisfaction of taking 100 of the regiment prisoner, as well as killing or wounding twenty more.[8]

Also in the mounted brigade was the one squadron of the Natal Carbineers (raised as long ago as 1855) which was not locked up in Ladysmith. It was commanded by Major Donald MacKenzie, who formed at this time a Kaffir Intelligence Corps which became extremely useful as the war progressed.[9] The Brigade was completed by two companies of regular mounted infantry from the King's Royal Rifles and the Dublin Fusiliers and a detachment of the Natal Police.

In command of the mounted brigade was Lieutenant-Colonel (later Lieutenant-General) Douglas Mackinnon Baillie Hamilton Cochrane, 12th Earl of Dundonald, aged forty-seven. Known familiarly as 'Dundoodle', he was, according to Birdwood, 'full of verve' though 'a curiously sensitive man, living largely on his nerves'.[10] As Lord Cochrane, fame had come to him after he carried the dispatches announcing the seizure of the Gakdul Wells and the death of Gordon (see Vol III, pp. 322, 335). After the relief of Ladysmith the newspapers sometimes referred to him as 'the stormy petrel'. As a cavalry officer he was a zealous, forward-looking reformer. During his four years (1895–9) in command of the 2nd Life Guards (which he had joined in 1870) he had concentrated on improving his

the Border Scouts, raised in the Northern Cape in May, 1900, and consisting of Coloured men only.

troopers' shooting and their mounting and dismounting speeds. Further, he had a penchant for inventing military aids. He designed an efficient and very light ambulance cart as well as a waterproof bag in which men could cross rivers while keeping dry. He realized that the chief cause of the appallingly high incidence of disease in South Africa was the consumption of foul water. He caused one of the military barrel water-carts to be opened and found that 'it contained filthy black sludge at the bottom'. This was because the draw-off cock was above the barrel's base. As soon as he got home he devised a better model consisting of 'three oblong cylinders, separate and removable' so made that it was 'temptingly easy to flush each tank every time it is filled with water'. This seems not to have been officially adopted. His most successful creation, though, was the 'Dundonald Patent Attachment and Galloping Carriage' which was one of the few of his inventions accepted by the authorities. It proved, according to Thorneycroft, 'admirable in the open plain of the Transvaal'.[11] There were mixed views as to his capacities in the field. Hubert Gough, never patient of restraint by senior officers, dubbing him 'one of Buller's weak subordinates', condemned Dundonald as 'forever an alarmist, sending out troops on the flimsiest of reports. The moment he had his brigade in the field he could not decide what to do with them'. Gough also found him 'very pleasant' and well-meaning 'but he has not anything like the steady nerves a soldier wants to do any good'.[12] This was probably unfair. On the whole he seems to have done well enough, being quick-moving and clear-headed while not interfering unduly with his subordinates such as Thorneycroft and Bethune who were, fortunately for him, men of ability.*

*   *   *

Buller, having spent sixteen hectic days in Cape Town, during which he sent Lieutenant-General Lord Methuen† off towards

---

* From 1902 to 1904 he commanded the Canadian Militia and in 1915 he chaired the Admiralty Committee on Smoke Screens. His contribution to the development of these both at sea and on land was considerable. He died, aged eighty-two in 1935.

† Methuen, a Scots Guardsman, the youngest lieutenant-general in the army, commanded the 1st Infantry Division from 1899. He was unfairly blamed for his lack of success at Magersfontein (see p. 83) and served throughout the war in many capacities, ranging from commander of small columns to large groups, until he was wounded and captured by De la Rey at Tweebosch (see p. 269). He

Kimberley and French towards Colesberg, decided to go to Natal, ostensibly to judge the situation there for himself but in fact to direct the operations of the Ladysmith Relief Force. This, by the end of the second week of December, had swollen to over 18,000 of all arms, of which Dundonald's mounted brigade constituted about an eighth. The four infantry brigades which formed the hard core of the force had with them sixteen machine guns. There was no horse artillery, but there were over forty other guns, fourteen of which were supplied by the Navy.

Botha, with perhaps 5,500 burghers and ten field guns, had used his breathing space well. Using a mass of native labour he had dug fifteen miles of rifle pits and gun pits along the north bank of the Tugela. These he screened by dummy trenches and gun emplacements. He rightly supposed that Buller, depending upon the railway, would not risk a long flank march and that he would attack frontally at Colenso where the road bridge had been left purposely intact. Fought on 15 December, the battle of Colenso was a fiasco. It was inherently badly planned and grossly mismanaged. After committing only two of his infantry brigades, Buller withdrew, having suffered about 6% casualties, as against only forty inflicted on the Boers. He quite unnecessarily abandoned twelve of his precious guns. The action of the artillery commander, Colonel Charles James Long, in going too far forward was injudicious, but ironically, though Buller blamed his failure on that action, he was possibly saved by it from a far greater disaster. 'Colonel Long's action,' said Botha, 'exposed our plan and forced us to fight. [Consequently] Buller's army never advanced across the river by the road bridge, as it was intended, to where we had planned to crush it.'[13]

Dundonald, having detached two squadrons of the 13th Hussars to protect the right flank, where they saw no action, and the Royals to protect the left flank, was sent to attack the 550-foot hill of Hlangwane. From this, which was on the British side of the river, it might have been possible for the field battery which had been attached to the brigade to enfilade the Boer entrenchments, could it have been dragged to the summit. Using his men dismounted, as he did, he might conceivably have dislodged the 700 or so Boers who had only very reluctantly re-occupied it early that morning, had he

---

was Commander-in-Chief in South Africa from 1907 to 1909 and promoted to Field-Marshal in 1911. He died in 1932, aged eighty-seven. His first appearance in this history was as Major-General, commanding the Home District in 1892 (see Vol III, p. 84).

not been refused reinforcements.* When Dundonald received Buller's order to retire, he had to do so under heavy fire. Thorneycroft's, the South African Light Horse and the Natal Carbineers suffered as many casualties at this time as in the approach to the hill. These casualties totalled sixteen killed, sixty-seven wounded and thirteen missing.

On the left Burn-Murdoch's patrols of the Royals thrice sent warnings that the opposite bank of the river was strongly occupied. Major-General Arthur Fitzroy Hart, one of the most obstinate and old-fashioned of the army's generals, treated this intelligence with contempt. He proceeded to commit the closely-packed regiments of his brigade to be slaughtered in a salient formed by a loop of the river which was nowhere near the drift (ford) at which he had been ordered to cross. The Royals suffered no casualties.[14]

* * *

Buller, demanding massive reinforcements, remained stationary and stunned south of the Tugela for the next twenty-six days. 'Black Week', which had been Stormberg (see p. 85), Magersfontein (see p. 83) as well as Colenso, was over. So was the first stage of the war.†

It can rain in Natal

28·12·99

---

* Major-General Geoffry Barton commanding the 6th Infantry Brigade from which Dundonald asked for reinforcements gives his reasons for refusal in *R.C.*, II, 660–1. He states too that he did leave 'three companies with Dundonald'.

† A week after Colenso an amusing incident occurred which could have happened in no previous campaign. Part of a squadron of the 13th Hussars 'were ordered to turn out and were naturally disgusted when it was known that the sole reason was for them to be cinematographed'! (*XIII H*, 8.)

6

'The maps are of little value, the open country
plus Mauser rifles render reconnaissance impossible. People talk of making a detour, or sending
a brigade round the flank. There is no use talking
that way with 8,000 horsemen in front of you, a
river and a position not to be turned.'

LORD METHUEN to Sir Redvers Buller,
2 December, 1899

' "Want of frigates" was to be found on Nelson's
heart, as he said on some occasion, and I am sure
by this time that "want of cavalry" must be
written on poor Methuen's.'

One of Rimington's Guides,
26 November, 1899

'If Sir R. Buller had fully appreciated the value
of cavalry, he would have diverted to Orange
River some of the regiments now being sent up
to French, and replaced them by some of
Methuen's infantry battalions, or else have delayed
Methuen's start till his force could be properly
equipped.'

The Times History of the War in
South Africa

'Methuen seems to have been banging at them
magnificently. But they have not defeated them,
or out-witted them yet.'

GEORGE WYNDHAM, Parliamentary Under-
Secretary of State for War, 1 December,
1899[1]

*Boer War: Cape Colony: 9th Lancers arrive from India –
Rimington's Guides – Methuen's advance: Belmont, Graspan,
Modder River, Magersfontein – Gatacre's defeat at Stormberg*

In early September, 1899, when war looked imminent, the 9th
Lancers, one of the seven regular cavalry regiments in India at the
time, was warned for South Africa. On 19 September it left Muttra
with 491 of all ranks and 518 horses. As the three transports which
were to carry the squadrons to South Africa left Bombay 'three

cheers were given for the "Ladies of Bombay", who had most kindly sent the troops boxes of games and books.'[2]

Two days before war was declared the first ship arrived off Durban. She was at once ordered to sail on to Cape Town, as were the other two which arrived on 10 and 11 October. On the way the rudder of one of them was smashed during a severe gale. Some of the horses were housed in wooden stables on the upper deck (see illustration No. 1) and before long the woodwork gave way. Six horses were at once washed overboard:

> 'The deck was covered with one struggling mass of horses and mules, mixed up with the broken woodwork of the stables, the whole being hurled first to one side of the deck and then the other. All,' wrote one troop officer, 'were horribly wounded, most with broken legs and some with eyes torn out. . . . Things were hardly better between decks. On one deck a huge water tank broke loose and went hurtling about, killing two horses. . . . It was a horrible thing having to jump this way and that to avoid the horses that kept hurtling up and down, kicking and screaming. . . . Tuesday, October 10th, 1899, will never be forgotten by "C" Squadron, 9th Lancers, not if we live to be Methuselahs!'[3]

Out of 150 horses on that ship, ninety-two were lost.*

By 18 October the regiment was assembled at Orange River Station as part of the force under Lord Methuen. Buller ordered him 'to relieve Kimberley, throw in a large supply of provisions, clear out the non-combatants [especially Cecil Rhodes, who had been screaming for help by every means open to him] and return to Orange River'.[4]

---

* The efficiency of the Indian authorities is well illustrated by the fact that three cavalry regiments (of which the 9th was the first), four infantry battalions and three artillery batteries were fully mobilized in only four days from the time that notice was given. To transport them twenty-two ships (fifteen of them horse transports) were engaged and actually 'sent off in sixteen days'. During the course of the war some 11,850 white troops, including reinforcements, left India for South Africa. Of these 'from time to time about 3,000 or 4,000 returned to India'. The consequent weakening of the garrison in the sub-continent was calculated at between 7,000 and 8,000 white troops. Numbers of native soldiers and even more civilians were sent to help with non-combatant duties. There were native orderlies, remount depot assistants, some 500 in the transport corps, 1,000 in the bhisti corps, another 1,000 in the corps of syces, 'also a very useful corps of dhobies, or native washermen, sent in May, 1900'. (Evidence of Maj.-Gen. Sir Edwin Collen, Military Member of Council, India, *R.C.*, III, 496.)

The 9th remained in the vicinity of Orange River Station, under-taking, together with the mounted infantry, daily reconnaissance patrols,* till 15 November when Rimington's Guides (see below) arrived to share these chores. Three days later remounts arrived to replace the 9th's losses at sea. These were 'small Colonial horses', but the saddlery which had come with the regiment from India was far too big for them. To make matters worse, there had not been time before leaving India to change the old, worn-out saddlery, which was quite unfit for service. In no time at all, as a result, the incidence of sore backs increased alarmingly. Thus the only regular cavalry regiment in Methuen's force was much debilitated from the start.[5] Its horses' poor condition was exacerbated by the semi-starvation rations given them after landing, at a time when they should have been generously fed. Further, the summer grazing in the Orange River district and beyond was very speedily exhausted. Buller had been grossly mistaken when he said to Methuen, 'Mind you, you will find there is grazing up there, and you will make them graze; don't listen to anyone if he says they want more for their horses.'[6] The consequences of the short rations and this miscalculation were grave indeed. (See p. 349.)

Rimington's Guides, 'a corps of scouts supplying guides to the army', was a newly-raised unit. It consisted at first of some 150 to 200 colonials, 'men brought up free from caste and free of class'. They had been raised, chiefly in the Cape Town and Port Elizabeth districts, by Major Michael Frederick Rimington of the 6th (Innis-killing) Dragoons,† one of a number of special service officers, all

* One of the first of these, on 10 November, led by the 9th's commanding officer, Lieutenant-Colonel Bloomfield Gough, resulted in the deaths of two officers of the Northumberland Fusiliers and the wounding of two other officers and two privates, from long-range Mauser bullets. Gough believed himself responsible and, as a result of this patrol and the ineffectiveness of the cavalry pursuit at Graspan (see below), Methuen relieved him of his command and sent him back to base: one of the first of many officers to be 'stellenbosched'. Not long afterwards Gough blew his brains out. (Amery, II, 340.) As a troop com-mander he had distinguished himself at the action of the Chardeh Valley, 10–11 December, 1879 (see Vol III, p. 234). In September 1899, Rawlinson had described him as 'a dashing fellow [who] would charge home always, even if he did not always choose the best opportunity – popular and a gallant leader without much brains.' (Rawlinson, 29 Sep., 1899.)

† Rimington, who was knighted in 1921, eventually reached the rank of major-general and became Inspector of Cavalry in India. He published in 1912 *Our Cavalry* (see p. 393). He also produced two pamphlets: *Hints on Stable Management*, 1897 (2nd edn, 1905) and *The Horse in Recent Wars*, 1904. (*continued over*)

regulars, sent to South Africa as early as July. He was a man of strong will and force of character, respected by his men to a high degree. To help him Rimington had a small number of regular officers. Of his men 'a large proportion' were Uitlanders, many of them Rand miners. Others were fully 'Dutch' burghers while some had English fathers and Dutch mothers. Others were gentlemen from England. One of these, Lieutenant (later Lieutenant-Colonel Sir) Reginald Rankin (Bt),* who was promoted by Rimington from trooper in the field, wrote to his wife 'in Rimington's we are rank heretics from the orthodox cult of martinets. One or two of us have actually been known to consult a trooper as to a tactical movement, with the happiest results to all concerned.' 'The best man I had,' said Rimington, 'was sixty-three. He had five horses shot under him during the war.' Most of the Guides were fluent in Dutch and the native languages, some of them veterans of past African campaigns (as indeed was Rimington himself), all of them remarkably self-reliant. They were not, said one infantry general, 'men I should invite to bivouac on my estate'. Indeed they usually stripped bare any Boer habitation they came across. Some brought their own horses, 'in many cases race horses and racing ponies'. 'Others would not take that responsibility.' The Guides came to be known as 'Rimington's Tigers' from the puggarees (actually made of leopard-skin) which they wound round their Boer-type hats. A regimental ledger was kept showing which part of the country was particularly familiar to each man. Some of them were attached throughout the war to columns and units in special need of guides or interpreters; others were attached to the various staffs. In Methuen's force to begin with there were only about 100 under Rimington.[7] In January, 1901, when Rimington took command of his own regiment, his Guides became Damant's Horse (see p. 224).

One of his officers described him thus: 'An inch or two over six feet high, his figure spare but lengthy and muscular, has been so knocked about (by hunting and polo accidents) that it has rather a lopsided look. . . . His face, like Driscoll's (see p. 163), is sun-blackened rather than sun-browned. . . . When he is thinking and talking about the Boers his expression (stern and grim) deepens into something positively savage. . . . He has the Celtic sensitiveness and humour. He is an artist. His manner among friends is extraordinarily winning. . . . His grave, melancholy face has a way of breaking into a most infectious laugh.' (Phillipps, 197.) He died, aged seventy, in 1928.

* Rankin later became a distinguished *Times* war correspondent (Morocco, 1908; Bulgaria, 1912), a prolific author (one of his works was a blank verse translation of Wagner's *Nibelungen Ring*), big-game hunter and mountaineer (he climbed the 22,000 ft Aconcagua).

Out of some 8,000 troops, Methuen was provided with less than 1,000 mounted men. Beside the 9th Lancers and the Guides, there were twenty-eight officers and men of the New South Wales Lancers (see p. 137) and two and a half companies of mounted infantry.*

There followed four battles, inevitably fought chiefly by the infantry and artillery. The first, which in many ways resembled Talana Hill, took place at Belmont on 23 November. This was succeeded two days later by the action at Graspan, which was much the same on a smaller scale. Both were expensive victories. Neither was much more than 'an honest, straightforward British march up to a row of waiting rifles'.[8] Both were fought against Commandant Jacobus Prinsloo's Kroonstad burghers, posted atop kopjes. These men retreated in good order after inflicting severe casualties on the infantry as they advanced across the open veld. Before both engagements the small number of British mounted men exhausted themselves in extensive screening and in usually fruitless reconnaissance. 'To reconnoitre over a perfectly flat plain,' as Methuen later told the Royal Commission, 'with these modern weapons firing 2,000 yards, and give any good reconnaissance report, is an impossibility.'[9] Before Belmont many of the mounted men had covered forty miles in the day.[10] No wonder, then, that Methuen found that when he had taken the Boer position at Belmont he had at his feet 'about 2,000 yards off, the whole of the Boer laager, but I had not anybody to go for it'.[11] Those few of the 9th and the mounted infantry who did try to pursue found themselves ambushed by a new Boer force which arrived on the scene as the battle finished. This was the first appearance in the field of the fifty-three year old General Jacobus Hercules De la Rey. It was he, about to prove himself one of the most remark-

* These New South Wales Lancers, members of the senior mounted regiment of Australia, were part of some seventy or eighty who had been training in England when war broke out. They were soon reduced in number and played a distinguished part in the campaign, coming to be known as 'the Fighting 28'. (Wallace, 35.)

After French received reinforcements before Colesberg (see p. 107), which included the Inniskilling Dragoons to which the New South Wales Lancers were attached, a patrol of twenty-five men was cut off and forced to surrender. (Amery, III, 141.)

The mounted infantry companies were drawn from the Northumberland Fusiliers, the Loyal North Lancashires and the King's Own Yorkshire Light Infantry.

There were twelve fifteen-pounder field guns and four naval twelve-pounders. Four further fifteen-pounders joined just in time for the battle of the Modder River. Another seventeen had joined before Magersfontein.

able soldiers of the age and certainly the most progressive and doughty of the Boer commanders, who now decided that for his burghers to sit on top of kopjes was to invite the British artillery to smash them. Consequently at Methuen's third battle, known as the Modder River, fought on 28 November, De la Rey dug his burghers in along the low-lying banks of the twisting river.* In fact the cavalry's reconnaissance reports before the battle twice warned Methuen that the Boer position there was strongly held, but he refused to believe it. The result was 478 casualties. The 9th, who were on the right flank, proved marginally useful by warding off Boer reinforcements. Rimington's Guides were also of some assistance on the left flank.

Thirteen days after Modder River, at the badly bungled battle of Magersfontein, where De la Rey again entrenched his men not on the kopjes (which the British guns fruitlessly pounded) but at their foot, Methuen suffered a severe reverse. By then further Boers had arrived from the environs of Mafeking, making a total of some 8,200, of which, incidentally, as many as 2,200 were without mounts. Methuen, too, had been reinforced. He now commanded nearly 15,000 men, including 'some details of M.I.'[12] and the 12th Lancers, over 500 strong, who had arrived from England at Cape Town on 19 November and been transferred from French's force on 3 December. All the mounted troops were now placed under Colonel Babington (see p. 50). There were also thirty-three pieces of artillery including the twelve-pounders of 'G' Battery, Royal Horse Artillery.†

Only one infantry brigade, the Highland, was engaged at Magersfontein, but it suffered very severe casualties. The artillery was largely responsible for saving it from complete annihilation. The 9th, which lost two men killed and eight wounded, as well as the 12th, acted dismounted in co-operation with the mounted infantry and the horse artillery. This they did under the prompt and energetic

---

* General Cronje (see p. 125), commanding the Transvaal commandos on the western front arrived with other reinforcements at this time. Though senior to De la Rey, he was persuaded by him to take the bold (and extremely unconventional) course of digging in on the river bank.

The total Boer force was perhaps 3,000 strong. With it were six 75mm (3 in.) Krupp field guns and three one-pounder Maxims ('pom-poms').

† This battery, which had only landed thirteen days previously and was in action for the first time, was fourteen and a half hours under fire. It expended 1,179 rounds during the battle: this is believed to have been the greatest expenditure of ammunition by any battery in one day during the whole war. (Headlam, 351; R.C., II, 361 (where the number of rounds is given as 1,250), 369.)

leadership of Babington, much aided by the vigour of the Earl of Airlie, the 12th's commanding officer,* to such effect that they 'prevented', according to the official historian, 'the reverse from becoming a disaster for the whole division'. The two Maxims of the two cavalry regiments were employed alongside the horse artillery 'all day, practically in the firing line', performing as the *Times History* put it, 'some of the best work done on a day of failure'.[13]

Next morning Methuen withdrew to the Modder River. There he stayed, licking his wounds for two long months. He has been much blamed for poor generalship in his first four battles. The chief criticisms have always been directed against his frontal attacks and his ineffective reconnaissance. The extreme inadequacy of his mounted arm both in numbers and fitness for service (as regards the horses) accounted partly for the latter. The acute shortage of water during an exceptionally hot season,† added to the fear that his sole line of communication, namely the railway, might be cut behind him, was his chief reason for failing to attempt the turning of the enemy's flanks. He was unfortunate, too, in having before him as examples the recent engagements at Talana Hill and Elandslaagte. The obvious lesson at that time seemed to be that direct attacks carried through unflinchingly were likely to meet with better results than elaborate manoeuvres in face of such mobile opponents. Methuen can hardly be blamed for not foreseeing De la Rey's truly revolutionary change of tactics. Above all, though, he would have needed a far more numerous and much fitter mounted element to provide the extended reconnaissance, screening and mobility necessary for wide flanking movements. Concomitant with this need, a far greater supply of forage and water would have been essential.‡ As it was, his thousand or so horsemen were barely sufficient for minimal screening purposes. There were none left for threatening the enemy's rear,

---

* 'Lord Airlie deserves all praise for his unconventional use of his men, and for the gallantry with which he threw both himself and them into the most critical corner of the fight.' (Conan Doyle, 158.)

† As soon as French, who was holding the enemy in front of Colesburg, heard of Methuen's defeat at Magersfontein he offered to send all his cavalry to the Modder River, but this offer was turned down because of 'scarcity of water'. (Maurice, I, 283.)

‡ The large field artillery horses suffered at least as much from short rations as did the cavalry's. Further, the deep, sandy soil in the area was another deterrent to rapid sustained movement.

The force's mule and ox transports were probably only just sufficient to complement the railway's capacity.

speedily seizing advanced positions or, as has been shown, for effective pursuit.

The first three of Methuen's battles well illustrated the dangers of small numbers of mounted men attempting to pursue superior numbers of retreating but unbroken mounted infantry (which is what the burghers in effect were). After Graspan, for instance, a small detachment of the 9th succeeded in getting across the line of retreat of a large body of retreating Boers, some six miles in rear of the battlefield, when these

> 'suddenly turned inwards and made a spirited and at that stage of the war,' as the *Times History* puts it, 'most unusual attempt to ride down the Lancers in the open, an attempt only frustrated by the coolness and gallantry of the mounted infantry and New South Wales Lancers, who occupied a fold in the ground on the line of retreat, and poured a heavy fire into the advancing Boers.'[14]

It was all very well for Lord Roberts to say, as he had during the 1899 manoeuvres in Ireland earlier in the year, that 'under the existing conditions of war, which render a frontal attack over open ground impossible, reconnaissance is, perhaps, the most important of the many important duties that devolve upon commanders.'[15] This postulated a large mobile force and adequate maps. Poor Methuen had neither. Instead he was provided with an enormously ponderous mass of slow-moving infantry and field guns and only primitive apologies for maps.

* * *

Even more poorly equipped with mobile troops was Lieutenant-General Sir William Forbes Gatacre. Buller gave him the task of holding the rather half-hearted Boer invasion of north central Cape Colony. For this task his mounted force consisted of 300 mounted infantry and some local volunteers. With a small infantry force and a few field guns he attacked the enemy at Stormberg Junction on 10 December after a night march. Due to extraordinary misfortune compounded by extreme mismanagement he contrived to lose a third of his force, mostly taken prisoner. The excellent behaviour of the mounted infantry during the retreat proved the one redeeming feature of an otherwise lamentable failure.[16]

*   *   *

By this date the first of the overseas colonial troops had arrived at Cape Town. These, the earliest units of the Canadian and Australian contingents, had left for the front on 1 December. Almost two-fifths of all the British mounted troops employed in the war were colonial. The majority were, of course, South African units, but the other colonies offered contingents right from the very start. Canada, Australia and New Zealand provided just under 20,000 mounted troops (not including those who arrived as the war was ending).* As early as 13 October, 1899, the Canadian Government had offered 1,000 volunteers, and the first Australian contingent actually sailed for the seat of war on the day of Talana Hill (20 October). From the Australian colonies one out of every fifty men of fighting age volunteered for service in the war.

Virtually all the contingents' men were enlisted for one year's service. When the time came for them to go home the conflict, as will be shewn, was at its height and the need for mounted troops greater than ever. In an effort to get officers and men to re-engage, Kitchener (then in chief command) sent Birdwood, his Military Secretary (see p. 72) to Cape Town where the Australasian contingents were assembling for re-embarkation. He interviewed all the commanding officers and spoke to most of the men. He was able to report that 'quite a number re-engaged for a further year.' Fresh contingents never failed to take the place of those which were time-expired, but the time lag, the disruption and the training of the new units were all conducive to inefficiency.[17]

* Canada, 2,273; New South Wales, 5,291; Queensland, 2,242; Victoria, 3,182; South Australia, 1,162; Western Australia, 982; Tasmania, 617; New Zealand, 4,172. (Extracted from Amery, V, 607–11.)

7

'In sporting circles, there was a rush to abandon the fox and pursue the Boer.'

THOMAS PAKENHAM, The Boer War

'I never detected any particular aptitude for active service in old yeomen. The yeomanry training has not usually hitherto been of so severe a character as to resemble real warfare in any degree. The yeomanry, too, are cavalry armed with carbine and sword; the Imperial Yeomanry were mounted infantry with rifle and bayonet, so that it was a positive advantage not to be acquainted with the cavalry drill and its differing words of command.'

TROOPER THE HON SIDNEY PEEL, 40th
(Oxfordshire) Company, 10th Battalion,
Imperial Yeomanry

'I would rather command a regiment of yeomanry any day. They haven't had the common sense crushed out of them.'

'A distinguished cavalry officer,'
quoted by Trooper Peel

'Of course the life we had was a very dull, dragging one, with constant exposure and very great hardship, and men who had a certain amount of comfort at home, I think, felt it more than the Regular trained soldier who has lived a much harder life.'

LORD CHESHAM, Inspector-General of
Imperial Yeomanry

'Then hey to boot & horse, lads,
And to the front away!
"Young Bloods" must win their spurs, lads,
And "laurels" while they may.'

Imperial Yeomanry Song by LADY GLOVER,
1900

'It is good fun to see the Imperial Yeomanry ride, as they fall off at the rate of one a minute.'

An Australian Bushman[1]

*Boer War: raising of Imperial Yeomanry, 1899–1900, 1901:
1st, 2nd and 3rd contingents – Paget's Horse – Duke of Cambridge's
Own – Sharpshooters – Roughriders – Lock's Horse – Lovat's
Scouts*

One of the immediate consequences of the news of 'Black Week' was the formation of the Imperial Yeomanry.* The day after Colenso Buller telegraphed the War Office: 'Would it be possible for you to raise 8,000 irregulars in England? They should be equipped as mounted infantry, be able to shoot as well as possible and ride decently.'[2] As early as the beginning of October Honorary Colonel Alfred George Lucas, a wealthy businessman who commanded the Loyal Suffolk Hussars Yeomanry, had suggested to the War Office that the Yeomanry should be used in some way in the coming war. At that time and later he was told that there was no intention of doing so. Now, in response to Buller's plea, George Wyndham, the Parliamentary Under-Secretary at the War Office, reopened the question. 'The "Imperial Yeomanry",' he wrote to his mother on 20 December, 'is my child. I invented it after lunch on Sunday and it is already a fine banting. To bring it to birth has been a business.' Three days later he was describing it as 'the finest and most striking creation of all this storm and stress'.[3] He set up a committee of 'influential and patriotic gentlemen' which was constituted by an Army Order on 4 January. Its leading lights were Lucas, Colonel Lord Chesham of the Royal Bucks Hussars (who from 1901 became Inspector-General of Imperial Yeomanry) and Lieutenant-Colonel

---

* In late December, 1900, a War Office Committee was convened to report on the Organization, Arms and Equipment of the Yeomanry Force. Six yeomanry officers (and Lord Dundonald as the sole representative of the regular cavalry) reported on 2 January, 1900. One of the yeomanry officers and Lord Dundonald submitted a minority report in which they said that

'it would not be possible to train Yeomanry in the limited time available so as to be proficient both in the use of the *arme blanche* and the rifle, and as proficiency in rifle shooting is of paramount importance for such a force as the Yeomanry, any temporizing with the *arme blanche* would render the force less efficient for practical purposes. We therefore consider that the word "Cavalry" [the majority had recommended the title "Yeomanry Cavalry"] should be omitted from the title, and the force to be known as "Imperial Yeomanry".'

The minority's recommendation was accepted. (Harris Committee, Cd 466; Dundonald, 180.)

After the war, the title 'Imperial Yeomanry' was retained until 1908.

Viscount Valentia of the Oxfordshire Yeomanry. These and others were personal friends of Wyndham: 'men of affairs, and as Masters of Foxhounds, they are in touch with the young riding farmers and horse-masters of this country'.* Wyndham saw the raising of the Imperial Yeomanry as a 'singular opportunity' to revolutionize the existing Yeomanry, many of the best officers of which regarded their service as a 'farce' and a 'sham'.† Though the men were of a higher calibre than those recruited for the regular army, the Yeomanry was 'still too largely a theatrical reminiscence of the cavalry which fought in the Crimea'. Field-Marshal Viscount Wolseley thought the Imperial Yeomanry would be of 'very little use in the field'. He told the Marquess of Lansdowne, Secretary of War, that to go 'into the highways and byways' to pick up civilians 'quite regardless of whether they have learnt the rudiments of discipline' was a 'dangerous experiment'. To this Lansdowne retorted, 'The Boers are not, I suppose, very highly drilled or disciplined.'[4]

The organization which was set up resembled nothing so much as an amateur small-scale War Office. At the beginning, everything (even for a short period the engaging of sea transports) was effected by the committee, with the result that the provision of equipment

* The Yeomanry Committee consisted of Lucas (general supervision); Honorary Lieutenant-Colonel Ernest William Beckett, MP (later 2nd Lord Grimthorpe), Yorkshire Hussars Yeomanry (finance); Lord Valentia (enrolment and establishment); Colonel Thomas St Quintin, who had served with the 10th Hussars in the Second Afghan War, and Honorary Colonel the Earl of Lonsdale of the Westmoreland and Cumberland Yeomanry (remounts and saddlery); Captain the Hon. Walter Lewis Bagot, who had served with Kitchener in the Sudan, 1898, who soon became Deputy Assistant Adjutant General of the Imperial Yeomanry and who after the war settled in South Africa, becoming General Manager of the Victoria Falls and Transvaal Power Company Ltd (clothing and equipment) and Colonel Lord Harris of the Royal East Kent Yeomanry (transport and shipping), the famous cricketer who had been Under-Secretary of State for War, 1886–9 and Governor of Bombay, 1890–5, who in 1901 became Assistant Adjutant General of the Imperial Yeomanry and who died, aged eighty-one, in 1932. Others who in due course succeeded those who had gone to South Africa were Colonel Hon. (later Sir), Henry Crichton of the Hampshire Yeomanry Carabiniers, who had joined the 10th Hussars in 1868, commanded the 21st Hussars, 1874–84 and died aged eighty-eight in 1922, and Major Sir Robert Alexander Baillie, Bt, who was soon to command the Australian Squadron ('The King's Colonials'), Imperial Yeomanry.

† In the last dozen years the numbers of men in the Yeomanry had declined from 14,400 to 11,800. This was during a period when the population of the United Kingdom had risen by over four millions. This absolute and relative decline was in part due to the great agricultural depression. (R.C., I, 70.)

and of horses was undertaken in competition with the Government. At the start only rifles, camp equipment and ammunition were provided by the War Office. A capitation grant of £25, later increased by £10, was allowed for clothing and saddlery for each man.* If he brought a suitable mount, as only some did, he was allowed a further £40. Men under twenty and over thirty-five were excluded and preference was to be given to unmarried men. Their pay was to be at regular cavalry rates. Battalions were to consist of 526 all ranks, including four companies each with a machine-gun section.† The first, 1900, contingent numbered 550 officers and 10,371 other ranks. The professional, or regular, staff which the committee engaged to run the show was largely 'chosen from men of Indian experience – the Indian Staff Corps – and they brought to bear', according to Lucas, 'a very broad and open mind on all questions'. The initial enrolment was arranged through the county Yeomanry centres, except for a few independent units (see below). Though some officers volunteered from the Yeomanry, there were more from the Reserve, the Militia, ex-regulars and ordinary civilians. Early on there was a large number to choose from.

So also was there in the case of the men, many more of whom came forward than were required. Numbers of them were educated men who in due course took over responsible jobs as large areas of South Africa were occupied. After the war some of these 'rose high

* The breeches supplied by the Yeomanry Committee were much superior to those later supplied by the War Office. They were 'of twilled material or velvet cord, provided with two good cross pockets, and hip pocket, and all proved most serviceable'. The Government issue breeches were, according to Private J. B. Craik of the 19th (Edinburgh) Company, 'most unsatisfactory. . . . They were so tight round the thigh as to impede movement and to cause the seams and material to split readily. The stitching was extremely bad and they were prolonged with continuations to the ankle which made them hot and uncomfortable and cramped the leg.'

Private Craik also comments on the ration biscuits of which one pound per man per day was issued. 'These were hard but satisfying and good. They were carefully packed in 40 lb hermetically sealed tin boxes covered with wood (which was most useful for lighting fires). . . . Boer bread was occasionally issued, but was most indigestible.' (Craik, J. B., MS *Journal of Service with 19th Coy, Imperial Yeomanry, 1900–1901*, Appendix. (Catalogue 'The Great Boer War', Oct., 1979 (Wright, W. J. and Lloyd, H. L.).)

† Each company consisted initially of: 1 captain, 4 subalterns, 6 sergeants (including 1 colour sergeant), 1 farrier sergeant, 2 shoeing smiths, 1 saddler, 1 bugler, 115 rank and file, 'to include 6 corporals, 2 cooks, and officers' servants'. (Fitzgibbon, 6.)

in the civil administration of the Orange River Colony and Trans-vaal.' Colonel the Earl of Scarbrough, of the Yorkshire Yeomanry Dragoons, noted that of 450 men he raised for the first contingent, $12\frac{1}{2}\%$ were farmers, $9\frac{1}{4}\%$ grooms, 9% clerks, 8% 'engineers', 4% butchers, $2\frac{1}{2}\%$ shoeing smiths, 4% 'of no occupation'. There were also among the forty-eight occupations represented, a few 'travel-lers', drapers and labourers. Colonel John Palmer Brabazon (see Vol III, p. 331), who took overall command of the Imperial Yeo-manry in South Africa from March to November, 1900 (having been relieved of his command of a brigade in the Cavalry Division), thought the men, though they would not 'have stood for five minutes against regular troops', were 'the bone and the blood and sinew and the intelligence of the country'. He thought them excel-lent fighting material in South Africa because they were 'irregular troops fighting irregular troops; the Boers were yeomanry and there-fore they met on their own platform. There was a large number of gentlemen in the ranks. They were a vastly superior crowd of human beings to the men we have in the [regular] ranks, naturally. They were the men I want to see in our ranks as soldiers, which other countries have.' Winston Churchill, when he first came across them in the field, found them 'excellently mounted on smart, short-docked cobs, which they sat and rode like the sportsmen they mostly were'.[5] The non-commissioned officers who formed the permanent staff of the units of the first contingent were those who were attached to the ordinary Yeomanry from regular cavalry regiments.

The chief inconvenience which troubled the first contingent was the inadequacy of the battalion staffs. For instance, the Adjutant-General's department would not allow for a paymaster, a paymaster-sergeant or for quartermaster-sergeants. Indeed a general weakness of the whole Imperial Yeomanry was, as Major Wyndham Charles Knight of the Indian Staff Corps (see Vol II, pp. 250–1 and Vol III, p. 97), its Chief Staff Officer, told the Royal Commission,

'the difficulty of finding efficient regimental staffs. Generally speaking, from Commandant down to Regimental Sergeant Majors, it has been necessary to draw on the regular army. Where amateurs were given field rank it was frequently impossible to employ them in active operations, owing to their being senior to the Column Commanders, and when they attempted duties of quartermaster and adjutant they generally failed.'

Further, most of the units were sent out, without transport. Not long after arrival in South Africa, numbers of the great magnates and many of the richer and older officers began to trickle homewards to attend to their private or political affairs. 'I forbade them; I refused them leave,' Brabazon complained, 'but then they went to Lord Roberts, and if they had any family interest they got leave.' 'Luckily,' as Knight soon discovered, 'there were in most cases better men in the ranks to take their place.' These, according to Knight, became 'the backbone of the Yeomanry when the officers who had brought out the original contingent went home'. Nevertheless there were some officers 'socially rather above the average of regular officers', who 'showed great keenness and adaptability in the field.' But Major Knight also found that the most difficult of all his tasks was 'the getting rid of the large number of undesirable and incapable officers sent out from England'.

Whatever defects or insufficiencies there were which arose from official parsimony were usually made up for by large amounts of money subscribed from various sources. Chief among these was £80,000 raised through 'the County Funds'. Liberal sums came, too, from business, £50,000 being contributed by Wernher, Beit. In numerous cases, the local magnate, who was usually already in command of the yeomanry regiment of his county, contributed generously towards the equipping and comforts of the Imperial Yeomanry regiments sent to South Africa. The Earl of Harrington, for instance, who was Colonel of the Earl of Chester's Yeomanry Cavalry, and who helped to raise the 21st and 22nd Companies of Imperial Yeomanry, handed to their commanding officers as they left Chester, 'a sovereign for each trooper as pocket money'. The Committee over which he presided bought '250 Burning Glasses to enable troopers to light their pipes without the aid of a match, 250 Field Glasses from Mr Siddall, optician, Chester [the firm is still in the 1980s in business there], and 250 Compasses'. Two of the officers were sons of the Duke of Westminster, the 21st Company, known as 'the Eaton Troop', being largely raised on the Westminster estate. The Earl of Dunraven and Mount-Earl raised and equipped the 18th Battalion of Imperial Yeomanry, known as the Mounted Volunteer Sharpshooters Corps and consisting of four squadrons (67th, 70th, 71st and 75th), one recruited in Edinburgh, the others in London. In both the Cheshire and Sharpshooter units (of the first contingent), only thoroughly good rifle shots were accepted. The standard required for the Imperial Yeomanry generally was fifty points out of eighty-four at ranges of 200 and 500 yards, in both standing and kneeling positions. The Cheshires averaged fifty-four points and the Sharpshooters' pass mark was even higher. The 20th Battalion, known as the Roughriders, was raised by the Earl of Lathom.[6]

There were raised at the same time by private individuals a few special, independent corps affiliated to the central organization. These varied enormously in quality. The finest, probably, was Paget's Horse, known by some as the 'Piccadilly Heroes' and by others as 'Perfectly Harmless', initially 450 strong, raised in the London district by temporary Major George Thomas Cavendish Paget, a grandson of the first Marquess of Anglesey, Wellington's cavalry commander at Waterloo.* According to Lord Chesham the officers and men were of 'a superior class ... as good as any'. Trooper Cosmo Rose-Innes wrote: 'We were a pretty average collection of young men of good social position and public-school education – a gentlemen corps.' One of the worst of the special units, it seems, was The Duke of Cambridge's Own, raised by the Earl of Donoughmore; but its bad reputation applied only to the unit sent out with the second contingent in 1901 (see below). The original unit, a company only, was composed entirely of rich men who had put down a sum of £130 each to find their own horses, outfits and passage to the Cape. Their pay they donated to the Soldiers' Widows and Orphans Fund. For what happened to this company see p. 180 below.

Considerable numbers of the Imperial Yeomanry were from Ireland, where the ordinary yeomanry was virtually non-existent. Trooper Fitzgibbon of the 13th Battalion found his first appearance in uniform in Dublin's streets a 'time of trial. ... Whereas, in Lon-

* One of his very 'gentlemanly' troopers, Cosmo Rose-Innes, described Major Paget in the field thus:

'Unquestionably at home in the dining-rooms and smoking-rooms of Pall Mall, his portly frame could be seen any day in camp, bending over a torn garment, with busy fingers repairing a rent, or laboriously digging the thread at the eye of the needle. No length of march seemed to weary his frame, no stress of weather to affect his serenity. Equally unaffected by a storm of hail or a hail of bullets, the luxury of drawing-room and the langour of St James's could not conceal the traveller, soldier and man. I saw the smiling indifference with which he was wounded near Elands River, and heard him chaffingly rebuke an orderly for drawing the fire upon his post. He was wounded again at Lichtenberg.' (Rose-Innes, 60.)

Paget had seen service in the Russo-Turkish War, 1877–8, the Zulu War, 1879 and the Greco-Turkish campaign of 1912. He died aged eighty-six in 1939. He seems never to have been a regular soldier.

don, khaki served for the wearer as a passport to every theatre and place of amusement, in Dublin the uniform of active service was too frequently greeted with hooting and muttered cries of "Robber!" '. The 14th Company of the Imperial Yeomanry wore the initials 'N.H.D.C.I.Y.' (Northumberland Hussars and Durham Company, Imperial Yeomanry) on their shoulder-straps. This caused endless amusement 'amongst the Tommies at Kimberley, who very aptly', according to one of the yeomen, 'translated the lettering into "No Home, Dirty Clothes, for 1 Year".'[7]

There were a few other units raised by private persons at this time. Though not affiliated to the Imperial Yeomanry, they were organized on almost the same basis. Among them was Lord Loch's Horse, composed chiefly of men with previous experience in southern Africa. Another was Lovat's Scouts of which three successive contingents were sent out. The class of men from which Lord Lovat chiefly raised his units was that of Scottish ghillies and stalkers – 'men thoroughly trained in the use of the telescope'. They performed much good service throughout the war, being used 'in the main for advanced guard and scouting work'.[8]

The first contingent of Imperial Yeomanry sailed from home between 27 January and 14 April, 1900. In the following month the highly amateur, very British organization which had produced a private army within the public one was taken over by the War Office and the committee was dissolved. All the units henceforth were absorbed into the general system. One of the chief advantages of this was the cessation of competition for remounts and of the confusion which was undoubtedly caused by rival purchasing commissions and varying prices. There was much criticism at the time directed against the supposed extravagance of the Imperial Yeomanry's purchasing commission in Austro-Hungary (see p. 504). But Lucas countered by saying that the 3,800 bought there were of a much higher quality than those bought by the Remount Department and that therefore the extra money paid for them was in fact an economy. Lord Chesham could not say the same for the horse-buying at home. 'We had various people buying all over the country. There were Yeomanry Committees and Colonels of regiments, generally rather buying against the Regular Remount Office, which, of course, put the price up.' Lucas was very proud that for 10,000 men* there were produced 13,000 horses. But the

* The number actually sent out was nearer 9,000. (Maurice, IV, 34.)

resulting multiplication and duplication in South Africa of remount officers and depots, and such questions as to whether Imperial Yeomanry remounts were to be available for general purposes and *vice versa*, were obvious evils created by the parallel arrangements.[9]

The first contingent was fortunate in that most of its units and, more important, its horses, had a certain amount of time to get themselves organized and acclimatized before being thrown into battle. Their arrival more or less coincided with that period after the Boer surrender at Paardeberg (see p. 142) when the pressure for reinforcements was temporarily lifted. The time thus given for training in South Africa proved invaluable. Nevertheless, Trooper the Hon. Sidney Peel of the 40th (Oxfordshire) Company, 10th Battalion, states that 'most of us never discharged the rifles we carried in the field, until we fired them at the enemy'.* On arrival each unit was sent to Maitland camp, near Cape Town, for as much training as possible. Units were often put to continue their training along the line of communications. 'It was impossible,' reported Kitchener, 'at first to put into the field a large number of new Yeomanry recruits, many of whom were unable to either ride or shoot.' Twenty battalions were formed, the first six of which, under Brabazon, left to join Roberts's main army on 29 April, 1900. 1,000 men were designated for the Rhodesian Field Force. Of the remainder, four battalions, under the Earl of Erroll, were assigned to the Orange Free State, four, under Lord Chesham, to Kimberley, one to Lieutenant-General Sir Charles Warren's force in Griqualand and two to Beira. Three stayed in Cape Colony.[10]

The terms of service of the Imperial Yeomanry were for one year or the duration of the war.† When these were fixed it was generally supposed that the war would be over within twelve months. When this proved to be very far from the case there was great pressure

* Peel also gives examples of the ridiculous peacetime practices which were insisted upon during training. Typical was the order given to strike tents so as to get them into straight lines: 'Sergeant-Major,' he protested, 'don't you know that this kind of thing is the ruin of the army?' To which he received the reply: 'Do you think I've been in the army all my life without finding that out? But you must do it all the same.' (Peel, 29.)

† When the war was over, some of the first Imperial yeomen to reach home for discharge insisted that, although they had served for less than a year, they should be paid for a *whole* year, stating, as Haig put it, 'that they were enlisted to serve one year or to the end of the War!' Consequently an order was speedily promulgated to delay the repatriation of the remainder till they signed a new agreement! (*Haig*, 31 Aug., 1902, 289.)

from both officers and men to be allowed to go home after a year's service. There was even some legal doubt as to whether they could be forced to serve beyond that period. 'They had had a very hard time of it,' Lucas told the Royal Commission, 'and a large number of them were men of business and they wanted to come home.' After May, 1900, the War Office disallowed recruiting for the first contingent. Therefore no drafts arrived to replace casualties, which were calculated at between 20% and 30% from all causes. The consequence was that a second contingent had to be hurriedly raised at the worst man-power crisis of the war when 'the spur and incentive to patriotic feeling and action of 1900 was largely absent'.

Lucas and two other officers were appointed on 15 January, 1901, to raise the second contingent and given little more than two months in which to do it. Lord Kitchener and Lord Chesham decided that what came to be known as the 'New Yeomanry' must be trained exclusively in South Africa. 'Therefore,' said Lucas, 'these men were simply raised by us and they were sent down to Aldershot and practically shipped off as fast as transports could be found for them. ... They were simply medically examined and put through a riding and shooting test.' In fact, the exigencies of the war made it impossible in most cases for even a modicum of training to take place at the Imperial Yeomanry base at Elandsfontein – two months had been the original plan. Instead nearly all were 'drafted away to the various columns within a few days of arrival'. One battalion, three days after arriving at Elandsfontein, was sent to Standerton 'where', its commanding officer reported, 'our horses were served out, and I had two regimental drills before we went straight into the field, doing the advance work of the column. That was all the training my regiment had.'[11]*

The second contingent was 17,000 strong. The greatest difficulty experienced in its formation was the finding of officers. About 500 had to be appointed 'at the rate of three 2nd Lieutenants per 110 men'. On top of that one captain and one lieutenant had to be found for the same number. The War Office limited the field by denying selection from the embodied Militia and, in effect, from the remaining officers of the Reserve. Very few Yeomanry officers were left 'as most of those wishing to serve had gone out with the first force'.

* There was much confusion as to whether there were battalions or regiments, companies or squadrons in the Imperial Yeomanry. Some official papers speak of battalions with squadrons! Individual commanding officers probably adopted whatever titles they preferred.

Socially, therefore, the New Yeomanry's officers were much inferior to those of the first contingent. The chief sources were the un-embodied Militia battalions and the Volunteers, none of whose officers was likely to know much about horsemanship or horse-mastership. Another source was those other ranks of the first contingent and of other irregular units who had come home and were prepared to return to the seat of war if dignified by commissions. Lucas's committee made the mistake of advertising for these: men who had 'previous South African experience during the War'. The result, according to Knight, 'was, as seen in South Africa, startling. Some had never ridden, some had never been in decent society before. . . . Many were physically unfit. . . . It was necessary to get rid of over 100 of these officers. . . . In one week's *London Gazette* over twenty resigned or were dismissed. . . . Their ideas on money matters were so irregular that it became necessary for the Field Force canteen to refuse to cash Yeomanry officers' cheques.' 'I see with disgust,' declared the commanding officer of one of the original squadrons, 'that three of my most inefficient privates have been given commissions in the Yeomanry.' One of them was unable to hold his water when he thought he saw a Boer and another had fits. Knight told of one officer who had arrived drunk with his draft. He claimed to have served as a saddler sergeant with the Imperial Light Horse, having been a saddler in the 16th Lancers. His commanding officer now reported on him as 'an impertinent, incompetent coward'. To this the man replied, 'Well, he didn't ought to have said that.' 'We had one man,' Knight told the Royal Comission, 'who was a Maltese. The only thing we were ever able to find out he could do was to play the piano. He refused to get on a horse at all. He is now taking money at the door at one of the principal hotels in Pretoria.' Numbers of the officers unquestionably came out so as to get a free passage to South Africa, believing that the war was about to finish.[12]

The men of the second contingent, on the other hand, though not such good material as those of the first, were still, generally speaking, of a higher quality than the ordinary regular recruit.*

---

* Their terms of enlistment were altered. The most important difference was that a trooper's pay was raised from the ordinary cavalry pay of 1s 3d a day which men of the first contingent had received to 5s a day – the same as for most of the Colonials. The men were mostly 'mechanics and workmen, who, owing to slackness of labour, thought,' according to Colonel Lucas, 'it was a good opportunity to earn 5s a day. There was no doubt that was a great inducement, and they

There were notorious exceptions. Those picked up in Leicester and Reading, for instance, were said to be largely rascals. The worst of all were those enrolled in London by the Duke of Cambridge's Own (see above). Many of these were men rejected by others. The Sharpshooters, for instance, also recruiting in London, out of 3,762 applicants rejected 2,557. Most of these were at once snapped up for the Duke of Cambridge's Own, although 707 had failed the medical test, 373 the shooting test and 268 the riding test, the remaining 1,209 being so obviously unsuitable that they had not even been tested! More than 1,000 men of the New Yeomanry had to be sent home almost as soon as they landed. 'A large number could neither ride nor shoot in spite of having passed tests in both in England.' Something like 75% had never, said Lord Chesham,

'been on a horse before they passed the test . . . and about 25% had ridden very little. As an instance I can mention one man who was going on rather a dangerous trek to Rustenburg from Elandsfontein. The Squadron leader told me that none of them could ride, but he was perhaps one of the worst, because he was found with his left foot on his off stirrup trying to get on his horse, and a very good Canadian Scout with that contingent made the remark: "I am certain of one thing, the Boers in this part of the world are not hungry or they would have taken all of us long ago" – they were escorting a convoy!'

The story is told of a commanding officer who asked a New Yeomanry man who had been instructed that he was to be 'No. 2 double vedette of No. 3 picket', 'What are you?' He received the

---

also wanted to go out to South Africa with the idea of settling there. These men,' he told the Royal Commission, 'came forward, but when they were asked to go into an ordinary recruiting station and strip, huddled together with a lot of ordinary recruits who were being brought in by the sergeant, they would not do it, and they walked out. They were of a different class and they would not subject themselves to it.' (Report, *R.C.*, I, 74.)

All notions of county organization were completely lost. 'The men were mixed up at Aldershot and sent out in sections of 110. On board ship there might be six sections, each of which would have in it Leicester, Hampshire and Northumberland men.' Attempts were made when they arrived at the central depot at Elandsfontein to sort them out, but these were seldom successful. The second contingent, even more than the first, was employed 'as a mass of mounted troops of a plastic character, who might be distributed by squadrons in any way that appeared to be most convenient.' (Report, *R.C.*, I, 75.)

reply, 'I'm Oirish.' 'And who,' remarked the officer, 'could doubt it?!'

The sore backs, to say nothing of the awful general wastage of horses, incurred in teaching both contingents (but particularly the second) in the field are ghastly to contemplate. The horse question for the Imperial Yeomanry was not improved by the fact that initially its veterinary service was on a regimental basis. This obsolete system which had long ago been abolished in the regular army (see Vol III, p. 116), though workable in peacetime, had been proved a complete failure in war over and over again. Further, no provision was made for a single administrative veterinary officer. Each unit at first engaged its own veterinary officer on contract and he was supposed to be a qualified practitioner, but since the competition for them was so great either unqualified men were employed or none at all.[13]

Like the officers, the men of the second contingent were only allowed to be recruited from limited sources. This meant that the majority were civilians. Out of a total of 958 obtained in Yorkshire, for instance, only sixty-seven were Yeomen, while 243 were Volunteers and the rest civilians.[14]

As with all large organizations, some of the New Yeomanry were better than others. 'Can you enlighten me,' wrote Major Cecil Henry de Rougemont, commanding the 5th Battalion, on 1 October, 1901, 'as to why everyone crabs the New Yeomanry? I consider they are extremely good, and brave as lions. They have been highly tried, having to be alongside cavalry regiments doing the same work.' Major Percy Sykes of the 2nd Dragoon Guards, in command of the Montgomery Imperial Yeomanry and other Welsh companies, reported that in one minor action, in September, 1901, they did 'splendidly', while Brevet Lieutenant-Colonel William Bernard Hickie, who was commanding a mobile column in the Transvaal, wrote home on 16 September:

'I see that they have been asking questions in the House about the New Yeomanry. . . . The 103rd and 107th Companies have been with me now for nearly five months. . . . I would not change these two companies for any equal number of men from any corps in South Africa. The officers are excellent and the men are A1. . . . The men have improved wonderfully in physique, their morale is excellent and their self-confidence enormous. They scout well . . . and they look after their horses excellently.'[15]

For the third contingent of 7,000 men,* known as 'the 1902 Yeomanry', which was raised between September, 1901, and January, 1902, camps of instruction had been formed at Aldershot, in Edinburgh and on the Curragh where up to five months' instruction was given before embarkation. However, by the time they reached the seat of war, it was over.[16]

* * *

As happened with so many of the hastily formed mounted units, those of the second (like the first) contingent of the Imperial Yeomanry were not only often used piecemeal as each crisis dictated, but almost invariably 'the regiments were not composed of the original squadrons that started from England. . . . They were made up from four companies from four different regiments, and so sent to serve as the mounted troops of a brigade or column – a system,' as Knight pointed out, 'which I know all the Brigadiers found great fault with.' Since even when the regiments left home they were generally made up of single squadrons from four different Yeomanry regiments, any hope of *esprit de corps* or of reaping the advantages of officers and men being well acquainted with each other had to be foregone.[17]

The tactical uses of the Imperial Yeomanry varied enormously. Like the regular cavalry and the mounted infantry, as often as not the units were worked rather as mounted rifles, which can be described perhaps as something between the two. On other occasions they were employed like cavalry proper or as mounted infantry. French told Lord Chesham that 'he was perfectly certain that on several occasions if we had stuck to our swords and lances,† our men would not have been ridden down by the Boers with their rifles.' This may, or, more likely, may not have been true, but as Lord Scarbrough pointed out, it was anyway quite impossible to teach a yeoman, 'with the short training he has . . . the effective use of a sword or lance *and* the rifle too'. Even with firearms all were

---

* The total of all ranks of the Imperial Yeomanry who landed in South Africa was 35,625. The total of the auxiliary forces serving in the theatre of war was 101,256: of the Militia, 45,566; City Imperial Volunteers, 1,726; Service Companies, 16,891; Volunteer Artillery, 243, and Volunteer Engineers, 1,205. (Turner, Maj.-General Sir Alfred E. Turner *Sixty Years of a Soldier's Life*, 1912, 305.)

† For their removal, see p. 236.

agreed that the yeomen with few exceptions were very indifferent shots and 'utterly ignorant of judging distances, both officers and men'. In this skill they were given no training at all.* One senior vet thought that the Imperial Yeomanry of 1901, the second contingent, were 'in many cases an ordnance and remount depot for the enemy'. He was, alas, not far wrong. 'These Yeomen are useless,' wrote Major Allenby (see p. 138) in October. 'After being some months in the field, they learn a bit; but by the time they are of any use, they have probably been captured two or three times; presenting the Boers, on each occasion, with a horse, rifle and 150 rounds of ammunition per man.' As late as March, 1902, Haig, who incident-ally despised the leadership qualities of Lord Chesham, repeatedly noticed that 'whenever the Boers hear of a column of Yeomanry being by itself, it is like a View Halloo to the pack and they all rush in to have a worry at it – and in many cases their recklessness has been justified by results.' Trooper A. H. C. Waine of the 3rd New South Wales Mounted Rifles, wrote home that the Imperial Yeomen were 'called de Wet's Own'.

The establishments of Imperial Yeomanry units were especially hard to keep up after a year or more in South Africa. The 20th Company, for instance, according to Captain Gilmour, writing in early 1901,

'left Cupar as fine a body of men in health and proficiency as any yeomanry or indeed any troops. Of the five original officers one is dead, one wounded, two gone home. I am the only officer left, one officer added was killed. Now we have another added, so we are two officers. Of the 116 men seventy-four are now away, killed, died of disease, in hospital out here or invalided home, or have got civil employment. The list of sick is a heavy

* Some of the squadrons had a couple of Colt machine guns attached to them. A gentleman-trooper of the 13th (Irish) Battalion describes how these 'little mountain guns', as he called them, were considered in 1900:
'Known as Colt tape-guns, they carried the same cartridge as our rifles, but, owing to their greater calibre, possessed a range a thousand yards longer. They were fed by a long tape containing at a time 500 rounds, and were capable of discharging automatically a rapid hail of bullets, one after another, upon the same objective. Each gun was served by a hand brought out from Colt's Gun Factory, and the rapid "pop-pop-pop-pop-pop" of these little machines did much to strengthen our defence [at Lindley, May, 1900 (see p. 178) where one Colt jammed], lending as it did to our side a support as moral as it was effective.' (Fitzgibbon, 137.)

one, and we are not sure how many may come back, but not many I fancy.'[18]

*   *   *

One of the earliest engagements in which units of the first contingent of Imperial Yeomanry took part occurred under Lieutenant-General Sir Archibald Hunter north of Kimberley on 5 May, 1900. The action of Rooidam was a rare example of good co-operation between infantry, artillery and the mounted troops. Hunter's mobile troops consisted of the Northumberland Hussars and the Yorkshire Dragoons. Both were beautifully mounted on horses which had benefited by an exceptional amount of rest. The Hussars were able to sweep round the Boer left flank, while the Dragoons seized a kraal at the gallop. From this they were able to occupy a kopje enfilading the enemy's main position. Both regiments then pursued the fleeing burghers for three miles along the Fourteen Streams road, taking five prisoners, numerous horses and rifles and a quantity of ammunition. The total Boer casualties were probably over fifty, including a commandant. The British lost seven killed and thirty-eight wounded.[19]

The best-known of all the Imperial Yeomanry's engagements took place at Lindley, east of Kroonstad, at the end of May, 1900. It resulted in the surrender of over 400 officers and men of the 13th Battalion to de Wet (see p. 181). Rather more typical was the capture at Groote Zwarte Bergen, after a brief resistance, of a party of fifty Imperial Yeomen in late January, 1901, by the 'rebel' Gideon Scheepers (see p. 207) in Cape Colony. They were marching, almost unbelievably, without scouts or flankers. Scheepers overwhelmed another detachment of seventy-five men of the Imperial Yeomanry and the 5th Lancers at Zeekoegat on 6 April, 1901. A month earlier, when De la Rey invested Lichtenburg, 100 Imperial Yeomen saved their horses by stabling them in the Dutch church. On 24 August, 1901, the 74th (Dublin) Company, Imperial Yeomanry was commanded by Major James Frederick Humby who had been taken prisoner at Lindley and escaped. Together with some of the Northumberland Fusiliers, the company made a heroic and successful defence of a vital convoy at Rooikopjes, fighting, vastly outnumbered, throughout the night. Of forty-three in action, ten were killed, of whom five were officers, and twenty-four were severely wounded.[20]

The second contingent found itself severely tried for the second time since its arrival (the first was at Vlakfontein (see p. 266) in the valley of the Marico River in the first week of May, 1901.) The twenty-nine year old Vecht-General Christoffel Greyling Kemp, reinforced by De la Rey, one of whose chief lieutenants he was, there attacked Methuen's column. The bush was exceedingly thick. This made proper deployment impossible. The Boers poured in their rifle fire from concealed positions with virtual impunity. Further, the ox-transport much impeded speedy escape, while a gun got stuck in a spruit. For four hours the Imperial Yeomanry, most of it composed of Welsh units, fought off Kemp's burghers. It is said that the Boers lost eighteen killed and forty-one prisoners. Methuen lost fifteen killed and thirty wounded.[21]

The most unfortunate of all the engagements of the second contingent took place, entirely dismounted, near Tweefontein in the Orange River Colony on Christmas Day, 1901. As they had so often done before, the Boers – this time under De Wet – climbed the steepest side of a British-held kopje* (in their stockinged feet) and achieved total surprise. They virtually destroyed the 11th Regiment of Imperial Yeomanry, perhaps 400 strong: all men of Kent and Middlesex. Temporarily in command under Methuen was Major F. A. Williams. Discounting the possibility of such an attack at any time, let alone in the dark of early morning, he failed to post sentries at the kopje's base. When the burghers, eventually 1,000 in number, poured in their fire on the sleeping yeomen, something like a third of them 'gave way to panic and fled, half-dressed and in many cases unarmed, to the nearest British camps.'[22] Others stood their ground nobly. The killed and wounded numbered 145 and over 200 prisoners were taken. All the horses were either killed, wounded or captured. The Boers lost fourteen men killed and thirty wounded.[23] 'What the Boers did at Tweefontein, when my mounted men fled,' Methuen told the Royal Commission, 'was to put their rifles under the right arm, pointing straight to the front, and advance, firing shoulder to shoulder ... coming with a steady canter, firing the whole while.'[24]†

The very last action of any importance of the whole war saw some 200 Imperial Yeomen and mounted infantry ambushed at Moolman's Spruit, near Ficksburg in the Orange River Colony, on 20 April, 1902. They lost six killed (including Captain Sir Thomas Fowler, Bt, of the Royal Wiltshire Yeomanry Cavalry), fifteen wounded and twenty-eight taken prisoner.[25]

* Groenkop, since known as 'Christmas Kop' (De Wet, 340).
† For other instances of these Boer tactics see p. 266 et seq.

8

'French took the initiative ... the beginning of
those skilful operations which for nearly three
months were to cover the all-important railway
communication between Cape Town and the
front, to confine the spread of rebellion and drain
away an ever increasing number of Boers from
other parts to the defence of Colesberg.'

*The Times History of the War in
South Africa*

'There's a General of 'orse which is French,
You've 'eard of 'im o' course, Fightin' French,
'E's a daisy, 'e's a brick,
An' 'e's up to every trick,
An' 'e moves amazin' quick,
    Don't yer, French?

'E's so tough and terse,
'E don't want no bloomin' nurse,
An' 'e ain't 'ad one reverse,
    'Ave yer, French?'

A London evening paper

'The one thing required here is "Cavalry"! I
think the country ought to be alive now to the
fact (which we have already pointed out) that we
won't keep up enough of the arm in peace time!'
HAIG to his wife, 26 November, 1899

'The Boers have weakened their other forces in
order to check us here.'
HAIG to his wife, 13 January, 1900[1]

*Boer War: French's campaign before Colesberg, – arrival of 12th
Lancers, 6th Dragoon Guards (Carabiniers), 6th (Inniskilling)
Dragoons, 10th Hussars, Household Cavalry Regiment*

While Buller was stuck at Colenso, Gatacre at Stormberg and
Methuen on the Modder, there seemed to be little to stop the Boers
streaming into the heart of Cape Colony and exciting rebellion as
they went. Had they done this Methuen and Gatacre would certainly
have had to abandon their advanced positions. Five factors prevented this catastrophic situation: the ambivalent attitude of the

'Cape Dutch'; the enlightened self-government policy applied by the British to all colonies fitted for it; the general 'defensive-offensive' attitude of the Boers; the incompetence of their Transvaaler commander, General H. Schoeman, and the comparative energy and efficiency of the combination of French, Haig and (as highly successful intelligence officer) Captain the Hon. Herbert Alexander Lawrence, 17th Lancers.* These three officers arrived at Naauwpoort on 20 November, three days before Belmont, fifteen before Stormberg, sixteen before Magersfontein and eighteen before Colenso.

For the next forty-seven days French held the enemy to the north of Naauwpoort, with a force which at first was miniscule but which even when reinforcements arrived was never superior to the Boers in his front. His initial instructions from Buller were to do his best 'to prepare for a flying column, strength, say, nearly 3,000 men' in readiness for the resumption of the planned advance on Bloemfontein.[2] Over the next few weeks further orders came from the embattled Buller nearly 400 miles to the east: 'Maintain an active defence without running any risks'; 'worry without risk'. These commands French was wholly successful in carrying out. His 'front' extended to about 180 miles of broken country and the only way he could hope to keep the enemy from pouring through was to demonstrate actively against some point which the Boers could not afford to abandon. Thus he would force them to concentrate in its defence until reinforcements made it possible for him to capture it. This place was the town of Colesberg, where, incidentally, Kruger had spent his infancy.

At the beginning French found himself with less than 1,600 men for surveillance of a front of at least thirty miles around that town as well as the protection of his lines of communication right back to Port Elizabeth though later on he was relieved of this responsibility. One and a half battalions of infantry were complemented by a battery of Royal Horse Artillery and a mounted force of twenty-five Cape Police, 200 men of the 2nd Mounted Infantry and some seventy-five

---

* Lawrence (later General the Hon. Sir Herbert) was the son of Lord Lawrence (see Vol II, p.150 et al.), Governor-General of India. He had joined the 17th in 1882. Towards the end of the war he commanded a column formed of ninety men of his regiment and a company of Imperial Yeomanry in the Fraserburgh–Sutherland district. He commanded successively a brigade and two divisions in the Dardanelles campaign and was in charge of the Cape Helles evacuation. In 1916 he was responsible for the victory at Romani in Egypt. In 1917 he took the 66th Division to France and became in January 1918 Haig's Chief of General Staff. He died, aged eighty-two, in 1943.

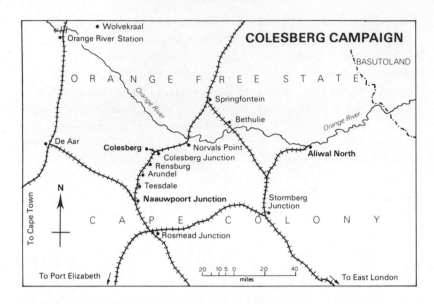

Map 4

regular cavalrymen. These last consisted of a few men left at the
remount depot at Stellenbosch by the 5th Lancers and the 18th
Hussars ('more farmers than soldiers,' according to Haig), and about
forty of the New South Wales Lancers who could 'scarcely be called
efficient cavalry'. The mounted infantry, Haig soon discovered,
'*evidently* know nothing of this kind of reconnaissance work. Moreover they cannot ride.' Their commanding officer reported that in
many cases two years had elapsed since they had last ridden a horse.

> 'Others have never been taught to ride before; some have been
> grooms to infantry officers and are thought therefore not only
> to know about horses, but also to be able to ride them! It is
> murder to send such men in their present condition out to meet
> the Boers. They fall off if the pace is faster than a trot. . . . It
> would be better,' wrote Haig in his diary, 'to call up all reserv-
> ists of the cavalry and send them out here to ride horses of the
> country.'

'This M.I. craze,' he informed his wife, 'is now I trust exploded. . . .
You had better not give these views to Sir Evelyn [Wood], for both
he and Lord Wolseley are the parents of the M.I.' The men of
French's 2nd Mounted Infantry were all specially selected from various regiments, and those who had had previous training at home

had been 'taught in all kinds of ways and on different systems'.[3] Nevertheless they represented at this date the cream of mounted infantry in the British army. This should be borne in mind when considering the enormous increase in the mounting of infantrymen which was to take place over the next two years in South Africa. That they were almost without exception very poor horsemen and horsemasters compared with the Boers is not surprising. Nor does it surprise to find Haig telling the Royal Commission that for the future he

'would not have mounted infantry at all; I think a well trained cavalry ought to supply all the requirements of mounted troops . . . .

'Given the fact that the amount of money to be spent on mounted troops is limited, those mounted troops ought to be cavalry. Cavalry can do everything that mounted infantry can do, and other duties in addition . . . .

'[Another] objection to M.I. is that you take away the picked men from the infantry, so that the residue is not so efficient; moreover it is difficult to get recruits for infantry – cavalry is always up to full strength.'[4]

Haig tells of two incidents which illustrate what tyros so many of the cavalrymen were. On Christmas Eve he was

'surprised to find many officers in a fit of the funks and the whole garrison standing to their horses at 3 a.m. *expecting* an attack. When a Boer patrol of some twenty or thirty men went out for an afternoon's ride, those on outpost duty reported an advance in force, and the whole of our troops turned out! Of course horses cannot be got fit under those conditions!'

Twelve days later

'it was found that during the night the Boers had occupied some kopjes close to the Inniskilling squadron whose duty it was to patrol during the night and protect their flanks. The squadron was at breakfast when the Boers opened fire! Luckily a sensible young gunner officer was at hand.'[5]

French now telegraphed for reinforcements. He must, he said, have at least a few squadrons of cavalry: 'most necessary for reaping fruits of victory in this country'.[6] The first to arrive were two squadrons of the 12th Lancers and a second battery of horse artillery. On 29

November, the 12th, which had only disembarked ten days previously, went out on a reconnaissance which established that Arundel Siding, fifteen miles from Colesberg, had been evacuated by the enemy. 'It was a sort of cavalry exercise,' wrote the Earl of Airlie, its commanding officer, 'with just the off-chance of a "brush".' Airlie, during this time, would, according to French, 'take two or three of his picked lancers and ride straight through the enemy lines, bringing back the most important information. I never knew he was gone until he came back.'[7] But on 1 December the 12th was sent off by rail to the assistance of Methuen. It was replaced on 5 December by three squadrons of the 6th Dragoon Guards (the Carabiniers), under Lieutenant-Colonel Thomas Cole Porter, whom a fellow commanding officer particularly liked: 'He is quiet.' This welcome reinforcement came as a result of Haig's telegraphed plea of 2 December, just after the 12th had left: 'There being now no reliable mounted troops here, General French considers that at least one squadron of cavalry be sent here soon to enable to reconnoitre Colesberg. Enemy might leave any day without our discovering it.'[8] That same day there arrived 200 men in two companies of the New Zealand Mounted Rifles who had left home with their horses on 21 October. Haig found their officers 'superior to the New South Wales lot' and the men 'a sensible lot, dressed like Boers. They were not armed with swords – a pity – so the General made them fix bayonets in their carbines and practice using them as lances. They worked all right.'[9]

On 12 December Haig wrote to his wife 'in our front are some 4,000 to 5,000 Boers about thirteen miles this side of Colesberg. Our task is to bluff them with the few cavalry we have. So far we have been successful in hemming them in, although today they got reinforcement from the East (friend Grobler* from Burghersdorp). If only we had sufficient cavalry with fit horses, we could do anything we liked with the Boers.'[10] The chief reason for the horses' unfitness was shortage of food. The myth that sufficient grazing was always available persisted. Even those animals near the railway never received more than eight to ten pounds of grain and twelve pounds of hay. Those acting away from the railway generally received the same grain ration but only five pounds of hay. As there was never a single day throughout this anxious time when French's mounted troops

---

* General E. R. Grobler, head-commandant of all Free State forces south of the Orange River. At about this time he became ill and was replaced by General Piet De Wet.

A further reinforcement under De la Rey arrived later. (Amery, III, 139.)

did not have by sheer audacity to hold the Boers to their position, the wear and tear on the horses was prodigious. Not until 16 December was there a single veterinary surgeon with French's troops. On that date there opened at Naauwpoort a Field Veterinary Hospital under a major. This had landed complete from India five days earlier and been rushed up the line. On its second day it had to deal with over 100 sick animals. Since its personnel was only sufficient for 'nursing' and dressing, men had to be found for feeding and watering, which further depleted the numbers available for fighting. Eventually kaffirs were engaged for this essential work.[11]*

Two squadrons each of the 6th (Inniskilling) Dragoons and the 10th Hussars arrived on 10 and 11 December. The 'policy of worry' now became easier to pursue. On the 17th French divided his outpost line into two brigades, the first to act to the east of the railway, the second to the west.† On 28 December Major Rimington arrived with some 170 of his Guides (see p. 80). A third squadron of the 6th (Inniskilling) Dragoons appeared on 18 December and the squadron of the 10th Hussars which had been wrecked at sea (see p. 302) turned up three days later. The final substantial reinforcements arrived on 5 January, 1900. These included one and a half squadrons of the Composite Regiment of the Household Cavalry (see p. 113) and a company of 'Colonial M.I.'. In spite of these mounted additions, at no time did French's mounted troops form even half his total strength.

---

* The hospital had been moved so quickly that no provision was made for the rations of the Indian natives, most of whom required special food to be prepared by themselves or their co-religionists. 'Fortunately, the foresight of the officer in charge had caused him to provide himself with ten days' rations for these men, or they would have starved while negotiations on the question were proceeding.' (Smith, 19.)

For more about Veterinary hospitals in the war see p. 334.

† 1st Cavalry Brigade: (Porter)	3 sqns, 6DG 40 N.S.W. Lancers Northern Coy, 2M.I.
2nd Cavalry Brigade: (Lieut-Colonel Ralph Bromfield Willington Fisher)	2 sqns, 6D 2 sqns, 10H Western Coy, 2M.I.
Divisional Troops:	Brigade Division, R.H.A. ('O' and 'R' Batteries) N.Z. Mtd Rifles ½ bn Berkshire Regt

What he achieved with his small mixed force, against one of the four Boer invading columns, three of which had already been victorious, was the successful formation of a screen, both protective and aggressive in character. By resource, stratagem and dash he solved a multitude of minor tactical problems. In each encounter, it should be noted, the rifle and carbine, not the *arme blanche*, governed the tactics. For all the use he made of swords and lances, his cavalry might as well have left them in store. Signalling by heliograph (though there was a chronic shortage of trained men and of instruments), and, later, by telegraph, played an important part in French's success. 'By using Coles Kop (a hill standing some 800 feet above the plain) as a central transmitting station, practically every post and camp was connected together.' By mid-January, 1900, no less than eighteen stations were in touch with each other, including Naauw-poort Junction, some thirty-five miles in rear of the fighting line.[12] The inevitable price which French had to pay was the wearing-out of many of his underfed horses. In view of the results, this was perhaps an acceptable price.*

By the time he was recalled to take over the Cavalry Division for Roberts's great advance, and much of the Colesberg force had been withdrawn to take part in it, the enemy had been sufficiently intimidated not to take immediate advantage of the fact that, under Major-General Ralph Arthur Penrhyn Clements, there remained only a skeleton force. However, in mid-February, at the time of French's flank march, Clements was pressed by large numbers and had to fall back on Arundel. The enemy opposite him had received considerable reinforcements from Natal.[13]

A chief interest of this small-scale Colesberg campaign is that it afforded Haig his first real opportunity to demonstrate what one of his junior officers called 'his extraordinary ability to express in concise form capable of being copied into a notebook on the field important orders for the movement and disposition of troops. In this he was an absolute master.'[14]

* Incidentally, French told the Royal Commission that it would have been quite possible 'somewhere about the middle or the end of January' to have turned the Boers out of Colesberg and driven them across the Orange River, had Roberts not ordered him to avoid all action which might involve many casualties. (*R.C.*, II, 304.)

9

'Nothing but the gravity of the situation and the strongest sense of duty would induce me to offer to place my services at the disposal of the Government.'

LORD ROBERTS to Lord Lansdowne,
8 December, 1899

'I hope we shall manage it all right out at the Cape, but it is a big business badly begun, and the difficulty of unravelling the tangled mess will be very great.'

LORD KITCHENER in a letter from Madeira,
28 December, 1899[1]

Boer War: Roberts and Kitchener arrive — strength of army in South Africa – Colonial Division formed

When the news of Colenso arrived in London the Cabinet decided to send out not only large reinforcements, but also Earl Roberts of Kandahar. He was to take chief command, while Buller remained in Natal. 'Bobs' Roberts, five foot three inches high and sixty-seven years old, had some six years before returned from India where he had made his reputation (see Vol III, p. 263). On the Duke of Cambridge's retirement from the post of Commander-in-Chief he had hoped to succeed him, but his arch rival Wolseley had gained that post and Roberts had been fobbed off instead with the chief command in Ireland. In 1896 he had proposed himself as commander of the abortive expedition to South Africa of that year. Now, in 1899, eight days *before* Colenso, he suggested that he should succeed Buller, whom he claimed to believe had lost his nerve. The day *after* Colenso he cabled London recommending Methuen's withdrawal to the Orange River and stating that Kimberley and Mafeking would have to be abandoned to their fate. He added: 'Ladysmith ought not to have been retained but as White's force especially the Artillery and Cavalry portion would not easily be replaced it should be relieved. ... Meanwhile Buller should be ordered to act strictly on the defensive' until reinforcements arrived.[2] The defeatist attitude of this telegram did not make the Cabinet think again. Perhaps its realism was appreciated. Roberts's appointment went ahead, though neither the Queen nor Wolseley was informed till after it had been made.

Major-General Lord Kitchener of Khartoum, Governor-General of the Sudan and still Sirdar of the Egyptian Army just over a year after his victory at Omdurman (see Vol III, p. 373), was ordered from Cairo to act as Roberts's Chief of Staff. He soon proved himself, with his enormous energy, what Haig soon found him: 'really the *working man* of the Obercommando!' This he had to be, for there was much to be done:

> 'We are getting along a little bit,' he wrote home on 30 January, 1900, 'but we have not a single saddle for love or money (see also p. 367); all our water-bottles are so small as to be useless. It was exactly the same in the Sudan, when I had to fit out the whole of the British troops with water-bottles which they had to pay for. Not a single emergency ration, so the men have to fight all day on empty stomachs. I could go on, but what is the use? I am afraid I rather disgust the old red-tape heads of departments. They are very polite, and after a bit present me with a volume of their printed regulations generally dated about 1870 and intended for Aldershot manoeuvres, and are quite hurt when I do not agree to follow their printed rot.'[3]

Wolseley expected Buller to resign on hearing that he was to have Roberts placed over him. In fact, five days after Colenso he wired home that for some time he had been convinced that it was 'impossible for any one man to direct active military operations in two places distant 1,500 miles from each other.'[4]

Roberts and Kitchener arrived in Cape Town on 10 January. At the end of the month Roberts assessed his actual fighting strength as 100,000 men with 270 guns. Of these nearly 40,000 with 120 guns were in Natal with Buller. Beside these there were certain Colonial corps. The massive reinforcements which were all the time pouring into Cape Town from home contained a smaller proportion of mounted troops than the original force. This was due to the reluctance of the War Office to send out the remainder of the cavalry regiments from home.* The deficiency was meant to be remedied by the creation of numerous units of mounted infantry. This was achieved by the simple process of ordering each infantry battalion to produce a mounted company, a practice which in peacetime had always been pursued in South Africa. In this way some 3,000 mostly

---

* Lansdowne telegraphed to Roberts on 9 January that another cavalry brigade was being mobilized. It could embark at once. 'If, however, it is sent, only the remainder of the Household Cavalry and five line regiments will be left at home.' (Maurice, I, 414.)

inefficient mounted men were furnished at a stroke. These were formed into eight battalions, each of four companies: the fore-runners of many thousands more mounted infantry.[5] How they were provided with a perpetual supply of mounts is shewn on pp. 289, 504. At Enslin the formation of a mounted infantry regiment of recently arrived Australians was attempted, but 'the troops remained spread up and down the line of communication ... so the idea never,' in the words of the historian of the Australian contingents, 'really came to anything.'[6]

The most important body of colonials was formed a few days after Roberts's arrival. It was named the Colonial Division and was commanded by Colonel Brabant whose regiment of horse had been formed earlier (see p. 73). Not until this independent division had been created was 'real activity', according to Amery, 'infused into the movement for ridding Cape Colony of its invaders'.[7] Within the division which eventually became 3,000 strong there were initially eight regiments of varying quality and size. These were the Cape Mounted Rifles, the Kaffrarian Rifles, Driscoll's Scouts,* 1st and 2nd Brabant's Horse, the Border Horse, the Frontier Mounted Rifles and the Queenstown Rifle Volunteers. The division's artillery consisted of eleven guns of different sorts.[8]

The regular cavalry regiments from home which arrived in time to be available to Roberts in his great advance were the 2nd Dragoons (Royal Scots Greys) who had arrived as early as 7 December; the Composite Regiment of Household Cavalry (known as the 'Compos'), made up of one squadron each of the 1st and 2nd Life Guards and one of the Royal Horse Guards,† which, as has been shewn, had

---

* Raised by Captain Daniel Patrick Driscoll, a British resident in Burma. One of Rimington's Scouts described him as 'a thick-set, sinewy man ... of an absolute sooty blackness; hair and moustache coal-black and complexion so scorched and swarthy that ... you might almost take him for a nigger. ... He looks and is a born fighter, but is apt to be over headlong in action.' (Phillipps, 197.)

† Each squadron's other ranks were:
  2 corporal-majors (sergeant-majors)
  10 corporals of horse (sergeants)
  1 farrier
  8 corporals
  3 corporal shoeing-smiths
  158 troopers
  2 trumpeters
The composite regiment's establishment of officers was twenty-nine. It had arrived in the last week of December. (Arthur, II, 698.)

been sent to French in the central district (see p. 109); one squadron of the 14th (King's) Hussars – (the other two had gone to Buller in Natal) – and the 16th (Queen's) Lancers which had sailed from Bombay and arrived in Cape Colony on 21 January, 1900.* How these regiments fared will be recounted later. It is necessary now to return to Buller in Natal.

* The 11th Hussars then in India were first on the roster for overseas service, but an outbreak of glanders put the regiment in quarantine for four months and prevented it going to the theatre of war. However, a dismounted detachment of two officers and 108 other ranks arrived in South Africa in time to be bottled up in Ladysmith. These were distributed among the four cavalry regiments there. Later on, the 11th sent out over 200 drafts chiefly for the 8th Hussars, but thirty of these were volunteers for the South African Constabulary. In the autumn of 1899 the regiment relieved the 21st Lancers in Egypt, where they took over that regiment's horses, many of which still bore marks of sword and spear wounds from the Omdurman charge.

10

'Of the whole British manoeuvre, indeed, the dash by the cavalry upon Potgieter's Drift alone had surprised the enemy.'

The official *History of the War in South Africa*[1]

(i)

Boer War: Natal: Buller's second attempt to relieve Ladysmith – Acton Homes – Spion Kop

After a month of inactivity awaiting reinforcements, Buller, in the second week of January, decided to make a renewed attempt to get through to Ladysmith. He came to the sensible conclusion that the best thing to do was to turn the extreme right of the Boer line of entrenchments. Unfortunately he entrusted the operation to Sir Charles Warren, who had been sent out after Colenso 'under such auspices', as Buller told Lord Dundonald, 'that I did not like to interfere with him'.[2] Warren was a disaster.

With the total failure of Buller's schemes and the catastrophes of Spion Kop and Val Kraanz which followed, this history is not much concerned, since mounted men were scarcely engaged. Only at the

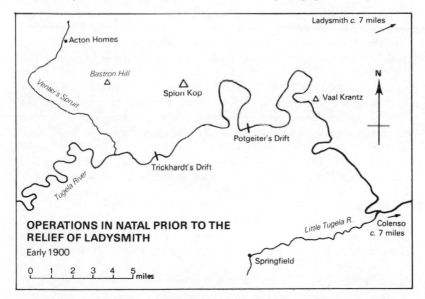

Map 5.   To be consulted in conjunction with Map 1, p. 40

outset did Dundonald's force of about 1,000 men play an important part.* On 10 January he received orders to secure the bridge over the Little Tugela River at Springfield, which he found intact, and then to await Warren's infantry division on the next day.[3]

Dundonald 'determined to exercise some discretion'[4] with regard to his orders. He correctly assumed that the position around Mount Alice on the south bank of the Tugela which the Boers had occupied during the recent dry season would now be evacuated by them, for during the last two days heavy rains had fallen. These would have swollen the river behind them, creating an obstacle to their retreat in case of a reverse. Leaving, therefore, part of his force to defend Springfield Bridge, he seized Mount Alice and on 11 January found the south bank entirely free of the enemy. Six volunteers from the South African Light Horse stripped and swam to the north bank to bring over the Potgieters ferry boat. They came under fire but all survived it. On 17 January the infantry crossed the Tugela at Potgieter's and at Trickhardt's Drifts against little opposition. Dundonald now had under him over 1,500 men, the Royals (412) and two squadrons of the 13th Hussars (260) having been restored to him. His orders from Buller were to protect 'the wheeling force from flank attack' and to 'act according to circumstances'. Consequently, also on the 17th, he crossed by a drift about half a mile west of

---

* A considerable part of the mounted troops was attached, quite unnecessarily, to the infantry brigades. The 1st Royal Dragoons and Thorneycroft's Mounted Infantry were thus denied to Dundonald. So were the 13th Hussars who were employed as divisional cavalry. This left only the Composite Regiment (made up of various parts of mounted units, mostly mounted infantry) (see p. 73), Bethune's Mounted Infantry and the South African Light Horse.

'The Basuto tribe furnished practically all the boys for grooms, etc. They were reliable and brave. One incident will show you how faithful they were: our scouts were advancing and suddenly they were fired upon by concealed Boers. Two or three fell; amongst them a young officer was wounded, and his horse shot dead. His Basuto boy who was in the rear saw what had happened and at once galloped forward his master's second horse which he was riding. His master mounted and returned, but the boy was shot by the enemy in the mouth. I visited him in hospital later on in the day; he had a terrible wound, the whole jaw being smashed to pieces. Had the boy been a British soldier I would certainly have told him that I would recommend him for the V.C.; but I promised the poor boy, instead, some oxen as a present, which in this part of the world is the price of an extra wife to do rough work. He died, however, three days afterwards, cheerful to the end.' (Dundonald, 169–70.) Compare this action of Dundonald's with Scheeper's diary entry quoted in a footnote on p. 207.

Trickhardt's. 'This crossing was by no means pleasant. The current ran strong and the water was up to our saddle flaps. Also the river-bed was uneven. A poor fellow of the 13th Hussars was swept away and drowned.'[5]

Dundonald's idea was 'to try and get to the west of the Boer right flank before it was entrenched, and secure and hold a position commanding the Acton Homes – Ladysmith road. All,' he wrote in his autobiography, 'was going well and I continued my advance, feeling sure that the infantry would be following.' Not only had Warren made certain that the infantry were *not* following, but Dundonald was astounded to receive a message from him saying that as far as he could see 'there are no cavalry whatever round the camp [which was miles in the rear], and nothing to prevent the oxen being swept away. You are to send 500 mounted men at once to be placed round the camp.' Having no alternative but to obey so peremptory an order, even if it was a truly dotty one, Dundonald nevertheless continued his unopposed advance with what was left to him. Having sent back the Royals, as ordered, and posted Thorneycroft's on Venter's Spruit kopjes to protect the infantry's advance, he was left with only about 800 horsemen.[6]

There followed on 18 January a minor action which is notable from its being the first success of any sort to attend the arms of the Relief Column. Dundonald's leading scouts were from the Composite Regiment, led by Major Herman Witsius-Gore Graham, 5th Lancers. Near Acton Homes they saw some 200 burgher reinforcements about to take up position on some low kopjes which commanded the way to this small hamlet. Accounts differ as to what happened next. It seems certain, however, that the Boers, though they had probably seen Dundonald's main body, were completely unaware of the presence of Graham's men. These, keeping themselves invisible behind the undulations of the ground, just managed to gain the kopjes before the Boers. So unsuspicious were the burghers that their scouts rode only a few yards in front of the main body which advanced carelessly in close formation. They were but seventy yards from the British rifles and on the point of falling into the trap set by Graham when some 'excited irregular' let off his rifle prematurely. There followed a general fusillade from both sides, the surprised Boers galloping away as fast as they could go. Some were shot dead, others lost their mounts. These took up a position on a hillock and fought gallantly for nearly an hour. They were eventually forced to surrender by superior numbers when Graham's supports, consisting of more mounted infantry and a squadron of the South African Light Horse, arrived on the scene. The majority of the burghers managed to escape. Twelve were killed, ten wounded and twenty-three made prisoner.* Graham lost only six men, including two wounded.[7]

The moment he heard that his advanced squadrons were engaged, Dundonald asked Warren to return the Royals to him. This in the shape of three squadrons he did (though they were soon withdrawn again), but, misunderstanding Dundonald, he signalled: 'I did not intend you should force on an action,' adding unbelievably next morning: 'Our objective is not Ladysmith. . . . By detaching your cavalry from me you are hampering all my movements and forcing me to alter my plans. . . . I require your mounted men to act as part of my force.' The following day, 19 January, Dundonald was summoned to see Warren who was supervising in person the crossing of his precious oxen at Venter's Spruit. 'I want you close to me,' was virtually all he said when the cavalry commander 'spoke of the importance of the outflanking movement of the Boer right by cavalry, and asked him for all the mounted men possible and some guns. Sir Charles Warren was obdurate,' wrote Dundonald later, 'and insisted on keeping the Royal Dragoons, and also requested that Thorneycroft's Mounted Infantry should be sent to him.'† After this one-sided conversation, Dundonald's transport officer told him that on arrival at Venter's Spruit Warren had asked 'Whose wagons are those?' 'Mounted Brigade, sir.' 'Can't pass,' said Sir Charles. 'If I let them go, Lord Dundonald will try and go on to Ladysmith.' Being 'an old hand', the transport officer managed to slip his wagons across the stream before Warren noticed.[8]

With so diminished a force and being assured that Warren did not intend to support him, Dundonald was, of course, quite unable to exploit the splendid opening which his disobedience had created.

* The estimates of casualties vary widely. Dundonald in a signal to Warren says 'about 20 Boers killed and wounded, 15 prisoners'; the official history says 'some fifty burghers, killed, wounded and captured'; Amery gives a total of forty-five Boer casualties. Dundonald gives the British loss as 'only six, but two of our wounded had ghastly wounds caused by soft-nosed bullets.' The official history gives the British casualties as 'numbering but three'. (Maurice, II, 361, 632; Amery, III, 222; Dundonald, 125.)

† Amery says that the interview was stormy and that Warren 'explained his view of the function of the mounted troops, which was to keep within half a mile of the infantry on both flanks, and between them and the enemy.' (Amery, III, 224.)

Warren, indeed, now decided to call a halt 'for two or three days' and ordered Dundonald to abandon his position and come in closer to him.* On hearing this even Buller became alarmed. From Roberts on 16 January he had received a message which stressed that 'rapidity of movement is everything against an enemy so skilful in strengthening defensive positions.' Warren, alas, was the last man to understand this. Never for a moment did he show the slightest comprehension of the chance of victory which Dundonald's minor success had brought within his grasp. The thought of having to alter his stolid plans appalled him. There can be little doubt that had he pushed his infantry should have attacked the salient which Dundonald's success been turned. He would have got behind the enemy's entrenched positions and there would have been little to stop him relieving Ladysmith. Buller told the Royal Commission that he had been 'dissatisfied with Warren's operations, which seemed to me aimless and irresolute', adding 'Dundonald's movement was a decided success, and should have been supported by artillery, while Warren's infantry should have attacked the salient which Dundonald's success had left exposed.' This was all very well, but it is difficult not to blame Buller for not taking over from Warren at an early stage.[9]

With the awful series of blunders which followed Buller's decision to occupy Spion Kop and its abandonment twenty-four horrible hours after its seizure and the consequent calling off of the whole operation on 25 January we are not concerned, since no mounted action took place. But the subsequent state of Thorneycroft's Mounted Infantry which formed part of the force engaged is well illustrated by Dundonald's description of it 'as it marched away to bivouac. It was a sad sight, half of the horses were led horses with empty saddles, their riders lying dead on Spion Kop, or mangled in hospital.'[10] Significant, too, for the use of regular cavalry in the future was the report of the Royals' commanding officer to Dundonald on 27 January: 'I have been saddled up for the last five days. My horses have not had their backs even looked at, and I have much shoeing to be done. My men are so tired that I have cases brought before me of men asleep on their posts. My horses want hay, or if not that, grazing.'[11] This was the state of the regiment after days of marching and countermarching without being in contact with the enemy!

* On 20 January a dismounted squadron of the South African Light Horse seized Bastron Hill, the Boers on it giving up their advanced trenches with little resistance. (Maurice, II, 368–9.)

'We all joined in a great gallop, never to be
forgotten: a mad gallop into Ladysmith.'
CAPTAIN WILLIAM BIRDWOOD[1]

(ii)

*Boer War: Natal: Buller's third attempt to relieve Ladysmith –
Vaal Kranz – relief of Ladysmith*

The third and penultimate attempt to relieve Ladysmith which involved the occupation and evacuation of Vaal Kranz by the infantry
was less costly than its predecessor but just as futile. The mounted
troops were not engaged. It was followed on the day of its abandonment by Buller's heliograph message to White saying that he intended
to try again, this time by taking Hlangwane.

There followed a fortnight of almost uninterrupted infantry and
artillery fighting, the 'painful prototype of modern warfare', as
Thomas Pakenham has put it, 'squeezing out the Boers, step by step,
hill by hill'. Here was first seen the creeping barrage. Here, for the
first time, the British army endured 'a series of interlocking engagements' spread over a long period.[2] The one-, or at most two-, day
battle had become a thing of the past.* The cavalry and mounted
infantry, formed into two independent brigades, were employed
protecting the army's flanks, a mostly passive role. They took
advantage of their comparative inactivity to feed and rest their
mounts, so that when, on 27 February, the six-hour 'battle of
Pieter's' eventually broke the Boer resistance on the Tugela, they
were in good condition and ready for the pursuit.

But Buller was determined that there should be neither pursuit by
the mounted troops nor harassment by the artillery. 'I watched the

---

* When an action was over and done with in one or two days there was
never a problem about watering and feeding the horses. Now with fighting
spread over fourteen days, there being very little hay available, the horses of
the artillery suffered considerable loss of condition from being unable to leave
their guns for periods long enough to enable them to be regularly watered and
grazed. Though in this instance the cavalry and mounted infantry were in an
exactly opposite situation, in prolonged battles over large areas in the future,
this new problem was to become acute.

Boers for four hours the other day,' wrote the American war correspondent, Richard Harding Davis, 'escaping from the battle of Pieter's and I asked . . . "Why don't you send your cavalry and light artillery and take those wagons?" The staff officer giggled and said, "They might kill us." '3 'It was lucky indeed,' wrote Deneys Reitz whose commando was among the mass of demoralized Boers, 'that the British sent no cavalry in pursuit, for the passages across the [Klip] river were steep and narrow, and there was frightful confusion of men and wagons struggling to get past. . . . Had the British fired a single gun at this surging mob everything on wheels would have fallen into their hands.' 'Instead of this,' wrote a German observer with the Boer forces, 'everything went off smoothly, and one only sees faces as contented as if a battle had been won. The homeward movement appears to be welcome to most of them. They have not yet clearly grasped that the Relief of Ladysmith is bound to ensue tomorrow.'4

The fact is that Buller was resolved that he should not be responsible for any more casualties in his army. He further conceived his task solely as the relief of Ladysmith, not the destruction of the enemy's forces. However hard his defenders may try to excuse him, it is impossible to deny that his attitude in this case is inexcusable. There would certainly have been some tough resistance from individual burghers forming the rearguard, but it was clear to everyone at the time that demoralization had set in. Even if Buller believed that no very large number of Boers could have been killed or made prisoner, he could certainly have captured or destroyed considerable amounts of supplies. To possess an enormous superiority in guns, to have at hand two entirely fresh mounted brigades and not to employ them against an enemy in rout is surely to gravely misunderstand the art of war. That Buller was most unfairly made a scapegoat for the failures of the Natal campaign is a fact. It is very unlikely that any other available general would have managed much better faced with the awful problems set by the terrain, by the particular Boer genius and by the severe limitations of his army's training and of his subordinate generals. But it is clear that he lacked that essential toughness which marks a superior commander, and in no instance did this weakness emerge more clearly than in his failure to pursue and harass his broken foes on 28 February, 1900.*

* On 12 January Roberts had told French that if Buller succeeded in relieving Ladysmith, Joubert's force would then be free, 'and he is almost certain to hurry his men to the south-west in order to try and block our way into the Orange

At first it seems that Buller was going to allow Dundonald and Burn-Murdoch to have their head, but not long after the mounted troops had crossed the pontoon bridge and Burn-Murdoch had got within five or six miles of Ladysmith, he was peremptorily ordered to withdraw behind the line of infantry outposts and to return to Nelthorpe. The most Buller allowed his mounted brigades to do was to find out, as he signalled to White, where the enemy had gone to.

Dundonald seems to have been jumpily cautious, possibly with good reason until he was quite certain that no serious opposition still remained. Hubert Gough, a twenty-nine year old captain in the 16th Lancers (see p. 264), led the advance guard of one squadron each of the Imperial Light Horse and the Natal Carbineers, consisting of about 120 men in all. He 'went to Dundonald and asked leave to ... push patrols into Ladysmith. First he said, yes – then, no – then, yes – in the space of five minutes recalling me to his side to repeat or contradict his orders. At last I escaped,' wrote Gough, 'with permission to proceed.' When the Boer 'Big Tom' opened on the advance guard, Dundonald ordered Gough to retire, but, seeing his way ahead unbarred, the intrepid Captain crumpled up the order, sent back to say that he had received it and went forward. It was now 6.15 p.m. Gough in the failing light set his two squadrons in two parallel columns of half sections so that neither should have the honour of entering the town before the other. Without more ado they galloped into Ladysmith to be greeted with joy by the emaciated forms of those who had withstood a siege lasting 118 days.[5] Meanwhile, during the next thirty-six hours, the Boers, 'dispirited by defeat, encumbered by a huge train of wagons' with only one bridge over the Sunday River by which to escape, were allowed to retreat unmolested. Lieutenant-General the Hon. Neville Gerald Lyttelton,* Buller's best infantry commander, said of him 'few commanders have so wantonly thrown away so great an opportunity'.[6] Even the entraining by the Boers of the heavy seige guns at Modders Spruit railway station was carried on without interruption. Rawlinson believed that 'Buller made a great mistake in stopping his

Free State.' (Maurice, I, 434.) This is exactly what happened. Had Buller pursued and harassed there would have been fewer of them, and more important they would have had fewer supplies.

* Lyttelton joined the Rifle Brigade in 1865 and saw much service in different parts of the world. He was present at Tel-el-Kebir in 1882 and commanded a brigade in the 1898 Nile Expedition. At the end of the war he succeeded Kitchener in chief command in South Africa. From 1904 to 1908, as a General, he was Chief of the General Staff. He died in 1931 aged eighty-six.

cavalry. They might have captured three trains and many prisoners at Modders Spruit.' The last train did not leave there till next day, 1 March, and the railway bridge was blown up as soon as it had crossed.[7]

11

'Even the muddy waters of a sluggish stream
were a blessed sight to the tired men and animals,
withered and worn by the scorching sky and
burning sands of a remorseless South African
day.'

Eye-witness account of the crossing of
De Keil's Drift, 12 February, 1900

'Considering the fearful heat, the absence of all
water for the horses and the enormous weight of
the British cavalry equipment, this march was a
feat of which the cavalry had every reason to be
proud.'

The *Times History*, on the march to the
Modder on 13 February, 1900

'There seemed to be only one thing to be done if
we were to get to Kimberley before the Boers
barred our path, namely charge through the gap.'

HAIG of the 'charge' at Abon's Dam,
15 February, 1900

'It was a magnificent dash – the finest I've ever
seen.'

LIEUTENANT WALTER HOWORTH GREENLY,
13th Lancers, of the Abon's Dam 'charge'.[1]

(i)

Boer War: Roberts's plan for advance on Bloemfontein – forma-
tion and composition of Cavalry Division – the 'charge', Abon's
Dam – relief of Kimberley

'There is a general move going on of the whole Cavalry Division
from Rensburg towards Orange River. Great efforts are made to
keep this move secret. We telegraph about the different parts of the
division as A. B. C., etc.' Thus Haig to his wife from the Mount
Nelson Hotel, Cape Town on 4 February, twenty-five days after
Roberts's arrival and twenty-five days before Buller relieved Ladysmith. The Cavalry Division to which he referred was in fact no
more than a collection of units which, as Haig told the Royal Commission, 'lacked that cohesion which is essential to success against

any organized military force.' As was the case throughout the war 'no organized, well-trained and complete staff took the field with any brigade or division.' For staff jobs officers were usually taken from regiments in the field, while the same applied to non-commissioned officers and men who were required to fill places as clerks, orderlies and servants for divisional and brigade staffs.[2]

The 'general move' to which Haig referred was part of the plan with which Roberts, being now so massively reinforced, hoped to march upon Bloemfontein, the capital of the Orange Free State, and from there upon Pretoria, the capital of the Transvaal, thus ending the war. In the course of preparation, his plan had to be altered as to one important detail. The chief reason for this was that Cecil Rhodes, cooped up in Kimberley and now being bombarded by 'Big Tom', appeared to threaten to make the garrison commander surrender if absolute priority were not accorded to its relief. It was quite untruthfully represented as being on its last legs. The tremendous influence of Rhodes is a thing hard to understand today, but the power of his fabulous riches and as a great builder of empire in the last year of Queen Victoria's reign was more or less accepted as irresistible. At any rate Roberts felt constrained to oblige him. The Commander-in-Chief's object now was to deceive the Boers under General Pieter Arnoldus ('Piet') Cronje (entrenched at Magersfontein opposite Methuen), as to the route he would take. Cronje, very understandably, believed that the British army was incapable of leaving the line of the railway. 'The English,' he is believed to have said, 'do not make turning movements; they never leave the railway, because they cannot march.' At the end of 1899 Buller had written to Roberts: 'There is no such thing as a rapid advance anywhere in South Africa, except by railway.'[3] Roberts was about to prove both men wrong, but, as will appear, at appalling cost in horseflesh.

His plan was to outflank Cronje's Magersfontein position to the east by means of a 'cavalry dash' upon Kimberley, closely followed and supported by three infantry divisions. This large army corps consisting of nearly 26,000 combatants with about a hundred guns*

* Figures vary enormously: totals, including non-combatants, from 37,000 to 33,000, mounted troops from 11,000 to 7,795, infantry from 25,000 to 18,000. The number of artillery pieces varies from 92 to 118. Roberts's despatch of 16 February puts his total force at 45,000 with 118 guns.

Cronje's forces at the very most numbered 11,000 with twenty guns. These numbers include the burghers investing Kimberley. Probably less than 7,500 men were under his immediate control. He was barely a quarter as strong as Roberts. Had all Cronje's men been mounted and available they would just

was to be massed behind Methuen as secretly as possible. The scale of the operation can be gauged by the fact that more than ten miles of sidings had to be constructed in the concentration area. In the meantime, by every possible means, the Boers were to be led to believe first that the plan was to advance by the direct route via the Norval's Pont and Bethulie crossings of the Orange River, and then, when the immense concentration could no longer be concealed, that a frontal attack was to be made on the Magersfontein entrenchments. On the whole the double deception was remarkably successful. Among the deceits practised were fictitious orders, later cancelled by cypher telegrams. The very minimum of officers was let into the secret.

The first troop movements started as early as 28 January, while French was in Cape Town, whence he had been summoned from Rensburg to see Roberts who was rightly very anxious about the expenditure of horses during the Colesberg operations.* On that day the first details from Cape Town started on their journey north-eastwards. A day or two later, as soon as French got back to his headquarters, most of his mounted troops began their transfer to the Modder River Camp. Some went all the way from Naauwpoort by rail, taking nineteen hours, but most, because of the fearful congestion on the railway, had to detrain at Orange River and march the rest of the way.[4] Their place before Colesberg was taken by all sorts of odd, comparatively immobile units. These succeeded in concealing their weakness very successfully. Indeed, by sending to Naauwpoort the 6th Infantry Division as soon as it arrived, by attempting to restore the railway connection with Stormberg and by sending the newly formed Colonial Division (see p. 113) to Gatacre before Stormberg, Roberts succeeded in drawing Boer reinforcements to Colesberg. Seven hundred and fifty of these, in spite of the imminence of Buller's next attack, were brought round from Natal in early February.[5]

---

about have equalled the total of Roberts's mounted troops. It is likely that not much more than a quarter of the burghers were well enough mounted to perform long and rapid marches. A number were without mounts. Cronje's force depended upon heavy ox-transport, just as Roberts's did, but, of course, the requirements of a Boer force were always very much less than those of a British one.

* Two days after he arrived at Cape Town, Roberts had telegraphed to French to 'save the horses as much as possible, for, until we can get hold of some of the regiments now in Ladysmith, yours is almost the only cavalry we have to depend upon.' (Maurice, I, 434.)

French's scratch cavalry division which was to be the first sizeable 'flying column' to be seen during the war, was in fact the largest mounted division that had ever worked together in the history of the British army. What its actual numbers were is in dispute. Haig says that on 15 February the total strength was '4,890 horses including the R[oyal] H[orse] A[rtillery]'. How many of the mounted infantry are comprised in that figure is unknown. He says that French had been promised 8,500 horsemen by 11 February. Certainly nothing like this ever materialized. [See Appendix for details of the force.] From that date till 31 March, a period of forty-eight days, the number of horses which could be put in the field by the cavalry regiments in the three cavalry brigades alone decreased to 840, a horrifying loss of something like 2,000 horses.

The number of horse artillery guns, all 12-pounder breech-loaders, weighing 12-cwt, was forty-two. From overwork around Colesberg or too short a time for acclimatization, combined with continual underfeeding the horses of the division were very far from fit for a gruelling campaign. Further, many of the horses were 'not shod up, the shoes on their feet were too heavy for the country, and one particular type of nail, which represented the bulk of the stock, was so brittle that it was not uncommon for all the nails in one shoe to break at the neck.'[6]

Roberts, probably on French's advice, got rid of two of the cavalry generals. Brabazon was 'said to be too old for real work'. As he was only fifty-seven, what really ruled him out was that he was, as Roberts told Lansdowne, 'too fond of comfort'. He was given the task of organizing and training the Imperial Yeomanry as it arrived in Cape Town (see p. 91). Babington initially commanded one of French's brigades. In the first week of February he seems to have made rather a mess of a considerable demonstration which Roberts ordered to be carried out as part of the deception process in the Koodoesberg area to the west of Methuen's position. At one point he ordered the Household Cavalry to charge, which they did – straight into a wire fence. The brigade lost three officers killed and some sixty other casualties, the Boers being supposed to have lost thirty burghers. Roberts sacked Babington, telling Lansdowne that he was 'so "sticky" that the regiments have lost all their go'. The fact that he was a protégé of Buller's may conceivably have had something to do with the matter.[7]

The country over which the 'dash to Kimberley' was to be made was mostly absolutely flat veld. It was perfect cavalry country.

Water, though, was very scarce. Particularly was this so in February, the hottest month of the year. Rain had not fallen for many weeks. The few wells and dams were therefore very low, but, more vital, grazing prospects were poor indeed. It was the very worst time of year to launch something like 5,000 large English cavalry and artillery horses and 10,000 oxen and 12,000 mules into what was virtually a desert.* But as Haig wrote, 'There was no good waiting, so French decided to push on, as all depended on "surprise".' In what one commanding officer called 'such a glorious little speech' Roberts addressed the division's commanding officers in the evening of 10 February. 'You are to get the greatest chance cavalry has ever had. . . . You must relieve Kimberley if it costs you half your forces,' he said. Kitchener told Haig that if the mission failed 'neither he nor the Field-Marshal could tell what the result in the "Empire" might be!'[8]

Next day the cavalry division marched due southwards, men of Rimington's Guides leading, getting out of sight of the Boers at Magersfontein before daylight. All tents were left standing which helped to fool Cronje. Six days' rations for the men and five for the animals were carried partly on man and horse and partly by the supply column.† The day's march of twenty-two miles took the division to Ramdam, a well-watered farm, forty miles as the crow flies from Kimberley. Here Colonel Ormelie Hannay's mounted infantry brigade was meant to join from near Orange River station. However, as most of his men had never been astride a horse before and they had become engaged with the enemy at Wolvekraal, they were a day late.

On 12 February a twelve-mile march eastwards was to lead to the Waterval and De Kiel's Drifts over the Reit River. An interval of 80 to 100 yards was kept between brigades, which were formed in

---

* Roberts and Kitchener during their month of preparations set in train a revolutionary reorganization of the army's transport arrangements, literally impounding all regimental transport so as to centralize it in transport companies. The system might have been successful had there been sufficient Army Service Corps officers and men to operate it, and assuming that there was time for people to become accustomed to it. These conditions did not pertain. Consequently near chaos often reigned during the next few months. French stood out against the changes and was able to keep his own division's transport safe. Indeed under the new arrangements each cavalry brigade was allotted an extra mule company of forty-nine wagons – probably by mistake. (Amery, III, 353; Maurice, I, 419–20.)

† About 5 % of led horses accompanied the division. (Maurice, II, 12.)
There was no hay ration. (Smith, 31.)

1. 'How the Horses of the 9th Lancers were taken to Africa' (see p. 78)

2. 'A Charge of Lancers, from the Boer point of view' (see p. 57)

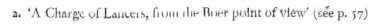

3. 'Ladysmith Garrison: Major E. C. Knox and remnants of the 18th Hussars' (see p. 66)

4. Lord Dundonald's galloping gun-carriage with Maxim gun (see p. 75)

column of regimental masses with 'fifty yards interval between columns', a close order but one which had a wide front and was of considerable length.

> 'We marched at 2 a.m. as long as there was a moon,' wrote Haig. 'Luck and the ground enabled us to get our many odds and ends away from camp in three groups without a hitch. When the moon went down we halted till morning, then pushed on to the Reit river. We threatened it in three places and got across at De Keil's drift with the loss of a few men.'[9]

By noon both the fords had been secured and the whole division began crossing. The idea was that the infantry divisions should follow on the cavalry's tail so as to take over the various river

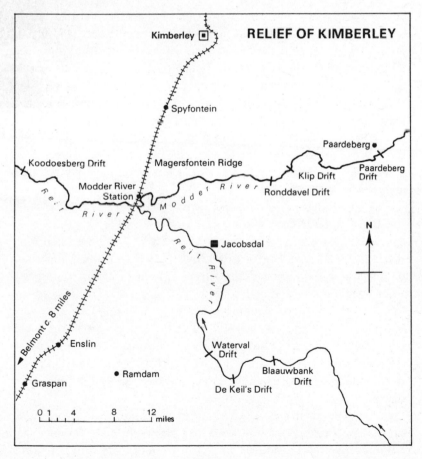

Map 6

crossings, thereby allowing the cavalry to proceed to the next ones. This, however, could not happen until the cavalry supply column came up. Haig tells why on this day it never appeared.

'We left our baggage at Ramdam till we knew whereabouts we could cross. . . . Tucker's [7th Infantry] Division . . . marched about 7 a.m. and he brought on *all* his bullock transport, passing it in front of ours. So that at 8 a.m., when I sent for our transport, it could not move, and did not get away till 5 p.m. . . . We had arranged to keep well back from the river bank [at De Kiel's Drift, "a very steep and bad one"] so as to let the wagons have a clear run; but Tucker's people coming up jostled and crowded till the drift got into an indescribable state of block!'

An eye witness saw 'a medley of wagons' swaying 'backwards and forwards in a lumbering helpless mass of obstructed traffic. Rumblings, creakings, shouts of the coloured team-boys, the cracks of their long whips, and all the noisy confusion of campaigning filled the air with clamour and left the night no peace.' Such appalling chaos was there that most of the cavalry's wagons 'were not seen again till Paardeberg' on 23 February! The most urgently needed supplies had to be drawn by hand, led horses with sacks being sent across the river to draw the rations. This crossing and re-crossing the river meant severe extra work for the horses thus employed. This day the poor animals had only a limited corn ration, no hay and no grazing.[10]

The small amount of resistance which had been met with at the two drifts came from inferior forces under Piet De Wet (not to be confused with his brother, Christiaan). There is reason to suppose that even if *he* had begun to realize what was really happening, Cronje was still convinced that the true point of attack would be a frontal assault on his Magersfontein position. This situation, so fortunate for French's outflanking movement, continued over the next few days. No pursuit was possible on 12 February as men and horses were too exhausted by the heat. Two squadrons of the 10th Hussars managed to go out in search of water, which they failed to find, but they were able, most usefully, to cut the Boer telegraph lines in six places.

Next morning it was 10.30 a.m. before the division could move off, having breakfasted and with two days' supplies for men and horses carried on the saddles. There were twenty-five miles of almost waterless sandy veld to cover before the Ronddavel Drift on the

Modder was reached. The line of march was now almost due north-ward.* 'We took no wagons,' wrote Haig to a friend, 'except four ambulances and a cable cart. The country was open and we advanced in line of brigade masses, and then opened out to squadron columns [line of squadron columns at deploying intervals, the guns between the intervals].' The whole front eventually covered nearly five miles. It must have been a very impressive sight, in spite of the vast clouds of dust.

'We were sniped at from positions on our flanks, and had to detach squadrons to turn them. This was again a very hot day, and several heath fires sprung up and burned our cable! [The wind luckily carried the fires away to the rear. Two horses were nevertheless burned to death.] About 2 o'clock about 1,000 to 2,000 Boers occupied a farm and hill on our right flank, and gave us some little trouble, but we took them in satisfactorily! We left the 1st Brigade to play with Boers and pushed the other two quickly for the Drifts which were about eight miles off.'

When Haig says 'we took them in satisfactorily' he refers to French's ruse whereby he made the enemy think that he was heading for the Klip Kraal Drift, nearly ten miles to the east of Ronddavel Drift. This meant marching part of his force for an hour and a half in the wrong direction, which added to the exhaustion of the horses. In fact the number of Boers thus 'taken in' was very small indeed, but French, having lost touch the evening before, was not to know this. By 5 p.m. the brigades were over the Modder. Haig proudly stated that 'the cavalry arrived alone at the drifts, the R.H.A. could not keep up.† The 12th Lancers,' he added, 'attacked Klip Drift, dismounted and pushed across and held the kopjes beyond . . . . The Boers were completely surprised. We got all their supplies, hot bread and peaches sent up by the friends of the Boers in Magersfontein.' Amongst the loot were gold and silver watches, clothing and rifles and ammunition. 'Fortunately,' reported an officer of the 9th Lancers, 'there was any amount of forage, our horses having practically had nothing to eat all day.' This was quickly snapped up and the Inniskillings' squadron, 'coming in late from guarding the

* Most of the M.I. had still not joined and the Carabiniers and the New Zealanders had only just arrived from Ramdam. These were left to bring on the transport.

† Two of the batteries had only been landed about ten days before. (Smith, 30.)

right rear of the division, only secured a little flour, which was made into paste for the horses.'[11]

On this day there was seen 'the all too frequent sight of a gun horse dropping in his traces as though he had been shot, or a troop horse pitching headlong and helpless.' A heart-breaking spectacle it was indeed. The 12th Lancers alone lost twenty-one horses dead, twenty-five missing, which presumably meant that they were left to die on the veld, and thirty-seven 'unfit to go on'.[12]*

On 14 February no further advance could be made. The delay at the drifts meant that the infantry were unable to take over from the cavalry in time and anyway it was 2 a.m. on 15 February before a part of the cavalry's baggage at last made its way into camp. 'We had no supplies,' wrote Haig, 'except what we carried in our wallets.' This was not quite true of the men's rations, for 'any amount of sheep' had been captured the previous day. Nevertheless, it was necessary for fatigue parties to wade waist deep across the river for rations and forage. Between 11 and 13 February inclusive, the divisional horse casualties totalled 460 of which fifty were dead, fourteen strayed and 396 'unfit to proceed'. There was no question of any sort of reconnaissance, for the rest of the horses were too exhausted. This was unfortunate as Cronje for some unknown reason had just moved his headquarters to within six miles of Ronddavel Drift where they were virtually unprotected. During the day some 900 Boers with two guns were added to the enemy's strength opposite the cavalry division's camp. At last, but too late, Cronje was beginning to perceive that he was being outflanked.[13]

At first light on 15 February three days's forage supplies (36 lbs of oats) were issued to the division. One of these was for the previous day, but, as Haig reported, 'several regiments could not carry more than oats for two days. The regiments from India had no "Corn Bags, 8 lb." (carried as rear pack on saddle), consequently only as much oats as could go into nosebag were taken.' This meant that sacks of oats had to be loaded on any spare horses available. These were inevitably the most exhausted of those still capable of work, as the stronger ones were required for the men. Most of these involuntary pack horses had dropped out by the end of the day and the

---

* The feebleness of the staff work at this period of the war is well illustrated by the fact that on this day, 13 February, sixty men of Kitchener's Horse were left to guard the water supply at Blaauwbosch and that on 16 February, *three days later*, this unsupported and apparently forgotten detachment was made prisoner by a Boer force under De Wet. (Amery, III, 401.)

grain they carried was left on the veld. The men were issued with one-and-a-half days' ration to be carried on the horses. So many of the gun horses were not up to their tasks that some of the horses from the wagons had to be pressed into service, the wagons being left behind.[14]

In the course of the day De Wet made the first of many raids which he was to carry out in the course of the war upon the British lines of communication. The transport oxen were so done up for want of rest and food that they were unable to accompany the infantry divisions. Consequently they were left with inadequate protection to graze at Waterval Drift. Valiant attempts were made to save the transport during most of the day, but in the end De Wet managed to stampede the oxen, most of which fled to the enemy's side. Roberts made the tough decision not to send any troops back to try to save the situation and in consequence 2,880 oxen, 176 wagons, 500 slaughter cattle and immense quantities of supplies had to be abandoned. Worst of all 38,792 rations of grain were lost. In a very real sense this catastrophe helped to seal the fate of the cavalry division.[15]

*   *   *

'I promise faithfully to relieve Kimberley at six on the evening of the 15th if I am alive.' Thus French is supposed to have addressed Kitchener on 9 February. Would he be able to fulfil the promise? He started off at 9.30 a.m.

> 'We had not gone three miles ... northwards,' wrote Haig, before our advanced squadrons were heavily fired on from some hills in their front – at the same time some Boer guns opened on us from a hill to our left .... The situation seemed to me to be that our friends of two days ago were holding the hills in our front to stop us going towards Bloemfontein, while Cronje from Magersfontein had extended his left to prevent us outflanking him.'

The horse artillery came into action as soon as the two Boer guns opened up from the left and the 9th Lancers, who were leading the advance, came to a halt. The Inniskilling squadron and a squadron of Scots Greys dismounted and tried to keep down the Boer rifle fire from the right flank.[16]

French was now faced by a sort of amphitheatre about two and a

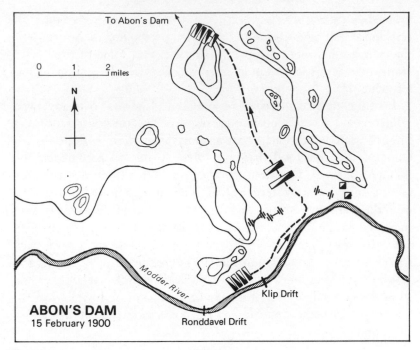

Map 7

half miles wide with two sides of it held by the enemy. Between the two sides, due northwards, was a lightly held low ridge which formed a kind of gap. He at once decided to brave the Boer fire and make for that gap as fast as possible. This 'charge' was to be covered by a bombardment from five of the horse artillery batteries, moving under escort provided by the mounted infantry. 'The ground rose from the river,' noted Haig, 'so we could not see whether there were wire fences or not.' While the leading squadrons of Gordon's brigade were deploying he sent forward a party of eleven men under Lieutenant A. E. Hesketh of the 16th Lancers to act as ground scouts and to cut any wire fences there might be. There were none, but Hesketh was soon killed and two of his men were wounded.

The first line consisted of four squadrons, two of the 9th Lancers on the right and two of the 16th Lancers on the left.* They deployed in extended order, with between five and eight yards between files,†

* One squadron each of the two regiments was still scouting on the right flank or actually engaged dismounted with the Inniskillings and Scots Greys. (Maurice, II, 35.)

† Goldmann (83) says five, while Maurice (II, 35) says eight yards. Haig diaries (3155 33/170) say 'about five yards'.

with their rear ranks forming the second line about twenty yards behind. Gordon led off at a pace which he guessed to be not more than fourteen miles per hour. This he judged to be the very fastest the enfeebled condition of his mounts could contrive. The distance to be covered was a little over one and a half miles. At that rate the 'charge' must have taken about six and a half minutes. Going up hill this must have been pretty gruelling in the extreme heat and amidst a vast cloud of dust. The lancers, exposed to a heavy cross-fire, had not been gone long when, in Haig's words, 'for a minute it looked in the dust as if some of our men were coming back, but they were only extending to a flank.' The 16th's right-hand squadron, as its commander recorded that night,

> 'got rather jammed up with that of the 9th. . . . I had no room to form line till near the top [of the incline]. We then advanced under a shower of screeching bullets. It was most unpleasant but very exciting. Directly we were on the top the fire ceased and the Boers began to bolt on their ponies. The only ones we speared with lances were those whose horses had run away and were on foot. These fellows shot at us till we were 100 yards off and then pulled out a white rag in hopes of having their lives spared. We killed them all. The lances seemed to knock them over stone-dead.'[17]

Some 800 yards behind the lancers the whole of Broadwood's brigade, with French and his Staff, now followed on. Not far behind them were Porter's brigade and the mounted infantry. However, by the time these were launched the enemy fire had virtually ceased. The Boer riflemen seeing that their fire was not stopping the 'charge' and no doubt puzzled and not a little alarmed at the extraordinary sight before them, sprang to their ponies and galloped off.

It is an astonishing fact that though on the right flank the cavalry came within 1,200 yards of the riflemen the casualties in men, beside those of the ground scouts, amounted to only twelve wounded, one of whom later died. The loss in horses was much greater. The 16th Lancers alone lost sixty, some shot, but most dead from exhaustion. The 9th Lancers had five killed, fifteen wounded and ten dead from exhaustion. It is supposed that the Boers lost fifteen men, a few of them made prisoner.*[18]

* Haig wrote in his diary: 'There being only six squadrons in the brigade, the officer commanding was unable to retain a squadron in close order in hand. The enemy would have lost more heavily had this been done, because many Boers

This remarkable 'charge', which became famous as the 'Klip Drift Charge', has been called by Thomas Pakenham a 'quite unnecessary dash to self-destruction across the veld'.[19] But it was only one comparatively small factor among numerous others responsible for the cavalry division's 'self-destruction', while it was considered absolutely necessary to get through to Kimberley at all costs so as to prevent its supposedly imminent surrender. The fact that this later proved not to be at all the case does not invalidate French's decision. With the orders he had received it was not for him to consider whether the horses of his division, the only large mobile force in South Africa, were being destroyed or not. Further, unless he were to allow another day to pass, during which many more Boers would have assembled to oppose him, he was surely right to take the risk involved. He thus undoubtedly saved men's lives even if he gravely impaired his future mobility.

One unique aspect of the 'charge' is that it was not launched against an enemy already engaged or retiring in disorder. It was no instance of shock tactics for, as the *Times History* puts it, 'there was nothing opposed to it on which a shock could take effect.' The minimal casualties were due to the open order adopted, to the prodigious amount of dust and to the scale of the horse artillery's covering fire. When after the war the great tussle between the shock and fire schools (see p. 389) was at its height, Roberts, the chief proponent of the latter, wrote that

> 'French's admirable movement at Klip Drift was essentially a rapid advance of fighting men carried out at extended intervals. It was a rapid advance of warriors who possessed the ability, by means of horses and rifles (not swords or lances), to place their enemy *hors de combat*. It was an ideal Cavalry operation, but it was not a "Cavalry Charge", as this term is generally understood, and the arme blanche had nothing to say to it.'[20]

There could not be, of course, any question of a pursuit. Even if the overloaded cavalry horses had been a great deal fresher they would have had no chance of catching burghers riding fourteen

---

escaped to a flank or passed through a gap in the lines towards the flank.' (Haig, diaries (3155 33/170).)

In the 'charge' were two veterinary officers, both of whom had also been in the 21st Lancers' charge at Omdurman – an extraordinary coincidence, considering how few charges were ever made, and how few veterinary officers there were. (Smith, 34.)

stone on fresh ponies. Though the last five days and those which were to follow up to the fall of Bloemfontein virtually destroyed the cavalry division's horses, it did not perhaps matter quite as much at at first appears, for, as will be shown, until the British took to ponies of the same small size as the Boers' and learned to place upon their backs reasonable weights, there was never any hope of overtaking the enemy's horsemen.

French now slowly covered the remaining few miles to Abon's Dam where, mercifully, there was water though hardly enough even for the men and the water-carts, which meant that the horses got none. He reached it at about 11.45 a.m. It took some time to cover the open country between there and the outposts of the beleaguered town. 'We got to Kimberley about 6 p.m.,' wrote Haig. 'The garrison made not the slightest attempt to assist us. Alone we cleared all the Boers investing positions in the south and took two laagers. The people in Kimberley looked fat and well. It was the relieving force which needed food!! For in the gallop many nosebags were lost.'[21] The first men in came from Rimington's Guides and the Scots Greys. Some of the besieged ladies were so excited that they nearly pulled the dust-covered troopers off their horses in attempts to hug them.

It was noted that when the horses reached water many of them fell down on their knees to drink, while a considerable number collapsed while watering. This was because it was very difficult to prevent them over-drinking. Equally, when after a long fast horses were fed, they often ate too much which gave them laminitis, a disease causing inflammation of the laminae of the hoof (for a fuller description see p. 358).

Next day the 9th Lancers, who had over 420 horses when they left Modder River Station, mustered only 105 fit for duty. Major Edmund Henry Hynman Allenby's squadron of the Inniskillings on arrival in Kimberley managed to assemble forty-two.* Another squadron did better. Of the ninety-four horses with which it started an eighty-mile, three-day march, five were lost from bullet wounds and ten, of which six had sore backs, were reported sick on arrival.

---

* To make the squadron up to 120 horses the squadron of the New South Wales lancers was attached to it. Most of the officers and men of this Australian unit had come direct from England where they had gone in 1897 to represent the Colony at the Queen's Diamond Jubilee. They had stayed on to attend a cavalry course at Aldershot. The unit remained with the Inniskillings until it eventually returned home. The arrangement worked well, the Lancers hero-

It was said that one regiment had 'but twenty-eight horses which, under the stimulus of the spur, could work up a trot'.[22]

'Roberts had to operate on exterior lines with a hastily improvised army, deficient in staff arrangements, transport, commissariat and, above all, trained and experienced mounted troops.'

ERSKINE CHILDERS in *War and the Arme Blanche*, 1910

'Even were I not detained here by Cronje, I should be unable to move on account of the crippled state of my horses.'

LORD ROBERTS to Cecil Rhodes, 27 February, 1900

'French has nicked in ahead.'

One of Rimington's 'Tigers' on 17 February, 1900[1]

(ii)

Boer War: French's actions around Kimberley — march to Koodoosrand Drift — Paardeberg — Cronje's surrender — machine guns

The whole of the day after his entry into Kimberley French spent in trying to pursue and outflank the investing force to the north and east of the town. At the same time he hoped to capture the train carrying 'Long Tom' before it could escape northwards. The exhausted state of the division's horses, which were 'absolutely reduced to a walk', made both tasks impossible to achieve. Nor could the rearguard around Dronfield, which numbered at most 100 burghers, be shifted by the chiefly dismounted efforts of the 1st and 3rd Brigades, supported by twenty-four horse artillery guns. The chief result of the operations of that day, except for twenty-nine casualties,

---

worshipping Allenby as much as did his own men. The squadron proudly christened itself 'Allenby's Own'. (Yardley, 43, 47; Gardner, 33.)

For earlier references to Allenby, who became Field-Marshal Viscount Allenby of Megiddo for his services in the First World War, having been Inspector of Cavalry from 1910 to 1914, see Vol III, pp. 107, 113 and 114.

including two officers killed, was the further prostration and crippling of the horses. It was one of the hottest days of the whole war and the lack of water was total. The 3rd Brigade which covered over thirty miles in fruitless outflanking movements, left sixty-eight horses dead from exhaustion. The 9th Lancers alone lost forty troop horses. In his haste to get started, French had left insufficient time for the horses to be watered in Kimberley before setting out at first light. As the weary regiments returned to the town at nightfall, they were delighted to see that Cecil Rhodes had come to their rescue. He sent them forage for the horses, soup, firewood and even cooking pots for the men: so much for the dire straits of the recently besieged!* During this day, the infantry captured at Bosjespan a Boer laager complete with seventy-eight wagons, tents, a hospital and much food. This to some extent made good the loss of the convoy at Waterval Drift.[2]

Owing to the breakage of the telegraph cable, there had been no communication between French and headquarters from the previous evening. Now, at 8 p.m. an officer of Rimington's Guides brought him news and orders. Cronje was retreating from his Magersfontein entrenchments eastwards along the Modder with a five-mile long train of wagons.† French was to make for Koodoosrand Drift, over thirty miles to the east, first thing next morning in an effort to overtake him. Kitchener's orders told French: 'Our mounted infantry and field artillery are too sticky for words and the Boers fight an excellent rearguard action. . . . I fear we can do nothing really serious unless you can come we are too slow [sic].' The only troops at all capable of the necessary exertion were those of Broadwood's‡ 2nd

---

* 'The ambulance mules of the Cavalry Division were so done up with the long marches of previous days, that they were unable to accompany the troops today. Some ambulances were accordingly borrowed from the garrison today and an ambulance train moved out a short distance in the direction of Macfarlane's station.' (Haig: diaries, 16 Feb., 1900 (3155 33/184).)

† During 16 February the 2nd Brigade had been left to the south of Kimberley, but it had failed to keep in touch with the enemy. Otherwise, surely, its patrols would have discovered Cronje's retreat and reported it to French. When headquarters received no acknowledgment from French by telegraph because the line was broken, no effort, it seems, was made to communicate by other means. French at midday, on the other hand, had asked for orders by using the heliograph station at Enslin. This route was equally open, of course, to Roberts's staff.

‡ Brigadier-General Broadwood who had joined the 12th Lancers in 1881 was at this date only a substantive major. He had distinguished himself in the Sudan and particularly at Omdurman (see Vol III, pp. 367–80, 388). It seems

Brigade which had enjoyed a comparatively restful day. Yet even these were very short of serviceable horses. Again the resources of Kimberley were brought into play: considerable numbers of remounts were supplied by the Diamond Fields Horse (232 of all ranks) and the De Beers Company.* Altogether, with two squadrons of the Carabiniers, the brigade mustered just over 1,200 cavalrymen.† With them were twelve horse artillery guns.[3]

Between 3 and 4 a.m. on 17 February this small band set off. At about 10 a.m. it had reached Kameelfontein Farm, some four-and-a-half miles north of the Koodoosrand Drift. This was an astonishing feat with starved, leg-weary horses. An average pace of 5 m.p.h. for seven successive hours, most of them in excessive heat, places this march high among the achievements of cavalry. From Kameelfontein Farm French could see to the south-west the dust cloud which indicated that he had indeed overtaken Cronje's great convoy. Finding a good position for his two batteries, French at once ordered his guns to fire at a range of just over 2,000 yards. The first of Cronje's wagons were actually on the point of crossing by the Vendutie Drift while others were being outspanned and the oxen driven out to graze, when, at about 11 a.m., the first shells burst upon them, not from their rear as they might conceivably have expected, but from their left front. This was one of the few occasions on which the horse artillery attached to the Cavalry Division proved itself really valuable. Another was at Abon's Dam.

The amazement in the Boer laager at seeing the cavalry and horse artillery which they supposed to be in Kimberley was unbounded. Nevertheless they reacted speedily, sending out one party to outflank the right of the guns and another with two guns to a position from

---

that Roberts blamed him for the disaster to Clements at Nooitgedacht (see p. 243) on 13 December, 1900. In consequence he was later sent home. 'We are all very sorry for him,' wrote Lieutenant-Colonel Clowes, commanding the 8th Hussars. 'He is a very good fellow and soldier too.' (27 Dec., 1900, Clowes.) See also p. 160 for Colvile's opinion of Broadwood after Sannah's Post.

He held commands in South Africa from 1903 to 1906 and died aged fifty-five in 1917. An American war correspondent found him 'an excellent type of the self-possessed soldier. Tall, lithe, with the lean face of a man in perfect condition, he never lost his poise.' (Howland, F. H. *The Chase of De Wet* . . ., 1901, 137.)

* When next day Gordon's Brigade left Kimberley to join French, it too had received remounts from the town: 107 from the Cape Police mounted section (355 of all ranks) and the Kimberley Light Horse (427 of all ranks). (Goldman, 109.)

† Household Cavalry, 398 all ranks; 10th Hussars, 344; 12th Lancers, 277; Carabiniers (6th Dragoon Guards), approximately 200.

which to shell French's headquarters. A squadron each of the 10th Hussars and 12th Lancers, dismounted, frustrated the first attempt, while another squadron of the 12th, some of whom remained mounted, supported by two guns, put a stop to the second. It seems that some of the lancers 'showed a reluctance to use their lances on a dismounted enemy'. For the rest of the day all the cavalrymen, dismounted (including those of the Carabiniers who did not arrive till the afternoon), 'scattered among the kopjes in the fashion they had learnt so well in front of Colesberg', held their own. At about 4 p.m. the fire on both sides slackened. A squadron of the 10th Hussars, about seventy strong, then went forward in open order to see whether the Boers were holding the river bank in force. Six hundred yards from the river they were met with heavy rifle fire. They instantly lost two men killed and three wounded. At this considerable cost it was established that the river bank was strongly held. The guns, meanwhile, continued to make sure that the Boers could not effect a crossing or collect their oxen.[4]

For French it was an anxious time. Had Cronje discovered how small was his force, it could surely have been swept aside. There was no rest that night, for a cavalry net had to be spread out to prevent Cronje's convoy escaping in the darkness. Not until just before dark did a distant dust cloud announce that the mounted infantry, preceding the infantry divisions, had reached the Paardeberg Drift from the west. During the night the only provisions French's men could

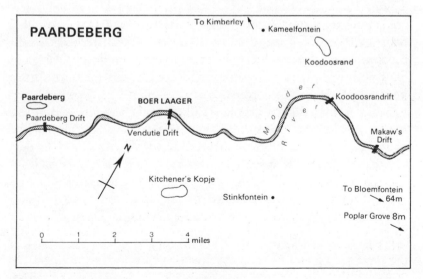

Map 8

get hold of were a few sheep 'taken in exchange for receipt' and what they could find in neighbouring farmhouses. The horses had no forage, except a 'small supply of oat hay found in Kamelfontein farm', and little enough shrivelled grass to allay their hunger. Not till after dark could they be watered at Kamelfontein Farm.

Cronje, due to French's speed and resolution, was now 'squeezed', as Thomas Pakenham has put it, 'between the upper millstone of French's surviving cavalry at Koodoosrand, and the nether millstone of two infantry divisions at Paardeberg.'[5]* There were two bodies of burghers who might have been able to join up with Cronje and provide him with a means of escape from the trap: those under Head Commandant J. S. Ferreira which had formed part of the Kimberley investing force (and with whom French had been in touch on 16 February) and Christiaan De Wet's commandos which were hovering in the south near Koffyfontein. Ferreira's thousand or so men had marched eastward intending perhaps to turn south so as to join up with Cronje. By the early morning of 17 February they had reached Bothashoek where they learned of French's march. This so alarmed their commander that he retreated northwards and was not heard of again for some time. This unintended result of French's move – the prevention of a junction between Ferreira and Cronje – was a bonus unknown to him till later.

De Wet, less cautious than Ferreira, hearing the thunder of the British guns as they poured lyddite and shrapnel into Cronje's laager, appeared from the south-east at about 5 p.m. next day, 18 February, accompanied by two pieces of artillery. He arrived as the so-called battle of Paardeberg was drawing to a close. This had been fought by Kitchener, Roberts being ill with a severe chill. The Chief of Staff with his infantry divisions supported by his numerous guns persisted all day in ill-coordinated attacks upon Cronje, whose men had dug in along the river bank. At all points he was repulsed. It was the most severe reverse suffered by the British on any day of the entire war. The casualties numbered 1,270. Kitchener's defenders say that he might have succeeded in assaulting the laager had not De Wet intervened. That, however, seems very doubtful.

De Wet immediately attacked a farmstead and a kopje (later named Kitchener's) to the south from Vendutie Drift. There he

* Baden-Powell, in 1906, when he was Inspector of Cavalry, made much of the use of the mounted troops at Paardeberg to illustrate how they should be employed 'tactically, to cut off and hold the enemy for the infantry to attack' (Baden-Powell, R. S. S. 'What Lies Before Us', *Cav. Jnl*, I, 9).

found only some 100 uitlanders of Kitchener's Horse. Taken utterly by surprise, their horses stampeded. They had no choice but to surrender. Before dusk De Wet had seized enough ground to provide an escape route for Cronje. 'It is true,' he wrote in his *Three Years War*, 'that he would have been obliged to leave everything behind him, but he and his burghers would have got away in safety. . . . General Cronje would not move.'[6] It seems that many of the burghers were demoralized and that they could not bear to abandon their womenfolk, amongst whom was Cronje's wife. Further, so many of his horses had been destroyed by the bombardment that it is doubtful if very many burghers could have in fact succeeded in escaping.* In fact a few – less than 100 – did gallop out to join De Wet. For three days against tremendous odds the escape route was held open. De Wet only retired when his gun ammunition had almost run out. Kitchener's troops now closed the ring around Cronje and awaited his capitulation. The cavalry played little active part in the investment. In fact it could hardly have done so even if required to, for, as French wrote to Kitchener this day: 'My horses and men are nearly worn out.'[7]

The first corn ration for four days was issued on 19 February. The horses were so ravenous that when they saw the corn being distributed bits had to be placed in their mouths to keep them under control. Until 23 February there was no sign of the missing parts of the division's transport, which had last been seen trying to cross the Modder at Klip Drift on the 15th! To make matters worse the heat and the drought were now succeeded by rain and cold. The horses, on the verge of starvation, shivered and died. Their ration was limited for part of the time to a single pound of oats for each horse.† During the eleven days that the cavalry occupied its position near Paardeberg, the average amount of corn issued was not more than four pounds per animal. On 24 and 26 February two convoys of sick horses were sent back to the railway. Thus there were 243 less equine mouths to feed. The remounts which arrived at the same time from Modder River were unshod. Both material and time for shoeing were in short supply. Consequently large numbers were hoofsore. The men scarcely fared better. 'We are not allowed tents,'

* The dead Boer horses were thrown into the river. On 22 February they were observed floating down at the rate of 100 an hour. (Smith, 37.)

†When in March the division left Paardeberg, it was found that more oats had been accumulated than could be carried on the supply wagons. The excess had to be burned! (Smith, 38; Stewart, 202.)

wrote Trooper Walker of the 12th Lancers to his parents, 'only one blanket and that is simply soaking wet, day and night, and to make matters worse we are only on half rations ... sometimes not even that.' Lieutenant Granger of the same regiment noted in his diary that 'the greater majority of the men had never known before what it was to be really hungry and many a stout and beefy reservist looked as if his clothes had been made for a man twice his size.'[8]

On 27 February, the nineteenth anniversary of Majuba and the day before Ladysmith was relieved, Cronje, the sixty-five year old 'Lion of Potschefstroom', with over 4,000 Free Staters and Transvaalers, surrendered.* During the nine days' siege which preceded this first considerable British victory and for many days after it, the soldiers drank from the increasingly polluted waters of the river – 'dead horse soup' they called it. Ironically during the next few weeks the resulting disease caused more casualties than all the bullets which had been fired by the Boers.

The losses of horses in the Cavalry Division, not including the mounted infantry brigades, between 11 and 27 February were 1,581. This represents a daily wastage of over eighty-five and a total loss of over 30% in eighteen days.

* * *

Just before the Paardeberg surrender there arrived in Lord Roberts's camp the first three 'pom-pom' machine guns to take the field. These large-size Maxims fired 1 lb steel shells† from a heavy 1.457-inch calibre barrel. The cartridges were contained in belts, each holding twenty-five projectiles, and the rate of fire was 150 rounds a minute. Before the war the only purchasers had been the Germans, the Chinese and the Boers, from whom the British captured a number in the later stages of the war and used attached to some of the mobile columns. Seeing that these guns were quite effective in the enemy's hands, the War Office at once placed an initial order for fifty, having before the war refused to do so. They were normally operated in sections of one or two guns, each under a Royal Artillery officer.

---

* A pet hen emerged from Cronje's laager. It was adopted by the ammunition column of the 3rd Cavalry Brigade and travelled in a box on a limber. It became so famous that someone suggested that 'the Zoological Society should find it a home'. (Farwell, 371.)

† This was the smallest weight of an explosive projectile allowed by the Geneva Convention.

They were really of the class of light artillery and required a carriage almost as heavy and prominent a target as that of a field-piece. Even when they worked properly, which was not often, the shells they fired, though alarming, were less effective than the small, rifle-calibre Maxim. When in quotations later on in this volume the name Maxim is used it usually means the small gun and not the pom-pom. (See, for example, p. 262, where both weapons were used at Klip-fontein.) The small Maxim was, of course, the familiar .303-inch calibre machine gun which had seen service on numerous occasions in the 1890s (see, for example, Vol III, pp. 365, 368 and 374). Other, larger, quick-firing guns such as the Hotchkiss and the 'Elswick'* were also occasionally employed in the course of the war.[9]

* The so-called Elswick gun was a quick-firing (about six rounds a minute) 12-pounder. Six of them were presented to Lord Roberts by Lady Meux, who had bought them in October, 1900 from the manufacturers, the Elswick Ordnance Company, for £45,000. They had been destined for a Japanese warship. They were manned by men from the company. An officer of the 8th Hussars found the gun 'very useful' at Olifant's Nek, a minor engagement which took place on 3 November, 1900. An officer of the 17th Lancers, four months before, had been much impressed by two of these guns used in certain engage-ments at that time. They were 'drawn by teams of ten mules to each gun, and driven with wonderful skill'. Their field carriages, though, were very heavy (200 lbs), which told greatly against their mobility. ([Official] *Textbook of Service Ordnance*, 1900, 358; information from William Reid, Director of the NAM; Morton, 73; Micholls, 36; Headlam, 498.)

'French, for some reason unknown, was quite "off his game".'

> J. G. MAYDON of the action at Poplar
> Grove, 7 March, 1900

'We should have had a good chance of making the two Presidents De Steyn and Kruger prisoner if French had carried out my orders.'

> LORD ROBERTS to Lord Lansdowne

'It was fortunate for us that the advance of the English was not very rapid. Had it been so, everything must have fallen into their hands.'

> CHRISTIAAN DE WET

'They are masters of the art of rearguard actions, and carried out their retreat in the most perfect order.'

> LORD AIRLIE, commanding the 12th
> Lancers

'We see with disgust that we have been bluffed and fooled and held in check all day by some sixty or eighty rifleman.'

> One of Rimington's 'Tigers'[1]

(iii)

Boer War: Poplar Grove – entry into Bloemfontein

On 24 February, three days before Cronje's surrender, French had to tell Roberts that his horses were too unfit for a projected cavalry raid on Bloemfontein. Consequently, though the brigades had been re-organized and the transport collected, it had to be called off. Partially for the same reason, but also because of the difficulty in bringing up necessary supplies of all sorts, there had to be a further week's delay after the Paardeberg surrender before the general advance could be continued. During that week, though the horses managed to get some rest, they got little more than a starvation diet. On this they were, of course, quite unable to build up their strength.*

* On 25 February, Haig stated that the fodder ration was 8 lbs per horse. (Haig: diaries, 3155 33/220.) Some authorities imply that this ration was reduced to 3 lbs by 6 March, but Haig again says on 7 March: 'They have been having only eight lbs of oats a day' since leaving Modder River Station on 11 February. (*Haig,* 207.)

On 28 February French inspected the remounts – 180 had come in on the previous day – as well as ninety-four newly arrived men of the Kimberley Horse. Haig reported that all the horses were 'poor, some lame, most want shoeing badly, several so lame as to be unfit to march'. The 126 remounts that arrived on 4 March were also 'a bad lot' and equally 'in no condition for marching'. That same day the drought was succeeded by torrents of rain. 'The shelters,' wrote an officer of the 9th Lancers, 'were blown away like paper; things were floating about in all directions. The men kept up their spirits by singing "Home, Sweet Home".' At about this time an order was issued that junior officers were to cook their own breakfasts. It lasted only two days. 'For two days,' complained a subaltern of the 12th Lancers, 'we started breakfastless except for chocolate and ration biscuits. After a bit we were allowed to have a cook per squadron. It is after all a bit difficult for officers to look after the comfort of their horses and men and at the same time collect stuff for a fire and boil water, etc.'[2]

French had another reason for being upset at this time. On 25 February Colonel Wodehouse Dillon Richardson, Director of Supplies, complained to Roberts that the Cavalry Division's units were drawing more rations than there were men and horses present. Roberts, who, it seems, had recently been upbraiding French for the poor horsemastership of his regiments,[3] became extremely angry. He sent for the commander of the Cavalry Division and in front of his three brigadiers gave him 'a real dressing down'.[4] It is not surprising that French 'left the interview hurt and embittered, feeling that he had been unjustly reprimanded, in intemperate language, in front of his subordinates.'[5] It was not until after 7 March that Richardson confessed to Roberts that he had made a gross mistake. He had failed to remember that sick horses, as much as healthy ones, and the men who tended them, were also entitled to rations and of course there was a large number of them! It was excessively deplorable that relations between Roberts and French should have been thus unnecessarily strained at this moment, for Roberts's next move depended for its success upon the wholehearted co-operation of the cavalry commander.

In the afternoon of 6 March Roberts addressed all his general officers thus:

'The enemy occupy a strong, but somewhat extended position in our immediate front. Their object is, of course, to block the road to Bloemfontein [at what is] apparently the only place . . . where our progress could be checked. . . . My intention is to send the cavalry division, with Alderson's and Ridley's Mounted Infantry and seven batteries of Royal Horse Artillery to threaten the enemy's line of communication with Bloemfontein. To avoid coming under the enemy's fire throughout this distance the cavalry will have to make a detour of about seventeen miles.* This would bring them to the south bank of the Modder River, probably some two miles above the Poplar Grove Drift. It is very likely, however, that General French may find some vulnerable points which it would be desirable for him to attack before he reaches the river. The destruction of their laagers practically cripples the Boers, as we have learnt

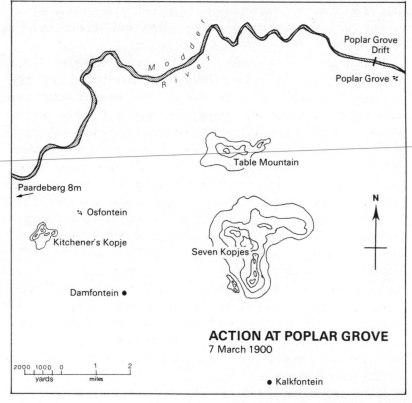

ACTION AT POPLAR GROVE
7 March 1900

Map 9

* In the event, most of the regiments covered over thirty miles in the course of the day, the horses being fourteen hours under saddle, mostly without water. (Goldman, 135.)

from experience. There are three or four laagers ... and it would be well worth General French's while to bring the fire of his forty-two guns to bear on them. It is intended that the Sixth Division ... should follow the route to be taken by the Cavalry Division for about six miles. It will then be on the south-east of the "Seven Kopjes", the southernmost limit of the Boer position, ... and will not have much difficulty in driving the enemy off these kopjes. ... The first position to which the Boers can retire from the "Seven Kopjes" is "Table Mountain", distant $4\frac{3}{4}$ miles. ... The "Table Mountain" is the key of the enemy position, and with that in our possession they will have to retire into the Modder River, as Cronje did, or force their way across it. ... .'[6]

Should the Boers try to cross to the north of the river they were to be deterred by the two other infantry divisions. It was a simple, bold plan designed to bring about a second Paardeberg. It was nevertheless riddled with flaws. These, it seems certain, were clear to French – at any rate in part. One of them was the fact that 2 a.m., the starting time which Roberts gave him verbally, was nothing like early enough to enable the decision to get well behind the Boer position in time and without being seen. It seems that French actually suggested starting overnight but that Roberts rejected the proposal.[7] In the event, the orders which Haig issued at 6.30 p.m. on 6 March gave 3 a.m. as the starting time. Whether this was a misunderstanding of Roberts's verbal instructions, or whether, as the *Times History* states, French changed it on his own initiative 'from a dislike apparently of long night marches', is not clear.[8] What is clear is that Major-General Thomas Kelly-Kenny, commanding the 6th Division, who was to follow the Cavalry Division, correctly understood Roberts to say that he was to start at the same time as French, namely 2 a.m. This, of course, he did. The consequent confusion can be imagined. It partly explains why French with his 2,700 officers and men (followed by a host of mounted infantry) had covered only about two and a half miles by 5 a.m., all the time moving very slowly without benefit of moonlight. Tired of 'struggling with emaciated horses in the darkness', he now halted at Damfontein to await the dawn three-quarters of an hour later. At about 6.45 a.m. he reached Kalkfontein, where he spent another three-quarters of an hour watering most of the horses at 'a large muddy pan', an operation which he considered absolutely essential on a day which was intensely hot. He had taken more than three and three-quarter hours to cover twelve miles.[9]

Another of the flaws in Roberts's plan was the seventeen-mile route specified. It was demonstrably too short to be an effective pincer arm. To make sure that the cavalry was unseen by the enemy a much wider sweep was necessary and neither time nor the state of the horses would allow this. It appears that Roberts did not sufficiently realize that once the cavalry was observed the Boers would suspect the trap and most likely retreat as fast as they could. This is exactly what happened. The leading scouts came under fire at about 6.45 a.m. and very soon afterwards the Boers started to withdraw. At 7.30 French sent a message to headquarters saying, 'I have quite turned enemy's left flank'. This was scarcely true for he could not be said at that time to be thoroughly 'in rear' even of Seven Kopjes. His message went on to say that he was 'following' the Boer withdrawal with 'horse artillery fire. . . .* I am moving round to attack a laager in rear of Table Mountain.' Half an hour later he sent a second message: 'Long line of wagons moving towards river from laager in rear of Table Mountain. Am following them with artillery fire. They are too well protected by riflemen in neighbouring kopjes and positions to enable me to attack them mounted or dismounted. I am watching for every opportunity.'[10] Few opportunities in fact presented themselves. 'The Boers,' wrote Haig, 'left their trenches and some took up new positions to try and check our advance. We lost fairly heavily in turning some Boers out of a farm and off a ridge [by chiefly dismounted action].'†[11] In short French decided that it was too dangerous to attempt to cut off the fleeing burghers. It is certain that he would have suffered considerable casualties had he tried to do so, for the enemy's rearguard actions were extremely well handled. As Dr Holmes, French's best biographer suggests, 'French appears to have believed that his task was impossible, and he was naturally disinclined to get his division lacerated in what he regarded as a fruitless battle.'[12] This reluctance is well illustrated by his reaction to what happened when the scouts of the 12th Lancers,

* Four extra horses were added to some of the horse artillery gun teams. Even then it was difficult to get them near enough to do any damage. Further there was a very real risk that the horses which dragged the guns forward would not be strong enough to drag them out of action again if compelled to retire. (Smith, 39; Goldman, 133.)

† Haig added characteristically: 'but nothing of course compared to what Infantry would have suffered had they tried to dislodge the Boers.' (Haig, 207.)

which was the leading regiment of the leading brigade (Broadwood's), were 'stopped by fairly heavy fire from the top of a gentle rise some 1500 yards away'. Broadwood at once ordered the regiment to 'form line' for a charge, but before this order could be carried out French sent another for the brigade to 'come in'. As this was not immediately obeyed he sent a second to the same effect. An officer of the 12th, who was acting as a galloper to the brigadier, tells what then happened:

> 'Broadwood said, "Tell the General I am just going to charge". The fire was getting hotter and the Boers could be seen galloping up to reinforce the few holding the rise. . . . Just before the word "Charge" was given, a third message from French came: "If General Broadwood does not come in at once he will be relieved of his command." Broadwood gave the word, "Troops left wheel" and we rejoined the rest of the division in a hollow under heavy fire.'[13]

The potency of De Wet's rearguards is shown by the British casualty figures: eight killed and forty-nine wounded. The loss in horses was 213 of which only some sixty were killed or wounded by enemy action. The highest estimate of Boer losses is fifty. No prisoners were taken. Virtually all the 5,000 or so Boers escaped, though they had to abandon considerable quantities of supplies. 'There was enough fodder jettisoned from the flying wagons,' wrote one witness, 'to find the greater part of the animals a feed of corn.' This was fortunate indeed for the wagons which arrived next morning carried no forage. 'Despair!', exclaimed Lord Airlie. 'You cannot move an engine without coal. . . . You can move the horse for a bit, but he dies.'[14]

Roberts was, of course, furious. More than two years later he told the Royal Commission that

> 'the Poplar Grove day was a most disappointing one for me. . . . Notwithstanding the comparative rest the horses had had after Cronje's surrender, they were in extremely poor condition, added to which the ground was very heavy owing to recent rain. Had the mounted troops been able to move more rapidly, they could undoubtedly have intercepted the enemy's line of retreat, for when I reached Poplar Grove late in the afternoon with the infantry and heavy artillery their rearmost troops were still visible. Immediately on sighting them I hurried off a staff

officer to tell General French what a short way off the enemy were, and to urge him to follow them up. The reply I received was that his horses had come to a standstill.'[15]

'I have never seen horses so beat as ours on that day,' wrote Haig. He went on to point out one of the major reasons:

'So many Skallywag Corps have been raised that the horses of the whole force could not have a full ration. The Colonial Corps raised in *Cape Colony* are quite useless, so are the recently raised mounted infantry. They can't ride, and know nothing about their duties as mounted men. Roberts's Horse and Kitchener's Horse are good only for looting and the greater part of them disappear the moment a shot is fired or there is the prospect of a fight.'[16]

In the course of the controversy following Poplar Grove, which soon became a *cause célèbre*, it was suggested that French ought to have told Roberts about his doubts as to the feasability of the plan. Even had he not been labouring under a profound sense of indignation, even had he been Roberts's bright-eyed boy, French would very like have been speedily 'stellenbosched' had he dared to question the Commander-in-Chief's scheme. Roberts was notorious for his ruthlessness with those who obstructed him. Further, the cavalry commander was still only a substantive colonel.

Whether the plan, even if carried out by totally fit and fresh cavalry, could ever have succeeded is doubtful. What is manifest is that it never had a chance with the starved horses unable to move, at most, above a trot 'for even a few yards'.[17]

On 13 March Roberts entered Bloemfontein. Since leaving Modder River the Cavalry Division alone had lost 42% of its horses in thirty days. The total horse losses for the whole army amounted to 5,169.[18]

'Little Bobs has curled himself up at Government
House here and given orders that he is not to be
called for a fortnight.'

> One of Rimington's 'Tigers' soon
> after the fall of Bloemfontein

'No one who had not personally witnessed the
despondency that existed after the taking of
Bloemfontein can realise how great and deep it
was .... The Transvaalers left in great numbers,
and the Free Staters had turned their faces to
their homes.'

> PRESIDENT STEYN in his memoirs

'The blasted waggons ... hurried out of the
shell fire only to fall into the frying-pan of an
ambuscade.'

> WINSTON CHURCHILL, on the action at
> Sannah's Post

'Sannah's Post was the first occasion, I believe,
where the Boers rode into close quarters in the
course of pressing a rearguard.'

> ERSKINE CHILDERS in *War and the*
> *Arme Blanche*

'I still wonder why [Lieutenant-General Colvile]
refused to march straight to the scene of the
disaster, which was bang in front of us, instead of
going on a wild-goose chase to Waterval Drift.
We must have saved men and possibly some
guns.'

> BRIGADIER-GENERAL HORACE SMITH-DORRIEN
> in his memoirs.[1]

(iv)

Boer War: Driefontein – Kroonstad Krijgsraad – Sannah's Post

The last action before the fall of Bloemfontein was fought at Driefontein on 10 March. The cavalry took hardly any part of it. The
12th Lancers, for instance, spent the day 'trotting backwards and
forwards under shell fire. Beyond killing a horse or two the shelling
did little harm.'[2] The entry into the Free State capital followed on
13 March. It was virtually unopposed. That the end of Boer resistance was but a short time away was the almost unanimous feeling
in the British camp. Many Boers felt the same. Numerous burghers,

dispirited, slunk off home. Others took advantage of the clemency proclamation which Roberts now issued. They handed in some sort of weapon and swore not to take up arms against the British again. An Australian newspaper correspondent, the poet A. B. ('Banjo') Paterson, wrote that the burghers

> 'handed in their old worn-out muzzle-loading rifles with which their grandfathers shot lions and zebra on the plains where they are now breeding from imported merino sheep and English stud horses. These old weapons they solemnly deposited and went back to the laager again, with brand new Mausers in their hands.
>> "Back to the laager again,
>> Back to the laager again,
>> It was only in fun that I gave up my gun,
>> I'm back to the laager again."
> One can imagine some festive burgher humming some such parody as he gaily rides back to the fighting lines after giving up his weapons.'

Trooper Ben Strange, a West Australian in Roberts's Horse, thought

> 'the old Boer on his farm deceptive indeed. A squadron rides up and he innocently hands over his firearms. You would not imagine the old "haysee" had ever been with a commando as he potters around. But as you ride away along the spruit and across the veldt – ping – comes a bullet from away among the rocks. You instinctively know that the man who is potting at you is the quiet-looking old farmer whose second rifle you didn't secure.'[3]

Roberts foresaw very little more fighting before the start of peace negotiations. Neither he nor the vast majority of the burghers had counted upon the determined leadership of President Steyn, Christiaan de Wet, De la Rey and Louis Botha. The war had lasted less than six months. These remarkable men and a few others were to ensure that it continued for another twenty-five.

Four days after the fall of Bloemfontein the leaders of the Free State and the Transvaal held a *Krijgsraad* at Kroonstad. It was unanimously agreed to prosecute the war more energetically than ever. A higher degree of discipline would be enforced and the commandos would form themselves into real 'flying columns'. The slow, speed-inhibiting wagon trains would from now on be eschewed.

Roberts, chiefly for reasons of supply, was compelled to delay his advance north-eastwards from Bloemfontein for no less than fifty-one days. This fact alone was a considerable boost to Boer morale.

* * *

While Cronje was still trapped in his laager at Paardeberg a number of commandos, in what they considered a national emergency, had come flocking north-eastward in the vain hope of helping him. Those that came from Colesberg enabled Clements to occupy that place on the day of Cronje's surrender and to reach Norval Pont a week later, while the burghers who left Stormberg so weakened that sector that Gatacre was able to enter the town on 5 March and Burghersdorp on the day after Poplar Grove. In due course the Colesberg and Stormberg burghers joined up near Smithfield. Under Commandant General Ian Hendrick Olivier, they numbered about 5,500, nearly all mounted and accompanied by over 700 wagons.[4] Keeping close to the Basutoland border they lumbered northwards unmolested to take up safe positions to the east and north-east of Bloemfontein.* With a view more to the distribution of his 'kill-Boer-rule-with-kindness' proclamation and at most to observing Olivier's movements, the Commander-in-Chief belatedly despatched French to Thaba 'Nchu. After a while, recalled so as to secure the Glen crossing of the Modder north of Bloemfontein,† French left

* This was a remarkable forced march undertaken with an extraordinary amount of impedimenta – the baggage train covered over twenty miles. It is a good example of how skilful the burghers were in the management of their oxen and their horses.
'The convoy marched from 2 a.m. to 5 a.m. each day and rested for two hours. It then marched from 7 a.m. to 11 a.m., and the oxen were out-spanned and grazed, for not a blade of food is carried for these animals in South Africa. From 2 p.m. to 5 p.m. they marched, then there was another rest till 7 p.m. when they marched until 9.30 or 10 p.m. . . . . So excellent was the discipline maintained among the 1,000 Kaffirs employed driving the wagons, that it is said that fifteen minutes from the time the order was given to start, everything was ready to move off. The Boer and the Kaffir understood each other; we', says the veterinary historian of the war, 'who ruined the latter by so-called kindness were badly and expensively served throughout the war.' (Smith, 51.)
† On 29 March an action took place at Karee Siding in which the Boers were driven on to Brandfort. The cavalry brigade mustered only 650 horses in four regiments. It marched about forty miles in the course of the day and performed a double flanking movement which, because of the exhausted state of the horses,

Broadwood at Thaba 'Nchu with an entirely mounted force something over 1,300 strong: a typical mixed force of all the various classes of mounted troops then in South Africa, 'formed from the strongest horses still remaining'.[5]*

Meanwhile Christiaan De Wet, relying on speed and secrecy, determined to swoop upon the waterworks at Sannah's Post, twenty-three miles east of Bloemfontein, upon the pumping station of which the town depended for much of its water. With 1,500 burghers, six guns, a pom-pom and a Maxim he speeded southwards. His intention was to post most of his force and all his guns on the east bank of the Modder opposite the waterworks while concealing himself and some 350 of his men in the Koorn Spruit two and a half miles to the west of the river. The larger force would drive the enemy into the lap of the smaller. This is more or less what happened except that the enemy turned out to be instead of a post of 200 men the whole of Broadwood's force. Olivier's approach had compelled

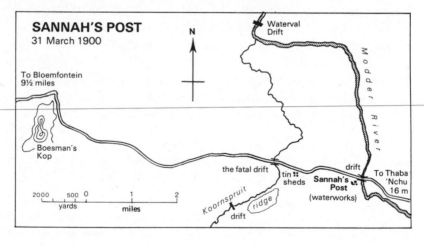

Map 10

was not very effective. (*Haig*, 210; Smith, 52.) I have dealt with Sannah's Post in detail and only touched on Karee Siding as being the less instructive of the two engagements.

* Household Cavalry (130), 10th Hussars (160), Alderson's MI Brigade (800) and 'Q' and 'U' Batteries, RHA (299). These figures are very approximate. For example, the two cavalry units only had 332 horses when they set out from Bloemfontein (Maurice, II, 275), while about 100 cavalrymen, whose horses had died or become useless since then, marched with the baggage column at Sannah's Post.

Broadwood to leave Thaba 'Nchu. On 30 March he telegraphed headquarters that he was about to retire some twenty-four miles to the waterworks where he would be 'within supporting distance of Bloemfontein'. There he bivouacked that night.

Soon after daylight next morning heavy shell fire was opened upon him across the river from north and east, 'at a range', as he wrote in his despatch, 'to which my Horse Batteries could not reply. ...I ordered the force to retire out of shell fire, and directed Roberts's Horse and "U" Battery to reinforce [the small detachment of mounted infantry] at Boesman's Kop, on which point I proposed to withdraw.'[6] These two units, followed by 'Q' Battery, in fact escorted Broadwood's large baggage column, which nevertheless, rushed pell-mell ahead of them. It consisted of ninety-two wagons in some of which were women and children – 'British refugees from the disturbed sections of the Free State' – and a few sick and wounded. With the convoy marched a few men leading sick horses and about 100 men whose horses had broken down, including troopers of the Household Cavalry and 10th Hussars.[7]

Not for a moment suspecting De Wet's trap which was now about to be sprung, Broadwood never thought to send scouts ahead, the road home being supposed to be clear of the enemy. As it was, the leading wagons quickly descended the fifteen-foot, crumbling banks of the drift across Koorn Spruit. There, with myriad rifles imposing silence upon their drivers, they were boarded by burghers who forced them to drive on and up the far side of the drift so that those wagons which had not yet entered it should suspect nothing untoward, the Boers appearing at a distance much the same as the other occupants of the wagons. To the following mounted and unmounted men the burghers concealed in the river bank shouted 'Hands up!' 'We had disarmed 200 of them,' exulted De Wet, 'before they had time to know what was happening.'[8] Similarly, since it was inextricably intermingled with the wagons, the whole of 'U' Battery, except for one gun,[9] stumbled into the trap.

But one artilleryman contrived to escape. Tearing up to Major Edmund John Phipps Hornby, 'Q' Battery's commander, who was only 300 yards from the spruit, he yelled: 'We are all prisoners! The Boers are *there*,' pointing to the spruit. 'They are among the convoy and among the guns.'[10] Hornby instantly gave the order 'Subdivisions left wheel – gallop!'[11] At much the same moment Lieutenant-Colonel Harry Leonard Dawson (9th Bengal Lancers) in command of Roberts's Horse, coming up on the batteries' left, saw what was happening. His men, in extended order, were within 200 yards of the spruit when 'a number of Boers stood up and made signs to them to go to the drift'. Dawson at once roared out the order 'Files About! Gallop!' This was the moment for De Wet to give the order to shoot. The resulting Mauser and Martini-Henry fire was devastating. Roberts's Horse alone lost seventy-nine officers and men of whom fifty-two were made prisoner, for most of the men whose horses were shot under them were captured.[12]

In retiring, two of Hornby's six guns had to be abandoned. With the help of some mounted infantry volunteers the remaining four guns were manhandled into the cover of a cluster of tin sheds about 1,200 yards from the spruit. Here, under intense fire, the guns were fought hour after hour, until eventually they retired with the rest of the force, covered by mounted infantry.* Eighty-seven horses belonging to the battery and to Roberts's Horse had taken shelter under the sheds. Of these eighty-five were killed or disabled.[13] Hornby† and three other ranks of the battery were awarded the Victoria Cross for their splendid courage.

While these distressing results of Christiaan De Wet's admirable ambush were being enacted, Alderson's Mounted Infantry Brigade was holding off the main Boer force under, amongst others, Piet de Wet. This was 'pressing vigorously across the river'[14] in the water-works area. The Household Cavalry and the 10th Hussars during this time hovered somewhere about halfway between river and spruit.

The moment Broadwood realized his predicament he acted swiftly. Messages were sent off to headquarters, one of them carried by an officer of the 10th Hussars.[15] Next, at about 7 a.m.,[16] he ordered the Household Cavalry

'to occupy a point higher up the spruit, and to work down it, one company mounted infantry to work along the ridge on the Household Cavalry's left, and the 10th Hussars to swing round the left of this company and operate against the rear of the enemy in the spruit. As soon as the movement was under weigh I relieved the Household Cavalry by two companies of Burma

---

* The mounted infantry were so impressed by the bravery and skill of the gunners that they actually rose to their feet under fire to cheer them as they passed.

† Hornby went home in 1901 to become ADC to Roberts. He died just before his ninety-first birthday in 1947.

Mounted Infantry,* and ordered the former to join in the movement of the 10th Hussars.'[17]

To make this turning movement possible a practicable drift across the spruit sufficiently south of De Wet's men had to be found. Lieutenant Richard Chester-Master of Rimington's 'Tigers' galloped off to find one.[18] This he did about two miles south of the fatal drift.

'As soon as the turning movement should have had the effect of checking [De Wet's] fire,' Broadwood, according to his despatch, ordered all the mounted infantry and the remains of the horse artillery to retire by this newly found passage of the Koorn Spruit.[19] Unhappily the turning movement was a total failure. It seems that as at Poplar Grove a sort of paralysis came over the small cavalry force.† It first took an unconscionable time crossing what was admittedly a very steep and awkward drift,[20] and then, even when joined by part of Lieutenant-General Cyril Godfrey Martyr's 600 mounted infantry, which had come out from Bloemfontein, it was completely held up by a handful of De Wet's burghers. In its defence it must be said that these Boers on a ridge to the west of the fatal drift were, as the *Official History* says,

> 'exactly in the kind of position to give ample scope to practiced riflemen. The ground before them lay open to the full range of their weapons, while they were completely hidden from view . . . .
>
> 'The cavalry had failed to produce any impression . . . and as they had not even gained any information about the enemy, the General was still ignorant of the strength of his immediate antagonists, and did not know how far up and down the spruit they extended. As Colonel Martyr . . . had omitted to report himself, Broadwood did not know that a fresh brigade of mounted infantry had arrived upon the battlefield.'[21]

* So called because it consisted of officers and men drawn from British units in Burma. (Maurice, II, 219.)

† 'No one seems to have been specifically placed by Broadwood in command of the various units detailed for the turning movement. Though Lieutenant-Colonel Fisher, 10th Hussars, was the senior officer . . . he did not take charge . . . probably because he was unaware of his responsibility.' (Maurice, 286.) The Household Cavalry was commanded by Brevet Lieutenant-Colonel Henry Thomas Fenwick, Royal Horse Guards. Both the commanding officer and the second-in-command were in hospital. (Arthur, II, 723.)

Unaware of this or any other help from the west and getting no news of how the turning movement was going, Broadwood, pressed hard by Piet de Wet's now reinforced burghers, had no choice but to order the general retirement to proceed. By 11.15 a.m. it had been completed. In the course of it the Boers were seen to be firing from the saddle, the first time since Stormberg that they had done so.[22] 'We fired at them as they passed us,' wrote Christiaan De Wet, 'and took several more prisoners.'[23]*

Why was Broadwood so feebly supported from Bloemfontein, only two hours' ride away? Partly because Roberts seems to have over-reacted and to have thought that the town itself was in danger. Instead of at once sending off French with parts of his division, he apparently allowed that general to waste 'the whole morning and afternoon hunting for Boers around Bloemfontein'.[24] Beside Martyr's weak mounted infantry brigade, Roberts ordered out Major-General Sir Henry Edward Colvile's 9th Infantry Division. Its arrival at Boesman's Kop was announced to Broadwood at 'about noon'.[25] This was the very first message about supports that he had received.

Strange to relate, Colvile now halted his men for an hour's rest and sent for Broadwood so that he could learn the situation from him in person. Broadwood at this critical moment of the engagement wisely decided that his place was with his troops. He sent a message back suggesting 'that a direct advance on the spruit offered the best chance of assisting'.[26] Two of Colvile's brigadiers urged him to 'go and see Broadwood, instead of waiting for him . . . ;† but he assured us,' wrote one of them (Horace Smith-Dorrien (see p. 419)),‡ 'that in any case he would get nothing out of Broadwood, as he believed he was in a state of collapse, and, after waiting for some twenty minutes, he ordered the Division to march to Waterval Drift.'[27]

As soon as Broadwood had succeeded in extricating his force, he reported to Colvile. 'I was surprised,' wrote Smith-Dorrien, 'to see him looking particularly active and well.'[28] Roberts in his Despatch considered that Colvile 'would have done better if . . . he had pro-

---

* De Wet says that the 'troops came hurrying through Koorn Spruit both on the right and on the left of our position.' (De Wet, 91.) No British account mentions any troops retreating to the left, i.e. the north, of the fatal spruit.

† 'The gunner officers in Colvile's division heard their comrades' guns in "section-fire" and knew it to be the sign of a desperate situation. Officers and men chafed at the deplorable delay.' (Conan Doyle, 382.)

‡ 'One of the few generals,' reported a trooper of Imperial Yeomanry, 'whom all men speak well of.' (Peel, 143.)

5. 'One of Rimington's Horse' (see p. 81)

6. 'An Old Transvaal Boer'

7. The first Boer horse captured by the Inniskilling Dragoons

8. 'Condemned to Death'

9. An officer of the 2nd New South Wales Mounted Rifles with 'supplementary' rations

ceeded at once to the scene of the engagement, and ascertained personally how matters stood, before deciding on the flank movement towards Waterval Drift.'[29] Certainly had he done so, he would have stood a chance of recapturing some of the lost guns and wagons with which De Wet was lumbered. It has been suggested that Colvile, a proud, not very brilliant man, was piqued that Broadwood, his junior, failed to obey at once his order to report to him and that he therefore denied him assistance.[30] His behaviour next day was equally unpleasing. He forbade Smith-Dorrien to evacuate eighty-seven wounded who had been left in and around the tin sheds. He said that as they belonged to the cavalry they were not his concern. Smith-Dorrien paid no attention and was able to bring away all the wounded 'in spite of heavy fire of the Boer guns at our carts, ambulances and stretcher parties'. The cavalrymen were extremely grateful.[31]

The total casualties at Sannah's Post came to 571. Of these 428 were prisoners, 113 were wounded and thirty killed.[32] No attempt was made to re-capture the waterworks till 23 April. Their denial in the meantime to Bloemfontein, (soon to be dubbed 'Blooming-typhoidtein' by Kipling),[33] meant that inadequate wells in that town and water brought in by the already over-loaded railway were the only sources available. The former contributed to the incidence of enteric fever (typhoid and paratyphoid) and the latter to the length of time before Roberts could resume his advance. Within ten days of the capture of Bloemfontein 1,000 men had gone into hospital. In the Cavalry Division the mounted infantry suffered more than the regular cavalry regiments and of these the two which had come from India, the 9th and 16th Lancers, were 'almost entirely free' from the fever.[34] When on 3 May the advance continued there were 4,500 men out of the whole army in hospital. At that time, thoughout South Africa some 15,000 men were out of action due to illness: seventy-five per thousand.[35]

The moral effect of Sannah's Post was considerable. It confirmed the steadfastness of those Free State burghers who were still in arms and it rallied the waverers. It was in some ways the prototype of the innumerable guerrilla actions which were to follow the fall of Pretoria.

'The army which marched into Bloemfontein had expended every military requisite except its own spirit and physical fitness.'
Official History of the War in South Africa

'We may soon have a good division together again.'
FRENCH in his diary, 13 April, 1900, at Bloemfontein

'You wouldn't know the regiment now if you saw it. The men have grown beards and are as dirty as niggers. The horses look more like costers' nags than Dragoon Guards' troopers. We are not allowed to carry anything but what we stand up in, except a shirt, a towel and a pair of socks in our wallets. I had a wash this morning, the first time for five days, so you can guess what we smell like.'
SQUADRON SERGEANT-MAJOR COBB, 7th Dragoon Guards, late April, 1900

'14 [May]. Only 93 horses in the regiment fit to travel . . . . 15 [May]. Cannot proceed. No forage.'
Regimental Diary, 8th Hussars

'Battles cannot be fought or victories won in the field if the enemy does not stand.'
The Times History of the War in South Africa[1]

(v)

Boer War: Reddersburg – Wepener – Fischer's Farm horse hospital opened – Roberts resumes advance – Kroonstad occupied – Welkom Farm – Zand River – relief of Mafeking – Johannesburg and Pretoria occupied – Lindley – Diamond Hill – Buller's advance – Buller joins up with Roberts

Christiaan De Wet, after his splendid success at Sannah's Post, now committed the only major mistake of his brilliant military career. Having with ease, on 4 April, after a twenty-four-hour fight, made prisoner over 500 infantrymen at Reddersburg, he went on to lay siege to the garrison of Wepener. This, numbering over 1,800 in all, consisted almost exclusively of the mounted troops of the Colonial

Division.* With more than 5,000 burghers De Wet squandered sixteen days, from 9 to 25 April, attacking the excellent defensive positions taken by Lieutenant-Colonel Edmund Henry Dalgety of the Cape Mounted Rifles. The juicy thought of capturing a large bag of the specially hated colonials undoubtedly warped De Wet's judgment. With Roberts's line of communication so long and vulnerable, the decision to go for the Colonial Division instead of sabotaging the inadequately guarded railway, lost him a splendid chance to discomfit the British. As it was he only just managed to retreat northwards in time to avoid the troops sent to relieve the Wepener garrison. The British lost thirty-three killed and 133 wounded.[2]

* * *

'Whenever there is an alarm Lord Roberts at once orders out French and the cavalry,' wrote Haig on 7 April. This was particularly true at the beginning and towards the end of the long wait at Bloemfontein when the alarms were chiefly due to De Wet's activities. Had it not been so, the Cavalry Division might have been better able to get itself into something like fighting order. As it was, the essential rest needed by both the surviving horses and the constantly arriving remounts, was almost invariably denied them. On 31 March the total available strength of the whole division was no more than 830 men and horses. Next day the Scots Greys reported that they could muster only eighty-six horses. On 14 April Haig complained that 'our great trouble is to find horses. Only underbred Argentine ponies are arriving here, and few of them are in condition for hard work. . . . We want about 2,500 horses to make our three brigades up to strength again.' Between 28 March and 4 May the remount depot in Bloemfontein alone issued 4,500 cavalry horses and cobs as well as 3,000 transport mules. Remounts from home were only just beginning to arrive at the beginning of May. 'The English remounts,' wrote Haig, 'are a fine lot. They ought to have been in the country two months ago! We must work them now at once, with the result that many will soon be useless from laminitis.'[3] Each Royal Horse Artillery battery was able to horse only four guns.

In March and early April there arrived from home the 7th Dragoon

---

* Cape Mounted Rifles (427); 1st and 2nd Brabant's Horse (804); Kaffrarian Rifles (393); Driscoll's Scouts (56); C.M.R. Artillery (93); Royal Scots Mounted Infantry (81).

Guards, 589 strong (garbed for the first time in khaki service dress), and the 8th Hussars. With the 14th Hussars, two squadrons of which had come round from Natal, there was now formed the 4th Cavalry Brigade, under the unpopular Major-General John Baillie Ballantyne Dickson, known to some of his officers as 'the old beast'.* At the same time the 17th Lancers, who had landed at the Cape on 10 March and were described by Haig on 10 April as 'a well mounted corps – horses in good condition', joined the 9th and 16th Lancers in Gordon's 3rd Cavalry Brigade, while two squadrons of the Inniskillings, which had been left at Rensburg, joined the rest of the regiment in Porter's 1st Cavalry Brigade†.[4]

*　*　*

The lengthy interruption to Roberts's great advance was caused by the need to receive not only remounts, but also all other forms of supplies. The broken bridges and culverts along the railway line had to be repaired before anything could begin to accumulate in Bloemfontein.‡ Replenishment of boots and other clothing was a first

---

* Dickson had joined the Bengal cavalry as a cornet in 1860, when only eighteen, becoming adjutant of the 18th Bengal Lancers. He later exchanged into the Royal Dragoons. He saw service in the Zulu War, 1879, was severely wounded at Abu Klea, 1885 and became lieutenant-colonel of the 5th Dragoon Guards. He died in 1925, aged eighty-three.

† On 19 April, while the horses of the 7th Dragoon Guards and the 8th and 14th Hussars were out grazing near Bloemfontein, there suddenly appeared three squadrons of the 17th Lancers,

> 'at full gallop, practising the "Advance in Line". Unable, or unwilling, to change course,' according to the 7th's historian, 'they thundered with reckless gallantry straight through the [4th] Brigade's grazing area. . . . It was several days before the [scattered] fugitives could be located and sorted out, and in fact some were never recovered. Those that were did not necessarily find themselves back with their rightful owners: "A horse is a horse on active service, and unnecessary questions about previous ownership are not asked." ' (Brereton, 279.)

Ian Hamilton described the officers and men of the 17th as 'those brave but rather unsophisticated warriors'. (Sampson, 31.) This was after the regiment's unfortunate action at Elandsrivierpoort on 17 September, 1901 (see p. 231).

‡ Towards the end of March the main supply bases were switched from Cape Town to Port Elizabeth (450 miles from Bloemfontein) and East London (402 miles), though it was some time after the occupation of Kroonstad (870 miles from Cape Town) before the switch was fully effective. Much, of course, still came direct from Cape Town.

priority. The men of the 12th Lancers, for instance, 'after five weeks in the clothes in which they stood up, were issued a complete change, their underclothes being, most wisely, burnt immediately.'[5]

'Some awful smells about! Enteric very bad – many funerals every day.'[6] Thus wrote Haig in mid-April. There is some evidence to show that the men of the cavalry suffered less from the awful scourge than those of the infantry. Nonetheless, considerable numbers succumbed, a fact which contributed to the inefficiency of the Cavalry Division.*

*　　*　　*

Two organizational changes affecting the mounted troops were made at this time. Early in April French asked Roberts 'what he thought of the mounted infantry. He said he was a great advocate for their use but that he was sure they could never in any sense replace cavalry. He has a strong idea,' confided French to his diary, 'that the value of their fire is much greater than that of the cavalry. I think we ought to combat this idea very strongly.'[7] Roberts very soon after that interview removed all the mounted infantry from French's command. 'We don't regret this,' wrote Haig, 'for the MI are a useless lot, and seem as soon as mounted to cease to be good infantry.'[8] This was a view which was proved wrong on a number of future occasions. The separate division into which the 11,000 mounted infantry were now formed never in fact existed as a separate entity for any practical purposes. At Bloemfontein a row soon developed between French and the commander of one of the new division's two brigades. This was Major-General Edward Thomas Henry Hutton, the father of the mounted infantry at Aldershot,† who now tried to get his men relieved on outpost duty by the cavalry. 'Hutton,' wrote French in his diary, 'has been behaving like an ass as usual! I had to go and see him and get his little game stopped . . . . My cavalry must have complete rest.'[9] Hutton before long took nominal command of all the mounted infantry in South Africa.

* The historian of the 12th Lancers tells how at the end of a long day three officers, finding no water other than from a pool in which lay a dead horse, could not curb their impatience to drink before the water was boiled and drank it 'with a liberal dash of whisky'. All three contracted enteric fever and only one survived. (Stewart, 209.)

† Hutton raised and commanded the mounted infantry there from 1888 to 1892.

The other organizational alteration involved the provision in future of four instead of two days' forage for the Cavalry Division, though to say that it made much difference, except to increase the weight on the horses' backs, would be to exaggerate.

*   *   *

At Fischer's Farm, 'a pretty spot' outside Bloemfontein, a very rough and ready depot for sick horses was now opened. An officer of the Inniskillings describes conditions there: 'The dead and dying horses scattered about were a painful sight; many were too weak even to graze, and some ten were shot daily. It was impossible to bury more than the entrails, so that hundreds of carcasses were lying about putrefying, the atmosphere for miles round being redolent and most nauseating.'[10]

When the advance from Bloemfontein was resumed Roberts's main force and Ian Hamilton's on his right flank (see below) contained about 17,200 horses for some 44,000 men. To supply all these, 40,000 oxen and 22,000 mules were required. In transport animals alone this meant that there were 1.4 animals for every fighting man. To attend to the health of these 79,200 animals there was a minuscule number of vets, only one of whom was even a major. All animals that could not keep up were abandoned, as had been the case ever since leaving Modder River. It was no one's duty to collect this debris of war and try to deal with it. Nevertheless the chief vet at Bloemfontein, when he heard of the appalling wastage going on, sent out a salvage party in the wake of the army. Over 500 horses left on the veld were thus recovered, many of which were later re-issued to the troops.[11]

*   *   *

When Roberts started off on 3 May, French and most of his cavalry had only just ceased from thrashing fruitlessly around in the Thaba 'Nchu area pursuing the will-o'-the-wisp De Wet brothers. Between French and Bloemfontein a force of 14,000 men, mostly mounted infantry but including Broadwood's 2nd Cavalry Brigade, under the command of Ian Hamilton, was ready to march parallel to the central force. The fact that this large semi-independent command was given to an officer much junior to French and that one of the cavalry brigades was included in it was a clear indication of the Field-

Marshal's diminished faith in the cavalry commander and his troops.*

French left Bloemfontein on 7 May, proposing to Roberts that in view of the softness of so many of his newly acquired horses, he should catch up the main army by easy stages. But in his anxiety to push on and, as he supposed, finish the war by seizure of the Transvaal's capital, Roberts ordered the cavalry to join him immediately. With great reluctance French obeyed. The 3rd and 4th Brigades marched sixty miles in two days. In consequence over 180 horses had to be abandoned or sent back. Many hundreds more were rendered virtually useless. 'The Field-Marshal,' wrote Haig on 14 April, 'faulted French because so many men were missing! But what can you expect to happen if horses stop from exhaustion and one covers sixty or more miles in two days.'[12]

Up to 9 May the cavalry horses received twelve pounds of corn daily, but no hay was provided. There was no time of course for grazing, nor was there much available, for, from the crossing of the Vaal onwards, the Boers had burned virtually all of it; 'not a blade of anything was left. The whole country in all directions was blackened by fire.'[13] For the next three days the supply column failed to reach the brigades at all. They had therefore to live off the country. This led, fortunately, to 'an abundance of oat hay being obtained from the various farms, together with mealies, though but few oats'.[14]

* * *

Though Boer morale, which had sunk so low on the fall of Bloemfontein, had been to some degree restored by De Wet's exploit at Reddersburg and by Roberts's lengthy stay in the Free State capital, there was no really serious opposition to Roberts's and Ian Hamilton's advance to Pretoria. During it there took place at least twenty-six minor engagements, but nothing approaching a real battle. Enormously superior in numbers, the British military machine trudged relentlessly forward, ever vexed and harassed by an adroit and mobile foe. In the *Volksraad* held at Kroonstad not long before its occupation, the Boer leaders unanimously agreed that the war should be carried on.[15]

* On 6 May the cavalry division numbered, very roughly, 6,000 of all ranks, including the horse artillery (twenty-four guns), eight 1-pounder quick firers and twelve other machine guns, as well as the staffs, Royal Engineers, Army Service Corps and Royal Army Medical Corps detachments. The actual horsed cavalrymen probably numbered little over 4,500. The total number of horses was probably less than 5,000 (Maurice, III, 536; Amery, IV, 112; Smith, 71.)

On 12 May Roberts occupied Kroonstad. By then the cavalry in both parts of the army had ridden between 120 and 160 miles in seven days, losing in the process (not at all surprisingly) just under a quarter of its strength in horses.[16] Even long acclimatized animals in perfect condition would have been hard put to it to emerge from so gruelling an ordeal unscathed. As it was the losses in this case were due less to starvation than to sheer want of condition, producing exhaustion, laminitis and sore backs.

A scratch horse hospital was opened at Kroonstad. By 20 May there were over 900 sick horses in it. To attend to these were

'400 war-worn men, the odds and ends of regiments, not under their own officers or non-commissioned officers, but under strangers for whom work is always grudgingly given by any soldier, especially at this time,' wrote the veterinary historian of the war, 'when discipline had visibly slackened. It is true a combatant officer was in command of the men. He was an unfortunate who had not done well in the field. In his misery at failure he sat all day deeply wrapped in thought . . . .

'Lord Kitchener, finding 400 dismounted men in a veterinary hospital, saw at once that it was a potential cavalry regiment. He directed a Cavalry Depot to be formed, took all the men and left their officers behind. . . . Native labour was decided upon. . . . The negro does not love work, and when he wanted money it was better to go with the troops as driver of a team of oxen, on a stipend that would make a curate's mouth water, rather than accept the local rates of the town. So the resources of the gaol had to be tapped, and its inmates were converted into hospital attendants.'

The 128 miles of railway between Bloemfontein and Kroonstad had been cut by the Boers in seventeen places. The blown bridges and culverts and the thousand-yard stretches of torn-up track took time to repair. Consequently all remounts were marched by road. On 17 May 352 arrived in Kroonstad. Even before they were issued, though most carried no weight on their backs, one-third of them were pronounced useless, through exhaustion, laminitis and injuries such as rope galls and sore backs.[17]

*   *   *

Roberts's invariable tactics throughout his advance depended upon the cavalry outflanking on both sides whatever positions the Boers took up, while the infantry held them in front. Almost without exception, all the way to Pretoria, the burghers escaped even partial encirclement. So slow were the cavalry's pincer movements that the enemy had but to stroll away to avoid them. This did not disturb Roberts unduly because he was always less anxious to fight battles than to reach Pretoria. This he did on 5 June, having crossed the Vaal on 24 May and captured Johannesburg, in some ways the very kernel of South Africa, on 31 May.*

Before entering Johannesburg Roberts negotiated a short truce, allowing Louis Botha, who had now become the supreme Boer commander, to extricate, with the help of Jan Smuts (see p. 230), his best burghers, his heavy guns and massive supplies, as well as much gold, in exchange for a guarantee that the gold mines would not be blown up. Whether as some historians have said this was a supreme blunder on the Field-Marshal's part or not it is hard to say. Certainly the charges for blowing up the mines were actually in place and certainly very important sinews of war were vouchsafed to the enemy which, but for the truce, would have been a spectacular catch for Roberts.

By the time of the fall of the Transvaal capital, some 300 miles had been covered in what must be rated one of the more memorable marches of military history. The main army had achieved it in thirty-four days, of which sixteen were rest days. This represented an average daily distance on marching days of sixteen-and-a-half miles. The forces on both flanks marched, of course, considerably further. Hamilton's men covered about 380 miles in thirty-seven

* The 7th Dragoon Guards were the first to set hoof and foot in the Transvaal. Its commanding officer, Lieutenant-Colonel William Henry Muir Lowe, obtained as a memento the town bell of Parijs where the regiment crossed. It was stowed with the regimental baggage and today it hangs outside the guard room wherever the 4/7 Dragoon Guards happen to be. (Brereton, 238.)

At the crossing of the Vaal men of the Household Cavalry used their 'strong arms' to help the Royal Engineers to cut 'a fine broad road up and down the steep river banks.' (Churchill: *Hamilton*, 234.)

On entering the town, a trooper of the 9th Lancers produced a lance flag which he had carried specially for the occasion. The commanding officer promptly appointed him his orderly. (Colvin, 116.)

By now the forage ration was reduced to five pounds of corn a day, sometimes supplemented by five pounds of maize. (Morton, 34.) On 27 May some forage was discovered: 'small stacks of curious fluffy grass called manna, and certainly heaven-sent – on which the horses subsisted and did not actually starve.' (Churchill: *Hamilton*, 235.)

marching days, averaging ten miles a day, while much of French's division (chiefly on the left flank) covered not less than 350 miles with hardly a day's rest: all this, as the official historian puts it most eloquently, 'over apparently endless prairies, in blazing sun and bitter cold, swept now by hot and choking dust storms, now by rushes of icy hail, fording rivers and floundering through sand, with scanty food and shelterless bivouacs.'[18]

*   *   *

Of the many minor actions in which the cavalry were engaged the first – a very typical one – took place at Welkom Farm on 4 May. Broadwood's brigade was leading Hamilton's force intending to secure the drifts south of Winburg when General Philip Botha's burghers, some 3,500 strong and perhaps 1,000 others from Brandfort, were seen to be converging. Broadwood was quick to see that if they met he would be encircled. He therefore ordered Captain Viscount Sudley's squadron of the Royal Horse Guards to seize the ridge which intervened between the kopjes for which the Boers were making. A race followed. It was only just won by the Blues at a gallop. They almost immediately came under artillery and rifle fire. Two squadrons of the 12th Lancers, with one Maxim supported by Kitchener's Horse and some mounted infantry, came speedily to their aid. After a time the infantry appeared and the burghers retired virtually unharmed. The Blues and the 12th suffered several casualties including one officer killed.[19]*

Six days later, the only engagement of any great significance during the advance took place at the Zand River on a bitterly cold morning. Dickson's brigade on the left came under a very galling fire and lost fourteen men killed and thirty-six wounded. French personally at one point ordered the 8th Hussars to charge.

> 'What a "charge" it was! The horses had not been fed or watered that morning,' wrote one who took part in it. 'We had come a good distance at a good pace, and, equipped in full marching order, carrying rations for horse and man, we could barely raise a decent gallop. With cool effrontery, the Boers mounted, and riding back some distance, dismounted and fired

---

* After the Boers had retired an excited infantry colonel came up, shouting, 'Where are they? Where are they?' Told that they had gone, he said, 'Gone again! Why, I've been trying to get a shot at them for three months and I thought I was going to this time.' (Hobson, 225.)

several rounds each, and once more repeated this performance. Eventually our best mounted reached a few of their stragglers, who paid the penalty of their temerity.'

The 8th killed two burghers, took two prisoners and wounded six.[20] Towards the end of an otherwise unsatisfactory day, Broadwood, on the right, managed to capture five wagons and twenty-eight prisoners. The total cavalry casualties in the three brigades engaged amounted to 161, including one officer killed and two made prisoner. The distance covered by most units was not less than thirty miles and the losses in horses for the day were 224. Due, Broadwood contended, to muddled orders, he had failed to turn the Boer left as Hamilton had desired; but Hamilton told the Secretary of State ten years later that the brigadier's performance had been lamentable. His unenterprising behaviour, he wrote, was a decisive factor in prejudicing Hamilton against conventional cavalry.[21] It also injured his reputation with Roberts (see p. 140). Almost unbelievably French at the height of the post-war controversy about the use of the *arme blanche* as against fire action, wheeled out the action at Zand River as a splendid example of 'the moral force of the cold steel'. Writing in 1910 he stated that when

'the Boer mounted riflemen attacked the flank brigade and began to drive it back, I galloped to the outer brigade with the thought that either every idea which I had ever formed in my life as to the efficacy of shock action against mounted riflemen was utterly erroneous, or that this was the moment to show that it was not. On reaching the outer brigade I ordered it to mount and form for attack. All ranks were at once electrified into extraordinary enthusiasm and energy. The Boers realized what was coming. Their fire became wild, and the bullets began to fly over our heads. Directly the advance began, the Boers hesitated, and many rushed to their horses. We pressed forward with all the very moderate speed of tired horses [!], whereupon the whole Boer force retired in the utmost confusion and disorder, losing in a quarter of an hour more ground than they had won during three or four hours of fighting. A cavalry which could perform service like this . . . can afford to regard with equanimity the attacks of those who have never led, trained, nor understood the arm to which I am proud to have belonged.'

Wishful thinking and self-deception can seldom have gone further.

It is totally clear that the 'charge' at Zand River produced insignificant enemy casualties, that it had no appreciable effect on the fortunes of the day, that the cavalry on the flank where it took place suffered serious checks and losses from a greatly inferior force and that both French's and Broadwood's turning forces completely failed to carry out Roberts's explicit orders to surround and destroy the enemy on both flanks.[22]

The Zand River action was the last of the war in which the Transvaal and Free State forces were organized as a more or less united army. The era of the guerrilla war was not far off.

* * *

Throughout the advance without exception there was never anything approaching a successful pursuit by the cavalry. Typical of the attitude of the officers towards the situation they found themselves in was that of a lieutenant of the Inniskillings:

'11 May. We advanced again as day was dawning, French's orders being that the enemy were in full retreat and the cavalry must pursue. A genial smile spread over everyone's countenance at the word "pursue", for, alas! who had a horse that could raise more than a trot? No wonder that we were losing our horses wholesale, from want of food and water, with eighteen to twenty stone on their backs, saddled from morning to night and perhaps all night, and then on again next day!'[23]

During that week of May alone, the Cavalry Division marched some 170 miles on the direct route. This meant that far greater distances were covered by those who were reconnoitring ahead and working on the flanks. On top of this there was the strain of night outpost duty. Often after marching and probably fighting all day, at nightfall the order would come: ' "Hold the hill you are on, keeping touch with so-and-so on your flank, fresh troops not being available." Then comes a night of anxious watching.'[24]

On at least two occasions Hutton's mounted infantry showed themselves to possess mobility superior to the cavalry's. On 16 May, at his own request, he was allowed by Hamilton to undertake a wide reconnaissance which began with a rapid night march and ended by the capture of several commando leaders and other prisoners. Then, on the day before the fall of Johannesburg on the plain below the Witwatersrand, neither the 1st nor the 4th Cavalry Brigades managed to even start upon the pursuit of the burghers as they retreated towards Pretoria. Hutton, however, in the words of *The Times History,*

'obtained French's permission to cut off the Boers without waiting for the cavalry. Sending Alderson with the 1st Corps [of Mounted Infantry] to circumvent the fugitives, and pursuing them in a direct line with [Lieutenant-Colonel Thomas David] Pilcher's* 3rd Corps supported by "G" Battery [Royal Horse Artillery] and the New Zealanders, he was rewarded for his enterprise by the capture, after a sharp skirmish, of a 3-inch Creusot gun, an ammunition wagon, twelve loaded supply wagons and fifty-four prisoners, including Commandant Runck of the German legion.'

This was one of the few instances during the whole war in which a direct pursuit resulted in a sizeable capture – and it was not made by the cavalry![25]

* * *

Meanwhile preparations had been made to relieve Mafeking, Cape Colony's most northerly town, under siege since the beginning of the war. A 'flying column' was formed at Barkly West, about twenty miles north-west of Kimberley. It was commanded by Brigadier-General Bryan Thomas Mahon, an 8th Hussar who had served on Kitchener's staff in Egypt, being present as Broadwood's second-in-command at Omdurman (see Vol III, p. 377) at which battle he had been erroneously reported killed.† His force included some 770 men of the Imperial Light Horse, 122 of the Kimberley Mounted Corps (not to be confused with the Kimberley Light Horse (see p. 140)), four Royal Horse Artillery twelve-pounders, a couple of pom-poms

---

* Pilcher, an infantryman, was much disliked by a number of his officers. One of them, Captain Gilmour of the Imperial Yeomanry thought him 'one of the worst men in all South Africa. He is quite too dreadful, a temper like a fiend, a blind, plunging, uncomfortable commanding officer, never rests and does no real work. . . . He is one of these dashers, but I do not think he often knows what or where he is dashing at. . . . We long for Clements or Benson.' (10, 14 Apr., 1901, Gilmour, 141, 150.)

† In November, 1900, he returned to Egypt, to govern Kordofan. He commanded the Salonika Army, 1915–16 and was Commander-in-Chief, Ireland, 1916–18, becoming a Senator in the Irish Free State in 1922.

and a few infantrymen.* It took fifty-two wagons, each drawn by ten mules, to carry the column's supplies.

On 4 May it started off. On 12 May it was attacked near Vryburg and drove the enemy off. Three days later, having marched 230 miles in eighteen days, Mahon's column joined Brevet Colonel Herbert Charles Onslow Plumer's force of some 800 Rhodesian levies, all mounted rifles.† With these Plumer, commanding all the local forces north of Kimberley, had for long been conducting numerous minor engagements so as to defend Rhodesia and to take the pressure off Baden-Powell in Mafeking. To the siege of that town there had been drawn during the first month of the war some 7,700 Boers, nearly a fifth of all those then in the field. Since that time of crisis only some 1,500 burghers had been conducting the investment.

On 17 May, after considerable opposition, Mahon and Plumer entered the town. The first men in were Major Karri Davies (see p. 48), second-in-command of the Imperial Light Horse and eight of his troopers. Mahon's column had marched a daily average of eighteen miles for little over a fortnight through a difficult and poorly watered country during which two actions had been fought. The siege had lasted 217 days. Its relief occasioned delirious rejoicing in Britain, thereby giving the language the verb to maffick.

From the point of view of the lessons to be learned from the war, it is interesting to compare the work of Mahon's 900 colonial mounted riflemen in relieving Mafeking with French's 'flying column' in the 'dash to Kimberley' with some 3,000 regular cavalry (see p. 128). Taking into account the numbers employed, the oppo-

* Mahon is said to have sent a coded message to Baden-Powell and to Plumer (see below): 'Our numbers are Naval and Military Club multiplied by ten [94, Piccadilly × ten = 940]; our guns the number of sons in the Ward family [The Earl of Dudley and five brothers = six guns]; our supplies, the Officer commanding the 9th Lancers [Lieutenant-Colonel Little = few].'

† Plumer had been joined on 14 May by 100 Queensland Mounted Infantry and a battery of Canadian artillery. These had been sent up to Beira in Mozambique from where they had made their way by rail, mule and horse to Plumer in Western Rhodesia. Plumer had raised his levies as early as 1896. His defence of Rhodesia over a long period of the first phase of the war was little short of brilliant. It is worth noting that it was carried out exclusively by men who were equipped and trained as mounted riflemen.

He became one of the best of the First World War generals, rising speedily to command 2nd Army. Between 1925 and 1928 he was High Commissioner for Palestine. In 1919 he was promoted Field-Marshal and in 1929 created Viscount Plumer of Messines. He died, aged seventy-five, in 1932.

sition met with and the distances covered, the contrast reflects most unfavourably upon the cavalry's performance.

* * *

Beside Roberts's and Hamilton's columns, the great advance towards Pretoria was intended to be co-ordinated with others: Buller, with his 45,000 men and 119 guns, from Ladysmith in the east; Hunter, with 10,000 men and eighteen guns, through Fourteen Streams into the Transvaal from the west, and Methuen, with 10,000 men and twenty-six guns, through Boshof* and Hoopstad to the left of French. All these, with the exception of Buller, managed to go forward more or less as Roberts wanted. Even Buller, when he was at last convinced that the Boers in his front had virtually melted away, ventured forward (see p. 186). Behind Roberts's main push, attempting to clear the country in wide swathes, were other bodies of troops. Their chief mobile components consisted of the Imperial Yeomanry, which on arrival in March and April had been distributed among the various commands. Trooper Peel of the Oxfordshire Imperial Yeomanry describes how such bodies conducted their painfully slow, unwieldy marches at this stage of the campaign:

'Far ahead are the advance-guard skirmishing in a long line on both sides of the track, then the general with his staff, marching probably, as his custom is, on foot, a custom which endears him to his infantry soldiers . . . . Then comes a little group with some mysterious packages wrapped up in cloth; these they unfold and screw together a couple of little looking-glasses on a tripod. It is the heliograph; they try flashes all round the compass . . . . At last it comes from right in front thi time . . . . A long conversation begins, but not one that a casual bystander can understand: only that he can be sure that we are marching towards our friends. After the heliograph comes a battery escorted by two or three companies of yeomanry, then a long

---

* At Boshof, on 5 April, Methuen surprised a foreign corps of some 100 Germans and Frenchmen under Colonel de Villebois-Mareuil. Unlike the few Boers with this force who wisely melted away before Methuen's 750 mounted men and a gun battery, de Villebois-Mareuil stayed and fought. He himself was killed and Methuen buried him with full military honours.

This little engagement was the first of any consequence in which the Imperial Yeomanry were in action. There were 500 of them commanded by Lord Chesham. In support were 250 of the Kimberley Mounted Corps.

train of waggons headed and flanked by a battalion of infantry. Then the ambulances – they would be in front if we expected an action today; then more guns and more infantry, till we get back to the yeomanry rearguard; on both sides of course are flankers of infantry and beyond them, a long way out more yeomanry.'

Peel also explains how a scouting patrol was carried out: 'Perhaps some little way from a ridge you draw rein, make a feint of seeing something and turn quickly to gallop back. Ten to one if an enemy is there he will think you have seen him. If you do not hear the crack of a rifle in the first few yards, you may ride on again pretty confident that the crest is clear.'[26]

One of the secondary bodies not directly involved in the great advance was the 9th Division commanded by Colvile, who was last seen failing to support Broadwood at Sannah's Post. On 22 May he received orders to march on the 26th with the Highland Brigade to Lindley, 'a straggling town with the usual corrugated iron roofs and a church in the centre', forty-seven miles to the east of Kroonstad. Lindley had already been captured by Ian Hamilton and then re-captured by the Boers. It was soon to become a storm centre of Boer resistance in the Free State, changing hands a further seven times in the next few weeks, showing how free were the De Wet brothers' and others' commandos to roam behind the British advance. Colvile had been told that on his way to Lindley he would be reinforced by the 13th (Irish) Battalion of Imperial Yeomanry, consisting of about 470 of all ranks and intended to provide him with virtually his only mounted troops.* The 13th Battalion, it so happened, was the flashy show-piece of the volunteer movement which had swept Britain after 'Black Week'. It quickly became known as the 'Millionaires' Own'. It consisted of four companies or squadrons:† The Duke of Cambridge's Own (see p. 93) raised by The Earl of Donoughmore which contained, chiefly, very wealthy men-about-town who had insisted on paying their own passage out to South Africa, and three

* Without them, all he had were 107 odds and ends, mostly from the Eastern Province Horse (which had been formed less than four months earlier and never numbered much more than 100 men). He certainly did not have enough for both scouting and protecting his three-and-three-quarter miles of guns and wagons. (Colvile, 158.)

† Early in 1900 an Army Order had been issued directing that all companies of the Imperial Yeomanry should in future be designated squadrons with four troops each. Each division of four men was to be referred to as a Section.

Irish squadrons. One of these, known as the Irish Hunt Contingent, was officered for the most part by Irish Masters of Foxhounds. It was commanded by Captain the Earl of Longford and included Lieutenant Viscount Ennismore. Its ranks were chiefly filled with Dublin men. The two other companies were of Ulster Protestant Unionists and included Sir John Power, a whisky baronet, the Earl of Leitrim and James Craig, later Lord Craigavon. All the officers gave their pay to the Widows and Orphans Fund.[27] Within eleven days of landing at the Cape the battalion had been 'deemed efficient for service'. 'We had established,' wrote one young yeoman, 'a record for the Imperial Yeomanry Base Camp at Maitland.' The same man was full of praise for the 'hardy and sure-footed Hungarian horses' with which the battalion was issued.[28] The 13th's commanding officer was Lieutenant-Colonel Basil Edward Spragge, a forty-eight year old infantry officer with considerable experience of active service in India.

When on 25 May Spragge at Kroonstad received the order to join Colvile at Lindley,* he had to reply that due to delays in procuring forage he would only be able to reach that place 'as early as possible on 27th'. This message seems never to have been passed on to Colvile,[29] who even denied that he had been made aware that Spragge had been ordered to join him on 26 May.[30]† It is clear that there was a lamentable lack of communication between Colvile and Spragge, due chiefly to inefficient headquarters staff work. In consequence, when Spragge arrived outside Lindley at 1 p.m. on the 27th, he not only did not find Colvile or any message from him, but instead soon discovered that the Boers had re-occupied the place.

* There is considerable confusion about this order. Spragge himself says that on arrival at Kroonstad he was 'shown a telegram to the Commandant, Kroonstad, from General Colvile, directing him (Spragge) to join him (Colvile) at Lindley.' (*R.C.*, IV, 416.) There are those who believe that this order was not addressed to the Commandant, but to Spragge by name, and that it was sent by the Boers in Lindley to lure the 13th into a trap. Colvile certainly denied that he ever sent the message. However, the present author tends to believe Spragge. (*R.C.*, II, 299, Appx VI. See also Reckitt, 37–8.)

† Further, Colvile, in *The Work of the Ninth Division*, says that Kitchener sent him a message on 24 May which also never reached him, saying: 'Yeomanry are so late they cannot catch you at Ventersburg. You must march without them; they will join you later via Kroonstad.' (Colvile, 222.) See also *R.C.*, II, 299, Appx IX, where this message is given as being received on 20 June and sent on '19th May' and in which the 13th I.Y. is called the '24th'. Clearly the '24th' must be the date, not the unit's number. How '19th May' is to be accounted for it is impossible to say.

Further, they were ready for him. Two days earlier, on his way from Kroonstad, where he had obtained two days' supplies, Spragge had met some surrendering Boers who told him that Colvile was at Lindley. Instead of taking them prisoner Spragge accepted the surrender of their rifles

'which included those of the Snider, Martini and Steyr makes, but,' as one yeoman pointed out, 'only one Mauser. This fact should have aroused suspicion. Our colonel ordered the names of our visitors to be taken, and then directed them to be given a good meal, after which *they were permitted to return whence they came.* . . . On learning that one of the Dutchmen came from a place called Paradise, "Tell him," said Colonel Spragge to the interpreter, "that if he doesn't go home and stay quietly upon his farm, he'll find himself in the real Paradise sooner than he expects." To put the matter shortly, the scouts of the Boer commandos at Lindley had been permitted to enter our lines to find out our numbers, our armaments and the amount of our supplies, had even had lunch with us, and all this information and hospitality at the expense of a few out-of-date rifles and a few perjured oaths.'[31]

As soon as Spragge realized that in Lindley itself, lying as it does in a hollow, he would be trapped, he withdrew to a more easily defended position two and a half miles to the north of it. There, not unreasonably, since at any moment he expected to hear from Colvile, he prepared to defend his battalion against the not very considerable Boer force (without, at first, any artillery) which was sniping at him. Even before the sniping started Spragge sent off two messages, one to Colvile who was eighteen miles on his way north to Heilbron and received it at 7 a.m. next day, and the other to Lieutenant-General Sir Leslie Rundle whose division was further south.* In both messages Spragge said that Lindley was 'a nasty place to retire from', that there was only one day's food left and that he would 'want help to get out without great loss'.[32]

---

* When Rundle received Spragge's plea at 10 a.m. on 28 May he was forty miles away at Senekal. He, like Colvile, was being harassed, but, belying his nickname of 'Sir Leisurely Trundle', at once decided to try to draw off the commandos around Lindley by advancing on Bethlehem. Unfortunately his telegram was intercepted. The Boers were ready for him. He was forced to retire after an engagement (Biddulph's Berg) in which he suffered 180 casualties to the Boers' forty. (See, especially, Kruger, 311.)

Colvile's first reaction on receiving the two orderlies who brought Spragge's message was to ask them, not surprisingly, 'Who is Colonel Spragge?' On questioning the men he was told that the yeomanry had retired five miles towards Kroonstad – (incorrect and merely, of course, the orderlies' judgment). This, and the fact that two uniformed men had been able to get through to him with ease, that one day's rations were well known in emergencies to last up to four days* and that he himself was being harassed by the enemy, decided Colvile not to do anything to help Spragge. To that officer he wrote the following message: 'The enemy are between me and you and I cannot send back supplies. If you cannot join me by road to Heilbron you must retire on Kroonstad, living on country, and if necessary abandon your wagons.'[33] By evening the three messengers by whom this order was sent returned, saying that they could not get through. Thus Spragge never received it. By then Colvile was still further on his way to Heilbron, at which place Roberts had ordered him to be by 29 May. Though he had not been specifically told so, he believed that his arrival there on time was an important part of Roberts's grand design. This was, of course, a chief factor in his decision not to go back to Lindley. In fact, as it turned out, it would not have made an ounce of difference if he had been a week late, but he was not to know that.

Meanwhile, hearing that the famous yeomanry unit which contained so many politically and socially important British gentlemen was in difficulties, numbers of commandos rushed to the scene, including Piet de Wet's, together with four artillery pieces. These last arrived on 30 and 31 May. The position Spragge had taken up was not a bad one, though he admitted that it was too extensive for the size of his force. This was due to the need to gather forage. He

---

* The battalion did in fact hold out for more than four days. Trooper Fitzgibbon says that an arrangement of rations was being contemplated which would have enabled the battalion to hold out for eight days:

'For breakfast, 1/8th ration of bully beef and one spoonful of jam per man; for dinner, a quarter-ration of mutton, derived from the sheep we had fortunately captured on the Sunday night; for evening meal, a quarter-ration of biscuit. This last would, however, hold out for two days only; and against the time when the biscuits should be exhausted, the Kaffir boys who had driven our wagons were set to work to mill the oats which we had brought for our horses, in order that from it porridge might be made, and thus supply a necessary article of diet. To this end a small mill had luckily been found at the farmhouse which lay within the radius of our ground.' (Fitzgibbon, 142–3.)

was sniped at all through 28, 29 and 30 May. On the 29th he drove the enemy out of several positions: but a party of sixteen men which he sent out to reconnoitre and, if possible, occupy an outlying position called the 'Stone Kopje', was surprised and nearly all were captured. Next morning, to remove, as Spragge later put it, 'the bad effect of this contretemps', he sent Lord Longford with forty men to occupy the hill which he regarded as the key to his position. This was accomplished 'at the point of the bayonet'. On 30 May the battalion's investment was completed. Next day, after some bitter fighting, Spragge surrendered. What happened, according to his own account, was this:

> 'About 2 p.m. I saw the picquet on the furthest advanced point on the "Stone Kopje" retire without any warning. I tried to reinforce the position, but it was too late. Just then a white flag was put up on the kopje by a quite irresponsible person, Corporal Jacques. The enemy took the hill and our position was now completely commanded. One Colt gun jammed and the kraal became untenable.'[34]

According to one yeoman the fear-crazed corporal was at once shot down by two of his men.[35] But the damage had been done. Trooper Thomas McCrea told the Court of Inquiry:

> 'I was one of a party under Captain Humby (see p. 102) who went to reinforce the company on the advanced Stone Kopje. I was following that officer up the hill when we met Captain Robin. I heard Captain Robin ordering the "Cease Fire", and saying that some of his men [in fact Corporal Jacques] had put up the white flag. Captain Robin asked Captain Humby if he would see him through it, and Captain Humby said he knew nothing about the white flag . . . . Captain Robin said he might as well blow out his brains. I would not allow him to do this and Captain Humby sympathized with Captain Robin. There was a heavy shell and rifle fire at this time. Captain Robin went away to a farmhouse at the foot of the kopje, waving a white handkerchief, and was shot in the hand while doing so.'[36]

Both Spragge and Longford, seeing the Stone Kopje overrun and the two white flags raised, had no alternative but to surrender. 'I say, old boy,' shouted Lord Ennismore to his captain, Lord Longford, 'it's no good. We must not sacrifice more lives.' 'Go on,' replied Longford, by now himself seriously wounded, 'until I give the order to cease fire.' Five minutes later, after two more men had been killed, he gave the order, and the last men of the battalion surrendered. 'Handkerchiefs which had once been white were raised on bayonets.' After the surrender 'a few Boers came up to us,' wrote Trooper Fitzgibbon, 'and to our wonderment seized us by the hand saying "Well done! You fought well, right well." "By George," one of us replied, "you're sportsmen, anyhow".'[37]

It was later decided at headquarters that poor Captain Robin should have his war gratuity and medal withheld from him, but on appeal a three-officer committee decided that he had hoisted the second white flag 'under a misapprehension that he was bound to respect the white flag hoisted by Corporal Jacques. Considering his want of military knowledge and his subsequent good service' both gratuity and medal were in due course awarded him.[38]

The casualties before the surrender show the respectable total of seventy-eight. Two officers and nineteen men were killed, forty-two officers and men wounded and twenty taken prisoner. About 390 surrendered and were marched into captivity.* The Boers were said to have lost seventy killed and wounded.[39]

Roberts, as soon as he learned of Spragge's situation by telegram from Rundle, ordered Methuen (who had arrived at Kroonstad on 28 May so as to fill the vacuum left by Roberts's departure from that town), to march to the yeomanry's relief. On 30 May he set off. On 1 June he was eight miles from Lindley when he heard of the surrender the day before. Later in the day his advance guard, the 3rd Battalion, Imperial Yeomanry, having marched forty-two miles, actually became engaged with the rearguard of the convoy with the prisoners. It only just failed to rescue them. It did, however, capture sixteen wagons and two guns. These last, in the words of its commanding officer,

'held us off for a time. Then we made a detour round to our left, and taking ridge after ridge, found ourselves on the flank of the retreating Boers . . . . Just as we were turning inwards to make our charge, we suddenly came across a precipice, about twenty-five feet drop, down which was apparently no path, and the face of which was fully exposed to the Boer fire. Our blood

* When Dundonald entered Standerton on 22 June he discovered that, had he arrived two days earlier, he almost certainly could have rescued a part of the Irish Yeomanry prisoners from Lindley who were passing through the town. (Amery, IV, 399.)

was up, and somehow or other thirty-six of us scrambled down the sheer wall on foot, and had our horses shoo-ed down after us. At the bottom was a nullah which gave us welcome shelter for a moment's breather; then mounting our horses we formed in single rank with a good interval, and issuing from the nullah, charged four hundred yards across the open, cut off the convoy and guns, and took the kopje beyond.'[40]

* * *

The public's reaction to the surrender was, as one historian puts it, 'as great as the pedigree of the defeated battalion was long'.[41] Roberts 'stellenbosched' Colvile whom he considered 'mainly responsible for the surrender'. This seems unfair, but Colvile's behaviour at Sannah's Post, taken with his general arrogance, perhaps almost justified his being made the scapegoat. Amery, in *The Times History*, ever the armchair critic, lashes out at Spragge: 'He could easily have retired to Kroonstad . . .'; but Colvile defended him: 'Having sent a messenger after me,' he wrote, 'it was only natural that he should wait, first for the return of the messenger and then for the force which he was hastening to join – only natural, and fully accounts for his delaying till it was too late to retire.' The *Official History* also supports Spragge, adding that 'his animals, soft from a train journey, had come forty-five miles in forty-eight hours. Most of his men had already marched far and fast. He had found a good position for his force, one well provided with water and grazing.'[42] The sad irony of the Lindley Affair is that had Corporal Jacques not shown the white flag, thus sparking off the surrender, the yeomanry might very well have held out another twenty-four hours and been relieved in the nick of time by Methuen's force.

At a stroke, the Boers (taking Rundle's Biddulph's Berg casualties into account) had inflicted more losses on Roberts's army than they themselves had suffered in the whole of their retreat from Bloemfontein to Johannesburg. Nevertheless the 13th Battalion had drawn to it Boer forces which would otherwise have been employed, several days earlier than they actually were, in cutting the railway line at one of the most critical moments of all for Roberts.[43]

* * *

Roberts's fighting force at the front five days after his entry into

Pretoria was down to not much more than 14,000. To this was almost immediately added a further 3,000. These were the prisoners of war, mostly other ranks, who were released under fire from their cage near the city by a force the advance guard of which was a squadron and a half of the Greys.[44]*

Negotiations were at once set in train for the surrender of Louis Botha's forces, but they came to nothing, for the news of Christiaan De Wet's remarkable successes against the British line of communication contributed enormously and instantaneously to the restoration of Boer morale. Botha scraped together some 5,000 Transvaalers and took up a strong position, fifteen miles to the east of the capital, covering a wide front near Diamond Hill. Here Roberts felt bound to attack them so as to remove the threat they posed to his eastern flank. In the course of the two-day battle the British losses of 180† far exceeded those of the Boers, but Roberts's object was attained.

On the first day, 11 June, the cavalry under French, ordered to turn the enemy's right flank (which it failed to do), fought amongst the hills mostly dismounted, with intervals of twenty or thirty paces between the men. Little was achieved, but their positions were held. Ian Hamilton's force, required to turn the Boer left flank (which it, also, failed to do), contained Broadwood's and Gordon's Cavalry Brigades. These, much attenuated 'from lack of horse-flesh',[45] numbered about 700 with nearly 650 mounted infantry and some of the guns of three horse artillery batteries.

One of these, 'Q' Battery, the same that had, in Conan Doyle's words, 'plucked glory out of disaster at Sannah's Post',[46] escorted

---

* According to one account, as the Greys were seen approaching by the prisoners, a 'great yell went up'. They thrust their guards aside, cut through the barbed wire and streamed towards the cavalry. De la Rey who had come to remove the prisoners out of British reach pointed his guns at them as they emerged from a dip in the plain.

'They were utterly caught in the open. It was an extraordinary opportunity for [De la Rey] to inflict the greatest single disaster of the war on the British. By the rules of war he was entitled, and by his duty as a general bound, to mow down the mob scattering wildly below him. But it was not butchery he cared for, and he was spared it by a misconception, for at the same moment the Greys, now reinforced, threw themselves at him. He thought the whole British cavalry was attacking. And while his attention was distracted the prisoners rushed madly to a train waiting to whisk them to Pretoria before he discovered his mistake.' (Kruger, 318.)

† Among the dead was Major the Hon. Lionel Fortescue, 17th Lancers, whose brother, the future Sir John, was then writing the third volume of his *History of the British Army* (Brereton, 285).

by a few troopers, was at one point pushed forward by Hamilton who had perceived a gap in the enemy's line. The guns were immediately attacked from right and left by two bodies of the enemy* who boldly rushed in firing at short range. Gunners and escort were on the point of being swept from the field with the loss of the guns when Broadwood sent a galloper to the 12th Lancers, ordering them to charge without a moment's delay. Many of the 12th were scattered about, patrolling. Consequently all that could be got into line were some fifty or sixty, including eleven officers. These were joined by ten men of the 10th Hussars. Lord Airlie, commanding the 12th (see p. 458), whose roan had just been shot under him, cantered up at this moment remounted on a white pony. 'Which direction are we to charge?' he asked. When told, he took place at the head of his men and gave the orders: 'The regiment will attack. Trot, gallop, charge.' The men brought their lances to the engage, stuck in their spurs and 'let out yells of every description'. Their enfeebled Argentine ponies were scarcely able to raise more than a canter, but the Boers for the most part, having emptied their magazines, melted away. A few – possibly twelve in all – were caught. Sergeant Thompson was confronted by an old burgher who had just shot dead a lancer officer. Throwing down his rifle, the old man pleaded for mercy. 'I'll give you mercy, you bloody bugger,' shouted Thompson, as he put his lance through the Boer's throat. 'Steady with your language there,' Airlie is believed to have shouted. One burgher was seen to fall off his horse with a lance sticking between his shoulders. Another was persistently hit over the head by the sword of a lancer officer, but only wounded.[47]

> 'We went on and on,' wrote Captain Gerald Walton Hobson, 'till [Lieutenant Walter Howorth] Greenly [the Adjutant]† rode up to the Colonel and said "I think we have gone far enough, sir." Airlie had previously told him to do this. "Very well. Files About, Walk" was the order. I knew what we were in for. It was obvious. I saw the Boers literally fall off their horses in their hurry to shoot at us now our backs were turned.'[48]

Airlie told the Adjutant to get the men 'to ride in more open order',[49]

* Some of whom were from a German unit. (Amery, IV, 283.)

† Hobson wrote two books: *Some XII Royal Lancers*, from which this quote is taken, and *The Story of the XII Royal Lancers*. He died, aged eighty-nine, in 1962. Greenly became Colonel of the 12th Lancers in 1917 and commanded the 2nd Cavalry Division, 1916–18. He died in 1955, aged eighty.

for they were bunching, making a mark for the enemy's fire. Trained to be as slow in retreat as swift in advance, the lancers at first retired walking, as ordered, but their walk soon became a trot which for those capable of it developed before long into a slow gallop. The very heavy Boer fire concentrated on Airlie and his white pony. He fell at once, shot through the heart. The total casualties numbered about seventeen officers and men and some thirty horses. There seems no doubt that the charge was successful in saving the guns.

Nevertheless the enemy pressure on Broadwood's right continued to increase. When a body of Boers crept up under the shelter of some mealie-fields and began pouring an enfilading fire on the retiring guns, he ordered Lieutenant-Colonel Thomas Charles Pleydell Calley, commanding the Household Cavalry, to 'clear them out' with one squadron of the 1st Life Guards, and another of the Blues. One account states that 'the troopers began immediately to dismount with their carbines, and the General had to send a second message to them, saying that it was no good firing now, and that they must charge with the sword.' The men thereupon pounded over the mealie-fields 'shouting with delight at the prospect of really getting in a blow' and, apparently, 'flogging their gaunt horses with the flat of their swords'.[50] But after losing one man and twenty-one horses, and riding for nearly a mile, they were disappointed in their attempt to close, for the enemy, as was his wont, dispersed in all directions.

Conan Doyle summed up these two charges thus: 'Cavalry as cavalry had vindicated their existence more than they had ever done during the campaign.'[51] Whether this was saying much, or not, he does not go on to say. Out of the 2,937 horses with which the Cavalry Division's four brigades started the battle of Diamond Hill, 675 were casualties by its end. Of these only twenty-one had been killed in action and fifty-five wounded.[52]

Though Ian Hamilton thought that Diamond Hill marked 'the true turning point' of the war because it proved that 'humanly speaking, Pretoria could not be retaken', Jan Smuts found that for the Boers the battle had 'an inspiriting effect which could scarcely have been improved by a real victory'.[53]

*　　*　　*

For two months after the relief of Ladysmith, Buller's army remained inactive. A fortnight later Captain Slocum, an official observer for the United States Army, found 'the slowness of General Buller's advance' 'inexplicable'.[54] In fact 'Sitting Bull', to use his new nickname (which alternated with another, 'Trek Ox'), had been ordered to stay 'strictly on the defensive' throughout March and April. Roberts had then wanted him in May to take part in a converging thrust towards Pretoria, but he 'insisted on the need to cross the Biggarsberg and clear the main railway northwards. Eventually Buller had got his own way.'[55] In the event Roberts received no assistance whatever from him during his march to the Transvaal capital. Indeed Buller only occupied his first town in the Transvaal, Wakkerstroom, a week after the fall of Pretoria.[56] When on 7 May at last he moved, he left behind his six regular cavalry regiments. (Most of these joined the advance on 23 May but saw little action.) In view of the mountainous nature of the country ahead this was a wise decision. Nevertheless some authorities believe that had the 1st and 2nd Cavalry Brigades been up, the burghers' enormous transport train would not have escaped capture. With him Buller took only one brigade of mounted troops, that of Dundonald and now called the 3rd Mounted Brigade. It consisted of the South African Light Horse, Thorneycroft's and Bethune's Mounted Infantry, Gough's Composite Regiment and 'A' Battery of the Royal Horse Artillery. The Composite Regiment had over the months lost some of the Natal volunteers and the Imperial Light Horse squadrons. In their place came two companies of mounted infantry, one Scots and one Irish.

' "I'm not trying to turn you into cavalry," Gough told his companies at the end of a day's hard training, "but some of you have already seen how much of our work is done as light horse and we must be good at it. Equally, when we dismount for infantry work we must be good at that too and I want to see you employing all the infantry skills, starting with musketry. We must be able to shoot whether on or off our horses." '[57]

Buller's campaign in which his infantry scrambled over the Natal passes into the dusty plains of the Transvaal and on to Standerton was, as he himself put it, 'an almost perfect' one.[58] Dundonald showed energy and his men great endurance.

'I enveloped the whole Force with a screen of mounted men well out on the front, flanks and rear. The main body,' he wrote in his autobiography, 'moved along unmolested, guarded by us from enemy sharpshooters who took their deadly aim and then bolted by a safe line of retreat. The work of cavalry in this

difficult country was arduous in the extreme; without the excitement of a general action there were daily losses. The Colt
machine guns were with the detached parties and did good
work; the enemy did not like them.'[59]

One of the least pleasant aspects of the advance was the burning
of the grass on the veld by the retreating burghers. Not only did this
reduce the grazing ground, but it nearly always acted as an effective
smoke-screen forbidding pursuits and concealing the direction of
retirement. On the other hand there was one pleasing fact to note.
For the very first time in the army's history, Buller's force was
accompanied in the field by some properly organized machinery for
the treatment of sick and injured horses.[60]

Buller twice outflanked and outmanoeuvred large numbers of
Boers. That his chief opponent was Lucas Meyer (see p. 39), one
of the least competent of the Boer commanders, certainly helped
him. Nevertheless the taking of Laing's Nek, the 'Gibraltar' of Natal
(see Vol III, p. 206), without the firing of a shot was no mean feat.
It entailed climbing very steep hill-sides in an audacious turning
movement which met with total success. An officer who took part
especially remembered the intense cold. The difficulty of watering
his horses was great for the water was everywhere frozen.[61]

On 20 June Strathcona's Horse, which had sailed from Halifax, Nova
Scotia, in mid-Match, came under Dundonald's command. Raised
especially for the war by the Canadian financier and imperialist,
Donald Smith, first Baron Strathcona and Mount Royal, it was commanded by Colonel Sam Steele, formerly of the North-West
Mounted Police. It consisted of 'Canadian-born men and young men
from home of the adventurous type, all mixed up together and held
together in a discipline of iron by Colonel Steele.' They brought
their own horses with them. Dundonald was pleased with them,
particularly as, being 'accustomed to be rounded up on the prairie',
they did 'not readily stampede when left under the charge of a few
men.'

The regiment was equipped entirely at Lord Strathcona's expense, and very similarly to the Canadian Mounted Rifles which had
been sent out by the Canadian Government in the first Canadian
Contingent. After it received its first draft from Canada it consisted
of twenty-nine officers and 568 other ranks. Pay was more than
twice that of British cavalrymen. The difference was made up by
Lord Strathcona.

A True Patriot.

Mr. BULL (to Lord Strathcona): "Four hundred men, fully equipped, at your own expense; Egad, my lord, yours is something like an offer—it will put to the blush some of my wealthy ones at home!!"

One squadron was raised in Manitoba, another in North West Territory and the third in British Colombia. Colonel Steele wrote later that

> 'the whole of the saddlery, clothing, transport wagons and many other articles of equipment had to be manufactured. The horses had to be purchased at the very worst time of the year, and were to be cow-horses, that is animals trained in round-up and all range work. Recruits were not wanting. One could have got thousands of the best men in Canada. I had an offer from 600 first-class Arizona stockmen. They were prepared to supply their own arms, pay for any class of rifle that I desired, furnish their own horses, spare and riding, if I would take them for Strathcona's Horse.... I had to decline.... I could have had the assistance of thousands of the finest horsemen in the US.'

During its year of service the regiment suffered twenty-six deaths, of which twelve were in action. Its first serious engagement took place on 11 July, 1900, when it helped to turn out the enemy from his position on Van Kolder's Kop. In the pursuit several casualties occurred and eight of the enemy were also killed.

On 18 June, at Zoutpans Drift, other Canadians had had a remarkable success. A lieutenant of the Manitoba Dragoons, guided by a sergeant and two of Hutton's Scouts, with a small detachment of the 1st Canadian Mounted Rifles, captured without loss two field guns, one of which was believed to have been taken from the Jameson raiders of 1896. Among the twelve men in the successful party there were representatives of ten different regiments of the Canadian Militia.[62]

* * *

The important railway centre of Standerton fell to Buller on 23 June. A little later Dundonald's mounted brigade was much reduced by the need for numerous garrisons on the lines of communication. He was left with Strathcona's Horse and Thorneycroft's Mounted Infantry, some 800 men, and his horse artillery battery. For the next four weeks, 'though there were no pitched battles to record,' as Dundonald put it, 'there was constant contact with the enemy, and I regret to say constant unavoidable loss.'[63] This might well describe the nature of much of the rest of the war.

First contact with Roberts's army took place close to the Zuikerbosch Spruit near Heidelberg on 4 July. Thus the two armies which had started their campaigns from bases more than 1,000 miles apart, joined hands after ten months of marching and fighting.* When a little later Buller met the little Field-Marshal it was for the first time in their lives. How they got on is not recorded.

The most important result of Buller's advance was the opening of the railway between Durban and Pretoria. From now on there were two main supply lines and one of them was only 511 miles in length as opposed to the other's 1,040 miles.

During these next few months, the regular cavalry of Buller's force performed, in the words of Lieutenant-Colonel Gore of the 5th Dragoon Guards, 'a great deal of perhaps thankless, but nevertheless hard and necessary work. I fancy,' he added, 'few people in the world know the frontiers of Natal . . . more thoroughly than the 5th Dragoon Guards!' There was also time for training.

> 'We had some useful *practical* musketry (such as my soul loveth),' wrote Gore in September, 'and *not* as taught at Hythe. The men shoot wonderfully well now at any object you like to point out to them *in the field*. My "words of command" are most unorthodox! I say to a man, "Do you see so-and-so?" "Yes." "Then hit it for me." And it is wonderful how they judge the distance, adjust their sights, fire, "observe" the strike, alter their sights again, and *hit* the mark! They didn't do this at first, though; they have never been taught to think for themselves.'

Thus under the pressure of experience did the British cavalry learn the lessons of the Boer War!

At the end of July the 5th Dragoon Guards found itself split up into five different detachments:

'Kotzee's Drift	one ½-squadron
Ingogo	one squadron
Laing's Nek	one ½-squadron
Volksrust	Headquarters and one ½-squadron
Zandspruit	one ½-squadron.'

This was very typical of what was to happen to cavalry regiments from now onwards. The life of the officers and men consisted of 'many alarms and false alarms; sham "turn outs"; "standing to

---

* When, later on, the men of the 8th Hussars first clapped eyes on Buller's troops, they 'all remarked what splendid condition his horses and cattle were in.' (Morton, 50.)

horses" at 3 a.m.'. ('Who,' wrote Gore, *'enjoys* getting up at 2.45 a.m.?') The regiment continued to be engaged in guarding the lines of communication until the end of April, 1901.[64]

For the 5th Dragoon Guards and for others, like the 13th Hussars, life was appallingly dull. For the last six months of 1900 most of the 13th, for example, was employed protecting the railway between Standerton and Newcastle. Kipling well conveys the men's feelings:

> 'Few, forgotten and lonely,
>   Where the empty metals shine –
> No, not combatants – only
>   Details guarding the line.
>
> Few, forgotten and lonely,
>   Where the white car-windows shine –
> No, not combatants – only
>   Details guarding the line.'[65]

There was great excitement in early July when a troop of the 13th was sent to escort rations for some of the Yeomanry prisoners captured at Lindley now released by De Wet. Seventy-eight of them were attached to the regiment for a month, 'during which time,' according to the regimental diary, 'endeavours were made to instruct the majority of them how to ride the quietest of the worn-out horses that were issued to them from the Remount Department in comparative safety.' A less pleasant incident took place in late August. Sparks from an engine set the grass alight where twenty-four horses were picketed. They stampeded and although all were recovered next day most were badly cut by barbed wire.

Throughout these weary months the men's health was poor. At the end of June 126 and at the end of July eighty-one men of the 13th Hussars were ill, chiefly from enteric or dysentry. During July alone fifty-eight of the regiment were invalided home.[66]

As with the regiments of French's Cavalry Division, Buller's managed to get through horses at great speed. The 18th Hussars, for instance, between 23 May and 7 August expended 200 or so. Typical of the cavalry's experiences at this time was that of this regiment in late July when it collected 'some forty remounts. ... We might almost as well have left them alone,' wrote one officer, 'as in three weeks' time there were only two of them left. They had come direct from the ship to Paardekop and, having immediately to take part in heavy work on indifferent food, had no chance whatever of keeping alive.' When the regiment was called upon to furnish the divisional cavalry of an infantry division it had to break up one of its three squadrons to make up the other two to a decent strength This was because there were only 302 fit horses for 436 men.[67]

*　　*　　*

At about this time two very irregular units were formed to assist in the task of dealing with the bands of burghers at large in the horribly inhospitable country of the Northern Transvaal. These were Steinaecker's Horse and the Bushveld Carbineers.

Major Francis Christian Ludwig Baron von Steinaecker was a German aristocrat who became a British citizen when he settled in Natal in 1890. At the beginning of the war, aged forty-five, he had enlisted as a private in the Colonial Scouts, a five-squadron corps raised by the Natal Government (and disbanded in March, 1900). He quickly rose to be squadron quartermaster-sergeant, but was soon promoted to lieutenant and transferred to the Intelligence Department. In April, 1900, with six men, he rode, walked and swam for over 500 miles through Zululand and Swaziland to blow up an important bridge at Malelane. This he achieved with 100 lbs of dynamite on 17 June. On his return he set about recruiting for and equipping his new corps, 'in', to use his own words, 'the enemy's country without base to draw from, without transport or provisions'. The historian of *The Colonials in South Africa* tells how

> 'he and his corps embarked on a warship and were landed through the surf at Kosi Bay, in the north corner of Zululand, not, however, without the loss of a boatload of arms and saddlery, the boat upsetting on the dangerous bar. Steinaecker's force now made their way to the Transvaal border, south of the Delagoa Railway. On 20th July 1900 he and a party of his men were successful in capturing Commandant Van Dam and another leader.'

As soon as Roberts and Buller reached the eastern confines of the Transvaal, Steinaecker's Horse, now consisting of some 450 men, all enlisted for three years, using Komati Poort as their centre, raided for great distances in the wild, pestilential country lying west of the Portuguese border. The area was extremely unhealthy for white men. Regular regiments when stationed there usually lost at least

10. Private (later Corporal) R. H. Renshawe, 19th Battalion, Imperial Yeomanry (Paget's Horse), Mafeking, 1901

11. Corporal Bowers of 22nd Company, Imperial Yeomanry, showing the equipment of a mounted yeoman

12. 'With French in Cape Colony: Scenes in camp at Naauwpoort' (see p. 105)

13. Shoeing-smith at work on the veld, c. 1901

50% of their strength from various fevers. Lions claimed more than one of Steinaecker's men and one was taken by a crocodile. Some of the wounded had to be carried 150 miles to the nearest hospital.

In due course the regiment became so self-contained that it possessed its own workshops, transport and intelligence. For more than a year its men ran the Selati railway unaided. It fought numerous small engagements, some more successful than others. It was especially skilled at stopping Boers and, more importantly, ammunition entering from Portuguese territory. Early in 1902 an extra squadron was raised. It fought under Colenbrander with Kitchener's Fighting Scouts (see p. 270).[68]

The Bushveld Carbineers (for a short time known as the Bushveld Rifles) were, according to Amery, raised 'by a well-wisher named Levi, the proprietor of an hotel at Pienaar's River'. It was very much a 'scallywag' corps made up of all sorts including local colonials, Cape Dutchmen, time-expired volunteers from the Imperial Yeomanry and numbers of Australians. It never numbered more than 350 men. Though they did useful work under Plumer and independently, particularly in the Zoutpansberg region, during 1901, the regiment is best remembered because of its five Australian and one English members who were had up for multiple murders of Boers. The Australian Lieutenant H. H. 'Breaker' Morant (so nicknamed because of his ability as a horse-breaker) and Lieutenant P. J. Handcock, in spite of recommendations to mercy, were shot on Kitchener's orders, after what was, to put it leniently, an unsound court-martial. It is clear that the Commander-in-Chief was determined to make an example, for there was mounting evidence of indiscipline in the numerous irregular units. 'Breaker' Morant became and has remained a folk hero in Australia. The regiment was disbanded in March, 1902, and immediately re-born as the Pietersburg Light Horse. Beddy's Scouts was another unit raised for service in the extreme north of the Transvaal.[69]

12

Botha to De Wet: 'What I desire from Your Honour, now that the great force of the enemy is here, is to get behind him and break or interrupt his communications. We have already delayed too long in destroying the railway behind him.'

3 June, 1900

' "The Transvaal is annxed", "the war is over", "sailing orders may be expected at any moment", and yet I am writing this with a loaded rifle by my side and with the sound of rifle fire in my ears; also with the happy consciousness that at any minute a "sniper" may honour me with his attentions, and yet "the war is over", for do not the month-old papers we receive from home persistently call our attention to this, to them, patent fact? It is not quite so obvious, however, out here.'

A trooper in Paget's Horse,
26 September, 1900

'By September the Boer army had been pursued to the boundary with Portuguese East Africa; the Transvaal had been formally annexed to the British Crown; 12,000 Boer troops were inside prison camps and a host of their fellows had taken the oath of allegiance to the Queen. The war appeared to be almost at an end.'

ANTHONY FARRAR-HOCKLEY in his biography of
Sir Hubert Gough[1]

(i)

Boer War: Prinsloo's surrender – De la Rey attacks from W. Transvaal – Onderste Poort – Zilikat's Nek – Middelburg entered – Buller marches from Paardekop – Bergendal – Komati Poort and Lydenburg entered

The Cavalry Division received its first batch of remounts on 23 June some twelve days after Diamond Hill. They were 'fat, sleek Hungarians', landed just before being sent up from Cape Town. They wore 'a fine summer coat' with which to face the South African mid-winter. The Division's senior vet thought they might just be fit for work in a month 'but not the work demanded from a soldier's horse'. The first consignment of veterinary medicines and dressings arrived on 5 July. The lack of these had been particularly felt because the incidence of mange had been increasing alarmingly in recent weeks. It was soon to become 'a veritable plague' which remained in all operational areas until the end of the war and, indeed, long after.[2]

*　　*　　*

'There is not much going on here,' wrote Haig from Pretoria a fortnight after Diamond Hill, 'except trying to get together some horses, men and saddles! We started polo yesterday. So things seem gradually quieting down, though Botha is still close by – and De Wet is still able to defy some 70,000 odd of British troops with possibly 2,000 men at most!'[3]

There was also De La Rey, 'the Lion of the West', who, over the next twenty-three months was to make himself in effect absolute ruler of the western Transvaal. He, too, with the 6,000 or so burghers whom he had been quietly collecting together, would have to be dealt with. But Roberts recognized that his most pressing tasks were to deal with De Wet, to provide for the security of the railway south of the Vaal and 'to capture or disperse the enemy's forces to the east of that line and in the north-east angle of the Orange River Colony'. At more or less the same time he would push eastwards from Pretoria towards Komati Poort 'defeating and dispersing the troops under Commandant-General Botha'.[4] Yet, though he remained convinced that 'he had only to capture the last 250 miles of railway, on which Botha and Kruger were perched, to end the war,'[5] the task of hunting down De Wet (accompanied as he was by President Steyn and his Cabinet) must take absolute precedence.

A large force was got together for the first step towards that end. When Ian Hamilton broke his collar-bone, its command was given to Hunter. In a fortnight's campaign Hunter's three divisions, with Broadwood's 2nd Cavalry Brigade and Ridley's Mounted Infantry as their most mobile element, forced the surrender of General Marthinus Prinsloo with 4,314 prisoners, two million rounds of ammunition, three of the guns taken at Sannah's Post, much livestock and, perhaps best of all, more than 4,000 ponies.* This had been

---

* The classifying and selection of these was carried out with 'the willing aid of the prisoners of war. . . . All were looking rough and poor,' reported Lieutenant A. H. Lane, senior vet of the 8th Division, 'but they soon recovered and

achieved – the greatest haul of prisoners during the whole war* – by containing the men of the various commandos, perhaps some 9,000 in number, collected along the Basuto frontier, within the huge mountainous horseshoe-shaped area which was known as the Brand-water Basin. The burghers, many of them tired of the war and led, with the exception of De Wet and Olivier, by indecisive leaders, had fled to this as a refuge. It turned out to be a trap. But even before all six of the wagon roads which were the sole exits from the trap had been closed, Det Wet (with Steyn in tow) had escaped. His column, 5,000 yards long, passed within a mile of a sleeping British camp. He had with him some 2,600 burghers, five guns and 400 wagons.† The failure of the chase which followed – and which came to be known as the First De Wet Hunt – will be related later (see p. 208).

* * *

In the meantime De La Rey had struck out from his stronghold in the Magaliesberg only some thirty-five miles from Pretoria. On 11 July three engagements took place – all involving the defensive chain round the capital provided by the Cavalry Division. At Onderste Poort the officer commanding the advance troop of the 7th Dragoon Guards, expecting the co-operation of a squadron of

---

made excellent remounts for mounted infantry and others who knew the value of this hardy animal, and were not above riding a pony. No contagious diseases were detected among this large collection of animals. Mange was apparently absent, and sore backs were not common.' (Smith, 90.)

It is said that 'a pattern maker from Armstrong Whitworth's works at New-castle,' whose scouting proficiency was unlikely but famous, 'located Prinsloo's army and gave General Hunter information of such value that the Boer general did not realize he was checkmated until he was attacked. The scout worked his way to the commando disguised as a Kaffir driving cattle. He had picked up a few words of Zulu, but fortunately never needed to use them on that occasion. The unit he belonged to was the Northumberland Hussars, a delightful crowd of scallywags, who did tremendous damage to the enemy after they had got used to the country.' (Digby, E. (ed.) 'An Imperial Yeoman's Service Memories of South Africa', *Indian Ink, being splashes from various pens in aid of the Imperial Indian War Fund*, 1914, 32.)

* The greatest single coup to be effected since Prinsloo's surrender occurred eighteen months later. On Majuba Day, 27 February, 1902, Rawlinson received the capitulation of 648 men with 1,078 horses at Lang Riet in the Orange River Colony (see p. 243). (Maurice, IV, 429; Rawlinson's diary, quoted in Pakenham, 548–9.)

† A further 1,500 Boers, with eight guns, two Maxims and one pom-pom, under Olivier, escaped *after* Hunter had accepted Prinsloo's surrender.

the 14th Hussars, seeing some 'khaki-clad and helmetted figures', waved to attract their attention only to find too late that they were part of a 200-strong commando with two guns. In the ensuing fight two officers and two men were killed and when all the ammunition had been expended, most of the troopers were forced to surrender. The reason why the 14th had not turned up was that they, too, had been attacked and forced to retire.[6]

At Zilikat's Nek to the west of Pretoria on the same day, due partly to a failure of communication between Lieutenant-Colonel the Hon. Walter Philip Alexander, commanding the Scots Greys, and the officer commanding three weak companies of the Suffolks, but chiefly to the tardiness of the headquarters staff in responding to warnings of De La Rey's attack on this important nek, a twelve-hour engagement ended in disaster. Greatly outnumbered, the Suffolks and 'C' Squadron of the Greys (about eighty strong), commanded by Major Henry Jenner Scobell (see p. 248),* numbering in all not more than 240 men, were compelled to surrender. Two guns of 'O' Battery of the Royal Horse Artillery were also captured. The Greys' casualties were two officers and one man killed, one officer and sixteen men wounded and sixty-nine taken prisoner. Amongst these was Scobell who managed to escape during the night.[7] Roberts at once 'stellenbosched' both Alexander, who had certainly shown a lack of initiative, and the commander of the Suffolks, who had

---

* Scobell, who died aged sixty-three in 1912, had joined the Scots Greys in 1879. In 1903 he was promoted Major-General and took command of the 1st Cavalry Brigade at Aldershot. After the war, in spite of a justified reputation as a column commander of the better sort, he

'imagined,' according to Hubert Gough, his Brigade-Major, 'that military thought and training could go on, exactly as he had been brought up to think of it as a young officer. . . . As a commander in peace he was only interested in the daily office routine. . . . If a complaint was levelled at his office for some slip or omission in the mass of returns called for by regulations, he regarded it as a very serious reprimand and became quite angry.

'Scobell arrived on the first day of cavalry training where at great public expense four cavalry brigades were drawn up in mass in front of him on Salisbury Plain. He was a fine horseman, riding a thoroughbred horse, and he cantered up – accompanied by at least four ladies of title, and just looked at the cavalry in mass in front of him. I think it was the first moment's consideration which he had given as to what lessons he intended to inculcate. After some thought, he ordered the cavalry to advance "in column of troops". . . . No wonder French dismissed him.' (Gough, 92; see also Farrar-Hockley, 72.)

In 1909 he returned to South Africa to take command in Cape Colony.

failed to occupy two hills which overlooked his position. Yet the chief blame lay with his own staff.[8]

These unexpected forays by De La Rey forced Roberts to delay the start of his main attack against Botha along the railway to Komati Poort, the Boers' life-line to the outside world. Indeed French had already started preliminaries for this eastern offensive* when he was urgently called to defend Pretoria. Roberts, with so many columns chasing De Wet in the south, was short of troops to defend the capital. The Field-Marshal's 'funk', as Haig called it,[9] was soon over, but the general advance was now delayed until 23 July.

French had grandiose ideas for 'a very wide turning movement' which would cut the road and railway well to the rear of Botha's army. Roberts vetoed the move and substituted a much less ambitious outflanking movement. He telegraphed French that his chief reason for insisting on very limited outflanking movements was that 'as we have no other cavalry with the force, I do not like you being so far away'.[10] French was furious but had to submit. The result was that two days later Botha's force crossed the Olifant's River 'in much disorder' but unpursued. French admitted that the horses were too tired by their long march. Whether, therefore, 'the sweeping and decisive character' of the great turning movement he had designed, involving far longer marches, would have resulted in the encirclement he envisaged, must remain highly doubtful.[11]†

* The Imperial Light Horse, during these operations in the Tigerpoort mountains to the south-east of Pretoria, suffered a reverse at Witklip on 7 July, when one of their squadrons was pinned down dismounted by a superior Boer force and fired on by its own supporting artillery. When eventually the survivors managed to retire, they found that many of their horses had been shot. Nine days later at Witpoort, Viljoen, one of the few swashbuckling Boer leaders, in independent command for the first time, launched a series of simultaneous dawn attacks with about 2,000 burghers. Both the New Zealand Mounted Rifles and the Canadian Mounted Rifles suffered considerable casualties before, after a six-hour fight, reinforcements drove the Boers off. (Gibson, 197–207; Maurice, III, 310–11, 316–17.)

† Amery, however, always pro-French and sometimes anti-Roberts, says that had French

'been allowed to carry out his plan, at the worst the Boers would have escaped too quickly for him to be able to get behind them; but the chances were against this, for Botha's own flight was hampered by the train of women and children who had suddenly been thrust upon him.'

He refers here to Roberts's action in expelling from Pretoria all the women whose husbands were still fighting for the Boers, together with their families. (Amery, III, 405; Farwell, 296.)

Especially is this so as, of the 4,023 horses* of his mounted troops with which he set out, 104 were actually unfit and, though the wastage of June had been replaced, very few of the remounts provided were capable of the hard marching the advance entailed. Indeed, during the first four days of it, the two cavalry brigades alone had lost on average about 130 horses a day.[12]

In pushing Botha nearly eighty miles westwards of Pretoria – (Middelburg was entered on 27 July) – Roberts had done so virtually without bloodshed. The elements, however, had not been kind. On 25 July, for example, the troops in their shelterless bivouacs were assailed by an icy tempest. One officer actually died from exposure, while the transport animals perished in their hundreds: 'in many places whole spans of oxen and mules lay heaped together, killed by the severity of the weather.'[13]

Roberts now decided to halt the advance while the railway behind him was made operational. During this enforced halt Captain Layton John Blenkinsop, Senior Veterinary Officer of the Cavalry Division,† opened a veterinary hospital:

> 'All the rope in the town was commandeered; the farriers made picketing pegs in the local forges, the chemist of the place helped to eke out the regimental supplies; spades, pickaxes, lanterns, buckets, etc. were purchased in the town, and a site selected near the station where there was a good water supply and store accommodation. ... Attendance on the sick was furnished by the Cavalry in the proportion of one man to every four horses.'

In its first four days the hospital admitted 451 horses of which 276 were sore back cases. Of these, twenty-eight had to be destroyed because of the severity of their injuries. What an appalling indictment this is of the regular cavalry's horsemastership! What a nonsense it makes of French's frequent complaints that he was not

---

* 1st Cavalry Brigade 1,531; 4th Cavalry Brigade 1,537; Mounted Infantry, Brigade 955. The rest of French's force consisted of about 1,500 infantry and twenty-four field and two heavy guns.

† Blenkinsop had served as Kitchener's chief veterinary officer in the Sudan where he gained the DSO. From September, 1901, till December, 1902, he was Senior Veterinary Officer, Remounts in South Africa. He was appointed Director of Veterinary Services in India in 1916 and next year, promoted to Major-General, he became Director-General, Army Veterinary Services, War Office. On retirement in 1921 he was appointed KCB and for the next eleven years he served as Colonel Commandant, RAVC. In 1942 he died, aged eighty.

allowed to make wide turning movements! The casualties among the horses of the mounted infantry were probably at least as horrifying, but they sent very few animals to hospital because they would not spare men from the fighting line to look after them. In consequence their sick horses were in most cases merely abandoned.[14]

By the time Roberts was ready to assume the advance his available force numbered over 18,700 of all ranks with eighty-two guns and twenty-five machine guns. To join Roberts at Middelburg, Buller had made a 100-mile march due north from Paardekop with some 7,851 men, of whom 1,800 were mounted.* He had had to march through country bare of supplies, remote from a railway and occupied by the enemy. There were numerous skirmishes but no serious actions. The 11th Infantry Division under Major-General Reginald Pole Carew, numbering some 8,017 men, and French's 2,708 of all ranks (of which 2,441 were mounted) completed Roberts's considerable army. Opposed to it were Botha's 7,000 burghers, nearly all mounted, with twenty guns.[15] These the Boer Commandant-General disposed along a twenty-mile front in mountainous country with virtually impregnable flanks. There followed, on 27 August, the penultimate set-piece engagement of the war. The cavalry took little part. Yet it was a report from the scouts of the 19th Hussars which told Buller that Botha had left a small gap in his defences. By switching his attack upon this weak spot in the Boer centre Buller made it possible for Roberts to gain his last victory. The battlefield was generally unfavourable for mounted movements. The official historian remarks that 'such a terrain, but a few months earlier, might have kept mounted troops tied fast to the infantry; but French's men, inured to resigning and resuming almost hourly the roles in turn of cavalry and mounted infantry, threaded their way amongst strong positions with confidence.' Nevertheless at the end of the day, when the Boers had caved in all along their front, the mounted troops and the guns failed to push forward in pursuit. It

* These included three companies of MI commanded by Major Henry King ('Bimbashi') Stewart, whom Hubert Gough thought 'an eccentric and dressy ass' but not a bad fighter. He was much liked by Dundonald: 'I can see him now as we were riding along in the direction of the enemy, without a coat and with shirt-sleeves rolled up to the elbows.' Later on in the war he was the first commander of the Johannesburg Mounted Rifles, raised on 12 December, 1900, 600 strong. This unit was known as the JMRs or 'Jews, Mostly Russian'. An old friend of Stewart's thought them 'the biggest lot of horse thieves in the country, and their C.O. was as bad if not worse than any of them.' (Farrar-Hockley, 58; Marling, 293.)

is almost certain that some of the Boer guns and wagons would have been discarded when the drift at Machadodorp was reached had they been followed up. Indeed one of their six-inch guns was actually abandoned some two miles beyond the battlefield. Its gunners, though, finding that there was no pursuit, returned in the night and dragged it away.[16]

With the battle of Bergendal regular operations virtually came to an end. Botha's burghers broke up into three main parts, scattered north and south of the railway. Some went towards Lydenburg, some clung to the line towards the frontier and some 2,000 marched to Barberton. Buller marched on Lydenburg, which he entered on 6 September,* while by 25 September Pole Carew had entered a deserted Komati Poort from which place well over 800 Boers and foreign volunteers had crossed into Portuguese territory and where he found vast quantities of rolling-stock – 'eight miles of the line are nothing else but rolling-stock'[17] – and other stores, much of which had been set on fire.

* There was some confusion when Buller entered the sphere of operations outside Natal, for Natal time differed from Cape time by over thirty minutes. (*XIII H*, 42.)

'We that saw Barberton took
When we dropped through the clouds on their
  'ead,
An' they 'ove the guns over and fled.'
RUDYARD KIPLING,
'English Irregular: '99–02'

'I am beginning to dislike De Wet. He is keeping
the war alive.'
MAJOR ALLENBY, 14 June, 1900

'During the eleven months I was commanding in
South Africa, I got rid of five generals of divisions for incompetency, six brigadiers of cavalry
and eleven out of 17 commanding officers of
cavalry regiments.'
ROBERTS to Brodrick, 2 September, 1901[1]

(ii)

*Boer War: French takes Barberton – Van Wyksvlei – First De
Wet hunt – Roberts succeeded by Kitchener – Komati River –
Rhenoster Kop*

French, at about the same time as the entry into Komati Poort, was
marching on Barberton, the terminus of an important branch line,
which had once been South Africa's greatest gold-mining centre.
The town had become in recent months a chief railway and commissariat centre for the Boers because its position, hidden in a valley
surrounded by lofty hills, was thought to render it practically
inaccessible to a hostile force.

French's column comprised the 1st and 4th Cavalry Brigades as
well as Mahon's Brigade and an infantry brigade, numbering in all
perhaps 5,000 of all ranks.* He left from Machadodorp taking nine

* Mahon's Brigade which joined French on 6 September at Carolina, consisted of the Imperial Light Horse, three companies of the New Zealand
Mounted Rifles, the Queensland MI and Bushmen, the 3rd MI, 'M' Battery,
RHA and about forty-five of Lumsden's Horse. This regiment of volunteers,
raised by Lieutenant-Colonel Dougald M'Tavish Lumsden, chiefly from indigo-,
tea- and coffee-planters from all over India, was paid for by public subscription
in the sub-continent. The Indian Government was only responsible for transport to Africa, rations, weapons and pay of 1s 2d a day. Lumsden himself
contributed 50,000 rupees. Other gifts ranged from fifty Arab chargers with
saddlery from the Maharajah of Bhownagar, to 'two horses, a mule, a donkey
and two small sleeping tents' ('They are all I have to help to conquer the enemies
of the Great White Queen') from Mohammed Mazamullah Khan, and 7,000

days' supplies,* since his route was not to be along the as yet un-
cleared railway (see endpaper map). It is reckoned that it took five
and a half hours for the column, stretching for thirteen miles, to
pass a given point and this excluded most of the actual cavalry which
was, of course, usually extended towards the front, flanks and rear.
Much of the way was over practically unknown, roughly mapped,
mountainous country where the men had to 'lead their animals in
single file, picking their way along sheer and broken ground.' In the
course of the march numerous horses were lost, 161 in Mahon's
brigade alone. French took the defenders of the town by surprise.
'With a daring that was almost recklessness he decided on a manoeuvre which would take [some of] the cavalry and a hundred of
Mahon's mounted men over heights well-nigh inaccessible and along
narrow ledges, with a steep fall into the valleys far below.' At one
point there was a stretch of 800 yards with a gradient of 35°, or
'10% less than the slope of the wall of a horse's foot at the toe'.
'It's the worst hill I ever saw,' wrote Lieutenant-Colonel Clowes of
the 8th Hussars in his diary. 'All vehicles have to be trebly horsed,
and then it's a job. They go on thro' all night and day, one getting
on top every ten minutes. It's wonderfully managed – an endless
string with a few breakdowns.'

French had had to contrive a means of drawing the enemy away
from an area where a handful of snipers could have delayed him for
days on end. This he achieved by giving out that he was 'going to
Ermelo and Standerton, meaning of course,' as Haig put it, 'that the
rumour should reach them and it has! For we find telegrams here
[Barberton] to that effect.'[2] French then actually marched due south
to Carolina, seventy miles as the crow flies from Barberton, before
darting eastwards so as to be able to descend upon the unsuspecting
town. There is no doubt that French took enormous risks. There
was a time when some 700 dismounted troopers were 'strung out
on a line probably extending more than three miles . . . completely

---

boxes of matches from one thoughtful gentleman. The regiment was armed with
short-bayoneted Lee-Metford rifles and there was a Maxim gun detachment. The
senior officers, senior non-commissioned officers, farriers, saddlers and signallers were all regulars from the Indian Army and the unit numbered at most 250
men. It had first seen action under Ian Hamilton. The remainder of the regiment
was now left behind at Pretoria awaiting remounts. (Pearse, 12–37, 316.)

Lumsden had been a tea-planter in Assam. Just before he raised Lumsden's
Horse, he had been appointed to command the Assam Valley Light Horse.

* These included 10 lbs corn and 2 lbs bran per horse each day. After Carolina,
though, these rations had to be reduced to 7 lbs corn and 1 lb bran.

at the mercy of fifty good men posted on any one of the positions commanding the track . . . . But "French's luck",' wrote the author of *With French in South Africa*, 'which had come to be firmly believed in by the whole division, stood by his men, and they reached the open ground without a shot having been fired or a Boer seen.' There were, though, a few times when isolated parties of burghers had to be brushed aside. Two squadrons of the Greys under Scobell now scrambled off north-eastwards. When their heliograph told French that the railway to the north of Barberton had been cut, so that none of the priceless railway stock could be carried away,* he dropped down on the town from the heights to the west. At the same time so did Allenby, who with the Inniskillings and the Carabiniers had led the flanking movement. The Boers admitted to total surprise.[3]

In Barberton, which was entered amidst much sniping on 13 September, 100 prisoners were taken, as well as forty locomotives, two complete trains, many rifles and much ammunition, seventy wagons, £13,000 and numerous sheep and oxen; but, alas, no forage. The telegram which French sent to headquarters caused much amusement there. It read: 'Have captured forty engines, seventy wagons of stores, eighty women all in good working order.'[4] French's Barberton march was the last of the considerable exploits of his Cavalry Division (though only part of it was present). It is ironical that it should have been achieved over country as unfit for mounted operations as any in the world!

Eighty-two officer and non-commissioned officer prisoners were released as well as many Boers who had been imprisoned by their erstwhile comrades for taking the oath of neutrality. The Inniskillings under Allenby a few days later captured six more engines at the Sheba mine. Further seizures along the line brought the total of engines captured to 105.

> 'Crewe station,' wrote an exultant Haig, 'is not in it with our engine yard and sidings here!! Fine heavy engines most of them are: from Orange Free State and Transvaal mail services. We have now to feed the infantry columns with our supplies from here. We gave Pole Carew five days', and today [19 September] we are sending a week's supply for 5,000 men to Ian Hamilton in our trains which we captured here!'[5]

* It is believed that a farrier-corporal used a pickaxe to break up the rails. (Smith, 102.)

*   *   *

On 3 October French left Barberton for Machadodorp. With the 1st, 2nd and Mahon's Cavalry Brigades he was to march from there diagonally across the 'high veldt' to Heidelberg, so as to clear the district of 'hostile inhabitants'. The march, 173 miles from railway to railway, over a country destitute of supply depots, was 'one long-drawn physical and mental strain. . . . The horses [were] under saddle day and night, and the men practically without rest. . . . The enemy,' wrote one who was there, 'hung on our flanks and rear, constantly harassing us, always to be seen on every sky-line.' 'The entire regiment,' wrote a sergeant of the 8th Hussars, 'was on out-post duty night after night, men in many cases being on sentry as often as five consecutive nights. This march was the most trying time the regiment experienced in South Africa.'[6]

Most of the remounts which had arrived in time for this march were colonials, small with plenty of muscle. At last the cavalry was beginning to realize that these little animals did 'better than other remounts on the long and weary marches'. There were one or two fights on the way. On 13 October, for instance, Mahon was attacked at Van Wyksvlei near Geluk by 1,000 Boers with four guns under General Tobias Smuts. These were deterred from making a dash on to the railway so as to capture or blow up the column's supply trains, but the cost was high: nine British killed and twenty-nine wounded.* On 16 October a reconnoitring squadron of the Inniskillings came into collision with 700 men and two guns with a pom-pom com-

* Major Edward Douglas Brown, second-in-command of the 14th Hussars and later to command the regiment as Lieutenant-Colonel Browne-Synge-Hutchinson, gained the Victoria Cross in this action: 'When the enemy were within 400 yards and bringing a heavy fire to bear, Major Brown, seeing that Sergeant Hersey's horse was shot, stopped behind the last squadron as it was retiring, and helped Sergeant Hersey to mount behind him, carrying him for about three-quarters of a mile to a place of safety. He did this under a heavy fire. Major Brown afterwards enabled Lieutenant [John Gilbert] Browne, 14th Hussars, to mount by holding his horse, which was very restive, under the heavy fire; Lieutenant Browne could not otherwise have mounted. Subsequently Major Brown carried Lance-Corporal Tumpeter Leigh out of action.' (*London Gazette*, 15 Jan., 1901.)

Lieutenant Browne later commanded the 14th Hussars, 1921–5 and from 1925–33, as a Brigadier, the Iraq Levies, the history of which he published in 1932. He was part author of the 1900–22 volume of the *Historical Record of the 14th (King's) Hussars*, 1932. He died at the age of ninety in 1968.

manded by Tobias Smuts, who drove in the squadron with considerable losses: five men killed and twenty-three wounded. In his diary that night Trooper Alfred Russell of the Inniskillings wrote: 'The Boers were so close behind us that they were riding in amongst our men, firing at the same time as they were galloping.' This is an early instance of the use of this tactic by the burghers. On 17 October Gordon's 1st Cavalry Brigade had a minor success when eight burghers were killed.[7]

During the march 1,230 out of 2,400 oxen died. This necessitated the destruction of no less than fifty-five wagons. With some 100 men and 320 horses lost, the whole operation was a dismal failure. It demonstrated with awful clarity the uselessness of the regular cavalry in the sort of warfare which the Boers were to impose upon the British army in South Africa for the rest of the war. There is little doubt that the mounted infantry or even horseless infantry could have carried out the task which French had been set at least as well as the cavalry, and at less cost. Big men on increasingly under-sized mounts, too heavily equipped and armed with carbines much inferior to the enemy's rifles, prevented from conforming to their traditional tactics, yet loath to abandon them for new methods, were now shown without any doubt to be powerless to exert any real influence on the course of the fighting.

*　　*　　*

Three months before this futile, expensive march, when Christiaan De Wet had escaped from the Brandwater Basin (see p. 196), his chief object had been to convey President Steyn and his ministers to a meeting with President Kruger who was then still with his cabinet at Machadodorp. For this purpose De Wet, whose escape was first discovered on 16 July, zig-zagged back and forth for some thirty-five days chased by ever increasing columns sent after him. His evasion of these for most of the time and his success in getting Steyn to his destination seem almost miraculous. Especially do they when it is considered that at this time he was hampered by an enormous transport train of some 450 wagons three miles in length, the average pace of which was 2½ miles per hour.[8] Though he and his men knew intimately the areas through which they marched; though virtually every farm they passed was on their side; though they could from time to time obtain fresh food supplies as well as horses with ease, it is clear that a chief reason for their ability to escape from what seemed impossible positions time and again was the consummate skill of the burghers in animal management.

Another reason was the brilliant intelligence-gathering of De Wet's two corps of scouts. One was commanded by the twenty-two year old Scheepers, whom the British claimed, though he was born in the Transvaal, to be a 'Cape rebel', but who himself claimed Orange Free State citizenship.* His 'men' numbered no more than thirty, most of them still in their teens. They were distinguished by wearing yellow puggarees. The other, known as Theron's *Verkenningskorps*, was led by D. J. S. ('Danie') Theron, an attorney from Krugersdorp, said to be as great a disciplinarian as De Wet himself. He was killed in a skirmish on the Gatsrand on 5 September. His scouts numbered about eighty hand-picked men including Hollanders, Germans, Russians, Frenchmen, a Bulgar, a Greek, a Levantine, a Turk and an Algerian Arab as well as a handful of burghers. They travelled light, with one Maxim gun and three trollies for carrying their equipment. Each man had at least one spare horse.[9]† With these scouts De Wet usually managed to know

---

* Later in the war Scheepers got to within striking distance of Cape Town itself. The town guard at Willowmore prevented him from entering the suburbs.

Described as handsome and dashing, he was shot on 18 January, 1902, one of the 700 'Cape rebels' condemned to death as traitors. In the event only fifty-one were actually executed. During his short career he became a living legend. He once occupied an unguarded town, released all the Afrikaner prisoners, jailed the local magistrate, burned all records and hoisted the Vierkleur, having hauled down the Union Jack. This he proceeded to tie to the tail of his horse as he galloped down the main street in celebration. After his death he was enshrined as a martyr. Among the numerous charges which were brought against him was that of 'barbaric' treatment of kaffirs. In his diary he wrote: 'We Afrikaners will never find justice under the English. Everything is for the kaffirs; their own soldiers go short and the barbarian, the kaffir, gets all the benefits'. (Meintjes, Johannes *Sword in the Sand*, Cape Town, 1969, 177; Cmd 981, 1423; Farwell, 331–3.)

† Even before the war had started, Theron, together with a Transvaal cycling champion, had raised a bicycle corps (the *Wielrijders Rapportgangers Korps*). This, which consisted of just over a hundred men, mostly of the upper classes, was useful in the early phases of the conflict. But Theron soon lost interest in bicycles and none was incorporated in his *Verkenningskorps*. (Maree, D. R., 'Bicycles in the Anglo-Boer War of 1899–1902', *Military History Journal*, June 1977, 15–21; Caidin, M. and Barbree, J. *Bicycles in War*, 1974, 63; Breytenbach, J. H. *Des Geskiedenis van die Tweede Vryheidsoorlog in Suid-Afrika 1899–1902*, 1969, I, 69, 105).

The Boers had other regular corps of scouts, among which were Edwards's and Ricchiardi's (Amery, II, 84).

exactly where his pursuers were, while so feeble was the British scouting system that the 3rd Cavalry Brigade, which on 17 July had been diverted to Lindley to cooperate with the 2nd Cavalry Brigade, did not learn *for some days* that the latter was but fifteen miles from it! On 19 July the 3rd came into contact with the enemy and lost twenty men but is believed to have caused considerable casualties among De Wet's burghers. On the same day the 2nd also struck De Wet's rearguard near Palmietfontein, losing twenty-one officers and men in a very sharp engagement. Neither brigade was aware that the other had been in action!*

On 21 July De Wet crossed the railway line at Honing Spruit, snapping up in the process an ammunition train with its escort of 100 men, thus indicating his contempt for the mobility of two British cavalry brigades! But two days later Broadwood captured five of the Boers' wagons. Almost immediately De Wet counter-attacked, causing thirty-nine British casualties.

Roberts had just entered Middelburg (see p. 199). He now felt strong enough to concentrate every available man upon what came to be known as the First De Wet hunt. On 4 August he sent Kitchener to coordinate the various columns which were supposed to be driving the enemy into the arms of Methuen's troops brought for the purpose to the north bank of the Vaal. De Wet, meanwhile, for a fortnight from 23 July, was established in a strong position between Vredefort and Parijs on the south bank of the Vaal. The forces immediately enveloping him on the south bank numbered some 11,000. There were six cavalry regiments, 1,000 mounted infantry, the Colonial Division, five and a half battalions of infantry and four batteries of artillery, two of which were horse artillery. Methuen's force included two regiments of Imperial Yeomanry and two battalions of infantry with six guns. Available not too far away in the Western Transvaal were a further 18,000 men.

The hunt was truly on when De Wet finally broke cover on 6 August. Two unfortunate blunders prevented what, but for them, might have resulted in the demise of the fox. First Kitchener, acting

---

* Lieutenant-Colonel Malcolm Orme Little of the 9th Lancers had now succeeded Gordon in command of the 3rd Cavalry Brigade. He was able to mount only about 400 men at this time. Broadwood's 2nd Cavalry Brigade had recently been made up to about 700 men.

Little had seen service as a Second-Lieutenant in the Afghan War, 1879–80. He was H. Gough's Orderly Officer in the battle of Kandahar. For his account of the action near Sherpur, 14 December, 1879, see Vol III, p. 239.

on false information, interfered with Methuen and ordered him to
concentrate on the wrong river crossing. Then Ian Hamilton, quite
inexplicably, but possibly relying erroneously upon instinct, failed
to stop the last remaining means of escape from the Maliesburg
mountains. These, from where he had sent off Steyn in charge of
De la Rey, De Wet had reached after an eight-day march. Rawlinson, Roberts's Assistant Adjutant General, confided to his diary:
'We ordered Johnny [Ian Hamilton] to go to Olifant's Nek but he
did not go there and in consequence De Wet has eluded us.'[10]

One general who comes well out of this abortive chase is Methuen.
He marched at very considerable speed, leaving behind his infantry
and transport. On 12 August he engaged De Wet's rearguard. On
that day the 10th Imperial Yeomanry captured a gun and sixteen
ammunition wagons, while sixty prisoners with De Wet's convoy
were set free. Methuen made his men march throughout the night
on more than one occasion. Some of the Imperial Yeomanry rode
eighty-one miles in fifty-nine hours with a fight in the middle. Both

cavalry brigades also managed to march considerable distances. One marched 115 miles in 125 hours.[11] All this wear and tear proved fruitless, exhausting for the troops and devastating for the horses.

*　　*　　*

On 11 September Kruger had left for Europe. On 24 October Buller was recalled to England and the Army of Natal, as such, broken up. On 25 October Roberts held a ceremonial parade in Pretoria to proclaim the annexation of the Transvaal, at which he bestowed numerous rewards for gallantry in action. On 31 October French was informed that the Cavalry Division would cease to exist and that, while nominally commanding all the cavalry in South Africa, he was to take command of the Johannesburg area.

'At present,' wrote Haig on 14 November, 'all is at a standstill waiting for Lord Roberts's daughter to get well [she was critically ill in Pretoria with enteric fever] and his departure!!'[12] Fifteen days later Kitchener succeeded as Commander-in-Chief. On 11 December 'Bobs' sailed for home. Once again there was a general feeling that the war was at last about to come to its end. The Boer 'army' had broken up on the Portuguese frontier and the burghers had made their way home by tortuous, circuitous routes.

It was not long, though, before the Transvaal Boers, inspired by Botha's and Viljoen's energy and faith, had started the work of reorganization. An early sign that this was proving effective was furnished when, on 7 November, 1900, the Boers gave a demonstration of an alteration in tactics which they were to practice a number of times before the war's end.* It was the precise antithesis of the tactical policy of concealed rifle-fire which under different circumstances had served so well and for which the burghers were so celebrated. It was a policy which was to prove formidable in the hands of skilled riders who knew their ground. In an action on the

* Some examples are: Dullstroom, 13 Feb. 1901; Geduld, 22/23 Mar. 1901 (see p. 49); Vlakfontein, 29 May 1901 (see p. 266); Kleinfontein, 24 Oct. 1901 (see p. 267); Bakenlaagte, 30 Oct. 1901 (see p. 255); Onverwacht, 3/4 Jan. 1902 (see p. 266); Yzerspruit, 24/25 Feb. 1902 (see p. 267); Boschbult, 31 Mar. 1902 (see p. 270) and Rooiwal, 11 Apr. 1902 (see p. 272).

The very first occasion on which, so far as the present author can establish, any considerable body of burghers charged firing from the saddle was on 16 January, 1900, when against twenty men of the Australian Horse, a body of Boers, probably a good deal fewer than 100 in number, 'suddenly appeared riding at full gallop firing as they came' near Norval's Pont. (Wallace, 104.)

Komati River, near Carolina, about 200 men of two commandos on two separate occasions suddenly deserted their concealed positions, mounted their horses, got into some sort of a line – one observer thought it 'a mile long' – and, firing from the saddle, charged down at a headlong gallop upon two troops of the Royal Canadian Dragoons which were escorting the guns. The first time they came to within seventy yards of their objective. The dragoons' casualties were thirty-one out of ninety-five engaged. Of these, sixteen were made prisoner, but later released, a practice which the Boers were increasingly prone to follow, having neither escorts nor destinations for prisoners. Lieutenant H. Z. C. Cockburn, the dragoons' commander, was one of three officers who were awarded the Victoria Cross for their part in this action. It is said, but to be doubted, that the enemy's casualties, among which were the two commandos' leaders, were greater than the British.[13]

Further evidence of the revitalization of the commandos in the Eastern Transvaal came on the day that Roberts relinquished his command, 29 November. There then occurred what was the last orthodox pitched battle of the war. Major-General Arthur Henry Fitzroy Paget (see p. 254), in command of a considerable force of infantry and with over 1,000 Imperial Yeomanry, Australians and New Zealanders under Plumer, attacked Viljoen's 1,200 burghers in a position of great natural strength at Rhenoster Kop, fifty miles from Pretoria. After some ineffective pounding by the British artillery and much destructive rifle fire by the burghers along a four-mile front for over twelve hours, Viljoen withdrew after dark. He lost twenty-four men, but Paget's casualties numbered eighty-six of which thirty came from Plumer's mounted force. The whole futile action was fought dismounted.[14]*

* An officer of the Tasmanian (Bushmen) Contingent at one point made his men trim their hats 'with grass or leaves to make them less conspicuous'. (Lieut. A. A. Sale, quoted in Wallace, 295.) This is the sole occasion on which the present author has read of the use of camouflage during the war.

13

'It is not like the Soudan and disappointments are frequent.'

> KITCHENER to Brodrick, the Secretary of State for War, 15 October, 1901

'One column by itself does no good. The Boers merely move out of the road until it has passed, sending out a few snipers to worry its flanks and rear.'

> HAIG in a letter, October, 1900

'The Boers are as unyielding as they ever were, and I don't see what can stop this guerrilla fighting for a long time. Some day, I suppose, they'll run out of ammunition.'

> ALLENBY in a letter, October, 1900

'It is an extraordinary thing when we think of it that the Boers depend almost entirely for their ammunition on captures they make from us.'

> CAPTAIN DAVID MILLER, the Gordons

'It is like trying to catch quicksilver in one's fingers!'

> HAIG in a letter, July, 1901

'It was certainly not an inspiring sight to see a Lieutenant-General of the British Army [Lord Methuen] sitting on the stoep of a dingy farmhouse saying he hoped the war would soon be over, to a group of women wringing their hands in his face.'

> An American correspondent, at a farm burning

'It is not a glorious job lifting women and getting potted by the husband.'

> CAPTAIN JOHN GILMOUR, 20th Company, Imperial Yeomanry

'*We* could have no thought of giving up the struggle, whilst the pride of England would not allow her to turn back.'

> CHRISTIAAN DE WET[1]

The guerrilla phase starts

(i)

Boer War: guerrilla phase starts — formation of columns — farm-burning — drives — blockhouse system — concentration camps — qualities of the column commanders

During the year which ended in September, 1901, the railways held by the British were cut by the Boers in one way or another 195 times.[2]* Those troops who were now being sent home because the war was thought to be over or because their term of service had expired — many of the first Imperial Yeomanry and of the colonial mounted formations — must have wondered what sort of victory they had won. It was unsafe for them to travel by rail at night virtually anywhere in the conquered territory; by day they were often forced to leave their trains to fight off enemy attacks and in an increasing number of cases their sailing orders were revoked.

From the end of November, 1900, when Kitchener succeeded Roberts, for nineteen tedious, irksome months — during the final, most protracted, guerrilla phase of the war — the Boer leaders, some of them proud to be known as 'bitter-enders', led chiefly by Botha, De Wet, De la Rey and Jan Smuts, caused more British deaths *in action* than in the first eleven months of the conflict.[3] Yet, except for the monumental *Official History* and the at least as lengthy *Times History*, none of the chronicles of the war gives anything like as much space to this last, longest of its stages as they do to its first year. The present work follows their example to some degree. The reason is simple. Lieutenant-Colonel Sir George John Younghusband,† commanding a battalion of Imperial Yeomanry, remembered the guerrilla period as 'on the whole a weary, dreary nightmare, and not worth writing about.' Duff Cooper, in his life of Haig, wrote that 'Guerrilla warfare is ... as tedious as it is inglorious.'[4] Even to list the numberless small-scale engagements, or to name the hundreds of mobile and not-so-mobile *ad hoc* columns which fought them is a wearisome exercise. Yet, paradoxically both

---

* The practice of placing one or two 'dummy trucks' in front of the engine to take the blast of dynamited rails was common throughout 1901. (See, for example, Russell, 102.)

Some of the less respectable Colonial units are said to have placed rounded-up Boers in these trucks. (Cutlack, F. M. *Breaker Morant*, 1962, 51.)

† Younghusband became Colonel of the Corps of Guides and wrote the history of that regiment as well as his memoirs: *Forty Years a Soldier*, 1923. He died in 1944, aged eighty-five.

militarily and socially, there is to be learned from them much of real interest, especially in connection with the influence they exerted on men and policies post-war.

Why did the Boer leaders continue for so long what in retrospect appears to have been such a hopeless struggle? In part it was because they remembered Gladstone's weak policy after the short-lived First Boer War of 1880–1 (see Vol III, p. 204), a policy similar to which the pro-Boer, anti-war voices in England were now loudly demanding. The Boer leaders argued that if they fought on long enough the British might well agree to quit on not unfavourable terms.

Further, the war had now deteriorated into what Birdwood called 'a whole series of minor engagements in which our men were worsted; insignificant little affairs in themselves, perhaps, but having an unpleasantly cumulative effect on morale.' So extensive had this effect become that fifteen months before the war ended, Kitchener, ever politically unsophisticated, even begged St John Brodrick, who had recently become Secretary of State for War, to send out native cavalry from India, men who would 'forget their stomachs and go for the enemy', to fight in what was supposed to be a white man's war!* 'The men,' he added, 'are getting indifferent. The Boers treat them very well as prisoners and I believe they are not always pleased when they are released.' In the following month, March, 1901, Kitchener was impelled to write to Milner: 'Our soldiers can't be trusted not to surrender on the smallest provocation. . . . Consequently disaster is not even now impossible if the Boers stick to

---

* The Viceroy of India (Curzon), who, immediately on the outbreak of war, had virtually denuded the sub-continent of white regiments, in December, 1899, offered a contingent of native ones. Lord George Hamilton, Secretary of State for India, refused it on the grounds, among others, that the use of coloured men against the Boers might 'combine the European powers against us'. The Cabinet was split on the issue, the majority being in favour, as were the Queen, the Prime Minister (Salisbury) and Curzon. There was no native unrest in India, incidentally, despite the events of 'Black Week' being fully reported in the press. (Dilks, I, 202.)

In a small skirmish near Grootvallei in the Orange River Colony on 1 August, 1901, a sowar of the 15th Bengal Lancers was killed. He was orderly to Captain John Stuart Mackenzie Shea of that regiment, who was in command of 300 South Australians. The sowar, according to the *Official History*, 'rather than forego the adventures of a campaign in which his colour forbade him to draw sabre, had voluntarily ridden unarmed behind his officer.' Captain Shea, incidentally, held important commands in India in the 1920s and 1930s and died, a full general, at the age of ninety-seven in 1966. (Maurice, V, 257; see also, Wallace, 335–6.)

it.' The Boers, of course, were not slow to appreciate the situation.

Morale was lowest, perhaps, in the Imperial Yeomanry. Writing to his father on 23 March, 1901, Captain Gilmour of the 20th Company reported that sixteen of his men had applied for leave to go home. 'Four, I think, is the most that will be allowed to go. I wish the authorities would say all or none and give some fixed date. It is really high time these men were away; though I would only say so to you, it is a fact that many have lost their nerve and need a good deal of leading.' A month later he wrote that 'all the old men are slack and disheartened and all the new men raw and hard to work in many ways'.[5]

In his despatch of 8 July, 1901, Kitchener described the Boer approach to the new phase of the conflict:

'Divided up into small parties of three to four hundred men, they are scattered all over the country without plans ... and on the approach of our troops they disperse, to reassemble in the same neighbourhood when our men pass on. In this way they continue an obstinate resistance without retaining anything, or defending the smallest portion of this vast country.'[6]

A captain of the 7th Dragoon Guards summed up the average soldier's frustrations: 'No form of warfare [is] so trying to the nerves and temper as that in which an enemy has no definite plan, but continually manoeuvres so as to avoid action, one day in front of one, the next day behind.' 'As you can imagine,' wrote Haig in July, 1901, 'people get rather stale always hunting an enemy who vanishes into space ninety-nine times out of 100, just when one thinks he is in the bag!' Nevertheless he found that 'men get so keen when there is a chance of catching De Wet. . . . The next best fox is Kritzinger (see p. 230).'[7]

'What is wanted now,' wrote Haig as early as 29 October, 1900, 'is to form detachments all about the country without having to take wagons with them.'[8] It was an ideal that was never more than partially realized. Certainly, as we shall see, considerable numbers of columns, known to the men as 'circuses', became vastly more mobile and independent of the heavier pieces of artillery and transport than anything dreamed of before. They were no longer 'nothing but escorts of their own supply columns'.[9] Yet even the later 'elite', 'extra-mobile' columns (hardly ever, incidentally, composed of regular cavalry), were a long time in matching the best of the commandos.* One reason for the column's inability to get to grips with the commandos was the comparatively poor intelligence network available to the British operating in a hostile environment. Another was the large number of unsuitable, unacclimatized mounts and the poor markmanship and above all horsemastership of most of the troops; but Conan Doyle points most cogently to a more important reason:

'The chase during two years of the man with two horses by the man with one horse, has been a sight painful to ourselves and ludicrous to others . . . .

'Even up to the end, in the Colony the obvious lesson had not yet been learnt that it is better to give 1,000 men two horses each, and so let them reach the enemy, than give 2,000 men one horse each with which they can never attain their object.'[10]†

* Kitchener did not issue the following order till 31 August, 1901:
'The enemy are now so reduced in numbers and dispersed that greater mobility is required to deal with them. Each column should therefore organize within itself well-mounted and lightly-equipped bodies of picked officers and men prepared to go long distances with a minimum of transport. The rate of captures can only be maintained by the more extended action of extremely mobile troops freed of all encumbrances, whilst the remainder of the column clears the country and escorts transport.' (Amery, 322.)

As late as March, 1902, a young officer could describe the Royals, in the column of Major Lord Basing, 2nd-in-command of that regiment, as certainly doing
'themselves royally. . . . The veldt was littered so far as the eye could see with Cape carts. . . . When this column halted and outspanned . . . the scene closely resembled the Israelites entering the Holy Land. I have never witnessed anything quite so immobile in my life. . . . My scouts going over its camping ground gleaned a full harvest – several ponies which apparently had broken loose and could not be caught, a rifle in a bush, two saddles near the drift, numerous odds and ends – rope, straps, nails, horseshoes, etc. – and several hundred rounds of rifle ammunition. This column . . . might well have been named "De la Rey's mobile Ordnance Department".' (Fuller, 243–4.)

† *The Times History* states that 'at one time, in imitation of the Boer practice, Kitchener tried the experiment of furnishing the columns with a quantity of spare horses. The result was only to encourage waste.' (Amery, V, 248.) This is contradicted by the experience of the 7th Dragoon Guards in July, 1901. At the end of twenty-four days of arduous driving (including the action at Reitz (see p. 247)), their strength was the same as when they started. The 12th Imperial Yeomanry, on the other hand, who had accompanied the 7th all the time, without spare horses, finished up with 150 dismounted men. (Thompson, 145.) Yet

Almost invariably each burgher moved with one or two and sometimes as many as five spare horses, all under the charge of Kaffir 'boys'.

*   *   *

Kitchener's policy throughout the guerrilla war was a mixture in one form or another of chasing 'every wandering band'[11] while at the same time denying supplies to the enemy by farm-burning and confiscation or destruction of the means of subsistence over wide areas.

During a single week in March, 1901, Haig's columns alone 'captured' over 120,000 head of stock.* 'Some grand cattle! ... I have a couple of beautiful cows which come along with the Camp for my own use. So,' he wrote home, 'we are well supplied with milk when moving slowly.'[12]

By the time peace came it was estimated that 30,000 farms had been burned and over $3\frac{1}{2}$ million sheep slaughtered. Ironically, Botha, as early as 6 October, 1900, had told his subordinate commanders that if they failed to 'prevent the burghers laying down their arms', he would be forced 'to confiscate everything movable and to burn their farms'.[13]

The heart-breaking nature of farm-burning is again and again referred to in letters and diaries. Typical is Lieutenant L. March Phillipp's description:

'The people thought we had called for refreshments and one of the women went to get milk. Then we had to tell them that we had come to burn the place down. I simply did not know which way to look. One of the women's husbands had been killed at Magersfontein. There were others, men and boys, away fighting; whether dead or alive they did not know.'[14]

In one farm the 18th Hussars found two girls in their twenties 'in a huge bed. The girls were given five minutes to dress whilst our

---

again, the commander of the Scottish Horse 'tried giving a 40 % extra supply of horses to one squadron for a short time, which turned out very expensive in horse flesh, as the men took no care of their horses, knowing they could always get another one.' (Tullibardine's evidence, *R.C.*, II, 450.)

* An officer of the 10th Hussars was one of many who complained of the 'awful business' of driving cattle and sheep. Ten men from each squadron were usually detailed for this purpose. It was deadly slow work for 'sheep travel at about half a mile an hour.' (9 May, 1901, Davies-Cooke.)

party explored the rest of the building. On their return they found the girls nearly dressed and, on looking under the mattress, found two Mauser rifles and a lot of ammunition, and beneath the bed two Boer men. Good old Bojer!'

At another farm an important commandant's wife was brought away by the regiment. The guide employed was a 'hands-upper' or Boer traitor (see p. 234). To him the enraged woman screamed, 'You blasted coward. If my husband catches you he'll kill you, and if my husband surrenders, I'll never sleep with him again.' 'Quite a lady!' commented the officer in charge. The same officer a few days later

'found an awful fat farm, which I burnt, and got eleven wagon-loads of oat hay for the horses, 2,000 lbs mealies for horses and mules and 3,000 rounds of ammunition concealed in the roof. We also got fowls and eggs. There was trouble over this, as it was the farm that a certain general got his butter, eggs and fowls from for his mess, and he was extremely annoyed and ordered me to assemble a court of enquiry, as he said he had given the Boer a letter of protection. I then remembered that a Kaffir had come and given one of my subalterns a note, which was almost illegible. We duly held a court of enquiry, and found that nothing was known about the farm. The general then got furious, and ordered a Column Court of Enquiry to be held, composed of officers not in the 18th Hussars. Major Philip Chetwode, 19th Hussars [later Field-Marshal Lord Chetwode and Commander-in-Chief, India, and one of the finest First World War cavalry leaders], was President of the Court and played up well. He sent in the following finding:

1. The farm had not been burnt.

2. If it had been burnt it had not been burnt by the 18th Hussars. The affair fizzled out as the general went home!'

Captain John Edmund David Holland of the 7th Dragoon Guards discovered that 'both officers and men had become very handy at carrying Boer ladies about' for they often staged 'sit-downs'. One of these hurled an over-ripe water melon at her would-be captor, which burst on his head 'like an exploding shrapnel shell'. Lieutenant Wickham Frith Chappell was later borne down upon by a lady carrying a hot iron. 'He handled them very carefully after this,' noted a fellow officer. When Mrs Jan Smuts was evicted, Corporal Gregory of the 14th Hussars offered her a cup of tea. 'Mr Gregory,' she said, 'you are the only gentleman in the whole British army.'[15]

*   *   *

Early in 1901 Kitchener stepped up his sweeping operations, converting them into systematic 'drives', ever increasing in scale. These were conducted on the principles of the sporting shoot. Success was measured by the 'bag' of killed, wounded, captured and surrendered men and by the numbers of horses, cattle and sheep removed or destroyed; in May, 1901, for instance, the 'game' accounted for in human form, including voluntary surrenders, amounted to 2,585, in June to 2,277 and in July, 1,820.

The columns taking part were to sweep everything before them until the enemy was brought up against some actually or supposedly impenetrable barrier or 'stop' such as a line of blockhouses (see below), a fortified railway line, a mountain range, the Zulu or Basuto frontiers or the sea. It took Kitchener a good twelve months to reduce the Boer forces to about 25,000, which was roughly half what their strength had been when he took over.

Among the more distinguished generals brought over to command these unwieldy operations were two who had seen much service in India. One was Lieutenant-General Sir Bindon Blood, who had achieved fame as Churchill's commander in the Malakand Field Force and was supposed to be an expert in mountain warfare. (See, also, p. 500.) He lived to the age of ninety-eight and to see his brash subordinate become Prime Minister. The other, whose successes in some of the great 'drives' were considerable, was Major-General Edward Locke Elliot. He later became Inspector-General of Cavalry in India.

The final, most sophisticated development of the drive technique was the blockhouse system, thought up by Milner. As early as January, 1901, it started life as a few lines of fortified posts protecting the railways. It eventually expanded into a series of gigantic, contiguous grid-meshes of barbed wire joining up the blockhouses, each of which was a miniature fort within rifle range of the next. The most spectacular line was that which extended from Victoria West, through Carnarvon and Clanwilliam, to the sea at Lamberts Bay. It became known to the troops as 'the Great Wall of China' or, alternatively, to the historically minded, 'the Lines of Torres Vedras'. On the day the war ended more than 8,000 blockhouses had been constructed (at an average cost of £16 each). Over 3,700 miles of fencing connected them. At least 50,000 white troops, supported by some 16,000 armed African 'scouts' (known by the troops as 'The Black Watch')[16] were required to man them. The extended lines of the drives within the grid-meshes might be, as were those on 23 March, 1902, as much as ninety miles in length, the distance from Birmingham to Cambridge. The line in Ian Hamilton's final drive of the war extended even further. Over 17,000 horses were used. These formed the largest body of mounted troops ever before placed in the hands of a British general. The control of such a line was particularly difficult when the advance was interrupted by bush or kloof. Loss of direction, overcrowding and gaps were impossible to prevent. Of these the Boers were never slow to take advantage. When railways were available as 'stops', armoured trains were employed. There were over twenty in operation before the war ended. They were equipped with guns and searchlights.

A valuable secondary function of the system was the protection of supply lines. This enabled columns to dispense with those imped-ing strings of slow-moving wagons. It meant that large supply depots, such as that which was set up at Ermelo, could be provided far from the railways and provisioned by convoys which were able to travel in comparative safety along the blockhouse lines.

The ineffectiveness of the system in its earlier days was demon-strated by the ease with which the hunted bands, either at night, or when driven up to the wire by day, broke through it. On one occa-sion De Wet (who, incidentally, was never caught, always managing to break through), boasted that he had merely used a pair of wire-cutters! In the great 'New Model Drive' of late February, 1902, more efficiency was achieved when men (including those of two squadrons of the 14th Hussars), were dismounted and entrenched at intervals along the wire *between* the blockhouses, while the driving troops (some of them from the 20th Hussars), advanced in extended line, ten paces between each man. 'We have been having it very hard lately,' wrote Trooper Duncalf of the Cheshire Imperial Yeo-manry on 18 February, 1902. 'We have been lying on the veldt about five yards apart for three or four nights to stop the Boers from breaking through.' To such extravagant lengths did the columns have to go to ensnare the wily burghers! Yet as late as early May they still managed to break through on at least two separate occa-sions! On one of these the burghers, whose clothes in many cases had been reduced by now to sacking, actually went on to blow up a train load of remounts, killing or maiming most of them.[17]*

* Perhaps the nearest historical counterpart to the 'New Model Drive' is the use by Darius, nearly 3,000 years before, of the human drag-net in the islands of

The blockhouse system might not have operated as well as it did had the Boers still possessed any artillery. The fencing could have been breached by shellfire with ease and the blockhouses themselves, being only proof against bullets, were equally vulnerable. As has been shown, it took some time for the Boers to lose their artillery, but its loss was not much felt, for it became increasingly clear to them that guns, like supply wagons, were becoming an anachronism in the era of guerrilla war. For the same reason, the British columns also soon abandoned first their field and later their horse artillery guns. In mid-December, 1901, Kitchener decreed that the growing numbers of superfluous artillerymen, some of whom were about to be sent home or returned to India, should be converted into the Artillery Mounted Rifles and the Horse Artillery Mounted Rifles. Thus, at a stroke, he created a number of new mobile columns. Each, commanded by a Royal Artillery lieutenant-colonel, was self-contained with its pom-pom section, scouts and signallers and numbered roughly 750 of all ranks. At the war's end the total strength was about 2,000. Both officers and men were, of course, of a superior stamp. Their horsemanship and horsemastership were well above the average. With a little practice, it did not take them long to become skilled at musketry too. At one point Kitchener actually applied to the Indian Government for 1,000 gunners to augment the Artillery Mounted Rifles.[18] This was refused, but in the end the War Office agreed to supply them.

The only large area where blockhouses could not be maintained, due to lack of water, was that inhospitable region of the Western Transvaal over which De la Rey exercised so overweening a sway. There early in 1902 Kitchener deployed numbers of elite columns, under nine separate commanders.

*   *   *

By the end of July, 1901, the size of Kitchener's army was not less than a quarter of a million. Of these something like 60,000 to 70,000

Chios, Lesbos and Tenedos. 'In every one of these islands,' wrote Herodotus, 'they took the inhabitants in a net. And they do it in this way:—Taking one another by the hand and forming a line from the north to the south side, they march over the island, hunting the inhabitants.' The sea, of course, was a much more effective barrier than lines of blockhouses. Darius never used the drag-net on the mainland, 'for', according to Herodotus, 'it was not possible'. (Herodotus, Bk VI, Ch. 31.)

more or less mobile men,* in anything up to 100 columns at a time, were pursuing less than one-third that number of Boers. Well over 170,000 were guarding the railways and chief towns, serving at the bases and in supply columns or languishing in hospital.

The most intractable problem connected with the drives policy was what to do with the non-combatants evicted from their homesteads. The construction of compounds in which to concentrate them caused a furore at home. Sir Henry Campbell-Bannerman, the leader of the Liberal Opposition, spoke of 'methods of barbarism'. Certainly the authorities devoted insufficient resources to the running of the concentration camps. The death rate within them from under-nourishment and consequent disease was unacceptably high. Yet the motive behind the scheme was purely humane. It also lacked military wisdom, for when, later, the policy was reversed and the Boer leaders were driven to look after their own women, children and black retainers, the burden they proved to be, and the far greater plight they were in, became weighty factors in urging their menfolk to give up the struggle.

*   *   *

The burghers' leaders' chief reply to Kitchener's not very complete scorched earth policy was to carry the war into the British territories

---

* Nearly all figures of combatants are likely to be inflated. Very rarely would a regimental state take into account the full number of men not actually available for fighting. The 6th New Zealand Regiment, for example, had 121 'ineffectives' out of 560 men even before it had fired a shot. These were distributed as follows:

'General's orderlies	4
Column commander's orderlies	3
Supply Column	2
Transport duties	10
Officers' orderlies	34
Hospital corporals	2
Quartermaster's establishment	9
Orderly room clerks	2
Left at depot with unfit horses	30
Sick	25'

It took the regiment's Commandant 'four months' writing and wiring' to get a sergeant and three men out of the mounted infantry depot at Pretoria. He only succeeded then by appealing direct to the General Officer Commanding, Pretoria District. 'In some regiments,' he found that the 'number of men who quietly left their units and lived along the line for months was appalling.' (Andrew, 107.)

of Cape Colony and Natal where such a policy would be politically unacceptable and, in the case of Cape Colony, where new sources of plentiful supplies would be certain. Further, from Cape Colony they had great hopes of adding large numbers of 'rebels' to their depleted commandos. The significance of this depletion was in fact more apparent than real. After one year's fighting a large part of the Boer forces was still intact. More importantly, those who had disappeared from the fray had been far from the better part. As the war dragged on the quality of the burghers still in the field became progressively finer. The weaklings, the 'traitors' and the pseudo-regular formations were progressively ousted. With a few conspicuous exceptions the opposite was true of Kitchener's troops. The Government, encouraged by Roberts's false optimism in releasing so many seasoned colonials and Imperial Yeomanry, could now only supply new, half-trained drafts of lower quality. Most of their officers of field rank found that the unglamorous grind of trying to round up the slippery, intangible guerrillas was unrewarding, painful and dull. Further, Roberts had made the mistake of distributing honours to these officers on a carelessly lavish scale. In consequence they were too often loath to take risks, thereby jeopardizing their past reputations or future decorations. As Kipling put it:

'The General saw the mountain-range ahead,
  With the 'elios showin' saucy on the 'eight,
So 'e 'eld us to the level ground instead,
  An' telegraphed the Boojers wouldn't fight.
For 'e might 'ave gone an' sprayed 'em with a pompom,
  Or 'e might 'ave slung a squadron out to see –
But 'e wasn't takin' chances in them 'igh an' 'ostile kranzes –
  He was markin' time to earn a K.C.B.'

'The moment an officer commanding a column gets a [newspaper] correspondent and half a day ahead of another column,' grumbled Haig in April, 1901, who at that time was commanding all the columns in the midland area of Cape Colony, 'he seems to feel quite satisfied and forget about the enemy.' In October, Allenby believed that he was one of the few commanders 'that do not play to the gallery and tell lies to push themselves'.[19] Hubert Gough, who like so many of the soldiers in his family, was apt to be too impetuous, lamented that most column commanders 'move about in solemn masses down the main roads, expecting and usually fearing (!!) a *battle*, which the Boers would not and could not fight.' He, poor man, not much later, fought a battle and lost it disastrously (see p. 265).[20] For most column commanders excessive wariness went hand in hand with growing weariness. There were, of course, notable exceptions. During the last eight months of the campaign, Kitchener introduced new tactical methods in the form of raids by single columns to supplement his massed, multi-column drives within the blockhouse system. During this period the exploits of the more enterprising column commanders, largely freed from headquarters' irksome interference, sometimes came to match those of their opponents in vigour, skill and intrepidity.

Men such as Benson (see p. 250), Damant,* Dartnell (see p. 259), Garratt (see p. 73), Rimington and Scobell became, fleetingly, household names at home. Others, notably Allenby and Plumer, went on to greater fame in the First World War. There were many less distinguished. Nearly all acquired nicknames. 'Velvet Ass', 'Nasty Knocky' and 'the Lunatic at Large' are among the more flattering.[21]

---

* Lieutenant-Colonel Frederick Hugh Damant, a native of Kimberley, came of Flemish stock. He was 6 ft 4 ins in height 'with side-whiskers down to the jowls of his grim and powerful face'. (Kruger, 467.) He took over Rimington's Guides in January, 1901, from when the unit changed its name to Damant's Horse.

14. Outside Kroonstadt: Haig and French

15. 'Menu of our first night's mess after a three months trek'

16. 'Buying supplies', August, 1900

17. 'Comparisons are odious: a contrast in mounted troops' (see p. 347)

'The "War" was the easiest part of the campaign.
We've had more fighting since the "War" ended,
more trekking, and much more discomfort.'

ALLENBY in a letter, 11 February, 1901

'Guerrillas are like fish swimming in the sea of
the population.'

MAO TSE-TUNG

'Not William the Conqueror himself created a
more complete desert between Tyne and the
Humber in the 11th century than Lord Kitchener
has created in South Africa in the 20th.'

JAN SMUTS

'There is so much sameness about this trekking
that it bores one nearly as much to write about
as to carry on.'

MAJOR HUBERT GOUGH, late winter, 1901

'An' I don't know whose dam' column I'm in,
nor where we're trekkin', nor why. . . .'

RUDYARD KIPLING, 'M.I.'

'I cannot say how long it will go on. . . . It is a
most difficult problem, an enemy that always
escapes, a country so vast that there is always
room for escape, supplies such as they want
abundant almost everywhere.'

KITCHENER to Brodrick,
10 February, 1901[1]

(ii)

*Boer War: De Wet's, Kritzinger's, Hertzog's and Smuts's
'invasions' of Cape Colony – Botha, De la Rey and Viljoen in
the Transvaal – National Scouts – Boer treatment of prisoners –
withdrawal of swords and lances from regular cavalry*

At the end of 1900 and in January, 1901, parallel with the disband-
ment of time-expired colonial corps, the formation of new ones,
under the pressure exerted by the incursions into Cape Colony, went
on apace. Probably the best of them was the Western Province
Mounted Rifles, 500 strong, which Haig found to be 'quite a smart,
well-disciplined corps of irregulars'. Raised chiefly in the Cape
Peninsula by Captain Chester Master (see p. 159), an aide-de-camp

of Milner's, it was later commanded by Captain Charles Herbert Rankin of the 7th Hussars. As soon as a squadron could be got ready, it took the field, for early in 1901 there were commandos within a day's ride of Cape Town (see p. 257). One troop was composed almost entirely of amateur cricketers. In many cases the men found their own horses.

The other units raised as part of what was called the Colonial Defence Force were the Colonial Light Horse, the Frontier Light Horse and the Midland Mounted Rifles. Of the men of this last an Imperial Yeoman remarked that 'some had the seamed and hardened faces of veterans of many a fight, others were boys of upwards of fifteen with high-pitched feminine voices.' He saw

'a company of them being instructed in the "manual exercise". It seems as though these later colonial corps are first brought into the field and then taught their rifle exercises and other drill when the interval between the trekking and fighting leaves them leisure to do so.

'One of the sergeants, a Swede, was a great swell. He was clean-shaven, save for two small whiskers at the side, and looked something between a young cabby and a waiter from a third-class restaurant. His dress was as follows: black shiny Hessian boots reaching to the top of his calf; tight black breeches à la Cape Police; khaki serge tunic, with gold stripes on shoulder-strap (and I never saw him without his polished leather bandolier); a still white linen collar one inch above the collar of his tunic; and a khaki field-service cap set very much on one side of his head, with the thin leather chin-strap coming down his cheek and round the point of his chin. And this in the midst of the guerrilla fighting in the snow-covered Sneeuwberg Mountains.'[2]

Other corps hastily cobbled together at this time included the Prince of Wales's Light Horse, with a strength of 500, recruited in January, 1901 in the Cape Town area. It saw action in the great De Wet hunt. Another was the Rand Rifles, chiefly employed in the defence of Johannesburg. Later in the year two units composed almost exclusively of Coloureds were formed: the Bushmanland Borderers, initially some 100 strong, but raised to 600 in 1902, and the Namaqualand Border Scouts, numbering 362. An officer who knew them well said that in the course of 'several stiff brushes with the enemy they were conspicuous for consistently refusing to surrender when surrounded, as patrols were at times. They would keep up a fight till dark, and although half of them were killed, the survivors of the party would escape. They made wonderful marches without water in their desert country.'[3]

Among other local corps raised in Cape Colony at this time of crisis were Warren's Mounted Infantry, which by June, 1901, was 180 strong, and the Cape Colony Cyclist Corps which by mid-February numbered 500 men.* These were much split up, sections being attached for scouting and despatch-riding duties to numerous columns. At about this period, too, for use in the Eastern Transvaal, there were raised Menne's and Morley's Scouts. These two units' chief task was to protect the railway between Pretoria and Natal. Another corps, the Heidelburg Volunteers and Scouts, commanded by Major Vallentin (see p. 266) and consisting entirely of surrendered Boers, was formed early in 1901 in the South-Eastern Transvaal.[4]

Perhaps the most interesting of all the irregular bodies raised during the war were the two regiments of the Scottish Horse. Their historian, the wife of its founder, described them as

'a corps composed of men of all classes, upbringings, professions and occupations – farmers, soldiers, lawyers, businessmen,

---

* Before the war cycling had been made a part of training at Aldershot. Among units which had cycling sections were the City of London Imperial Volunteers (C.I.V.) and the Royal Dublin Fusiliers. Of the local regiments the Rand Rifles (see above), the Durban Light Infantry and a troop of the Southern Rhodesian Volunteers (with Plumer's Mafeking relief column) all possessed sections of cyclists. A cycle corps of 102 men served during the siege of Kimberley. Not often during the guerrilla stage of the war, but often up to the fall of Pretoria, formation commanders had one or more cyclists as orderlies. There were others carrying mail, despatches, money and, in their alpine rucksacks, groceries, whenever a camp was established near a town. Another use to which cyclists were put was the carrying of carrier pigeons. It was found that they got upset on horseback! Scout Callister of the Cape Colony Cyclist Corps gained fame by 'cycling 120 miles, gaining a vantage point, lying "perdu" for several days and then releasing birds whenever he saw Boer activity.' (Parritt, B. A. H. *The Intelligencers*, 210, 211.) On the veld, cycles were not of much use as it is usually covered with thorny scrub which makes punctures inevitable and frequent. Special 'War Cycles' were made for use on railway lines. Some were constructed for eight men, others for only two. The Royal Australian Cycle Corps introduced them to the war. A detachable rim was fitted to the pneumatic tyres. This could be removed for work off the railway. These cycles were especially useful for checking the line for demolition charges and rail breaks. At one point in the war it was estimated that some three per cent of the active British forces were on bicycles. (Maree, D. R. 'Bicycles in the Anglo-Boer War of 1899–1902', *Military History Journal*, June 1977, 15–21.)

Highlanders, Lowlanders, Australians, South Africans, moulded together and united partly by a semi-feudal idea, partly by a semi-clannish instinct, partly by an excellent organization, primarily by a stolid sense of duty to their country.'

The thirty-year old Captain the Marquess of Tullibardine* was given permission by Kitchener in November, 1900, to raise a body of chiefly local Scotsmen 'as a kind of town guard in Johannesburg'. But it grew speedily into much more than that. By mid-February, 1901, four squadrons were already in the field. Soon, having scoured Johannesburg, Cape Town and Pietermaritzburg for high quality recruits, Tullibardine obtained sanction to recruit from the Yeomanry at home, as well as from Australia. His father, the Duke of Atholl, the Highland Society of London and the Caledonian Society of Melbourne acted as his agents.† Time-expired and other Australians, not all of Scottish extraction, were also picked up at the South African ports. Eventually the first Regiment consisted of six squadrons and the second of five. In all, 157 officers, twenty-two of them regulars, and 3,252 other ranks served with the two regiments. A maximum strength of 1,843 of all ranks was reached in February, 1902. The men's average age was 22½ and their average height 5 ft 7½ ins. The earlier recruits were enlisted for only six months, the later batches for a year or till the war's end. All wore blackcock's feather hackles in their slouch hats and cartridge loops on the breast of their jackets.

Tullibardine asked his father to send from home 'men who could shoot, and not to bother about riding, as I could soon,' he told the Royal Commission, 'teach them enough of the latter, and I found I got better class men from Scotland this way.' He observed that 'the Australians were magnificent scouts, but a little apt to romance' and that the South Africans were

---

* Lord Tullibardine, who had joined the Royal Horse Guards in 1892, was now given the local rank first of major and then of lieutenant-colonel. In the Nile Expedition of 1898 he had served on Broadwood's staff and in the Natal campaign he was aide-de-camp to Burn-Murdoch (see p. 69). He succeeded his father as 8th Duke of Atholl in 1917 and died in 1942, aged seventy-two. Lord Esher (see p. 378) thought him 'as clever as possible'. (Esher to Brett, M. V., 21 Feb. 1905, *Esher*, II, 75.)

† 250 men, 'very fine riders and all Victorians', sailed in one batch. Most of them were men who had passed the tests for the 5th Victorian Contingent, sent officially by the Australian Government, but who had found themselves eliminated by the final ballot. (*R.C.*, II, 447; Wallace, 338.)

'very apt to romance, and in consequence, their reports were treated with suspicion. The Scotsmen – if you could get any who rode well enough – were the most reliable of all, but . . . owing to his fine horsemanship, the Australian was far and away the best scout . . . .

'The men from Midlothian and Glasgow knew a little too much about strikes and that sort of thing, and they were a little more difficult to manage, but they did very well as far as fighting went.'

Fifty of the best Australians were armed with lances from the butt ends of which 2 ft had been cut off, the end shoes then being re-placed. They were employed as 'pig spears. We used them often,' said Tullibardine, 'but we never used them into people, because the Boers put up their hands the moment they saw them.'

The Marquess managed to gain very exceptional independence from headquarters. He was allowed to set up and retain exclusively regimental depots for remounts and for men, as well as his own hospital and convalescent camp. He seems, too, to have had absolute control over the appointment and promotion of his officers, subject only to Kitchener's formal ratification. All the officer casualties suffered in the Scottish Horse's three main engagements were made good by the promotion of forty-six men from the ranks. This shows of what high calibre were the other ranks.*

To each regiment was attached a troop of about twenty-five specially selected scouts who drew extra pay and were excused all guards and pickets. With each of these troops were some fifteen Zulus 'provided with Boer ponies'. These came under their own Chief who 'undertook to have a certain number of men always with the regiments, and as he was made responsible for their behaviour and could enforce obedience, the work done was admirable.'† There was also a troop of fifty picked cyclists.

During the guerrilla stage of the war, both regiments were very fortunate for part of the time to be under Benson (see p. 250) and Kekewich (see p. 65), two of the finest and most successful column

---

* One of the troopers of the regiment was a qualified dentist. 'I found him,' Lord Tullibardine told the Royal Commission, 'of great use in the convalescent camp in Johannesburg, as the want of dentists is one of the great drawbacks in the medical organization of the army.' (*R.C.*, II, 448.)

† The only other regiment that adopted this system was the 5th Dragoon Guards at the beginning of the war. It is likely that Tullibardine got the idea from that regiment.

commanders. The 1st Regiment distinguished itself at Moedwil on 30 September, 1901, when De la Rey attacked Kekewich's camp at dawn, causing 192 casualties of which seventy-three were from the regiment. Exactly a month later the 2nd Regiment took a prominent and gallant part in the disaster at Bakenlaagte (see p. 255), while both regiments were very actively engaged at Rooiwal on 11 April, 1902 (see p. 272).[5]

*　　*　　*

In mid-December, 1900, Commandant Pieter Henrick Kritzinger and Judge James Barry Munnik Hertzog ('Hedgehog' to the troops, 'a thin high-cheeked man with angry eyes: a fierce hater',[6] who was later to become South Africa's most anti-British Prime Minister), made their initial entry into Cape Colony.* These two men were, in effect, forerunners of De Wet's first, short-lived 'invasion' of mid-February, 1901. Kritzinger, one of the finest of the Boer leaders, a massive, moustachioed man of thirty-one, re-entered Cape Colony in mid-May and was not driven out till three months later. Both leaders re-invaded later. On 3 September, Jan Smuts, Kritzinger's exact contemporary, made his famous incursion into the Colony. In spite of all that French's and Haig's energy could do he was still there when peace came nearly nine months later. In the course of his prolonged foray he passed through twenty-eight districts, some as large as Wales. His single greatest march covered 700 miles in five weeks. This was a record march for any commando. 'Day after day, week after week, month after month,' said French when he was welcoming Smuts's assistance in the First World War, '[he], with every disadvantage in the way of numbers, arms, transport, equipment and supply, evaded all my attempts to bring him to decisive action.' French, in his speech, then quoted Marius's reply to Sulla's challenge: 'If you be a great general, compel me to fight you.' The greatest number of men Smuts ever had at his disposal (by the end of April, 1902) was about 3,000. Of these six-sevenths were 'rebels' (or British subjects). The columns trying to trap him were some three times that number. These Kitchener would dearly have liked to be able instead to launch against De la Rey at a time when Botha and De Wet were monopolizing the remainder of his striking power.

* On the eleventh day of one of the prolonged chases after Hertzog, an Imperial Yeoman wrote that 'the horses want pushing and at night the light of the camp fires shines red on blood-stained spurs.' (Gilbert, 152.)

That he was not able to do so was Smuts's great achievement.[7]

On 17 September at Elandsrivierpoort, a most unfortunate placing of the 17th Lancers by Haig, who had just been given command of the regiment, led to Smuts and 250 men passing into the midlands of the Colony 'which were soon, under his influence, aflame from end to end'.[8] An isolated squadron of the regiment guarding a crossing of the river was overwhelmed by Smuts's burghers. These in the early morning mist and on account of the captured khaki uniforms which they were wearing were mistaken for friendly troops. The lancers fought with the greatest resolution for a good hour before their camp was taken. Out of the 140 officers and men of the squadron, eighty-five became casualties.* One burgher was killed and six were wounded. Smuts captured more than 250 horses and mules and managed to drive off with two wagonloads of ammunition and rifles, 'the enemy thinking,' as he put it, 'that the waggons were loaded with our dead and wounded.'[9] By the time this loot – absolutely essential to Smuts's success – was being removed, a second squadron of the 17th had come on the scene; but Smuts and his men got clean away.[10]

Various other, smaller scale sallies into the Colony, some of them of respectable duration but none of them greater than some 250 in numbers of men, were also made from time to time, notably those of Commandants W. D. Fouchée, whose men were distinguished by wearing white puggarees, W. Malan, C. Myburg, General W. Wessels, Theron and Scheepers, all of them demanding debilitating treks by the long-suffering British columns. Spectacular and alarming though these forays were, the strenuous efforts of the British, making increasingly skilful use of the railways,† to prevent any large

---

* Four officers and twenty-eight men, killed; two officers and fifty-one men, wounded.

2nd Lieutenant Lord Vivian was among the wounded. In February, 1918, Smuts wrote to him after they had met in London:

'I still see you lying on the ground, badly wounded, on that morning when the 17th Lancers were rushed at Elands River. How gallantly those boys fought against us, many being killed because they knew not how to surrender. That fight, although a defeat, ought surely always to be reckoned among the most precious records of that great regiment. I only regret that in this war [World War I] the mounted arm has had so few opportunities of distinguishing itself.' (Smuts to Vivian, 4 Feb., 1918, Micholls, 52.)

† The speed of rail travel was invariably slow, seldom more than twenty miles an hour. In the height of the winter of 1901, for example, the 5th Lancers took five days to reach Naauwpoort from Pretoria. The officers were conveyed in

force crossing the Orange River frontier, were completely successful. Nevertheless, the effort, the numbers of troops required to make it, the casualties and the wear and tear involved were totally out of proportion to the numbers of the enemy employed. The all-pervading fear that a general uprising would be the invasion's result proved in the end quite unfounded. The numbers of 'rebels' induced actually to join the commandos, as opposed to those who afforded them sustenance and information, were never very large.

*   *   *

The situation six months after Roberts's departure (four months before Smuts's incursion) was that Kitchener was prosecuting three major campaigns at the same time across a territory not less than half the size of Europe. Botha, though unable to realize his dream of invading Natal in force, was still at large in the Eastern Transvaal. So, too, more to the north, was Viljoen. De la Rey, in spite of some reverses, continued to harass in the Western Transvaal and De Wet having survived the so-called second or 'Great' De Wet Hunt remained in the field as the most ubiquitous of gadflies, darting about, ambushing convoys here, disrupting communications there. Both men were to continue to be Kitchener's chief enemies right up to the bitter end.

*   *   *

It is impossible to follow in an orderly manner the fortunes of each of the cavalry regiments, regular or irregular or, indeed, of the mounted infantry and rifles. Each was more often than not split up into numerous parts and distributed, *ad hoc*, amongst the various

---

goods vans and the men in open trucks and flats. 'The cold was intense and the men, taking every advantage of the slow rate of travelling, fastened their stirrup leathers to rings on the sides of the trucks, and catching hold of them, ran along-side the train.' (Willcox, 279.)

On one occasion, at the height of Haig's chase of Smuts, two columns were being rushed round to try to entrap 'Oom Jannie' as his burghers called their youthful leader, but

'the engines ran out of water . . . . The water tanks at the station ran quite dry so that we had to turn the troops out to fill the engine tanks with water. They had buckets, nose bags and indeed any kind of vessel which would hold water. In this way,' wrote Haig, 'we have managed to get the trains on, but it has been slow work.' (*Haig*, 251.)

columns. For example, 'D' Squadron of the 5th Lancers was separated from the rest of the regiment for the last ten months of the war.[11] Further, like all the fighting units, portions were also often relegated to guard duties. In the case of the 5th Dragoon Guards, the whole regiment, in detachments of half a squadron or less, was employed exclusively on the lines of communication for a nine-month period, sending out some twenty patrols daily. The 14th Hussars in July, 1901, were split into nine detachments, posted along a line of blockhouses. A regular mounted infantry officer, who spent some months garrisoning Lydenburg in mid-1901, tells of

'work of a most trying kind .... Besides the day-picquets, grazing-guards, escorts to convoys and fatigues on the defences, half our men and an officer were on picquet each night. By day a picquet would be sniped, or a stray cow driven off by a Boer, and the whole Company turned out; by night a shot from some sniping Boer or jumpy sentry frequently turned the whole garrison out. There was all the hard work and risk of being with a column in the field, with none of the chances of getting your own back.'[12]

In Natal alone there were no less than thirty-seven garrisons. Within Cape Colony, as the conflict dragged on, more and more loyalist South African colonials, mostly untrained levies, took over static duties chiefly as Town Guards, thus setting free more seasoned men for column work. By the end of 1901 there were over 20,000 of them, some of whom were mounted and known as District Mounted Troops.*

A lieutenant of Canadian artillery describes what campaigning could be like during one of the tedious and exhausting chases after the elusive commandos:

'[November 1900]. The rain was falling in sheets, and the wind blew swirling clouds of clammy mist through a struggling column of as wet, worn-out, muddy and oddly garbed men as you ever saw .... The dripping, shivering horses staggered along through the mud and storm with hanging heads and trembling limbs, their riders with faces so pinched and drawn with

* On one occasion in mid-October, 1901, according to Haig, '187 of these creatures, Dutchmen by parentage and also at heart, surrendered to the enemy without making a fight or suffering a single casualty! But for [this] most of [Smuts's] commando would be walking by now.' (*Haig*, 252.)

hunger and fatigue that you could hardly recognize men that you knew and met every day. They were wrapped up in all sorts of grotesque ways. . . . Cavalry with numnahs (blankets) strapped to their stomachs, white rubber sheets swathing their legs, and horse blankets over their head and shoulders.'[13]

* * *

During the last twelve months of the war the army acquired some more or less useful reinforcements in the shape of Boers who had surrendered voluntarily – traitors (or, as the British thought of them, loyalists). They were universally known as 'tame Boers', 'hands-uppers', or, by the Boers, as 'ensoppers' or 'yoiners'. They were the very antithesis of the 'bitter-enders'. In the Transvaal they were officially known as National Scouts and further south as the Orange River Colony Volunteers. By the time peace came they numbered nearly 5,500.[14] Many were impoverished 'bywoners' or white farm labourers. These acted chiefly as transport drivers. Others were much superior, influential men, who had taken the oath of allegiance and who passionately believed that to continue the war was madness. Numbered amongst these were such distinguished officers as ex-General Piet De Wet, Christiaan's brother (see p. 108) and the young Andries Cronje. Well mounted, armed and paid, they acted as intelligence agents, guides and scouts. Others formed an auxiliary burgher police force.[15] At the war's end something like one-fifth of all the fighting Afrikaners were on the British side.

* * *

The Boers' methods of dealing with prisoners, once they were unable to hold on to them, varied. There are very few instances of bad treatment beyond what the exigencies of the war dictated. As the burghers' need for replacements of clothing increased, the 'uitschuddings' (stripping) period was entered. 'We gave them our rags,' wrote Smuts, 'our torn clothes and our unwearable boots and took their uniforms and boots instead.' Sometimes prisoners were, in Kipling's words, made to 'walk man-naked in the 'eat' back to their units.* As

* 'He's shoved 'is rifle 'neath my nose
      Before I'd time to think,
   An' borrowed all my Sunday clo'es
      An' sent me 'ome in pink;

(continued over)

early as October, 1900, when a man of the Inniskillings ran into an enemy patrol, he was relieved of his arms, boots and £27 which he had in his belt. 'With two hearty kicks' he was then sent on his way. Others were returned less their trousers as well as their boots. Two men of the 14th Hussars were told by their captors: 'Now we are going to shoot you because of our women and children you are starving at Potchefstroom' concentration camp. But in the end they were merely deprived of their boots and told to get out. There are numerous examples of very special consideration being shown. For instance, when a wounded New South Wales Lancer prisoner died in Carolina, he was buried 'most reverently, numbers attending his funeral in tall hats and frock coats'. His grave was later found to be 'beautifully decorated with flowers'. French tells how

'on Christmas Day, 1900, a young Boer officer came to him under a flag of truce, asking on behalf of Commandant [C. J.] Beyers that they might bury their dead. French agreed. As, however, there were important movements on hand, he regretted that he could not let the officer return to his own camp until next day, when having made him comfortable during the night, he gave him a small box of cigars and a bottle of whisky as a Christmas present to Beyers. A few days later two cavalrymen taken prisoner by the Boers marched back to their own camp, with horses, arms and equipment complete, and they had a note from Beyers to French thanking him for the Christmas box and saying that, as he unhappily had no cigars or whisky to give in return, would he accept the liberation of these men as a Christmas gift.'

An' I 'ave crept (Lord, 'ow I've crept!)
  On 'ands an' knees I've gone,
And spoored and floored and caught and kept
  An' sent him to Ceylon!
    Ah there, Piet! – you've sold me
      many a pup,
    When week on week alternate it was
      you an' me "ands up!'
    But though I never made *you* walk
      man-naked in the 'eat,
    I've known a lot of fellows stalk a
      dam' sight worse than Piet.'
(Kipling, R. 'Piet', *The Five Nations*, 184).
  Most Boer prisoners were sent to camps in Ceylon.

It is revealing of Smuts's character that when French later told this story to him, he commented that Beyers had made an improper use of property which belonged to his country![16]

*　　*　　*

The roles played by the regular cavalry from now onwards differed in hardly any respects from those of the colonials, the Imperial Yeomanry and the mounted infantry. Nor did its weapons. In late October, 1900, the process of making the cavalry nearly indistinguishable from the mounted infantry was begun. The *arme blanche* was to be disavowed and abjured. First, carbines and lances were withdrawn. Then all regular regiments, other than those under French's command,[17] soon also lost their swords, though, for some unknown reason, the 16th Lancers seem to have been divested of theirs even before the march to Kimberley, and the 5th Lancers not until June, 1901.[18] The infantry pattern Lee-Enfield rifle of .303 calibre, with bayonet, was issued in their place.* It was carried in a short bucket, was heavier than the carbine and much nearer to being a match for the Boer Mauser. It was sighted up to 2,800 yards, whereas the extreme range of most types of carbine was only about 1,200 yards.† 'The rifle,' stated the order from headquarters, 'will henceforth be considered the cavalry soldier's principal weapon.'[19] The first regiment actually to use rifles instead of carbines was probably the 18th Hussars. When the official Australian contingents arrived in Cape Town, even the officers had their swords replaced by rifles 'in the same way as every trooper'.[20] The temporary demise of the *arme blanche* was little to the taste of the chief cavalrymen.

'When the sword and lance were taken away from the cavalry,' lamented Haig in his evidence before the Royal Commission,

---

* This was the forerunner of the SMLE (Short Magazine Lee-Enfield) which was the army's standard rifle well into the middle of the century. That weapon did not appear till 1903 (see p. 398).

The 7th Dragoon Guards had last carried bayonets in the 1820s. (Brereton, 287.)

† A trooper of the 14th Hussars had his collar-bone smashed by a Mauser bullet which had travelled 1,800 yards. (Oatts, *14H/20H*, 307.)

'The Martini-Metford carbine [see Vol III, pp. 402–3] is not a fit instrument to put in the hands of a soldier,' wrote one young subaltern. 'You might as well give him an arquebus or a Brown Bess. What can he and his popgun hope to achieve against an enemy armed with a Mauser?' (Rankin, 179–80.)

'we did miss them. It was a great mistake, and moreover,' he added, 'General Smuts, who arranged the details of surrender with me in the west of Cape Colony, said that it was the greatest mistake to take away the sword and lance from the cavalry, because he said that they always estimated that if they got within 200 yards of a position they could take it, owing to the bad shooting of the British, but he said that if cavalry had been there he would never have attempted to go near the position, because the cavalry would have charged down upon them with the *arme blanche*. That opinion he volunteered.'[21]

'My men were forced to take the field without their valises, consequently they had to make the shirt, drawers and socks last six months without a change; and as opportunities for washing them seldom occurred, they became infected with vermin, which nearly distracted them. It was no uncommon sight to see a whole regiment, when halted for a few minutes, take their shirts off and go ahunting for the little pests.'

BREVET-MAJOR A. W. ANDREW,
Commandant, 3rd New Zealand Brigade[1]

(iii)

Boer War: living conditions, officers and men – food and drink – entertainments – recreations – looting – clothing

'I am travelling quite in luxury!' Thus Haig from Stormberg in June, 1901. 'I have a saloon with my cook on board, and also brought two of my horses, etc., etc., and attach the whole to an armoured train. So I halt where and when I like.' Ten months earlier Squadron Sergeant-Major Cobb of the 7th Dragoon Guards was writing:

'The whole Brigade looked perfect scarecrows, our clothes were all in rags, and dirty isn't the name for it. We had been in pants and puttees* for over three months and as we had not any tents we had to sleep and work in the same clothes . . . . The only time we can get undressed is when we have to wash our underclothing – which is not very often.'²

These contrasts were typical of conditions not only between senior officers and their long-suffering men, but also between the earlier and the later stages of the war. One hardship shared by all ranks, especially prior to the entry into Pretoria, was the lack of tents. The Inniskilling Dragoons actually went, as did many other units, for eight months without any. Lieutenant Marling of the 18th Hussars reported on 14 May, 1901 that with 12° frost and 'an inch of ice on my bucket this morning' his men were suffering badly without tents. They were 'only allowed two blankets and a waterproof sheet'. Five days later, when the 18th and 19th Hussars marched

'about thirty miles with six guns and one pompom, we took no transport with us, only two ambulances, and we only had what we carried on our horses, no shelters, no nothing. Fortunately we found a good farm full of loot. We tore off all the doors and rafters for firewood and got five pigs, eleven chickens and seventeen geese, so we slept round a roaring fire all night, but the cold was intense. Drank whisky and cocoa. 10° frost.'³

How arduous life on trek could be is well illustrated by 2nd Lieutenant Aubrey Davies-Cooke of the 10th Hussars:

'22 March, 1901. Marched at 5 a.m. and without a single halt did twenty-one miles. . . . Horses absolutely dead beat. Several had to be shot. Got into camp about 1 p.m. – eight hours without a halt and crossing five drifts. . . . Our turn for night pickets. No rations issued to men tonight, so that they had to go on picket in pouring rain after a long march with nothing to eat since 4 a.m.!'

The difference between life in the field and when out of the line – (a word which is used only metaphorically!) – is well illustrated by the following opposed accounts. An Imperial Yeoman found that

* There was current at this time a delightful story about an Imperial Yeomanry sentry who 'bolted back to his picket, pursued, he averred, by a large snake. On investigation the snake turned out to be the man's puttee, which, becoming un-rolled, trailed along after him as he moved and was difficult to shake off!' (Macready, I, 99.)

'one got dreadfully hungry trekking and could eat anything. An army biscuit was a priceless luxury. Bully beef was not so bad, provided one could cook it up with a few vegetables. Fires were easily improvised with dried cowdung which was to be found everywhere. Ant heaps made excellent ovens. They burned with a deep glow and would boil a mess tin or fry a chunk of trek ox admirably.'[4]

By contrast Trooper Alfred Russell of the Inniskilling Dragoons gives a vivid picture of life in Dundee on 3 April, 1901 between treks: 'There were a great number of Indians, in fact I saw more Indians than Kaffirs. Bread could be bought at 6d and 1/– per loaf, lemonade 6d, cigarettes 3d and 6d packet, sugar 4d lb. In fact you could buy almost anything at a very reasonable price.' This was certainly not always so. In Johannesburg at the beginning of 1901, for instance, butter was selling at 5/6d a pound and eggs at 9/– (not 9*d*) per dozen. When on 3 April the regiment arrived at Glencoe Junction:

'Everything was carried out in a systematic way. As soon as the horses were entrained, so many men were told off for carriages, the forage and rations drawn. Afterwards an issue of tea made by the Refreshment bar, 1 pint of tea per man, then an issue of biscuits, jam and Maconochie about 6 o'clock, also an issue of rum. We then fed the horses, wagons were put on the trucks by natives, two wagons on each truck, also Cape Carts, etc., and about 7.30 o'clock p.m. we steamed out of the station. . . . A number of men rode in open trucks and on the wagons, everybody seemed to be in pretty good spirits as all kinds of eatables and drinkables could be bought, beer 6d pint.'

Five days later, from Belfast, he reported that the troops were 'on corned beef and fresh bread'.[5]

One officer wondered

'what we should have done without canned foods. As the war lengthened out, more and more varieties made their appearance. I remember tinned eggs and bacon, tinned camp pie, tinned apple pudding, tinned slabs of bacon (good for greasing boots) besides the normal tinned foods ... The only official drinks were raw rum and raw lime juice, the latter so sour and bitter that it had to be administered on parade, otherwise the men threw it away.'

Depending on place and season, supplies of food could be plentiful, even on trek. In mid-February, 1901, an Imperial Yeomanry captain wrote home to say that he and his men were

> 'living well on chickens, ducks, geese, sheep, potatoes, cucumbers, pumpkins, peaches, apricots, figs and grapes. Every farm you come to has a hedge of peaches. A lot of them are not ripe. ... They make a capital dish stewed. The green figs are capital. ... Chickens or hens – and some are very ancient hens – are all to be cleaned up, so we do have some rare sport catching them. ... Any pigs are to be caught and killed, and as bayonets are now a thing of the past, any penknife is used.'[6]

After the relief of Ladysmith, as Sergeant-Major Burridge of the 5th Lancers discovered, 'we were limited in the food line, as our tummies wouldn't stand up to real good feed of peace time rations. But one thing there was plenty of: "Bergoo", so called by the men – really Quaker Oats with tinned milk; not a very satisfactory feed compared with what we had pictured revelling in on relief.'

Kitchener told the Royal Commission, with some truth, that one of the successes of the war had been the supply of food: 'I consider that the soldier was better fed than in any previous campaign.' He said that the 'chief criticism made related to the package of much of the tinned meat in the inconvenient shape of 6-lb tins, too large for soldiers to carry with ease.' He might have added: especially on horseback.[7]

On special occasions, great efforts were made to supplement rations. On Christmas Day, 1901, Lieutenant Marling wrote that 'with much trouble [he] had got up about 800 lbs of plum pudding for the men [of the 18th Hussars] and thirty-six hams, and we gave them a lot of rum, so they did pretty well, poor devils!' Whenever possible, some sort of special entertainment was arranged for important dates. On New Year's Eve, 1900, the Inniskilling Dragoons held a 'camp fire from about 7 o'clock till 10 o'clock. A very musical evening,' reported Trooper Russell. 'Sentimental and Comic singing.'[8]

On a different level, Lord Airlie, commanding the 12th Lancers (see p. 184), who was a highly religious man and a finely conscientious officer, wrote on 26 January, 1900: 'Opened such a beautiful Christian Soldiers' Association tent yesterday evening. So nice for the men. Stationery free. Tables and chairs. No religion till 7 p.m. and then undenominational.'[9]

As for recreation, Haig played 'bridge nearly every night when not on the trek,' while, when on the line of communications, the 8th Hussars 'to vary the monotony played the 14th Hussars a cricket match, using pick handles for bats. Scores: 14th Hussars, 45; 8th Hussars, 59.' Rounders was another game often played. Football was constantly played, as it increasingly had been since the 1880s when cavalry regiments first got up proper teams. The 9th Lancers in mid-July, 1900, found themselves 'in the middle of a large herd of blesbok.* Needless to say, nearly every officer went after them, not to mention a good many irresponsible men, and soon there was a great battle raging, often more dangerous to the brigade than the buck!' We are not told how many of the latter were bagged![10]

For the men when at base there were three roller-skating rinks in Pretoria. Trooper Seed of the 3rd Hussars joined there a photography class and one evening enjoyed 'a marvellous entertainment . . . a combination of gramophone and cinematograph', during which he saw 'moving pictures of singers in opera and heard songs' simultaneously. ' 'Ouse (Clicketty-click . . . Lizzie's legs . . . Kelley's eye . . . Top o' the 'Ouse)' was universally played, particularly aboard ship both coming to and going from South Africa. On those voyages of comparative idleness, while the officers played baccarat, whist and poker, the men played ' 'Ouse'. Private enterprise thrived. Young Lieutenant Fuller remembered 'a vendor of Sarsaparilla [a syrupy tonic made from the roots of the *Smilax* plant] or some other effervescent fluid which he carried in a bucket yelling 'Oo sez a cooler? . . .'Oo sez a Bombi-bi fizzer?'[11]

It is difficult to tell how much looting took place, though it is likely that the regulars had a better record than the colonials. In April, 1900, Roberts published an order about looting by the 3rd and 4th Cavalry Brigades. 'But we were starving,' wrote one of the 4th Brigade, 'and sheep were all over the place, so we just took them – their owners were fighting against us.'[12]

Many of the items of clothing, as they always do in every army, came under heavy criticism. Not least to be abhorred were the so-called waterproof capes which were issued to all mounted troops. According to one commander of New Zealand troops, they 'were not worth drawing, as they would not keep the rain out for five minutes.'[13]

* The South African bubaline antelope (*Bubalis albifrons*). It has a large white spot on its face, divided by a dark crossbar between the eyes.

The guerrilla war

'One does not fight because there is any hope of winning. It is much finer to fight when it is of no use.'

CYRANO DE BERGERAC

'Our Sergeant-Major's a subaltern,
   our Captain's a Fusilier –
Our Adjutant's late of Somebody's
   'Orse, an' a Melbourne auctioneer;
But you couldn't spot us at 'arf a
   mile from the crackest caval-ry.
They used to talk about Lancers once,
   Hussars, Dragoons an' Lancers once,
'Elmets, pistols, an' carbines once,
      But now we are M.I.'

RUDYARD KIPLING, 'M.I.'

'We have spent two hundred million pounds to
   prove the fact once more,
That horses are quicker than men afoot, since two
   and two make four:
And horses have four legs, and men have two legs,
   and two into four goes twice,
With nothing over except our lessons – and very
   cheap at the price.'

RUDYARD KIPLING, 'The Lesson'

'That the third year of the war should dawn without the British forces having yet got the legs of the Boers, after having penetrated every portion of their country and having the horses of the world on which to draw is the most amazingly inexplicable point in the whole of this strange campaign.'

CONAN DOYLE

'A bluebottle is more mobile than an oak, yet the oak holds the ground in the end.'

TROOPER PEEL of the Imperial Yeomanry

'We must fight to the bitter end.'

STEYN to Kruger, 1 June, 1901[1]

(iv)

Boer War: engagements during the guerrilla war: Bothaville – Dewetsdorp – Springhaan's Nek – Braakpan – Vryheid – Reitz – Wildefontein – Bouwer's Hoek – Bethel – Zeerust – Gruisfontein

– Schweizer Reneke – Middeldrift – Bakenlaagte – Cyferfontein – Tiger Kloof Spruit – Vrieskraal – Klipfontein – Spyfontein – Quaggafontein – Armstrong Drift – Blood River Poort – Onverwacht – Vlakfontein – Kleinfontein – Yserspruit – Twee-bosch – Boschbult – Boschmanskop – Rooiwal – end of the war

During the last eighteen months of the war, innumerable very minor actions occurred. These resulted for the most part from isolated attacks on small garrisons and convoy escorts. The numbers of men involved were small. So, except in their total, were the casualties. In the same period there took place numbers of more important engagements, though none of them was on a scale large enough to warrant the name of battle. Elements of the twenty-one regular cavalry regiments in South Africa took part in at least sixty-five identifiable combats in this category.* There is space here to consider only a few of the more significant or typical skirmishes (for they were seldom more) which occurred in the course of the protracted guerrilla phase of what came to be known, increasingly inaccurately, as the 'last of the gentlemen's wars'. Their chief interest lies in the sometimes surprising developments in tactics which characterized them. Of those which bore some small resemblance to the larger affairs of the first year's campaign, nine stand out.† The first was the considerable British victory at Bothaville on the Valsch River in the Orange River Colony on 6 November, 1900, while Roberts was still nominally in command. It was fought at a time when the second De Wet hunt was in full cry and when both sides still possessed artillery. Though no cavalry were engaged, it is described here, as it affords a good example of the use of the mounted infantry:

'The time had now come,' wrote De Wet in his memoirs, 'to

* 1KDG, 3; 2DG, 1; 3DG, 1; 5DG, 3; 6DG, 2; 7DG, 3; 1D, 1; 2D, 4; 6D, 5; 5L, 6; 7H, 1; 8H, 2; 9L, 3; 10H, 5; 12L, 1; 13H, 1; 14H, 2; 16L, 3; 17L, 5; 18H, 9; 19H, 4.

† Bothaville, 6 Nov. 1900; Rhenoster Kop, E. Transvaal, 29 Nov. 1900 (see p. 211); Nooitgedacht, W. Transvaal, 13 Dec. 1900, where, in the worst reverse since Sannah's Post (see p. 140), De la Rey and Jan Smuts overwhelmed Major-General Clements's camp, killing eighty-eight, wounding 186 and capturing 368 men and losing 900 animals; Lake Chrissie, E. Transvaal, 6 Feb. 1901 (see p. 508); Vlakfontein, W. Transvaal, 29 May 1901 (see p. 266); Moedwil, West Transvaal, where Colonel Kekewich, the hero of Kimberley, lost 214 officers and men and 514 animals killed, at the hands of De la Rey, 30 Sep. 1901; Lang Reit, Orange River Colony, 27 Feb. 1902 (see p. 196); Tweebosch, W. Transvaal, 7 Mar. 1902 (see p. 269), and Rooiwal, W. Transvaal, 11 Apr. 1902 (see p. 272).

make another dash into Cape Colony. President Steyn had expressed a wish to go with us. . . .

'On the morning of the 5th we arrived at Bothaville. . . . Without suspecting any harm we went into camp about seven miles from the English. . . .

'[Suddenly] I heard the report of rifles. . . . The English were within three hundred paces of us. . . .

'It was early morning. . . . Many of the burghers still lay asleep rolled up in their blankets. . . .

'I had heard a good deal about panics – I was now to see one with my own eyes. Whilst I was looking for my horse to get him up-saddled a few of the burghers were making some sort of a stand, but all those who had already up-saddled were riding away at break-neck speed. Many even were leaving their saddles behind and galloping off bare-back. . . . I called out to them: "Don't run away! Come back and storm the enemy's position!" But it was no use. A panic had seized them. . . .

'The leader of the enemy's storming party was [Lieutenant-] Colonel [P. W. J.] Le Gallais, without doubt one of the bravest English officers I have ever met.'[2]

What De Wet omits is the fact that a patrol of the 5th Mounted Infantry, sixty-seven strong, had stumbled upon his main picquet of five men fast asleep and taken them prisoner without a shot. Realizing that the Boer laager must be near, this patrol galloped up to some rising ground. From there they saw below them the laager in which were some 800 burghers. They opened fire upon them, thus causing the Boer panic. Nor does De Wet mention that Steyn's adjutant had kept the President's horse saddled so that he was able to gallop off, losing nothing personal except his cuff-links.

Only now did the action become truly fierce. Some 130 Boers whose horses had disappeared in the stampede took up position behind cover. For four long hours they held off the rest of Le Gallais's mounted infantry numbering about 150 at the start. These came speedily into action, as also did two guns of 'U' Battery, Royal Horse Artillery. There developed at close range a deadly rifle duel. 'It was Tommy's battle,' observed Sergeant Jackson of the 7th Mounted Infantry. 'Single men and little groups manoeuvring on their own,' many of their officers, including Le Gallais, having become casualties. All the time the couple of guns (reinforced later by the battery's remaining two), and one pom-pom exchanged shots across only forty yards with the three guns (and one pom-pom) which the Boers were capable of bringing into action. Meanwhile, as the rest of the mounted infantry appeared (bringing their total numbers up to about 600), many of the burghers who had fled also returned to the fray and tried but failed to turn the British left. Eventually, reinforcements which had been heliographed for, arrived on the scene. Whereupon 'one of the Malta M.I. shouted "Fix bayonets!" and it was passed on. It is on record,' says Sergeant Jackson, 'that just four men *could* fix bayonets, as the majority had been used for picqueting pegs so often that the socket was knocked flat! But the Boers did not know this and stood up in a body waving anything white they had.'

Le Gallais found himself, together with other officers, trapped in a farm house. He died that evening. Roberts called him 'a most gallant and capable cavalry leader, brought up in the very best of schools, the 8th Hussars, . . . whose career has closed with his finest and best achievement.'[3] The total British casualties were thirty-eight killed and wounded. The Boers lost about thirty-four killed and wounded and ninety-seven taken prisoner. The spoil included De Wet's entire artillery of six guns, one of which had been captured at Colenso and another at Sannah's Post. More welcome were large numbers of horses, saddles, carts and spare arms with ammunition.

Great heroism was displayed on both sides in what was one of the more grimly ferocious little engagements of the war. 'Unlike a good many well-known fights,' wrote Sergeant Jackson, 'Bothaville *looked* like a battle-field, dead horses everywhere. . . . The guns looked chipped about and the wagons and Cape carts were in splinters. Every here and there little hollows had been scraped in the sand, most of them with blood marks in them.'[4] British victory though Bothaville undoubtedly was, within ten days of it De Wet, already known as 'The Swooper'[5], was marching south to invade Cape Colony, a project he was forced to abandon by mid-December. On 23 November, after four days' siege, the lightly garrisoned town of Dewetsdorp, named after his father, capitulated to him. A relief force, which included 600 men of the 9th and 17th Lancers, arrived too late to save the place.[6]

Twenty-one days later, at Springhaan's Nek, near Thaba 'Nchu, Major G. W. Forbes of the Montgomery Yeomanry learned from a Kaffir scout that the men of one of De Wet's commandos were 'off-saddled and cooking their evening meal some four or five miles away'. He immediately galloped 'A' Squadron of the 16th Lancers and a party of his 9th (Welsh) Battalion of Imperial Yeomanry to surprise the laager. This they did. 'The Yeomen galloped on to a kopje overlooking the camp, while the 16th's squadron,' claims the regimental historian, 'charged right into the middle of the enemy, *shooting off their horses* and scattering the Boers in all directions.' The *Times History* states that the troopers laid about them *'with clubbed rifles'*. Whichever version is true – and probably both are – the charge met with a surprisingly great measure of success. Eight burghers were killed, thirty-three wounded and seventeen captured. Relatively unimportant though this skirmish was – (it marginally helped to prevent De Wet invading Cape Colony at this time) – it is significant as the earliest instance of regular cavalry charging with the rifle, after the *arme blanche* had been replaced by it. Further, it was rare, until much later on, for a piece of intelligence to be so accurate and timely. The lancers lost six horses and had one man wounded. What the yeomanry lost is not known.[7]

*　　*　　*

In May, 1901, a young burgher reported that 'the enemy is adopting our methods of fighting. At one time it was said an Englishman was like a chicken. He retires at sunset, and nothing need be feared from him after dark. Now, however, he is making night raids all over the country, and practising our own stratagems upon us.'[8] One of the earliest night raids was carried out against Smuts's commando near Braakpan in the Western Transvaal on 14 April. It was highly successful. Parading at midnight, Rawlinson's mounted column which was led by Kitchener's Horse, completely surprised the Boer laager at dawn, after a fifteen-mile ride. All the enemy's impedimenta, two guns and twenty-three prisoners were taken. Sixteen Boers were wounded for three of Rawlinson's men.[9]

One of the terrors attendant on sudden attacks at dawn was the stampeding of the horses in the camp attacked. This, not surprisingly, happened more often when the Boers night-raided than when the British did. On 11 December, 1900, large numbers of Botha's men swooped upon the mounted infantry forming part of the defences of Vryheid in the Eastern Transvaal. Their defence was rendered totally futile by the stampede of their mounts. The mounted infantry were virtually destroyed, the burghers actually employing the rows of saddles lying in line on the ground as cover from which to pour in their murderous fire.[10]

The most famous of the British night raids ended in the town of Reitz, north-east Orange River Colony. In early July, 1901, a document was found there which showed that the Boers habitually left the place on the approach of a column and then returned to it when the danger had passed. Elliot, in command of three mobile columns engaged in a major drive, therefore ordered Broadwood, commanding one of them, to double back upon the town during the night of 10 July, and take by surprise the small commando which was known to have recaptured it. Broadwood took with him two squadrons of the 7th Dragoon Guards and two of the 12th Imperial Yeomanry, perhaps 400 mounted men, with one pom-pom. Marching at 11 p.m., he covered some twenty to thirty miles of badly broken terrain, reckoning to surround the place exactly at first light. But the straying of one of the connecting files made him late. Dawn saw his main body still three miles short of the target. There was no times therefore to stop up the town's exits. Consequently he at once ordered the advance guard, Second-Lieutenant Cecil Arthur Shaw's leading troop of the 7th's 'B' Squadron, to gallop into the town. By the time the bewildered Boer picket dashed in, shouting 'the English are on us!', the calvarymen were pounding at their heels. The surprise was nearly complete. To Broadwood's astonishment, though, the Boers who awoke so rudely to find themselves prisoners or shot at as they tried to mount and escape, were no everyday, ordinary burghers. They were instead 'the headspring of the Orange Free State' – the whole of President Steyn's Government staff, military and political. Yet Steyn himself, helped by his faithful Coloured servant, Ruiter, escaped. So too, in other directions, did seven of his bodyguard. Sergeant Cobb and another man of the 7th, actually pursued the hatless, coatless and bootless President, unaware, of course, of his identity. His pony, being fresh, soon got away from theirs, exhausted as they were by the night march and final gallop. Cobb, one of the regiment's best shots, seeing the uselessness of further chase, dismounted at some eighty yards from his prey and aimed his rifle.

'But,' as the *Official History* puts it, 'the oil on the sliding bolt and striker-spring had become frozen and clogged in the long night ride, disabling the weapon. Thrice the man pulled trigger harmlessly, the quarry sped on, and when shooting and further pursuit alike became hopeless the pair turned towards Reitz, regretting not overmuch the loss of a single ordinary burgher. Thus Steyn made his escape by a miracle.'

Not only Steyn, but also De Wet, evaded death or capture. The latter had decided to sleep at a village some distance out of the town. Broadwood's captures included two generals and twenty-seven officials, the remaining guns which he had lost at Sannah's Post, £11,500 (including 800 sovereigns) and all the government papers. There were no British casualties.[11] A fortnight after Reitz, Steyn's wife heard from her husband's private secretary that he had received, as a temporary prisoner in Pretoria, 'every consideration' and that he would 'long remember the kindness of the Seventh Dragoon Guards who captured' him.[12]

In Cape Colony, two months later, the first real success there came about as a result of a night march. Scobell of the Greys commanded a column of just over a thousand mounted men. Among them were 'A' and 'D' Squadrons of the 9th Lancers and Captain J. F. Purcell's company of the Cape Mounted Rifles. There were also twelve men mounted on bicycles. It was an exceptionally mobile body. It had no wagons. All its supplies were carried by pack mules: but its chief source of food was what the men could loot. Scobell (see p. 197) was proving himself one of the most successful and dashing of all the column leaders. Aged forty-two, he lived really hard, sharing every discomfort with his men. He was thought of by them as 'a rattling good man'.* On 6 June he had caught Kritzinger's men asleep at Wildefontein after another night march. Now on the fifth night of a six-day trek in vile weather over mountainous terrain, he called upon his almost starving men and horses for a supreme effort. The commando which they had been hunting, that of Commandant Johannes Lötter, a Cape 'rebel', who had originally entered the Colony with Kritzinger, was ripe for destruction. It was a truly elite force of about 130 rebels – Afrikaners from the Cape. Yet Lötter's intelligence was, surprisingly, inferior to that which Scobell's highly trained Africans brought him. These had now located the commando in a gorge called Bouwer's Hoek or Groenkloof near the village of Pietersburg, some nine miles away.

'The column,' recorded one of the 9th's officers, 'marched at 1 a.m. in pouring rain, lumbered up with cloaks or mackintoshes, and just before reaching Groene Kraal Farm turned to the left

* In May, he had given a ball at Cradock. Champagne was lavished on both officers and men. (Trooper S. Edingborough, CMR, MS 26 Jul., 1901, quoted in Pakenham, 527.)

For his failure in high command in peacetime and his old-fashioned views on cavalry see pp. 197 and 410.

through the prickly pears and reached the foot of the kloof [narrow valley]. Up this we struggled and stumbled, sliding away in the wet mud until the top was at last reached. The Colonel here explained his plans to C.O.s and squadron leaders. The farm, where the Boers were supposed to be, was behind a ridge, which could be seen near the far end of the plateau, and a donga [ravine] ran from it, passing pretty close to the left edge of the rise and then into a steep kloof. The "A" Squadron was told off to get round this flank, the C.M.R. were to go direct for the ridge, while the "D" Squadron were sent round the right flank and rear [where they saw no action].'

Unfortunately most of Lötter's men were sheltering for the night in a stone sheep-house or kraal a few hundred yards from the farm. As dawn broke on 5 September, the very day on which Smuts first bivouacked in the Colony, 'A' Squadron, commanded by Captain Lord Douglas James Cecil Compton,* rode towards the farmhouse, passing right by the door of the kraal. From there the suddenly awakened Boers were quick to fire at the Lancers at almost point-blank range.

'Thinking those [Boers] he saw only an outpost, Lord D. Compton called to Lieut [Robert Vaughan] Wynn† in front, who was commanding the advance party of half-a-dozen men, to gallop on. This he did with his party.

'Lord D. Compton himself had a narrow escape, for dropping his pistol at the gate of the kraal he dismounted, picked it up, mounted and galloped on after the advance party unscathed, but several other unfortunate men who then tried to get past the kraal were knocked over. However, a certain number of the squadron managed to get to the kraal walls and others behind some sort of cover.

'While this was going on the C.M.R. had made good the ridge, so that the Boers, cooped up in the kraal, were having a bad time of it, but like fools kept on firing. Wynn's party had got on beyond the farm, from which only five Boers came out, and they were all subsequently shot in the donga . . . .

* 4th son of the 4th Marquess of Northampton. He commanded the regiment, 1908–12. In *Who's Who* he entered under 'Recreations': 'fond of almost all sports and most games'.

† Wynn became the 6th Lord Newborough in 1957 and died in 1965, aged eighty-eight. The present author knew him well.

'The Boers thought they were so safe that they had no outposts out, and had only sent out one patrol to look for forage.
The work was most complete, for the whole of Lötter's commando, with everything it possessed, with the exception of the
patrol, . . . had fallen into Scobell's hands. He well deserved his
success for the dogged way in which he had stuck to his game.
The real hard week's work was soon forgotten.'

Lötter and his men, 'fighting,' as Scobell put it, 'with a rope round
their neck', though outnumbered nearly ten to one, put off the
moment of surrender until thirteen of them had been shot dead and
forty-six wounded. A further sixty-one were taken prisoner. Over
200 ponies and 30,000 rounds of ammunition were also captured.
Seven men of 'A' Squadron were killed and five wounded. The Cape
Mounted Rifles had two fatal casualties and one officer and two men
wounded. Lötter and seven of his commando were later court-
martialled and executed as Cape rebels.[13]

One of the best known of the earlier exponents of the night march
was forty-year-old Lieutenant-Colonel George Elliott Benson of the
Royal Artillery.* He had started the war as Deputy Assistant
Adjutant-General and had distinguished himself at Magersfontein.
He was a noted horsemaster who turned out to be a born guerrilla
leader. Kitchener considered him a model independent column commander. Over a period of seven months in 1901, twenty-one of the
twenty-eight night raids which he undertook were successful. How
difficult they were to carry out and how headlong was the culminat-
ing gallop into the sleeping Boer laagers is shown by the fact that his
men suffered more casualties from falls than from bullets. But they
developed under Benson's instruction that high degree of discipline
which was necessary to protect themselves and their horses from 'the
irregularities which occur in the dark, even under skilful control'. A
regular mounted infantry officer who joined Benson's column found
'everything much stricter' than in the other columns in which he had
served. Standing orders were printed and, most revolutionary for
the period,

'before starting each man was told the object of the [night]
march, so that all started keen. At every drift, wire fence or
other obstacle there was a staff officer to superintend. The

* In 1898 he had commanded Arab levies in the Eastern Sudan, nearly capturing Osman Digna (see Vol III, p. 309). (Headlam, 241.) The Boers christened
him 'the mad Englishman'. (Crum, 178.)

column was frequently halted, and straggling reduced to a minimum, and connection was always systematically kept up. No dogs, no talking or smoking; no rattling of wheels or accoutrements was allowed.'

One of the more perplexing tasks to be undertaken in the dark is that of 'saddling up'. Even in daylight it is not simple with heavy kits. At night, for instance, the loose end of a strap, which by day would be seen, is easy to miss and can badly injure a horse as, also, can anything resting unseen on its spine. Benson's men, like Rimington's at the same date and later, became adept at 'saddling up' in the dark. A North Country Imperial yeoman gives a good account of what it was like to take part in a long night march:

'Very trying, as the air is frosty and you sit in the saddle with your feet like ice and your hands numbed with cold, the only comfort being to stick them deep down into your pockets, taking the reins in your teeth or dropping them on the horse's neck, letting him go. Food you may have in your haversack, but that has to be carefully husbanded. No smoking allowed, no lights to be struck! What can a man do? Why, chew and be happy!'

What he chewed was 'cake tobacco, served out especially on a long night march'. Hard though night marching was on the men, it was rather less so for the horses. It had the priceless benefit of allowing the daylight hours for grazing.[14]

What constantly happened when intelligence was poor and an unwieldy cluster of columns was employed on a night raid is well illustrated by Allenby's description of 'the most ill-arranged night march' he had ever seen.

'A monumentally futile operation. Yesterday Bruce Hamilton* heard of a party of Boers, from thirty to ninety, who were vaguely supposed to have been at some farms about twenty miles from here [Bethel]. He therefore ordered 300 men per column – 900 in all – for a night surprise. He took command,

---

* Major-General (later General Sir) Bruce Meade Hamilton, an infantryman whom Kitchener placed in command of groups of mounted columns in the Orange River Colony, Cape Colony, Zululand and Eastern Transvaal during the last year or so of the war. Rawlinson thought him 'a good fellow as generals go though not brilliantly clever'. (Rawlinson, 14 Dec. 1901.) He died, aged seventy-nine, in 1936.

but the column commanders had to come too. The result was one general, three column commanders and five or six regimental commanders to run this band of 900. We sallied forth at 7 p.m.; luckily, a lovely night with a ¾ moon. We marched on, steadily, till 3 a.m. Then we began to try farm after farm. At 6 a.m., having seen no signs of a Boer, we off-saddled for two hours, had some breakfast and came back here, having done fifty miles in twelve hours fruitlessly and foolishly. The Dutchmen had gone thirty hours before; naturally, seeing that columns were all around their haunts. If it had been advisable to send out, one regiment under its own C.O. could have done the job quite as effectively. And yet you people at home,' he wrote in a letter on 4 December, 1901, 'wonder why the war goes on.'[15]

On 9 December, by contrast, Bruce Hamilton's three columns (Rawlinson's, Brevet Lieutenant-Colonel Frederick Drummond Vincent Wing's, and Brevet Lieutenant-Colonel Edward Charles Ingouville Williams's) effected a successful dawn surprise.

'At 3.45-a.m.,' wrote Rawlinson in his diary, 'as we came over the rise, the whole of the Boer laager lay at our feet only some 800 yards off. The M.I. [2nd and 8th] let go a cheer and a whoo-hoop which must have been a rude awakening to the laager. A few odd shots, the whining of one or two bullets and the whole of our line of over 2,000 mounted men set off at a gallop, yelling with delight. We never waited to shoot – the more the Boers shot the more we yelled. My orders were that none of the men were on any account to stop at the laager. There was to be no looting of wagons or waiting to shoot. Our objective was to be the mounted Boers and the gun we heard was with them. I don't think I have ever seen a prettier or more exhilarating sight than that was in the grey of dawn. The M.I. all streaming away just like a pack of hounds and giving tongue like red indians. We had a good long gallop of nearly seven miles. The horses did well and we were rewarded by collecting 53 prisoners to our own check – only six got away. We killed 21 and had one officer of 8th M.I. slightly wounded in the leg. . . . Having stopped the hunt and collected the "game" we went back to the laager to rest for a few hours. There we found 67 more prisoners, about 3,000 cattle and some 30 carts and wagons. . . . 57 miles in the 21 hours. . . . Woolls-Sampson [see p. 48 and below] deserves the utmost credit for having led us so well. . . . We got about 57 horses from the Boers which will fill up casualties.'

*   *   *

Time and again it was made clear by results that small mobile bodies were more likely to succeed than ponderous masses. The experience in August of Captain Oswald Buckley Bingham Smith-Bingham, 3rd Dragoon Guards (later to become Inspector-General of Cavalry), affords a pointed contrast with that of Allenby. With one squadron of his regiment, after a full day's march, he rode from Zeerust through the night to pounce on a convoy at dawn. He captured seventy-five wagons with supplies, seventeen men and thirty ponies.[16]

Even more profitable was the rush made on 5 February, 1902, by the four squadrons of the 1st Scottish Horse upon one of De la Rey's laagers at Gruisfontein, near Lichtenburg in the Western Transvaal. They were led by their newly appointed commanding officer, Major Henry Peregrine Leader of the 6th Dragoon Guards (Carabiniers), who had fought in all French's campaigns from Colesberg onwards.* With his 634 men and a 'pom-pom' he arrived within charging distance of Commandant Sarel Alberts's camp just in time to surround it before first light. Surprise was total. The burghers were sleeping in various scattered kraals. The whole group was completely encircled and though some of those who had been so rudely awakened managed to fire at their attackers at a few yards' range, not one contrived to escape. Seven were shot dead: Leader lost twenty-eight horses killed but only eight men wounded. Alberts surrendered together with seventeen of his officers and all his surviving men, numbering 131, of whom ten were wounded. Tullibardine, who founded the Scottish Horse, told the Royal Commission that it was 'my scouts who were mainly responsible' for the success of Gruisfontein. A troop of scouts, about twenty-five in number, was attached to each of the two regiments of Scottish Horse. Those who so dexterously located the laager were a mixture of Scotsmen and Afrikaners, aided by a few Zulus provided with Boer ponies.[17]

One of the last successful night raids was undertaken by elements

---

* Born in Detroit and educated in Canada, Leader had joined the Carabiniers in 1885. From 1905 to 1909 he commanded that regiment. As a Major-General he commanded the 1st Indian Cavalry Division from 1914–17. In 1917 he became Inspector of Cavalry in India, retiring in 1920.

of five columns commanded by Colonel Alexander Nelson Rochfort, Royal Horse Artillery, who had been wounded at Sannah's
Post. After much careful preparation, he surrounded the township
of Schweizer Reneke, one of De la Rey's chief bases in the Western
Transvaal,* entering it at daybreak on 16 April, 1902. The surprise
was almost total. Fifty-seven burghers were taken. These included a
brother of De la Rey and an adjutant of De Wet. There were no
British casualties. By this late stage of the war it had been learned
that where practicable it was important to start well after dusk, so
that the Boer scouts would be unable to see evidence of preparation.
In this case, Rochfort started at 6.30 p.m., rode about forty-four
miles mostly through bush country and arrived at 5.30 a.m. If these
figures are correct, the average speed must have been four miles per
hour, a truly swift rate of march for some thousand horsemen.[18]

Night raiding seldom succeeded except when the column leader
was well served by efficient, physically tough mounted troops and,
more important, by first-class local intelligence. Benson (and, later,
Rimington and Rawlinson) had both. In Benson's column were some
of the best of the mounted infantry and the 2nd Scottish Horse. He
had no regular cavalry. About one-third of his 1,400 men consisted
of infantry, but these were as a rule used exclusively as escort to his
movable supply depot. He was, though, burdened with a battery of
field guns. His intelligence officer was the extreme uitlander, Aubrey
Woolls-Sampson, chief begetter of the Imperial Light Horse (see
p. 48), who had been wounded at Elandslaagte. His knowledge of
Afrikaans, the native languages, individual Boers and Kaffirs, as well
as of the terrain, was exceptional, as also was his skill in training
'loyal' Boer and native agents, scouts, guides and spies and in gather-
ing information from the kraals. As the war drew to a close, other
intelligence officers came to emulate Woolls-Sampson's skill. The
columns commanded by Major-General Arthur Paget, especially,
had an efficient scouting service. A local Englishman, Mr W. Car-
lisle, proved invaluable in the Western Transvaal. The success of
Kekewich at Gruisfontein was partly due to his detective work (see
above).†

* Schweizer Reneke had been invested on 19 August, 1900, and its garrison
not relieved until 9 January, 1901. It was then reoccupied by the Boers.

† The central Field Intelligence Department expanded enormously under
Colonel (later Lieutenant-General Sir) David Henderson (whose book *The Art
of Reconnaissance* was published in 1907). When Kitchener took over it consisted of 280 officers and men. At the war's end, beside thousands of Africans, it

Typical of Benson's and Woolls-Sampson's successes were two lengthy marches on the nights of 5 and 15 August, 1901, in the Ermelo district of the Eastern Transvaal. These resulted in complete surprises and the capture of sixty burghers with their horses and wagons. Three equally profitable night raids on 10, 15 and 16 September (for one of which Benson marched fifty-two miles in twenty-four hours), were followed on 17/18 September by a ride of forty miles which brought the column at dawn to a laager at Middeldrift, on the Umpilusi River. Fifty-four Boers, with 240 horses and numerous wagons and cattle, were taken. Other minor night raids succeeded this one which marked the climax of the column's successes. So alarmed by Benson had the Boers in the area become that their laagers were kept constantly on the move. They never pitched camp in the same place for two successive nights. They learned, too, to be saddled up by 3 o'clock each morning. Not only were the commandos becoming more circumspect and wary, they were also combining for a supreme effort to destroy what Louis Botha called Benson's 'restless column'.[19] By fast marching and brilliant deception, they now decoyed away from him two columns (Rimington's and Rawlinson's) which had been within supporting distance.

On 30 October, as Benson made his way back to base for fresh supplies, marching with his supply column, some 2,000 burghers smashed his rearguard of about 280 of all ranks, near Bakenlaagte. Benson was mortally wounded, sixty-six other officers and men were killed and 165 wounded.* The action is particularly interesting because some of the commandos, so as to effect their junction with sufficient speed to outwit Woolls-Sampson's spies, had to march seventy miles, riding the last thirty miles at one stretch, arriving on the field at exactly the right time.† They then made one of their increasingly common charges, yelling at the top of their voices, firing from the saddle and, when twenty or thirty yards from the

---

was employing 132 officers and over 2,300 men.

Armed native scouts usually accompanied columns in the last months of the war. (Warwick, 21, 23.)

In January, 1902, Haig reported that he found Abe Bailey, who had ridden with Jameson in 1896 and who was one of the principal Transvaal mine-owners, 'of great assistance in helping me to get men for Intelligence work ever since I came to [Cape] Colony a year ago.' (Haig, 262.)

* The vets with the column, as they also did on other occasions, helped to tend the wounded men. (Smith, 172.)

† These were brought by Botha himself, who had just returned from his abortive invasion of Natal, and numbered between 250 and 500. (Childers, 245.)

guns, dismounting and shooting at the closest range. But this charge, executed with perhaps 900 or even 1,200 men in two lines over the rolling veld, was on a scale hitherto unknown. 'There's miles of 'em, begob!' exclaimed an Irish soldier. The charge which swept over a mile and a half of ground was the more effective as the streaming rain raised a thick steam from the ground, limiting visibility and providing a natural 'smoke' screen. Benson's rearguard of mounted infantry, seventy-nine of the 2nd Scottish Horse (of whom sixty-seven became casualties) and his artillery, was completely outflanked on both sides of the position which he took up. These devoted men stood their ground nobly, sacrificing themselves to save both the main part of the column and the convoy.* The Boers, whose casualties numbered nearly 100, including one general, were so exhausted that they decided not to press the attack. They had to be satisfied with the guns they had captured and the casualties they had inflicted. It was not until dawn on 1 November that the reliefs sent for by Woolls-Sampson (who took command on Benson's death) arrived on the scene. Allenby's and Brevet Lieutenant-Colonel Henry de Beauvoir de Lisle's† columns, totalling some 2,000 mounted men, marched fifty-two miles in sixteen-and-a-half hours, while Lieutenant-Colonel Charles St Leger Barter's column rode thirty miles from dusk to dawn.[20]

Such noteworthy forced marches were becoming more frequent as some of the better columns learned how to manage their horses. The most astounding marching record of any single column's was

---

* The commander of the 2nd Scottish Horse, Major F. D. Murray, was killed, so were five other officers and twenty-eight men of the regiment. Four officers and thirty men were wounded. Lord Tullibardine says that there were only ninety-six of the regiment engaged. 'They stuck it out until only six were left unhit or prisoners.' (R.C., II, 455.)

† He became General Sir Beauvoir de Lisle, who in the First World War commanded the 1st Cavalry Division. In the 1890s in India 'not to know De Lisle was to argue oneself unknown.' He was then adjutant of the Durham Light Infantry. His polo team beat every other and was the first from an infantry regiment to do so. (Gilbert, 253.) He was the author of Polo in India and Tournament Polo.

He (as also did Rimington) trained unbroken horses with his column. He placed them in the ranks at the rate of three or four a day. He was a great equestrian enthusiast and first-class horsemaster. In his column he was lucky to have a number of Australian horsemen to whom the handling of unbroken and troublesome horses was a pastime. (Smith, 177b.)

An officer in his column wrote that his
'plan of attack differs from that of most of the commanders. When he

18. A railway scouting cycle (see p. 227)

(see p. 227)

19. 'The Empty Saddle'

20. Sir Redvers Buller

21. The Earl of Dundonald (see p. 74)

22. Brig.-Gen. J. R. P. Gordon (see p. 134)

23. Brig.-Gen. T. C. Porter (see p. 108

24. Maj.-Gen. Sir Edward Brabant (see p. 73)

25. Major Charles Briggs (see p. 49)

achieved by a little known artilleryman, Major Hugh Sandham Jeudwine (who as a lieutenant-general became Chief of the General Staff of the British Army of the Rhine in 1919). The winter of 1901 saw his 400 mounted men chasing, but never catching, Commandant Salomon Gerhardus ('Mannie') Maritz's commando which at one point got to within thirty miles of Cape Town. In fifty-four days he marched 1,150 miles: an average of over twenty-one miles every twenty-four hours. This he accomplished in the outlying Calvinia district of Cape Colony in the face of appalling difficulties of supply and over the roughest of tracks. He on one occasion marched all night through rain for forty-eight miles to relieve a besieged post, and on 8 July his column rode sixty-eight miles in twenty-four hours: an average speed of over 2.8 miles per hour. More than three months later, Maritz, described by Reitz as a man 'of enormous strength, cruel and ruthless in his methods, but a splendid guerrilla leader', was still at large. Major Frank Wormald, 12th Lancers (who later commanded the regiment) found himself, with one of his squadrons, co-operating with the columns which were successfully barring Maritz from entry into Cape Town. On 31 October, hurrying to save a convoy, he arrived too late to do so, but marched with his 150 troopers a staggering sixty miles in seventeen hours, largely in the dark: an average of three-and-a-half miles an hour. Rimington contrived two excellent forced marches in August, 1901. On the 23rd his column marched forty-eight miles and during the night of 24th rode a further fifty-seven. Of the regular cavalry, parts of the 7th Dragoon Guards managed in December fifty-eight miles in one day and forty-seven in another, while the Royals, in March, 1902, after riding some ninety miles in forty-eight hours were not surprised that seventy of their horses were no longer fit to carry their riders.[21]

The most stunning of all the marching feats of the war was performed not by a handful of picked men but by a body of four conjoined columns* numbering some 4,800 assorted horsemen in the heat of an African midsummer. In one of Elliot's vast drives in the Lindley area, this mobile mass had actually by 4 January, 1902,

wishes to attack a Boer position he gallops at it, his men extended fifty paces apart.... The theory is that a long line of galloping men, fifty paces apart, can hardly be hit. If one portion of the line is checked, the rest, by their rapid movement, automatically as it were, outflank the checking force.' (Gilbert, 253.)

* Broadwood's, de Lisle's, Byng's and Major Robert Fanshawe's. These commanders had all become outstanding horsemasters, adept, too, at living off the country.

covered nearly 250 miles in five consecutive days – an average of fifty miles a day! These marches are probably the most extraordinary distance rides ever performed by a large body of troops under service conditions. At long last there had been brought together thousands of horses, thoroughly conditioned and properly fed, with well trained riders. The lesson had taken an inordinate time a-learning.[22]

*　　*　　*

The sorry catalogue of ambushes during the guerrilla war, nearly always due to poor scouting, includes Cyferfontein in the Western Transvaal on 5 January, 1901. The culprit in this case was Woolls-Sampson who had contrived to take command of his Imperial Light Horse and on this occasion was leading two of its squadrons. His record as a hot-headed commander was as deplorable as his prowess as an intelligence officer was pre-eminent.* Though requested by Major Briggs (see p. 49) 'in unmistakable language to slow down and send out scouts in advance', he first trotted and soon galloped off to occupy a hill in 'quarter column' without a pretence of reconnaissance, wrongly believing that a troop of the 14th Hussars had declared the hill clear.

'He had barely given the order to deploy,' records the regimental historian, 'when suddenly 700 or 800 [of De la Rey's] Boers who were practically invisible in the long grass, opened a tremendous fire at from fifty to 100 yards range .... Those who survived the first volley dismounted, their panic-stricken horses plunging madly, and returned the fire .... Many of the surviving men took cover and fired from behind their dead horses; others, to get a better target, knelt, returning the fire in that position; a number of them had the tops of their heads shot off. The fire was maintained for approximately ten minutes.'

The Boers now, according to an officer who was present, galloped down between the two squadrons firing from the saddle. Woolls-Sampson soon realized that the situation was hopeless and screamed 'Retire! Retire!' His regimental sergeant-major, a regular of the 5th Dragoon Guards, took up the cry, galloping along the whole line,

---

* After Cyferfontein Kitchener wisely removed him to the Intelligence Department, where in Ian Hamilton's view, he became 'at one leap the second figure in the war, second only to Lord Kitchener himself'. (Gibson, 159.)

'hat in hand, waving the men away'. Neither he nor Woolls-Sampson was hit. Fifteen men of the regiment were killed, some being hit three and four times. Thirty-two were wounded. Eighty horses were killed outright and twenty had to be destroyed later. Many of the saddles were shot to pieces and could not be salvaged. The belief that colonials were better at scouting was badly shaken after Cyferfontein.[23]

It was somewhat restored, though, eleven months later. On 18 December, near Bethlehem, De Wet, with some 700 men, made an uncharacteristic mess of an ambush which he planned against the 1st and 2nd Imperial Light Horse, also about 700 strong. With them were some 300 of the 11th Imperial Yeomanry escorting two 15-pounders and two pom-poms. In command was sixty-three year old Major (acting Brigadier-General) John George Dartnell, a Canadian and one of the few Indian Mutiny veterans active in the war. At the age of twenty he had been promoted brevet major after leading the only successful escalade attack on the fortress of Jhansi (see Vol II, p. 192). Since 1874, having retired from the army in 1869, he had commanded the Natal Mounted Police, seeing service in the Zulu and First Boer Wars. In 1899 he had marched with Yule from Dundee and been present at Talana Hill (see p. 41). He was a heavily built man of irrepressible ebullience with a smart imperial beard. He now found his column, as had so many before him, isolated and face to face with De Wet. By good fortune he was informed by a surrendering burgher that seven commandos in ambuscade were awaiting his arrival. When De Wet's warning signal gun was fired, Lieutenant-Colonel Duncan Mackenzie, commanding the 2nd Imperial Light Horse, which formed the advance guard, was prepared:

'He suddenly saw the enemy riding out of the Tiger Kloof Spruit, where they had been concealed [in long grass]. They formed up in line like a British regiment and charged over the flat ground. I galloped through a long hollow in front of us, dismounted my men and lined the crest of the ridge, at the same time shouting: "Now, 2nd I.L.H., you have the chance of your lives!" We opened fire at the approaching enemy and soon checked them. [The closest they got was 150 yards.] A few took refuge in a little stone kraal on our left front, and others swerved to our right and worked round our flank. I noticed a high ridge on my left front which commanded my position and quickly sent Captain Jack Duff with his squadron to occupy it. Only just in time, for he sent a message back saying that about 500 Boers [an exaggeration] were riding up to occupy the position, but on seeing him and his men and no doubt concluding that the position was strongly held, returned to the valley. The Boers whom we first drove off went round the right flank and attacked the 1st I.L.H. inflicting a good many casualties.'

This attack on the rearguard was a more determined one. It lasted for nearly four hours before De Wet disengaged on the imminent arrival of reinforcements. These came just in time for, although each man possessed three bandoliers containing 135 rounds, ammunition was beginning to run short. De Wet accused some of his men of cowardice:

'What,' he wrote in his memoirs, 'was now my bitter disappointment when I saw that only one-third of my burghers were charging. The others were keeping under cover, and do what I would I could not drive them out.

'Everything went wrong.

'When the burghers who were charging the English discovered that the greater part of their comrades had remained, they turned round and retreated. ... So I thought it best to retreat, swallowing my disappointment as best I could.'

He admitted to two killed and nine wounded, of whom two subsequently died. The British losses were one killed and fourteen wounded. An Irish doctor, Captain Thomas Joseph Crean, who acted as medical officer to the 1st Imperial Light Horse, gained the Victoria Cross, less for his ministrations to the wounded than for his dare-devil bravery in the line.[24]*

*   *   *

At Vrieskraal in the Eastern Transvaal, on 16 August, 1901, General C. H. Muller's Johannesburg Commando, part of Viljoen's command, ambushed two squadrons of the 19th Hussars. Advancing through thick bush country without proper scouts, these made the

* Crean had been twice wounded at Elandslaagte. He served with the 1st Cavalry Brigade, 1914–15 and finished his career as Medical Officer to the Royal Enclosure at Ascot. In the mid-1890s he had been a member of the Irish International Rugby XV, and of the English rugby team in South Africa. He died aged fifty in 1923.

cardinal blunder of breaking ranks so as to round up cattle, which had in fact been placed as bait by the Boers. Fortunately the 18th Hussars were not far behind, both regiments being part of a so-called 'flying' column of Kitchener's brother, Major-General Frederick Walter Kitchener. After a time the 18th drove the enemy off. The 19th left behind them 'helmets on the ground and bits of clothing hanging on the thorn bushes'. They lost three killed, two wounded and one missing. The 18th had three men wounded. Thirty-five horses, thirty rifles and 2,000 rounds of ammunition were also lost. Thus was it that the commandos were able to keep in the field so long! The Boers at Vrieskraal lost one officer killed and a few men wounded. They took, and released the same day, twenty-four of the 19th. One of the Boers who was present records that he

'found a few of our Irish Americans swapping clothing with the captured soldiers. Some of the Tommies who were relieved of their boots had rolled puttees around their feet as a protection against the thorns (*dubbeltjies*) with which the sand was strewn. I met Joe Wade, neatly dressed in a uniform of one of the 19th talking amiably to a soldier who was wearing in exchange Joe's tattered trousers patched and torn to ribbons. ... Where modesty decreed that clothes should be soundest, the trousers were most at fault, and Joe remarked "I suffered much from sunburn and exposure in those parts". ... A little distance away stood a young Hussar, wearing the limp and greasy hat of his captor. ... One man was allowed to retain his trousers, because, it was thought, he had received too great a fright.'[25]

* * *

The regimental historian of the Inniskillings wrote of the action at Klipfontein, near Camden, in the Eastern Transvaal on 12 February, 1901:

'In this fine charge the regiment lost only one man, Private H. Love, killed and two wounded, Privates J. Leary and M. Clear. It was one of the few instances of a successful cavalry charge during the war, and only proves what can be done by cavalry well handled and well led. ...

'About mid-day the advanced guard [of Lieutenant-Colonel William Pulteney Pulteney's column], one squadron 14th Hussars, with a pom-pom, became engaged with the enemy

and could advance no further. . . . The Inniskillings were at
last sent on to clear the ridge, supported by artillery fire. We
moved in column of troops to the front. . . . "A" Squadron,
under Major [Arthur Rowland] Mosley, extended, supported
on its right rear by "C" Squadron, under Lieutenant [Cuthbert
Francis] Dixon-Johnson, and "B" Squadron, under Major
[Thursby Henry Ernest] Dauncey [who had charged with the
21st Lancers at Omdurman]. Trotting on, the whole came
immediately under rifle fire from front and both flanks, and
drew swords. "A" Squadron, cutting a wire fence, kept
straight towards this fire, until pulled up by a second wire fence
in front of a deep ravine which ran down the far side of the
ridge. Here they dismounted and kept the enemy occupied
with a good return fire.

'In the meantime "C" and "B" Squadrons had inclined to
the right, cut two wire fences, and were approaching a third.
Here "C" Squadron was joined by one troop of "A" Squadron. As soon as the last fence was cut, the charge was sounded
by the Commanding Officer. "C" Squadron giving a cheer
extended and charged straight at the left flank of the Boers who
were opposing Major Mosley. The Boers immediately fled . . .,
"C" Squadron getting right amongst them. The Maxim at once
opened fire and made good practice. After crossing the valley
this squadron was recalled. The pom-pom soon after came into
action and threw 348 shells into the midst of the Boers galloping up the hill opposite. . . . The Boer losses, not counting those
inflicted by the pom-pom, were five killed, fifteen wounded and
ten prisoners.

'The pursuit was carried on, "C" Squadron being again
pushed forward and capturing over 1,000 head of cattle, fifteen
wagons, twenty Cape carts, and thirty to forty saddle horses. . . .

'It had been a long day on the horses – from 5 a.m. to 10 p.m.,
saddled throughout.'[26]

Nine months later, at Spyfontein on 30 November, a troop of the
Inniskillings, led by the most recently joined subaltern, Second-
Lieutenant L. M. Oliver

'gallantly charged a hill of which the Boers had got possession
and from which they were shooting into the flank guard [of the
supply wagons of Rimington's column]. They galloped straight
at the ridge. . . .

'Lieutenant Oliver topped the ridge twenty yards in advance of his men, and was immediately pierced by four bullets (he was hit nine times); another of the troop, Private Tremayne, was killed and another wounded. . . .

'The Boers, although about 100 in number [almost certainly an exaggeration], fled when they saw the troop coming, but were rallied by their leader, and drove it back. Our guns then opened fire and the New South Wales Mounted Rifles charged the hill in flank, driving the Boers off.'

At the same time as Oliver's troop charged, another 'went round the right' and 'although under very severe fire, got through scot-free'. It seems that Oliver's charge may well have been a foolish piece of recklessness on the part of a very green young officer.[27]

On two occasions at the end of 1901 parts of the 7th Dragoon Guards charged with bayonets. On the first, Captain Moreton Foley Gage, whose squadron was being severely sniped at from a kopje near Quaggafontein on 8 December, ordered his troopers to fix bayonets. Using their rifles like lances at the 'engage', they charged the kopje, 'whereupon the Boers, though in superior number, turned tail and fled'. One private was wounded. On the second occasion, three days after Christmas, a flying column of the 7th with a battalion of the 6th Mounted Infantry,* commanded by Major Charles William Thompson of the 7th, found themselves under heavy shell and pom-pom fire at Armstrong Drift. The 7th had not experienced such a bombardment since the battle of Belfast in August, 1900. Nor would the Boers have been able to deliver it had they not three days before captured the guns at Tweefontein (see p. 103). Major Thompson ordered his trumpeter to sound 'Draw Swords', which was obeyed, of course, by the fixing of bayonets. Line was formed in a good old-fashioned manner and the column, some 600 strong, thundered across perfectly open, unobstructed ground. The Boers wisely fled without firing another shot. Two mounted infantrymen were wounded and two of the 7th's horses were killed.[28]

*   *   *

A combination of vague intelligence and youthful impetuosity (or, as some might say, a misapplication of 'the cavalry spirit') was the

---

* One of the best mounted infantry regiments. It was known by the Australians as 'the galloping 6th'. (Wallace, 290.)

cause of a minor disaster on 17 September, 1901. Louis Botha's long-awaited descent into Natal with nearly 2,000 secretly collected burghers had at last been set in motion.* As he expected, the news of it caused a 'commotion' at Kitchener's headquarters.[29] Among the four columns which were hurriedly sent to block his way was one commanded by Hubert Gough, now a brevet lieutenant-colonel, who had last come to prominence leading the way into Ladysmith (see p. 122). His 'Composite Regiment' consisted of 585 mounted infantrymen in four companies with two 15-pounder guns. During the long waiting period after the relief of Ladysmith, Gough had trained his men rigorously (see p. 186). Each company (one of them was of the 60th Rifles) engaged twice a week in firing live bullets, a thing much scoffed at by his fellow commanding officers. Gough's[30] reputation as a horsemaster was well deserved. He held a daily sick parade for his horses and inspired his officers to pay special attention to the prevention of sore backs.[31] In the few months during which the column had been in the field, it had already achieved a reputation for daring escapades. Now, near Scheeper's Nek, at the mouth of a gorge not far from the meeting of the Buffalo and Blood Rivers, its commander indulged in one too many. 'People have been saying,' wrote Allenby a few days after Gough's debacle, ' "I wish these Dutchmen would concentrate and give us a show." Now they have done so, have mopped up a column . . . and we are not in a position to hit them back. At this rate the war will go on for years.'[32]

What happened at Blood River Poort was this. In spite of Natal Intelligence's reports that Botha with up to 700 men was in the neighbourhood, when Gough saw some 200 burghers carelessly, as he thought, off-saddling at a farmstead, he assumed that they were all that he had to contend with. He decided to attack. To 'Bimbashi' Stewart (see p. 200), who was a few miles behind with another body of mounted infantry, Gough sent a message asking him to follow on speedily.

> 'It seemed,' as Gough's biographer puts it, 'that his chance had now come. The ground was such that they could begin their approach to the valley unseen. They must then ride hard for a thousand yards over open grassland to seize a spur overlooking the river bed, but once this was gained, even if the sentries gave the alarm, there was an excellent chance of bringing the enemy

* His orders were almost identical to those of Joubert's at the war's beginning.

under close fire before they could escape. Orders were given; three of his four companies made ready; the advance began. On a signal, the regiment broke into a gallop over the skyline to cross the open ground. Behind the centre companies raced the battery . . . .

'Unfortunately for Gough, his dashing plan was based on a fallacy. The 200 men were . . . but a detachment of a much larger force. The main body of this force . . . were also approaching the point of attack at the same moment from the opposite direction but were hidden by the rock walls of Blood River Poort. The pace of events began to quicken.

'The Boer sentries gave the alarm and men began to rush up to support them from the river. Simultaneously, the main column of Boers came into sight of the charging British companies. As those from the river bed began to open fire to the front, 500 enemy horsemen galloped out to Gough's right flank from which, almost at once, they began to envelop him.'[33]

In less than twenty minutes of a 'bitter fire-fight'[34] four officers and nineteen men were killed and five officers and nineteen men wounded. Gough and 235 men as well as the two guns, 200 valuable ponies, 180 Lee Metford rifles and 30,000 rounds of ammunition were captured. What the Boer casualties were is not known. After numerous adventures, Gough escaped that night and the other prisoners were later released half-naked. Stewart, who had with difficulty saved some of Gough's transport, wisely kept out of the fray.

The action is especially interesting as being one of the rare occasions on which both the British and the Boers in their initial charges fired their rifles from the saddle.[35]*

* Blood River Poort may be the first instance where mounted infantry thus charged. The first occasion on which regular cavalry did so was when the 16th Lancers charged with rifles blazing at Springhaan's Nek on 14 December. (See p. 245.)

During the great post-war cavalry controversy, a minor point of debate was the question of firing from the saddle. Erskine Childers, the chief civilian apostle of the 'fire' school, put forward the view that one of the elements in the rifle's superiority was that it could 'be used both from horseback and on foot. The first-class mounted rifleman . . . will be at home in both. He will use saddle-fire mainly in its unaimed or roughly-aimed form,' thus producing 'great effect in daunting aim and nerves alike'. Colonel William Balck of the German Army disagreed, 'because of the danger to officers and men in multi-rank formations'. (Childers: *War*, 32; Balck, Col. W. *Tactics*, trans. Krueger, Walter, 1914, II, 166–7.)

Another was at Onverwacht (or Bankkop), also in the Eastern Transvaal. There, on 4 January, 1902, Major J. M. Vallentin, newly in charge of one of Plumer's two columns,* made exactly the same mistake as Gough had done. Seeing a group of some fifty burghers, apparently isolated, he 'formed the impetuous decision to gallop them down' with what men of his advance guard he had at hand, blazing away from the saddle. They had gone but a small distance when first 300 and a little later another 200 Boers appeared as if from nowhere. Firing at the gallop, they completely enveloped Vallentin's flanks. Again, as at Blood River Poort, the 'desperate *mêlée*' which followed lasted less than twenty minutes. Vallentin and nineteen men were killed, forty-five wounded and about fifty to sixty captured. Among the otherwise unknown Boer casualties was Opperman, one of Botha's best commandants, who was killed leading the first Boer charge.[36]

One of the more spectacular of the earlier Boer charges took place at Vlakfontein, near Naauwpoort, on 29 May, 1901. Kemp (see p. 103) added a highly successful refinement to the Boers' new technique of firing from the saddle whilst charging. By means of a trail of gunpowder the burghers, most of them the same men who had charged at Geduld two months before (see p. 49), set fire to the dry veld grass. Masked by the curtain of smoke blowing towards the unsuspecting rearguard of a British column, some 500 burghers abruptly burst out of the flames. Most of them were firing from horseback, but others were seen leading their mounts and shooting as they ran either with the rein dropped altogether or with it over the arm. So successful were they that the casualties in Brigadier-General Henry Grey Dixon's column† numbered no less than forty-nine killed and 130 wounded. Kemp lost forty-three burghers, mostly in a successful counter-attack undertaken by Dixon.[37]

Almost exactly five months later, on 24 October, at Kleinfontein

* About 100 Queensland Imperial Bushmen, Imperial Yeomanry and some mounted infantry.

† About 800 men, half on foot and half mounted. The 7th Battalion, Imperial Yeomanry, suffered most. These yeomen and 200 men of the Scottish Horse were seeing action for the first time. Lieutenant William John English (aged nineteen) won the Victoria Cross in this engagement. Dixon, an infantryman, was described by a doctor in the Scottish Horse as 'a charming man – ADC to the King – but his generalship is beyond argument – there is none.' (Julius M. Bernstein Papers, NAM, 7706-51, 22 Jul., 1901.) He was knighted in 1902, but did not rise above the rank of Brigadier-General. In *Who's Who* he actually gave as his recreations: 'hunting, shooting, fishing'.

in the Western Transvaal, De la Rey's commandos, about whose whereabouts and numbers intelligence, as was so often the case, was silent, attacked one of Methuen's columns. Lieutenant-Colonel Stanley Brenton von Donop, quite unsuspecting, was marching his column,* with 100 wagons in attendance, along a road fringed by thick forest, through which his Imperial Yeomanry scouts could see nothing, when the blow fell. Three divisions of Boers, those of Kemp, Commandant Piet Steenekamp and Acting-Commandant O. Oosthuizen, each two or three lines deep,† some 500 in number, charged down 'like a regiment of European cavalry straight for the centre of the convoy'. A very confused and bloody action followed, from which the Boers eventually drew off. They left, it is said, as many as fifty bodies on the field, including that of Oosthuizen. Von Donop's casualties numbered eighty-four Europeans and forty-nine native drivers.[38]

The next occasion on which De la Rey's burghers charged, shooting from the saddle, was on 25 February, 1902. Near a stream called Yzerspruit, on the road from Wolmaransstaad to Klerksdorp, they ambushed one of Methuen's convoys, consisting of 151 wagons. This was one of the very few which by this late date still had to travel across open country as opposed to along a blockhouse line. It was in charge of Major William Campbell Anderson, 15th Hussars, who commanded the 5th Imperial Yeomanry. Two hundred and thirty men of this battalion formed the mounted part of the convoy's escort.‡ Once again De la Rey's intelligence, based on ubiquitous scouts and the heliograph, far outmatched that of Methuen. Every movement of the convoy was at once known to the Boers. Anderson, by contrast, had not the slightest inkling that some 1,200 burghers were awaiting him in ambuscade. Well before dawn, these carefully hidden Boers burst forth, attacking first the front (Kemp), then the rear (General Jan G. Celliers) and finally, hoping (in vain as it happens) that front and rear would have drawn the escort to their defence, one flank (General P. J. Liebenberg) of the convoy. All three attacks were stoutly and skilfully resisted. As day broke, De la Rey, seeing that the native drivers and conductors were in a state of panic, ordered a general charge. The official historian

---

* 680 of the 5th Imperial Yeomanry, 330 infantry and seven guns.

† The first action in which there is mention of the use of successive lines of Boer horsemen for charging.

‡ The rest of the escort consisted of 260 foot soldiers, two field and three machine guns.

describes its progress:

> 'Nine hundred horsemen appeared on the left. Having advanced in unbroken line to within 500 yards, firing from the saddle as they ambled forward, the whole body suddenly charged impetuously down upon the flank. A fire which was not to be faced met the stormers; three times they came on, wavered and fled back out of range. Once under shelter they were steadied by their officers, and twenty minutes later advanced and charged again. For the fourth time they were hurled back by a terrible fusillade from the men of the flank guard who lay immovable, in the face of what were virtually repeated rushes of cavalry. ... Soon after the second repulse of Kemp from the flank [Celliers] galloped on to the field with 500 men and immediately rode against the British rearguard. .... Like Kemp, Celliers met with a shattering reception; his men refused to face the fire, and scattering backwards and outwards, contented themselves for the next two hours with bringing a cross-fire to bear upon the rearguard, which suffered considerably but replied with vigour.'

It was to no avail. The escort was outnumbered at least three to one. By 7 a.m. when at last the firing ceased there could be no doubt that there had been suffered an unmitigated disaster. De la Rey, though he found most of the wagons empty, got what he so badly needed. Among the booty were three ammunition carts with half a million rounds in them. He also captured most of the 170 horses and 1,450 mules which were with the convoy. He lost, though, which he could very ill afford, fifty-one burghers, including an outstanding young general called Lemmer. The British casualties numbered 381, of which fifty-eight were killed and 194 taken prisoner. These were released next day.[39]

De la Rey's men again charged firing from the saddle in the course of an action near Tweebosch on 7 March. This was the greatest reverse for British arms in all the guerrilla period. It came about as a result of shockingly poor intelligence and the disgracefully cumbersome column commanded by Major Archibald Paris* which formed the force with which Methuen was attempting to seek out and destroy the victors of Yserspruit. It was burdened with four field guns, about 300 regular foot soldiers and eighty supply wagons. In it there were parts of fourteen different units, numbering about

* Paris, a Royal Marine, commanded the Royal Naval Division at the defence of Antwerp in 1914.

1,250 men, of whom under 900 were mounted. Of these a few were surrendered Boers. There were also 257 men of the Cape and British South Africa Police; 126 of Ashburner's Light Horse, a Cape Colony unit; ninety-two of the Diamond Fields Horse; sixty-four of Cullinan's Horse, a Bechuanaland unit; forty-eight of Dennison's Scouts, another unit formed at Vryburg in the North Cape;* and 294 of two Imperial Yeomanry units (5th and 86th) of the second contingent. Methuen was hoping to be joined by the purely mounted column of Brevet Lieutenant-Colonel Harold Maxwell Grenfell,† but De la Rey, knowing exactly where both were, got between the two bodies long before they could unite. Paris's column was easy prey for De la Rey's burghers, nearly 2,000 in number. Though the regular infantry and the artillerymen fought with magnificent valour for five hours, they were totally abandoned by the majority of the motley bands of horsemen who were meant to support them. Many, but not by any means all, of the men of the Imperial Yeomanry, untried, untrained and undisciplined, vied with the colonials in the panic flight. Paris managed to rally some forty men including a few from the Cape Police and the Imperial Yeomanry. These fought off repeated attacks from a cattle-kraal until De la Rey shelled them with the guns he had captured at Yserspruit, forcing their surrender.

* In September, 1900, by Captain, later Major, Charles George Dennison. The unit initially consisted of only fifty men, but was later expanded to 200. It was part of the Kimberley column in mid-1901, and saw much action under Major Paris. Dennison had pursued an active South African Colonial military career, serving as second-in-command of the Border Horse in the Zulu War, 1879, and in the First Boer War, 1881. In his book, *A Fight to the Finish*, published in 1904, he was strongly critical of 'that curse of the British Army, jealousy', giving this as the reason why De Wet was never caught. He gives, more usefully, an account of how his Scouts worked:

'. . . extended order: my front covered by my screen, which usually extended about three or four miles; the distance between two men of a half-section was always about fifty yards, and between each half-section about 300 yards. Thus four men covered a front of 400 yards, but in wooded or rugged country the men were much closer together. The screen was supported on either flank by the remainder of the corps riding in open skirmishing order, myself in the centre with a section of gallopers; besides which individual scouts in advance were often used, and always connecting links in my front to the officers in charge of the screen.'

Dennison was not himself present at Tweebosch. (Dennison, C. G. *A Fight to the Finish*, 104, 106, 108; Stirling: *C*, 222.)

† Grenfell, 1st Life Guards, was in command of a regiment of Brabant's Horse although only a Captain in his regiment. He commanded the 3rd Dragoon Guards, 1908–12.

Most of the mounted men 'thundered to the rear. . . . The limit of their flight seems to have been the wind of their horses.'[40] All the gunners and many of the infantry were killed or wounded in the course of a series of 'last stands'. The total casualties were sixty-eight killed, 132 wounded and about 600 prisoners all of whom were soon released. Two hundred and forty horses were killed or wounded. Methuen himself, senior even to Kitchener, was severely wounded towards the end of the fight and forced to surrender. He was the only British general to be captured during the war. De la Rey behaved towards him with exemplary chivalry, sending him off to the nearest British hospital in his own wagon.[41]*

There were only three more actions in which the Boers employed their charging-and-firing tactics. The first was on 31 March, at Boschbult, some sixty miles west of Klerksdorp. Here a mixed, but mobile reconnaissance in force† (a rare and dangerous anachronism at this stage of the guerrilla war) under Brevet Lieutenant-Colonel George Arthur Cookson, 16th Bengal Lancers,‡ was, as so often, led on by a decoy force into the arms of a much superior one, led by Kemp. Cookson's men fought back strenuously and even managed to entrench themselves, using sacks and carcasses of dead horses to thicken the parapet. In the course of the hotly fought engagement which raged from 10 a.m. to 5.30 p.m. the Boers charged, firing from the saddle, usually at a well-controlled canter,

---

* Civil Veterinary Surgeon D. T. Tamblyn, who was in charge of the Mobile Field Veterinary Hospital which accompanied Paris's column,

> 'made several trips with boxes of ammunition from the waggons, and distributed it along the bullet-swept line. . . . Two horses were killed under him early in the fight, and he was captured but escaped, to be again taken at the surrender. . . . The whole Indian and Kaffir establishment of the F.V.H. were butchered. One Farrier Sergeant of Indian Native Cavalry and two Indian Veterinary Assistants (men carrying no arms) were ruthlessly shot dead after the surrender, and nine Hospital Kaffirs were either killed in action or murdered later.'

De la Rey strongly deprecated this behaviour of his burghers, and was known to have some of them flogged for maltreating prisoners after Yzerspruit. (Smith, 213b; Amery, V, 507.)

† About 1,000 strong: Canadian Mounted Rifles; Damant's Horse; Royal Horse Artillery Mounted Rifles; 28th MI; 2nd Kitchener's Fighting Scouts (one of two corps of about 400 men each, raised in December, 1900, by and commanded by Colonel Johann William Colenbrander, a famous hunter, who described himself as 'one of the best Zulu linguists in South Africa'. (*Who Was Who*, II, 213)); two weak companies of Imperial Yeomanry; four field guns and two pom-poms.

‡ In the First World War Cookson commanded the 2nd Cavalry Division.

on more than one occasion. The Royal Horse Artillery Mounted Rifles, about 200 strong, distinguished themselves by abruptly checking one of these with 'a steady volume of fire reserved till the enemy was at point-blank range'. In the most spectacular of the charges, the line is said to have extended 'nearly four miles from flank to flank'. All were to no avail. Kemp failed to dislodge Cookson and when De la Rey came on the scene, he ordered him to give up trying to. In the course of the tricky retirement into the entrenchment, a party of twenty-two of the Canadian Mounted Rifles, who were undergoing their baptism of fire, were cut off. They fought on until only four men were left unwounded. Private C. N. Evans displayed especial gallantry. Though mortally wounded, he fired two full bandoliers before breaking his rifle into pieces 'with his dying hands'. Cookson's casualties numbered 106 killed, wounded and missing. He also lost 364 horses and mules killed. These died as a result of Boer field guns shelling the entrenchment area. That De la Rey still possessed and was using four guns and had the ammunition for them, all captured from the British, is a cause for wonder. What the loss in burghers was is not established. The official historian believed them to be 'considerably more' than the British, but the *Times History* says less than ninety. The action is particularly interesting in that Cookson's force had ridden some thirty-five miles before it started; yet this did not prevent the advance guard chasing the decoy Boers at speed for some eight miles. By some, at least, the arts of horsemastership and horsemanship had at last been mastered.[42]

Next day, near Boschmanskop in the Eastern Transvaal, due to very inaccurate intelligence, three squadrons of the 2nd Dragoon Guards (the Bays),* towards the end of a night raid, were drawn into what may have been a deliberate trap. The Boers made two charges firing from the saddle in semi-darkness just before dawn. Outnumbered nearly three to one, the 295 officers and men of the regiment extricated themselves as best they could. It is certain that the Bays, under Lieutenant-Colonel Hew Dalrymple Fanshawe,† conducted their six-mile retreat falling back by alternate squadrons with real skill. A squadron of the 7th Hussars eventually arrived on

---

* The Bays and the 3rd Dragoon Guards, the first arriving in South Africa in December, 1901, and the second eleven months previously, were both thrown into action with no more than ten days in which to acclimatize.

† Fanshawe, who married the daughter of F-M Sir Evelyn Wood, commanded the British Cavalry Corps in 1915. He was Colonel of the Bays from 1921 to 1930 and died, aged ninety-three, in 1957.

the scene and covered the final phase of the withdrawal to camp. One account (Conan Doyle's) says that they 'galloped in with such dash that some of them actually got among the Boers with their swords.'* In this action, alternatively known as Leeuwkop, Fanshawe's casualties were twenty killed, sixty-one wounded and three missing. The Boers suffered considerably fewer though they were still heavy.[43]

*   *   *

De la Rey was away pourparlering with Kitchener when his lieutenant, Kemp, with a rashness his commander would certainly have censured, led the most spectacular charge of the war executed by either side. It took place at Rooiwal, very near to where he and Cookson had fought the action of Boschbult twelve days previously. (See p. 270.) It occurred in the course of the last large-scale drive of the campaign, which Ian Hamilton had been sent by Kitchener to co-ordinate. His groups of columns, which incidentally included not even a troop of regular cavalry, numbered some 11,000. Kemp, wrongly believing that the two columns under Kekewich and commanded by Von Donop and Grenfell, numbering perhaps 1,750, constituted the weak point of the twenty-seven-mile-long line, concentrated against them. In all he had summoned practically all the still procurable fighting burghers in the Western Transvaal: seven commandos, numbering somewhere between 1,700 and 2,600 – a singular feat at the war's eleventh hour.

When Kemp in broad sunlight led some 800 of these, formed in orderly and compact lines, two, three and even four deep, riding, it is said, knee to knee, against the British advanced screen, Von Donop mistook them for part of Grenfell's column and Grenfell mistook them for part of Rawlinson's. Von Donop actually ordered his signallers to open communication with them. Kemp's men, having started a good mile and a half away, were less than 1,000 yards off, topping a slight ridge in what was otherwise totally flat, open veld and already firing from the saddle, shouting in a blood-curdling manner, before their real identity was established.† An irregular dismounted defensive line was speedily formed: there were but a few

* If they still carried them, which is extremely unlikely. Certainly the Bays did not. Some of the latter, it is said, complained that 'they had been crippled by the removal of their swords'. (Childers, 247.)

† Numbers of them were dressed in khaki, as were so many burghers at that date. This never helped with speedy identification.

seconds in which to do it. Kemp, whose Intelligence had led him to believe that the right flank of the drive comprised no more than 300 troops,[44] was amazed to see over 1,100 dismounted men* with two field guns and a pom-pom hastily making a rough semi-circle to oppose him. Nearby were many more dismounted troops, including the Imperial Light Horse in Rawlinson's column, with a further four field guns and two more machine-guns: something approaching 3,000 men with rifles, supported by six guns and three machine guns, arrayed against 800 burghers firing at random from magazine rifles.

> 'To continue the charge,' writes Thomas Pakenham, 'seemed folly, if not madness. Yet Kemp and [Commandant F. J.] Potgieter [who appears to have been leading the central section] both accepted the challenge; in their attempt to out-do De la Rey's achievements, they threw his tactics to the wind. They cantered on, forming a massed phalanx. ... The six British guns began to tear holes in the column. Still they came on, gambling everything on the chance that the British would turn and run.'[45]

A few of the raw, untried Imperial Yeomen did, in fact, turn and run,[46] but the mass of Kekewich's men stood firm. Considering that so many of them were only half-trained, it is perhaps to their credit that they did so, faced by such an alarming spectacle as what one of the Scottish Horse called 'the transmigration of the soul of the Dervish into the heart of the Dutchman'.[47] Men were indeed reminded of Omdurman. Certainly such a perfect target had not presented itself to British troops since the charge of the dervishes in that battle. Others' minds even went back to 1854, for at one time Kemp's centre checked its pace to allow his flanks to swing forward into line just as the 'black-looking mass' of the Russian cavalry had done when bearing down on the Heavy Brigade at Balaklava. 'The sonorous charge of European cavalry,' wrote the official historian, 'the chanting onset of the Zulu impi were less impressive than the slow oncoming of this brigade of mounted riflemen.'[48] Potgieter, 'conspicuous with his neatly trimmed beard and his blue shirt',[49] got to within seventy – some say thirty – yards of the British line before he fell with three bullets in his head and body. At the same moment those behind him spun round and cantered away. 'I am by no means sure,' wrote Ian Hamilton a week later, 'that the Boers would have

* 460, 1st and 2nd Scottish Horse; 420 Imperial Yeomanry; 290 South African Constabulary.

actually fled, had it not been for the promptitude with which Briggs, of Rawlinson's column, threw the Imperial Light Horse in a direction by which they must fall on the flank of the Boers, unless they cleared right back.'[50]

Now, at last, it seems with hindsight, was the supreme opportunity for a speedy follow-up pursuit. Hamilton had arrived on the scene just as Potgieter dropped dead from his horse, a little after 7 a.m. It was 9.30 before any pursuit began. Large numbers of horses had been killed – 150 in Grenfell's column alone, exclusive of those in the advanced screen – and probably another 150 had been wounded, while many more had stampeded. But another reason for the delay was Hamilton's fear of a counter-attack on Kekewich's convoy,[51] the capture of which had no doubt been high on Kemp's list of priorities. Further, the terrain was largely unknown and a swarm of locusts caused an exhausting distraction by seeming like the dust of a large commando. When at last, in Hamilton's words, 'our scouts began to gallop towards the Boers, they stood firm at first, thinking they were only outposts sent to make the camping ground secure. As, however, the long line of some eight miles in width came rolling up over the veldt, they thought it was time to be off.'[52] For three hours the chase went on, covering eighteen miles, but only twenty-three stragglers were picked up, though two 15-pounder guns and a Maxim which had been taken at Tweebosch were recaptured.

By far the most interesting aspect of what was in effect the last engagement of consequence in the South African War is the question of casualties. The counted loss in burghers was only fifty-one killed, of whom virtually all fell in the great charge, forty wounded and thirty-six unwounded prisoners, making 127 in all. There were undoubtedly a few more wounded carried off during the fight. The British on the other hand lost twelve killed and seventy-five wounded, a total of eighty-seven. Practically all these casualties must have been inflicted by the inevitably unaimed fire from horseback of the advancing phalanx. That so few of the Boers in that phalanx were hit argues that the firing of the British riflemen was abysmally inefficient. At least two and probably six 15-pounders and two machine guns were in action and it seems that these last did 'most of the actual execution'. Numbers of the burghers were seen to have received two bullet wounds in the abdomen 'where machine-gun fire caught them just above the pommel of the saddle'.[53]*

* Erskine Childers reckons that, during the last year of the war alone, the

Rooiwal was unquestionably a major defeat for the Boers. Its repercussions in Pretoria where the peace talks were in progress were not slight. Kemp's rash onset had in effect gambled away the last considerable fighting force left in the field. De la Rey (unlike de Wet who was a real 'bitter-ender', and Botha who was ready for peace), had been wavering uncertainly. Rooiwal made him more ready for an end to the fighting.*

* * *

It was Kitchener's refusal any longer to admit the burghers' wives and children to the comparative humanity and security of the concentration camps which was probably the chief reason why their leaders came to the negotiating table, prepared to agree to terms previously unacceptable. Another reason was proffered by Smuts when he got there. 'The veld throughout the entire Cape Colony,' he told his fellow delegates, 'is overgrown with scrub. ... Where you have no forage the horses cannot exist. ... On account of this deficiency of horses, we cannot expect a general rising.'[54]

The negotiations lasted sixteen days. Prince Francis of Teck, who had recently rejoined the Royals from the staff, had a friend in Pretoria who kept the regiment cryptically informed of progress by telegraph. '269' referred to the hymn of that number, the first line of which is 'Christian, seek not yet repose.' When eventually the number was changed to 135: 'The strife is o'er, the battle done', there was general rejoicing which was intensified by the next wire which gave the number 537: 'Peace, perfect peace.'[55]

With the details of the terms offered by the British and accepted by the Boers, this work is not concerned. It is enough to say that the burghers agreed to lay down their arms and recognize King Edward VII as their lawful sovereign. In return, among numerous other comparatively minor but remarkably generous concessions, none of them would lose his freedom or his property and as soon as circumstances permitted 'a representative system tending towards

Boer mounted charges inflicted in killed, wounded and prisoners, some 2,500 casualties, as well as the capture of eighteen guns. (Childers: *German*, 23.)

* Kitchener's despatch mentioned two National Scouts 'for good service' at Rooiwal. Of 'General Andries Cronje' it says that 'in pursuit of enemy's guns' he 'outstripped his men and captured them single-handed. He afterwards pursued and captured three men single-handed.' (Kitchener's *Despatch*, 1 June, 1902, Cmd 986, p. 14.)

autonomy would be introduced.' The surrender document was signed at Vereeniging on 31 May. There was a separate document dealing with the rebels. This disenfranchized them, but where there were to be trials for high treason the death penalty was not to be exacted. In all 21,256 burghers and rebels surrendered. The bitter end had come at last. The subsequent history of South Africa is well known. It needs no repetition here.

Most of the regular cavalry regiments were soon sent home, to India or to Egypt to join the only five which had never been sent to the theatre of war.*

The returns for 31 May, 1902, show that there were 65,275 horses in the field and 66,453 in remount depots and veterinary hospitals at the war's end. Over 24,000 which had been requisitioned in Cape Colony were said to have been returned to their lawful owners. This seems to be a very remarkably high number, reflecting on the care with which the officers in charge of the 'protection' farms kept their records, but in fact, almost certainly included in that figure are some 18,000 which, being registered in coastal districts considered safe from the enemy, never left their owners![56]

For one regular cavalry regiment,† meticulous records kept by Lieutenant Alfred Searle Head, its veterinary surgeon, show that from November 1899 to June, 1902, it

'used up 3,750 horses. The distance travelled in a straight line was 6,116 miles; but, as this does not include reconnaissances and scouting, these would in all probability double the mileage, bringing it up to 12,232 miles. On this basis, which is a liberal one, we used up one horse every 3½ miles during the campaign. I hope next time we may do better.'[57]

The general feeling of disappointment and frustration which the regular cavalry felt about its performance during the war is well summed up by Goldman:

* The 4th, 11th and 15th Hussars and the 21st Lancers had remained at home. The 4th Dragoon Guards was the only regiment that had been left in India. All of these regiments had from time to time supplied reinforcements to those in South Africa. Those that now remained there 'settled down to a fairly leisurely routine during which all ranks went home in batches on four months' leave.' (Oatts: *14H/20H*, 315). The men of those regiments which returned soon after the war's end and which had been in South Africa for long periods were allowed varying degrees of furlough. Those of the 13th Hussars, for instance, were granted just over two months. (Barrett: *13H*, 214.)

† Almost certainly the 6th (Inniskilling) Dragoons. Lieutenant Head nowhere in his account discloses the name of his regiment.

Some views on the part played by the regular cavalry

'The only part of the recognised duty of the horseman which has fallen to the cavalryman's lot has been the reconnaissance under conditions exceptionally dangerous, the extended patrol, the quest for a cunning enemy, and the swift and hazardous flank movements, or surprises, after a hard day's scouting. . . . On the battle-field itself he has ordinarily fought on foot. . . . Of old he was generally held in hand to finish brilliantly what artillery and infantry had begun. . . . With no corresponding arm to meet and oppose him, he was deprived of those chances of action and stimulus that are vital to his purpose and being.'

Baden-Powell, like so many of his confreres, drew comfort from the fact that, to quote his evidence to the Royal Commission, 'of course, there was no cavalry opposed to us. . . . This war does not apply really.' Erskine Childers only told the brutal truth when he wrote that the hearts of the cavalrymen 'were never wholly in it. There were *arrières-pensées*; vain longings for situations which obstinately refused to recur; a tendency to throw the blame on the horses, on the higher command, on anything but their own inability to read the signs of the times and vitalize their own traditions by recognizing the uselessness of the steel weapon and the preponderance of the rifle.'

The attitude of the average upper-class officer to the end of the war is perhaps well summed up by Captain Gilmour of the Imperial Yeomanry:

'War if it be cruel,' he wrote while it was still waging, 'is yet the only way to gain peace; and I am sure all of those who go home after this or any other war will make far better citizens, because they *know* the value of peace, their love of Queen and country is intensified and they will not take the same narrow views of life they would have done had they remained at home in ease and luxury in their own small world. We have had to give up much personal comfort, have had to subordinate priv-ate aims and ambitions to the common cause – the protection and strengthening of our Empire. We feel we have a bigger stake in it, we feel an increased pride in it.'[58]

*　　*　　*

From Victoria Road in the Cape, Haig in early September, 1902, wrote home that he was 'now living in the Mess of the 17th Lancers. . . . Troops go out, each under its own officer, every morning except Thursday which we keep as a sort of holiday after the Indian fashion. But on that day we have sports for the men, tent-pegging, line cutting, etc., etc. though indeed almost every afternoon there is something going on for the men, either football or shooting at bottles (6d a break, 1d a shot!) or something or other. . . . The "Institute" has three marquees fitted up with tables, etc., where they can write, play cards, etc. and read the papers; here they get coffee or tea. There is also a wet and dry canteen in a tin shanty adjoining, which we had erected for them so the men are having quite a comfortable time now. We officers play polo, course hares, etc. and I find the time pass pleasantly enough.'

Above all, Haig found it 'quite a pleasure to be back at Cavalry work proper again, and to do whatever one thinks right in the way of training the squadrons.'[59]

Another sure sign that peace had really come was given by the Treasury official who attended every meeting of the Royal Commission which sat at home to enquire into the Veterinary Department. 'Every time,' wrote an officer of the 18th Hussars who was a Commissioner, 'we proposed anything that would cost money, he vetoed it.'[60]

14

'I trust you will make arrangements to supply us
with horses from Australia, India and America.
Our wants will, I fear, be considerable.'

LORD ROBERTS to the War Office,
4 Feb., 1900

'The fundamental question which has to be faced
in connection with Remounts for the Army lies
in the difficulty of creating a department upon the
basis of so small an annual demand, sufficiently
elastic to obtain at very short notice ... any
quantity up to 250,000 during a year under war
conditions.'

*Report of the Secretary of State for War's
Committee on the Supply of Army Remounts,*
1902

'The efficiency of the cavalry depends upon their
horses ... so it is necessary to get purchasers who
are specialists in buying horses ....

'In time of war we take horses with broken
knees and short tails and various blemishes ...;
but it would not be a credit to our army to
mount them on blemished horses in time of
peace.'

CAPTAIN W. II. FIFE, a Government
remount buyer, in 1901

'To buy a horse in one's own country is quite
difficult enough, and requires no little tact,
patience, knowledge and confidence. But it is
infinitely more difficult to buy many thousands
in a hurry in a strange country.'

L. S. AMERY in *The Times History of the
War in South Africa*

'For every horse that had been bought in a
leisurely way through accustomed channels from
recognized dealers, a score were now called for in
urgent haste from all sources; the field of purchase
was extended from the British Isles to four con-
tinents; the Inspector-General, whose presence
had been rarely required in Pall Mall, became an

official on those personal exertions, and on the
result of whose administration the successful
prosecution of the war largely depended.'

*Report of the Court of Enquiry on the
Administration of the Army Remount
Department, 1902*

'They were dealing with an operation involving
the raising of the business of horse-buying . . .
by 6,000 per cent above the ordinary purchase.'
ST JOHN BRODRICK, Secretary of State for
War, January, 1902[1]

(i)

*Boer War: remount question: home supplies – remount department
– Inspector-General of Remounts – Horse Purchase Scheme –
buying abroad: in South Africa – U.S.A. and Canada – Austro-
Hungary and Russia – Australasia – Argentina – sea transports:
remount fittings – losses at sea – purchasing officers – conducting
officers – cattle men*

Having studied in some detail the ways in which the mounted troops
of Britain and her Empire were employed in the Great Boer War, it
is time to consider how it was possible to produce the vast number
of animals without which they could not have operated.

Since 1815, in a normal peacetime year, the number of remount
horses required for the whole army at home was never more and
generally less than 2,500. There was not the slightest difficulty in
procuring this modest number. Major-General William Robinson
Truman, the Inspector-General of the Remount Establishment at
the War Office,* told a War Office Committee in 1901 that it would
be almost as easy, without having to buy abroad, to get the 25,000 a
year which, in 1891, it had been calculated would be needed on the

---

* Truman, who was fifty-eight in 1899, had joined the 7th Dragoon Guards
as a Cornet when he was twenty-one. Eleven years later he exchanged into the
13th Hussars as a Captain. The following year he exchanged into the 5th
Dragoon Guards. By 1883 he had reached the rank of Lieutenant-Colonel. In
1887 he was appointed Colonel of the 7th Dragoon Guards. Between 1878 and
1883 he served as adjutant to the Warwickshire Yeomanry. From 1891 to 1893
he was Officer Commanding No. 14 (York) Regimental District, although he
also became Assistant Inspector of Remounts in 1891. He succeeded Major-
General Ravenhill as Inspector-General on 1 January 1899. He died aged sixty-
four in 1905.

mobilization of two Army Corps and a Cavalry Division.* Indeed, in the first twenty months of the war, over 49,000 had been obtained in Britain alone.[2]† Hitherto, nothing like that number had ever been required. During the war scare of 1878, for instance, 2,250 horses were bought in a period of four weeks, while for the 1882 Egyptian campaign 1,700 had been bought in seventeen weeks.[3] These were the sort of maximum demands for which the Remount Department was geared.

Increasingly, over the years, most of the animals bought in Britain (outside Ireland) were in fact imported. Truly indigenous horses of the sorts required by the army were becoming very few indeed.[4] Every week something like 1,200 foreign horses were landed at London, Liverpool and Glasgow docks. Most were from the United States and Canada. 'They are quiet and very rarely kick,' said Truman. 'They are handled very young, and a good many [of the dealers] sell them with a guarantee for one month. . . . They are trained mostly in American buggies.'[5] It was horses such as these, very few of them branded at their place of origin, which formed the majority of 'English' remounts towards the end of the nineteenth century.

In peacetime buying was generally confined to a month or two in the autumn. The required number was usually obtained before the winter set in.[6] It so happened that the 1890s were a good period for buying horses in Britain. Increasing numbers were being thrown on the market due to 'the extensive use of electric power in the streets [i.e. trams] and of mechanical means of progression'. The demand consequently fell and so did prices. In October, 1899, it was estimated that in the coming year the average cost to the army of horses (as opposed to cobs) would be £55 a head. In fact over the first year and a half of the war it turned out to be only £43 6s. Some of the tramway companies, for example, as they switched over to electric traction, allowed their stables to become virtually empty. By 1902, though, the drain had been so great that one of the leading dealers complained that neither he nor foreign government buyers could get

* It seems certain, if almost incredible, that the question of transport animals was totally overlooked at the time of the Stanhope Memorandum (see Vol III, p. 31). For the force envisaged, some 34,600 extra ought to have been provided for. (Smith, 121.)

† 35,000 horses, and 3,149 cobs from England, Wales and Scotland; 7,000 horses and 4,000 cobs from Ireland. (Stanley, 1.)

Early in 1902, about 2,800 remounts were purchased in the British Isles alone each *month*. (Biddulph, 22.)

any more horses in England. Everyone, he said, 'is buying horses in Ireland now.'[7]

Beside the duty of purchasing horses for all the mounted corps at home, the department was also responsible in theory for remounting one cavalry regiment and one field battery in Egypt and one cavalry regiment and three field batteries in South Africa. In practice the horses for Egypt were mostly bought in Syria and those for South Africa at the Cape.

The long-standing and approved method of providing remounts at home was by purchase from dealers who had been accustomed by long practice to procure horses for army purposes and who knew the classes required. Virtually all the troop horses for the cavalry of the line were bought in Ireland. In that country there were five or six so-called Government dealers (each employing twenty or thirty buyers) who entered into arrangements with the Remount Department to provide animals at a fixed price. They were bound to take back within six months any horse that proved unsatisfactory and supply a fresh one. The laid-down average cost of these before the war was £40. Most of the horses were between five-and-a-half and nine years old. Before it reached five-and-a-half a horse was reckoned to be too immature for full cavalry work. Animals bought for the cavalry were never less than 15.2 hands in height, which was the minimum laid down in Queen's Regulations.[8]

Major Prince Francis of Teck, who was the Remount Department's Staff Captain in Dublin between July and December, 1899, gives a good picture of how horses were bought in Ireland.

'If we buy in a fair, we employ a man who is termed in the trade a "blocker", who hangs about outside the fairs before any of the horses come in, and if he sees a horse likely for our purposes, he brings it up to whoever the buyer may be.* Because of competition with the big dealers we get very few horses at fairs. Therefore we go straight to the big dealers. When we got big orders, say, to ship 150 or 200 a week, we would give one or two of the dealers perhaps four or five days' notice, and we might take 100 from one man, perhaps fifty from another and fifty from another, and take Monday, Tuesday and Wednesday

* James Daly, a horse dealer in Ireland who had been supplying the Government for fifty years told the Biddulph Court of Enquiry that it was 'the understood thing that if a blocker gets in before me then I give him a sovereign and he gives way.' (Biddulph, 85.)

for buying these three lots. They would come into our depot in Dublin and be trained down to Cork, and then shipped from Queenstown.'[9]

Considerable numbers of horses were bought every year by buyers for foreign armies, but these were not usually in competition with the Remount Department because they only bought three- and four-year-olds, which were then, once exported, looked after and trained (at great expense) until they were ready for the ranks. 'By waiting,' Truman told the Stanley Remount Committee, '*we take only the survival of the fittest.* ... 15% of the four-year-olds the foreigner buys suffer from ailments such as coughs, curves, spavins,* and they go wrong in the wind.' One of the biggest dealers in Ireland, on the other hand, believed that foreigners buying three- and four-year-olds got 'the pick of the horses'; but he admitted that the Government got a good bargain buying the older horses at the prices given. The three regiments of Household Cavalry were the only ones for whom four-year-olds were bought. For the cavalry of the line 'the great difficulty of getting horses trained at that age is that we have not the men to train them.' But even if that problem had not existed, it was uneconomical to buy young animals because by the time they had become 'made horses' each would have cost not less than £90, their keep costing something between £25 and £40 a year.[10]†

*   *   *

Truman's tiny headquarters staff‡ was housed in a fourth-floor flat in Victoria Street, next door to the Veterinary Department, while the Quartermaster-General's department under which it came was in

---

* Hard bony tumours in the legs, produced by inflammation of the cartilage.

† A fully trained six-year-old would, as often as not, last in the ranks at full efficiency up to the age of fifteen or sixteen. (Stanley, 3.)

The best time for mares to breed was reckoned to be between the ages of three and eight. After nine the limit was soon reached. (Stanley, 38.)

‡ In April 1899, the Remount Department's establishment was as follows:

Headquarters: 1 Inspector-General
                1 Assistant Inspector-General
                1 Deputy Assistant Adjutant-General (not on the HQ Staff)
                1 Superintending clerk
                4 Clerks
Woolwich: 1 Assistant Inspector (for Royal Artillery, Royal Engineers and the transport services)
               1 Staff Captain   *(continued over)*

Pall Mall. The Victoria Street premises were so small that not even Truman himself had a separate room. This, according to Colonel Richard Charles Bernard Lawrence,* who joined as Chief Assistant Inspector in December, 1899, was

> 'a constant source of trouble, because we have crowds of visitors; we have had as many as forty or fifty a day; one officer has to see a visitor, and naturally the interview disturbs the work of the man sitting next to him, and the visitors overflow into the passages; there is no getting rid of them. [They are of] every sort and kind; stockbrokers who want to get a contract for Russian horses, Germans, Frenchmen, and any number of horse dealers, ladies who come and want to know when their sons, who are conducting officers [on ships bringing remounts from abroad] are going to arrive at the Cape.... Cattlemen also come up sometimes.'

This was still the state of affairs twenty-eight months after the war began! The Victoria Street staff was increased by one officer eight months after the outbreak and by the end of the war by three more.† To have obtained further aid would have been, according to Colonel Lawrence,

> 'a hindrance; I could not get another officer into my room. I do not know where I should put him. This question of the office

---

<table>
<tr><td></td><td>2 Veterinary Surgeons and a company of the Army Service Corps</td></tr>
<tr><td>Ireland:</td><td>1 Assistant Inspector of Remounts</td></tr>
<tr><td></td><td>1 Staff Captain</td></tr>
<tr><td></td><td>1 Veterinary Surgeon and a company of the Army Service Corps</td></tr>
</table>

There were also two small remount depots in Ireland, one near Dublin and the other at Lusk, where a few 'cheap three-year-olds' were kept. (*R.C.*, IV, 231–2; Stanley, 50.)

The total annual cost of the department in peace time was £16,460. (Stanley, 56.)

   * Colonel Lawrence had entered the 5th Dragoon Guards from Sandhurst in 1876 at the age of nineteen. He saw service in Egypt in 1882 and served on the Staff in Bengal for some years before commanding the 1st King's Dragoon Guards from 1894–8 when he became a Professor at the Staff College. He served with distinction as a Brigadier-General on the General Staff in France during the First World War.

   † Two extra HQ clerks were employed soon after the outbreak, and by the beginning of 1902, a further two, making a total of nine. (*Hansard:* (*C*), 1902, 985.)

has been represented continually to the Secretary of State for War. .... In July, 1900, the Quartermaster-General wrote: "I believe it has at last been settled that your office is to be moved up here to Pall Mall", but we are still down in Victoria Street.'

Nor should there have been difficulty in finding accommodation, for when the Imperial Yeomanry organization was set up, it was given the whole of Cleveland House, a large building close to the War Office. But of course the comparatively glamorous nature of a patriotic voluntary movement had priority over one of the most vitally important departments of war!

There was a private telephone line between the War Office and the Remount Department, but, as Lawrence put it, 'the heads of the Departments do not come and speak to us on it.' It seems that the chief means of communication were by telegraph. 'We have to send telegrams down to the telegraph office, which is quite close to us, and they find their way through in the ordinary way.' There was insufficient room in Victoria Street to store the Remount Department's records. Consequently they had to be kept in Pall Mall and sometimes it took four days to get a paper out of the War Office. Further, the clerical staff was not large enough for copies of any but the most important communications to be taken.[11]

*   *   *

For some years past the Government had possessed the power by Section 115 of the Army Act and through the Horse Purchase Scheme established in 1897 to requisition for payment every horse in the country, but in effect this applied only in the event of a threatened invasion. For other, lesser national emergencies there had been set up in 1888 a system of voluntary registration of horses with a view to forming a reserve. (See Vol III, p. 390.) Under this scheme owners of twenty or more horses could register a proportion of their animals. The agreement into which they entered stipulated that they should produce that proportion of suitable horses for sale when the occasion demanded. In the meantime they were paid an annual retaining fee of 10s per horse. An officer of the Remount Department was then supposed to inspect the horses annually. When the emergency arrived and the Government took an animal it paid a price which took into account the cost of replacement and the estimated loss which might accrue before replacement. Only horses

which were 'practically serviceable' of from five to ten years of age
and from fifteen hands to sixteen hands two inches in height were
registerable.* A fine of £50 was liable to be paid for every horse
which was not forthcoming, though in fact there were no cases of it
ever being exacted. Early in 1899 14,105 horses were thus registered
in the horse reserve.[12] When it came to the crunch less than 10,000
were actually taken up in the whole course of the war. Most of them
were harness as opposed to riding horses, and they cost, on average,
£52 10s each. The fact was that the same classes of horse could be
bought cheaper from dealers.

Generally speaking it was discovered that riding horses registered
in the stables of Masters of Hounds and of private owners proved
unsatisfactory.† On the other hand the class of horses kept in large
numbers by omnibus companies and other similar concerns, which
were chiefly of use for draught purposes, proved very serviceable in
South Africa. As has been shown, it was soon realized that the
mounts most in demand for the war were cobs not exceeding fifteen
hands. Such small animals had only been used at home in limited
numbers, chiefly for the training of mounted infantry. Not a single
one had been registered for the horse reserve.[13] Colonel Charles
Colvile, a director of the Road Car Omnibus Company, thought
the registration system 'about the smartest thing and the most
businesslike thing the War Office ever did, because you can select
six-year-old horses, all of which are the survival of the fittest. . . .
You register horses that never grow older, and never get worse.
You take the plums.'[14]

* The classes of horse were:

'Cavalry,	Officers'
"	Heavy
"	Light
R.H.A.,	Riding
"	Draught
R.A. and R.E.,	Riding
"	Draught
Infantry, A.S.C., etc.	Riding
" "	Driving
" "	Heavy Draught
Pack'	

(Stanley, 59).

† The department gave as much as £100 for hunters. All of them according
to Truman were 'unsatisfactory. The hunter, as a rule, is an unsound animal
and is no good in the summer.' (Stanley, 5.)

*   *   *

Neither the diminutive Remount Department nor the inadequate registration system bore any realistic relation to the needs of the war upon which Britain was now embarked. The army which had to be supplied with means of mobility was by far the largest that had ever sailed from the British Isles. It had to operate 6,000 miles from its base and over a much larger extent of country than any other over which a British army had ever before been called upon to act. Above all, no force in modern history had ever before included such a vast proportion of mounted men. Early on in the conflict it became apparent that all previous estimates of remount requirements were hopelessly unrealistic. Even before Lord Roberts went out in chief command and telegraphed on 24 February, 1900, to the Secretary of State: 'Please arrange for early and steady supply remounts. . . . Without mobile force I can do nothing in this country,'[15] the need for vast numbers of remounts was becoming daily more obvious. As mobility away from the railway lines entirely depended upon horses, mules, donkeys and oxen, it is obvious that the department responsible for providing these was at least as important as any of the other supply departments.

That Truman from his two or three rooms in Victoria Street was able to tackle the task which confronted him at all is almost miraculous. Yet during the whole war, of horses alone, 518,800 were provided. This number, it has been calculated, if stood in a straight line touching each other side by side, would extend from London to Manchester! Of these something like 347,000 (67%) were 'expended during the campaign', an average *daily* loss of 336 over the thirty-two months of the war.* The total expenditure for which Truman's department was responsible in one way or another came to the

---

*Apparently in conflict with these figures, Colonel Thomas Deane (see p. 328) told the Royal Commission: 'the estimates of the losses during the Crimean campaign were 80%, while the losses during the past war were 120%.' (*R.C.*, II, 44.) As with so many statistics where their bases of calculations are unknown, it is hard to discover the truth.

About 470,000 of the total provided, as well as 149,600 transport mules, were found by the Remount Department, two-fifths of them from countries outside the Empire. The rest were procured by the Imperial Yeomanry's first contingent (see p. 94), by the colonies or sent from India. (*R.C.*, I, 97; Amery, VI, 418.)

Neither the Royal Commission nor General Biddulph's Court of Enquiry more than touched upon the whole question of losses in the field.

staggering sum of £15,339,142 which in today's money is well over £555 million.[16]*

Not surprisingly, Truman was not an officer of outstanding character and drive. It would have been extraordinary if he had been. The department over which he presided was considered of hardly more consequence than the much despised veterinary department. It would scarcely appeal to ambitious men either socially or militarily. Its small-scale peacetime business largely consisted of transactions with horse dealers, a breed of men not very highly regarded. Even in purely War Office terms it was only one of a number of departments which came under the Quartermaster-General. Further, the average cavalry colonel almost certainly much regretted the old days before the Remount Department was created in 1887 when each regiment bought its own remounts. He was apt therefore to resent the impersonal system which had been imposed upon him from above.

In 1902 a row was kicked up in the House of Commons about the scandals supposed to have occurred in the course of the remount operations. Ill-informed attempts were made to place blame upon Truman's shoulders. All the cases turned out in the end to be connected with corruption on the part of officers employed by the Imperial Yeomanry Committee, to which body in February, 1900, the War Office had delegated the buying of their own remounts. Truman's department had nothing whatsoever to do with them. One or two other accusations concerned minor corruption by individual officers employed in the purchasing commissions abroad. These comparatively unimportant speculations were severely dealt with the moment they came to light. One result of the Commons row was that Truman was officially asked to resign. This he resisted. Instead he was offered a Court of Enquiry. This he accepted. From the reports and evidence supporting the Court's findings and from other enquiring bodies set up before and after the Court, much of the contents of this and the next chapters has been derived. (See Appendix, p. 504.)

Truman, never very articulate when testifying before these tri-

* The remount department in South Africa which started the war with one clerk, ended it with thirty-four, of whom four were civilians.

Throughout the war the department's accounting was in the sole hands of a regimental major with no departmental or financial experience, no departmental regulation to guide him and no check on his operations. After the war he was responsible for the sale of 120,000 animals. (Amery, VI, 443–4.)

26. Colonel James Babington

27. Major William (later F-M Lord) Birdwood

. Lt-Col Michael Rimington (see p. 80)

29. Colonel Robert Baden-Powell
(see p. 52)

. Lt-Col A. Woolls-Sampson (see p. 47)

31. Lt-Col W. H. Birkbeck (see p. 296)

32. Lt-Col Edmund Allenby (see p. 138)

33. Lt-Col E. D. Browne-Synge-Hutchinson, V.C. (see p. 205)

34. Lt-Gen. Edward Elliot (see p. 219)

35. Colonel G. E. Benson (see p. 250)

36. Colonel Lord Chesham (see p. 88)

37. Major Karri Davies (see p. 48)

bunals, failed to do justice either to himself or to his office. Yet reading the mass of evidence produced, it is clear that he was largely responsible for a feat of organization 'unparalleled,' as Mr Balfour put it, 'in the military annals of the world'. If its scale was comparable only to the remount operations connected with Napoleon's invasion of Russia, its complexities were infinitely greater. Further, after General Robert Biddulph's long and searching enquiry into the department's administration, the Court rightly stated that the unprecedented demands made upon the department had been met

'with extraordinary success. The number of horses actually despatched to South Africa was in excess of the demand. When horses were deficient at the front it was not due to the failure of the Remount Department to land them on the coast, but to the many other demands on the railway systems, and to the exigencies of the war which compelled the issue of Remounts before they were acclimatised or fit for work, and the consequent excessive wastage.'

It was argued – and the argument has some force – that Truman's amazing success in exceeding demand was actually responsible for some of the cruel wastage which occurred, though the blame was clearly not his. Lieutenant-Colonel Arthur Middleton stated that during the fourteen months of his command of the Natal remount department (from the beginning of 1901), there was never any dearth of imported remounts.

'The enormous wastage I consider was due entirely to the readiness with which they were supplied. There was always such an influx of horses into Natal that anybody who wanted a horse got him next day whether he was really entitled to one or not . . . . There was a certain proportion of men who if they got quiet horses would do their best with them, but if the horses were not all perfectly broken and perfectly amenable to their sort of treatment, they took no care whatever of them, they knew so well they could get another one.'

'A new horse,' wrote one veterinary officer, 'appeared to be the Army panacea for meeting casualties. New horses meant getting rid of the war-worn in order to keep down the forage bill and that for attendants. The new horse only led to further wastage, and so readily available was the supply that it actually increased the waste and diminished efficiency. The moral obligation of looking after an animal is neglected when it can be changed tomorrow!'[17]

The chief shortcoming for which the department could be said to have been responsible was the pre-war failure to collate and keep up to date intelligence about numbers and types of horses available throughout the world. Yet with such a miniscule staff, this would surely have been beyond the capacity of the department.

The same would have applied to the related question of the supply of horses procurable in South Africa itself. Truman was much criticized for not insisting that more use was made of these. In the *Secret Handbook* published by the Intelligence Division of the War Office a couple of months before the war began, the number of horses known to exist in parts of Cape Colony alone in 1896–7 was stated to be 201,535.* However, the political decision not to declare martial law until late on in the war's progress ensured that this large reservoir remained untapped for a very long time (see p. 291). Moreover the Cape Dutch were often hostile. Their pastors directed them to deny supplies to the British. Nevertheless local horses, even before the imposition of martial law, were occasionally bought for the locally raised units, usually at inflated prices. Another reason for the initial neglect of this promising source is well illustrated by a letter of 3 January, 1900, from the officer in charge of Remounts in South Africa, Colonel Robert Stevenson (6th Dragoon Guards). He reported to Truman that the horses imported from the Argentine were 'undoubtedly better than the country bred, and land here cheaper, in excellent condition, and no change of hemisphere, which is what kills the English horses.' This early view of the merits of the Argentines soon evaporated with experience. Eleven months later, Stevenson was writing: 'No one who has seen the Argentine at the front has a good word to say for him except the 10th Hussars.' By September, 1901, his view was that the colonial horses were the best of all! This extraordinary turnaround is explained in part by the fact that most of the early importations of Argentines were of much better quality than the later ones. Further, as virtually all the larger types of animal were gradually supplanted by small cobs, the local horses, which were nearly all of this sort, found increasing favour. Acting-Veterinary-Major Arthur Henry Lane summed up what was certainly a far-reaching error when he complained that

'thousands of hard little horses could have been procured. But

* Seven of the Colony's districts, including five which were supposed to contain a large horse population, furnished no returns.

these were allowed to be taken by the enemy, and we imported a comparatively useless animal at about double the cost. . . . During the first year or so of the war, it was ridiculous to see columns mounted upon played-out horses, passing close to farms which contained good seasoned ponies, and yet making no attempt to remount themselves.'

It has been said on good authority that had martial law been declared at the start there would have been sufficient horses in Cape Colony to supply all the remount needs during the first year of the war. As it was, once the Boers began the invasion of the Cape at the end of 1900 and in early 1901, there were captured or brought in for safe custody, as the veterinary historian of the war puts it,

'thousands of horses, among which were useful, hardy animals, immune to local diseases, from which every imported horse suffered. . . . On arrival it was no one's duty to look after them excepting the overworked Station Commandant. . . . He as a rule had no knowledge of horses or their requirements, his chief concern being to prevent them being recaptured by the enemy. . . . These animals died in large numbers.'

They became known as 'Protection Horses'. In April, 1901, Kitchener ordered all columns operating in the Cape to be re-mounted solely from this source 'on payment and on requisition from the inhabitants'. By July, 75,000 had been obtained. To accommodate these several new remount depots were opened, the largest being at Cradock, the centre of a famous horse-breeding district.

Over and above these there were thousands more, some useful, many useless for military purposes. A few isolated, uncoordinated efforts began at this time to be made to train and make fit for service as many as possible. Thousands, though, including the brood mares and foals which formed a large part of the whole, were left to starve on remount farms. These 'wretched creatures were herded at night inside infantry entrenchments,' as one witness put it, 'and each day marched solemnly to grazing grounds a short distance away, bare of everything but the bones of those which had died. No rations were allowed them. How could they be when our own horses in the field were on a semi-starvation diet?'

Nothing resembling a coherent scheme for solving this problem was attempted until October, 1901, when a 'Protection Branch' was created. By then more than half of the protection stock had died.

Only 22,700 remained alive, many of whom were past recovery. In spite of a monthly cost of £3,000 the new branch failed over the remaining six months of the war (during which small numbers were being added from time to time) to save more than some 54% of all protected animals on remount farms. It is horrifying to think of the numbers that must have perished from neglect, disease and starvation in the nine months *before* October, 1901.*

Horses brought in from the Transvaal and the Orange Free State were categorized as 'Captured Horses'. After an order issued in mid-winter 1901 there were vast numbers of these, perhaps as many as 125,000. That order stated that the Boers were reduced to riding mares and foals. To prevent this all such animals which were useless as remounts were to be collected and destroyed.† 'There must be no hesitation,' read the order, 'about destroying useless horses and young stock on the ground that they can be no use to the Boers, cost nothing to feed and that it is a pity to destroy them. That they should grow up to carry an armed Boer ... is exactly what it is desired to prevent.'

Another order, though, established a 'Live Stock Recovery Department'. This was charged with the duty of collecting strayed and abandoned animals from all sources and of forming depots for their reception and re-issue. This horse salvage service put an end at last to the cruel and inefficient practice of destroying most strayed and abandoned horses on the spot so as to deny them to the enemy. What little stock recovery there had been during the first fifteen months of the war had been effected by the occasional employment of natives, first at so much a head and later at a daily rate of pay, as 'stock collectors'.

In the Phillopolis province, which was noted for its horses, an officer of the 17th Lancers says that many

'were found wandering about the veldt. These were driven into kraals at the farms, and many useful remounts were acquired.

* Animals living in coastal districts considered safe from the enemy were registered and remained with their owners. Of these there were 18,000 in October, 1901. The figures of horses returned to their owners in May, 1902, given in Amery, VI, 444, almost certainly include these and are therefore very misleading. (See p. 276.)

† Before the war a Boer would have thought it *infra dig* to ride a mare. (Biddulph, 232.)

The task of deciding which animals to destroy could not of course be satisfactorily carried out while troops were on the march day after day because there

They were nearly all brood mares and young horses; several three-year-olds were impressed, some of which lasted for months. The breaking and backing of these horses had to be performed in a rough and ready manner, but was accomplished with few accidents: the chief difficulty was to get a bridle and saddle on, a feat which was usually performed by the transport Kaffirs, who were adepts in the art of handling a horse.'

Seven months before the war ended a further horse-saving reform was introduced. Regimental rest camps for 'war-tired' horses of every class were authorized. Column commanders were actually *ordered* to leave men behind to look after them. This meant reducing the number of combatant soldiers in favour of producing less wastage of mounts. Had this principle been followed much earlier, the columns' efficiency would without doubt have been dramatically increased.

* * *

For the tardiness in utilizing local South African horses and for all the awful muddles and unnecessary misery connected with protection, captured, strayed and 'derelict' horses, Truman can hardly be blamed. Grappling as he was from his tiny office with the insistent demands for more and more remounts at any cost, from anywhere, he could not have been expected to deal with remount matters in the actual theatre of war.*

His task and that of the Remount Department in South Africa were made infinitely more difficult in 1900 by the belief held both at headquarters and in London that 'the march to Komatipoort had practically finished the war.' In the first burst of confidence the supply was actually ordered to be halted altogether. It was thought that there were enough animals in the country or on their way to carry on till November. The numbers fell from 34,000 in the second quarter of the year to 10,000 in the fourth. As the true situation began to emerge, the demand for horses gradually increased again. When Kitchener took over in December, it was becoming horribly clear that the vast numerical superiority which Roberts had enjoyed while the Boers contested possession of the railway lines had disap-

---

was no time for the 'careful draughting' necessary. It was therefore excessively wasteful. (Smith, 161.)

  * During the war, remounts for four reserve cavalry regiments and sixty-six 'new batterys of artillery' *at home* had also to be found. (Amery, VI, 417.)

peared once they had opened a new campaign on the open veld. The Commander-in-Chief immediately raised his requirements to 3,000 cobs a month, then to 5,000, and before long he was calling for 35,000 a quarter. Truman by then, in obedience to orders, had actually withdrawn some of his buying commissions. They had to be rushed back to their posts, and of course it took some weeks before the department could catch up again. In the first quarter of 1901, the supply, therefore, fell 10,000 below requirements. For this the ignorant and the guilty, of course, blamed Truman most unfairly. The supply only caught up in the second quarter. In the meantime, consequently, horses had to be issued the moment they arrived, regardless of their condition. Early in the year the situation was further exacerbated by the need to mount numbers of newly raised corps, such as the 2nd Imperial Light Horse, the Johannesburg Mounted Rifles, the Scottish Horse and Kitchener's Fighting Scouts, as well as certain colonial corps which had been disbanded in 1900 and which were now hurriedly resuscitated.[18]

* * *

It ill became French, searching for a scapegoat to explain the uselessness of his horses, to write in his diary on 17 May, 1900: 'The Remount Dept at home have not done well by any means. . . . This I think is the main cause of the waste of horse flesh in this campaign.' Until now this has been almost universally accepted as gospel. The chief actual causes were, in fact, starvation (see p. 349) and shockingly poor horsemastership (see p. 356).

Few historians of the war have devoted much space to the vital remount aspect of the campaign, known at the time as the 'Horse Question', and none has gone into it in detail. It therefore gives the present author real pleasure to be able to pay posthumous tribute to the Inspector-General's unflappability and steady, plodding hard work which induced the Director of India's Remount Service to declare to the Royal Commission that Truman 'was mainly responsible for the successful operations of the war'.[19]

* * *

When, on 9 October, 1899, eight cavalry regiments and nineteen artillery batteries were among the troops warned for service, they were all completed to their full establishment of horses by transfer from other units. After weeding out such animals as were unfit for active service, this entailed providing about 30% more horses. The registration scheme, of course, had not by then got under way, though sanction had been given for the employment of three cavalry lieutenant-colonels to assist in purchasing under the scheme. As there were no depots available, the horses thus bought had to be sent direct to the nearest regiments. In due course, though, depots were established at Canterbury, Colchester, Norwich and Southampton, with a resting depot at Cork for embarkation purposes only.[20]

As long ago as 1879 the policy in peacetime of buying small numbers of horses for the army from overseas had been adopted. In that year a few had been bought for the 3rd Hussars in Hungary. These had later gone to the Cape and were reported upon as very good horses. In 1886, Buller, when he was Deputy-Adjutant-General, had recommended the purchase of 300 in Canada, but a proposal to buy a limited number each succeeding year so as to keep in touch with that source of supply was later turned down. For Kitchener's 1896 campaign in Egypt a few Hungarians were bought, and in 1897 and 1898, Colonel Truman, as he then was, apparently on his own initiative, bought 2,059 cobs in the Argentine for the mounted infantry then at the Cape and in Natal.[21] Why this purchase was made when South Africa abounded in cobs remains obscure. Incidentally they were badly reported upon both as regards 'bottom' and 'go' as well as medically.[22] In July, 1899, three and a half months before the war started, three officers were sent out to the United States 'to make inquiries as to the possibility of obtaining horses and mules should war break out'.[23] Beyond this precautionary step almost nothing was done till the war had started to sound out the possibilities of horse and mule buying overseas except in South Africa itself, in Argentina and in Australia, where a purchasing commission was despatched in September. This was ordered to buy cavalry and artillery horses 'in anticipation of the remount requirements for 1900–1901'.[24]

Colonel Stevenson, with one Staff Captain, four veterinary surgeons and four farrier-quartermaster-sergeants was sent out in July, 1899, to report on horse supply in Cape Colony and Natal and to create a remount department from literally nothing. He at once set about buying cobs. At first these were solely for Baden-Powell's Protectorate Regiment of mounted infantry which was then forming. By the end of August he had purchased some 900 at an average price of £19 10s from 'up-country men' and from 'a great number of Dutchmen [i.e. Boers]. Mr Cecil Rhodes,' Stevenson added, 'who was a friend of mine was kind enough to lend me a large farm belonging to the De Beers Co, about eight miles from Kimberley, where I congregated the horses I bought in the different districts.' In September he had set up remount depots at Stellenbosch and Pietermaritzburg and had managed to horse all the mounted troops then in Natal, as well as their transport, 'before they left their stations for the front'. He also mounted the troops which came from India on their arrival. From this point onwards it was reported that it would be impossible to obtain large numbers of cobs in South Africa. In fact, by the end of 1901, as has been shown, over 126,000 had been bought. By then some initial obstacles had been overcome. One of these was that the Basutos at first refused to sell any of their thousands of ponies,* and, more important, that it was considered politically dangerous to risk an uprising of Boers living within Cape Colony by requisitioning animals. However, when, in May, 1900, martial law was declared there, an extensive new source of supply opened up.[25]

* * *

The realization that unprecedented numbers of remounts from countries outside the Empire were going to be needed was, of course, a gradual process.† The war had started before, in mid-October, a purchasing commission was sent out to the Argentine to buy cavalry

---

* Lieutenant-Colonel William Henry Birkbeck (1st Dragoon Guards), the Assistant Inspector of Remounts in South Africa, reported in June, 1900, that 'until the occupation of Bloemfontein, hardly a pony could be bought [in Basutoland], even by the Resident Commissioner himself; but as soon as the tide of victory turned, purchase became rapid and easy, and 2,000 ponies were purchased in three weeks, at an average of £15, including the £2 commission to the agents, Messrs Fraser & Co, who collected them for us.

'During the period of tension on the frontier, owing to the presence of the Boers round Wepener, not a pony could be got, and again, after the relief of Wepener, the supply flowed in, but not for gold. Cattle was the form in which the Basutos preferred payment, and another 1,000 were obtained by this means.' (Birkbeck, 8.)

Haig much approved of Birkbeck. 'No one,' he wrote in December, 1901, 'could have done this remount work as well as Birkbeck has.' (*Haig*, 261).

† The buying of transport mules had begun in Spain, Italy and the United States as early as August, 1899. (*R.C.*, IV, 231.)

In the United States in 1901 there were 1,089,418 agricultural and 422,073 unbroken horses. (Sessions, 32.)   (*continued over*)

horses and cobs for the mounted infantry, and it was not till January, 1900, that the three officers in America were ordered to form themselves into a purchasing commission and to start buying cavalry horses. Another month went by before they were told to buy cobs. In fact, up to the end of February, 1900, all the cavalry and artillery horses in South Africa came almost exclusively from the United Kingdom and Australia. Purchasing commissions were not sent to Canada and to Austro-Hungary (where, according to the Military Attaché in Vienna, 'there was a very strong pro-Boer feeling') till the end of April, 1900.[26]

In certain countries there were obvious political difficulties about buying horses. Holland, where the price of cobs was low, was clearly out of the question. The French Government would not allow the export of horses. Nor would the governments of Morocco and Algeria. From the tone adopted in Germany, Truman 'did not think it desirable to purchase there.' In Scandinavia the prices asked were prohibitive. Polish horses were reported to be unsuitable. Those in Italy were said to be of poor quality. Mexico could only provide animals which were 'very thin, very small and very few'. In 1900 a consignment from Chile was shipped, but the crossing of the Andes combined with a long, expensive sea voyage made further purchases unacceptable.

Enquiries of all these countries were made during the course of the war* because the countries which were then providing large numbers of horses, other than those in the Empire, might at any moment prohibit export. The United States, for instance, had relaxed a total prohibition only a short time before the war, while at the beginning of 1902 embargoes were imposed upon export from seven provinces in Russia.[27]† There was a constant fear that the

---

In the United States, where 86% of horses were still on farms, the total number of horses was 18,280,000. In Canada the total was 1,478,700. (*R.D.A.*, 37–8, 44.)

* The Remount Department in India was very much larger than that in the United Kingdom, and beside keeping a permanent reserve of 2,000 horses for immediate work in the ranks, it maintained up-to-date tabulated information about possible foreign supplies. If this had been available to Truman he would have been saved a great deal of trouble. (*R.C.*, II, 42, 44, 97.)

† Count Eugene Zichy, a well-known traveller of the day, suggested that Mongolia would be a good source of supply for hardy small horses at a few dollars a head. They could all be obtained a few weeks' march from the coast, and it was said that the voyage was no worse than that from Canada. In the event, the war was over before this source could be tapped. (*R.D.A.*, 63.)

Austro-Hungarian Government would forbid exports from Fiume. However, it was decided to treat the purchases there as a purely private business matter. All British officers were warned to keep strictly 'to their role as private gentlemen'. On one occasion a senior officer found two veterinary surgeons 'dining in khaki uniform' in Fiume's principal restaurant. He ordered them out 'to get into mufti'.

India, Australia, New Zealand, Canada and South Africa itself were the only totally safe sources of supply, but all these together were unable to meet the inordinate demands which from the spring of 1900 soared ever higher week by week. Indeed, before the war was over more horses and mules had been sent from the United States alone than from the United Kingdom and all the Colonies put together.

Before the opening of hostilities the General Officer commanding in Cape Town estimated that the need would be 5% of the total strength each month. On 17 November, 1899, only 125 cavalry horses and 250 mules per month were thought to be necessary. After that date, as more and more units were ordered out, as more and more infantry regiments were converted to mounted infantry and as more and more new irregular regiments were formed and the wastage in the theatre of war reached outrageous proportions, the requirements increased by leaps and bounds. By January, 1902, when the war had been waging for twenty-six months, about 14,000 horses and 2,000 mules were being despatched monthly.[28]

*　　*　　*

The immense task of carrying men, animals and stores to South Africa not only from the British Isles but also from all over the world, was, as in earlier wars it had always been, the responsibility of the Admiralty, employing chiefly, the ships of private firms.* To

* From the beginning of the war till 31 December, 1902, the totals carried by 1,027 ship voyages to and from South Africa were:
804,692 persons
459,336 animals
1,374,070 tons of stores.
Every one of the ships was British registered. (Maurice, I, 108–9.) The force carried by sea to South Africa was 'much larger than any which had ever crossed the seas before in the service of this or any other country'. (R.C., I, 125.)

There were two types of Admiralty charter: transport and freight. A transport was a vessel wholly taken up by the government on a time charter. A

this, as will be shown, there was to be one exception. Since 1876 the Admiralty's transport department had been so organized as to be able to convey a large force overseas from Britain at short notice. Particulars of suitable ships and their whereabouts were always kept up to date. In late September, 1899, without waiting for formal requisition, the department started engaging ships world-wide. Thus, when mobilization came, there was no delay in embarking the troops sent initially from home. By the middle of November they were all on their way.* This commendable achievement was made easier by the fact that the Admiralty always kept in stock considerable numbers of such things as troop bedding and horse fittings.

Of these last there were 10,000 in 1899, but they were all of a type known as 'the Admiralty Fitting' which was on the point of being superseded by a more efficient and much cheaper specification, soon to be known as the 'Remount Fitting'. The Admiralty fitting consisted in the main of a narrow, short, close-fitting 'crate' in which the horse was slung on a horse hammock. Much experience had recently been gained on the comparatively new large-scale trans-Atlantic horse and cattle trade carried in steamships. This showed that the high mortality which had always in the past resulted from the old fittings could be avoided by using the new ones in the cattle boats which had been specially designed for the trade. Technical experts of the Houlder Line and the Admiralty had been working on the details of the new fittings with Truman for more than a year before the war started. These, which were based on the commercial

---

freight ship was one in which the whole or a portion of the accommodation was engaged at a rate per head, or for a lump sum for a specific voyage. Freight ships, unlike transports, were not at the Admiralty's disposal for as long as they were required. (Maurice, I, 98–9; Smith, 254–5.)

The Colonial contingents were mostly carried by freight ships engaged locally by their own governments, though passage for some was provided by Admiralty transports sent from the Cape. (Maurice, I, 97.)

Within the sphere of India, the Indian Marine Department, not the Admiralty, was responsible for army sea transport.

* Nevertheless, Haig heard from 'an old sea captain' in Cape Town 'that the Admiralty are the laughing stock of the Mercantile Marine for the way they have hired transports. Certainly the cavalry seem to have been sent out in the slowest old tubs when of all the troops it was essential to have the horses here first to let them get over the voyage before moving.' On 16 November he was writing that not one of the transports 'had arrived yet, and several are now four days overdue – horses should be sent out always in the fastest ships: it is economy to do so.' (Haig to his wife, 15 Nov. and to his brother, 16 Nov. 1899, *Haig*, 177–8.)

specifications, did away altogether with the horse hammock, it having proved positively harmful. There were many other structural alterations, but the most important, indeed revolutionary, aspects of the Remount fittings were those which enabled far more horses to be carried in each ship. This was in spite of the length of each stall being increased from six-and-a-half to eight feet thereby giving the horse a far more secure foothold with which to counter the roll of the ship.

Mr Frank Houlder, Managing Director of Houlder Brothers, gave evidence to the Court of Enquiry which showed that one of his ships, had he 'planned her out according to the way the technical advisers of the Admiralty required, would carry 550 horses, whereas the same boat loaded for the Remount Department . . . took 870.' It was because of this enormous saving, because Houlder and Truman had worked out an entirely new contract system which was much cheaper than any of the Admiralty's,* because fewer horses died with the new fittings and because the Admiralty had its hands full with other work, that Truman gained permission immediately after war was declared to take over from the Admiralty responsibility for all remount ships. He employed the Houlder Line almost exclusively, chiefly as brokers and hirers, their own ships numbering only a dozen. The Admiralty did not resume responsibility till February, 1901, and by then the Remount fittings had been universally adopted. In the seventeen months of the Remount Department's control, fifty-seven ships had been engaged. These made 107 voyages.[29]† Though the extra work which this thrust upon the department's diminutive staff was colossal, the economy effected and the extra numbers of horses which could be carried were vital to the solution of the whole remount problem.

There was, however, one drawback to the new system. Unfortunately, the extra length of the horse stalls meant that there was no

* At the beginning of the war, the Admiralty were engaging ships on what was known as a time charter. A steamer thus engaged and fitted up for horses cost for the voyage between England and the Cape about £41 10s per animal. The same boat chartered under the Remount regulations cost only £25 per animal. The saving came out at about £16 10s a horse, which totalled about £1,250,000 for the 84,000 or so carried in the first fourteen months of the war alone. (Biddulph, 77.)

† The Admiralty during this period still dealt with ships for carrying transport mules. (Biddulph, 54.)

On average, the proportion of tonnage required for a man was four and for a horse twelve-and-a-half tons. (Maurice, I, 109.)

longer an alleyway behind the horses from which their dung could be cleared. Because in the trade, where nearly all the voyages were of short duration, and usually confined to the finest season of the year, the standings were never cleaned out during the passage, it was supposed that the same procedure would suit the carrying of army horses in wartime. But as one witness pointed out,

'this showed a want of knowledge of the amount of excreta a horse produces in a voyage of thirty days; behind mares it was a foul pool of pultaceous faeces fetlock deep; behind geldings it was a mound which raised their hind quarters considerably above their fore hand, and threw considerable strain on already tired fore legs. . . .* On transports which also carried troops the putrid mass *had* to be removed, as its overpowering stench cannot be described.'

This state of affairs which very materially decreased the condition of horses aboard ships was only partially overcome in the course of the war. It took less time to put right two other initial defects. Early on bad wounds caused by frightened horses biting each other were common. In some cases there were 'great pieces out of bitten horses' necks'. This was because there was a shortage of muzzles for habitual biters. Until zinc troughs were universally provided on ships, the wooden ones were 'nearly always eaten away or broken by the animals before the end of the voyage, and the nails which projected from the broken parts,' reported one officer who went out on a remount ship, 'are a source of great danger, many cases of badly lacerated lips and faces having to be treated after the arrival of the animals.'

The historian of the 14th Hussars says that on the voyage to Durban in December, 1899, the regiment's horses were got out of the hold 'in batches and exercised round the decks on coconut matting'. It is interesting that he goes on to state that 'nothing like this had ever been attempted before'.[30]

*   *   *

The total losses of horses and mules at sea for the whole period of

* Numerous cases of laminitis (inflammation of the laminae of the hoof) and of thrush (inflammation of the lower surface of the frog of the hoof) resulted from animals standing up to their hocks in muck. (Biddulph, 90.)

the war worked out at about 3.5%. Lord Roberts, when he was told this, was much surprised, having heard, rightly, that in some instances there had been heavy loss. 'In horses shipped from Australia to India yearly,' he wrote in 1902, 'the percentage is quite as high, if not higher.'[31] In fact the passage from Australia was one of the roughest and most trying. The loss during the war on remount ships from there amounted to over 5.5%. But the greatest losses occurred, remarkably enough, on the run from home to the Cape. On five ships with exactly the same fittings which between March and November, 1901, carried horses both from the United Kingdom and from Fiume to the Cape, the average loss on the passage from home was 9.23%, while that from Fiume was only 0.97%. This wide difference was probably almost entirely due to the practice of making every ship which left Britain embark horses at three ports, London, Southampton and Queenstown. This prolonged the voyage by four days in what was often its severest part and entailed the ships remaining at anchor in rough seas. Frequently the worst time for the horses was when they were rolling about in or outside harbours. The Atlantic crossing usually produced only 2.65% losses. Of 69,000 shipped from New Orleans, for example, only 1,828 were lost. Even on passage from Montreal to Durban, which sometimes took forty days, the average loss was not much higher.

The only really serious losses of ships were those of a cavalry transport, the *Ismore*, carrying part of the 10th Hussars with guns and 315 horses in St Helena Bay on 2 December, 1899, and the *Suffolk* which lost 928 out of 930 remount horses when she was wrecked off Cape St Francis, near Port Elizabeth, in 1900.* Incidentally throughout the vast operations not a single man was lost at sea from causes due to the ships which carried them out. In total over

---

* Excepting these two wreckings, there were less than thirty voyages on which loss of horses exceeded 10 per 100 embarked. One of the more horrifying of these was that of the *Rapidan* which encountered a gale in the Irish Sea soon after leaving Liverpool. At the same time a fire broke out in the engine room. For hours the ship was nearly stationary rolling in the trough of the sea. The animals lost their footing and their weight smashed the boards of their fittings. Many fell to be kicked to death by their neighbours. Others had their necks broken by their halters or were suffocated by their nose-bands pressing on their nostrils as they lay suspended by their head ropes. Yet others were badly gashed by the nails used in the fittings coming loose. Some were subsequently found wedged between the stanchions, which had to be sawn away to free them. Most of the attendants were seasick and could render no assistance. The nails in the

13,140 horses were lost 'on voyage': only 2.5 % of the total of horses supplied from all sources, including South Africa, and less than 3.7% of the total losses from all causes.[32]

*   *   *

To operate the enormously expanded activities of the Remount Department, numerous officers of various sorts had to be found with great urgency. On the whole it was not too difficult to get hold of honest officers for the various purchasing commissions, though, since the time when cavalry officers used to buy their own regiments' remounts, there were very few who had been able to get any experience of horse buying. Further, the attractions of active service or more lucrative employment tended, as the Stanley Committee reported, 'to operate against the permanence and continuity of purchasing appointments'. Most of the purchasing officers, being, as it were, thrown in at the deep end, learned their job pretty fast.* At the peak crisis periods, purchasing officers worked incredibly long hours. Ten or eleven hours' were normal. Eighteen, nineteen and even twenty-two hours at a stretch were not unknown.

Whether there were many cases of dealers taking advantage of the inexperience of untrained, hastily appointed purchasing officers is not clear. There were almost certainly some, but very few ever came to light. One Member of Parliament said that he had heard that in an Exeter dealer's establishment horses had been seen, 'some with wet bandages on them, and some with a pipe over their shoulders squirting water on a splint.' His informant had said to one of the employees: ' "Holloa, is your master setting up a veterinary establishment?" "Oh, no," was the reply, "we are preparing for the Government buyer who is coming down tomorrow." ' It was well know, added the Member, 'that horse dealers fake up horses in this

---

boots of the rest gave them no grip on the iron-sheathed decks. The ship had to return to Liverpool to refit, where she disembarked 109 of the worst injured. 156 out of a total of 460 had been killed or had to be destroyed. (Smith, 264–5; Biddulph, 179, 329.)

* Included in the forty-four employed overseas and at home were nine seconded cavalry officers and six officers from the Reserve. Two were general officers, twelve colonels, ten lieutenant-colonels, ten majors and ten captains.

Each military district at home kept lists of possible horse-purchasers among officers on the active list. It was some time before Truman was allowed to select any but active list officers. (Biddulph, 13, 302–5.)

way and unless the horses are tried very severely one cannot detect for a few days whether they are sound or not.'[33]

Far more difficult than securing purchasing officers was the task of finding Military Conducting Officers for the remount ships. The total employed was over 260 and it is significant that only about 33% of these were employed on more than one voyage. The job was a very unattractive one, entailing onerous responsibilities under pretty foul conditions. 'There were practically no experienced officers available,' wrote Harold Sessions, a veterinary civilian serving on a purchasing commission. 'Combatant officers who were of any use at all were required in the army in South Africa, and if a useful man happened to go out, he was immediately secured at Cape Town to work up country, and his services were not available a second time.'[34]

> 'At one time,' said Colonel Lawrence, 'I was sent out when we were running short of conducting officers to try to get them hurriedly in Pall Mall. . . . The Military Secretary seemed to get quite annoyed, and told me I must not try to rush the names of officers through, so I had to go away and try somebody else; then I found a friend in Major-General [Alfred Edward] Turner [Inspector-General of Auxiliary Forces], who got us a number of Militia officers, more particularly some officers of the Irish Militia, who were excellent men, accustomed to horses and ready to rough it. . . . We were not allowed to call up Yeomanry adjutants, and at first the employment of Reserve officers was objected to.'

Every ship was supposed to carry, beside the conducting officer, one Military Veterinary Surgeon. Here, as in the case of the purchasing commissions, where veterinary surgeons were even more vitally essential, the greatest exigency existed. The supply afforded by the Army Veterinary Department was soon exhausted. As early as November, 1899, civil members of the profession at home had to be resorted to, but of these the number that could be persuaded to help was quite insufficient to meet the demands of both the army in the field and the Remount Department. In America and Australia the purchasing commissions were allowed to engage local veterinary surgeons. In due course the great majority of those employed came to be foreigners. To induce British vets with proper qualifications to take on the arduous job, £50 a voyage with first-class passage back as well as out-of-pocket expenses were offered. Before long there was

added to this a sliding scale of bonuses for animals safely landed.*
Early on there were cases where either no conducting officer or no
veterinary surgeon could be found before a ship sailed. The work
then forced on to the shoulders of a single officer was strenuous
indeed. For instance, as many as eighteen of the earliest batch of
remount ships which left the United Kingdom sailed without any
veterinary surgeons aboard.[35]

What made the work of conducting and veterinary officers so
particularly irksome was the poor quality of the horse attendants or
'cattle men' on remount ships. They were all civilians engaged by the
shipping firms at the ports of embarkation. The scale was from one
to four foremen per ship† and one man for every fifteen horses. It
was not always possible to find enough men for even this inadequate
number. More often than not they had never dealt with horses in all
their lives. Many of them were 'the riff-raff of the New Orleans and
Liverpool slums'.‡ At Fiume, however, where the Hungarian and
Russian cobs were embarked, there was little trouble in getting the
numbers, but there the language problem was a hindrance. 'The
semi-Italian population of the place,' wrote Lieutenant-General Sir
Montagu Gilbert Gerard,§ who was sent out in early 1902 to report
on the Austro-Hungarian remount operations, 'are eager to go out,
for they get £3 a month and their food, there and back .... They are
not allowed to land at the Cape.'[36] From every other port, especially

---

* For example, the bonus for a voyage mortality of less than $2\frac{1}{2}$ % was 3s a
head; for 5 % to 7 %, 1s; for over 7 %, nil. (Smith, 262.)

† Most ships managed to secure foremen who had been to sea with animals
before. (Sessions, 233.)

‡ 'At New Orleans it became necessary to search every man as he came on
board, and to take away from him any long knife, razor, pistol, knuckle-duster,
or similar article which he might be in the habit of using for offence or defence.'
(Sessions, 233.) Mr Owen Williams, a civilian veterinary surgeon, says that they
had to apply for police protection 'and we had continually to watch the men.'
(Biddulph, 263.)

At Fiume 'the scum' sent out from Liverpool on one occasion mutinied,
refusing to embark the horses from the jetty. Sixty willing Hungarians ('who
would work the whole day for half a glass of wine') took over the job. (Welby,
59.)

§ Gerard, who published *Leaves from the Diary of a Soldier and Sportsman* in
1903, had served with the Central India Horse from 1870–95, seeing service in
the 2nd Afghan War (see Vol II, p. 212), and the Egyptian campaign of 1882.
He became Military Attaché at St Petersburg, 1892–3. He was commanding the
Hyderabad Contingent when called upon to report on the Austro-Hungarian
remount operations.

those in the United States, Canada and England, the cattle men were, according to Harold Sessions, 'the most dissolute on the face of the earth'. An officer of the 8th Hussars, who was conducting officer on a mule ship out of New Orleans, found that the men

'we had to look after the mules were not muleteers as they were supposed to be – in fact only about twelve out of them had ever seen a mule! The remainder were composed of loafers from New Orleans with a Life-Guardsman, a novelist, a telegraphist, a private secretary, a baker, a miner, a short hand writer and an American man-of-wars thrown in. Also two Germans who could not speak a word of English and a nigger. The deaf Life-Guardsman was a long way the most useless of the lot. They are all coming out with a view of getting something out there [in South Africa] to do, and a good many of them were through the American [Civil] War.'

'It is not,' wrote Harold Sessions, 'a particularly tempting job to look after animals at sea, particularly when the work is of an uncertain and temporary nature, and men who can get anything to do on land are not available for transport work.' Mr W. C. Scrivener, Houlder Brothers' shipping manager, found that it was 'not a question of payment; you cannot get them to go for a casual job.'[37] Mr Stephen John Graff, the Admiralty's Assistant Director of Transports, found that even those owners who paid the men well did not succeed with them. 'They have tried all kinds of ways; they have even got them from the Church Army.' So that they should be legally entered on the ship's articles, cattle men were bound to be paid a token 1s a month, but 'again and again £3 and £5 for the voyage has been paid'. Captain Pitt, Naval Assistant to the Admiralty's Director of Transports, reported that many of the attendants from foreign ports 'deserted and have gone over to the enemy in some cases when they got out to the Cape.' A reliable authority asserts that 'a Boer recruiting agency existed in America whence men were shipped under the guise of cattlemen in boats bringing animals to South Africa, where they slipped ashore and either joined the nearest Boer commando, or enlisted in one of the British irregular corps with the intention of deserting with their arms and ammunition on the first favourable opportunity.' There were numerous instances when the American cattle men's engagements ended on arrival in port, 'and Kaffirs,' according to the Assistant Inspector of Remounts in South Africa, 'had to be sent on board to feed the animals till they could be landed, while the "American citizens" smoked and looked on.'[38]

* * *

As soon as the war broke out the contractors selected by the United States purchasing commission got working. The chief ones were at St Louis, in Texas, Wyoming and further west. In December, 1900, when Colonel Ulick George Campbell de Burgh, commanding the 3rd Dragoon Guards,* went out to relieve Colonel Scobell of the 5th Lancers (see p. 248) in chief command of the commission, he speedily extended the operations even further westwards. The chief purchasing point became Ogden, forty miles north of Salt Lake City. From there the States of Utah, Washington, Montana, Oregon and Nevada were tapped. At no time was the commission anything but undermanned. There was a perpetual shortage of men of the classes of non-commissioned officers and stud grooms. But the American dealers, seeing that they were on to a good thing, were immensely helpful. Some of them 'gave up their permanent ranches and their ordinary occupations as cattle dealers or horse breeders at these ranches, for the purpose of taking up the trade of supplying the British Government with war horses.'

It is fascinating to see how, as the war progressed, the type of horse demanded in South Africa became smaller and smaller, till the numbers of large cavalry and artillery animals almost vanished altogether.† In the summer of 1901 the purchasing commission in the United States was ordered to buy no more cavalry horses, and in February, 1902, Kitchener reduced the standard height of the cobs he wanted to 14.1 from 14.3 hands, 'the bigger horses,' he wired, 'however good of their kind, not being what we require'. This, incidentally, had the effect of bringing the price down dramatically, for Class 'A' (15 to 15.1 hands) cost 100 dollars, Class 'B' (14.3 to 15 hands), 85 dollars, while Class 'C' (14 to 14.3 hands) cost only 37 dollars a head. Yet it was already becoming difficult in America to obtain cobs of 14.1 hands and less in height. This was in spite of

---

* His elder brother, Lieutenant-Colonel Thomas John de Burgh, 5th Dragoon Guards, commanded the 17th Battalion, Imperial Yeomanry in the later stages of the war. He had been wounded on 22 December, 1900, at Matjesfontein.

† In December, 1901, a telegram from the Cape read: 'Well-bred weight-carrying polo pony is the ideal required for all mounted troops, who now carry little on saddle.' (GOC, Cape to QMG, 11 Dec. 1901, Birkbeck, 54.)

the fact that only six years earlier small cobs had been a drug on the market. In Texas, for instance, ranch owners had been shooting them down, while in Portland, Oregon, there was a factory for making them into German sausages. Large numbers, too, were used in the cotton-growing districts around St Louis.[39]

At the height of buying by the American commission, which had become the largest horse and mule purchasing business the world had ever seen, between £200,000 and £300,000 was being spent each month. Six ships, each calculated to carry nearly 1,000 horses, arrived at New Orleans every four weeks or so and sometimes more often.

The stream of telegrams which came from South Africa altering the specifications of the animals required were very upsetting both to the dealers and to the purchasing commission, but generally speaking there was little delay in filling the ships the moment they docked.[40] Nevertheless, it might take weeks before the news of a reduction in height of two inches or of a relaxation of some aspect of soundness could penetrate to the remote mountain districts.

'Probably,' wrote Harold Sessions, by now a much harassed purchasing officer, 'the first way in which the horse owner would get the news would be when a buyer rode out to his valley to see what he could buy. He would then have to tell him that the specification had been altered since his last visit, that half the horses that he had broken were now not suitable, and for future selling he must break in some of another size. This, unless the dealer purchased some horses that he didn't want and which he knew under the new specifications could not be sold to the British Government, would dishearten the horse owner and he would not break in any more.'

The profits of the dealers were greater than they would otherwise have been, because the war was always expected to be over at any moment, and the Government naturally wanted to avoid having to fulfil long-term contracts once the need for horses had ceased. Proper economic contracts would have had to be made three or four months before delivery. As it was the orders were given only a very short time ahead. The dealers therefore took the risk of numbers of horses which they had gathered for sale being thrown back on their hands. To cover this eventuality, they were clearly entitled to extra profit. The big dealers 'made it a custom', as Mr Malcolm Moncrieffe, one of the largest of them, said, 'to buy in advance of orders given by the Government, otherwise we could not at any time have supplied the rush orders that came from at ten to twenty days' notice.' This was especially necessary because it took time to break in wild horses. 'Our system of purchasing,' said Mr Moncrieffe who was buying in eleven States, 'is simply to go into the open market and buy every suitable horse that is presented for sale, making arrangements with the breeders and others to break in a certain number for future delivery.' But, as Mr Rhodes of Denver, Colorado, pointed out, 'three or four weeks doesn't break a horse, three or four months is necessary. Nothing breaks a horse like taking him on a round-up for a season. Just riding him up and down a lane he doesn't learn much.' Major the Earl of Fingall who was the purchasing officer in the Colorado Springs district found when he took up the post in October, 1901, that 'it was customary to take horses that were only partially quiet'. This he continued to do until in the spring of 1902 he received orders to 'take nothing except what was absolutely quiet'. He found, however, that 'the thoroughly trained horse in the west is very seldom a thoroughly sound one' and here he came up against the unnecessarily stringent requirements as to soundness which many veterinary surgeons were still insisting upon.[41]

When the huge operation was at its height the purchasing commission consisted of four main departments. There were the headquarters in Kansas City; a large number of small commissions in various localities each under a 'combatant' officer, supported by a veterinary surgeon, and a number of depot ranches, the central one of which was formed in the spring of 1901 at Lathrop, Missouri. Here the contractors had acquired 7,000 acres extending over eleven miles of country, and here the animals were tested for glanders by a staff of six veterinary surgeons, kept whenever possible for some weeks, fed on corn and sorted out in readiness for forwarding to New Orleans as the ships required them. Between 3,000 and 7,000 were usually in stock at any one time, and during the fifteen months of its existence, over 80,000 animals passed through the ranch. During the great drought of 1901 in one of the hottest summers ever known in the central and southern states of America, the contractors provided pumps and oil engines to fix to the almost dried-up wells that were worked by windmills. Gangs of labourers were also set to work digging new ones. Where supplies on the spot could not be found enormous water wagons were kept going round the fields. In preparation for the winter the contractors built in a few weeks gargantuan barns capable of holding thousands of animals, not only at Lathrop but in other parts of the country too. Lastly there was the embarking organization at the New Orleans docks, where the fitting of ships, provision of forage for the voyage and all the multifarious business connected with shipping animals were carried on. Conditions at New Orleans were at first poor and the accommodation very cramped, but as time went on new pens were erected. As a rule the animals were given four days' rest before being put on board. Each ship as she arrived was inspected and all the fittings were thrown overboard so that anything at all which could possibly carry contagion was removed. Brand new fittings made of pitch pine (which itself acted as a disinfectant) had to be put up for each voyage. Most of the men employed at New Orleans were, of course, negroes. None of them, said Captain the Hon. Reginald Marsham of the 7th Hussars,* who was in charge at New Orleans, would work for 'under a dollar a day, and the system was, the first time you spoke to [i.e. criticised] him was the last time. The second time he got his dollar and went.'[42]

*   *   *

Horses constantly had to travel 3,000 miles or more before reaching the embarkation depot at New Orleans. An officer leaving his purchasing ground in the North-West for New Orleans would have a continuous train journey of four days and nights. Trains carrying horses might well take two or three times as long. Some were snowed up for days at a time, while during the summer, with shade temperatures up to 106° Fahrenheit, numerous watering halts had to be made. By American law, no animals were allowed to travel over a certain time without being unloaded, watered and fed. Where railway competition existed, it was sometimes possible, at a price, to get special horse trains which went as fast as passenger ones. Between 300 and 400 were carried on each train. The covered cattle-cars each carrying twenty-four horses were well designed and spacious, the railway companies being used to carrying large numbers of livestock over long distances as were also, incidentally, those in Argentina.[43]†

* As a Brevet Lieutenant-Colonel, Marsham commanded a squadron of the Remount Service, 1917–19. He died, aged fifty-seven, in 1922.

† In Canada, where over 12,000 horses were bought, the purchasing commission relied on large contractors to supply chiefly cavalry and artillery horses. In the Toronto area these cost between 140 and 150 dollars, while in the North-

In Austro-Hungary, on the other hand, the business was new to the railway authorities. Not only were the trucks provided unsuitable, but there were virtually no places en route where animals could be detrained for food and water. Therefore the commission which was buying for shipment from Fiume (from where some 6,400 were being sent away every month in late 1901 and the spring of 1902), had to work out all such arrangements beforehand. Often, early on, forage had to be sent ahead and rough unloading platforms and temporary corrals erected.[44] Before long the contractors actually had to 'take into their employ' certain station masters every 100 miles or so along the line to ensure adequate feeding and watering and to stop the attendants selling the forage en route. In late summer 1901 the purchasing grounds within reasonable distance of the coast became exhausted. Thereafter cobs had to be brought from areas further and further away. Russia – even some of her northern and north-eastern provinces – soon became the principal buying region.*

In an increasing number of cases these Russian cobs, which proved more suitable for South Africa than the Hungarian ones and of which nearly 28,000 were bought between mid-September, 1901, and the end of March, 1902, alone, had to travel for ten days or a fortnight before they even reached rail-head. Then they had to face some 2,000 miles in what came to be known locally as the 'Boer trains' before reaching the quayside at Fiume where, until the contractors improved matters, the gangways were often so badly arranged that the horses had to *slide* down into the holds.[45] In due course halting and purchasing points were established at Stryj, just over the frontier from Russia (where all horses had by law to change wagons), and at Agram where stables for 4,500 were provided. In these the animals were given three days' rest. At Agram a veterinary hospital was established by the Austro-Hungarian authorities. There munici-

West Territory and British Columbia the price was only 100 dollars. The former, though, included a new set of shoes and delivery on the wharf at Montreal, which was not the case for the latter. The distances were often immense. For instance the journey from Calgary to Montreal is over 2,250 miles, and the cost per truck-load of eighteen horses was 200 dollars. The wages of the men in charge of the horses were also very high. The headman on each train received five dollars a day. Of the 787 horses shipped from Calgary, only two died in transit. (Biddulph, 11.)

* The cobs came from 'near Odessa to Warsaw on the west and from Wiataka to Orenburgh on the east, a space roughly of 1,000 by 700 miles'. Ever since the great famine of 1891–2 there had been a scarcity of horses in southern Russia. (Lieut-Gen. Sir M. G. Gerard's Report, 12 Mar. 1902, *R.D.A.*, 49, 50.)

pal veterinary surgeons carried out their inspection so as to guard against the introduction of disease. Every sort of illness was dealt with most efficiently.

At Fiume sheds lit by electric light were built for 1,400 horses and in them all animals were kept for not less than twenty-four hours before being embarked. The contracts specified that any horse could be finally rejected by the British officers at Fiume. Indeed at one time there were 2,000 rejections on hand there. A rumour that rejects were sent to Hamburg and then to Antwerp 'to be shipped for the Boers' seems very unlikely to have been true. All expenses were borne by the contractor until the animals were actually aboard ship. Their cost per head on board varied between £26 10s and £28 10s. By the time they reached the Cape the cost had risen to about £43. Their initial cost, according to Veterinary-Colonel Alfred Ernest Queripel,* who had been sent out to report on the operations, 'was absolutely nothing; it could almost be left out of the question altogether. It was the contingent expenses that were important.' Buying was quite easy during the ice-bound winter months when very large fairs were held and 'the peasantry have nothing to do but sell'. In the rest of the year, though, the peasants 'being very busy with their land, the difficulty of collection was very much greater.'

Queripel reported that he 'had never examined such wonderfully sound animals as they were'. There was a certain percentage of nine-year-olds of which he 'never found an unsound one. Their legs were as clean as the day they were foaled and their feet as hard as iron.' Few of them, indeed, even required shoeing. Gerard, who reported in March, 1902, found that nearly all of them fed 'freely as soon as berthed . . . . They, as is typical, have ugly heads and most are extremely shaggy, with their long winter coats often caked with mud, as in some cases they pass the winter with no better shelter than the lee side of the haystack which supplies their forage. They seem absolutely free from vice, and almost without exception are quiet, good tempered and not timid.'

Many Russian cobs, unlike those in Hungary† ('Hungarian people do not ride'), were accustomed to the saddle, though those from south-east Russia, known as Khirgishes, were 'a little wild . . . but as soon as you have ridden them for two or three days they are

* Queripel, since 1894, had held the post of Inspector General, Civil Veterinary Department, India.

† Most of the Hungarian cobs came from the Kolosvar and Klausenburgh areas. They were chiefly hill ponies known as Heklars. (*R.D.A.*, 60.)

perfectly docile'. Some came from other Russian districts where peasants practically never rode. Yet they, too, were so quiet 'that anyone could mount them'.[46]

After the buying for the Imperial Yeomanry had been taken over by Truman, the whole business of purchasing animals from eastern Europe for embarkation at Fiume came into the hands of one powerful contractor. This man was a remarkable Jew called Hauser. He was said by the Imperial Yeomanry's chief buyer to be 'about the best dealer in Hungary'.[47] Lieutenant-Colonel John Hotham, the first head of Truman's Purchasing Commission, believed that Hauser had 'more capital than anybody there . . . and if you want to buy horses quickly you want a big dealer with capital. I went to see the Austrian Remount people in Vienna. They told me that the horse trade is in the hands of the Jews. There is nobody else to buy from.'[48] Two attempts were made by Truman to break Hauser's monopoly. In both cases, it seems, Hauser at once gobbled up his competitors (themselves Jewish), who appeared happy to become his partners.[49]

> 'I have been positively assured,' wrote Gerard early in 1902, 'particularly at the Vienna and Pesth Jockey Clubs, that we have been terribly "done", particularly at first, and that, though in their own interests the contractors have been serving us much better during the past twelve months, they are still making exaggerated profits. One must, however, bear in mind the universal suspicion and dislike of the Jews prevalent in this country, as well as in Russia; whilst, on the other hand, our remount officers, from want of knowledge of the country and language, are apt to drift into relying for everything on the contractors' people and into associating with them more than is socially customary in this Empire.'[50]

Whether Hauser made exorbitant profits or not – and Gerard thought that he was making between £10 and £14 on each horse[51] – he was certainly enormously efficient. Even early on, when the Imperial Yeomanry were still buying their own mounts, he had stabling for nearly 4,000 horses in Szabadka alone. Before long the whole complex organization was firmly in his hands. 'Our Remount officers,' wrote Gerard, 'would be powerless if called on to ship a consignment sent from any other quarter.'[52]

Hauser's method was to sub-contract to 'local – always Jewish – dealers, for the required supply: e.g. Mr Kashkin of Kiev; Isaacs and

Hutaffer of Warsaw; Pimka Magodow of Orël; Labell and Weissman of Koslow; Abram of Tambov, etc.' Each of these, whose buyers numbered well over fifty, had under him numerous commission agents 'with about £50,000 in ready cash in their hands, scattered through the districts'.[53] Captain Hartigan, a retired veterinary surgeon, one of the original buyers employed by the Imperial Yeomanry, told the *Committee on Horse Purchase in Austro-Hungary* (the Welby Committee) (see Appendix, p. 504) how as soon as Hauser received a contract these men swarmed round him

'like bees, and he gives them great satchels of money, and they go into the different districts. It is a custom there – as it is in Ireland – directly a horse is bought, to put a piece of mud on his croup; that signifies that that horse is sold, unless, of course, the man wants to resell him. In Hungary the man who is paid a guinea for finding the horse brings it up to the dealer, and it is marked in that way.... The horse is brought to this fellow, one of the men that Hauser employs – the fairs are chiefly on Saturdays, Sundays and Mondays – the bargain is made, and this fellow has to get his note, which is equal to a sovereign, for having found him. He will put it in his pocket and run away again to see if he can find another. The dealer is looking out at the same time. The horses are bought, and they come back in droves into the place. They will be tied together, as many as ten in a line, with a man riding on one, and they come in from the different fairs.'[54]

Hotham was soon able to identify Hauser's buyers.

'One would have a green ribbon, another a purple ribbon, and so on. After a week or so I could recognize whether it was Fisher had bought them or it was another man.... If I cast ten horses belonging to the green-ribbon man Hauser would hear of it. I think his system was a good one.... All dealers are the same. I have dealt with Arab dealers and dealers of many countries. If you take a dealer in the right way you can do very well. They all work and try to make about the same profit. If you have a strong man to look after them you get a fairly good horse; but if you have a weak man you may get anything.'[55]

Hauser's methods were much superior to those employed by 'a great Italian buyer' called Ranucci, by a gentleman called Lewison who bought Ranucci's contract, and by the shipping firm of Van

Laun and Co. in whose hands the Imperial Yeomanry had found themselves at the very beginning. Hartigan wrote that Van Laun thought that he could get horses

'like books off a shelf. He would say: "Ship alongside off Fiume; take 800 horses." When the horses came from the fairs they were all draggled and all over mud and they were rushed into a place, docked, given a drink of water and a feed of hay. They then came before us with a man on their backs with a rug or a carpet. Then the horses came into a shed, where I examined their eyes and feet, and they were walked out and branded, and sent to the train. In most cases there was no time to put shoes on. It was most scandalous.'[56]

*   *   *

In Australia, from where over 25,000 horses were bought, there were special problems. The horse market was restricted and there was much competition. Truman's purchasing commission (never more than two or three officers at a time) had to compete with buyers for the South African Constabulary and with private shippers who were hoping to make a killing when they landed their purchases at Durban by selling them to speculators and even sometimes to the Government.* The commission also had to compete with buyers for the Australian contingent in South Africa and with the regular buyers for the army in India who purchased on average 1,600 large walers for cavalry and artillery a year at £50 a head. Prices in consequence soon escalated. Many of the horses were bought c.i.f. (cost, insurance and freight) to South Africa, which meant that all losses on the voyage fell upon the seller who had also to submit to final approval on disembarkation. The initial cost of a cob grew from £10 to £12 a head, while the c.i.f. contracts grew from £31 to £33 a head.

The proportion of horses which were quiet enough to ride was small and there were difficulties as in America about procuring properly broken horses at short notice from the interior. Many hundreds of miles had to be covered before they reached rail-head.

* 'Everybody was buying horses because one man had sent a lot [to Durban] and had got £42 [a head], and, therefore, butter merchants, linen-drapers, members of Parliament, and everybody, were sending horses too.' (Col Hotham, Biddulph, 275.)

At only one port were there any horse yards. This was Pinkemba, near Brisbane. At Bowen, for instance, the animals had to be driven along a jetty three-quarters of a mile long. Both there and at Sydney they had to be kept in their railway wagons until the ship was ready to embark them. It became therefore a matter of importance to try to synchronize the arrival of the horses with that of the transports. Further, every hour that a steamer waited, the cost of demurrage increased. The typical walers, such as were supplied to the Indian cavalry, were generally a failure in South Africa, but the Australian cobs, known there as 'nuggets', were comparatively tough and not easily tired. Their numbers, however, were limited.[57]

* * *

Of the 25,800 horses bought in the Argentine a few were cavalry and artillery horses costing £20 each, but the majority were cobs at about £8 a head. These prices included all expenses incurred up to delivery at Buenos Aires. There a daily charge of thirty centavos (about 6d) was made for each horse until it was embarked. Sessions describes the method of purchase (which would have been much the same elsewhere):

'The horses were ridden up singly, so that we could see how they behaved while being ridden. Afterwards we trotted them to see if they were sound in wind and action; they were then brought back to us, and if in shape and make they answered the required description they were then examined in detail to see if there were any defects in limb or body which might interfere with their work. Their age was next ascertained by looking at their teeth, their height was taken, and if they appeared satisfactory, their age, height, colour and markings were put down in a book opposite a certain number. They were then branded with a broad arrow on the right hoof to show that they belonged to the British Government; and on the left hoof they were branded with a number corresponding to their description in the book; while a letter was also branded on the hoof to show which of us had purchased the horse. After the branding they were brought back to a gaucho who with a long knife trimmed their manes and tails, which always seemed to me a pity, but which was according to Government orders.'[58]

* * *

316

From India, beside the mounts required for what was known as the Indian Contingent (three cavalry regiments, four infantry battalions and three artillery batteries), many other horses were sent. The total was about 7,000. Most of the animals were drawn from native cavalry regiments. Others were given by the native states 'with great loyalty and generosity'.[59]

'Where the horse, exhausted by a month's sea voyage, was allowed no rest, but at once put into the ranks, moved up to an altitude of 5,000 or 6,000 feet above the sea and made to endure long marches on short rations, it is not surprising that he was found unequal to the demands made on his strength, demands which the best of horses would be unable to meet under such adverse conditions.'

Report of the Court of Enquiry into the Administration of the Army Remount Department, 1902

'At an early stage the Remount Department was rather looked down upon ... but latterly there were a good many applications from different regiments by men who had got weary of trekking.'

LIEUTENANT-COLONEL W. H. DARBY, D.A.A.G., Remounts, Johannesburg

'In the Transvaal and Free State operations, half the strength employed would have done the work in a shorter time had the horses been fit and well fed. To bring the enemy to action it was essential to gallop them down. On no single occasion during the guerrilla war was this accomplished on a large scale.'

* * *

'Had South Africa been a country where the wear and tear of horse shoes was considerable, nothing would have prevented an entire collapse of the military arrangements within three months from the date of taking the field.'

MAJOR-GENERAL FREDERICK SMITH in the *Veterinary History of the War in South Africa*

'It was sad to hear the constant reports of revolvers putting an end to the miseries of worn-out horses.'

An officer of the Inniskilling Dragoons, autumn, 1900[1]

(ii)

Boer War: remount question: acclimatization – coat shedding – lack of rest on landing – rail transport – depots in South Africa – veterinary department in South Africa – veterinary hospitals – debility farms

There was a particular reason why horses from northern climes were not as fit as might have been expected on arrival in South Africa. It was the consequence of their rapid transfer from one hemisphere to the other. For instance, a horse leaving Fiume with his winter coat on would shed it when crossing the tropics. If he reached the Cape at the beginning of winter there, he would (or ought to) throw out another winter coat only a few weeks after shedding his first.* Equally, a horse coming down from Canada or, say, Montana, would have a very heavy coat which was hardly suitable for the climate of New Orleans. Even if there were time, men and machines enough for clipping, which there often were not, the strain of extreme changes of temperature and of as many as three changes of coat in as many months was always debilitating. The President of the Horse Commission for India told the Stanley Committee that in his experience the average horse which has to undergo a double change of coat coming from Australia to the northern hemisphere finds it 'such a drain that he is not fit for work for a year'. There were many horses who 'refused to change their coats for several weeks'. These, of course, suffered shockingly from the cold. Equally those animals which arrived from the north in South Africa during the summer suffered enormously from the heat because, until near the end of the war, there was a chronic shortage of clipping machines. Veterinary-Surgeon Robert Pringle† thought that he could have saved 25% of deaths in his hospital had he been able to clip his patients.[2]

Another tiresome cause of enfeeblement was the initial requirement that every remount ship from wherever it came must call at Cape Town for orders.‡ From there, as often as not, it would be required to proceed to another port for disembarkation. These prolongations of the passage, especially the hanging about waiting for instructions, added to the unfortunate animals' ordeal. All contracts, incidentally, stipulated that there should be no extra charge for such extended voyages. As late as the end of April, 1900, the congestion in Cape Town harbour was overwhelming. On 24 April, for in-

* If as constantly happened the luckless animal was almost immediately rushed by train to the uplands, perhaps 6,000 feet above sea level, before he had re-grown his winter coat, he was apt to die of cold. In one place the railway rises 2,400 feet from the coast in twenty-seven miles; in another, 1,000 feet in fifteen miles.

† As a major-general Pringle became Director-General of the Army Veterinary Service, 1910–17.

‡ Soon after the reopening of the Natal–Johannesburg line, nearly all ships were ordered to discharge at Durban. (Smith, 87.)

stance, there were 3,000 horses on board ship in the roads awaiting disembarkation. Priority was not accorded horse-ships. They had to take their turn with all other transports. The Principal Veterinary Officer begged that these horses might be taken off in lighters as was being done at the more easterly ports, but it turned out that there were no lighters available! Those animals which were disembarked in the next few days were at once rushed up the line to Bloemfontein, 750 miles away. By 7 May they were marching daily and carrying some twenty stone under campaign conditions![3]

*　　*　　*

A principal cause of the horrifying wastage of horses once they had been landed in South Africa was the lack of time for rest and acclimatization allowed them before they were despatched to the front and immediately set to the most exacting of work. Even horses brought from Ireland to England recovered from that brief passage only after weeks and sometimes months. Horses transported the short distance from Brighton to London frequently required two or three weeks before they thoroughly adapted themselves to the change of air and food. 'It has been proved by long experience in India,' wrote Lord Roberts in 1902, 'that, if the horses from Australia have any strain put upon them before they have had ten months' or a year's acclimatization, they break down.' It is obvious, therefore, that there were very good reasons why every horse, from wherever it emanated, should have a considerable acclimatization period on arrival at a South African port. Lieutenant-General Sir William Francis Butler (see Vol III, pp. 40, 133, 300), who had commanded at the Cape just before the War, 'would certainly never think of doing much' with his own horses for peaceful let alone war-like purposes under two months after arrival from home. Though experts, as is their wont, differed, all were agreed that less than eight weeks was not enough. The heads of the veterinary profession thought 'a year not too long a time' for the larger horses, if not for the smaller cob. The need for such lengthy acclimatization was partly because of the notoriously delicate digestive functions of the horse. Sudden changes of food, and even more of water, much of which on the veld was brackish or very hard, produced intestinal irritation and enervating 'alterations in the physiological process of urine-secretion'.[4]

From the point of view of this history it is especially interesting

38. (*Above left*) Louis Botha

39. (*Above right*) Christiaan de Wet

40. (*Left*) Ben Viljoen

41. (*Below left*) Jan Smuts

42. (*Below right*) Pieter Kritzinger

43. Kitchener and French in Pretoria

44. Maj-Gen. William Truman (see p. 28

45. Lt-Col Sir Henry Rawlinson

46. Maj.-Gen. Sir Ian Hamilton

to consider the case of the comparatively small number of cavalry horses which were already in the ranks of regiments when they were sent from home. In Haig's evidence to the Royal Commission on the war he says 'hitherto there has been too much pampering in peacetime.' Some of the casualties at manoeuvres in England, he added, were attributable to 'lack of hard condition'. The veterinary historian of the war who was himself a witness states with eloquence what happened to such animals:

'The stabled and pampered troop horse found himself in South Africa suddenly exposed to scorching sun by day and drenching dews by night. His long English winter coat was burned brown or came away in patches, and was clogged with sweat and dirt. His rest on shipboard had robbed him of such muscular fitness as he possessed, and he groaned under his 20-stone load. . . . He was turned out to graze but did not know the meaning of it, and abused his freedom by stampeding. Prevented from stampeding by knee-haltering, applied by ignorant men, his leg was cut. . . . He shivered and shrunk up in the rain, and the absence of generous feeding, hay and water, soon left him a shadow of his former self.'[5]

The exigencies of the war were of course the reason always given as to why horses were denied essential rest. These were exacerbated by the lack of sufficiently large depots at the ports for them to rest in.[6] The failure to erect these till late on in the conflict was, as with so much else, a result of the belief which was universally held that from the moment Pretoria fell the war would almost immediately end.

The war had been waging for twenty-six months when Mr Brodrick wired to Kitchener that reports were reaching him 'from many quarters that . . . unconditioned horses are being issued to columns and sent at once on long treks. . . . Surely it would be better to rest some columns for a time than to waste horses.' To this Kitchener, who like most of his Staff remained resolutely ignorant of the realities of the remount question, replied on 25 November, 1901, asking for Truman and 'some thoroughly practical officer' to be sent out to look at the problems. He added

'till the recent operations in Natal, which drew heavily on remounts, the best horses arriving had average of three weeks at ports, and weak or in any way unfit horses, longer. I hope I shall soon be able to return to this scale of rest, but in view of strain on remounts to replace losses and increase of mounted troops, as well as preparation for Cavalry coming dismounted I should be glad if you could send me 2,000 riding horses at once, and a monthly increase of 2,000 riding horses.'

Brodrick retorted next day:

'The question of resting horses seems to us of the first importance. We will certainly send officers to help you [Colonel Viscount Downe, (10th Hussars), one of Roberts's aides-de-camp, and Colonel Hotham were ordered to make a report]. But no change of hand will be effective unless you lay it down authoritatively that columns must rest till horses are in proper condition. We cannot continue indefinitely to send 10,000 to 12,000 remounts per month to be used up by Column Commanders in a few days.'

Eleven days later he added: 'Several reports have recently reached me of horses from oversea being sent up country and sent on trek unshod, and consequently becoming unserviceable in two or three days. Cannot you issue an absolute prohibition of such practice?' Kitchener had, in fact, already before the end of 1901 issued instructions which should have ensured time for proper shoeing.* His orders then were that horses were to remain in the port areas for not less than ten days 'before going to the high veldt'. There they were to be exercised for a further ten days 'before issue to dismounted details at Base Depots'. Nevertheless, as late as 28 April, 1902, less than a month before the end came, Downe was informing the Quartermaster-General that 'very few officers I found knew of this order, and horses were continually sent to depots up country with no description of them or *date of their arrival in the country*.'[7]†

A concrete example of lack of rest is provided by the case of the Inniskilling Dragoons. A few days before they left Bloemfontein in early May, 1900 (having lost numerous horses from all causes since arriving in South Africa six months previously), remounts were issued so as to bring the regiment up to strength. Some of these had just arrived by train; others had been trekked up from the Orange

* But see p. 332.

† Kitchener's Deputy Assistant Adjutant General, Major Birdwood (see p. 72), used to plead with him 'that more time should be allowed for the acclimatization of imported animals – without, I fear, much success. He was the most persevering man in the world, but also one of the most impatient.'

River, a distance of 150 miles. Many of them were recently shipped, half-broken Argentine ponies, fed during their sea voyage on hay. Now, given literally no time for grazing, they were offered oats which they had never seen in their lives before and which they refused to touch. Their condition was soft indeed and it is not surprising that, having to carry twenty stone, many of them died of exhaustion and sore backs in the course of a few days. In its two-and-a-half years of active service, the regiment, which landed with 406 horses, was issued with 3,884 remounts, of which 823 were either picked up on the veld or transferred from other units. The expenditure which this represents was equivalent to the re-horsing of the regiment ten and a half times. Out of the 4,170 cases of sickness only 163 were due to bullet wounds and three to shell fire (3.9%). The Royal Dragoons did rather better in some respects. In the three years from November, 1899, to October, 1902, they got through 3,275 horses. This represents the replacement six times of every horse taken out from home. Of the total only fifty-six were killed or captured in action. Three of the original animals actually survived the campaign. Another example of inordinate wastage is furnished by the record of the 1st Mounted Infantry which was completely rehorsed over three and a quarter times in fourteen months. Of its total losses of 1,031 only fifty were lost in action, while ten were killed by lightning.[8]

From time to time, as has been shown, Truman managed to send out 'many more horses than were demanded in the hope that by their getting ahead of requirements we might,' as he told the Court of Enquiry, 'ensure a rest after landing, but it was in vain. No sooner did fresh shipments land than new corps were formed.' Captain Edward Pennell Elmhirst, who had been for thirty years hunting correspondent of *The Field*, spent the first six months of 1900 as a remount officer. During that period he was constantly being harried by peremptory orders from headquarters 'that all but the sick and inefficient were to go up at once. . . . In very few cases indeed were the horses at Cape Town more than ten days. In very many cases they went up three or four days after arrival.' Captain Duncan Vernon Pirie, Liberal Member of Parliament for Aberdeen and an ex-officer of the 3rd Hussars,* went out as a conducting officer from home with a troop of the Greys. They left Port Elizabeth for

* Pirie had served with the 4th Dragoon Guards and as extra aide-de-camp to Graham in the 1882 Egyptian campaign. He made rather a fool of himself at the action of Kassassin on 28 August (see Vol III, p. 286).

the front 'the evening of the day they landed with remounts immediately after thirty-one days at sea. The life of the horses,' he added,
'was entirely put in the background in order to obtain immediate
military ends.'[9]

*   *   *

The fearful squandering of horseflesh, especially during the first half
of the war, was in part accounted for by the appalling conditions on
South Africa's railways. All narrow gauge, all single line, the strain
placed upon them by the military demands for which they had not
been designed was overwhelming. Virtually all troops and supplies
had to use them, a proper system of roads being conspicuously
absent. Distances from the port bases to the front were vast. For
instance, Bloemfontein is 450 miles from Port Elizabeth, Kimberley
647 miles and Mafeking 870 from Cape Town, while Pretoria is
649 miles from East London and no less than 1,944 from Cape
Town.[10]*

A Staff Officer of Remounts on the Midland line which started at
Port Elizabeth said that horses were treated 'very much after the
style' in which coal was treated. Indeed in Natal the long iron coal
wagons were throughout the war the chief conveyances of remounts.
In the Cape they were shorter in length, but in neither did facilities
exist for watering and feeding during journeys. Typical of the attitude of the regimental authorities to the care of horses in transit is
the case of a troop officer of the 12th Lancers who, three days after
the regiment had landed at Cape Town, was

> 'ordered to load eight horses per truck; twice I reported I could
> not do so and received nothing but abuse. On the third report I
> was told if I did not do so I should be put under arrest. I did it.
> At 9 that night the train stopped at a wayside station. The guard
> reported many horses down in my troop! Of the thirty-two
> horses I had taken such care of, nine were dead and many
> injured; the train was like a shambles.'

At first the horses were placed across the wagons with their heads
tied to the sides, but later, following the peacetime practice of the
Cape Government Railway, tying up was abandoned. The result

* The colossal scale of South Africa is vividly demonstrated by the fact that
Durban is as far from Cape Town in a straight line as London is from Naples;
from Port Elizabeth to Cape Town equals Munich to London and from East
London to Cape Town is the same as from Venice to London.

was beneficial for now the animals were better able to rearrange themselves so as to resist sharp curves, steep gradients and shunting jolts. The narrowness of the wagons meant that the larger horses became badly rubbed both back and front, while the peculiar construction of especially the Natal wagons caused other injuries from projecting bolts and rails. Very few trains arrived from the coast without a number of injured horses. When the 7th Dragoon Guards soon after arrival were entrained in March, 1900, their mounts were 'packed eight or ten at a time in trucks far too small for English horses. . . . During the journey up-country,' wrote Lieutenant Noel Dawson Henry Campbell, 'two horses were killed outright, crushed to death by their companions, and twenty so badly injured that they were unfit for any work, a heart-rending state of affairs after all the trouble we had taken to keep them fit for active service.' On the way to Bloemfontein in early April, an officer of Lumsden's Horse (see p. 202) wrote: 'The horses – poor devils – are packed ten, eleven and twelve in a cattle-truck, and the way they kick at times is a caution. All along the train the trucks are broken and splintered. Oh! for the luxury of our Indian horseboxes!'

Iron trucks did not, of course, lend themselves easily to alterations. Their worst aspect, though, was that their iron floors gave no grip. It was useless to put down a carpet of sand or cinders as the first considerable incline or sharp bend shifted it to one end or one side. On steep hills the horses themselves gravitated to the lower end of the trucks. In more than one case the pressure proved so great that animals were forced over the end of the wagon to fall on the single buffer behind. From the covered-in cattle and ordinary goods trucks, of which, incidentally, there were few enough for troops and stores, let alone for horses, all animals had to be taken out to be watered and fed, an enormously time-consuming process. This was complicated by the lack of platforms. The roofless wagons (the low freeboard of which was raised by a wooden railing) were better, for men could clamber along the railing to put nosebags on and to attempt to water by the use of pails (a slow and wasteful method, especially where water was a valuable commodity and often not laid on at stations in sufficient quantities). An officer of the Imperial Yeomanry found that to feed 120 horses in open wagons never took less than two hours, 'and that was with 130 men!' (See illustration No. 54) Not until well into 1902 were a certain number of wagons arranged on the pattern generally adopted on the Indian railways. In these the horses were placed parallel to the railway lines in two rows facing towards the wagon's centre. There was a bar fixed between each batch to which the heads were secured, and between the rows of heads there was space for fodder and attendants. This obviously cut down the stowage space since only six animals could be taken in each wagon as opposed to eight or nine when they were stood side by side across the wagon. This was why no serious attempt was made to bring the system into universal use during the war. Nevertheless, the amount of time that it must have saved would have been enormous.[11]

*　　*　　*

A major problem was the chronic shortage of officers and men to accompany remount trains and to man the fixed feeding stations which were hastily established along the line. Until well into March, 1900, according to Colonel Stevenson, the whole system, such as it was, depended entirely upon 'stray officers waiting to join their regiments or battalions who were lent to me but were moved on to the troops at the front as soon as a chance offered or their services were required'. When the pressure was at its height, soon after Lord Roberts's arrival, when troops, stores and remounts were being rushed to the various fronts as fast as trains could be made up, as many as 300 horses in a train were despatched without a single officer or soldier. 'When each train was in charge only of a [civilian] conductor and twelve or fifteen nigger boys,' said Captain Elmhirst, who early in 1900 was stationed for two months at Stellenbosch depot to which every horse landed at Cape Town was sent, 'it was impossible that the horses (nine or ten in a truck or box) could be adequately fed or watered, or even watered or fed at all, during their three days, and sometimes more, of journey up-country.' Even as late as mid-July, 1900, when an officer at Krugersdorp near Johannesburg took over 500 remounts, he found that 'they had been eleven days on the journey, and there were seven men in charge of the whole train: soldiers and no officer. . . . Horses very weak. Some of them were hardly able to stand up.' This was perhaps an exceptional case, for by June, 1900, on most of the railways, arrangements had been completed whereby the animals were taken out of trains every twelve hours or so for proper watering and feeding and a little stretching of their legs. Nevertheless, there were occasions when breakages of the line or heavy concentrations of troops in a particular area placed too great a strain on the railways, when horses were left longer than twelve hours without water, when only damp hay could be hurriedly thrown into the wagons or a few hard-won mouthfuls from a pail given to them. In war such things cannot be avoided. For example, there was a longish period when, because a railway bridge was broken at Norval's Pont on the Midland Railway, none of the remounts for the army at Bloemfontein could be carried beyond it. They had, instead, to be walked alongside the railway a distance of 130 miles. More than 5,000 were sent thus in various batches averaging about twenty-one miles a day. Some of these lost up to 30% of their number due chiefly to exhaustion but also from straying because there were insufficient men to look after them. Virtually all of those that did arrive were unfit for issue to troops for a considerable time afterwards. There were, nevertheless, remarkable feats of railway organization. For example, when in September and October, 1901, troops were being concentrated to repel Botha's invasion of Natal, over 32,800 animals were moved in thirty-five days over immense distances.[12]

Time and again horses would be issued to units the moment they had been detrained. Sometimes they would set off on trek the very same day. It was a constant practice, too, for horses to be issued from a depot still in poor condition and unshod. In May, 1900, for instance, the 16th Lancers, having lost two-thirds of the walers they had brought from India less than four months before, were remounted with 'mostly English horses' from the Bloemfontein depot. Their orders were so categorical that they were given 'no time to fit saddles or get things into order in that way. Many of the horses were not shod up. Some of the horses,' reported the commanding officer, 'arrived late on the Sunday afternoon and were marched to the north early on Monday morning.' Largely responsible for this state of affairs was Kitchener himself. Neither when he was Roberts's Chief of Staff, nor as Commander-in-Chief, until well into the guerrilla stage of the war, did he begin to show the slightest knowledge of or indeed interest in the limitations of the horse. As Lieutenant-Colonel Middleton, the officer commanding the remount department in Natal, told the Court of Enquiry:

'Lord Kitchener would send down a peremptory order – he would see on the return how many horses we had got at the different depots – that they were to be at a certain point at a certain hour, without knowing anything about the local circumstances. Both General Lyttelton and General Hildyard wrote several letters, and I wrote to the Military Secretary protesting against such callous indifference to horseflesh, but he would not see it or would not alter it until recently [early in 1902].'[13] (See also p. 321.)

*   *   *

At the outbreak of the war there were only two small remount depots in South Africa. One was at Stellenbosch outside Cape Town and the other was at Nottingham Road, seventy miles inland from Durban. By the end of the war there were twenty-four, each one considerably larger than the original two, ten of which were manned exclusively by civilians and natives.* Eventually there were three classes of depot: landing, issuing and resuscitating. The issuing depots were also in effect resuscitating depots 'because,' as Colonel Deane put it, 'the horses that reached [them] were in such poor condition as to be mostly unfit for work.' The resuscitating depots were chiefly employed, of course, in nursing back to health worn-out and incapacitated horses sent in from columns. In association with most of them, large farms were rented. The Mooi River depot, for instance, had 8,000 acres of good pasture on the high veld of Natal. These were later called debility farms (see p. 336). The Stellenbosch depot, which was technically a base and not a resuscitating depot, had on occasions as many as 1,400 horses in one day sent in from the front worn out. Most were re-issued after about six weeks of proper care and attention.

* At the beginning of the war the regular cavalry's reserve squadrons had to be made into emergency remount depots. This was a serious disadvantage since it put a stop to the men's training. (Maj.-Gen. [later General Sir] Henry Fane Grant, son of F-M Sir Patrick Grant (see Vol II, p. 164), Inspector-General of Cavalry, in Biddulph, 251–2.)

The Imperial Yeomanry sent out 550 of all ranks to man their own Base Depot. (Biddulph, 176.)

The Commandant of the 6th New Zealand Regiment found that if he had had a regimental depot in South Africa, he could have kept his

'regiment mounted at enormous saving to Government. As it was, I was able to establish a reserve of sixty horses in the field which I led about with me. If I had sent them into the remount department, I should never have seen them again.'

'The 1000s of ponies caught on the veldt were wasted. Out of every 100 captured, about twenty were good ones. If I could have sent these into my depot to be handled quietly for a couple of months, I could have kept my regiment mounted, without drawing on Government at all.' (Andrew, 110.)

It took a long time before the number of depots began to match the need. It took even longer before they were anything but grossly undermanned in officers, other ranks and civilians. To obtain a sufficient number of trained officers was always impossible, but even to get hold of officers of a reasonable quality was difficult. 'Those who were worth anything,' said Middleton, 'managed to secure berths at the front, and those who were no use at the front were sent down for what they thought would be a loaf in the remount department. When they got there they found it was not so much of a loaf, and away they went, and we were glad to get rid of them too.' The shortage of officers available for and willing to undertake non-combatant jobs was chronic. In Johannesburg, for instance, one major was placed for a time in charge not only of the remount depot, but also of 'the banks and the liquor traffic'. A tragic case, not perhaps typical but illustrative of the problem as well as of the attitude taken by the authorities towards the importance of the remount department, is that of Colonel the Hon. George Hugh Gough, grandson of the first Viscount Gough (see Vol II, p. 220). Gough, who had commanded the 14th Hussars from 1891 till 1896, went out in October, 1899, as Assistant Adjutant-General of the Cavalry Division. Buller, however, considered him 'unfitted for work in the field on account of his great excitability and sent him to the Remount Depot at Stellenbosch.' What happened next is best told in Lord Roberts's words. Writing to Lord Lansdowne on 1 April, 1900, the Field-Marshal said:

'The poor fellow committed suicide by shooting himself with a revolver on the bank of the Orange River at Norval's Pont. . . . [He] wrote to me more than once to give him some berth nearer the front. Nothing suitable offered until a few days ago, when I appointed him to command the depot to be formed here [at Bloemfontein]. I heard that this pleased him greatly. On his way to join he was ordered to remain for a few days at Norval's Pont, where there was a great collection of troops and stores owing to the bridge over the river having been destroyed. This apparently unhinged his mind, for he shot himself the following morning. . . . It is a terribly sad business, but I hear that Gough showed signs of insanity as far back as 1885 [in which year he had been promoted Brevet Lieutenant-Colonel].'

If Roberts's information was correct, it is a little alarming to find that he had served as private secretary to Wolseley, the Commander-in-Chief, for two and a half years from 1897. Before that he had seen much active service. He had been Evelyn Wood's ADC in the 1881 Boer War, Edward Hamley's in the 1882 Egyptian campaign, where his horse was killed under him at Tel-el-Kebir, and he was wounded at Abu Klea in the 1884 Sudan expedition when in command of the mounted infantry. In Ireland he had enjoyed a great reputation as a point-to-point rider, 'no day being too long and no fence too big for him'. He was said to be 'the beau-ideal of a light cavalry officer'.[14]

The official War Establishments laid down for base and advanced remount depots were in fact not sent out when the 1st Army Corps left home. This was probably because they were designed for an European not a Colonial war. In consequence the personnel was 'added as it could be found'. In November, 1899, five transport companies of the Army Service Corps were detailed to man the five depots then being established. These men were assisted by civilian rough-riders, farriers, clerks and native boys. When Lord Roberts arrived, just as it became clear that dramatic increases in mounted troops were imminent, he ordered the transport companies' men, both white and black, back to their legitimate work.*

'Within ten days,' reported the harassed Birkbeck, 'a scratch civilian and native establishment was made up, which, with the help of the Indian native non-commissioned officers and syces then arriving in charge of Indian remounts [of whom 2,100 had arrived by April], filled the breach until the arrival from England of seven base remount depots. Of these, two only had men;† the other five, of which two were sent to Natal, were skeletons, comprising officers and non-commissioned officers only. These depots arrived 15th to 31st March [1900].'[15]

How inadequate the staffing was is illustrated by Captain Elmhirst: 'The utmost I had for feeding and watering and exercise was eighty-four syces.' Much of the time he had no British non-

---

* This was an unfortunate result of the new Commander-in-Chief's wise decision to remove the remount department from subordination to the transport department, an arrangement which had proved both unwieldly and the cause of much friction resulting from an obvious conflict of interest.

The initial provision of horses for the South African colonial corps was left in their own hands, but the remount department still had to find remounts for them. (Amery, VI, 432.)

† Within two months of landing most of the men of these two complete depots 'had joined the Cavalry Division, and no one,' said Birkbeck, 'regretted their departure.' (Birkbeck, 21.)

commissioned officers. What few soldiers he had were chiefly engaged in breaking in half-wild Argentinians. The depot had only four officers and three veterinary surgeons. One vital disadvantage of the perpetual undermanning of depots was touched on by Middleton. The remount department, he told the Court of Enquiry in April, 1902, 'never could undertake or pretend to supply a fit horse from anywhere even if they kept him for a month, because they had not the staff to exercise them. Keeping a horse grazing about did not make him any fitter.' As late as mid-1901 there were only fifty rough-riders at the De Aar depot for 1,000 completely unbroken horses. At the Germiston depot near Johannesburg where, in the war's later stages, it was not uncommon to have as many as 13,000 horses at a time,* added to on occasion by large numbers of captured horses, only about 5 % of the broken animals could actually be ridden. This was partly because of a shortage of saddles, but chiefly for lack of riders.

'The others were driven round and round. . . . This,' according to Honorary Lieutenant and Quartermaster John Edward Darby, 'was the only way to try to condition them. We did not condition them to the saddle. . . . We have tame Boers [see p. 234] in the depots breaking them. [They] could always ride them in about three or four days' time after catching and breaking them. . . . Sometimes we got Zulus, who were frightened to go near a horse. Occasionally we got a certain number of Basutos that you could utilize for riding purposes.'

At one time all the rough-riders belonging to regiments were re-moved from every one of the remount depots and returned to their units. Nothing shows more clearly than this how little the head-quarters staff understood the remount situation. Those depots, which were controlled by

'the average Colonial Corps,' reported Lord Tullibardine of the Scottish Horse (see p. 228), 'would become a source of con-stant peculation, not only in horseflesh, but also in grain. With cavalry regiments' depots, too, I noticed that horses and ponies which were not worth their keep were often kept going because they were old friends, or because some NCO wanted to show

* The Port Elizabeth depot often had 5,000 horses at a time, while from the Bloemfontein depot on one occasion 3,000 were issued in two days. (Birkbeck, 21.)

how he could bring a horse round after it had been given up by a vet. . . . Also ponies suitable for polo were very often allowed to remain in the depots longer than was otherwise necessary.'[16]

The chronic shortage of farriers and shoeing-smiths was a crucial factor in the wastage of horses. Fortunately there were virtually no metalled roads while there was a great deal of soft going on the veld. In consequence, shoes which lasted barely a month at home, even during the idleness of winter, in South Africa lasted three months and sometimes till they dropped off. The basic reason for the shortage was the very small number of trained men in the Reserve. This of course inhibited speedy wartime expansion.* Until the war had been going five months the whole of the remount department had only *two* military shoeing-smiths for the entire theatre of war. When numerous infantry units became entirely horsed and when scores of irregular mounted units were being hastily raised, there was scarcely a trained farrier among them. The shoeing problem then reached major proportions.† Stevenson had to engage large numbers of civilian farriers in an effort to shoe his charges before sending them to the front. He found that nearly all the American and Australian horses arrived unshod. This meant that they landed with 'the hind feet worn down to the heels'. Set to work within a few days of landing it was not surprising that they soon went lame. Thorneycroft found that in many instances it was 'impossible to shoe such a horse, there being no hoof left to nail on'. Fifteen shoeing-smiths arrived with the base depots sent from home, but 'nearly all, for various reasons, became ineffective in a few months.' To cope with the work that had to be done at least forty were necessary for the Natal base depot alone. Wages for civilian farriers in the country were very high: 'for what we call a fireman, £17 10s a month, and for the doorman, the man who fixes shoes on to horses, £15 10s'. The army farriers evinced no little discontent at seeing their civilian brethren earning in a day what they could hardly expect in a week. At one depot the officer in charge paid civilian farriers by piece-work, thinking to economize. In fact some of them netted in consequence as

* On mobilization there were *meant* to be three sergeant-farriers and eighteen shoeing-smiths for each cavalry regiment. Beyond these there was a variable number of men who were induced by a small premium to qualify after a few weeks' instruction as 'cold shoers'. These could nail on a shoe even if they could not fit one. (Smith, 241.)

† On one occasion it took seventy-four telegrams to get hold of a farrier for a regiment of mounted infantry. (Smith, 242.)

much as £42 a month! By the end of the war 175 civilians were being employed in remount depots alone. They worked alongside sixty army farriers and shoeing-smiths, as well as 104 Indian shoeing-smiths. Employed at the front with columns and in the veterinary hospitals were over 200 more. At the same time the depots were shoeing some 35,000 animals every month, while over 100,000 sets of horses shoes (and 70,000 mule shoes) were being imported monthly. The supply from home proved totally inadequate and therefore many had to be bought from Sweden, Germany and America. Most of the horses – 'especially the Australians' – had to be shod in stocks as they were so wild. All the clerks, also, were civilians. It was not until August, 1908, that Stevenson had an Army Service Corps staff sergeant-major accredited to him.[17]*

In view of the weakened state of so many of them it is surprising how disease-resistant the horses employed in the South African War proved to be, especially as African horse sickness (*Paard-ziekte*) at the lower altitudes and during the summer months of February to May was a special hazard, particularly in Natal. Nevertheless disease played a significant part in the abominable expenditure of animal lives, and when the veterinary historian of the war wrote of 'one of the greatest veterinary disasters of modern times', he was certainly exaggerating but not all that much. There was little African horse sickness in the 1899–1900 hot weather, but in the following two seasons at least 5,700 fatal cases among horses and over 2,000 among mules were recorded. The disease is a highly malignant one which only attacks solipeds (horses, asses and mules). A young Boer officer described the symptoms: 'The first is coughing; then the flanks heave heavily owing to its painful breathing. Ultimately it suffocates, dropping heavily to the ground, often with a leap and a plunge. Immediately after it falls a head of snow-white foam gathers at the nostrils. ... The horse is often carried off within an hour of diagnosis.' Beside sore backs and heel galls, veld sores, very similar to those which afflicted the men, quittor, a suppurative disease of the feet, caused largely by neglect in shoeing, and glanders (see Vol II, p. 38)

---

* The Boer commandos often carried a small forge with them. When they had used up all the fencing wire in an area for heating and beating into horseshoe nails, the burghers would go out at night 'near the enemy's lines and interrupt his communications in order to clip telegraph wire for our use'. Not only horseshoe nails were made on the forge. Young Roland William Schikkerling made 'forks by flattening an end of the wire and splitting it into three prongs' and also 'spurs by twisting and bending the wire to fit the boot.' (Schikkerling, 121, 164.)

were the other chief diseases prevalent. A subaltern of Imperial Yeomanry was told by the vet at one of the veterinary hospitals that 'the whole country was poisoned with glanders' but that 'people don't think so much of it out here as they do in England.'[18]

Readers of the preceding volume of this work will remember that in 1887 veterinary surgeons were finally withdrawn from cavalry regiments (except the Household Cavalry) and transferred to the Army Veterinary Department which had been formed nine years earlier (see Vol III, p. 116). Concurrently one would have expected non-regimental veterinary hospitals to have been created. This, in fact, did not happen, with the consequence that sick horses still to remain with their units, not only at home, but also on active service abroad. However, the Field Army Establishments of 1888, 1891 and 1892 provided for one 'Sick Horse Hospital', with a capacity of 300 horses, to accompany an Army Corps (with a cavalry division) on mobilization. Yet this hospital, which was to be located immediately in rear of the army, was also to serve as a remount receiving and issuing depot, while the remount depot at base was to receive both remounts from ships and sick animals for the hospital. In short, as the army's veterinary historian has put it: 'Veterinary Hospitals were utilized to hold healthy remounts, while Remount Depots contained both healthy and sick animals. Had it been desired to ensure the general infection of the army with contagious diseases, no better arrangement could have been devised!'[19]

Astonishing as this may appear, even more so is the fact that in 1898 the new edition of *War Establishments* (drawn up without consultation with the heads of the veterinary department) made no provision of any kind for the care of sick animals in the field. The single Sick Horse Hospital had been swept away.

'The only indication of the existence of a Veterinary Service was a Base Depot of Veterinary Stores, and an Advance Depot of Stores under a Farrier Sergeant! Further, *every V-Lieut-Colonel had been abolished from the Army in the Field*; the Principal Veterinary Officer alone remained, with no administrative staff to carry out his orders!

'... Thus the outbreak of war in 1899 found the Veterinary Service without the shadow of an organization, nothing more indeed (save for the P.V.O.) than the British army took with it to Flanders in 1799.'*

* In 1898 the War Office had initiated a proposal for the formation of a

As regards the supply of veterinary officers, the mobilization plans laid down an addition of fifty to the peace establishment. Since there were only fourteen in the Reserve and since the establishment did not even meet the requirements of peace conditions, every single army vet at home left immediately for South Africa, while the extra fifty had to be supplied by engaging civilian practitioners. As these were not even given temporary commissions, their authority in the army was severely limited. By the end of the war there were 322 vets working in South Africa. This was over 10% of the whole profession.[20]

*　　*　　*

In India, ever since the Afghan War of 1879–80, the need for Field Veterinary Hospitals had been recognized. The moment war seemed inevitable, Colonel Francis Duck, who had become the Director-General of the Army Veterinary Service at the War Office in 1897,* recommended that one or more of these hospitals should be sent for from India. Throughout the first year of the war these represented literally the only real semblance of properly efficient veterinary organization which existed in South Africa. The first hospital (together with fifty veterinary chests) arrived promptly at Durban on 1 October and travelled to Ladysmith next day. There both they and the Principal Veterinary Officer in South Africa were soon stranded. A second Indian field hospital arrived in mid-December,

Station Veterinary Hospital at Salisbury as an experimental measure. The Director-General of the Army Veterinary Department, Colonel Francis Duck, opposed the proposal solely on the grounds that he was not to be allowed any trained staff from his department. He would have had to rely on the loan of odd bodies from other branches. Wolseley, on the other hand, supported the idea:

'The proposal,' he minuted in February, 1899, 'is a step in the right direction because the new system for peace would be a preparation for war. In war we could not allow Cavalry Regiments to take seriously sick horses about with them. Officers Commanding Cavalry will object to the scheme; that branch is more conservative in its instincts and prejudices than the officers of other arms. All Commanding Officers protested loudly when sick soldiers of many corps were collected into one Station Hospital, but firmness based on military knowledge carried the day, and now it is only a stray fossil here and there who would go back to the old expensive system of Regimental Hospitals.'

Of all this nothing had come by the time war broke out. (*H.R.A.V.C.*, 201–2.)

* Duck, who had joined the AVD in 1867, served in various South African campaigns from 1877 to 1885. In 1894 he was appointed PVO, India. He retired in 1902, was made KCB in 1911 and died in 1934, aged eighty-nine.

1899, to be followed by another in February, 1900. From then on-wards the *ad hoc* expansion of the service accelerated fast, but not fast enough to meet the demand, until emergency measures were taken more than two years after the start of the war (see below). By the end of the war there were fifty field hospitals, of which ten were entirely Indian.* The problem of establishing and administering these vital organizations was made more difficult because only those officers who had served in India since the introduction of hospitals there possessed any experience of their working. The others had to learn from scratch and to evolve their own systems. Further, except those in the Indian hospitals, virtually every man employed was borrowed and of course quite untrained. Some were deliberately 'hiding away' from their regiments, many not being recovered for months. 'If he was a useful dresser,' wrote one veterinary officer, 'it was not to be wondered at that no active steps were taken by the hospital authorities to find out where the man's regiment actually was.' The situation was improved when in 1901 large numbers of trained dressers were sent from India.

* * *

Concurrent with the growth of hospitals, more and more farms were being bought up or commandeered for what came to be called 'debilitates'. The idea was that these warn-torn horses could re-cuperate on such 'debility farms'. (See also p. 328.) Their effective-ness, however, was impaired by a number of important defects. Due to lack of personnel to sort out the contagious sick (mainly cases of glanders and mange) from the merely exhausted, thousands of the latter became infected by the former. Again because of lack of super-vision, when the available grazing became exhausted (which con-gestion constantly ensured), horses were not infrequently left to starve. Even in the case of those farms where proper feeding and

* On the day peace was declared the staff of these fifty hospitals was an follows:

Army veterinary officers	63
Civilian veterinary surgeons	113
European dressers	79
Indian dressers	528
Civilian farriers, conductors and clerks	217
South African natives	3,547

On the same day there were 9,200 sick horses and mules on debility farms and 28,700 in the hospitals. (Smith, 224.)

adequate organization existed, few horses left them hardened enough for active service. The only way to have achieved this was to *ride* them and there were seldom enough even local boys, let alone rough-riders, to effect this. Horses never become really fit unless exercised with a man on their backs. In no other way can the backs and loins be conditioned properly. If not so conditioned, when suddenly required to carry heavy weight over long periods partial paralysis of their hind quarters soon follows. Large numbers of horses were abandoned or destroyed from this cause. None of these grave faults in the system was fully corrected throughout the war. This was largely because, as in so many other spheres, 'the war will soon be over' was the attitude which permeated all thinking.[21]

*   *   *

Until near the end of 1901 veterinary hospitals, their personnel and their necessary water-troughs, mangers and, above all, shelters for the bad cases, formed a very low priority indeed. Neither men nor material could be diverted from what were supposed to be more pressing military needs. The building of block-houses, of accommodation for sick men and for stores, and a host of other requirements took priority. This meant that the increasingly urgent cries for help of the veterinary officers in charge went unheard. By the autumn, though, when there were between 20,000 and 28,000 fresh cases of sickness occurring *every month,** the congestion in the hospitals reached crisis point. Even Kitchener could no longer ignore the gravity of the situation. Consequently on 1 December, 1901, Brevet Lieutenant-Colonel Arthur Long was appointed Inspector of Veterinary Hospitals, Remount Depots and Farms. He was

'authorized *to order in Lord Kitchener's name* everything he considered necessary. . . . Quite a feverish activity prevailed in carrying out improvements, and in building stabling. Money was poured out like water. A new hospital, costing thousands,' wrote a senior veterinary officer, 'could be obtained without hesitation, and not always with due discrimination as to the requirements of the place, or the oscillating centres of the campaign. The work was carried out under conditions approaching panic, which is always extravagant.'[22]

---

* The regulation width allowed a horse in the ranks is three feet. On this basis, 20,000 horses in line would extend over eleven miles! (Smith, 275.)

*   *   *

The excellent idea of mobile veterinary hospitals or detachments with each considerable column was occasionally adopted by individual commanders. An example is the rough and ready system which was adopted with some success during the long drive across the Eastern Transvaal in the spring of 1901. Another instance is the mobile hospital, provided with proper transport, which accompanied the columns of General Blood's operations in the Eastern and North-Eastern Transvaal in July and August, 1901. This hospital received the sick which were no longer under regimental care. These were quietly driven along in mobs of fifty, each with a white superintendent and three natives. The animals grazed as they travelled. Each day the hospital moved with the supply column, thus lessening the difficulty of feeding. From time to time the sick were evacuated to the base hospital at Middelburg. The chronic shortage of trained staff at all levels too often made such arrangements as these impossible. The war had been waging for over two years before an order directed that each column should be accompanied by a mobile hospital. Ironically, within a few days of this directive being issued, with the appointment of Colonel Long, veterinary personnel were largely withdrawn from columns. They were placed instead in the Field Hospitals on the lines of communication, thus leaving no one to take charge of the mobile hospitals.[23]

*   *   *

There is ample evidence that throughout the campaign horse stealing was not only common but almost universally prevalent. Even the most respectable and best-disciplined units seem to have thought it smart to filch any animals which seemed superior to their own, so long as they could get away with it. Lieutenant-Colonel Clowes of the 8th Hussars, for example, found that 'any horse that gets loose and is not well marked gets snapped up by another regiment at once. Its no use only branding feet.' He had $^{VIII}_{H}$ cut with scissors in 'the hair of each of my horses' quarters'. Another trick which Clowes learned was to picket his horses 'by one foreleg on to an iron peg. I find that they don't break away at nights at all with that fastening.' It also enabled them 'to lie down if they wish'.[24]

Types of horses used in South Africa

'A good, strong, well-made, hardy polo pony
was the type of animal that was wanted.'

HAROLD SESSIONS, F.R.C.V.S.

'The *raison d'être* of the heavy man and horse has
gone .... A light man, armed with a rifle, on a
hardy, wiry and enduring cob, is the cavalry
soldier of the future.'

LIEUTENANT-COLONEL W. H. BIRKBECK,
Assistant Inspector of Remounts,
December, 1900

'Only a London bushorse, that's what he was last
    year,
When he worked from Highgate Archway to the
    Strand,
A good run for his collar work, not difficult to
    steer
And pulling up quite suddenly he was grand.

Some said he came from Suffolk and was one of
    Gilbey's strain
But I think he hailed from far across the sea.
A Canadian by the colour of his coat, his kind
    of tail and mane
But they didn't give him no straight pedigree.

Only a London bushorse, but they picked him for
    the front
Without asking him if he would like to go.
When they want a slave who's willing and in a
    fight to bear the brunt,
They don't give him a chance to answer No!

So they packed off poor old Whisker and about a
    hundred more
In a transport bound for Table Bay
And they say he wasn't sea-sick on his passage
    to the war,
But was ready for his breakfast every day.

      *   *   *

Only a London bushorse by the Modder river
    lay,
A hero unremembered in the strife,
Forgotten in the shouting of the loud triumphant
    strain,
Yet he gave his all for England with his life.'

' "Whisker", a warrior, by one who knew him':
                popular music hall song

'The merits which go to make a useful horse for campaigning are infinitely more common in small horses than in big ones.'

SIR WALTER GILBEY, Bt, in 1900

'Small horses are so easy to nip on and off in a hurry.'

THE EARL OF SCARBROUGH,
Imperial Yeomanry

'A native-born pony will avoid any dark or suspicious-looking spot as by instinct, and will even pass a hole in a moment without pressure of rein or leg, but an English horse, fresh from smooth pastures or hard roads, will put his nose in the air and give his rider tumble after tumble, unless he keeps a constant lookout for holes, which is not consistent with good scouting.'

TROOPER THE HON. SIDNEY PEEL, 20th
Company, 10th Battalion, Imperial Yeomanry

'One day a couple of De la Rey's men came riding up on race horses from Sir Abe Bailey's stud farm in the district which they had commandeered .... De la Rey spoke in fatherly tones: "On commando these beautiful creatures will be dead within a week. How would you like that?" .... Crestfallen the lads rode the horses back to their stables and returned on their scraggy but hardy ponies.'

JOHANNES MEINTJES in *De la Rey –
Lion of the West*[1]

(iii)

Boer War: remount question: types of horses used in South Africa

Towards the end of the war reports were officially called for upon the qualities of the different national types of horses supplied. Over thirty generals and other senior officers in the field sent in their assessments. The chief characteristic which these reports share is their contradictory nature. Here are some typical examples. Of the imports from Russia one colonel declared that they were 'very suitable for mounted infantry work' while another thought them 'too heavily built for mounted infantry work'. Colonel Cecil William Park, commanding a mounted infantry column, considered them 'delicate feeders', but Rimington found that 'they will eat anything and pick away at the grass at every chance.' An officer of the Johannesburg Mounted Rifles averred that they had 'good feet', yet another mounted infantry officer announced that their feet were 'quite deformed'. Of the horses and cobs from the Argentine, Rimington found the cobs 'most suitable for mounted infantry', only to be contradicted by Major-General Elliot, commanding the Mobile Division, who regarded them as 'quite unsuitable, even for mounted infantry'. Of the walers sent from India, one regular cavalry commanding officer reported that they had 'done very well indeed'. French on the other hand considered them 'in every way unsuitable for campaign work'. Of course these officers were more often than not assessing completely different articles. One would have seen a certain number of a particular nationality which had been given virtually no time to acclimatize, while another would see a group from exactly the same type, even from the same batch, which had been rested for many weeks. Similarly one shipment from one of the exporting countries would be quite different in origin, size, quality and even kind from another shipment.

Nevertheless there was substantial agreement on specific points. When Thorneycroft wrote that 'too much cannot be said in praise of the Colonial-bred horse'* his opinion was almost universally echoed. 'Of course,' he added, 'in the South African horse we find a considerable strain of Arab and Thoroughbred, a combination which is hard to beat.' He might have added that the colonials – exactly the same, of course, as the class used by the Boers – were the only animals of which it could be said for certain that they had not endured a long sea voyage, suffered an unseasonal change of coat or an inadequate acclimatization period. Further, all the imported horses, with the exception of some of the Australian cobs, were unable to cope with the rocks, boulders, shale and the innumerable holes caused by ant bears and rodents which quite suddenly punctu-

---

* Of which 158,816 had been provided by the war's end. (Amery, VI, 419.)

In Natal it became common practice to send to the remount depots captured cattle not required for food. From there the animals were exchanged and bartered for horses from the local inhabitants. In 1901 alone some £60,000 of cattle were thus disposed of. (Biddulph, 126.)

At times forced requisitioning took place. In June, 1900, when 2,400 remounts were required in a hurry, picquets and sentries were placed around areas of Pretoria and 'two lines of beaters, one of cavalry and M.I. . . . and one of Colonial M.I.' produced 424 horses and 163 mules. (MacDiarmid, D. S. *The Life of Lt-Gen. Sir J. M. Grierson*, 1923, 162.)

ate the normally good going of the grassy surface of the veld. The local horses, on the other hand, were as 'nimble as goats over such a ground'.

An officer serving with Rimington's Scouts gives the best description of

'the South African pony, wretched little brute as he looks. [He] will tripple and amble on, week after week and month after month, with a heavy man on his back, and nothing to eat but the pickings of sour, dried-up veld grass and an occasional handful of Indian corn. . . . All the imported breeds will gradually languish and fade away and droop and die, worn down by the unremitting work and the bad, insufficient food; but your ragged little South African will still amble on, still hump himself for his saddle in the morning, and still, whenever you dismount, poke about for roots and fibres of withered grass as tough as himself, or make an occasional hearty meal off the straw coverings of a case of whisky bottles. With an action that gives the least possible exertion*; with the digestion of an ostrich and the eye of a pariah dog for any stray morsel of food; with an extraordinary capacity for taking rest in snatches and recouping himself by a roll whenever you take his saddle off.'

Halfway through the war, when at last the value of small native South African horses was beginning to be fully appreciated, some newly arrived cavalry regiments found, as did the Carabiniers in January, 1901, that most of the mounts which they had brought with them were 'exchanged for Boer ponies' commandeered from Cape Colony. It was not long before their worth was proved. On 25 May, 1901, two squadrons of the regiment made a considerable capture of Boers, wagons, livestock and 'a Colt gun complete with carriage'. 'A good capture,' wrote the regimental diarist, 'and impossible if we had not had better horses than we had ever had before.' In the following July the regiment did nearly seventy miles in forty-six hours with 'only two halts of half-an-hour and one hour, and with a good deal of hard fighting into the bargain. . . . Certainly,' he added, 'nothing wrong with the horses.'

At the end of January, 1901, the 7th Dragoon Guards 'commandeered 238 excellent Cape horses . . . an ideal lot for the work,' wrote Captain William Stobart Wetherly, 'by far the best horses

* 'The pace is between a trot and a canter, almost a run, and is easy for both man and horse.' (Spurgin, 13.)

the regiment had been mounted on throughout the campaign.' Among this batch and a later one were enough greys to mount a complete squadron. This proved to be a mistake for, during an action on 3 February, they 'made a splendid mark for the enemy, as the waning light and burnt veldt showed them up tremendously.' Three were killed on that occasion. At about this time, incidentally, this regiment collected 'a mob of about 100 *driven* horses with which casualties could be temporarily replaced [thus keeping] the fighting strength of the regiment up to its standard. . . . The regiment was for the first time really mobile and able to move long distances at the gallop.' The South African pony had the advantage over most of the imported animals of being virtually inured to the torments inflicted by the horse-fly, which was especially active in parts of the country. It took a long time for the English horses to become accustomed to its attentions. Those from America had known it at home. But perhaps the most useful attribute of the local ponies was their capacity for abstinence. They were 'quite satisfied with one feed of corn per day, whereas the average English horse required three, and would not touch the bushes of tough grass which were to be found on the veldt.' The Cape ponies in one Cheshire company of Imperial Yeomanry, during a fortnight's trekking 'did twenty miles and more every day on eight lbs of oats only – this is an unusually bare ration – and they did fifty miles into Colesberg in twenty-two hours, carrying the man, his arms, food, bed and horse food as easily as possible.' When unbroken, though, they could be extremely refractory. In one yeomanry unit 'some well-known steeplechase jockeys' were seen to be 'thrown heavily to the ground whilst trying to break in these animals.'

French was the only senior officer who found fault with the local mounts. Even the larger colonials, he stated, were 'not suitable' for regular cavalry. It was true, of course, that very heavy men needed larger horses than the average cavalryman needed. In part, indeed, the reason why the Household Cavalry were sent home early was the dearth of big enough horses to mount their especially heavy troopers. An advantage of the large officers' chargers and the English and Irish troop horses was their ability, denied to the Boer pony types, to carry two men out of action in an emergency.

Considerable numbers of the Colonials were, in fact, natives of Basutoland. During the first six months of the war, the Basothos were disinclined to sell their horses to the army, probably because of the uncertainty as to who was going to win (see p. 296). After the occupation of Bloemfontein sales increased speedily and continued on a large scale for the next eighteen months. In the rest of 1900 alone, 4,419 were sold to the value of £64,032. This averaged out at £14 10s for each animal. In 1901 the average price went up to £16 15s, as much as £50 per horse sometimes being paid. In that year 15,684 were sold for £262,991. As early as June, 1900, numbers of Basothos employed by the army were deserting their picket duties because their chiefs had ordered them home 'to get their horses fat'. More often than not Basotho horses could only be obtained in exchange for cattle. Sometimes as many as four or five cattle were required for one horse. These consisted chiefly of stock confiscated from the Orange River Colony.* 'Towards the end of the war,' wrote Rimington, 'everybody who could get a Colonial pony rode it in preference to any other horse.'

Strathcona's Horse (see p. 187), previous to their return to Canada early in 1901, handed over their horses – mostly Canadian 'cow-horses, that is, animals trained in round-up and all range work' – to French, whose officers thought them the very 'best seen in the country'.

> 'The animals from Canada,' reported the regiment's commanding officer, 'did not enjoy the change. Several of them bucked so badly that I had, at the request of the remount officer, to send some of the men over to remind them that they had to behave themselves. These horses had not bucked for months, yet, strange as it may seem, no sooner did they change masters than many of them began their old tricks.'

Rimington thought the Canadians 'were good. As a rule they were hardy and had been used to living on very little. They were, however, often longbacked and more suitable for draught than for riding. I think we may attribute that to the preponderance of trotting blood in Canada.'

* * *

Though the Russian cobs were usually said to possess some useful characteristics, such as docility and hardiness, their slowness was widely deplored. One divisional commander wrote that 'so long as

---

* As a result of so many of the best horses being sold during the war, the post-war stock declined alarmingly. (Warwick, P. *Black People and the South African War 1899–1902*, 1983, 70.)

they are not asked to go more than six miles an hour, they keep their condition well on Service rations.' On an occasion in 1902 the sluggishness of one of the Royals' Russian cobs led to its rider being captured. A few days later a patrol of the regiment chased and rode down a Boer mounted on the same horse. The unfortunate man relieved his feelings by shaking his fist at the miserable animal 'and cursing it fluently and vigorously'. One of the most enthusiastic comments upon the Russian cobs came from Major Maurice Hilliard Tomlin, commanding the 9th Mounted Infantry. They marched, he wrote, 'over fifty miles within twenty-four hours of being received from Remounts, and none were knocked up'. Haig found them to be 'extremely hardy; stand heat equally well as cold and keep their condition on very little food'. Two months after the war's end he found that 'the local people are all very anxious to buy Russians at the sales'. Rimington found them 'common, under-bred, straight-jointed, bad-footed, hardy brutes. I do not think,' he added in a lecture to the Military Society of Ireland, 'anybody would want to ride a Russian if he saw him, as he is an ugly brute.' Everyone was agreed that the smaller the Russian cob the better. Major-General William George Knox touched on a likely point. 'They cannot be of the best class of horse obtainable,' he wrote, 'as the military register in Russia must prevent the exportation of good horses on a large scale.' Plumer, nevertheless, found that the Russians 'came around quicker after the fatigue of a long day's trek than other re-mounts except the South African ponies.' The Scottish Horse, late in the war, was issued with 'very large quantities of Russian ponies which had had a good rest after landing and were given light work' in the regiment's Johannesburg depot before joining their squad-rons. Lord Tullibardine, commanding the regiment, told the Royal Commission that he had 'no better ponies. . . . They were too small and slow for cavalry, but suited the Scotsmen to perfection, while I issued my bigger horses to the Australians.'

Most of the Hungarians were unpopular. Colonel Birkbeck sup-posed that the breed had been spoiled over the years 'by the use of Hackney stallions'. According to Knox the Hungarian horses were 'not a patch on what was bought about 1880 for the 3rd Hussars, who were all mounted on them. Unless the breed has since deterior-ated a better class horse might have been produced for South Africa. The breed has many points in its favour for military purposes.' A distinguished veterinary surgeon found that in all his 'two and a half years' trekking, not 10% of all the Hungarian horses issued to the regiment have lasted to do any work. They are mostly weak, flat-sided, light-boned, round-jointed, long-bodied animals, which look pretty when fat and sleek, but tuck up and go to pieces with one day's work – in fact, they are what are called "Flat-catchers".' He found that 'the N. Americans were a decided improvement on the Hungarians. . . . [They] did good service, although more fitted for draught than cavalry work.' Though Haig considered that the Hungarians were 'a bad lot, but not worse than the Argentines,' he nevertheless 'rode all the way through on an Hungarian. . . . He was an exceptional one, and many people who saw him would not believe that he was an Hungarian. That shows,' he told the Royal Commission, 'that there are some Hungarians that are good.'

The Argentinians were not favoured by many: 'underbred, cowardly brutes'; 'slow, clumsy'; 'evidently sired by a cart horse; they are slow and stubborn'; 'when tired they lay down, and it was impossible to move them, even with a bayonet'. Rimington, always fair and thoughtful, reported that the Argentinian horses 'got a bad name at the beginning of the war because they were not given a chance to acclimatize, were ridden half-broken, and compelled to go on long journeys with little or no food.' Further they 'died from neglect from the Mounted Infantry'. On the other hand, French thought the Argentine *horses* quite good for regular cavalry. Colonel Birkbeck, though, maintained that 'no one who saw [the *cobs*] at the front had a good word to say for them, except the 10th Hussars.'

Of the remounts sent from home, Rimington discovered 'amongst horses branded E [for English] many which I think may be Hungarians and Canadians imported into and sold in England.' (See p. 281.) Most 'English' horses, as opposed to cobs, were condemned as being too big and requiring too much looking after. Another minor disadvantage was that their thick necks were apt to prevent them from getting their heads down to graze without breaking their breastplates.* The officer commanding the 1st Royal Dragoons reported that unless 'English' horses 'get corn and hay, and lots of it, they stand exposure badly.' Two other regular cavalry commanders thought the 'English' cob satisfactory. One mounted infantry commander said that it 'proved to be the most suitable of all imported animals'. Knox found the 'English' import 'a bit of a fool as a remount when put immediately in the field. . . . He takes

---

* The breastplate is the strap round the horse's neck, fastened to the front of the saddle and between the forelegs to the girth, which has the purpose of preventing the saddle from slipping backwards.

time to adapt to strange conditions of service . . . and is a bit like his British rider in that respect.' Some officers found that the Irish cobs and the English polo ponies stood the work better than the others. Of all the mounts imported to South Africa those which came from the London and provincial omnibus companies were probably the ones which needed least rest on arrival. This was chiefly because they were in hard condition before they left home and consequently, as Lord Roberts put it, 'benefited by the three or four weeks' rest on board ship' unlike most other imported horses which were 'principally purchased off grass runs' and which it was 'essential on board ship to keep low [so as to minimize the risk of laminitis and colic]; the result being that when they landed they were in soft condition and quite unfitted for immediate hard work.'

Many of the Australasian horses which were sent to South Africa were inferior to the well-bred among the walers which were regularly imported into India. This was because the breeders 'could not break faith with the Indian purchasers' both military and civilian. When the 1st Australian Horse marched from Paardeburg to Bloemfontein, only fifty out of 140 of their horses were fit for duty, 'the rest had died on the way, or were unserviceable.' One lieutenant-colonel, reporting in 1900, nevertheless thought them the best imported horses for South Africa. Kitchener, however, in February, 1902, noticed a 'marked deterioration in those imported since September, 1901'. A peculiarity of Australian horses was noticed by more than one officer. They proved to be less willing or accomplished swimmers.

A certain number of ponies were brought from Burma, mostly only about thirteen hands in height. Captain Francis William Mussenden of the 8th Hussars saw mounted on these some big mounted infantrymen. They looked 'very funny with their legs almost touching the ground, but they can carry any amount of weight and go on for ever.'

After Poplar Grove, Roberts asked some of the Cavalry Division's commanding officers what sort of remounts they would prefer. 'We plumped,' reported Lord Airlie, commanding the 12th Lancers, 'for Indian country breds. . . . We got thirty-five the other day, part of a present of 1,000 from (who was it?) Pathala [the Maharaja of Patiala], I think. They have done well, though only just off the ship. . . . They want less food.'[2]

* * *

There are numerous examples during the war of horses of all breeds exhibiting exceptional physical toughness. In September, 1900, for instance, a horse of the Victorian Imperial Bushmen received a bullet which 'passed right under one eye and out an inch under the other, and he has not,' reported the commanding officer, 'taken the slightest notice of it, but takes his feed and works as well as ever.' At the very first action of the 7th Dragoon Guards one of the led horses was hit on the head 'and went head over heels like a shot rabbit. The bullet went in at one ear and came out at a corresponding place on the other side. Shortly afterwards the horse got up and when the fight was over was watered at the dam . . . and ate his feed as if nothing had happened. He trekked for months afterwards.'[3]

Lieutenant Head of the Army Veterinary Department, who served throughout the war with a cavalry regiment, remarked how wonderfully well

> 'Mauser-bullet wounds do if not interfered with. I have had horses shot through the bones of the leg, the abdomen and the lungs and in the great majority of cases they were able to be led along with the troops, and quite fit again in two weeks. The bullet wound seals itself at once with coagulated blood, and heals without the formation of any matter and without becoming septic if the blood clot is not washed or picked off. This is very important in a country of dust and flies. All a bullet wound really requires is a little iodoform dusted over it to keep off the flies, and not to convert a simple wound into a serious one by attempting extraction. . . . The horses with bullet wounds that accompanied us on the march were mainly those in which the wounds implicated the soft structures, and it is to these that my remarks about non-interference apply.'

His experience led him to believe that 65% of bullet wounds 'either cause death outright, or so seriously injure the animal that it cannot leave the field. In a small percentage of cases animals which can carry their rider out of action were found subsequently to be incurable' and had to be destroyed.[4]

Starvation of horses in South Africa

'This has been a dreadful war for the horses. I
have had in my squadron alone 500 horses since
we started.'

SQUADRON SERGEANT-MAJOR COBB,
7th Dragoon Guards, to his wife,
25 February, 1901

'There were greater difficulties with regard to the
distribution of forage in the field than with
regard to the distribution of food for the troops.'

*Report of the Royal Commission on the
War in South Africa*

'The pathetic sight of some unfortunate animal
too weak to move or even eat, gazing wistfully
after a retreating column, was only too frequent,
and could not fail to touch even the hardest heart.'

MAJOR N. D. H. CAMPBELL, 7th Dragoon
Guards, November, 1900

'A sufficiency of grain is necessary to enable
horses to stand hard work, but they will never
keep in condition unless they have an ample
supply of hay or some bulky equivalent.'

LORD ROBERTS, *Circular Memorandum,
No. 5*, 26 January, 1900

'The transport required for the food of 1,000
horses would suffice for that of 12,000 men.'

LORD ROBERTS's evidence to the
Royal Commission

'18 May, 1900. The grass is drying up fast and
then I don't know what will be done for forage.
Rains come in August.'

LIEUTENANT-COLONEL CLOWES,
8th Hussars[1]

(iv)

Boer War: remount question: shortage of forage and grazing

During February and March, 1900, the mostly 'English' troop horses
of the Cavalry Division were exposed to something approaching
actual starvation. They were ill-prepared to face it, largely because
of grossly inadequate feeding in the preceding months. It is a major
tragedy of the war that in November, 1899, Buller laid down a
forage ration which the Acting Principal Veterinary Officer in South

Africa condemned at the time as possibly enough for the light pony of the country in peacetime but nothing less than a starvation diet for the large cavalry trooper horse expected to work as hard day after day as any in military history. Buller and his chief staff officer both had first-hand experience of South African mounted warfare, for both had served in the Zulu War of 1879 (see Vol III, p. 187). They had then dealt almost exclusively with local horses of small breeds with no acclimatization problems, in the hands of comparatively small numbers of colonials fighting against natives in only one part of the country and for only a few days at a time.

This misleading experience was not the sole reason for the low ration scale. Government policy and parsimony, as has been shown, coincided to impose an initial inhibition against both commandeering and buying from the Cape Dutch farmers. Further, the difficulties of conveying hay and corn by the single line railways, though formidable, were often overestimated.* These causes were responsible for a daily ration which was much lower than that allowed for peacetime manoeuvres at home. It worked out at an average of eight pounds of grain and eight of hay. It nevertheless varied considerably depending upon the available supply. Very often hay, which was so important for bulk, and all of which according to regulations had to be found within the theatre of war, was almost non-existent, while the largest quantity of grain allowed was ten pounds. It was of course argued that a proper daily allowance of grain, which for the large horse in work ought to be not less than fifteen pounds, was impossible to supply. If that really was the case, it is obvious (and easy to say after the event) that a smaller mounted force would have answered better. 50,000 horses given fifteen pounds to thrive on are clearly to be preferred to 75,000 given ten pounds to starve on. On the march from Bloemfontein to Pretoria when the horses of the Cavalry Division died like flies, there was literally no hay available and sometimes only five pounds of oats a day could be issued. It is

* Considerable quantities were imported from various parts of the world. With that which arrived from South America, there came a noxious, foul-smelling weed, *Althermarathera achyrantha*. Known to this day as 'khaki weed', it still appears in the mealie fields, in spite of vigorous efforts to eradicate it. Another weed, known as tulip-grass (the common name for several herbs of the genus *Homeria*), indigenous to most parts of South Africa, is highly poisonous. It comes up with the first young grass and has a small yellow flower. Horses, unfortunately, will eat it ravenously. It is often fatal to them. Numbers died from eating it when care was not taken to stop grazing wherever tulip-grass was seen.

an astonishing fact that troop horses at home, standing in stables and working on average one hour a day, and that usually under a stripped saddle, were allowed twenty-two pounds a day. Further, on manoeuvres that ration was invariably increased.*

Remount headquarters at the Cape were constantly being pressed by commanding officers to ensure that only small cobs were asked for. 'The rations,' pleaded one officer, 'won't keep any animal over 14.2 hands alive.' An official report to the War Office near the end of 1901 stated that units 'keep demanding ponies, which are the only things they can feed enough to keep them alive.' The good effects of feeding up horses during their first few weeks after disembarkation were illustrated by the case of one Imperial Yeomanry regiment which was fortunate enough to spend some six weeks at base before being sent up country. During that time its horses received about sixteen pounds of forage a day. 'Those horses,' said Lord Chesham, Inspector-General of Imperial Yeomanry, 'lasted a long time and did very good work.'

There can be no doubt that the appalling magnitude of the hopeless struggle to deal with the many hundreds of sick and debilitated animals after the capture of Bloemfontein in early 1900 was the result of protracted under-feeding. One who took part in that ghastly struggle described what the wretched beasts looked like:

'They were living skeletons, covered with a tightly-drawn skin through which projected all the unshrinkable part of the frame. The head looked too big for the body, the sockets over the eyes were cups, the ears drooped, the lips pendulous, the eyes staring and anxious. Of the neck there was nothing but *ligamentum muchae* and the bones. The back was that of a skeleton, every rib distinct up to its head, deep gutters existed on either side of the vertebrae, and the latter stood up from the withers to tail as if subcutaneously cleaned of their muscular covering. The abdomen appeared not to exist; had the animal been eviscerated and sewn up no greater collapse would have been evident. The prominences on the pelvis stood out as in the actual skeleton, the hip joint was a rounded mass with deep cavities in front and behind; the anus was widely open, the tail powerless. From side to side this living skeleton swayed and crossed its hind legs if compelled to move. When tied up in batches they leant against each other, and the centres collapsed under the pressure. There

* For peacetime rations and frequency of feeding, see Vol III, p. 393.

were hundreds of such cases, and scores and scores of these complicated with sore backs of the most formidable character, the withers being as a rule affected and the bones hopelessly destroyed. There were hundreds lame, generally from laminal congestion rather than acute laminitis, and scores were foot-sore. The majority of the animals were past all chance of re-covery within a reasonable time, if ever; in fact, we cannot call to mind any case which had proceeded to the stage described which recovered. Food appeared to do them but little good, corn did harm, for it could not be digested, they died by scores daily. A cold or wet night settled for ever the fate of the weakest. Even those a little stronger were unable to rise in the morning, and unless assistance was at hand never rose again. Cases would drag on and then die when rest and grazing might have been expected to work recovery.

'These wrecks of a war, this flotsam and jetsam of human passions and strife, these helpless victims of a policy of the grossest cruelty and gravest injustice, were dying by hundreds, anywhere and everywhere: in camps, in the streets of the town, in any water supply,* and bodies could be found in every donga. The air was poisoned by their decomposition.'

During the thirty days of the operations between Modder River and Bloemfontein, the Cavalry Division alone, as has been shown, lost 42% of its horses, while roughly one-third of the horses of the entire force became useless. As late in the war as June, 1901, an officer of the 18th Hussars recorded that with 12° of frost, 'the wretched horses are absolutely starved with cold, besides which they only get eight pounds of oats per day, no hay, very little grazing and are worked daily often from 6 and 7 a.m. till 7 p.m.' The inadequate forage ration which was chiefly responsible for this disgraceful state of affairs was set at its low scale largely on the assumption that there would always be sufficient grazing to make it up to what was essen-tial for continuous hard work often under daunting conditions.[2] This assumption was fatally misconceived because in a war with an ubiquitous enemy armed with long-range weapons, animals can seldom be allowed to wander about in search of grass even if there is time for them to do so. Since it takes a horse about an hour to eat

---

* As soon as the troops left Kroonstad, where the Valsch River is dammed to furnish the town's water supply, the Medical Officer of Health began removing the carcasses of horses which had collected in the dam. After extracting 700 in a month he ceased to keep a record! (Smith, 118.)

47. Lt-Col The Earl of Airlie (see p. 84)   48. Lt-Gen. Sir Bindon Blood (see p. 219)

49. F-M Earl Roberts

John Charlton

50. The Boers charging at Bakenlaagte 1902 (see p. 256)

three pounds of cut hay, he very obviously takes longer to eat the same quantity when he has to find his fodder himself. Further, there are large stretches of the veld at certain times of the year, especially August and September, which yield very little grazing and many others where the grass is at best thin, tall and soon consumed. Then again English cavalry horses, used to manger feeding, 'were as helpless on the veldt as the town-bred soldier. They did not know what was expected of them; when they had purchased a little experience, the grazing had been eaten up by mules and herds of oxen.' What every good horsemaster knew from observation was, to quote Rimington who was one of the best of them, that for sustained hard work carrying heavy weights, horses 'must have a bellyful. I use wheat or even barley straw, or green mealie stalks to stuff their bellies out, and use bran when obtainable for the same reason.'

The war had been going on for many months before proper feeding troughs or mangers, even in the standing camps and hospitals, were anything like plentiful. Without them there was always a shocking waste of forage. 'I calculated,' wrote the veterinary surgeon in charge of the Middelburg hospital in the Transvaal, 'that in feeding horses off the ground, one-third of the grain ration was lost by being trodden under foot, and in wet weather feeding becomes impossible.' Nose-bags were only a partial answer to this problem, for even when they eventually arrived in quantity, there were never enough horse attendants in camps and hospitals to feed large numbers by this method.[3]

* * *

By the time Lord Roberts arrived, commanding officers' and veterinary surgeons' complaints about the low ration scale had reached large proportions. He himself, an experienced horsemaster, at once sent his Acting Principal Veterinary Officer to the front and almost immediately received the report that no grazing was to be had 'within reasonable reach of any of the camps occupied by the western and central forces' and that what there had been in the vicinity of the Orange River had been eaten by locusts. Unfortunately the urgency of the operations at that time required every locomotive and wagon to be used for concentrating the large force needed for the relief of Kimberley. In consequence nothing was then done to augment the forage ration. Had it been done six weeks earlier, the virtual prostration of the cavalry which followed would almost certainly have been avoided. That Kitchener when he assumed command never saw fit to make the increase was partly due to the continuing belief that the war would soon be over and partly because his understanding of equine problems was, as has been shown time and time again, manifestly slight.[4]

All too often the military programme exacerbated the forage shortage. On occasions columns were ordered to destroy the grass on the veld by burning* and even to throw captured grain into rivers. The policy of laying waste vast areas, destroying thousands of tons of grain and thousands of acres of growing crops, so as to deny them to the enemy, was often carried out by men on half-starved horses: a paradox indeed.[5]

Perhaps the most shockingly outrageous instance of cruelty through inefficiency which the present author has come across in his painful researches into the question of horse starvation is that reported by Lieutenant Rankin of Rimington's Guides. In 'a high-boarded railway truck' he witnessed 'a mob of gaunt horses kicking each other out of the way in their efforts to get at and eat their own dung.' These pitiable animals had not, it seems, been fed since leaving Cape Town more than forty-eight hours previously. 'Fifty yards away, across the line, huge stacks of trussed hay were looming heavenwards.'[6]

* Orders prohibiting this practice were published in April, 1900, and July, 1901.

" ABANDONED ! "

15

'The weapon which is of highest importance to the cavalryman – after the essential spirit of untiring keenness and "go" – is his horse, and practical horsemastership is his most useful qualification.'

BADEN-POWELL in 1906

'As a rule cavalry officers are bad horsemasters, having no idea of taking care of their horses. This important part of their duties is utterly neglected.'

THE EARL OF SCARBROUGH to the
Royal Commission

'Like a woman, a horse is subject to moods, and, to continue the analogy, it is necessary to coax them out of him with subtlety and a knowledge of what is likely to do the most good and at the same time do little or no harm.'

BADEN-POWELL in 1914

'What man who crosses a horse for the first time in his life would care to be handicapped by going out to meet in combat the finest natural mounted rifleman that the world has ever produced?'

A Veterinary Officer in South Africa

'It is absolutely impossible if Cavalry are to do their work that they can be laden as they were in the last campaign.'

SIR JOHN FRENCH to the *Royal Commission*

'The regular cavalry, otherwise admirable soldiers, looked upon a horse not as an aid to mobility but as a vehicle of transportation, lumbering it up with God knows what until it resembled a pedlar's mule.'

LIEUTENANT J. F. C. FULLER'S *Journal*, 1902

'The Mounted Infantry used to carry very heavy kits, and then came the order from Pretoria to reduce the kits, and the men threw away the pots and pans they used to carry.'

PRINCE FRANCIS OF TECK to the
Royal Commission[1]

*Boer War: the remount question: poor horsemastership – squadron
system introduced – amateurism of officers – sitting on horseback
too much – sore backs – saddles – cavalry weights*

Except at the very end of the war, horsemastership, or the art of
looking after horses, was, with one important and a few other exceptions abysmal in all branches of the army. Horsemanship, or the art
of riding, on the other hand, was rather better understood. Sir Ian
Hamilton rightly pointed out to the Royal Commission that 'horsemanship and horsemastership together spell mobility'. It is clear that
the British lack of mobility compared with the Boers' innate capacity
for it was a major reason why it took two and a half expensive years
to end the conflict. A study of the extent to which these two matters,
especially horsemastership, were dealt with is therefore of the first
importance. It was not to be expected that the thousands of infantrymen who were placed without previous training on saddleback (an
expression, incidentally, first used with this meaning in 1899) should
be anything other than indifferent horsemasters or horsemen.*
Rimington put it succinctly when he said that a foot soldier placed
on a horse 'did not know whether to feed it on beef or mutton'.[2] In
the last few months of the war, however, according to Kitchener,
they 'improved very much in the matter of looking after their
horses,' and, of course, with practice their riding ability improved
too. What comes as a surprise and a shock is to discover how feeble
was the horsemastership of most of the regular cavalry and of the
trained mounted infantry. 'It has been contended,' writes the historian of the 12th Lancers, 'that the British cavalry officer talked more
and knew less about horses than anyone else on earth.' Sir Evelyn

---

* Not only infantrymen were poor horsemasters. Lord Chesham, noticing on
two consecutive days that a certain private of an Imperial Yeomanry regiment
was leading his horse, rode up to him and congratulated him on the care he was
taking of his animal. 'The man shook his head. "Oh, it ain't that, sir," he
replied. "He ain't touched in 'is back, but I've lost my left-hand stirrup-leather."
Chesham, astonished, said, "Well, mount on the other side, then!" – to receive
the incredulous cockney retort, "Get along with you! Why, if I did that I'd be
faicing the wrong waiy!" ' (Birdwood, 112.)
    Another yeoman, belonging to the 24th Company, wrote in March, 1901:
'We got a draft of men and it was a pantomime when they got their horses
(rough horses off the veldt). The air was full of arms and legs and saddlery.
When the dust cleared there were men lying in all directions and they lost thirty
horses, saddles and all! Funniest sight I've seen since leaving Penrith!' (From a
MS letter in an anonymous scrapbook advertised in Booklist No. 50, Woodford
Bookshop.)

Wood believed that 'as a race' we were not good horsemasters compared with other nations. This generalization may or may not have been true, but to find out why so many otherwise highly trained men of the mounted arm, whose very lives depended upon their horses, should have been so callously and inefficiently indifferent to their welfare, it is necessary to look more deeply into the organization, training and outlook of both officers and men. The problem is to discover why 'the average non-commissioned officer or trooper', in Hamilton's words, 'does not possess a sufficiently intimate knowledge of or affection for his horse to enable him to nurse and save it when making an exceptional effort.' One answer came from an Imperial Yeomanry trooper in Paget's Horse, who believed, probably with justice, that the expression 'to swear like a trooper' originated with the horses.

'Those noble creatures,' wrote Trooper Cosmo Rose-Innes, 'are responsible. They spend their leisure time in devising new means of exasperating those whose duty it is to attend them. When hungry they will fight so hard to get at the food that it takes a quarter of an hour to fasten on the nosebag. Once on, they will endeavour to spill every grain of corn, so that one must stand and watch them feed, conscious that it means one gulp of scalding coffee for breakfast, a biscuit shoved in the pocket, and then "saddle-up". You have but to stand quietly beside them for a few moments and the fore hoof is carefully placed upon your toe, and when in your agony you strike at the horse he dodges the blow and you strike the bit.'[3]

A cursory look at most of the Continental cavalry of the time and at the native cavalry of India is enough to show that their horsemastership was greatly superior to that of the British regulars. It was universally agreed, too, that the men of the British artillery, both field and horse, were generally good horsemasters – infinitely better than the cavalry and mounted infantry.* There are, nevertheless, a very few isolated examples from the past of exceptionally good horse management on the part of the regular cavalry. One such is the

* Major-General Frederick Smith, the leading military vet of the age, thought the artillery without superiors as horsemasters. He nevertheless wrote of 'the Epsom salts, diuretic ball and tonic powder management so common in the artillery.... Unfortunately they love drugs and nostrums, and attribute to these results which are really the outcome of their own admirable care and supervision. Their weak spot is their love of a fat horse.' (Smith, 161.)

remarkable performance of the 19th Hussars in the Nile campaign of
1884–5 (see Vol III, p. 346) where operations were at least as testing
as, but considerably less prolonged than, any encountered in South
Africa. Another instance is the extraordinary feat of a squadron of
the 17th Lancers during the Indian Mutiny campaign of 1858–9 (see
Vol II, p. 218). This squadron marched some 5,000 miles in twelve
months, including one stretch of 176 miles, halting only to feed, and
another of forty miles a day for six consecutive days. They lost only
two horses in the year, not counting battle casualties. In South
Africa, by contrast, each regular regiment in one cavalry brigade
averaged during some 2,000 miles of marching, 70% wastage
monthly, including only a very small proportion of killed or
wounded in action. This was not at all exceptional. For example,
after the 7th Dragoon Guards' first week of trekking, half of their
horses were unfit for duty. 'Exhaustion, sore backs and laminitis,'*
writes the regiment's historian, 'had swept through the ranks like
the destroying angel, leaving behind on the veldt a long trail of
putrefying carcasses.' One troop of the regiment, three weeks later
had lost thirty-one out of its original thirty-six mounts, 'only a small
proportion having been killed in action'.

The Imperial Yeomanry's record is even worse. In two months
of 1901 600 remounts were issued to two companies of the second
contingent, although they were engaged in nothing more demanding than ordinary outpost and convoy work. The attitude of some
of the yeomanry is disagreeably shown by a North Country man's
confession that finding the coal truck in which he and twenty-five
of his comrades were travelling was too crowded, 'a few of us sat
in the horse-trucks. We found that to be perched on a rough, sharp-
edged rail was not so comfortable as could be desired, so climbing

* Laminitis, known as 'fever of the feet' is an inflamed condition of the fleshy
leaves which are found beneath the wall of the hoof and covering the coffin bone.
   'It is generally caused by over-exertion, particularly when the animal is in
   an unfit state to undergo it; horses which have been at rest for some time,
   especially if they have been overfed, being very likely to suffer if suddenly
   put to heavy work. In animals which are unshod it is often a sequel to foot-
   soreness, and after a sea voyage it is of frequent occurrence unless care is
   taken to graduate the exercise given immediately on landing.'
The treatment officially recommended included: 'Make the animal take a little
exercise several times a day, a few minutes at a time, and keep cold swabs over
the hoofs', hardly a prescription easy of achievement on active service! (*Official
Animal Management*, 1908, 339). (See p. 333 for other equine diseases suffered
in the war.)

down, we sat on the horses' backs. Luckily the poor animals were too sick of life to object much to this unexpected treatment.'[4]

Most of the colonial small wars where British regular cavalry was employed were of comparatively short duration and the enemy's cavalrymen, if they existed at all, were not in most cases notably better at caring for their horses. Further, the area of operations was infinitely smaller than it was in the South African War. The extra wear and tear caused by marching continuously over immense distances was virtually unknown. It can be said therefore that good horsemastership was not an important prerequisite for an army maintained chiefly for quelling backward peoples on restricted battlefields: or, rather, that such an army managed to get by without the deficiency being generally noticed. When, however, it came to longer-lasting wars against other so-called 'civilized' armies, it did not take very long for the weakness to became palpable. The most conspicuous instance was during the Peninsular War where the German Legion's horsemastership was again and again shown to be so much better than that of their British allies that Sir John Burgoyne could say with some justice that they were always able to put 100 horses in the ranks to the British ten. Captain Mercer of the Royal Artillery found during the Waterloo campaign that the German dragoon would sell everything he had to feed his horse, whereas his British counterpart looked upon the animal 'as a curse and source of perpetual drudgery to himself' and would 'sell his horse itself for spirits'.[5] Moreover it is notorious that in the Crimea the horses of the two cavalry brigades fared considerably worse than those of the horse artillery.

During the short Egyptian campaign of 1882 starving cavalry horses were seen on one occasion standing next to a growing corn crop. It was said at the time that those in command failed to recognize it as a forage plant. It seems just as likely, though, that the junior officer in charge was waiting for higher authority. In either case this is an example of a chief cause of the regular cavalry's poor horsemastership. Another example is given by Lord Methuen. When he was marching through the Marico district 'living from hand to mouth', he noticed that many of the regular cavalry's nosebags were empty, 'although the Yeomen and Colonials had theirs all full of mealies. The two latter [it is interesting that he found the Imperial Yeomanry (first contingent) better than the regular cavalry] required no telling; the Cavalry soldier, on the contrary, had probably received no definite instructions. He had not been trained to look out for himself and use his own intelligence.' Rimington's Scouts were a shining example of the exact opposite attitude. 'The moment a man gets off his horse he throws the reins over the horse's head,' wrote their commander, 'and the horse stands and grazes. . . . He is always nibbling whenever the man is dismounted.' Rimington also made his Scouts off-saddle at every opportunity, even if only for five minutes. Having light Colonial saddles with very little on them (see below), it was no great trouble for the rider to unlace the girth. It took him but a moment to slip the saddle on again. (But see p. 112.) 'In the retreat from Sannah's Post [see p. 160] my men were all off-saddled while the Boers were pressing us, but it was a good habit.'* In reply to questions put to him by the Royal Commission, Rimington said that horse management was 'absolutely the first thing in a campaign. It is 75 per cent of the campaign as far as I can see.' Asked by Lord Elgin, the Commission's chairman, whether he did not use 'rather drastic measures with the men who did not treat their horses well,' he replied 'Yes, we made their lives a burden to them.' He laid down that 'men who give sore backs should not be at once remounted or sent to a base, whether horses are available or not, but should be made to go on picquet on arrival at camp.' Lord Strathcona, a Commission member, asked Rimington: 'You do not mean that there should be any disregard of the health of the men?' Back came the answer: 'I disregard the men's health completely compared with the horses. A man can speak up for himself, and will no doubt do so and go to the doctor, but the horse cannot say anything.' In his written evidence he even went so far as to state that 'with all mounted troops extreme severity and absolute disregard for the men's health, feelings, or safety is necessary.'[6]

* * *

Shortly before the outbreak of war an important reform in cavalry organization had taken place. The troop was succeeded by the squadron as the basic unit. Under the old system, as has been shown

* A prime example of the *bad* habit is related by Birdwood. In the course of a long wait during which a ridge in front of Strathcona's Horse was being reconnoitred, he noticed that the men were 'sitting on their horses, leaning on the high pummels of their saddles. . . . I rode up to Colonel Steele and suggested that he should dismount his men. His reply was to turn round to his regiment and bawl: "Ye sons of ——! Why the —— —— are you sitting on your —— horses?" – whereupon the regiment dismounted!' (Birdwood, 113.)

in the earlier volumes of this work, the squadron and troop officers had no more than a slender control over their horses and the minimum of interest in their welfare. All questions of stable management and diet were strictly regulated from the top. In most regiments, indeed, no horse could be taken out of its stable without the commanding officer's express permission, while the ridingmaster was the only officer supposed to possess the expertise to train the whole of the various squadrons' horses. The troop officer was allowed only the smallest possible degree of initiative and given little more than nominal responsibility. He was not expected to gain practical experience of horse management, while the lifeless routine to which he was committed was just as well, indeed often better, carried out by his troop sergeant-major. Haig considered that the main lesson of the war was that 'modern conditions of warfare entail higher training of the individual'[7]. (See also p. 435.) This applied at least as much to the care of horses as to any other military matter. Lord Roberts told the Royal Commission that the average regular soldier's 'individuality had been so little cultivated that his natural acuteness was checked and his want of resourcefulness marked'. He added that the mounted troops' performances during the war

'would have been attended by less waste had the men been better horse-masters. It is not sufficient that Cavalry or Mounted Infantry should be able to ride, but they must know how to get the utmost out of their horses by good treatment and never-failing consideration of their wants. The discouragement of individuality and the practice of training men to work under all circumstances in numbers and to follow precise rules is to blame. A man should be taught to ride as an individual, and not as one of a squad, and the same with horse management. Until the soldier is held directly responsible for, and so takes a personal interest in, the condition of his charger, until he learns to rely on his own common-sense and experience, not merely on the orders of his superior . . . our horsemastership is sure to be indifferent.'[8]

The new squadron system was designed to give the squadron commander, at least, more responsibility than hitherto. Under it he was in theory held responsible for the training and welfare of both his men and his troops' horses to a greater degree than before. A reform of this sort, however, takes much time to become effective, particularly, as in this case, when a completely new outlook on behalf of the officers must be developed. Many of them were far from anxious to assume a greater degree of independence which carried with it increased responsibility and therefore expenditure of time. It is certain that by the autumn of 1899 the new system had not yet borne fruit.

The old system had grown up over many years and was the inevitable result of the amateurism of British cavalry officers. Unlike those in the artillery and engineers who had to prove a certain measure of expertise before being commissioned and unlike those in Continental armies who made soldiering a life's calling, the regular cavalry officer was very much a part-timer. He could, and more often than not did, come into the service for a few years (during each of which a number of months were spent on leave) and then retire when it suited him. Under these circumstances he could not hope to obtain the sustained training necessary for good practical, individual horsemastership which he ought to have been in a position to pass on to the men under him. French, who was naturally as uncritical of his cavalry as possible, told the Royal Commission that the training of regimental officers and men,

> 'especially in regiments from England, had been too narrow. They understood,' he said, 'stable management better than the care of horses in the field. . . . For example, at the commencement of the campaign, partly owing to strict orders re looting, many opportunities of foraging were neglected . . . . Few officers or men understand how to feed horses on maize, barley or wheat, which were often to be found in the farms; they either over-fed them, thereby impairing their digestions and giving them Laminitis, or refused to risk this evil, neglecting available supplies. Towards the end of the campaign officers understood better the moderate use of unaccustomed feed, and how to keep horses fit on whatever supplies were available.'[9]

Even under a more favourable, flexible peacetime system a proper understanding of the art of horsemastership was difficult to achieve unless prolonged manoeuvres, realistically simulating war conditions, could be carried out, which lack of training areas and paucity of funds always prevented. Nor was any improvement to be expected while horses and men failed to get out of stable and riding school often enough to experience the real difference between barracks and field. These desirable objects were always frustrated by government parsimony. Large-scale manoeuvres, which soon after the Crimean

War had been begun, largely at the insistence of the Prince Consort (see Vol II, p. 406), had been gradually dropped chiefly on the grounds of cost, while excessive mollycoddling of troop horses was encouraged so as to cut down the expense of having to replace them. 'Hitherto,' wrote Haig in 1903, 'there has been too much pampering in peacetime.'[10]

Further, a very important psychological factor which militated against good horse management was the *folie de grandeur* which made it a point of honour for the cavalryman to be seen off his horse's back as little as possible, lest he should be reduced to the status of a mere infantryman.* Rimington found that 'a great fault with most

L'homme propose   *mais le C.O. dispose.!*

troops' in South Africa was their determination to remain on horse-back. 'The ordinary cavalry soldier,' he wrote, 'gets into a habit of it at the Riding School.' Rimington's Scouts were always made to dismount when going down hill. Going up hill he found it an advantage for his men to remain mounted (because the saddle gets well shifted back, which is a good thing), [also] if you are scouting you want to be on the horse when you are going up hill because you do not know what is going to happen when you get to the top.' Lieutenant-General Rundle (see p. 178) found that it was almost impossible to get the men of the Imperial Yeomanry regiments to get off their horses when they halted. 'They would sit upon them for half an hour unless somebody told them to get off.' In April, 1900, an order from Government House, Bloemfontein, read in part: 'Lord Roberts has frequently observed that men remain

* Other minor reasons are suggested in Vol II, p. 431.

mounted when there is no necessity for it, and on the line of march he has never yet seen the horse being led.'[11]

The artilleryman's training, on the other hand, was exactly the opposite. It was driven in upon him from the very start of his career that without his horses he and his precious guns were useless encumbrances. He was taught that it was a crime to remain on horseback a moment longer than was really essential. The artilleryman's creed was that his horse was his first consideration. The cavalryman, on the other hand, too often thought that at best his horse was, in Rimington's words, 'a very weary and irksome necessity', that it was merely a conveyance, a machine that needed the minimum of maintenance.[12] There were honourable exceptions to this attitude, but under the conditions of the South African War, when it seemed that the supply of remounts was inexhaustible, there was little incentive for the average man to vary it. One veterinary officer who saw a great deal of the war said that 'the moment officers and men realized that another horse was forthcoming when the present one was ridden to a standstill, care was thrown to the winds.' Moreover, it was not easy for officers and men to keep up interest in the condition of horses whose rations left them half-starved. French went so far as to tell the Royal Commission that he thought horsemastership in the field was 'altogether a matter of feeding'.[13]

The same cavalier attitude which made so many cavalry officers consider that the boring details of horse welfare were beneath their notice existed among most staff officers and nearly all the generals. Lord Roberts, with his Indian experience behind him, was a shining example of the opposite. As soon as he took over, he issued ever more frequent and peremptory orders about the care of horses. But neither these nor those which came later and less often from Kitchener's headquarters seem to have had more than a minimal effect. Kitchener's policy of centralization in the last phases of the war did nothing to encourage obedience to his orders. It was a major cause of the terrible destruction of horses. As *The Times History* puts it:

'Lord Kitchener directed the movements of almost every column from Pretoria. . . . A column would start with soft horses straight from the depot, or come in with its animals entirely exhausted and find orders to be at some spot forty miles away at dawn. The commander might know that to obey would kill half his horses and make his column impotent for weeks; but to fail might wreck the whole combination and certainly wreck his own prospects, and so the horses were sacrificed.'

Rimington and Brabazon were two of the chief examples of senior officers who positively bothered about horse care. 'I really believe, although I say it,' Brabazon told the Royal Commission, 'that I was the only General Officer who tried to stop the abuse of horseflesh. I never saw such shameful abuse of horseflesh. . . . I never saw an irregular man go except at a gallop – he thought that was the normal pace for a horse. If he rode into Pretoria to get a tooth-pick or a glass of beer, he would gallop his eight or ten miles there and back.'[14]

The most shocking cases among the hastily mounted infantrymen occurred soon after Lord Roberts's arrival, when the overwhelming need to make all fighting troops mobile caused new mounted infantry battalions to be formed almost overnight. These were raised by the simple method of each battalion being required to furnish the men of one company and put them on horses as completely untrained, of course, as their riders. (See p. 112.) Well might Kipling's 'M.I.' say:

> '. . . We are the beggars that got
> Three days "to learn equitation" an' six months
> o' bloomin' well trot.'

On one night march during the advance which led to the relief of Kimberley, Colonel Hannay's column which included five batta-lions of these newly raised mounted infantry contained, in the words of the *Official History*, many 'rank & file [who] crossed a horse that day for the first time in their lives. In the darkness . . . the horses often stumbled, and their riders fell. The animals went on with the column, leaving their masters[!] on the ground. . . . To allow the stragglers . . . to rejoin it was found necessary to halt all day.' The night march covered ten miles. It took eleven and a half hours to complete. These unfortunate men and their mounts skirmished with the enemy a short time afterwards and not surprisingly forty became casualties. The enormity of trying to create horsemen, let alone horsemasters, without even a single day's training can only be appreciated when it is realized that even a skilled man with a trained horse found it difficult to mount and dismount from a military saddle with its mountain of impedimenta, when the leg had to be raised high and wide to avoid entanglement. Colonel Hannay's men, even if they managed to mount and to keep their seat, had to cope with 100 rounds of ammunition across their shoulders, weighing over eight pounds, as well as their rifle weighing ten pounds and a bayonet, water bottle and haversack. The commander of the Scottish Horse found that the Australians in its ranks

'knew most about horses, but owing to their being accustomed to getting a large supply of horses in their own home they were apt to use up their horses too quickly. Had they been less good horsemen they would have been better horsemasters, but the best Australians left nothing to be desired. . . . The South African enlisted man was a bad horsemaster and had none of that love of a horse which is so strong in an Australian. Scotsmen: Very fair horsemasters, owing to their ignorance about horses and their willingness to do exactly on all occasions what they were told to do; also they seldom had any ambition to gallop their horses, but preferred to go quietly.'[15]

*   *   *

The related questions of types of saddle and the total weight to be carried by horses were vitally important to the whole problem of horsemastership, the prevention of sore backs being perhaps the most important single aspect of it. In the seven decades following Waterloo very little serious, let alone scientific, thought had been given to the question of sore backs. It was an absolute maxim that every sore back resulted exclusively from the carelessness of the man who sat on it. Though this was certainly a part of the problem, it was far from being the whole of it. While every sore back was a punishable crime, the incentive to conceal it was enormous. There were numerous examples of this cruel practice during the war. Many were connived at by commanding officers, who would not allow cases to be reported to the veterinary officers till they were so terrible that the back was literally raw. Their usual reason was the desire to show a good paper strength at a time when remounts were temporarily hard to come by immediately before an advance. The Acting Principal Veterinary Officer in South Africa when he inspected the invalids on Fischer's Farm in April, 1900, was horrified less at the large numbers than at the excessive severity of the cases, all of which should have been dealt with long before they were actually reported. Very few of these miserable wretches were ever again able to take the weight of a rider. Not until the 1890s was the lesson which the veterinary department had been teaching for decades beginning to be learned by the cavalry. Only then did the design, and particularly the adaptability, of saddles at last become an earnest study.[16]

By chance, just in time for the war, a new, revolutionary cavalry riding saddle had evolved as the result of many a committee's deliberations. It was known as the 'Steel Arch Universal Pattern'. (For its predecessors see Vol II, p. 425–7 and Vol III, p. 403.) It was very strong, the arch standing a strain of six hundredweight, and though weighing 28 lbs it was lighter than any of its forerunners. One of its revolutionary features was that the stirrup was no longer attached by putting the leather through a hole cut in the sideboard, which in earlier types had been a prolific cause of sore backs. On the whole this saddle met with the cautious approval of officers and men, though Sir Evelyn Wood was not the only expert who still thought it 'too heavy and cumbersome'. Lord Tullibardine of the Scottish Horse found that the burrs in front of the side bars were quite unnecessary and that they interfered with 'the play of the shoulder'. These were removed in later models. When fully loaded with all the impedimenta normally attached to it, without which the British mounted man seemed unable to operate, it usually took two men to lift it on and off the horse's back. Consequently, 'no commanding officer worth his salt was going to unsaddle when he might be called upon to move at short notice.'[17] (For later improvements and the 1912 saddle see p. 448.)

As with nearly all items of equipment, there was a chronic shortage of saddles at the war's beginning. In mid-December, 1899, there were in South Africa only 500 cavalry sets* in reserve 'to meet the wear and tear' of 16,000 issued. There were a further 500 in reserve for the mounted infantry. At that time 11,500 sets were being demanded from home! (See also p. 112.) During the first few months of the war the Cape and Natal areas alone demanded 30,000 sets. On 12 April, 1900, Haig complained that there were not enough saddles to mount all the men in the Cavalry Division. 'Permission,' he wrote in his diary, 'received for an officer to go to Cape Town tomorrow with letter from HQ to enable him to bring the saddles straight through. 1,500 American saddles are in store in Cape Town.' Six days later he reported that an officer and fifty-two men 'left by train to bring up saddles'. Only the next day, though, he wrote: 'No American saddles because they are a sure cause of sore backs after even one or two days' use.' As late as September, 1900, an officer of

* A set of saddlery consists of bridle, stirrups, wallets, breastplate, numnah, shoe cases, rifle-bucket and straps, as well as the saddle itself.

the 17th Lancers said that though remounts were plentiful it was very hard to come by saddles for them.

'Eventually cartloads of various articles of saddlery, salved from various corps and gradually drawn into Kroonstad, arrived, and hours were spent in assembling the more serviceable parts and in completing losses. A small consignment of the Mexican pattern saddles was served out: though very light, they were not constructed for comfort with the British style of riding, being very short in the seat and having a very high pommel and cantel.'

By the end of the war, there had been sent out from home alone 76,100 sets. So many of all sorts from all over the world had been collected by Ordnance and were in use that a very large number had to be burned. There was no market for them.[18]

The Mark III of the new Universal Pattern, which had only begun to be issued in 1898, was, not surprisingly, far from being in universal use, even by regular cavalry regiments as they left for the seat of war in 1899. A number of different kinds of saddles had therefore to be found while the contractors at home laboured to fill the rush of orders. The commonest was the Colonial Saddle (or Cape Fan) which, from the mid-1880s, had been manufactured in thousands all over the Empire. It varied in design and even more in quality of manufacture. It weighed about 21 lbs, with wallets, girths and irons. There were complaints from some quarters that many of these saddles caused injuries to both withers and spine from not being wide enough in the front arch to prevent pinching, or curved up enough behind to clear the spine. Usually, though, the Colonial saddle was cherished for its lightness compared with the Universal Pattern, and because it was easier to make fit any size of horse. Nevertheless, no pattern of saddle existed which would fit every size of animal, and to place on the back of a thin Australian a saddle which fitted a fat Hungarian was to be certain of galling the Australian's back.* The Colonial seems to have given the fewest sore backs

* 'The shape and bulk of a horse's back depend upon his condition; with every variation in this there is a corresponding variation in the shape and size of the back . . . . The tendency on service is for the saddle to become large, for the reason that the horse's back is becoming smaller . . . . The saddle rests on the muscles and not on the bones: the muscles are growing progressively smaller but the bones do not waste.' (Smith, 248.)

The gaps caused by muscle shrinkage could be filled up with extra stuffing. The Colonial saddle made this comparatively easy. Almost anything would

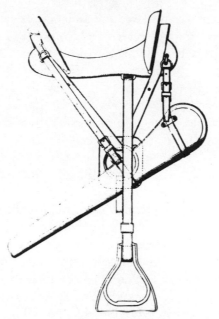

and it did 'not admit', as Baden-Powell discovered, 'of excessive extra kit being carried'. It was virtually the same as the saddles used by the Boers.

The 'McClellan Universal Pattern American Cavalry Saddle' (see illustration above), described by one authority as 'a sort of bad Mexican saddle' and by another as 'like a little wooden box', which was imported from the United States in large numbers, was liked more by the mounted infantry than by the regular cavalry. One day's fighting during July, 1900, produced in the 1st and 4th Cavalry Brigades no less than 229 sore backs. This was the effect of the American saddle placed on 'soft' Hungarians. On 20 July the 7th Dragoon Guards, after only two days on outpost duty, had eighty-seven horses out of action, most of them recently fitted with the American saddle.

The Australian stock-saddle which also appeared in numbers was not a general favourite, though it had its admirers.[10] Other types which were resorted to included the Austrian, Canadian, Cape Mounted Rifle (considered by Thorneycroft almost as good as the

---

serve. Wool was available almost everywhere in South Africa and was largely used. The difficulty, of course, was to get the men to notice when the gaps occurred. Further there was a certain amount of skill required to do the job properly. Colonel Thorneycroft found that restuffing caused no difficulty to the one saddler he had for each company. (*R.C.*, IV, 354.)

Colonial for mounted infantry) and Indian cavalry. It was this last type, old and unfit for service, with which the 9th Lancers left India for Durban, there being no time for the acquisition of new ones. By the time the regiment went into action at Belmont (see p. 82), though they had been in South Africa for thirty-six days, their horses were very far from fit. Numerous sore backs had resulted largely from the poor condition of their Indian saddles, and the ninety-three small Colonial horses with which their losses in a storm between Durban and Cape Town had been replaced were too small for the Indian saddles. Lord Tullibardine thought 'the Allan pattern' the best saddle he saw in South Africa. 'This is Allan of India,' he told the Royal Commission, 'the man who supplies the Indian Government. But it was capable of being lightened a good deal.'[20]

The loss of saddles throughout the war was appalling. When, through lack of acclimatization, starvation and over-work, animals were abandoned, so as often as not were their saddles. The Boers must have picked up many hundreds of discarded saddlery sets. For instance, in one trek of 175 miles the Inniskilling Dragoons lost seventy. When regulars could manage so shocking a loss, it is not surprising to find that an Imperial Yeomanry regiment – the Metropolitan Mounted Rifles – having just received 610 new horses, lost forty to the field veterinary hospital and had to destroy thirty-five others after marching only *fourteen* miles. Most of the seventy-five sets of saddlery were just left for the enemy to gather up.[21]

* * *

Our Prisoner.   Overloaded.

As for the ever-burning and closely related question of cavalry weights, the regular cavalry in peacetime and for a long time during the war continued to overload its horses. Veterinary opinion was agreed that the maximum weight the average cavalry horse ought to carry for any appreciable length of time was about fourteen to fifteen stone: roughly one-sixth or one-fifth of his body weight. In fact the ordinary troop horse in marching order carried a weight equivalent to that of two men: more than twenty stone was usual; less than eighteen very rare. 'You can get them to carry them for manoeuvres,' Prince Francis of Teck told the Remounts Court of Enquiry, 'but they are knocked up even over that. You would have to search the world over to get horses really strong enough to carry these enormous weights day after day, month out and month in.' On the march to relieve Kimberley, the weight carried by horses in one regiment was approximately twenty stone. This was made up thus:

'Heavy regimental saddle
Sword
Carbine
Full wallets
Picketing peg and rope } c. 9 stone
1 horse-shoe case with 2 shoes in it
20–24 lbs of oats
2 days' man's rations

Lance
150 rounds of ammunition } c. 11 stone
Man

Total weight c. 20 stone.'[22]

17 stone, 6 lbs, 10 ozs was the minimum weight which Haig believed possible 'after reducing it to the barest necessaries'. (But see below.) He went into great detail. On the man was carried:

	lbs	ozs
'Helmet (or slouch hat)	1	8
Frock	2	0
Pants	2	8
Braces (or belt)	0	5
Shirt and vest	2	4
Drawers	1	0

	lbs	ozs
Puttees and socks	1	5
Spurs and straps	1	0
Field dressing and description card	0	2
Ankle boots	4	0
Knife and hoof pick	0	8
Water bottle (full)	3	0
Two leather bandoliers, with 100 rounds ammunition	8	8
Sundries, such as pipe, tobacco, matches, towel, soap, etc.	2	0
	30	0'

On the horse was carried:	lbs	ozs	st.	lbs	ozs
'Colonial bridle and head rope	4	0			
Cavalry saddle (stripped)	14	6	[saddlery set]		
Stirrups etc.	8	0	2	3	2
Saddle blanket	4	12			
Nose-bag (with 6 lbs oats)	7	0			
Cloak – 8 lbs, or British warm 4 lbs 8 ozs (according to climate), and mackintosh or waterproof sheet, 2 lbs	10	0			
	48	2	3	6	2

Total weight to be carried by horse:—

	lbs	ozs	st.	lbs	ozs
As above	48	2			
Arms	14	8	17	6	10
Man (clothed)	182	0			

Too heavy!'

The average cavalry trooper weighed about 10 stone, 12 lbs naked, but it is an interesting social fact that the reservists were almost invariably heavier. Haig found that 'many of the Dragoon and Lancer reservists were far too big and heavy'.[23] From Australasia were sent out in the mounted units 'fine, tall, broad-shouldered men, half as big again as the average Tommy. Fine to look at,' wrote the Commandant of the 6th New Zealand Regiment, 'but oh, the poor horses! It was strange that the colonials, who consider themselves most practical in everything, should have allowed appearances to count. In one squadron the men averaged twelve stone; this meant [some] weighed nearer 13½ or 14 stone.' Haig believed that it might just be possible to bring the total weight down to near fourteen stone. This could only be done, though, if the weight of saddle and bridle were to be reduced in future designs, and, more important, if there were 'two classes of transport, one to accompany the squadron wherever it goes, and one to accompany the first line transport.' The squadron transport would carry such items as picket pegs, blankets, mess tins, cooking utensils, forage and rations.[24]

Rimington managed to reduce the weights of his Scouts to between 14 and 14½ stone all told. He did away altogether with wallets (in which the changes of clothes were carried and which offered a great temptation to riders, for 'anything and everything' found their way into them).* Discarded, too, were the breastplate, hoof picks, 'extra highlows strapped on wallets', picketing gear, hay nets (omitted by Haig, too, as so little hay was procurable), shoe cases and extra shoes (also omitted by Haig),† and grooming kit (Rimington found that a wisp of straw or rushes could do all that was needed and had the added advantage of not removing the coat's grease, the horse's natural waterproofing.) Before the charge at Abon's Dam (see p. 134), the regular cavalrymen, who were carrying '7 lb tins of bully beef', threw them away since, as Haig put it, they were 'an unsuitable adjunct to one's saddle in a charge'.[25]

One Imperial Yeomanry battalion left the base camp at Maitland with only

'such articles as man and horse could carry: the front saddle-

---

* Typically, as soon as the war was over, the cavalry resorted to what Lord Tullibardine called in 1903 'the enormous wallets now in use'. They were never used in South Africa, he told the Royal Commission, towards the end of the war. He found that 'very much reduced wallets . . . might be used, just large enough to hold tobacco and a pair of socks for the men . . . . Should a man carry anything else, it should be carried in his haversack or pocket. A shirt can always be carried in his great coat.'

Lord Tullibardine also said that the men's ammunition boots were 'very much too heavy and were conducive to bad riding, as the men practically lost all sensation in their feet and were slow to get on and off.' He also found, incidentally, that the stirrups generally served out were much too small to take the men's ammunition boot, many accidents occurring from this cause.' (R.C., II, 453.)

† 'Shoes drop off a good deal after horses are first landed, as then feet are soft, but in a month this is all right, the horn grows hard and the nails only require more than ordinary care on the part of officers, farriers and troopers'. (Rimington, R.C., II, 531.)

pack comprised a spare tunic, riding breeches and blanket, rolled in the waterproof sheet on which we lay at night. The near wallet contained a grooming brush, picketing peg and a knife, fork and spoon, wrapped in half a towel. The off wallet carried a change of underclothing, a piece of soap and as much tobacco as would fit in beside. Outside the wallets a spare pair of boots was strapped. The rear saddle-pack consisted of a cavalry cloak, a sweater for night wear, an empty sack and picketing gear. In addition to these, the saddle carried a leather case with a spare pair of horse-shoes, a rifle-bucket and a corn-bag with one day's ration of oats. Each man was girt with a bayonet-belt, haversack, water bottle and last but not least a bandolier carrying one hundred rounds, or nine pounds weight, of ammunition.'

In July, 1901, Trooper Duncalf of the 21st Company, Cheshire Imperial Yeomanry, wrote home: 'It is no use sending me anything to wear as our Captain will not let us carry it. He has made us take our wallets off our saddles and he will not let us carry more than a change of underclothing with us. He is a terror. He thinks no more about us than if we was dogs.'[26] In August, 1900, the kit of an officer of the Inniskilling Dragoons

'consisted of a pony and a pack-saddle, on which was packed my valise and a small tente de'abri that weighed only a few pounds. The valise contained my bedding, and in the saddle-bags I had a change of clothes and luxuries. The pack-pony was generally up when I wanted it; but, failing that, I was equipped as one of my men, except that I carried a small saddle-bag on my charger holding pocket lantern, razor, soap and a penny looking-glass. Whenever we halted the men would make a tente d'abri out of blankets with a sword at each end as poles. . . . [After the withdrawal of the *arme blanche* (see p. 236), this – perhaps the only good use of the sword – was, of course, no longer possible.] To compete with an enemy like the Boer, our system of a man carrying everything necessary for some days on his horse is ridiculous. He must ride like a Boer, with his saddle and ammunition only, and light two-wheeled transport should be provided to fall back on.' [This, as shown above, was adopted by most of the columns in the later stages of the war.][27]

The dilemma which faced the cavalry with respect to weight, and the attitude of many officers towards it, is well shown by the case of another officer of the Inniskilling Dragoons who was proud of inventing 'a good plan for carrying corn-sacks on the ordinary saddle with stirrup-leathers and reins. We thus,' he said, 'dispensed with wagons on our flank column for four days at least.'[28]

Only in the very last period of the war was it becoming common to leave all unmounted and spare men as well as all ailing horses at base.[29]

16

'At present half – more than half – of the troops we maintain are unfit to take the field. We are trying to meet others' "best" with our "worst" and that will spell disaster one day.'

ARNOLD-FORSTER to Curzon,
8 September, 1904

'A good deal of the time of the next ministry will be taken up with reform of the army. I don't envy the man who has got that job.'

HALDANE in 1905

'This is an army which ... asks for more efficiency for less money.'

HALDANE in the House of Commons,
8 March, 1906

'We have an Army in excess of our requirements for "small wars" – and wholly inadequate to demands of a great war.'

ESHER to Lord Knollys,
30 September, 1906

'I doubt whether the Secretary of State has any idea of the difficulties under which his schemes of reform have been carried through the War Office itself, and with which the General Staff still has to contend.'

HAIG to Esher, 11 October, 1909

'Not since the days of the Commonwealth had the British Army been so generally gripped with a sense of professional purpose in peacetime.'

CORRELLI BARNETT in *Britain and her Army*,
1970[1]

(i)

Army reforms, 1902–1914: abolition of Commander-in-Chief's post – creation of Army Council – reorganizaiton of War Office – creation of General and (later) Imperial General Staff – Haldane's great schemes – Haig's large part in them – expeditionary force formed – Territorial Army – Special Reserve – Field Service Regulations

Of the senior generals whose reputations survived the South African War, five stood out in the public's estimation above the others. Roberts and Kitchener, not for the first time in their careers, became national heroes. So to a lesser degree did French, Ian Hamilton and Haig. These three – two of them cavalrymen – were to achieve key positions in the army, first at home during the twelve years before the First World War, and then in the course of that horrible conflict. During the period between the two wars there was a vast amount of soul-searching in British military circles. Many were the hard-fought engagements between diehard conservatives and forward-looking reformers, between those reformers themselves and between traditionalists and iconoclasts.

These were presided over, as it were, by four Secretaries of State for War: Brodrick, who gave way in 1903 to Hugh Oakeley Arnold-Forster, both serving in Balfour's Conservative administration.* When that fell at the end of 1905, Richard Burdon Haldane, perhaps the most successful of all modern War Ministers, served first in Campbell-Bannerman's and, on his death, in Asquith's Liberal governments. In 1908 he was succeeded by John Edward Bernard Seely, whose chief claim to remembrance rests upon the way in which he dealt with the Curragh 'mutiny' early in 1914, his last year at the War Office before being succeeded by Kitchener. By the time he went there the leading reforms which his three predecessors – but chiefly Haldane – had effected were more or less complete, if not in detail, at least in outline.

The experience of the Boer War and the imminence of an European one demanded five major undertakings. Above all the central direction of the land forces, that is the War Office, required radical reorganization. Second, and concomitantly, a real General Staff had to be created. Third, there was a need for the military requirements of the Empire to be harmonized with those at home. Fourth, the feebleness of the auxiliary forces (the Yeomanry, the Militia and the Volunteers), had to be remedied, and lastly a compact, complete striking force had to be formed for use in Europe with adequate reserves. All these aims were accomplished to a remarkable degree just in time for the First World War. The chief but by no means all the credit must lie with Haldane, aided by his Military Private

---

* Balfour himself, more than his two War Ministers, was responsible for the 'collection of ideas, reforms, advisers and institutions' which Campbell-Bannerman and Haldane inherited from him. (Spiers: *Haldane*, 188.)

Secretary, Colonel Gerald Francis Ellison, Viscount Esher,* Haig and, later, Major-General Henry Hughes Wilson.

*   *   *

In the first year or so after the Boer War the paramount overseas threats to meet which it was thought that the army would be needed were still the old ones of a Russian incursion into India and its European consequences, as well as, though decreasingly, a war with France. But some time before these threats had been virtually removed by the Anglo-Russian Convention of 1907† and by the signing in 1904 of the *Entente Cordiale*, the menace represented by an increasingly bellicose Germany had begun to point to her, and not to her neighbours, as the most likely enemy to peace in Europe. The story of how the ties between France and Britain were strengthened in face of this new situation, both politically and, later, militarily,‡ is well known and need not be retold here. What it entailed for the army was a reversal of the main thesis of the Stanhope Memorandum of 1891. This had stated that it was 'sufficiently improbable' that a British army would be required to take the field in an European war. (See Vol III, p. 31.)

The task now, therefore, was to produce within the financial restraints imposed by a Liberal-dominated Parliament, as large and

---

* Reginald Baliol Brett, 2nd Viscount Esher, was offered but always refused high political office. Brodrick called him very aptly 'a potentate without portfolio'. (Brodrick to Curzon, 6 Nov., 1903, quoted in Dilks, I, 102.) He had been a Liberal Member of Parliament in the 1880s and joint secretary of the Hartington Royal Commission on Naval and Military Administration of 1889 which had recommended abolition of the post of Commander-in-Chief. Beside being Chairman of the War Office Reconstruction Committee (see below), he was a permanent member of the Committee of Imperial Defence from its inception. He died in 1930, aged seventy-eight.

† This Convention became possible partly because of the threat which Germany was already posing in Europe, and partly because of Russia's humiliation in the Russo-Japanese War of 1904–1905, which had been preceded by the Anglo-Japanese alliance of 1902.

Nevertheless, as late as 1908, Haldane had apparently 'defended in Cabinet a scheme for reinforcing India in case of a Russian invasion', but he almost certainly had an ulterior motive in this. (Harris, Sir C. to Haldane, 19 November, 1916, Haldane MSS, NLS, MS 5, 913, ff. 27–8).

‡ As a result of the Franco-German rift over Morocco, Sir Edward Grey, the Foreign Secretary, and Haldane agreed in January, 1906, that secret talks should take place between the French and British General Staffs.

effective an expeditionary force for co-operation with our ally across the Channel, as our colonial and home defence commitments, as well as the competing demands of the Navy, would allow.*

It is generally, if not universally, agreed that this daunting task was surprisingly well executed. In January, 1906, when Haldane first went to the War Office, he discovered that only 80,000 men were available to take the field and that it would be two months before they could do so. By 1910 what was to be known in 1914 as the British Expeditionary Force, some 160,000 strong, was more or less capable of crossing the Channel within fifteen days.† It was very small by Continental standards, yet in view of the peacetime criteria which determined its size, it is commendable that it was as large as it was. It undoubtedly constituted a neat and effectual fighting machine. In nearly every respect, except that of heavy artillery – a German speciality – it was superior in quality to any European army,

---

* Under Balfour and Arnold-Forster, in cabinet, in the Commons and in the newly formed Committee of Imperial Defence (which though founded by Balfour in late 1902 had come into being as a fully-fledged body with a secretariat in May, 1904, and was one of the chief fruits of Esher's three-man War Office Reconstruction Committee), the principal battle had been between the 'Blue Water' school, which believed that the navy alone could block any invasion, and the 'Bolt from the Blue' school, which fought for an adequate army at home to deal with surprise attacks on our shores. Balfour sided with the former. In July, 1906, he said that he could not envisage any circumstance in which the mobilization of six 'large' (three brigade) divisions, or 154,000 men would be necessary. (*Hansard*: (*C*), 12 July, 1906.)

A secondary, but relevant, conflict concerned the provision of reinforcements for India should the Russians still invade through Afghanistan. Kitchener thought that an addition of at least 100,000 men within a six-month period should be provided for. This, too, Balfour accepted – in theory. Roberts, unhappy that these two priorities, without some sort of universal compulsory service at home would leave the British Isles insufficiently defended (see below), resigned from the Committee in 1905.

† Railway time-tables and shipping schedules were not finally settled until 1912 and 1913 respectively. Recent research has revealed that it is unlikely that the mobilization plan could have been implemented 'without much confusion before 1913'. Some important, but not vital, details had not indeed been fully arranged until about May, 1914. (Spiers: *Haldane*, 159, 219.)

A Special Army Order of 1 January, 1907, was the first that proclaimed publicly that the regular army at home would, in time of war, form an Expeditionary Force of one cavalry and six infantry divisions. Its numbers on mobilization were fixed at 6,494 officers and 160,200 men. There was an establishment of 456 guns, 168 machine-guns, 62,216 horses and 7,938 vehicles. To maintain its strength for six months, 2,674 officers and 74,918 other ranks were required.

and probably the best that Britain had ever sent overseas at the start of a war.

Concurrent with this new responsibility was the need to create an ample pool of basically trained officers and men, not only to reinforce the expeditionary force, but also to provide for home defence, once that force had gone abroad. Conscription in peacetime being unfeasible politically, financially and to a large degree militarily, in view of the Empire's overseas commitments, there was no perfect solution to this long-standing problem of reserves. Haldane's creation of the Territorial Army (although Kitchener made little use of it when war came) and his other measures, like the Special Reserve, none of which came fully up to their creator's sanguine hopes, probably got as near to fulfilling the need as it was possible to do.

Roberts, especially after he had ceased to be Commander-in-Chief upon the abolition of that post, campaigned vigorously for the introduction of compulsory universal service and training for home defence. Only thus, he argued, could the regular army be freed for its commitments overseas and for the provision of that reserve of officers and men without which any sudden expansion would prove impossible. His campaign failed, as it was almost bound to do in the political climate of the times. Nevertheless, as the numbers of Territorials decreased, in 1913, to below the quarter of a million which Haldane had considered to be their essential minimum, more and more senior officers, including French who had become Chief of the Imperial General Staff the previous year, came to demand universal compulsory home service.

*   *   *

The abolition of the post of Commander-in-Chief, the creation of the Army Council* in its place in 1904 and the formation of a General Staff were more or less skeletal reforms which Haldane inherited. Though his two predecessors had introduced a number of other useful improvements, it was with the advent of Haldane that, for the first time since the days of Cardwell (see Vol III, p. 30), a truly dynamic grip upon the problems of the army was taken. This is especially surprising since he was a lawyer, a philosopher, an educa-

* Its members were the Chief of the General Staff, the Adjutant-General, the Quartermaster-General, the Master-General of the Ordnance as well as the Secretary of State for War, the Financial Secretary and the Permanent Under-Secretary to the War Office.

tional reformer and a Liberal.* Hitherto he had taken only an inter-
mittent interest in the affairs of the army. Fortunately his tact,
brilliance of intellect, grasp of detail and capacity for hard work
immediately endeared him to the senior soldiers in the War Office.
Haig, writing home from India, where in October, 1903 he had gone
as Kitchener's Inspector-General of Cavalry, heard that 'everyone
in the soldiering line at home speaks well of Haldane, so the advent
of the Radicals is certainly of great advantage to the Army.…
French seems to like him very much and "the Army Councillors",
Hubert Hamilton† writes me, "have now the spirits of schoolboys
home for the holidays".' (The majority of the Army Council had
strongly disagreed with and disliked Arnold-Forster.) At about the
same time that Haig was writing thus, Esher, that *eminence grise* who
did so much, more often than not behind the scenes, to help along
the progress of army reform, wrote to him to say that 'there is only
one change not yet made which Haldane *must* make. It is to put you
in Hutchinson's‡ place. I have never left him alone for a day since
he took office on the subject. If *you* get back here in that place for
two years the whole tone of army officers and their education will
have undergone a change which will recast the army.' Haldane acted
speedily on Esher's advice and put Haig, not in 'that place', but as
Director of Military Training. This post he held until 1908, when he
did replace Hutchinson as Director of Staff Duties. 'Although called
"Training",' wrote Haig of his new post, 'the Department also deals
with War Organization and Home Defence, so that it is the most
important Directorate in the General Staff at the present time.'[2]

At his first meeting with the new Minister, arranged by French,
who since his return home in 1902 had held the vital command at
Aldershot, Haig found him 'a fat, big man, but with a kind genial
face. One seemed,' he added, 'to like the man at once.… He seems
a most clear-headed and practical man, most ready to listen to and
weigh carefully all that is said to him.'[3] Later on, in 1909, the two
men 'discussed objects for which Army and Expeditionary Force

---

* Though, admittedly, one of the leading 'Limps' (the name given to the
'right-wing' Liberal Imperialists).

† Colonel Hubert Ion Wetherall Hamilton had just gone home from being
Kitchener's Military Secretary in India to command the 7th Infantry Brigade.
He was killed, aged fifty-three, in October, 1914, while, as a Major-General,
commanding the 3rd Division in the La Bassée-Armentières operations.

‡ Lieutenant-General Henry Doveton Hutchinson was appointed Director
of Staff Duties at the War Office in 1904 and remained in that post till 1908.

exist,' as Haig confided to his diary. 'He is in no doubt – viz. to organize to support France and Russia against Germany, and perhaps Austria.'[4]* Nevertheless, Haldane was quite unable to declare publicly that this was his line of thought. He still had to pretend, not least in the interests of not alarming his radical colleagues, that the size of the expeditionary force 'was relevant for the reinforcement of the North-West Frontier'.[5] (See fn. p. 378).

Brodrick's and Arnold-Forster's plans, particularly with respect to the provision of reserves and the question of the Militia and Volunteers, which usually clashed with each other, required large increases in the Army Estimates and were disliked by nearly all Members of Parliament, had left disarray and uncertainty in army circles. Further, in so far as their schemes were tried at all, they looked like failing lamentably in practice.† Realizing that he would have to father an entirely new approach to army reform, Haldane was confronted with two cardinal restraints. The first was imposed by the radical and pacifist factions in the Cabinet which wished to spend what monies there were on their social welfare measures and as little as possible on defence‡ and therefore fought against a foreign policy which included possible expensive military entanglements in the future. The second was the certainty that priority would always, and rightly, be given, in the face of Germany's massive naval building programme, to expenditure on the fleet. Haldane's method of getting round these basic obstacles was masterly. In the words of Edward Spiers, upon whose detailed and percipient study of Haldane and his reforms this account largely relies:

> 'Haldane had laid the groundwork for success by insisting, initially, on the need for economy within the War Office. By imposing arbitrary financial restrictions, a ceiling of £28 million,§

* One highly placed officer at this time wrote to Ellison: 'If you organize the British Army, you'll ruin it.'! (Cooper, I, 106.)

† But see p. 477.
The best concise account of these schemes is to be found in Spiers: *A & S*, 243–64.

‡ Considerable sections of the Conservative Opposition were, of course, equally keen to see the Army Estimates reduced.

§ This was nearly £900,000 lower than the 1904–5 estimates.
That Haldane kept the Army Estimates so low, year after year, is probably the most unexpected of his achievements. In 1906 they were 20 % of gross public expenditure. By 1912 this had decreased to 16 %. Only thus was he able to make his measures acceptable to his Party and the country.
It was significant that Haldane made it clear in his very first speech to the

he had ensured that future reforms would be based upon existing resources. . . . The army, whose *raison d'être* was effective
operation in war, had to remain for an indefinite period of peace
as a burden on the Exchequer: only if this burden was tolerable
could reform be accepted on a lasting basis. . . . Far from per-
ceiving a strategic objective and simply providing the where-
withal in men, arms and organization to meet it, Haldane had
set a mandatory financial limit and had hoped that the existing
forces, if better organized, would fulfil the strategic requirements.'[6]

Haldane's three greatest achievements were the creation of the
long-overdue striking force for a great war, the forming of the
structure of a second-line army, namely the Territorial Army, and
the making of the General Staff into a truly competent directing
instrument.

In all these Haldane came to rely more than on any other of his
assistants upon Haig, who when in November, 1907, he became
Director of Staff Duties continued to perform the chief functions
with which Haldane had entrusted him in his earlier post two and
a half years previously. He was now the senior officer holding a
General Staff directorate. By the time that he returned to India as
Chief of Staff in 1909, he had been largely instrumental in laying the
foundations upon which these momentous achievements could be
built.

Haig's chief drawback, which dogged him throughout his career,
was a combination of ineptitude when it came to expressing himself
verbally and a propensity for blunt brusquerie with those who disagreed with him. In spite of this, he got on well with his Minister.
'Douglas Haig,' wrote Haldane to Esher on 8 September, 1906, 'has
impressed me greatly by the change for the better initiated even in
his first fortnight.'[7] Having been relieved of all educational duties,
Haig was provided with, as he wrote in November, 1907, 'sufficient
officers to work out "Principles of employment of troops" and other
fundamental questions which hitherto have been ignored.'[8]

Haig's labours in the War Office were strenuous, his tasks
manifold. The first was the reorganization of the auxiliary forces and

---

Commons in July, 1906, that, though his proposals entailed the reduction of
both the infantry and the artillery by about 20,000 officers and men, only the
cavalry of all the arms was to be left untouched as to numbers. (*Hansard* (*C*),
12 July, 1906, 1075–1119.)

the provision of proper reserves. At the same time he was required to bring up to date and to standardize the manuals upon which all training was based (see p. 386). Later, in 1908, he was instructed to formulate specific proposals for making a reality of the Imperial General Staff, which had been brought into existence at the Colonial Conference of 1907. He also had a hand, of course, in all the complexities attending mobilization planning, while the responsibility for overseeing the Staff College was also his.

In preparing the Territorial and Reserve Forces Act of 1907, the very first passed by the Liberals, Haldane had to meddle with long-established and deeply treasured prejudices and traditions. From time to time he was disposed to give way to the protests of the fiercely independent commanding officers of the Yeomanry, Militia and Volunteers, many of them in Parliament. It was chiefly Haig who time and again persuaded his Minister to stand firm. The lynch-pin in the creating of the Territorial Army,* which it was intended should be embodied on the outbreak of war for six months' training, was the forming of County Associations throughout the land. Through these the building of a decentralized administrative structure, with the supply, above all, of training facilities, especially drill halls, was necessary. The associations, to be chaired by the Lords Lieutenant, would also be required to promote military drill in schools, cadet corps and miniature rifle clubs. 'The Volunteers,' wrote Haig to Esher, 'won't have the associations as proposed at any price!'9 But eventually Haldane and he, with the minimum of concessions, won them round. On an equally vital point the Militia stood firm. They were excluded altogether from the Act, for they would not undertake to be sent overseas in an emergency. Thus the hope that they could be employed as semi-trained drafts for the expeditionary force was for the time being dashed. Nothing daunted, Haldane and his assistants devised a new reserve body – the Special Reserve. This was to be a semi-professional force with terms of service designed to 'attract the men who would formerly have entered the Militia'.10†

---

* Which was to consist of fourteen divisions, fourteen cavalry brigades and very considerable service and specialist troops.

Haldane and Haig, especially, appreciated that in the German and French armies, all ancillary services were completely organized in advance of mobilization. They now tried to ensure the same for the British army.

† In 1910 Haldane launched the National Reserve as a part of the Territorial Reserve. This was open to any man who had served in the army, navy, the

51. 'Shipping Hungarian horses at Fiume for the Army in South Africa'

52. 'Catching wild horses'

53. 'Entraining horses at Cape Town'

Virtually all Haldane's reforms were expounded in seven memoranda, the first of which dealt with 'the present situation'.[11] It was upon these that Haig when he arrived from India depended as his brief. This is not the place to examine the details either of these papers or the many hundreds of others that resulted from them, particularly since most did not directly affect the mounted branch. Referring to those which dealt with the Territorials and Reserves, Esher well summed up their importance. The scheme's great merit, he wrote in early 1908, is 'that it provided *not* an Army, but Machinery by which, in the event of a land war . . . you could grind out an army in time.'[12] A large part of the credit for this lies with Haig – the great cavalryman. The unhappy facts that after he had left the War Office, the numbers of Territorials – already known as 'Terriers' – failed, right up to the war, to be maintained even at the accepted minimum, that large numbers of them omitted to attend their annual camps for the full fifteen days and that, in late 1913, only 18,800 had volunteered to serve abroad on mobilization,[13] do not detract from the excellence of the intelligent hard work which Haig put into the scheme's devising, at nearly all stages obstructed by his more diehard colleagues. Both he and Haldane had always said that the scheme would take a very long time to reach success. This it ultimately did, for when in 1920 the Territorial Army was re-born after the First World War, it was almost exactly the same as had been legislated for thirteen years before. It continued in similar form till well after the Second World War.

* * *

Beyond the broader issues for which Haig's assistance was so valued by Haldane was the vital question of the detailed organization and administration of the army in the field. Haig reminded those present at a General Staff Conference held in January, 1908, that during the South African War three different systems had been adopted

Volunteers or the Territorials. These veterans enrolled through their County Associations. If they were passed as fit, they were classed as reservists who were able to make good any shortage in the TA ranks. If unfit or too old, they were allocated to sedentary or ceremonial duties. The other parts of the Territorial Reserve were for technicians who had not before served in the armed forces and for ex-Terriers who had completed their four years' service. (Spiers: *Haldane*, 183.)

The part played by the Yeomanry in Haldane's schemes is discussed at p. 450.

concurrently by three different headquarters. For a large-scale Continental war, he argued, such an amateurish approach would spell disaster. Something vastly more methodical and co-ordinated was called for, 'hence the need for a "book of regulations" produced by the "War Staff".'[14] From soon after the end of the Boer War, a colonel in the Staff Duties Directorate had been intermittently compiling material for a manual designed to produce a unified staff system for war. It was to be different from *Combined Training*, published in 1905,* in both scope and scale. It was to be known as *Field Service Regulations, Part II – Administration*. Together with *FSR, Pt I – Operations*, which was the training manual for all arms, it would form the standard rule book for the conduct of a major war.† Its publication had been consistently obstructed by, particularly, the Adjutant-General's and Quartermaster-General's departments and by the Director of Military Operations, jealous of their own independence and prerogatives. They resented a directorate from the General Staff being imposed upon them. Lyttelton (see p. 122), who was Chief of the General Staff from 1904 to 1908, gave the project only tepid support. Haldane, however, threw his weight behind it. Eventually, on 23 December, 1908, the military members of the Army Council were persuaded by Haig to agree the proofs of *FSR, Part II*. 'It has been,' he noted in his diary that evening, 'over five years in the waiting!'[15] Its importance in the history of the army is hard to exaggerate. For the first time a common doctrine was prescribed throughout the land forces. It detailed what was required of every commander at all levels in the operations of war.

Haldane provided funds for exercises and manoeuvres as well as for war games and staff rides. These two latter, against stiff opposition from, especially, the Director of Military Operations, Haig now proceeded to organize on a truly professional basis. They showed up numbers of alarming weaknesses. Confusion, for example, as to the respective powers of the Quartermaster-General and the Inspector-General of Communications and Railways was revealed. The need for common standards and co-ordination of the several staffs was

* This and the *Staff Manual* had been largely the work of Rawlinson and Wilson, under Roberts's guidance.

† Haig, of course, devised the sections on the cavalry. 'The fact [that cavalry] is armed with a long-range rifle,' he wrote, 'has endowed it with great independence, and has extended its sphere of action; for cavalry need no longer be stopped by difficulties which can only be overcome by the employment of rifle fire.' (*FSR, Pt I – Operations*, 1909, 14–15.)

clearly demonstrated. Though for long after Haig had returned to India, strenuous efforts were made by his erstwhile colleagues to invalidate the principles embodied in *Field Service Regulations*, the army which fought the First Great War was largely administered and organized on the lines laid down in them. Not only Haldane's unwavering support, but also that of Sir William Gustavus Nicholson,* the first Chief of the Imperial General Staff, were largely responsible for this happy situation.

* Nicholson, originally a Royal Engineer, had served nearly thirty years in India before the Boer War. In 1900 he had become Director of Transport in South Africa, in 1901 Director of Military Operations at the War Office and in 1905 Quartermaster-General. In 1911 he was made a field-marshal and in 1912, on leaving office, a baron. He died, aged seventy-three, in 1918. Haldane thought that Nicholson had 'a great brain', but found him a difficult personality. (Spiers: *Haldane*, 74.)

'As well to think of using the elephants of the Emperor Porus [whose 200 elephants were defeated in 326 B.C. by Alexander] on a modern European battlefield as shock cavalry.'

LIEUTENANT-GENERAL SIR IAN HAMILTON,
writing from Manchuria in 1905

'It is evident that occasional perfunctory dismounting of a troop or squadron, which was formerly considered adequate training in fire tactics, is no longer sufficient for the development of the fire power of Cavalry.'

BRIGADIER-GENERAL BROADWOOD in 1906

'It must never be forgotten that it is only by the employment of "shock tactics" and the superior moral of the highly trained horseman wielding sword and lance, that decisive success can be attained.'

LIEUTENANT-GENERAL SIR JOHN FRENCH
in 1905

'The only possible logical deduction from the history of late wars is, that all attacks can now be carried out far more effectually with the rifle than the sword.'

FIELD-MARSHAL EARL ROBERTS in 1910

'The very essence of cavalry lies in the offensive. Mounted it is incapable of tactical defence, but, in order to defend itself, must surrender its real character as a mounted arm and seize the rifle on foot.'

LEUTNANT-GENERAL FREIHERR VON BERNHARDI
in 1910

'Our British regular cavalry are at least ten, if not fifteen years ahead of any continental cavalry in rifle shooting, fire discipline and the knowledge of when and how to resort to fire tactics.'

MAJOR-GENERAL RIMINGTON in 1912[1]

(ii)

'Shock' v. 'fire' controversy, 1902–1913: lance abolished and re-instated – Cavalry Training, 1904, 1907, 1912 – short rifle introduced – Cavalry Journal founded – lessons of Boer and Russo-Japanese Wars – 'cavalry spirit' – decline of mounted infantry – Continental views – effect of manoeuvres on training – increased excellence of cavalry's musketry

In September, 1903, Roberts presided over a conference convened to examine cavalry tactics for the future. Of it Haig wrote in his diary, 'I strongly maintain that the chief method of action for cavalry is the mounted role. [Roberts] hotly opposes me and the principle laid down by me in Part IV, *Cavalry Drill* [1898], "Collective Training".' In January, 1904, Roberts, who was still Commander-in-Chief, told Kitchener that he considered it 'quite a misfortune that Haig should be of the Old School in regard to the role of cavalry in the field. He is a clever, able fellow and his views have a great effect on French, Scobell [see p. 248] and some other senior officers.'[2] This was certainly true, but even without Haig's undoubted influence, the majority of cavalry officers were of the 'Old School'. In 1907 Haig published *Cavalry Studies: Strategical and Tactical*. This book arose out of the proceedings of five Staff Rides which he organized when he was Inspector-General of Cavalry in India. He foresaw an ever-increasing role for cavalry in the future:

'1. The extended nature of the modern battlefield would give the cavalry a greater choice of cover to favour its approach.*

2. The increased range and effectiveness of modern weapons and the greater length of battles would lead to moral exhaustion, which in turn will render cavalry attacks more likely to succeed.

3. Rapidity of movement for cavalry will become more necessary because of better weapons used by the infantry.

4. The small-bore rifle bullet had less stopping power against a horse than the older large-bore bullets did.'[3]

Except for the third, these paragraphs, with hindsight, seem to be almost nonsensical, especially the last one which, in the age of the machine gun, seems unbelievable. At the time these views were not seen thus at home or on the Continent. Elsewhere in the book he quotes approvingly from some articles in the *Revue des Deux Mondes* written as long ago as 1889: 'The value of the arm appears to be quite unaffected by the considerations habitually brought forward by its detractors. It is not regulated by the power of fire-arms.' Unable of course to foresee the fundamentally different nature

---

* Brevet-Major Andrew (see below) pointed out in 1903 that 'it is on the clear, open ground, that has hitherto been considered a cavalryman's ideal, that the rifle produces its greatest effect, and attains a superiority over the assailants beyond all our expectations.' (Andrew, 68.)

of the firearms of the 1880s and those being developed at the beginning of the twentieth century, the apparently anonymous French author goes on to ask, again with Haig's approval: 'Who ever raised cavalry higher than [Napoleon]? And yet muskets carried further and straighter in his time than in the days of Charles XII or Gustavus Adolphus.'[4] Haig, to be fair, goes on to say:

'A charge, though a very prominent part, is only one part of the function of the cavalry, and efficiency in the use of the rifle is absolutely essential, as it will be in more frequent use. On the other hand, now as formerly, all great successes can only be gained by a force of cavalry which is trained to harden its heart and charge home.'[5]

Though Haig *after* the Boer War seemed to be intransigently opposed to concentration upon training in fire-action, it is intriguing to look at what he wrote in his 'Tactical Notes' in November, 1899, when the war was a month old: 'The use made by the Boers of their ponies to carry them to a position or positions from which to deliver a flanking fire upon attacking troops should not pass unnoticed by us, and might sometimes be imitated by our Cavalry with good result in suitable country.'

He suggested that the cavalry should 'pay more attention to [dismounted action] in time of peace. Musketry training and field firing to be made more practical. Tactical schemes for Cavalry in *all* kinds of country; and check Cavalry Officers when in broken ground they sit still and complain that "they can do nothing in this damned country!" '[6] Even earlier, in 'Notes on Dismounted Action of Cavalry', 1892, he had expressed the view that dismounted work was not irreconcilable with an over-riding commitment to the knee-to-knee charge.[7]

Until, as a result of the Esher Committee's recommendations, Roberts was unceremoniously sacked, he was the chief proponent of the 'New School'. Kitchener in India supported him. In May, 1904, he wrote to him summing up pretty pithily the reformers' case: 'Cavalry should be able to seize and hold positions by rifle-fire and therefore assist the general scheme . . . instead of wandering about, sometimes aimlessly, seeking for the enemy's cavalry in order to charge them as their only role in war.'[8] There were, of course, wide variations of view ranging from the extreme conservatism which wanted virtually all training and armament to concentrate, as of yore, upon shock action, to those, like that of the thirty-year-old Winston

Churchill, who wished to totally abandon the *arme blanche*. In April, 1904, he spoke in the Commons thus: 'I hope the Government will go boldly forward and throw away "ironmongery" altogether. Modern war is fought with firearms, and if cavalry is to play a great *role* in the battlefield in the future, they will have to use modern weapons, and not the sharp sticks and long irons with which the wars of savagery and mediaeval chivalry were conducted.'[9] Another cavalry officer whose views nearly coincided with Churchill's was Lord Dundonald (see pp. 74, 76. See also illustration No. 4). While the war was still waging he wrote to Roberts:

'The subdivision of lands into fields by wire fencing is rapidly increasing. . . . A few strands of wire, or a bit of difficult ground, will delay a mounted advance quite long enough for the rifle to do deadly work amongst the horsemen, if even a few riflemen keep their morale. For the magazine, the flat trajectory, the great range and accuracy of the modern rifle all favour the man with the fire-arm as compared to the man with the sword. . . .

'To make the Cavalry into splendid shooting corps will take time and labour; to teach them to slide off their horses almost before they come to a standstill, and up with their rifles like the best Boer or Colonial game shots, will take more time, but it cannot be done if in the training we give most prominence to the *arme blanche*.

'I am convinced that to make our Cavalry into quick and good riflemen and to learn all else they ought to know for efficient dismounted work, will take all the training and all the time that can be given.'[10]

Roberts, who was never an extremist, struck the first important blow for the reformers when he issued Army Order 39 of March, 1903 (see illustration, p. 392). This abolished the lance 'on guard, in the field, at manoeuvres and on active service'.* Even more provocatively it stated (in exactly the same words that he had used in the order which he had issued during the war (see p. 236), when he removed the *arme blanche* from French's cavalry) that the rifle would 'henceforth be considered as the cavalry soldier's principal weapon'. At the same time he published a Circular Memorandum on 'Cavalry Armament' in which he drew from a number of lessons of past

---

* In at least some of the regiments of the German, French, Austrian and Russian cavalries, the lance was still carried up to and well beyond 1914.

A.O. 39.
March
1903.
Cavalry Equipment.—1. Regiments of Cavalry will, in future, be armed with the carbine (or rifle) and sword. Regiments of Lancers, Dragoon Guards, and Dragoons, will retain the lance as at present, but it will only be carried on escort duty, at reviews, and other ceremonial parades; not on guard, in the field, at manœuvres, or on active service.

§4
Cavalry
430

A.O. 39
continued.

March
1903.

2. Ten D.P. and ten exercise lances per squadron will be allowed for each Cavalry regiment for use at skill-at-arms practices, tent-pegging, &c.: and any lances in excess of that proportion now on charge under Barrack Schedules 30 and 31 will be withdrawn and returned to store. These practices will only be carried out as a means of recreation for the soldier, and time will not be devoted to them at the expense of training in equitation, shooting, swordsmanship, and field work.

3. In issuing these instructions, the Commander-in-Chief desires to impress upon all ranks that although the Cavalry are armed with the carbine (or rifle) and sword, the carbine (or rifle) will henceforth be considered as the Cavalry soldier's principal weapon.

cavalry work, especially during the Franco-German War, the conclusion 'that cavalry will generally act dismounted, but that small bodies ... may effect surprises against all arms by making use of shock tactics'. He then asked whether it was

> 'worth while to arm our cavalry with the cumbersome lance, and to detract from their efficiency as scouts and skirmishers, their primary and most important duties, in order that they may be able to take full advantage of opportunities which are of the rarest occurrence? The question,' he inferred, 'answers itself. For shock tactics, the armament of our cavalry should be the sword.'

Roberts, nevertheless, did not think it 'necessary, or even wise, that the lance should be entirely discarded. It is well,' he wrote in 1903, 'that a cavalry soldier should have a knowledge of all weapons which may be effectively used by the mounted man.' He added that

> 'lance practice, especially tent-pegging is ... a most useful exercise, improving the seat on horseback, giving the man confidence and strengthening his muscles. As military sports, tent-pegging and lance *v.* bayonet should be encouraged in every way possible. They are for the men what polo is for the officers, the best and most wholesome method of employing their hours of recreation. ... On no account should they be allowed to encroach on the time given to field exercises, the study of

ground and serious work.' He ruled that 'practice in handling [the lance] will be given on exactly the same system as practice in handling the bayonet in the infantry.'

In view of the later re-introduction (see p. 410) of the lance, it is interesting to note that in 1905 four of the most influential members of the Army Council, including Lyttelton, the Chief of the General Staff, agreed with Roberts that the lance should be abolished.[11]

The extreme conservatives affected to care not one jot what *arme blanche* weapon was carried. Such a one was Lieutenant-Colonel Frederic Natusch Maude, a Royal Engineer and a fertile writer on technical and military historical matters, who wrote in 1903:

'The closed squadron, regiment or brigade riding knee to knee in the attack has been the essential factor of success, and provided the horses could gallop side by side in good order it was practically all one to them whether the riders carried riding canes or tulwars, for the great cavalry leaders of the past knew that it was weight, cohesion and speed only which gave the decision, and what happened after that in the way of killing was a mere luxury in comparison. . . . The sword and the lance have their uses, but these become almost insignificant in proportion as the real object viz. cohesion is attained.'[12]

Rimington (see p. 80), whose experiences in the Boer War one would have expected to yield a less old-fashioned judgement, glorified the knee-to-knee charge, and also believed that the type of weapon was a secondary consideration.

'Your men and horses cannot turn; there is no room. Weapons,' he wrote in 1912, 'in this case may be ignored, the horses' weight and momentum is the weapon. Horse and man total upwards of 1,000 lbs in weight, they represent nine feet in height by three feet in width. The front extends for, say, seventy or eighty yards [one squadron]. The pace is ten yards per second. It is,' he added with relish, 'a rushing wall, there is nowhere any gap.'

He then advanced a modified interpretation of the extreme Old School view:

'The very fact that there are many more occasions suitable for fire action than of shock action must not make us lose sight of this, namely, that though we may use fire action when we meet the enemy nine times out of ten, it is on the tenth occasion, and then because shock action takes place, that something definite, something which affects the result of the campaign, is seen to happen.'[13]

In 1910 Roberts elaborated his reasons for wishing to retain some sort of sword or its equivalent:

'It is desirable that cavalry soldiers, equally with their comrades in the infantry, should have a steel weapon of some kind for use in the assault by night, in a mist, or on other occasions when a fire-fight might be impossible or inadvisable. Instead, however, of the present sword, the cavalry soldier would be more suitably equipped with a sword-bayonet for fixing on the rifle when fighting on foot.'[14]

Haig was, of course, unhappy about suppressing the lance. He had, perhaps, forgotten that in his 1899 'Tactical Notes', he had written: 'It is a question whether the Dragoon-lancer* is not a mistake! His lance hampers him.'[15]

'Personally,' he wrote on 2 April, 1903, 'I think our regiments of cavalry should be armed in equal proportions viz. half the cavalry should have swords, the other half lances – but I believe that a good hog spear would be better than the existing long lance.† There is no doubt that the latter is an impediment when scouting and when acting dismounted – but *I don't think it is wise to abolish the lance.* Strategical reconnaissance must culminate in a tactical collision if the enemy possesses cavalry; we want the lance for this.'[16]

That battle he was to win before long (see p. 410).

---

* By this he meant, perhaps, all types of cavalry except lancers.

† Haig told the Royal Commission that the hog spear which he wanted introduced would need 'a counterpoise at the end' which would 'get over the difficulty of carrying it when acting dismounted.' He added that 'whatever you taught a man to use, that weapon he would prefer'. (*R.C.*, II, 411.)

In 1903, in reply to Major Martin Archer-Shee, 19th Hussars, who had invented a folding lance, Baden-Powell wrote that he was 'very anxious to see a good folding lance introduced. I do not,' he added, 'set much store by the strength of it, as I regard the moral effect as its great feature.' (Baden-Powell to Archer-Shee, 8 Oct., 1903, letter in private collection.) Nothing ever came of this invention. Archer-Shee became adjutant to the Cavalry School at Netheravon in 1904.

*　　*　　*

To replace *Cavalry Drill*, 1898,* which had been largely the work
of French, a new official manual, which omitted much of the 'detail'
of its predecessor, had for some time been in preparation under the
guiding hands of Haig. It was to be known as *Cavalry Training*.†
Early in 1904 it was ready for publication. The Army Council, however, held up its issue because some of the more reactionary members
of that newly created body disapproved of the 'Preface' to it which
Roberts, disliking its very Old School tone, had taken the unusual
step of writing.‡ Arnold-Forster, in fact, admitted to Roberts over
lunch that the hold-up had been decided upon on the advice of
French, now commanding the 30,000 troops of the 1st Army Corps
stationed at Aldershot. Roberts protested most vigorously to the
Secretary of State and actually threatened to resign from the Defence
Committee if the Preface were suppressed. In consequence, at
almost the same moment as he ceased to command-in-chief, the
manual, Preface and all, was issued provisionally for six months. In
January, 1905, when he heard that the manual was to be issued without his Preface (once more, although he did not know it, at French's
instigation), he again remonstrated with Arnold-Forster, declaring
that what he had written 'provided the fulcrum of the entire argument' – which is of course why it was dropped! The Secretary of
State could only reply, feebly, that the Army Council had decided

---

* The immediate predecessors of the 1898 manual, were: *Movements of
Cavalry, provisionally approved for the Cavalry at Aldershot*, 1874; *Regulations for
the Instruction and Movement of Cavalry*, 1876, 1885 and 1887; *Cavalry Drill
(Provisional)*, 1891 (3 vols), 1896.

† All reference to 'foot parades' is omitted and the manual contains for the
first time an index.

‡ It is interesting to note that Henry Wilson vetted Roberts's Preface and
made some suggestions for improving it. (Roberts to his daughter, Lady
Aileen Roberts, 22 February, 1910, James, 439.) Wilson, true to his character,
later renegued, becoming a strong adherent to French's views (see p. 422).

Dundonald, who from 1902 till 1904 commanded and reorganized the
Canadian Militia, wrote in 1904 a Preface to the Canadian version of *Cavalry
Training*.

'It is not meant,' he declared, 'for cavalry who turn their backs, but for
those who, when they see the enemy preparing to charge with sabre and
lance, will coolly dismount, form up, and when he gets within reach, pour
in such a withering fire as will in five minutes kill as many of the enemy as
the same enemy with sword and lance would kill in five hours on active
service.' (Quoted in Rimington, 55.)

that 'the Preface had done its work'. One member of the Council pointed out that its omission 'would not be a slight to the late Commander-in-Chief, in that the *book itself* will be practically that drawn up under his direction.' Lyttelton thought that it would be 'rather anomalous to publish a preface by the late Commander-in-Chief under the auspices of the Army Council'. He pointed out that none of the other manuals ever had Prefaces. All this only went to show that the moment Roberts left office he also lost influence.[17]

The Preface so well expresses the moderate, commonsense view that it is worth quoting extensively:

'I desire most earnestly to call the attention of all ranks of the cavalry to the augmented importance of this branch of the Service, consequent upon the introduction of far-reaching guns and rifles.

'Cavalry must now be considered not only the eyes of an army, and the arm by which a demoralized enemy can best be destroyed, but equipped (as it shortly will be) with the new short rifle, it will take a part in war which it never has been able, or indeed expected to take, in the past.

'It is hardly too much to say that the change which has taken place in cavalry is as great as that which occurred to the infantry when the cross-bow and pike were replaced by the rifle and bayonet. When cavalry was first organized lancer regiments depended entirely – and other corps almost entirely – on the lance and sword, owing to the short range, inaccuracy and difficulty of loading of the smooth-bore musket and carbine. Tentative changes were made when muzzle-loading and breech-loading rifles were adopted; but it is only within the last quarter of a century that lancer regiments have had any firearm given to them save a pistol. . . .

'But what does the development of rifle fire consequent on the introduction of the long range, low trajectory, magazine rifle mean? It means that instead of the firearm being an adjunct to the sword, the sword must henceforth be an adjunct to the rifle; and that cavalry soldiers must become expert rifle shots and be constantly trained to act dismounted.

'Cavalry officers need have no fear that teaching their men to fight on foot as well as on horseback will in any way interfere with that *élan* which is so essential for cavalry soldiers to possess. It will, I am satisfied, only serve to increase their confidence in themselves and in their branch of the service. . . .

'I should consider that a leader who failed to take advantage of an opportunity for employing shock tactics when required to close with the enemy was unfit for his position. But I cannot agree with those military experts who hold that, in future wars, cavalry shock tactics will form as prominent a feature as heretofore. I think the improvement in fire arms will give the victory to the side which can first dismount on ground less favourable to a charge than an open plain. . . .

'I would beg of cavalry officers not to be led away by the feeling that there is something unsuitable to the mounted arm and detrimental to its prestige in employing dismounted men when cavalry is opposed to cavalry. . . . I confidently predict that the commander who makes use of his rifle fire in an intelligent manner will, *coeteris paribus*, beat the commander who despises, or does not know how profitably to avail himself of, the deadly weapon about to be placed in the hands of our cavalry soldiers.'

The rifle which Roberts introduced for the cavalry was virtually the same as that used by the infantry, except that it was shortened by five inches and lightened by one pound.* He stressed in his Preface the importance of the rifle being 'carried on the person of the soldier himself', as opposed to the sword which should be attached to the saddle. This was a battle which Roberts had been fighting ever since the Second Afghan War in 1879 (see Vol III, p. 235).[18] In his Introduction to Erskine Childers's *War and the Arme Blanche*, written in 1910 (see below), he lamented that 'the rifle is still being carried on the horse. . . . This is not the case in India [as a result of his orders when Commander-in-Chief there], where the rifle, supported by a small bucket, is attached to the man, so that when he dismounts the rifle goes with him.'† The 1907

* This was the 'Rifle, Short, Magazine, Lee-Enfield, Mark I' (see illustration p. 398). The Mark III was generally substituted in 1912. In 1913 the 11th Hussars and two infantry battalions were selected for trials of the experimental .275 rifle. It is possible that, had the First World War not intervened, this rifle might have been adopted. (Lumley, 10.)

From now on the infantry musketry course was adopted by the cavalry.

† In 1907 a new 'equipment for carrying the rifle', made by Squadron Sergeant-Major Dove of the 14th Hussars, was demonstrated to Kitchener in India. This was probably similar to what was officially introduced in India soon afterwards and known as the Taylor equipment (see below). The official report

PLATE I.

RIFLE, SHORT, MAGAZINE, LEE-ENFIELD. MARK I

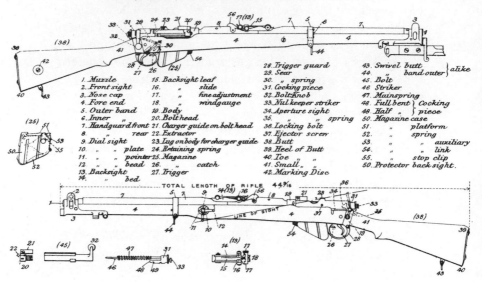

1. Muzzle	15. Backsight leaf	28. Trigger guard
2. Front sight	16. „ slide	29. Sear
3. Nose cap	17. „ fine adjustment	30. „ spring
4. Fore end	18. „ windgauge	31. Cocking piece
5. Outer band	19. Body	32. Bolt knob
6. Inner „	20. Bolt head	33. Nut keeper striker
7. Handguard front	21. Charger guide on bolt head	34. Aperture sight
8. „ rear	22. Extractor	35. „ „ spring
9. Dial sight	23. Lug on body for charger guide	36. Locking bolt
10. „ „ plate	24. Retaining spring	37. Ejector screw
11. „ „ pointer	25. Magazine	38. Butt
12. „ „ bead	26. „ catch	39. Heel of Butt
13. Backsight	27. Trigger	40. Toe „ „
14. „ bed		41. Small „ „
		42. Marking Disc

43. Swivel butt	alike
44. „ band outer	
45. Bolt	
46. Striker	
47. Mainspring	
48. Full bent	Cocking
49. Half „	piece
50. Magazine case	
51. „ platform	
52. „ spring	
53. „ „ auxiliary	
54. „ „ link	
55. „ „ stop clip	
56. Protector back sight.	

TOTAL LENGTH OF RIFLE 44⅞

LINE OF SIGHT

edition of *Cavalry Training* (see below), which differed considerably
from the 1904 edition (not even, as in that edition, listing the word
'rifle' in the index), applauded the fact that the rifle was to continue
to reside in buckets attached to the horse since it was only to be used
on exceptional occasions to 'supplement the sword or lance'.[19]* How
dangerous and ridiculous this arrangement was is well illustrated
by this 1910 description of it in the 17th Lancers:

> 'Sword in scabbard on the near side, rifle in rifle-bucket on the
> off side, lance slung or held by the right hand with its butt in a
> lance-bucket on the stirrup. To dismount it was necessary to
> take the rifle out of the rifle-bucket, replacing it with the lance,

made on the 14th in 1908 stated: 'With the new equipment for carrying the rifle,
combined mounted and dismounted action is being constantly practised. This
equipment seems to be very satisfactory.' (Browne, 246.)

 * Even Bernhardi, in his *Cavalry in Future Wars* (see p. 415), says that 'the
sword should be attached to the saddle, the carbine to the man, as is, in fact, the
practice of all races of born horsemen.' (Bernhardi, 176.)

The arguments as to how best the British cavalryman should carry his firearm had been going on since the days of Marlborough. They never ceased till
cavalry itself ceased to exist in the late 1930s.

which was left on the horse. It is hardly bearable to think what would have happened to groups of led horses under heavy fire.'

French, of course, was 'of the opinion that the rifle should be carried on the horse and not slung to the man'. In 1904, though, he announced a slight but obviously unsatisfactory compromise:

'A bucket, similar to the old carbine bucket, and adapted to the new rifle, has been tried at Aldershot with excellent results. It is lighter than the old carbine bucket, and is so fixed on the saddle that the increased length makes no difference. This bucket is constructed so that it will contain the rifle fitted with a sling, by which, when the cavalry know they are likely to be engaged in dismounted action, the rifle can be carried on the man's back.

'I consider it is of the greatest importance that, in the cavalry fight (mounted) the cavalry soldier should have perfect freedom to use his sword or lance.'[20]*

As early as September, 1901, Roberts had written to Sir Evelyn Wood that he would do all in his power 'to make cavalrymen understand that they must not think it in any way *infra dig* being trained to fight on foot.'[21] It was *obiter dicta* such as this from a man who, in spite of his subsequent career, was still likely to be thought of as a mere Bengal gunner by regular cavalry grandees and snobs, which were so offensive to them. One can imagine French or Haig muttering to themselves: how dare this 'Indian' heretic presume to interfere with 'the arm of the gods' of which we are the acknowledged high priests! This exclusive, anti-'Indian', closed-shop attitude was a significant element throughout the controversy.

One of Roberts's most potent allies was the infantryman Ian

---

* A number of attempts to devise better ways of carrying the rifle on horseback were made at this date. One which had an official life of four years was the 'Equipment, rifle carrying – mounted men (Taylor pattern)' bucket and 'carrier', which was discontinued in 1910. 137 sets were issued to each squadron of the 13th Hussars in India in 1908. Another was the 'Crocker Rifle Equipment', 100 sets of which were tried out in the same year by 'D' Squadron of the regiment. Various means of improving the charger of the new rifle were also attempted. In 1904, the same regiment tried out the 'Harris Charger'. Details of these experiments are hard to find. Some of them were the brain children of progressive regimental officers. (Barrett: *13H*, 221, 237, 241; *List of Changes in Indian Military Stores*, Sec. 6/6971 and 5322, 1910; information kindly supplied by the National Army Museum.)

Hamilton, who became Quartermaster-General to the Forces in 1903. In his evidence to the Royal Commission given in that year he said:

'I have heard it said that if the Boers had possessed cavalry, in the European sense of the word, our men would have had a chance of showing the advantages of a boot-to-boot charge over a looser formation admitting of greater individual initiative. It is difficult to answer this sort of argument [which was one of those most frequently put forward by the Old School]. If both sides were to agree to carry out their fight with punctilio and a chivalrous disregard of the requirements of scientific arms, then no doubt there would still be suitable scope in warfare for old-world methods .... Compared to a modern rifle, the sword or lance can only be regarded as a mediaeval toy. ... It must be remembered that sword and lance are still the same as they were in the days of King Arthur [not, perhaps, *quite* true!], whilst the firearm improves steadily, the latest step in this direction having taken place since the South African War. In scouting and reconnaissance especially, I hold that cavalry who use their rifles must beat back or pierce the cavalry screen of opponents who are thinking mainly of their swords or lances, and of how they can best come to close quarters so as to use them. ... I freely admit that on some rare occasions a determined charge by a swarm of horsemen with cold steel might have an effect on the morale of a shaken or surprised enemy which no rifle fire could produce. Therefore I say, arm the cavalry with the sword as well as the rifle; but let the rifle have the place which is its due under modern conditions.'[22]

French, of course, who was to become more and more influential as he climbed to the top of the army tree, disagreed fundamentally. He also complained to Arnold-Forster that Hamilton was 'behind' what he considered Roberts's harmful reforms.[23] He told the Royal Commission that he was 'absolutely certain that if we are opposed to cavalry anything like as good as we think our own cavalry, the leader who gets down off his horses and begins firing is lost .... In an ordinary campaign, say against France or Germany, cavalry forces will come together, and then the rifle is of no use at all .... I would make the sword or lance always the principal weapon of the Hussar or Lancer.'[24] Colonel Henderson [see Vol III, p. 400], on the other hand, writing in 1901, deplored how small was the number of military men who 'realized that the small-bore and smokeless powder have destroyed the last vestiges of the traditional *role* of cavalry.'[25]

Thus the great cavalry controversy got under way. In 1907 the 1904 edition of *Cavalry Training* was superseded by a manual which was hardly less conservative than its predecessor, though training with sword and lance was banished to an appendix. It went so far as to say that 'thorough efficiency in the use of the rifle and in dismounted tactics is an absolute necessity', but it then went on to make it unequivocally clear that 'it must be accepted as a principle that the rifle, effective as it is, cannot replace the effect produced by the speed of the horse, the magnetism of the charge and the terror of cold steel.* For when opportunities for mounted action occur, these characteristics combine to inspire such dash, enthusiasm and moral ascendancy that cavalry is rendered irresistible.' In 1910 the 1907 edition of *Cavalry Training* was republished with minor amendments. A new edition was issued in 1912 with a noticeable lessening of stress upon the paramountcy of the *arme blanche* but, of course, like the 1910 reprinting, without Roberts's Preface. Haig by that date had left the War Office. Under 'Shock and Fire Action' the 1912 manual states:

> 'The rifle endows cavalry with great independence in war, and numerous situations will occur when it can be used with greater effect than the sword or lance. But a bold leader will find frequent opportunities for mounted attack which will produce more rapid and decisive results than can be gained by even the most skilful use of the rifle. It is, however, by no means necessary when an attack is made that only one of the two methods should be employed, for fire action can create favourable opportunities for shock action, and a well-executed combination of the two methods will often present the greatest chances of success.'

*　　*　　*

Part of what looked like a concerted campaign by the 'shock' advocates was the founding in 1906 of the *Cavalry Journal*. It was specifically designed to defend and to spread the *arme blanche* gospel. Its inspiration came from Baden-Powell (with French's strong

---

* This entirely contradicted Roberts's 1904 dictum that 'the sword must henceforth be an adjunct to the rifle'.

backing) and that of Charles Sydney Goldman who had written a sycophantic book on the Cavalry Division in South Africa (from which quotations occur in earlier chapters of this volume). Its first editor was Colonel the Hon. Osbert Victor George Atheling Lumley of the 11th Hussars, a brother of the 10th Earl of Scarbrough. Beside articles by serving officers on tactics, organization and weapons, as well as sport, there was much space devoted to detailed accounts of mostly pre-Crimean cavalry actions. The early issues contained numerous reviews of whatever international military literature tended to be friendly towards *arme blanche* tenets. At first it was under the unofficial wing of the United Services Instititution, but the staff of the Cavalry School (see p. 428) took it over in 1908, and in 1911 the editorship became automatically one of the duties of the School's Commandant. It lasted until 1941.

Evidence of the importance which cavalry officers attached to the social exclusiveness of the arm was provided when, in 1909, the Cavalry Club enlarged its premises to about twice its original size. The Club had been started in 1890 by Captain Wetherall of the 20th Hussars rather against the Duke of Cambridge's wishes, 'who disliked the idea of confining its advantages to one branch of the service'.[26] It flourished nevertheless and in it is to be found an extensive library of books on the subject of cavalry. In 1976 the club was amalgamated with the Guards Club which joined it in 127 Piccadilly, and where both still prosper, horse and foot, as it were, joining hands most amicably.

*   *   *

A great deal of the ammunition used by both sides was derived from their different interpretations of the lessons to be acquired from the Boer War and from the Russo-Japanese War of 1904–5. The cavalry as such – that is in the sense that the Old School thought of it – in neither conflict had many opportunities to show its mettle or to influence the result. In both wars, cavalry neither incurred catastrophic reverses nor contributed to decisive victories. During the whole of the Boer War the British regular cavalry, with the exception of the very minor effort at Elandslaagte (see p. 53), never made a knee-to-knee traditional type of *arme blanche* charge. It spent most of its time, as has been shown, particularly during the first phase while it still had its swords and lances, waiting upon the occasion – and the occasion never came. The Old School could point to neither disaster nor achievement. It therefore fell back on the proposition that the South African experience was a 'one off' which would never be repeated. Consequently, it argued that for an European War the charge with the *arme blanche* should still be recognized, as it always had been, as the first object for which the cavalry should be trained. In spite of the evidence of the vastly increased power of the rifle which the Boers had provided, the Old School faced the future fully confident of its ability to effect the charge against European cavalry. As the Boers did not carry the *arme blanche*, their relevance for future wars did not exist. In thus urging that cavalry should be armed and trained so as to be able to oppose the traditional tactics of the French, German and Austrian cavalry, the conservatives were not entirely unrealistic, as is shown below (see p. 418), especially as they believed that the first and most important task in an European war would be to knock out the opposing cavalry (see p. 419). They argued that a guerrilla campaign against mounted riflemen gave no guidance to tactical thinkers. The lessons which the traditionalists claimed to have learnt from the war were, therefore, chiefly negative ones. During the later stages of the struggle, for instance, French complained to Roberts that the Boers 'never attempted to come on with the dash and vigour they display now [November, 1901] when the cavalry being deprived of their weapons for mounted attack have always to get off their horses and resort to firearms.'[27] This was a bizarre conclusion indeed, for, as has been shown, in so far as the mounted arm in South Africa was formidable at all, it was clearly the rifle which made it so. A vital argument against French's view was well put by Brevet-Major A. W. Andrew, who had commanded the 3rd New Zealand Brigade in South Africa. Writing of the 'Boer rushes' when '600 Boers could be dimly discerned galloping fast at us,' he commented, 'I have not the least doubt that a regiment of lancers would have scared the souls out of them, but could we afford to attach a regiment of lancers to each column and keep it intact, riding along for weeks and months waiting for such an opportunity? Fifty or sixty columns were in the field, and as many regiments would have been required, so this was impossible.'[28]

Another astonishing lesson which a number of the champions of the *arme blanche* derived from the war was that the Boers would have been even more successful had they possessed it. 'The Boers did all that could be expected of mounted infantry,' wrote Goldman in 1910, 'but were powerless to crown victory as only the dash of cavalry can do.'[29] Lieutenant-Colonel Maude went so far as to suggest that 'if the commando which attacked Benson at Bakenlaagte [see p. 255] had been able to charge home with cold steel, lance or sword, the result for us must have been considerably worse than, in fact, it was.' Although a Staff College graduate (see Vol III, p. 112) Maude seems never to have been on campaign. He certainly was not at Bakenlaagte![30] He was one of the most immoderate 'knee-to-knee' men. In his *Cavalry: Its Past and Future*, he wrote:

'Every hour spent on training men to skill in mounted combat tends towards mobility and cohesion; every hour on the range, in theory at least, detracts from it. Actually in practice there is ample time for both. The evil only begins when the soldier is taught to rely on the firearm, not on the sword; for then he begins to look on the horse as a mere means of locomotion, and not, as it really is, an essential part of the ultimate cavalry unit.'[31]

What men like French refused to contemplate was the possibility that 'cavalry in combat with cavalry', to use Erskine Childers's words, 'would have the bad taste to use their rifles'. They could not believe that mounted men in future conflicts might be tempted to impose fire-tactics on the cavalry, as the Boers had done in nearly every type of combat during the war. In 1904 French quoted

'several instances . . . in which a powerful attack by the Boers (employing dismounted tactics in the open) was conspicuously defeated and driven back by a few squadrons of Regular cavalry attacking mounted . . . . These mounted attacks were made with absolutely untrained horses, so used up that in order to get the semblance of a gallop out of them the men had to flog them with the flats of their swords, and yet the very instant such an attack developed, the enemy's fire became wild, for a few moments they wavered, and then the plain was covered with Boer horsemen flying for their lives. After they discovered that our cavalry galloped for them directly they appeared in the open, they never, within my experience, trusted themselves from under efficient cover. The operations of the Cavalry Division [on the march to Pretoria] generally took place so distant from the main line of advance, that such incidents as these were never seen by the Commander-in-Chief [a dig at Roberts!] or the Headquarters Staff, nor, so far as I know, have they ever appeared in any official report which has been made public.'

All this special pleading begs many questions the answers to which will at once spring to the minds of readers of earlier chapters of this volume![32]

In the Manchurian war between Russia and Japan, which was the first in which both sides enjoyed a complete array of modern technology, the chief reason why the cavalry of both sides failed to come into its own was that both armies 'had gone to ground in trenches behind barbed-wire entanglements because of the killing power of machine-guns and quick-firing artillery'.[33] It is not surprising, therefore, that there were very few cavalry actions from which lessons could be usefully deduced. Nevertheless, the cavalry controversialists at home searched avidly for clues which might help to advance their respective arguments. It was noticed that the Japanese, whose mounted force was vastly inferior in numbers to that of the Russians, were largely influenced by German models and believed in the cult of shock tactics, though they did not possess lances. The Russian cavalry, on the other hand, unlike all other European cavalries for the last quarter of a century, had concentrated largely on dismounted firepower. The Russians were generally better horsed and the better horsemen but they were on the losing side, and on the whole they put on a pitiable performance. This fact gave the British *arme blanche* school much ill-founded encouragement. It was ill founded because the Tsar's best regiments were held back in Europe for fear of an European war and because those that were present were equipped in most cases with inferior carbines* and, in spite of their training, were very defective marksmen. Disregarding these aspects, the anti-fire school put down the paltry performance of the Russians to their mounted infantry training which had 'emasculated their Dragoons'. Such was the view, for example, of Colonel Birkbeck (see p. 296), commanding the Netheravon Cavalry School (see p. 428), who had been attached to the Japanese 3rd Army.[34] Ian Hamilton had also been in Manchuria, as Military Representative of India with the Japanese Field Army. His view was diametrically opposed to Birkbeck's. Time and again he was not surprised to find that 'the cavalry, Russian and Japanese, did nothing. . . . Cavalry trained to act as good solid infantry when dismounted might,' he wrote, 'have done much, either on the Russian or Japanese side.' At

---

* Although the Russians since 1870 had placed much faith in machine guns – more so than any other nation – their cavalry were only armed with carbines and bayonets during the Manchurian War. (Hutchison, Lieut-Col G. S. *Machine Guns: Their History and Tactical Employment*, 1938, 33.)

the battle of the Yalu, as on other occasions, he noted 'that there was no place or opportunity where the horse could possibly have been of any value except to bring a rifleman rapidly up to the right spot.' Hamilton, as a result of his Manchurian observations, summed up the basis of the New School's reasoning thus: 'If one side is so unfair as to dismount and shoot, the opposing side must follow suit or be shot.' He added that he was not against the sword 'but only against those who would train cavalry so that they enter upon a field of battle thinking rather of where they may deliver a charge than of how they may employ their mobility to enable them to make use of their rifles with the best effect.'[35]

*　　*　　*

Another weird plank in the platform of the shock-action school was that each advance in the power of firearms would entail a matching enlargement of the 'friction' of battle which would demoralize infantry and gunners to such a degree that the cold steel charge would still often be possible. As long ago as 1893 the then Inspector-General of Cavalry had declared that 'with smokeless powder infantry will be able to see cavalry coming, and if their morale is not perfect the sight of a large mass of cavalry coming in the distance might have some effect upon them. Although,' he added, 'we shall not be able to so often surprise the enemy, our moral effect will be increased.'[36]

One of the saner and less controversial points of view was propounded by Brigadier-General Broadwood (see p. 140 and Vol III, p. 367), who could certainly claim to have had recent experience of cavalry leading:

> 'Given an efficiently trained force, victory,' he wrote in 1906, 'will fall to the leader who, untramelled by shallow generalization or by a false Cavalry spirit, is prepared to employ shock and fire in proportion that circumstances demand. If this be true of all Cavalry leaders, how much more is it so of our own service, called on to be ready to meet enemies in all parts of the world among the most varying conditions of ground, armament and tactics?'

Here Broadwood was touching on a problem which was unique to the British cavalry and which served to complicate and confuse the issues particularly with regard to training and armament. A chief reason for the tendency to ignore the lessons of the South African War was the undoubted fact that, significant though that campaign was, it bore little resemblance to the question of the defence of India, which was so much more vital to the interests of Britain. No one disagreed that there was a real place for the sword and especially the lance when dealing with, for example, civil unrest in India. It was therefore not unreasonable to suggest that these weapons should be retained not only in all native cavalry regiments as their chief armament, but also, since they took their turn of duty in the sub-continent, in at least to some degree, regiments of the line at home. Surprisingly enough, though, this case was not made a very great deal of by the *arme blanche* advocates. It was left to Roberts, in his 1903 Memorandum, to point out that 'occasions may arise, particularly in campaigns against savages, who are ill-armed, or who have an innate fear of horsemen, when the lance may be the surest and speediest means of demoralizing the enemy.'[37]

*   *   *

A 'middle-of-the-roader' with much South African experience was Lieutenant-Colonel Edward May, a gunner and a prolific writer on military subjects. While the war was still on he wrote that 'it will be well if for the future we aim at making our troopers at least as formidable on foot as on horseback.' At the same time he made a telling point which would not have displeased the Old School:

> 'To keep a certain force of cavalry in hand, husbanded carefully for the pursuit with which the day may culminate, is a wise provision. If the same regiments which have been at work all day are asked to pursue in the evening, the task set them is an impossible one. Be the officers and men as keen as can be wished, the horses at any rate are tired out, and rapidity of movement is with them out of the question.'[38]

*   *   *

Cavalry officers' worst nightmare was that they would never again be given opportunities to relish what Baden-Powell called the 'best sensation' he had ever enjoyed, namely 'leading a well-trained brigade of cavalry at a gallop. . . . It is the sensation that your chest is going to burst and your inside to fall out with pleasure. There is a tremendous feeling of exultation in moving that great, rushing, thundering mass of men and horses just by a wave of your hand.' Indeed the chief basis of the Old School's case was the fear that dismounted action would destroy what was believed to be the uniquely sacred 'cavalry spirit'. 'It is above all things important,' wrote Colonel Henderson in 1902 'that dash, the most precious possession of the cavalry soldier, should never be tampered with, either in training or in war.' In March, 1904, Arnold-Forster asked French for a report to put before the Army Council. French thought this document so important that he sent a copy to the King's Private Secretary. In it he wrote:

'Cavalry is an arm which none thoroughly understand but those who have served with it for some considerable period of their lives; the very soul and essence of its power lies in what is well termed the "cavalry spirit". It is difficult to define what one means by the "cavalry spirit", but it is a power which is *felt* and realized by those who have served much with the arm. Its attributes are "elan", "dash", a fixed determination always to take the offensive and secure the initiative. Such a spirit can never be created in a body of troops whose first idea is to abandon their horses and lie down under cover in the face of a swiftly-charging mass of horsemen . . . .

'Having served in the cavalry nearly all my life, I have formed the strongest opinion that if it is laid down by regulations that cavalry soldiers are to regard the rifle as their principal weapon, and that shock tactics are to be resorted to under very exceptional circumstances, we shall soon find that we have no cavalry in the British army worthy of the name; that our cavalry will probably be over-ridden by the highly-trained forces of that arm which are kept up by the Great Powers, and as a natural consequence, all great tactical combinations, whether in attack or defence, will be paralyzed.'[39]*

* It is only fair to point out that in the same report French stated that 'no stone should be left unturned to make cavalry soldiers the best possible shots, and thoroughly adept in all dismounted duties.

'The infusion in a body of cavalry of the true "cavalry spirit" will also have a marked effect on any enterprise such as making a dash for a position which it is most important to hold on to until the infantry can arrive, so that troops thoroughly imbued with that spirit will effect results which would be otherwise unobtainable.'
(French: *Role*, 2.)

Haig, in December, 1903, had written much the same: 'If we allow cavalry to dismount in season out of season . . . we shall ruin the arm for *war*, whatever use they may be at peace manoeuvres.'[40] In reply to these rather arrogant views on the special and superior standing of the cavalry, Roberts, in his Introduction to Erskine Childers's *War and the Arme Blanche* (see below), confessed that he could not

'follow the train of thought which insists upon cavalry requiring a "spirit" for "shock action", and a spirit different, it is presumed, from the soldierly spirit which it is essential for the other arms to possess if they are to behave with resolution and courage on the field of battle. The "charge" doubtless requires "dash", but no special "cavalry spirit"; the excitement of galloping at full speed, in company with a number of his comrades, is of itself sufficient to carry the cavalry soldier forward. . . . I have taken part in cavalry combats, and have frequently had occasion to scout and reconnoitre with two, three or perhaps half a dozen cavalry soldiers, at a time when capture by the enemy meant certain death. And I have no hesitation in saying that scouting and reconnoitring try the nerves far more seriously than charging the enemy.'[41]

This was written in 1910. So was the following by French, indicating that by then he was more prepared to admit that the *cavalry* spirit was not unique: 'Those who scoff at the spirit, whether of cavalry, or artillery or of infantry [can there have been many?], are people who have had no practical experience of . . . personal leadership in war.'[42] This statement was one of a number which show that French, as the years went by and as he had increasingly to face the awful responsibilities of the highest commands, was prepared to modify his extreme views. (For further evidence, see p. 420.)

It seems clear that not even a majority of junior cavalry officers agreed with Roberts. Most of the more senior ones certainly did not, from Sir Evelyn Wood who told Lyttelton in 1904 that he was very worried about the likely disappearance of the cavalry spirit and that he believed that Roberts lacked any real support, to Baden-Powell, who was Inspector-General of Cavalry from 1903 to 1907, and who wrote in a Memorandum in March, 1904: 'I fully agree with General Sir J. French's remarks as regards the role of the cavalry.'[43]

The next engagement initiated by the Old School was designed to achieve the official re-instatement of the lance. In 1907 that perfect example of the typically reactionary cavalry officer, Major-General Scobell, had openly sympathized with the regiments (all lancers) of the 1st Cavalry Brigade, which he commanded, when they flouted the suppression order of 1903 by carrying their lances not only at drill but also on field training. Worse still, French does not seem to have taken any notice of this breach of discipline within one of his brigades.* Long before this, enormous pressure had been applied to the Army Council to restore the use of the lance. The Annual Reports of the Inspector-General of the Forces in 1904, 1906 and 1907 had called attention to the alleged lack of 'effective steel weapons with which to oppose a continental opponent'.[44] As early as April, 1904, Roberts had written to Kitchener in India to use his influence 'since I understand that a great struggle will be made to get that weapon reintroduced now that I have left the War Office.' Kitchener did his best. Amongst other things he sent for Haig and 'lectured him on the subject'.[45] But the battle was lost when in 1909 an Army Order directed that 'regiments of Lancers will in future carry the lance not only on escort duty . . . but also on guard, during training, at manoeuvres and when so ordered on field service.' (See illustration below).[46] Roberts, furious but impotent, got in touch

.O. 158. **Cavalry Equipment.**—With reference to Army Orders 39 of 1903 and 258 of 1906, regiments of Lancers will in future carry the lance, not only on escort duty and at reviews and other ceremonial parades, but also on guard, during training, at manœuvres, and when so ordered on field service.

54
Cavalry
902

1909.

with Sir William Nicholson (see p. 387), who the previous year had succeeded Lyttelton as Chief of the Imperial General Staff and was usually inclined towards the New School. Nicholson could only reply, rather lamely, that 'the original order either went too far or not far enough'.[47]†

It is extraordinarily difficult today to grasp how vastly momentous, not only sentimentally and romantically, but also symbolically,

* It was not only at Aldershot that little notice was taken of the 1903 Army Order. 'It did not,' wrote the historian of the 17th Lancers, then stationed in Edinburgh, 'prevent both men and officers being trained as offensively as possible in the use of the abolished weapon. Probably,' he added, 'on cold winter mornings, bearing a dummy lance, cap, tunic and gauntlets, they wished that there had been a greater observance of army orders.' (Micholls, 59.)

† The lance remained in being until 1927 when Army Order 392 decreed that it should be retained only for ceremonial occasions.

were the lance and lancers to cavalrymen and to others of the time. Hubert Gough, with the 1st Cavalry Brigade at Aldershot, wrote in his memoirs that 'to motor down from London and elsewhere, just to see three Lancer regiments march out of church on Sundays, with their different plumes, blowing in the breeze, and different coloured tunics and facings, was almost as popular a way of passing the time as sitting on the Victoria Memorial in the hopes of seeing the Queen emerge.'[48]*

*   *   *

Way back in 1886 Buller had prophesied that 'the value of mounted infantry will be the most noticeable feature in the next great war'. Whether he meant an European war or not, it is certain that his prediction was correct with respect to the Boer War.[49] Twenty-seven years later, in 1913, eleven months before the First World War, the Army Council decided that mounted infantry would not be used in an European war. Consequently the two 'Mounted Brigades' then in being, which consisted of cavalry and one battalion of mounted infantry each, were broken up.[50]† What happened between 1886 and 1913 as to the organization, establishments and tactical training of mounted infantry is a complicated story. With its intricacies we need not be troubled. Its relevance to the great cavalry controversy lies in the fact that the 'fire school' failed, in the words of Edward M. Spiers, to 'organize an alternative mounted force able to exploit the advantages of the rifle'.[51] Nevertheless, shortly after the Boer war, the decision had been come to that mounted infantry must be trained on a far larger scale than before the war.‡ By 1906 there were the

* Except in India, tent-pegging, the lancers' favourite sport, was not encouraged post-war. It was permissible for recreation, but frowned upon by the War Office, if not by the lancer regiments, as part of training. To prevent the horses damaging their legs, the sport was to be limited to aged animals and carried out only on soft ground. Further, galloping was only permitted in the final forty yards before reaching the peg. (Sworder, Major J. C. C., Director Mounted Events, The Royal Tournament, letter to *The Times*, 19 May, 1982.)

† Repington of *The Times* (see below) applauded this decision to get rid of what he called 'the cavalry of poverty', and urged the formation of a second regular cavalry division for the expeditionary force. (Luvaas, 316.)

Already, in the 1907 edition of *Cavalry Training*, the single battalion of mounted infantry which in the 1904 edition had appeared as part of the composition of a cavalry brigade (together with three cavalry regiments and one battery of Royal Horse Artillery), had been omitted.

‡ For the 1898 Salisbury Plain manoeuvres, four companies were formed into a battalion, two trained in the MI School, Aldershot, and two at Hounslow. Three of the four companies were mounted on cavalry horses. When war came

equivalent of twenty battalions trained at permanent stations where three training centres of a sort were set up. This sounds much more business-like than it actually was, for the training was for only a few months a year for one company from, in theory, each of the eighty infantry battalions stationed at home,[52] and, anyway, two of the three schools were closed in the following year.[53] Even Colonel Alexander John Godley, Commandant of the Mounted Infantry School at Aldershot, was against the creation of a permanent force. Given its limited opportunities in war, he believed such a force to be an unnecessary hybrid.[54] He saw it, nevertheless, as an useful adjunct to the cavalry and as suitable for escorting the Horse Artillery. The Inspector of Cavalry's report on the 1905 manoeuvres stated that the 'roles of regular cavalry and mounted infantry were still in confusion, both as regards their individual duties and in combination with other arms'.[55]

Part of the argument against mounted infantry, and indeed against all dismounted action by any mounted troops, was that, since one man in every four was required to attend to the horses when the fighting was on foot, a quarter of every unit was unable to take part in it. Colonel Henderson pointed out that

'the led horses are a source of weakness, physical and moral. They form a most sensitive and most vulnerable point. It is not always easy to place them in security; and the fact that they constitute the sole means of retreat renders them a source of continual anxiety both to officer and man. The former is preoccupied with providing for the safe cover of a crowd of animals; the latter, fully realizing his helplessness and discomfort if deprived of his mount, is never quite happy when there is the slightest chance that they may become separated. In consequence there is always a tendency on the part of dismounted men to think more of getting into the saddle than of offering a protracted resistance; they are thus less stubborn in defence than infantry, and more inclined to give way when there is a danger of their being outflanked.'*

there were available only the two MI battalions trained at Aldershot. These were the only properly trained mounted infantry that went out to South Africa. (Godley, 52.)

* A trooper of Paget's Horse gives the drill which was used in the war when dismounted action was ordered:

'Upon receiving the order: "With carbines prepare to dismount – dismount!" those who ride numbers one, two and four when formed in

Haig, not surprisingly, felt very strongly that 'cavalry (properly trained) should fulfil all the requirements of mounted troops, and that mounted infantry should be abolished. No country can afford to maintain mounted troops of different values.'[56] As has been shown, he got his way.

Perhaps the chief reason why mounted infantry units, or any other similar bodies, were never seriously organized as an alternative to regular cavalry was the faintly surprising fact that nearly all the better known of the column commanders returned from the Boer War, where they had seen the advantages of mounted infantry at first hand, had promptly plumped, almost to a man, for the Old School idea that in future wars the traditional cavalry arm was superior in battle. The most they would allow was that there might be a role for limited numbers of mounted riflemen to fulfil subordinate protective duties so as to 'free cavalry for independent strategical action'.[57] When Lieutenant-Colonel de Lisle (see p. 256), for example, who had served with the mounted infantry during the whole course of the war, and was to command the 2nd Cavalry Brigade in 1911, declared to Roberts in 1910 that the cavalryman could become proficient with *both* sword and rifle, thus enabling him 'to charge home with the sword when the opportunity occurs',* Erskine Childers fulminated to Roberts, 'If an officer with his war record in the MI, can with such sublime tranquillity declare for the sword and lance which he has never used, and probably never seen

column of fours, pass the bridoon or snaffle rein [see p. 449] to the man who rides number three, in such a way that he can, while remaining mounted, control his own and lead the other three horses. When this has been done, the three dismounted men advance as ordered, while it is the duty of the sergeant-major to keep the horses in safety, but following as near as may be to the troop to which they belong.'
(Rose-Innes, 140.)

* De Lisle put forward a subsidiary argument for retaining some 'real' cavalry:
'So much ammunition is now used and the difficulties of replenishing it are so great, that we may expect to find armies in the future, towards the end of the battle, facing each other, but unable to bring matters to a conclusion for want of it. It is on these occasions that a cavalry, kept back as a weapon in the hands of the commander, and launched at the right moment, will achieve a decisive result.'
(de Lisle, Col H. de B. 'Mounted Troops in Co-operation with Other Arms' (Lecture arranged by GOC 2nd Div.), *Aldershot Military Society*, CXI, 21 Feb., 1911.)

used in war, what can one do? The superstition seems immortal, unconquerable.' This may appear to be a rather extreme reaction, but Childers *was* extreme (see below). Nothing could persuade him that, in Spiers's words, 'parity would ever be credible' while 'shock tactics were so elaborate and complicated to teach, and once taught so devoutly believed in.' Indeed, de Lisle's comparatively mild desire for equality in training time between rifle and sword might have led one to suppose that he was a traitor to and not an adherent of the Old School, for the astonishing fact is that by 1910 *80% of cavalry training time was being devoted to shock tactics, while only* 10% *each was given over to fire tactics and reconnaissance.*[58] These proportions hardly changed right up to 1913. The proponents of the 'charge home' side of the controversy seemed, unquestionably, to be winning.

* * *

A powerful figure at this time was Colonel Repington (see Vol III, p. 106, and, above, p. 72), the Military Correspondent of *The Times* from 1904 to 1918. He was unequivocally a French/Haig man and as such an invaluable propagandist for the Old School. His influence through his articles in 'The Thunderer' was sufficient for people to identify him so closely with army matters as to regard him as a sort of official spokesman. This he very nearly became when in 1911 he was appointed editor of the newly started *Army Review*, a quarterly published under the auspices of the War Office staff. His views on the great cavalry controversy can be summed up by his statement that cavalry armed only with the rifle 'is a chicken trussed for the spit' and that all cavalry should be armed with the lance, 'the best weapon to supplement the rifle'. He also commended with warmth 'the true cavalry spirit which scorns mathematical calculations'.[59] In other respects Repington was forward-looking, especially with respect to military aircraft and submarines.

The debate was carried on not only in articles and letters in the newspapers and periodicals but, more importantly, in full length books devoted entirely to the subject.* Most of them make intensely

---

* In 1902 there appeared Colonel Henderson's magisterial 'The Tactical Employment of Cavalry', one of two lengthy articles in a Supplement to the *Encyclopaedia Britannica*. It includes much material for both sides of the debate, but on some of the more vital points is generally progressive. He felt, however, that 'the cavalry soldier must be taught to consider himself as, first and foremost, the soldier of the charge and the mêlée. . . . If he is not sometimes allowed

dry reading today, but some included revealing prefaces and intro-
ductions from the two chief champions. First, in 1905, came
French's Preface to *Cavalry in Action in the Wars of the Future*,
written by an anonymous Frenchman using the initials 'P.S.'.*
Slightly disingenuously, French wrote:

> 'The controversy which has raged over the question of
> "L'Arme Blanche" *versus* "The Rifle", after becoming much
> involved by reason of each side misunderstanding the aim of
> the other, has now somewhat subsided.
>
> 'The two schools of thought are well harmonised and
> brought together in [this book].
>
> 'Put tersely and briefly, we are told that the first objective is
> the *enemy's Cavalry*, that everything must first conduce to its
> overthrow and defeat, and then a brilliant field of enterprise is
> open to the Cavalry soldier in his *role* as a mounted rifleman. . . .
>
> 'It must never be forgotten that it is only by the employment
> of "shock tactics" and the superior moral of the highly trained
> horseman wielding sword and lance, that decisive success can
> be attained.'

He added that 'Cavalry soldiers must, of course, learn to be expert
rifle shots.'[60]

A year later there came out Goldman's translation of Lieutenant-
General Friedrich von Bernhardi's *Cavalry in Future Wars*. This
influential work had first appeared in Germany in 1899 and had been
revised in 1902. It was therefore not, of course, right up to date. It
is a curious work based largely on the author's experience as a
Lieutenant in the Franco-German War of 1870–1. French in his
Preface to it fell fully for those parts which suited his views, much
commending the author for laughing 'at the idea held by so many
"amateurs" that "Cavalry duels" are superfluous'. He himself
sneered at 'the mischievous teaching which scoffs at . . . "tourna-
ments" and the "Cavalry spirit" ', which he feared proceeded

---

to lose himself in the exhilaration of a charge, his dash invariably deteriorates.'
At the same time he believed that 'a few cool and intelligent riflemen . . . can
easily hold at bay a far larger number of mounted troopers,' that 'fire is a far
better means of keeping the foe at a distance and of gaining time than shock'
and 'that a really good cavalry must be trained to use the lance as well as the
sabre and the rifle.' (Henderson, 51–69.)

* Almost certainly Colonel Breveté P. Silvestre, commanding officer of the
30th *Régiment de Dragons*, author of *Le Service à Court Terme et la Préparation
de la Cavalerie en Vue de la Guerre*, 1906.

'entirely from the pens and from the brains of men who have no practical knowledge of the handling of the Cavalry Arm'. French's Preface to Bernhardi's next volume, *Cavalry in War and Peace*, which appeared in translation in 1910, abounds in statements the veracity of which it is difficult to recognize, such as 'the Boer mounted riflemen acknowledged on many occasions the moral force of the cold steel, and gave way before it.'[61] Otherwise for the most part he repeats his earlier arguments.

In the same year, 1910, there appeared the highly polemical *War and the Arme Blanche* by Robert Erskine Childers, with an Introduction by Roberts.* Childers was a fiery Irishman who had written three years earlier the fifth volume of *The Times History of the War in South Africa*, under Leo Amery's editorship. He was also the author of a famous book, *The Riddle of the Sands*, the outcome of yachting expeditions to the German coast in 1903 in which he prophesied the menace of German naval power and imagined a German raid on England. During the Boer War he had served with the City Imperial Battery of the Honourable Artillery Company. He later produced a book of his experiences: *In the Ranks of the C.I.V.*† *War and the Arme Blanche* embodied most skilfully and disputatiously the whole of the New School's case: total abolition of the *arme blanche* and absolutely undivided attention to training with the rifle. Roberts in his Introduction, in effect, summed up its contents. He demolished the proposition that the abnormality of the Boer War made it inapplicable to future thinking.

'Are not all wars', he asked, 'abnormal?

'As the Boer War was the first in which magazine rifles were made use of, and as the weapon used in future wars is certain to be even more effective, on account of the lower trajectory and automatic mechanism about to be introduced, shall we not be

---

* Equally polemical and a great deal more muddled and unpleasant was Bernhardi's criticism of it in the *Cavalry Journal*. ('A Consideration of Opposite Views Concerning Cavalry', trans. by 'White Horse' from *Militär Wochenblatt, Cav. Jnl*, V, 1910, 466–83.)

† Childers, son of R. C. Childers, the pioneer of Pali literary studies in England, was a House of Commons clerk for fifteen years from 1895. He served in the RNAS and the RFC in the First World War. In 1922 he joined the IRA, was captured and executed by Free State soldiers. His son, also Erskine, became President of the Irish Republic in 1973 and died, aged seventy-nine, the following year.

54. 'Railway Transport. Illustrates the difficulties of watering and feeding horses in trucks'

55. 'Chargers of Five Nations – English, Argentine, Cape, Hungarian and Russian'

56. 'A veteran English horse after a year's service'

57. 'F.Q.M.S. Cowan doctoring a sore back'. 7th Dragoon Guards

very unwise if we do not profit by the lessons we were taught at such a heavy cost during the war?'

He went so far as to say that 'knee to knee, close order charging is practically a thing of the past' and that 'cavalry soldiers must not only be good shots, but they must be taught how to fight as infantry.'[62]

Childers followed up with another book in 1911. Entitled *German Influence on British Cavalry*, its first object was to act as a counterblast to Bernhardi's *Cavalry in War and Peace* with French's 'highly laudatory Preface'. He points out that Bernhardi was writing in both of his books 'as a German reformer, for what he regards as an exceptionally backward cavalry' and that therefore to think of them as pertinent to the British cavalry debate was both foolish and dangerous. He also shows that by selecting quotations from various chapters of *Cavalry in War and Peace* 'each party to our controversy could easily claim the General as an adherent to his cause'. For instance, on page 111, Bernhardi writes: 'We must be resolute in freeing ourselves from those old-fashioned knightly combats, which have in reality become obsolete owing to the necessities of modern war', only to follow on page 325 with: 'The crowning-point of all drill and of the whole tactical training is the charge itself, as on it depends the final result of the battle.'[63] Childers makes some other points worth recording. 'For all we know,' he correctly prophesied, 'even the mounted rifle charge may wholly disappear as science improves the firearm.' He states, too, and rightly, that the contradictions between the four official training manuals, *Cavalry Training*, *Mounted Infantry Training*, *Infantry Training* and *Combined Training*, 'are a public scandal'.* Possibly the most important sentence in the book is a plea to the British cavalry 'to have the pluck and independence to break off the demoralizing habit of imitating foreign models, and to build on our own war experience and our own racial aptitudes', thereby gaining 'the power of creating a cavalry incomparably superior in quality to any continental cavalry.'[64]†

---

* These and the other military manuals were gradually brought more into line with each other. By August, 1914, most of the contradictions which they contained had been reconciled.

† At Haig's first inspection of the Cavalry School which he founded in India, he was flabbergasted to see that a road had been named 'Childers Road'. The Commandant explained the matter thus: 'Ah, sir,' he said, 'that road is a cul-de-sac and leads to the cemetery.' (Terraine, 36.)

*   *   *

To a certain degree at the time, and certainly later, it was hard not to ridicule what seemed the stick-in-the-mud attitude of the old cavalry school in Britain. Nevertheless it was only necessary to look across the Channel to our potential enemies and allies to observe even greater, more visible conservatism. None of the continental powers, except Russia in Manchuria, had had any experience of the actual use of modern weapons in war. At least Britain had undergone the awful trials of the Boer War. As early as 1902, Roberts, who in September of that year had attended the German manoeuvres, told Brodrick that where 'drill, tactics, dress and equipment' were concerned, there was a considerable need for change in the German Imperial army. On all these counts he had no doubt that the British were far in advance, and would have nothing to fear.[65]

There were virtually no professors of the New School in Germany, Austria or France. Colonel Ludwich Koch was an exception. 'From my personal experience,' he wrote in 1908, 'I can assure the reader that the fire fight will become more and more interesting the more we occupy ourselves with it and that dislike and prejudice will disappear the deeper we go into the subject.'[66] There was also one Frenchman, General Francois de Négrier, whose experiences as an observer in the Russo-Japanese War led him to try to take the French cavalry into the twentieth century. He believed passionately that adherence to the *arme blanche* could only lead to useless and wanton sacrifice of life.[67] But as William L. Taylor, a leading modern American authority, has put it, de Négrier 'failed to reckon with the intransigent attitude of the military mind, the French being the most reluctant of all.'[68]

The official regulations of both the German and the French cavalries stressed the offensive spirit even more than did the British. The German regulations of 1909 read: 'Mounted action is the principal method of fighting for cavalry,' while the French manual laid down that 'the charge in close order is the principal mode of action for cavalry.'[69] The United States regulations also decreed that mounted action must be 'the main role of the cavalry arm, its organization and armament. The instruction should be with a view to rendering it effective in such action.'[70]* Even the Russians after

* Astonishingly, even after the start of the First World War, an American military writer could state that 'when an officer takes it upon himself to discard the mounted charge entirely, or even to pay little attention to it, on the theory

the Manchurian War believed that 'the duel between the two cavalries will, without doubt, be in favour of that one which is imbued with the greater offensive spirit.'[71] With few exceptions, the continental armies thought little of mounted infantry. A general view was that it was nearly as expensive as cavalry and not nearly as efficient.[72] A typical German view was that 'mounted infantry cannot hold the field against highly trained cavalry, for sooner or later they would be caught when in the saddle, and then before they had time to dismount and fire it would be all over with them.' After about 1905 continental thinking with respect to the charge was beginning to veer towards combining shock and fire by the use of horse artillery, machine guns and rifles before, during and after an action. The larger commands became, the less difficult was it to combine shock and fire tactics, because, as a rule, there would be too many men for all of them to be able to take part in a proper charge.[73]

*   *   *

As the great debate rolled on towards the fateful moment of truth in August, 1914, significant changes took place in the senior army posts. French succeeded the Duke of Connaught as Inspector-General of the Forces in November, 1907,* while Smith-Dorrien (see p. 160) succeeded French in the Aldershot command. For the old cavalry school this was a real blow, for not only was Smith-Dorrien an infantryman but he was a very forward-looking soldier endowed with determination and energy. Both he and French possessed vile tempers, and when Smith-Dorrien made sweeping changes at Aldershot, French was furious, especially when large numbers of trees were cut down to increase the ground for training.†
More seriously, Smith-Dorrien, in his own words, was

'not at all pleased to find that the Cavalry Brigade at Aldershot were low down in the annual musketry courses, and further, on field days and manoeuvres, hardly ever dismounted, but delivered perfectly carried out, though impossible, knee to knee

---

that it is a thing of the past, he is going squarely against the plainly expressed opinion of the War Departments of all nations, including our own.' (Hayne, Capt. P. T. *Lectures on Cavalry*, Kansas, 1915, 52.)

* From the previous year French had been officially recognized as Commander-in-Chief designate of the BEF.

† When the Great War came, the friction which had built up between him and French during the years 1907 to 1914 flared into a blaze.

charges against infantry in action. So on the 21st August 1909, ordering all cavalry officers to meet me at the 16th Lancers' Mess, I gave them my views pretty clearly, with the result that dismounted work was taken up seriously and the improvement in musketry was so marked that the cavalry went nearly to the head of the lists in the Annual Musketry. I submit that my action was justified by what happened in the Great War, but at the time I am aware that my attitude was resented.'[74]

The previous year, during Smith-Dorrien's first annual manoeuvres held in September, 1908,

'at the end of the first day's operations the cavalry brigade of one side went comfortably into bivouac, taking,' as 'Wully' Robertson, the Chief of General Staff at Aldershot (see Vol III, pp. 55, 114), put it, 'little or no precautions for security during the night, and being unaware that within a mile or two was the bivouac of one of the enemy's infantry brigades. Later on a battalion of this brigade discovered the presence of the cavalry, and at dawn next morning surrounded and took the whole of them prisoners. An umpire came to headquarters to ask for a decision as to what should be done, and was promptly told by [Smith-Dorrien] that the cavalry must be placed out of action until the operations terminated. The lesson thus driven home was not likely to be forgotten, and outweighed the disadvantage of depriving the captured brigade of an additional day's training.'[75]

An interesting development also took place at these same manoeuvres. French then began what was clearly an amelioration of his uncompromising stand on cavalry matters. In 1904 he had told Roberts that 'nothing can make me alter the view that I hold on the subject of cavalry.'[76] Now, four years later, at the end of the manoeuvres, he criticized the mediocre performance of the dismounted work. Haig lamented that French 'gave vent to some terrible heresies such as the chief use of the Cavalry Division in battle is their rifle fire: led horses to be moved, and men need not be close to them.'[77] The following year, French's Inspection Report not only said that led horses must be better concealed but pointed out most vigorously that 'cavalry officers require to familiarize themselves with methods to be employed in a fire-fight.' In March, 1909, Haig held a Staff Ride. In his report upon it he wrote: 'Occasions for charging will be few, but they occur – and the results from such action will be immense. The mounted attack, therefore, must always be our ideal, our final objective.' The following year he published, anonymously, *Cavalry Taught by Experience: A Forecast of Cavalry under Modern War Conditions*, basing it upon an imaginary battle between opposing cavalries. In it he wrote:

> 'Cavalry which is systematically trained in peace to resort to the rifle on each and every occasion may certainly not be so likely to take any of those risks in war which sometimes lead to a body of cavalry meeting with a disaster. They will adopt the safe and sure course [one might think this to be not a bad thing!], save their own skins and be *cautious* and *slow*. ...
> Cavalry which is taught in peace to have a belief in mounted action, the *arme blanche* and shock tactics will be likely, *now and then*, to take a reasonable risk to achieve a great end.'

It is possible to fancy that the reiteration of qualifications in these two quotes indicates a slight amelioration even of Haig's dogmatism.[78]

It was French whose energy and drive insisted upon more realistic manoeuvres in 1909 and 1910,* and his reports on the way the cavalry performed in them were little short of devastating.† When, in succession to Nicholson, he became Chief of the General Staff in 1912, his successor as Inspector-General was General Sir Charles Whittingham Horsley Douglas, who two years later was to succeed him as CIGS. Douglas was an infantryman who had served under Roberts in the Second Afghan War and with distinction in South Africa. His Annual Reports in 1912 and 1913 were equally critical of the cavalry. In 1912 he wrote: 'Our cavalry commanders are inclined to employ shock action whenever possible without reference to the circumstances of particular cases. ... Many of the

---

* In 1911, the Agadir crisis, a series of industrial strikes and the Coronation of King George V prevented manoeuvres on a divisional basis.

† In the 1909 manoeuvres a composite regiment of the Household Cavalry clashed with the 1st Cavalry Brigade.
'Simultaneously the scouts of either brigade sighted the enemy. Simultaneously each brigade was ordered to charge. So close were they that men could hear the orders shouted to their opponents. The charge was launched, the men could not be stopped, and they met with a crash. ... The superior weight of the Household Cavalrymen swept the 1st Cavalry Brigade back. ... Two men of a Lancer Regiment were killed outright, and casualties were numerous.' (Arthur, III, 10.)

manoeuvres showed disregard of the effect of fire that could not be justified by our regulations, and the attempts to combine shock and fire action were seldom successful.' The following year he reported his fear that

'the present training of cavalry shows tendencies that may lead to useless sacrifice of our available cavalry force in war. . . . It would be wise to impress on our cavalry commanders that while the mounted attack is the most effective method of obtaining decisive results . . . attacks of this nature which promise nothing but a useless sacrifice cannot be too strongly condemned.'[79]

It is interesting to note that Haig, who took the chief command at Aldershot in 1911, failed miserably in the 1912 manoeuvres. One staff officer remarked that he 'was so completely outmanoeuvred that the operations were brought to a premature end'. This seems to have been chiefly because his opponent made clever use of the new air arm.[80]* In 1913 he was no more successful. His dispositions were said to have left a three-mile gap in the 'British' centre.[81] On the other hand Haig much criticized French, who himself conceded that 'the manoeuvres taught *us all* many lessons.'[82]

In 1910 Henry Wilson, then only a brigadier-general, took over the vital post of Director of Military Operations which he was to hold until the outbreak of the war. In this position he became chiefly responsible for the planning of the mobilization and concentration of the British Expeditionary Force. He had been very much a Roberts man, but from 1907 when French had recommended him for the job of Commandant of the Staff College at Camberley, he had jumped on the French bandwagon. By 1912 he had become French's closest adviser. As French's view on the cavalry was gradually amended, so, in the opposite direction, was Wilson's. Behind the scenes in all that was going on, of course, was the slightly sinister figure of Esher. He, more than anyone, had the ear of the Kings, both Edward VII, who died in 1910, and George V. His influence with Ministers, too, was great. French and Haig were very much his protégés and he their patron. They probably owed their

* Allenby, who, as a Major-General, became Inspector of Cavalry in 1910, is also said to have performed poorly in the 1912 manoeuvres. Though more progressive than Haig, he had great faith in shock tactics and insisted on much practice of massed charges. (Gardner, 63.)

rapid promotion in some degree to his intercession. His son was taken by French as his aide-de-camp at Aldershot.

*　　*　　*

The *arme blanche* tradition of the British cavalry displayed, to use Brian Bond's words, a 'capacity for survival that bordered on the miraculous'.[83] Nevertheless even the most extravagant of the iconoclasts, Erskine Childers, could write with absolute truth in 1911, 'our cavalry, excessive as its reliance on the steel is, stands, of course, in the matter of fire-action, ahead of all Continental rivals.'[84] This was not actually as wonderful as it sounds, for as John Terraine has put it, 'the British cavalry was the only cavalry that *could* shoot'. He added: 'and that was prepared to get off its horses in order to do so.'[85] This would seem to indicate that in the end the French/Haig school had lost its fight, but perhaps the usual British genius for compromise coupled with the initiative of a few top-middle-rank cavalry officers, is more likely to be the answer to the conundrum. Surprisingly, some of the first signs of a real improvement in the cavalry's musketry training were to be seen in India.

17

'However much thou art read in theory, if thou
hast no practice thou art ignorant.'

SAADI, a Persian poet, in 1258

'More musketry field training under Service conditions, and always with horses. . . . Encouragement of shooting clubs. . . . It would be better if
musketry training could be spread over the whole
year, and not confined to one fortnight, as at
present.'

Report of Major-General Dickson's
Committee on Personnel and Organization,
1901

'Greatly increased facilities for *practical* musketry
are required.'

HAIG in 1902

'The Musketry statistics of [the 14th Hussars] are
a long way ahead in excellence of any other unit
in the [9th] Division [India]. The Regimental
average shows an increase of ten points on last
year and is so abnormally high as to be specially
remarkable. This doubtless is due to the fact that
the Musketry training of the Regiment in all its
branches is sound, systematic and consistent, that
the Regiment is equipped with the most modern
appliances for instruction, and to the zeal and
interest exhibited by all ranks.'

Official report by GOC, 9th Division,
1910[1]

(i)

*Cavalry training: musketry – signalling – Netheravon Cavalry
School*

In 1903 Private William Egbert ('Bertie') Seed of the 3rd Hussars,
aged twenty-one, gained the prize of 'a small carriage clock in a red
morocco case'. He had taken, as he proudly wrote to his mother,
'first place in all India at 600 yards'.[2] Again and again during the
next decade, members of cavalry regiments in India were to run off
with the top musketry prizes. Before the Boer War few cavalrymen

had competed, either at home or in India, for the various cups, shields and other prizes which were then usually won by the infantry. In the 1890s, when each cavalryman was allowed only forty rounds a year for practice with his carbine,* musketry was considered in the mounted arm as 'degradation and a bore'[3] or, as Roberts put it in 1902, 'a somewhat irksome business which has to be got through as quickly as possible'. Now, equipped with a truly useful rifle, there grew up far greater interest in its skilful use. Regimental rifle clubs and bodies such as the Southern India Rifle Association sprang into being. Annual musketry courses were held in regiments and the Schools of Musketry at Lydd in Hampshire and at Pachmarhi in India were patronized by cavalry regiments as never before. In 1904 the Khan of Nanpara in Oudh offered a Challenge Cup for competition in shooting. It was open only to the British cavalry serving in India. All the squadrons of each regiment that entered had to take part. In the first year thirty-six squadrons competed and the 15th Hussars won the cup as well as taking third and fourth places. In the years that followed the 15th often came at the top of this and other competitions, one of the most prestigious of which was that for the Empire Cup. In 1909, for instance, Sergeant A. Hanks and Corporal G. Voice were awarded the Gold Jewel and the Bronze Jewel for best and third best marksmen in India. Never before had a cavalryman won the Gold Jewel. In the same year, Corporal Voice won the Jubilee Shield presented by the Indian School of Musketry, which since 1897 had always hitherto been won by an infantryman.[4]

Two of the best shooting regiments were the 13th and 14th Hussars. The results of their annual musketry courses in India show that interest in the subject was not confined to a few outstanding shots. In 1906, for example, the 13th Hussars produced seventy-eight 'marksmen', 170 1st-class shots, 209 2nd-class and four 3rd-class shots. In 1909 the regiment's annual course results showed 271 'marksmen', 250 1st-class shots, twenty-seven 2nd-class shots and no 3rd-class shots. In 1908 the 14th Hussars had done even better with 354 'marksmen', 212 1st-class shots, thirty-five 2nd- and four 3rd-class shots.

The official reports by inspecting generals became increasingly adulatory as the years went by. In 1907 Kitchener wrote of the 13th: 'I am glad to see musketry has received due attention and improved.' In 1908 the Assistant-Adjutant-General, Musketry, India, in his report on the 14th, wrote: 'Several teams competed in a series of

* Ten years later 120 rounds was a normal ration. (Micholls, 66.)

Tactical Problems in fire discipline and fire control. ... The 14th Hussars are manifestly well trained and excellent in Musketry.' The official report on the regiment next year said: 'Remarkably good results have been obtained in Musketry, in which there is much emulation.' When a new and much stiffer musketry course was introduced in 1910, both regiments continued to excel.[5] In the 14th, one officer particularly was responsible for laying 'the foundation of the great shooting success of the regiment'. He was Major Edward James Tickell, a well-known Irish big-game shot, who amongst other similar achievements won 'the Disappearing Target Competition and was first in the Championship Stakes' at the regimental rifle meeting in 1907.[6] At home, too, the spirit of competition was very much alive. In 1903, for instance, the 11th Hussars 'carried off all three events for which it is possible for cavalry to enter' at the annual meeting of the Army Rifle Association. The regiment won 'The Queen's Cup for Cavalry (with the highest score ever made by Cavalry), The Young Soldiers' Cup (the first time it has ever been won by Cavalry), and the Inter-Squadron Team Match (tying with the highest score ever made)'. In 1905, 'A' Squadron of the 11th won the Association's Inter-Squadron Shield for Musketry, presented for regiments at home.[7] In some regiments, of course, keenness in musketry was less than in others. The historian of Haig's regiment, the 17th Lancers, states that at this time, 'though efficiency with the rifle was maintained, the tendency was ever increasing towards mounted manoeuvre and attack'.[8] But there was a good reason why rifle shooting had to be taken seriously in every regiment, for from 1902 onwards a man's proficiency pay had been made largely to depend upon it. Subject to character-suitability and (from 1906) possession of a 3rd-class certificate of education, attainment of a second-class standard of shooting qualified a man for 'service' pay of 6d a day. 3rd-class shots received 4d.[9]

Though men might become excellent shots at the increasing number of ranges which were being constructed, field firing bore little resemblance to war conditions. More often than not, for instance, horses, as the Inspector General of Cavalry complained in 1904, were 'not allowed on the range' and the chronic shortage of training grounds made realistic fire tactics difficult to practice.[10]

Indicative of changing attitudes was the newly sanctioned practice of sending complimentary notices to the local press telling of successes gained not only in musketry, but also in signalling and sports.[11]

*　　*　　*

The historian of the 5th Dragoon Guards tells how 'after the experiences of the South African War, signalling was the thing at which all regiments wanted to distinguish themselves.'[12] As with musketry, there was keen competition. For some years the 11th Hussars held the position of the best signalling unit of the cavalry.[13] The 1899 establishment of signallers in a cavalry regiment had been one trained NCO, twelve trained men and six 'supernumeraries' under one officer for whom signalling was only an incidental duty. By 1906 the establishment had been increased to three trained officers, four NCOs and twenty-four men. In 1899 the war establishment of heliographs in each regiment was one, with another kept at home for the reserve squadron. By 1906 each regiment was provided with eight. The moment the Cavalry Division arrived in South Africa, a Mounted Signalling Company had been formed for which twenty-nine other ranks were withdrawn from regiments. A further eighteen regimental signallers were taken for divisional and brigade headquarters.[14] All this led Haig after the war to recommend the formation of a permanent corps of signallers for peacetime.[15] Two War Office committees (in 1906 and 1911) recommended that a separate Signal Corps should be formed to provide communications for all branches of the army, but for financial reasons no action was taken on these recommendations. In 1911 an Army Order, among other reforms, for the first time defined the responsibilities of regimental signal detachments, 'which besides finding internal communications for their respective units were required to provide such visual stations as might be necessary to communicate with the higher formation headquarters and neighbouring units.'

In 1907 three telegraph cable sections were formed for the cavalry division and in 1912 a signal squadron for the division and a wireless signal company for communication from army headquarters to the division were set up. Towards the end of the war a new wagon for laying cables at the trot had been invented which much speeded up cable laying. By 1914 (except in telephones, of which senior officers were rather frightened, and wireless, still in its infancy), technical efficiency in signalling was greater than ever before, and more time was being devoted to training in the use of flags for semaphore signalling, heliographs (at night, Begbie lamps) and the telegraph.[16] The training of despatch riders, too, was taken more seriously than before the war. From 1902, when all officers on mounted duty with troops were ordered to carry whistles,[17] trumpet-calls and words of command both for drill and in the field became increasingly rare.

*   *   *

A major step in the direction of professionalism was taken in the spring of 1904 with the founding of the Cavalry School or College at Netheravon House on Salisbury Plain, presented by its former owner, Sir Michael Hicks Beach. The brain-child of Baden-Powell, its first Commandant was Colonel the Hon. John Edward Lindley of the 1st Royal Dragoons, who had been from 1901, until its demise in 1903, Commandant of the Imperial Yeomanry School of Instruction, and who was to command the 3rd Cavalry Brigade from 1907 to 1910. The School came about because the new system of entrusting the education of both men and horses from the first day of their service to their respective squadron leaders and sergeant-majors (see p. 360) lacked, in Lindley's words, 'the machinery at their disposal for carrying the system into effect'. Now that all training of the men and horses was taken out of the 'professional' hands of the adjutant and ridingmaster (whose post was abolished in 1906), it was essential that some of these officers' expertise should be transferred to the 'amateurs' who had taken it over. The 'Riding Establishment' at Canterbury was amalgamated with the new School, and at first the 'art of equitation' was its chief *raison d'être*. 'Tackling, backing and breaking' of the young horse 'and the instruction of the recruit in every progressive stage of riding and in the effective use of his arms when mounted' were the main subjects of the curriculum. Veterinary and 'cavalry engineering' courses were included in the syllabus, for passing the final examinations in which officers received certificates. Also taught were 'horseback sketching and reconnaissance, bivouac and billeting schemes, compass and despatch riding, tracking, etc.' Every regular cavalry regiment was required to send two representatives, one for the six-month officers' and one for the eight-month NCOs' courses. Each officer brought 'two unmarried soldier servants' and two trained horses, while each NCO brought one trained horse (and later two horses) with him. On the day of joining each officer and NCO was allotted one untrained remount, which at the course's end was inspected by the Remount Department and, if considered fully trained, passed into regiments as a charger or a trooper. There were also five six-month annual courses for some thirty officers and NCOs from the Yeomanry. Experts gave lectures on strategy and tactics and every officer was required to practice lecturing to his men.[18] After the First World War the School was closed and transformed into the Army Equitation School at Weedon in Northamptonshire, which became 'the Mecca of all military horsemen until mechanization'.[19]

*   *   *

Meanwhile in India, Haig was largely instrumental in founding a similar Cavalry School at Saugor in the Central Provinces. The premises consisted of converted barracks and were quickly made ready. The first course, lasting seven months, began in September, 1910. There were twice as many students as at Netheravon. Three officers who had attended a course there came out as instructors. Five officers were selected by the Commander-in-Chief to act as student instructors. There were also five non-commissioned officer instructors from European regiments in India and six from Indian cavalry regiments, as well as one Indian officer. The first course was attended by fifty-four subaltern students of which twenty were Indians. All were required to have served for three years and possess a good knowledge of field sketching and map reading. The amenities included capacious stabling, a veterinary hospital, a covered riding school, numerous lecture rooms and a fencing hall. There were no less than five polo grounds as well as lawn tennis courts and a golf links. The school was finally closed in 1939.[20]

'The full-dress parade was comparatively rare; the field day in marching order had largely taken its place.'

The historian of the 11th Hussars, in 1903

'Men must do much more riding in open country and less "show riding" in the riding house. Hitherto inspecting generals have devoted much time to the inspection of work done in the riding school, hence this kind of equitation has come to be regarded as the end and object of training, instead of only being a means to an end.'

HAIG's evidence to the *Royal Commission*

'[It is] not everywhere realized that the skill and aptitude of the scout and skirmisher are not less important than the steadiness and precision of the mass.'

ROBERTS's evidence to the *Royal Commission*

'I must explain for the benefit of the ignorant reader that cavalry manoeuvre in column and fight in line, and that cavalry drill resolves itself into swift and flexible changes from one formation to the other. Thus by wheeling or moving in echelon a front can always be presented ... almost at any moment in any direction.'

WINSTON CHURCHILL in *My Early Life*

In 1903 Roberts thought that the British cavalry-man was 'far from being proficient' in the use of the sword.

'There have been,' he wrote, 'in the past several reasons to account for this:

1. Insufficient training of the individual.
2. An unpractical "Sword Exercise", adapted to parade purposes only.
3. Insufficient instructors.
4. Steel scabbards.
5. An ill-balanced weapon.'

ROBERTS in a WO Memorandum[1]

(ii)

Cavalry training: duties of the arm – training times – encouraging of individual initiative – scouting and screening – manoeuvres – swordsmanship – preparation for charge – horse training – 'chin-strap affair'

It is interesting, when considering what proportions of training time were apportioned to which of the cavalry's duties, to learn what different officers considered those duties to be. Baden-Powell voiced in 1906 quite unambiguously what many a proud cavalry officer would have admitted only grudgingly that 'the infantry is the arm which does the fighting and wins the battles, and the cavalry assists the infantry to do this by destroying the enemy's cavalry as a first step, then by finding his main force, by co-operating on the battle-field, and eventually by turning his defeat into disaster.' Strategically, he wrote, the cavalry's functions are 'to cover the front of the army, and, by gaining full information of the enemy's main force and con-cealing their own, *to give their Commander-in-Chief complete liberty of action*; also to prevent the enemy's cavalry doing the same on their part. To threaten the enemy's communications and force him to waste strength in defending them, etc.' Tactically, Baden-Powell defined the cavalry's tasks thus: 'To destroy the enemy's cavalry; to keep the infantry informed and protected; to cut off and hold the enemy; to chip in where required on the battlefield; to smash up the enemy in pursuit or to protect one's own side from pursuit.'[2]

Henderson, writing the article on 'Cavalry' in the *Encyclopaedia Britannica* supplement of 1902, asserted that the 'Reconnaissance of the enemy's position is the foremost of [cavalry's] functions', and then, later, went on to contradict himself: 'But most important, per-haps, of all its functions are the manoeuvres which so threaten the enemy's line of retreat that he is compelled to evacuate his position, and those which cut off his last avenue of escape.'[3] What was, effec-tively, the official definition of the tasks of the cavalry was expressed by Haig in 1907, when he divided it into three distinct types: '*Independent Cavalry*, for strategical exploration, under direct orders of the Chief; *Protective Cavalry*, for the provision of the First Line of Security for the Army as a whole; *Divisional Cavalry*, for scouting in the close vicinity of the Infantry Divisions, for orderly work in the [Cavalry] Division, and for inter-communication between Divi-sions.'[4] Three years later he elaborated on 'the essential difference between the task allotted to an observation patrol and to a recon-noitring patrol.... Observation troops should usually remain quietly in concealment until their withdrawal and return are really threatened.... Whereas an observation patrol should be able to fulfil all its tasks by going to one spot and remaining there in concealment the whole time, a reconnoitring patrol will constantly be under the necessity of moving on, to fulfil its task properly.'[5]

*　　*　　*

Perhaps the greatest advance in post-war training was the increased amount of time allotted to real training as opposed to general routine parades, formal drills and all that is summed up in the phrase 'spit and polish'. Before 1900 only forty-two days a year were set aside for intensive instruction. In the winter squadrons were 'struck off all duties'(!) for twenty-one days during which the teaching of such things as 'post practice, sword and lance exercise, dismounted duty, pitching tents, picketing, digging kitchens, latrines and shelter trenches had to be hurried through.' The Order Book of the 9th Lancers laid down for the twenty-one days of spring training a syllabus which included 'mounted and dismounted duties in scouting, reconnaissance, commands and signals: *four days*; advance, flank and rear guards, defence of localities and obtaining and transmitting information: *four days*, and a march in the field, pitching and striking camp *en route*: *two days*, ending with the Commanding Officer's inspection'.[6] The instruction given in these ridiculously short periods was, of course, elementary and perfunctory in the extreme.

Though, as has been shown, by 1910 80% of the time set aside for training seems to have been usually spent in perfecting preparations for the charge, the total number of hours each year given over to *all* forms of training for war, especially scouting, outposts and general reconnaissance, was now immensely greater than pre-1899.* In the 11th Hussars, as probably more or less in all regiments, in a typical post-war year, January and February were devoted to troop training. In March squadron training began, while in April the annual musketry course was fired. Squadron training continued during May until mid-June. Regimental training and sometimes squadron training with infantry brigades took place until mid-July, followed by a month of brigade training with infantry divisions. Most of August and September was supposed to be devoted to manoeuvres with higher formations. In fact during some years there was no money for more than brigade training.[7] This was so, for instance, in 1905 and 1906.[8] Effective field training much depended, of course, upon a regiment's location. In Glasgow, for instance, the 17th Lancers found that there was 'scarcely an open field sufficiently

---

* It is an astonishing fact that the 1876 edition of *Cavalry Drill* nowhere mentions outposts and protective duties. The 1891 edition, however, devotes thirty-four pages to these subjects.

large to drill a troop', while less than a mile from the cavalry barracks in Edinburgh were the sands of Portobello.[9] Further, what was actually meant by troop and squadron training largely depended upon whether the commanding officer was a shock or a fire advocate. If the latter, he was still, of course, limited, though not as much as pre-war, in the number of rounds he was allowed to expend each year. By 1906 virtually every squadron possessed some sort of sand table, on which models of country were made and tactical schemes carried out. Increasing instruction in map-reading, for the men as well as the officers, was less uncommon than in the past.

> 'Our training now,' wrote Baden-Powell in 1906 when he was Inspector of Cavalry,* 'has to be effected by *instruction* rather than by mere drill. . . . The useless NCO who was formerly considered efficient if he was able to throw up his chin and to spout, parrotwise, a string of "aids" to a squad of men, no longer passes muster where "instruction" to each recruit is required in his own words and by his own demonstration. . . . *Cavalry Training*, in which general principles are inculcated while much of the former "detail" is omitted, gives an opening for initiative on the part of the keen instructor, and forces the less capable one either to think for himself – and therefore to improve – or else to be exposed.'

Baden-Powell, as became the Inspector of Cavalry, gave a glowing account of how recruits spent the first three months of their training. They were, he wrote,

> 'carefully trained in free gymnastics, swimming, map-reading, sword-fencing, semaphore-signalling, musketry and general theory, &c, before they go to the Riding School and Horse Management.
>
> 'They are then allowed to ride easy horses on saddles covered with a numnah, or on a numnah with roller and handles to give them confidence.
>
> 'They have competitions in wrestling barebacked and football mounted, &c, by which they very quickly learn to stick on, to mount and dismount quickly, and to guide their horses.
>
> 'After this they are taught the "grammar" of riding, not

---

* As a result of the War Office reorganization of 1904, the post of Inspector General of the Forces was created on 1 May. To avoid confusion the Inspector General of Cavalry was at the same time redesignated Inspector of Cavalry.

in big classes, but individually by an instructor who is also mounted and can thus demonstrate his teaching.'

Some of the 'circus tricks' on which a great deal of training time was spent were 'Prize Snatching', 'Horses taught to lie down', 'Tent-pegging', 'Sliding the Slope', which sounds alarming, 'Jumping and Charging Dummies' and 'Free Jumping-Lane', whatever that was. Riding instruction for recruits was more important than ever, since, as Amery complained in 1903, 'every day we get fewer men accustomed before they are recruited to work with horses, and the use of the horses as a means of locomotion by all ranks in Great Britain is

A trooper of the 7th Hussars in 1910

quickly dying out'. Nine years later Rimington was lamenting that 'nowadays only at most 15 % of the men in our cavalry have, before enlistment, had anything to do with horses.'[10]

To whatever 'cavalry school' officers adhered, there was among them an increasingly explicit feeling that, in Correlli Barnett's words, 'for the first time, barrack-square drill and battlefield tactics [had become] different things.'[11] At the lowest level, that is in the squadron and troop, more and more officers, especially those who had served during the war in inferior commands, were impressed with the need for the training of their men in individual initiative. *The Report of the Royal Commission* said that it had been pointed out by

'many witnesses, and with special force by Lieutenant-General Sir Ian Hamilton, that the conditions of modern warfare with long-range arms and smokeless powder involve an immense extension of lines of battle, diminish the power of control by Commanding Officers, and increase the degree of individual intelligence required in each individual private, both in attack and defence.'[12]

Lord Scarbrough told the Royal Commission that one of the chief reasons why the cavalry failed so wretchedly in South Africa was the 'unsuitable training on German lines . . . total absence of individual thought and action; too much polishing of bits and buttons, long stable hours, wearisome to man and horse'.[13] A committee set up by Roberts soon after the capture of Pretoria to report on the organization and equipment of the cavalry for the future, and chaired by Major-General Dickson (see p. 164), recommended 'much less parade drill in yard and school' and 'more individual training, in both mounted and dismounted work, both out of doors and by lectures'.[14] The cult of individualism, of course, could go too far – or be slightly misunderstood! Haig told the Royal Commission in 1903 that

'the country is flooded with half-trained Yeomanry officers [fresh from their experiences of active service] who proclaim everywhere that training is unnecessary, that the individual is everything, and the result is that the country believes that it has a really valuable asset in its half-trained auxiliary troops. In fact, any effort on the part of the War Office to obtain greater efficiency from the Volunteers, etc., seems to be looked upon by the country as another instance of red tape, and a deliberate attempt to destroy the intelligence and the individuality of the citizen army.'[15]

A number of the more intelligent officers had for some years been injecting into their training a sense of self-reliance. When commanding the 5th Dragoon Guards during the late 1890s in India, Baden-Powell had

'made it imperative for every man to go a ride by himself of about 120 miles, and to take a week doing it. This tended to make men self-reliant, reliable, intelligent and smart. At first it was feared that many of them, finding themselves away from all regimental restraint, would break out and make an orgy of it; but I have never heard a single complaint of the men on this head. They knew they were trusted to carry out this duty of riding off to report on some distant object, whether a railway station, a bridge or a piece of country, and they took a pride in themselves and their horses while away, because they knew that the good name of the regiment was in their hands. We found it in practice the very best reformer for a stupid man that could be devised.'[16]

This system was introduced at home by Baden-Powell when he became Inspector of Cavalry.[17] 'Men,' wrote Haig in 1903, 'must learn to move freely across country, and be instructed as ground scouts, to take cover, to carry verbal messages, judging distances, reconnoitring, etc., and their intelligence developed out of doors.'[18] A private serving with the Imperial Yeomanry during the war illustrates exactly the sort of thing which in action resulted from the mechanical training which was now, at long last, being eschewed:

'What a misleading title "Scouts to the Column" is! This generally means advance-screen, which is expected to do scouts' duty. A small party of men in widely extended order ride along in charge of an officer, who keeps to the centre of the roadway with an orderly in attendance close behind him. The "scouts" have strict orders to keep going forward in a straight line, not to get either in front or behind the centre men, and to keep their dressing. What is the result? If very rough and difficult country is encountered, instead of a man being allowed to use his brain and keep well under cover, so as to thoroughly scour the surrounding ground and look where he is going, he has to keep in line and ride blindly on. He may see mounted men moving about on a ridge in front and report the matter – 100 to 1 no notice is taken; on you go again straight ahead. Often remarks are passed such as "Cattle Grazing", "Loose Horses", etc. – as you get nearer the position the truth is known when the bullets begin to sing and whistle around your head. . . . Men gradually fall into a slack way. They may be as keen as mustard at first and keep a sharp look-out, but after being continually rebuked by an officer or "non-comm" for not keeping a line they lose heart and get absolutely weary of the whole game, and ride blindly on and locate the enemy by drawing their fire, so practically becoming human targets.'[19]

Both officers and men when they passed tests in scouting and despatch riding were now 'invested with a distinguishing badge, viz. a brass "Fleur-de-Lys" (North Point) on the left arm'. Their status as qualified scouts had to be contended for every eighteen months, when they had to compete 'with new men coming on'.[20]

After the combined manoeuvres of 1903* Roberts's report stated that 'one of the points brought prominently to notice was the want of sufficient training in scouting and reconnoitring – two of the most important duties of the Cavalry soldier. . . . Smokeless powder and repeating magazine rifles make it almost impossible to judge whether 50 or 500 men are in action.'[21]

Field-Marshal the Duke of Connaught acted as Umpire-in-Chief for the manoeuvres. He found that

'the work done by the Cavalry of both [opposing] forces, strategically and tactically was very faulty. I would call attention to cases of officers' patrols moving all together in one body with no military precaution; of want of individual reconnaissance and scouting, of want of initiative of superior officers . . . . At Lambourn . . . I found this village occupied by patrols of both forces without either taking any notice of the other. Generally speaking the manoeuvres were remarkable for the uncer-

---

* These were held 'about Newbury Downs' between 10 and 19 September. At one point a patrol of the 14th Hussars dined in a room immediately above the hotel room occupied by the commander of the 'enemy' force, who was Sir Evelyn Wood! (Browne, 231.)

It was whilst encamped in preparation for these manoeuvres that a massive stampede of the regiment's horses took place. This was caused by the fact that the horses were tethered by the foreleg only to 'a single peg and shackle', a system which the cavalry had been ordered to try out. The soil was sandy and the pegs pulled up very easily. The inhabitants of Southampton were much startled by so many horses careering through their streets in the middle of the night. Six horses were killed, ninety-one seriously injured and eleven went missing. (Browne, 234–5.)

tainty which prevailed to the end of the whereabouts of the main army of both sides. This would appear to reflect on the work of the Cavalry as a whole.'[22]

The results of inadequate training and old-fashioned concepts combined with the experiences of the war led to much doubt among the senior and middle-rank officers as to how to act in the field. Fear induced by ignorance often led to inaction on manoeuvres. In those of 1903 the senior umpire of one side, Lieutenant-General Lord Grenfell (see Vol III, p. 363), thought that its cavalry

'had forgotten their normal role – that of being the eyes and ears of the force to which they belonged. Instead of going boldly forward to obtain information and remaining well ahead in protection of that force, they came timidly back to it at night, as if to seek protection from it. . . . They were slow and timid, and the Commander* did not appear to have made up his mind as to the part which he ought to take in the operations.'[23]

It is interesting to note in passing, that, in spite of the severe strictures of the umpires, French's report on the cavalry during the manoeuvres reads thus: 'The work done by the Cavalry throughout the manoeuvres was excellent . . . great dash and energy'![24]

The sort of fiasco which could still occur as late as 1910 on manoeuvres took place when Haig was Chief Director of a divisional exercise (four cavalry brigades) in India. A 'determined effort' was made to drill the massed troops.

'The success of the effort,' records one who was there, 'was limited. Brigadiers, in a glorious effort to hear the first command and convey it to their troops, commanded nothing that belonged to them for the rest of the day. Regiments chased anything with crossed swords on its shoulder-straps, and the rear squadron of the rear regiment, after galloping for over an hour and a quarter to take up its position in divisional line, miraculously found itself near camp, on which it gave up the unequal contest and went home, there being nobody about.'[25]

---

* This was Colonel William Henry Muir Lowe of the 7th Dragoon Guards who had served throughout the war (see p. 169), having seen previous service in Egypt and Burma. He retired aged forty-seven in 1908, having been Colonel in charge of Cavalry Records, Northern Command, 1905–7. He was 'dug out' in 1914 to become Inspector of Cavalry. He died in 1944 at the age of eighty-three.

*   *   *

As Inspector of Cavalry Baden-Powell once again demonstrated how forward-looking he was by almost invariably making his regimental inspections by motor car and by initiating a series of exercises in embarking and landing men and horses.[26] At all levels he was instrumental in ensuring that exercises in the field conformed so far as possible to rigorous active service conditions. In England, unlike India, where, in effect, the whole sub-continent was open to field exercises, this was always excessively difficult.* Farmers had to be compensated for damage, large parts of the manoeuvre area were out of bounds and movement had to be mainly by roads. Even Salisbury Plain and the Curragh were hardly adequate for really large-scale operations. This meant that nothing approaching corps manoeuvres could ever take place, as they did constantly in Germany. The statement of an officer of the 18th Hussars that his regiment was billeted during the 1910 manoeuvres on large farms and that 'we made many friends among the large dairy farmers in the West of England' gives the un-warlike flavour of these exercises.[27] Of the 1903 manoeuvres it was reported that it was all too common 'for cavalry, after a hard day's work, to give up the positions won during the day in order to return to camp' and that the commander of one cavalry brigade did not know where 'a considerable cavalry force' which he had left on 'observation duty, but out of touch with the enemy' actually was. 'He thought it was on his right, whereas it was on his left. On the last day, after remaining for a considerable time inactive, the cavalry chose an inauspicious moment for delivering its attack, with the result that practically the whole brigade was placed out of action.'[28]

Two major difficulties which had to be faced when attempting to approximate large-scale manoeuvres to war realism were first the fact that, except at Aldershot and in Ireland, the cavalry was not organized into commands, and second, more vital, that even in those two places the higher formations lacked anything approaching permanent staffs. Unlike the great armies of the Continent, the notion

---

* In India, of course, ample facilities existed for all sorts of field exercise which invariably took place each year between 1 December and 30 January. 'Every description of country,' wrote Haig, 'is easily reached from the military cantonments and no difficulties present themselves in the matter of camping or marching to suit the supposed military situation.' Further, sufficient transport was usually obtainable 'without expense to those taking part in the exercise'. (Haig: *Cav.*, v.)

of always having in being a staff which would take into war each formation, certainly up to division and even up to corps level, was still largely foreign to the British army. This was chiefly due to parsimony, and meant that every year individual officers who had almost certainly never worked together before had to be nominated for each exercise to act as staff for the commanders of the opposing forces. When in 1907 the Cavalry Division for the British Expeditionary Force was being brought into existence, the appointment of a permanent staff under a nominated General Officer Commanding was turned down because it would have cost £2,300 a year.[29]

* * *

With the advent of the new sword designed for pointing or thrusting as against cutting or slashing (see p. 447), much time was consumed in teaching the technicalities of 'the new swordsmanship'. On foot, on the barrack square with the sword and in the gymnasia (numbers of which had recently been built) with foil and mask, and mounted in the riding-school or *manège*, the instruction went ahead day after day. To provide practice in the use of the sword and horse in the mêlée, 'dummy-thrusting' had taken the place of the 'heads and posts' of the days of the old cutting weapon. For the actual charge itself, the 'Straight-run Dummy' and the 'Galloping Dummy' were used. 'Dummy thrusting' was carried out on a figure-of-eight course with jumps. The dummies represented men, mounted and dismounted, in various positions. Each had a target disc attached to it. The 'Galloping Dummy' was towed towards the galloping swordsman. The idea was that man and dummy should meet at roughly the speed of the charge. The dummy was usually equipped with a can of sorts, representing the sword. This the attacker had to collect on his own blade as his attack went in. For 'mounted combat' practice, two mounted swordsmen were armed with foils and fought each other, protected by masks, as also were their mounts. Much was made of this exercise, the spirit of competition being constantly promoted with a view to 'squadron or regimental honours as a preliminary to competing at the Royal Military Tournament each year'.[30] Considerably less training time was now taken up with trying to ensure that the whole regiment went through the motions of the 'sword exercise' and the actual charge 'as one man'.[31]

The new, greatly simplified drill required to ensure that any formation from squadron to division could be made, in Churchill's

words, 'to present a front in an incredibly short time as the preliminary to that greatest of all cavalry events – the charge',[32] was
welcomed in most regiments, certainly by the other ranks.

'It is certain that in up-to-date cavalry circles,' wrote Lieutenant-
Colonel (later Sir Lancelot) Rolleston* in *Yeomanry Cavalry:
or Mounted Infantry?* in 1901, upon his return from the war,
'extreme cohesion in the attack by no means holds the leading
position it once had as a test of excellence ... The fact is that
although, in former days, the aim was to close cavalry so tightly
up that the men could neither turn round and bolt, nor accept
the opposing files, it is now recognized that, with men who
mean business, so long as alignment and pace are good, a too
rigid cohesion is no great benefit The best Indian cavalry,
indeed, who, above all others, may be said to ride to kill, prefer
room to use their weapons, and never attempt a knee-to-knee
charge on service.'[33]

Baden-Powell continued to cry in the wilderness about keeping
'the steel arm, whether sword, lance or bayonet' truly sharp. 'A
really good swordsman,' he stressed to the Royal Commission, 'is
most difficult to train. No amount of the usual barrack-square sword
exercises will ever make a swordsman, but an indifferent swordsman
with a sharp sword has the advantage over a fair swordsman with a
blunt one. Very few of our officers or men knew how to sharpen a
sword or how to keep it sharp on service.'[34] This aspect of swordsmanship, once slashing had, at long last, been succeeded by pointing,
was, of course, of less importance, but Baden-Powell, in 1903, was
still of the belief that a sword for both purposes was desirable.

*   *   *

As a result of the experiences of the war, the hitherto rigorous and
precise rules concerning the way in which men were to sit on their
horses were paid far less attention to. 'When galloping to deny the
enemy a point of vantage,' wrote an officer who had seen much
service, 'it is immaterial whether the men keep their heels down or
their elbows up.'[35]

* Rolleston had served with distinction in the Imperial Yeomanry during the
war in South Africa where he had been severely wounded. He commanded the
South Notts Hussars Yeomanry, 1896–1906 and the Notts and Derby Mounted
Brigade, 1908–11. He died, aged ninety-four, in 1941.

*   *   *

Another lesson of the war was the need for more sensible training of the horse. 'Under the old Canterbury system,' wrote Amery in 1903, 'much time was spent with a view to showing up a good ride of *haute école* animals, whilst the new system aims at training a horse which ... will be generally useful on a campaign. ... The horse is now trained a great deal in the open [instead of] almost entirely in a school or manège.'[36]

*   *   *

Of all the internecine battles fought after the war in the cavalry, the 'chin-strap' controversy was not the least painful, even bitter. Allenby, always a great stickler for details of discipline, expressed himself appalled at the way in which cavalrymen on manoeuvres ignored orders to use their chin-straps. 'He had watched as caps flew off in all directions, and all proceedings were brought to a halt while headgear was recovered. He now insisted,' his biographer tells us, 'on the observance of this order. ... Almost the entire cavalry and the Inspector-General' became involved in this unhappy, if perhaps rather trifling affair.[37]

'I think *he* [Lord Roberts] would understand my pet fads about bicycles and motors in war, i.e. means of locomotion and mobility which increase from day to day, versus the horse, which is becoming obsolete.'

LORD ESHER to his son, 1910[1]

(iii)

Impact of internal combustion engine – use of motor cars – use of aeroplanes

The impact of the internal combustion engine, which was to be the agent of the cavalry's eventual demise, was first felt upon the British army during the war. 'The motor lorries sent to South Africa,' said

Kitchener in 1902, 'did well. Thorneycroft's are the best. They will, in future, be found superior to steam road traction as field transport.'[2] A few motor cars as opposed to lorries were bought from France, but the war ended before they could be used. The intention was to employ them for carrying searchlights to illuminate the blockhouse lines.[3]

In 1900 the War Office had set up a Mechanical Transport Committee under the Royal Engineers. A year later, soon after his return home, Buller approached the Automobile Club, the forerunner of the Royal Automobile Club, to see whether any of its members would consider hiring out their vehicles for the manoeuvres that year. Three were taken on as staff cars for a week: a 7 hp. Panchard, a 12 hp. Daimler and a 16 hp. Napier.* In 1903 the Motor Volunteer Corps was formed – the first unit of its sort in the world. Wearing newly designed uniforms, the owners of forty-three cars and thirty-one motor cycles took part in that year's manoeuvres. 'The manoeuvres,' reported Roberts, 'would not have been so successful but for the work of the motor volunteers.' By 1904 the Corps consisted of twenty-four officers and eighty-nine other ranks. Later that year there took part in the manoeuvres the first men as combatants to use mechanical vehicles. Wearing rifles slung over their shoulders, six motor cyclists were attached to each of the opposing forces' head quarters as despatch riders. In 1906 the corps was disbanded and replaced by the Army Motor Reserve.[4] This body's first 'Permanent Staff Officer' was a retired 9th Lancer. In 1909 the Reserve consisted of 134 officers whose essential qualifications were

'that they shall be first-class drivers and first-class car-masters, that they shall be good linguists and good map readers, not only able to find their way, but to select the best roads by foreign as well as English maps, and that they shall have a thorough knowledge of army organization generally, and particularly of the composition of the force to which they are attached, as well as sufficient tactical knowledge to enable them to follow the operations and judge the whereabouts of units under all circumstances . . ., lastly, it is essential that they possess the virtue of being able to keep a discreet silence as to what they may see and hear in the course of their duties.'

* Motor staff cars had been used by the French army in its 1900 manoeuvres. (Crouch, J. D. 'The Use of Motor Transport in the Boer War', *Soldiers of the Queen*, Victorian Military Society, Mar., 1984, 6.)

These paragons were soon complaining that their services were 'not fully utilized' and that they were not given 'the opportunity of General Staff work for which their intelligence and training' fitted them. The officer 'administering' the Reserve assured them that 'such is certainly not the view of the authorities, who realize fully the value of these gentlemen who give their services and their valuable cars to their country'. Asserting that 'motor cars widen the Commander's range of vision', he added that the fact that these cars were 'driven by men intelligent, trustworthy and helpful as only a highly educated gentleman can be, adds enormously to their value and efficiency'. In 1909 the establishment of motor cars attached to the Cavalry Division was fifteen. These were all attached to Divisional headquarters, 'but doubtless two or more cars will be allotted when necessary to detached brigades or even Contact Squadrons.' In November, 1913, the Army Motor Reserve was disbanded.[5]

*　*　*

The first military use of aeroplanes in Britain took place during the 1910 annual manoeuvres on Salisbury Plain. Captain Bertram Dickson of the Royal Horse Artillery flew a Bristol machine on a reconnaissance flight for 'Red Force' which succeeded in locating the 'Blue Force' positions. His plane was one of three bought by the War Office for experimental purposes. Churchill, then Home Secretary, was present for part of these manoeuvres, and later made arrangements for the enlargement of 'the scope of the work hitherto carried out at the Balloon School . . . by affording opportunities for aeroplaning'.[6]

'You attach a great deal of importance to distinc-
tion of dress, and so on?'
  'I do.'
  'It is extraordinary how much our people think
of such things.'
LORD ELGIN questioning Ian Hamilton,
(Royal Commission) in 1903[1]

(iv)

*Changes in uniform – final evolution of the cavalry sword – horse
furniture*

Changes in non-ceremonial, working dress for all ranks which followed the war were an outward sign of the new professionalism.
That wonderfully decorative piece of cavalry equipment, the sabre-
tache, the supposed chief purpose of which was to keep the scabbard
from hitting the horse's flanks, was abolished in 1901 for officers, as
it had been for other ranks some seven decades earlier.* At the same
date the leather bandolier, worn over the left shoulder, was substituted for the pouch and pouch-belt for other ranks in the Field
Service Order. This bandolier held ninety rounds of .303 ammunition in five pouches in front and four behind, each carrying two
five-round clips. For officers what was called 'Universal Service
Dress' made of khaki serge was introduced early in 1902. A year
later it was made compulsory wear on all mounted parades, except
those rare ones held in 'Review Order'. By early 1914 all shoulder-
chains on service tunics had disappeared by order. This was pro-
foundly resented. Shoulder-chains were the sole remaining part of
the cavalryman's uniform in Dismounted Order which differentiated
him in the eyes of the common herd from the other arms. Their suppression finally all but removed all distinctions of service dress
between cavalry and infantry. The exceptions were spurs and the way
in which puttees were worn. These, as has been shown (see p. 238),
were a new invention during the war. At first cavalrymen wore them
fastened below the knee where the cord pantaloons were tied. From
there they were wound *downwards*, as was the infantry method. Before
long, though, it was found that they were apt to unroll themselves
on horseback. Consequently in the cavalry they came to be attached
to the top of the 'highlow' or 'boot, ammunition' and wound
upwards.[2]

* The shabraque, or decorative saddle-cloth, had been abolished in 1896.

There had been general agreement during the war that the helmets which officers had been handed out at the war's start were excellent. Lord Airlie thought them 'wonders', affording very good protection to the head. On the other hand, 'the men's helmets,' he wrote in January, 1900, 'are too horrible. Hideous, unserviceable, the cover over them coming over their ears makes it very difficult for them to hear.' Further, according to the Gordon Committee, 'a man cannot shoot lying down without shifting his helmet, and it affords very little protection.'[3] After a year or two of unsatisfactory experiments in headgear, such as the Glengarry type forage cap and the muffin-topped peaked cap for officers (which was very like the old Peninsular cap of nearly 100 years before), the present-day flat peaked cap with chin-strap, introduced on Arnold-Forster's initiative, was almost universally worn. The chin-strap was meant, but was certainly not always (see p. 442), to be worn 'down' when the man was on horseback. 'Down' in the cavalry soon came to mean on the point of the chin. Artillerymen, on the other hand, wore their straps under the chin.[4]

* * *

The seemingly endless search for a trooper's sword which for the first time in the cavalry's history would escape the harsh and nearly universal criticism which all its predecessors had had heaped upon them, came to an end in July, 1908. In that month the 'Pattern 1908, Mark I' was officially sealed. It had taken five years of the keenest discussion and research to produce. In 1903 there was set up the most important of all the scores of committees which had sat to consider the subject over the previous thirty years. French chaired it and its other members were Haig, Rimington and Scobell. It was the first sword committee to be given by the War Office complete liberty of action, and it speedily arrived at the basic decision that the sword of the future should be, primarily, a thrusting or pointing weapon. In its report of January, 1904, it recommended that the clumsy and much criticized 1899 pattern should be replaced by one with 'a narrow chisel blade'.[5] Experimental swords elicited from the troops who tried them out a considerable measure of approval of the thrusting-only principle, but there were many influential doubters and, further, the details of the five different types constructed in 1904 and 1905 were not considered satisfactory. Yet another committee was therefore set up in 1906. Scobell chaired it and there were seven other members, of whom one was a gunner. In spite of its terms of reference which spoke of a sword 'for thrusting but capable also of being used as a cutting weapon', which might have been expected to lead to yet another unsatisfactory hybrid, the committee came up with a truly revolutionary pattern. After numerous samples had been produced by the Wilkinson Sword Company and Mole & Sons, and tried out by regiments, the 1908 Pattern, Mark I, eventually received Army Council approval. Its last and rather unexpected hurdle was the King. He wanted to throw it out as 'hideous', asked why a new pattern was needed at all and why cutting had met its end. A high-powered deputation of senior officers had to hasten to explain the new weapon's merits and the Monarch grudgingly gave way. He insisted though that the Household Cavalry should retain their existing 1892 Pattern, Mark II, for ceremonial use.

The 1908 sword and its scabbard were, unquestionably, the most perfect ever produced for the army. The scabbard was made of sheet steel and lined with wood. The sword's chief revolutionary features were its narrow, tapering, rapier-like blade and its pistol-shaped grip. This had been designed by Colonel Malcolm Fox,* an infantry-man, who had experimented with gutta percha before getting the right shape. His grip, curved and with a depression for the thumb, was said to be 'a minor masterpiece inasmuch as when properly held it automatically brought the blade into position for thrusting'.[6] The cutting effect of the new blade, even when sharpened, was minimal, and this fact is what finally settled the age-old controversy of cut *versus* thrust.†

* Fox had been Inspector of Army Gymnasia in the 1890s and on retirement in 1903 had been appointed Inspector of Physical Training to the Board of Education, a post he held for seven years.

† There was a very considerable body of cavalry officers, chiefly but not solely of the old school, who were not happy with the abandonment of the cutting sword. The strongest argument against the single-purpose weapon was that those who in the past had supported the sword against the lance always reasoned that the double-purpose sword, possessing two modes of attack, was superior to the lance, possessing only one. The other argument most frequently put forward was the difficulty of extracting the pointed sword from the body of an assailant, leaving the attacker vulnerable to the weapon of the following assailant. The feeblest argument was that 'a Briton, a German, any man of Teutonic stock, will always naturally use a sword for cutting or slashing; a Frenchman, Spaniard or Italian will equally naturally use it to point and thrust.'! (Tyrell, F. H., Lieut-Gen., letter to *Morning Post*, 24 Apr., 1908.) There was a lengthy correspondence at this time in the *Morning Post*, *The People* (3 May, 1908), *Daily Telegraph* (18 Jun., 1908). (See also *The Army & Navy Gazette*, 25 Apr., 2 May, 1908.)

The overall length of the weapon was thirty-five inches. Its maximum reach with the arm fully extended just about equalled that of the 1868 lance, and, as will be shown in the final volume of this work, there were to be occasions in 1914 when men using it against the German lance did not find themselves out-distanced. It was a little heavier than its immediate predecessors, but its balance was so superior to theirs that it *seemed* lighter in the hand. Some very minor changes were made in 1910 and 1911. In its final Mark I* form it was studied by the United States army which produced an almost identical sword in 1913.*

In 1912 the officers' 1896 pattern sword was replaced by what was in effect a more ornamental version of the other ranks' 1908 sword. It is still the sword used on ceremonial occasions. So also, but only in the 10th Hussars (now the Royal Hussars), is an extraordinary, even grotesque, version which for an unknown reason that regiment insisted on adopting.[7]

* * *

After the South African War was over the new, slightly lighter type of army saddle which had evolved in its initial form just before the war (see p. 366) was adopted. It was known as 'the Universal Pattern Steel Arch, 1902'. For the first time in the cavalry's history this saddle was truly universal. Its three sizes – large, medium and small – within the next decade superseded all other types of riding saddle throughout the army, with the exception of those for the officers. These last, in virtually all cases, kept to the Colonial pattern. In 1912 yet another pattern was approved – the 'Universal Pattern' saddle (see illustration on p. 449). In this, which looked very similar to its predecessor, the seat was marginally longer and the hind arch slightly lower. Another improvement was that the front and rear arches were jointed to allow them to fit themselves automatically to the backs of animals of all sizes. Another advance was made by supporting the seat from front arch to rear by double webbing so as to stiffen it. This was important because in wet weather the leather unless stiffened was liable to stretch and become mis-shaped. There were other minor amendments, such as steel studs instead of screws. Sir Evelyn Wood, who had criticized the 1901–1902 saddles as too heavy, pronounced this final evolution of the army saddle

* Lieutenant George Smith Patton, aged twenty-eight, is credited with perfecting this sword. (Robson, 57.)

58. The Universal Pattern
    Steel Arch saddle of
    1902 with the deep
    rifle bucket

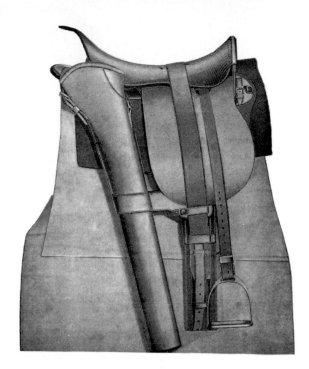

59. Viscount Haldane

60. 'Line will attack – charge!', 11 Troop, 'A' Squadron, 7th Hussars, 1913

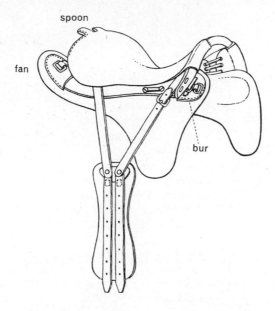

The 'Universal Pattern' saddle of 1912

'the acme of a soldier's saddle',[8] The major problems of strength *versus* weight had at last been solved so far as man's ingenuity could manage the task.

During the rest of the history of the mounted arm there were only minor alterations in the design of the other items of horse furniture such as bits and bridoons, general harness and bridles.* The cavalry and artillery went into the First World War with horse equipment little different from that of 1902.

* In 1902 there came about a small change in bridle design. In that year was introduced the 'Universal Pattern Reversible' or 'elbow' bit. This combined the action of the curb, which by itself was severe on the horse's mouth, and the snaffle, which was less painful but had less controlling power (see Vol II, p. 429). During the war, the snaffle alone, according to an officer of the 7th Dragoon Guards, was 'more than sufficient to hold a horse carrying eighteen stone for an average of twenty-five miles a day'. (Thompson, 81.) With it was used a white head rope which had replaced the steel collar chain in 1891. A minor, but heated, debate took place as to whether officers' chargers should also abandon the more glamorous collar chain for the white head rope. It was finally decided that they should. (Pomeroy, 231.)

449

18

'Whilst the flowers of Peace are blooming,
   Voice with voice, and soul with soul,
Be all kindly wishes flowing,
   Blithely round the wassail bowl:
Every Briton loves his country,
   Every soldier loves his Queen,
Every man loves darling woman,
   Loves his home hearth-fire's sheen.
      To our County Corps of Yeomen
      Drain the bumper o'er and o'er.
   Hip! Hip! Hip! Hip! Hurrah! Hurrah!
      To our County Yeoman Corps.'
         Song of the Yeomanry Cavalry[1]

*Yeomanry: unfitness for service – shortage of officers and men –
lack of staffs – pay and allowances – class of men*

'Military opinion is unanimous in holding that the yeomanry as at present constituted and serving under existing conditions are quite unfit to take the field against European troops.' Thus an official memorandum of 1907.[2] Four years earlier Lord Chesham (see p. 88) told the Royal Commission that in his view there was not 'a single regiment in England which, if you take it all through, is fit for service, and I don't think it ever could be. . . . The only way we shall get yeomanry to be of any use is to look upon each regiment as a depot for general service.'[3] In effect this is what some of them had become by August, 1914. Haldane's great scheme envisaged an additional 3,140 yeomanry (about six regiments) as part of the British Expeditionary Force.[4] These units were chiefly designed to act as divisional cavalry for the Force's infantry divisions, and, of course, were therefore obliged to serve overseas. The rest of the yeomanry, which numbered in total some 27,000 of all ranks, formed in part a nucleus from which the cavalry of a second line might be formed in time of war, and in part an essential element of the home defence forces.

There was much to be done to bring the regiments out of the excessive amateurism which had always hitherto characterized them. Under General Sir Henry MacKinnon, who was first Director of Auxiliary Forces from 1905 and then of the Territorial Force till 1910, and especially under his successor Sir John Cowans, giant

450

steps were taken to professionalize the yeomanry. Yet, even before their time, some vital measures had been taken. The strength of each regiment had always varied enormously and the whole system encouraged the enlistment of men, not because they were good yeomen, but because their enlistment 'swelled the regimental roll and brought money to the regimental exchequer'.[5] Arnold-Forster in 1904 braved a major outburst of displeasure on the part of many a yeomanry colonel and fixed a maximum establishment. This at first was 476 per regiment, and it was found, unfortunately, that a number of the best regiments were well above that prescribed strength, while others were well below it. There was an overall shortage of both officers and men. In 1905, for instance, there was a shortage of some 2,300 of all ranks, while two years later there was a deficiency of over 300 officers alone. In 1906 at the annual training, 4,600 out of the establishment of 27,638 were absent.[6]* Training was for a minimum of eight and a maximum of eighteen days a year and a great deal depended upon the preparations made before the period started. One of the major difficulties was the lack of proper staffs, brigade organization and administrative services. By 1914 much had been done to provide a semblance of these, making the annual training much more useful than hitherto.

There were some insuperable impediments to professionalism which remained. There is no doubt, for instance, that numbers of ex-cavalry officers would have joined yeomanry regiments if they could have been given commands commensurate with their rank, but the best commands, such as that of a squadron, were more often than not held by a local magnate, and it was rightly considered that for the purpose of recruiting that should continue to be the case. Lord Lovat (see p. 94) summed up the position thus: 'You have to take your officers from two classes, from the men of influence in the country and the men financially sufficient to be able to help your squadrons to go, and, secondly, you want to get the other officers who, if it comes to war, would be ready to help, and who would really do the work of the squadron, and who, as a rule, are not so rich.'[7]

There was the question of expense which was apt to inhibit recruiting. 'They give you £5 horse allowance,' Lieutenant-Colonel

---

* 1,948 were absent with leave and 357 without it. Of the 21,731 horses employed, 10,754 belonged to the yeomen or their relations, 550 were supplied by the Remount Department and 10,427 were hired. ('Imperial Yeomanry Training Returns' quoted in *Cav. Jnl*, I, 235.)

Weston Jarvis, who had commanded the 21st Battalion in South Africa, told the Royal Commission, 'but it costs in many instances more than that to hire a horse for the training, and the class of horse that is hired for £5 is not good enough; he is a broken-down cab-horse as a rule.'[8] There was a further allowance of £2 per man granted for each regiment. But this was usually insufficient to pay for uniforms, the band and maintenance of the permanent staff. As one authority has put it, 'the mere fact that some out-of-pocket expense was met by each trooper and/or the unit commander tended to turn the yeomanry into something of a hobby.'[9]

As for the men, there was a distinct change in the types who joined the yeomanry. In the last quarter of the nineteenth-century they came in large part from the farmers and the agricultural classes. Since the great agricultural depression a much larger percentage of recruits were now coming from the towns – even more than for the regular army – and that was an increasing tendency right up to 1914.

19

'It is often said that officers care about nothing but polo and hunting. I have known cavalry officers, several of them squadron commanders, men with large independent means, men who had horses at Melton and ponies all over the place, who would give up hunting, polo and everything simply to go and have their squadrons out in the morning, and then go into the barrack rooms and lecture them in the afternoon. I have seen them in uniform in barracks very often at 5 and 6 in the evening, having been working the whole day. That was the kind of work that was going on in the Cavalry Brigade at Aldershot for some time before the war.'

FRENCH in 1902

'An officer who [at Sandhurst] is recorded as "distinguished" in any subject, or who secures a "special certificate" of proficiency, derives no advantage whatever.'

The Akers-Douglas Committee on
Military Education, 1902

'Few [officers] read or study. Military science as such seems to be beyond them. A battle is in their eyes only a game of football. What is the good of heroism when you are picked off by an enemy three miles away? You want science.'

CURZON to Brodrick, 1900

'I fear that proficiency in games or in the hunting field will not help our poor lads much when they have to face the carefully trained and highly educated German officers.

'*Our* difficulty is that our lawyers and physicians are professional men, but until very lately our soldiers have been amateurs – and soldiering a pastime and not a "business". Even now, it is the exception and not the rule to find a clever and highly educated soldier.'

LORD ESHER in 1906

'Nowadays young officers begin work at daybreak and go on till midday, 1 o'clock, or perhaps

till 3 p.m. The squadron officer is now training a
succession of men for the Reserve. There is
winter training, then squadron training, regimental, brigade and possibly divisional training.
The men are trained to a much higher standard
and they are trained now by the squadron officers
and not by the adjutant and his staff.

RIMINGTON in 1912[1]

(ii)

*Officers: types – Royal Military College, Sandhurst – Staff
College, Camberley*

Soon after the start of the Boer War, one of the best known of the
military 'crammers', Dr Thomas Miller Maguire (see Vol III, p. 96),
wrote that it was extraordinary how deeply rooted in England was
'the delusion that mere physique is the first qualification for a commission in the army, and that next is money, the next skill in games
of ball, the next horsemanship, the next good breeding and good
manners, and the last general intelligence and culture.' He believed
that 'a large proportion of our young officers', and he should have
known, 'are by far the most ignorant persons of their social class in
Europe, Japan, our Colonies or the United States.'[2] There was quite
a widespread feeling that the standard of education of 'gentlemen'
had declined in recent years. Lieutenant-Colonel Arthur Williamson
Alsager Pollock, who had been a *Times* Special Correspondent in
South Africa, believed, for instance, that 'regimental officers of
former days not only quoted Horace, but were intimately acquainted
also with the English Classics, both prose and verse. Now we read
trashy novels and cheap magazines.' Lord Esher thought that some
young officers read books and 'improve their minds, but spasmodic-
ally and without real incentive. A lad will think, for a week,' he
wrote in his journal in 1907, 'that in order to be a general he must
"work at" strategy; so he will take real pains to master a campaign
of Napoleon. The following week it strikes him that he cannot command armies until he is forty, and he falls asleep in the anteroom.'
Haldane, however, told the House of Commons in 1906 that he
believed that 'a new school of officers has arisen since the South
African War, a thinking school of officers who desire to see the full
efficiency which comes from new organization and no surplus energy
running to waste.'[3]

At about this time particularly, snide remarks and jokes about the lack of brains of the average officer seem to have proliferated. It was said, for example, that the Boers inflicted the death penalty on any man who killed a British general.[4] The obituary of General Joubert in *The Times* was believed (wrongly) to have asserted that he had once said that 'British officers make the grand mistake of thinking their opponents are as stupid as themselves.'[5] When young Hastings (later Lord) Ismay joined the 21st Cavalry (Frontier Force) in 1907, his father, a distinguished Indian civil servant, was very upset 'and never tired of telling the story about the cavalry officer who was so stupid that even his brother officers noticed it.'[6] Julian Grenfell when he joined the 1st Royal Dragoons nevertheless found that he liked his fellow officers 'better than the Oxford people: I thought it would be the reverse.' On his way to India he had gone to see a silent film at Port Said with Lieutenant Sclater Booth, 'very ugly and very nice'.

> 'Booth could not understand, the words being by the nature of the performance left for the intelligence of the audience to supply. So I kept up a running commentary: Booth – What are they doing now, eh? Self – Well you see, they are trying to kill him; the cowboys are not sitting on him to try to keep him warm. Booth – Why have they put that rope round his neck, eh what? Self – They are going to *hang* him with the rope. That is why they have put it round his *neck*.'

A story told by General Sir George de Symons Barrow exemplifies the amateurish outlook of the average officer. In the days before cavalry drill was simplified there were certain movements, such as 'changing line on a new alignment' which required a preliminary order. A young lieutenant of the 4th Indian Cavalry, asked by the inspecting general, 'Why is it necessary to give preliminary order "A" before the second order "B"?' replied 'Ah! Why indeed, sir, why indeed!' In 1900 Captain William Elliot Cairnes, who later produced a hagiography of Roberts, wrote that 'the lad who joins a cavalry regiment with a school reputation of being a fine cricketer or racket-player is assured of a welcome which would possibly be denied to the lad who had passed at the top of the list into the service.'[7]

The end of the war saw no change in the social composition of the officer class. Indeed until about the year 1910 nothing faintly resembling 'democratization' could be discerned, and even then it was no more than an almost imperceptible glimmer. Before that year virtually none of the cadets who entered the Royal Military College at Sandhurst had lower-middle-class backgrounds. In 1900 only 1.7% were *not* 'gentlemen' (17%), businessmen and managers (12%), 'military professionals' (i.e. relations of army officers) (42.6%) or members of the professional classes (26.7%). Ten years later the figure was 3.4%, while the percentage of 'gentlemen' had actually risen to 20.5%.[8] It took the First World War to begin to reflect in the army that predominance of the bourgeoisie which had begun nationally in earnest during the last third of the 19th century.

*   *   *

An unattractive case of intimidation of an unpopular officer occurred in the 2nd Life Guards on 21 July, 1902. Four subalterns of the regiment, Lieutenants Sir George Lionel Lawson Bagot Prescott, Bt., Lord Montgomerie (later 16th Earl of Eglinton and Winton), Hugh Ashton and 2nd-Lieutenant Robert Duff, decided that a newly joined 2nd-Lieutenant, Charles Dalton Gregson, should have life made so unpleasant for him that he would leave the regiment. According to Captain Herbert Henry Spender-Clay, who was the senior officer present in the Mess that evening, 'a sort of bogus auction' was held in the course of which Gregson's uniform was 'roughly pulled off' and his overalls were destroyed. A coal scuttle filled with 'house refuse' was then emptied over the unfortunate fellow's head and he was forced to run round the green outside the mess, wearing only his boots and a pair of drawers – all within the hearing of the sentries. Spender-Clay, who took no actual part in the proceedings, then went to bed 'as there did not appear,' he said, 'to be any sign of bullying'. The others, however, had not finished with Gregson. First, they ducked him in the water-trough and then rolled him in the mud. Not satisfied with this, they followed him to his bedroom and threw all his furniture 'except one piece' out of the window. 'I suppose you know,' they then shouted at him, 'what all this means – it means we do not want you.' What made the incident worse was the fact that Gregson was Orderly Officer that night and was, of course, unable to go his rounds of the sentries, having nothing to wear. The Commanding Officer, Lieutenant-Colonel Sir Audley Dallas Neeld, Bt., who, like Spender-Clay and Prescott had fought in South Africa, was severely censured. 'If the officers of the 2nd Life Guards,' wrote Roberts, 'were in a proper state of discipline, such an occurrence could not have taken place.' Spender-Clay, although the King told Roberts that he thought the punishment a little too severe, was forced to resign, while the four subalterns had their leave stopped for six months. Poor Gregson was seconded to the Indian Army in 1903 and the following year transferred to the 20th Deccan Horse of which he became adjutant. Spender-Clay rejoined in 1914, was employed on the Staff and in 1918 became a lieutenant-colonel. He was Member of Parliament for Tonbridge from 1910 until his death in 1937. Ashton commanded the regiment from 1920 to 1922 and the Composite regiments of 1st and 2nd Life Guards from 1923 to 1925. Duff became adjutant of the regiment, but resigned in 1907, rejoined in 1914 and was killed in action in October of that year.[9]*

* * *

Osbert Sitwell just before the First World War was attached to the 11th Hussars. He found it agony: 'a life fit only for horses and dogs – which were, indeed, considered by the officers (and very rightly) as being by far the most important members of their community.' Another aspect of officers' attitudes at the time is well illustrated by Bernard Shaw's apocryphal story of the gallant captain whose visiting card bore the words 'The Celebrated Coward'. His superior had given him an order which would have put success in the operation upon which they were engaged against the Boers beyond doubt. This would have entailed his superior's and almost certainly his own promotion. But, as General Sir John Hackett puts it, 'the captain strongly believed that the British army should be officered by gentlemen. His superior wasn't one. Therefore the captain ran away. He was cashiered of course, but he had ensured the failure of the operation and prevented for ever the advancement of his superior. When this triumph of principle over self-interest was made known the captain was at once made an honorary member of several London clubs.'[10]

* The Earl of Athlone (Queen Mary's brother) transferred from the Royal Horse Guards to the 2nd Life Guards in 1911 at the request of the King who thought that the officers of the regiment 'were a poor lot and needed some new blood injected'. (Private information.)

In 1912 the *1st* Life Guards attained the distinction of being the most exclusive regiment ever. 70 % of its officers were of the aristocracy, 18 % landed gentry and only 12 % middle class. (Razzell, P. E. 'Social Origins of Officers . . ., 1758–1962', *British Journal of Sociology*, XIV (Sept. 1963), 256.)

By contrast, here is Lord Airlie (see p. 184) writing of his regiment, the 12th Lancers, a short time before he was killed at its head: 'How happy we have been in this dear, dear Regiment. . . . Such a happy home, I wish I had the eye of a hawk and the genius of a Murat for its sake. . . . Selfish as I am – and I am I know – dreadfully so very often, I don't think I have been selfish about the dear Regiment. I do so care for it for its own sake.' Airlie was of the sort that Private Corbett came across during the war: 'gentlemen a soldier could look up to with respect and admiration'. Another was Prince Alexander of Teck (later Earl of Athlone).

> 'He is a splendid chap,' wrote Trooper Seed of the 3rd Hussars, 'and all the men like him. . . . [During a post-war exercise] he made all the men laugh by the way he took my message. When I told him the enemy were coming towards him, he pretended to get excited and commenced jumping about and throwing his arms in the air, at the same time shouting "Where? Where? Oh tell me where they are! What shall I do?" He behaves just like a schoolboy at times, although he is a Prince.'

Amery believed that

> 'there is a good deal to be said from the purely military point of view for an aristocratic class of officers; there is absolutely nothing to be said for a military plutocracy. Good breeding and good brains will both tell on the battlefield. Money will not. . . . How many brainless sons of wealthy *parvenus* enter the cavalry simply and solely for the sake of the social connections they hope to acquire!'[11]

* * *

The Akers-Douglas Committee on Military Education had no doubt that in 1902 the young man wishing to become an officer was usually 'deficient in general education'. This does not say much for the public schools which provided most of them. Even during the Boer War 62% of all officers who joined the regulars came from public schools, 11% from Eton alone. Right down to the Second World War, the vast majority of new officers came from the public schools.[12] The Committee's chief and not very demanding recommendation was that every potential officer should have a proper general education before he went to either of the cadet colleges at

Sandhurst and Woolwich. Having entered, his instruction ought to be confined to those military and technical subjects which were necessary for efficiency.

The state of the Royal Military College at Sandhurst* at this time was deplorable. There was 'absolutely no inducement to work', even those cadets who failed to attain 'the low qualifying standard' being given commissions none the less. It was certainly clear that the instructors had 'no inducement to teach'. 'The best men,' said the Assistant Military Secretary for Education at the War Office, 'do not go into Sandhurst as instructors.' The pay was derisory. 'An officer is looked upon as taking a step downhill when he accepts such an appointment.' It was regarded as 'a shelf on which an officer may spend a few years comfortably, avoiding the monotonous routine of life in barracks and the constant changes of station which constitute such a serious tax upon the pocket of the married officer.' The junior officer, once he had left Sandhurst, was 'lamentably wanting in military knowledge'. The desire to acquire knowledge and zeal in the military art was minimal. 'Keenness is out of fashion. . . . It is not correct form; the spirit and fashion is rather not to show keenness.' The Committee believed that it made 'no difference to the subsequent career of the officer whether he passes with the highest possible distinction or merely succeeds in scraping through.'[13]

Training at Sandhurst in 1902 did not include musketry or revolver shooting, although there was a range nearby. Cadets who wanted to shoot had to join a club and pay £1 per term. In 1902 drill still included forming square to receive cavalry.[14] Signalling and veterinary science were not then included in the syllabus. On average during the one-year course cadets, whose average age on entry was nineteen and a half, only rode for thirty-nine hours. Each horse worked for a mere twelve and a half hours per week. 'No attempt is made to give cavalry cadets more instruction in riding than those cadets destined for the infantry.' Virtually all of it was done in the covered school and sometimes in a small paddock, as also were all gymnastics. Neither stable management nor horse-mastership was taught. The Committee also discovered that only about a fifth of the cadets had ever ridden at all before entering the

* Between 1876 and 1914 the College trained 55 % of all new officers (except those for the Artillery and Engineers who went to the Royal Military Academy at Woolwich). From 1862 the College also catered for a proportion of officers going into the Indian Army (Otley, 222).

college. Much time and effort were devoted to Military Topography, 'overmuch regard being paid to elaboration of highly finished sketches, finish appearing to be regarded as of equal importance with accuracy'. At the same time only sixty hours in the year were appropriated for the teaching of elementary tactics. Very typical of the sense of priorities was the fact that cadets were required to clean and pipe-clay their 'buff waist-belts', but had their rifles cleaned for them. The Committee, with justified if heavy-handed sarcasm, commented: 'This is remarkable, for while a cadet might acquire a familiarity with the mechanism of the rifle from being required to clean it, the educational value of pipe-claying a belt is extremely slight.' Nearly all activities were geared to the dreaded inspections of visiting generals. Practical work was seldom performed and this was reflected in the passing-out examinations. Out of a total of 3,800 marks, only 450 were for tactics, of which 150 were for non-theoretical work. If the general standard was low, that for the cavalry was even lower. 'In no branch of our service,' wrote Amery in 1903, 'are brains more essential than in the cavalry. Yet such is the deadly effect of the heavy financial demand made on the cavalry officer that the standard of marks which enables a man to get into the cavalry is many thousands below that of the infantry.' The Committee found that the cadet was led, throughout the course, to believe that his studies 'need not trouble him' once he had obtained his commission.[15]

How remarkably well things at Sandhurst had progressed by the start of the First World War will be shown in the final volume of this work. One cadet who was there not long before it found that the instruction by then had become

'superlative. We learned to fire the Vickers or Maxim gun, to signal with flags, we marched and had night operations. . . . We dug trenches on Hartford bridge flats in our canvas fatigue kit. . . . Sex talks was "taboo" and "*not done*". Food was excellent and we had free beer at lunch of a mild calibre.

'The riding school was under the old cavalry system. The riding master was an ex-ranker officer, Honorary Major Bill Sykes, assisted by sergeants from cavalry regiments. . . . The first morning in riding school, the riding master would call out as we paraded with all the horses drawn up in front and behind us: "Those G[entlemen] C[adet]s who have hunted on the right, those who can ride next, those who *can* ride next, those

460

who have ridden left" [it was presumed that there was no one who had not ridden!]

'Riding was taught under the system of survival of the fittest – quarter-hour trotting without stirrups, followed by jumping without stirrups and with arms folded at the third lesson on a slippery saddle. Few would deny that this method put numbers of pupils off riding altogether. It also upset the horses.'[16]

Another cadet, Sir John Smyth, who was to win the Victoria Cross in the First World War and himself become an instructor at Camberley, discovered that 'in direct contrast to Repton, and indeed most other public schools, at Sandhurst we worked very hard indeed. A certain number, who were destined for the Guards or the Cavalry, could afford to take things easily, though even they had to attain a certain standard to pass out at all – and some never managed to do so. . . . The régime at Sandhurst at that time [1911] was a good preliminary training for the young officer. The life was hard and discipline strict.'[17]

Though rugby football was said at this date to be the 'be-all and end-all of the College's activities', the cavalry company* never entered a team because rugger was not the game for horsemen, since it often involved serious injuries to knees and legs.[18]

*   *   *

What was basically wrong with the military training of officers, and, indeed, of other ranks too, was the exceedingly small amount of money set aside for it. In 1899 the post of Director-General of Military Education which had been founded in 1869 was abolished and the Military Secretary took over his duties.† Economy was the motive. So it was, too, where the subject generally was concerned. From the 1901–2 Army Estimates only 0.4% was allowed for the purpose. (This was a decline from the 0.63% of 1890–1.) Of the total estimates only 0.15% was provided for technical military education for cadets and officers. Further, the £4,000 given annually for proficiency in certain foreign languages, which had been reduced in 1898 to £1,000, had now dwindled to £550.[19]

Some of the first reforms which were implemented as a result of

* The organization of Sandhurst was that of an infantry battalion. (*Army Order* 220, 1904.)

† One result of the Akers-Douglas Report was the establishment in 1903 of the post of Director of Military Education.

the Akers-Douglas Committee's recommendations were the revision of regulations for examinations which reduced the number of subjects to those of a more practical nature,[20] the institution of one month's summer camp during the year's course and greater inducements to attract 'capable officers to take up instructional work'.[21] In 1903 Roberts issued a *Special Army Order* to do away with (for the entrance examinations) a 'separate list of candidates for cadetships in the Cavalry'. The reasons given were that 'in modern warfare the duties of cavalry officers of every rank are of so responsible a nature that it is essential they should be possessed of the highest professional attainments and be amongst the most capable, intellectually and physically, of those seeking admission to His Majesty's Army' and that the cavalry, under the new measures for reducing expenses (see p. 470), would now be open to 'many capable men' who had hitherto been debarred from entering it.[22] The 'separate list' was nevertheless restored not long before the outbreak of the First World War, under, presumably, the pressure of the continuing deficiency of cavalry officers of *any* calibre. (See p. 471.)

The system of examinations for promotion which officers had to take in the course of their careers and which the Committee said encouraged 'the custom of idleness with a brief period of cram',[23] were radically altered to produce more practical tests and greater efficiency.[24] By the outbreak of the First World War there were, as a result, many more officers who could face with some equanimity the challenge posed by Roberts in 1903: 'It is not too much to say that the fate of an engagement may rest upon the good judgement and reports of a cavalry subaltern; and the issue of a campaign on the recognition and seizure of some strategic position by a cavalry brigadier.'

After the Boer War it was estimated that the army needed about 800 officers a year. Sandhurst and Woolwich together could only produce a maximum of about 500. To help in remedying this situation and at the same time carry out the Committee's recommendation that the Sandhurst course should be extended from one to two years it was decided to double the College's capacity. A new block for an increase of 424 cadets and twelve officers was started in 1908 and opened in 1912.[25]

*   *   *

As was shown in Volume III (see pp. 110–13), the Staff College at

Camberley in the 1890s was not yet, in Colonel Frederic Maude's words, 'a true university, for experimental and original research'.[26] Brigadier-General Sir James Edmonds who was there in the last years of the century remembered that

'there was a written, marked examination at the end of the first year [of the two-year course], but nobody regarded it seriously. I was trying to help a lame duck (a nominee [i.e. an officer nominated by the Commander-in-Chief who had not had to pass any examination before entering]) when the invigilator came up. I expected trouble; all he said was, "It's no good prompting him, you must dictate to him," and proceeded himself to do so.'[27]

This gives the flavour of the standards then existing. It took a succession of remarkable Commandants and Professors after the Boer War to transform the College into a true school for teaching what a staff officer would actually have to perform in war and peace. Like the Royal Military College, and for the same reasons, on the outbreak of war the Staff College lost most of its pupils. In April, 1900, it was closed. Seven months later, though, it was reopened and the scope of instruction was at once widened. Though the instructional staff numbered only six, the number of students was increased to thirty-two each year, making a total of sixty-four. Short, emergency courses were given so that a small number of officers might gain the rudiments of staff work before being despatched to South Africa.[28]

Rawlinson became Commandant in 1903, Henry Wilson in 1907 and Robertson in 1910. Under their brilliant, energetic and realistic guidance both matter and method of instruction were revolutionized. The College not only expanded but came as near to emulating the great staff schools of Germany and France as such an institution could under British conditions. By 1913 there were as many as 185 candidates for the thirty-six vacancies available. General Sir Harold Franklyn remembered that in June of that year 'the examination was almost as much a test of endurance as of knowledge, for it was spread over a period of ten days and on nearly every day there were two papers, each lasting three hours.' He recalled that

'the most colourful personality among the students then at the Staff College [was] an officer in the 11th Hussars, who, in addition to his cherry trousers, wore his blue patrol jacket open to display a canary-yellow waistcoat. When one adds that he had thick curly black hair, the picturesque effect can be imagined. His father, a distinguished general, once asked a friend, "Have you ever met anyone with as much buck and swagger as myself?" The friend was frank enough to say "no", whereupon the general said, "Then you can't have met my boy Bertie." Yet Bertie was in fact a gallant and efficient officer with a keen intellect behind a foppish facade.'[29]

*   *   *

One of Kitchener's earliest actions when he got to India was to propose a Staff College there on much the same lines as Camberley's. His chief reason was that

'the best officers of the Indian Army will not go to Camberley, and it does not suit many officers of the British Army serving in India to go home for two years: (1) because they cannot afford it [it cost between £200 and £250 a year over and above an officer's pay to go to Camberley]; (2) because they are married and settled down in India; (3) because they feel that they lose touch with what is going on in India, where possibly their future lies.'

His plan met resistance in London on the ground that an Indian Staff College might 'create a separate school of thought and increase the existing diversities of military opinion', to which Kitchener replied: 'The Army has no military school of thought. I wish there was more thoughtful research, and more effort to base opinions on well-digested knowledge.' He said that no divergence of training methods would be permitted that had not been approved by Camberley. He won the battle and in 1905 the Staff College opened first temporarily at Deolali, and later in 1907 when new buildings had been prepared, at Quetta. In the nine and a half years of its pre-First World War existence 218 officers graduated from the College.[30]

*   *   *

In 1911 there died an officer of the old school, General Sir Baker Russell (see Vol III, p. 273), who had been in his time at least as colourful a personality as the Bertie of General Franklyn's recollection. Wolseley had thought Russell one of his finest discoveries. He had joined the 6th Dragoon Guards in 1855 and transferred to the

13th Hussars as a captain in 1862. From the Indian Mutiny to Tel-el-Kebir he had ignored both the drill book and danger. He believed that all cavalrymen should 'look pretty in time of peace and get killed in war'. A booming 'By Jove!' usually preceded his speedily-made decisions both in the field and at the War Office. He was seventy-four when he died.

Captain Lawrence Edward Grace Oates, who died aged thirty-two in 1912, was a very different sort of officer. Very shy, but a wit, he, like Russell, was vastly brave. In May, 1900, he had joined the 6th Inniskilling Dragoons from the Militia. In March, 1901, with a draft of fifteen men soon after arriving in South Africa and before joining his regiment, he found himself in charge of an officer's patrol fighting Scheepers (see p. 207). Caught in a river-bed and taking full advantage of cover

> 'he directed each man, as he finished his ammunition, to creep back to the town [Aberdeen] with his rifle; several were seriously wounded, but managed to crawl away. In the end, after four hours' fighting, only Oates himself remained; with one of the last shots fired by the enemy he was shot through the thigh, the bone being broken. Twice Scheepers sent a white flag demanding surrender, but on both occasions got the same reply – viz. "that they were there to fight, not surrender".'

At one point the enemy came to within twenty yards of Oates, but Scheepers eventually retired and did not secure a single rifle.[31] Oates, who later served in Ireland, Egypt and India, became adjutant of his regiment. His chief amusements were hunting, steeplechasing and yachting, at all of which he was very skilful.[32] He was serving in India when he read about Scott's preparations for the South Pole expedition. Scott accepted him and the War Office gave him leave. He was placed in charge of the expedition's nineteen sledge-drawing ponies. The circumstances of his heroic death are too well known to repeat here. His body was never found.

There died in 1908 one of the less typical and less distinguished cavalry officers. The Hon. Hugh Rowley, who was a product of Eton and Sandhurst, had served only a year in the 16th Lancers way back in 1852. His claim to fame was his literary output. In the 1870s he published *Puniana, More Puniana, Advice to Parties about to Marry* and *Sage Stuffings for Green Goslings*.

* * *

An officer joining the Indian Army found that he received better pay and a larger pension than he would have had at home. It cost him much less to play polo and his general standard of living was comparatively luxurious. This last applied, too, to the officers of the European army when their regiments were stationed there. Major Gregory of the 12th Lancers, for example, tells how, for his washing he paid the equivalent of 1s a month.

> 'The Dhobi would come every week and take as many articles as we liked to give him, and when one remembers that we had white uniforms in summer and drill khaki which required washing, not to mention socks, towels, shirts, sheets, bed covers and pillow cases, all of which were a personal issue and washed at our expense, it will be seen that the size of the laundry bundles was at times considerable.'[33]

The amazing number of different native servants who attended upon the most junior officer decreased not one jot up to 1914. For a bachelor establishment of perhaps two or three subalterns in a bungalow there was the *khitmatgar* or butler as top man and then the 'dressing boy' or bearer who cleaned, pressed and laid out all the different orders of dress. There were the full-dress uniform and mess dress 'and their equivalent in white linen'; undress, which consisted of a blue frock coat and overalls in the hussars, and field service dress, made up of serge and drill breeches and overalls. Each of these had its own helmet, cap, boots, spurs, belt and sword sling. Then there were the kits for polo and hunting as well as ordinary plain clothes. When it is considered that each officer changed his clothes four or five times a day and that camp kit, guns, sword and revolver all had to be kept clean, it will be seen that the dressing boy was busy. He was, however, assisted by the 'dog boy', whose other most vital duties were the carrying of the hurricane lamp which lit his officer's path between bungalow and mess, and frightened away snakes. The *bhisti* prepared the bath, morning and evening. The sweeper swept and also performed 'sanitary work'. This was the normal indoor establishment. The outside servants included the *sais* or groom for each horse or pony, the 'grass-cut' who procured fresh green fodder, the *mali* 'who tended the endless rows of potted crotons and cannas which did duty as a flower garden' and the *chokidar* or night watchman.[34]

The young Julian Grenfell, who went out with the 1st Royal Dragoons in 1910, found that to his pay as a subaltern were added

Colonial Allowance of 4s a day and a 'Customs Rebate' of 1s 2d. Yet his 'everyday living expenses' which consisted largely of his mess bill exceeded his total income (not counting his private allowance) by about £50.

> 'I love India,' he wrote home, 'and the Royal Dragoons (who are magnificent and yet friendly) and my clothes, especially my boots, and rice, and curry, and the entire lack of privacy – three men black as your hat sitting on your doorstep all day.
>
> 'It is horse and saddle and boots (Field Boots, Polo Boots, Gaiters, Wellingtons, Undress Wellingtons, Mess Wellingtons, Dress Wellingtons) all day and every day . . . riding to riding school, riding in riding school, riding back from riding school, changing into very tight black trousers with a yellow stripe and a very tight red tunic, riding to stables, riding back from stables, riding to luncheon, riding back from luncheon, changing into riding breeches, riding to foot drill, foot drill on FOOT, riding back from foot drill, polo (on horseback) or stalking (on or behind a horse), then tea, dinner and bed.'

Grenfell loved pigsticking which he compared to 'coursing with human greyhounds'. At Muttra in the summer the temperature rose to 117°F in the shade. This, too, he loved: 'punkahs, and a swimming bath, and a streaming face all day; and getting up at 4 and sleeping in the middle of the day.'[35] In almost every record of life in India mention is made of the high summer temperatures and by no means always were regiments or individual officers able to avoid it by moving to the hill districts. Its effects were worse, of course, where there was high humidity, such as pertained in so much of southern India, known throughout the army as the 'sloth belt'. The official hot weather invariably started on 1 April. This signalled the rapid disappearance of many of the officers and rather fewer of the men to the hills. If the regiment as a whole remained in the plains, as most did, it was reduced to about half strength, though all the troop horses remained. The fortunate half then exchanged sandflies, mosquitoes, prickly heat and fever for dinners, dancing, racing and polo. By the end of September things were back to normal, and the training season commenced.

Officers' pay

'A life of racing, polo, hunting, balls and parties required an income much greater than an officer's pay, which was in any case not competitive with those in other professions.'

CORRELLI BARNETT in *Britain and Her Army*, 1970

'The necessity of ample means bars efficiency. A rich man seldom remains long enough in the service, nor can he be said to make it his profession; he consequently lacks the necessary incentive to advance himself. Moreover, the chances for practical training for war in this country so seldom occur that an inevitable slackness pervades all his actions. As a rule officers are bad horse-masters, having no idea of taking care of their horses. This important part of their duties is utterly neglected.'

LORD SCARBROUGH in 1902

'The pay [of cavalry officers], though never adequate, was not too small when too much was not expected and when officers came into the Army to have a good time. But, now that more work is expected and officers have so much less time to themselves, they can no longer be expected to pay out of their own pockets for the privilege of soldiering.'

*   *   *

'The average English boy would prefer cavalry to other branches of the Service if he thought he could afford it, and this is confirmed by the fact that there is no difficulty in finding candidates for the Indian Cavalry.'

A War Office Report in 1905[1]

(ii)

Officers: reasons for post-war deficiency – minor reforms to reduce expenses – promotion from ranks

'The worst paid man in England is the young officer. He gets the work,' Wolseley told the Royal Commission on the War in South Africa, 'but he has not got the same pay that my butler has, when you take into account what the butler gets in the way of feeding, housing and clothing.'²* Rimington pointed out in 1912 that 'fewer country gentlemen can afford the requisite allowance to their sons. Expenditure all round has increased, whilst incomes, at any rate those derived from land, have shrunk. More youngsters go abroad to the colonies. "How hardly shall the rich man enter" the barrack gate now, when so much more work is to be done!' Poor pay was an important reason why after the war there was a chronic shortage of officers below the rank of major. The total deficiency in the whole of the army as late as 1907 was 4,419 out of a mobilization establishment of 10,666 – over 41%. The numbers required for mobilization in the cavalry at that date were 327 for the expeditionary force, 238 for depots at home, to which was added 'wastage for twelve months' of 227, making a total of 792. Including the Reserve (majors and below only) the number actually available at home was 632, a deficiency of 160 or 20.2%.³

In 1903 a War Office Committee was appointed to consider the expenses incurred by officers. The evidence it elicited provides the fullest and most authoritative details of a cavalry officer's actual expenses as they were during most of the latter half of the nineteenth and the first years of the twentieth centuries. His initial costs were estimated at a minimum of £600, which was £400 more than those for an infantry officer. But the Committee realized that the 'original expenses of joining are frequently run up by expensive uniform, horses and entrance subscriptions to approximately £1,000.' Once the subaltern had joined, the lowest estimate of his 'necessary expenses' was put at £281 13s 4d per annum. After taking his pay into account, he needed about £160 to meet the balance.†

---

* Cavalry officers' pay did not alter materially between the Boer and the First World Wars. In fact, in 1913 it was virtually the same as it had been in 1806. In 1913 it stood thus:

Lieutenant-Colonel	£392 7 6	(plus Command Pay of 3s)
Major	£273 15 0	
Major after two years	£310 5 0	
Captain	£237 5 0	
Captain having higher rank by brevet	£273 15 0	
Lieutenant	£139 18 4	
Second-Lieutenant	£121 13 4	

(Hutchinson: *Deficiency*, 4; Stanley: *Expenses*, 25.)

† 'Mess subscription, eight days' pay at 6s 8d   2 13 4
    Incidental mess expenses, at 12s 6d a month   7 10 0
    Share of mess guests   4 10 0

(continued over)

Further, it was 'considered practically essential for all cavalry officers to hunt as part of their military training'.* To pay for this at least another £100 a year was necessary, while the ordinary fee for entrance to Sandhurst was never less than £100. Extreme economy on a subaltern's part could make it just possible for him to exist on a private income of £300 a year. In practice, though, the 'general average' was £600 to £700 'upwards'.[4]

The Committee's proposals were wide-ranging. They aimed at reducing the theoretical minimum of £300 a year of private income to £120.† In this neither they nor the 1905 Hutchinson Committee (see below) succeeded, but considerable numbers of recommended improvements were almost at once implemented. These included the free issue of a field kit on joining; the provision of chargers, military saddlery, accessories and shoeing partly at public expense; the supply for a small rent of furniture for officers' quarters and messes at all home stations; the cessation of contributions to the mess on appoint-

	£	s	d
Messing, 365 days (less sixty days' leave) at 4s 6d daily	68	12	6
Moves and manoeuvres	10	0	0
Repair and upkeep of uniform	25	0	0
Washing and mending, at 25s a month	15	0	0
Shoeing two chargers	4	10	0
Brushes, cleaning articles for horses, saddlery, &c.	5	0	0
Repair and upkeep of military saddlery	5	0	0
Horse clothing, bandages, &c.	2	0	0
Two soldier servants, at 2s 6d a week	13	0	0
Clothes for ditto (including riding kit)	18	0	0
Subscriptions, regimental cricket club, &c.	3	0	0
Drink and tobacco	22	17	6
Other expenses: travelling, plain clothes, riding kit, &c.			
(say)	75	0	0
Total necessary expenses	281	13	4
Deduct 365 days' pay at 6s 8d	121	13	4
Balance to be met out of private income (say)	160	0	0'

(Stanley: *Expenses*, 9.)

* The cost of polo ponies for those who could afford to play at all, and in the smarter regiments every officer was expected to, was another heavy expense. In 1906 a beginner's pony cost about £55. By 1914, though, prices both at home and in India had doubled. (Micholls, 75.)

† In 1905 there were very few cadets at Sandhurst, according to the Commandant, who could expect even £200 a year, income or allowance. (Hutchinson: *Deficiency*, 3.)

ment as well as on promotion and of subscriptions to the regimental band fund.[5] None of these reforms seemed to make much difference for some years to come. Indeed, whereas there were twenty-three officer vacancies in the cavalry at home in 1903, by early 1905 there were forty-four. This was nearly equivalent to the number of officers required for two entire regiments on the peace establishment.[6] Another War Office committee (the Hutchinson Committee) which looked into the problem in 1905 decided that the three main causes which deterred candidates from joining the cavalry were 'the inadequate pecuniary and professional gains for work done; the uncertainty of the time at the disposal of officers for hunting and long leave, and the loss of prestige of the army in general, and of the cavalry in particular, owing to the constant belittling of officers by the press . . . and even by persons in high positions.'[7]

However relevant these last two causes might have been for the future recruitment of officers, the unsatisfactory nature of the immediate post-war situation was largely due to the fact that some 3,700 officers had either been killed, died of wounds or disease or been invalided in South Africa.[8] Further, several officers who gave evidence to the Hutchinson Committee of 1905 on the deficiency of cavalry officers pointed out that 'uneducated officers commissioned during the war and unable [after it] to pass promotion examinations' were a cause of 'the present gaps in the establishment'.[9]

The Akers-Douglas Committee of 1902 which had been set up to consider officers' education and training, concluded gloomily that there was

> 'nothing whatever to prevent the young man of very limited educational attainments from obtaining a commission in the cavalry if sufficiently provided with private means. . . . We may require from the candidates either money or brains; the supply is most unlikely to meet the demand, if we endeavour to exact both. . . . In fact, the supply not being equal to the demand, the military authorities have been compelled to accept almost any candidate.'[10]

During the war no less than 454 virtually untrained young men had been taken, long before completing a full course, from Woolwich, Sandhurst and the Militia and given commissions in South Africa.[11] These sources constituted in effect the only reserve of subalterns. But even that most inefficient reserve proved to be utterly inadequate. During the eighteen months between 1 January, 1900, and mid-summer, 1901, there had to be found over 3,000 officers in excess of the normal supply for the regular army alone. 'I had to get them from somewhere other than the usual channels,' the Military Secretary at the War Office told the Royal Commission. 'I got them straight from school or their families. I sent them out without even Gazetting them.' They were 'ordinary educated young gentlemen, knowing nothing, quite untrained'.[12] Now, in 1905, the situation in peacetime was so bad that a temporary scheme for filling vacancies had to be adopted of appointing totally untrained gentlemen as 2nd-lieutenants on probation.* Naturally, too, the question of promotion from the ranks was considered, but this could not be resorted to on any significant scale without a very considerable increase in pay (which the more radical Liberals liked even less than they liked the class from which officers were traditionally drawn). In fact there had been a marked decline in the numbers over the years.† The period 1885 to 1895 had seen one in eighteen such promotions (combat commissions only) for the whole army, while the proportion fell to one in forty-six between 1906 and 1910. In the cavalry there were none at all between 1903 and 1913.[13] No doubt this reflected the persisting expense of a cavalry officer's life style and the insistence in so many regiments upon exclusivity during the Edwardian heyday. In the course of the war, though, especially in

---

* The Hutchinson Committee of 1905 wrote to eleven junior officers who had resigned their commissions in the cavalry within the last six months, asking them to give, confidentially, their reasons for leaving. In summary their replies were:

(a) passed over for promotion (2); (b) 'enteric after the war and not fit to serve abroad' (2); (c) 'on account of expense' (2) (One stated that he had an allowance of £500 p.a.); (d) 'insufficient pay for quantity of work now required' and 'uncertainty of the time when the work was to be done'; (e) 'prospects of promotion remote. Left to farm in Transvaal'; (f) 'married and did not want to return to India'; (g) 'with regret, on account of age (subaltern)', and (h) 'disgusted with the way an average officer has to spend his time, tea fights, garden parties, &c. Soldiering not taken sufficiently seriously.'

(Hutchinson: *Deficiency*, 10.)

† 'Most men,' wrote Captain G. T. Younghusband in 1891, 'lose more than they gain during their term of service in the ranks: in self-reliance, in manner, in polish – even in speech. We have known for instance a born gentleman, who after three years in the ranks had utterly lost the proper use of the letter "h".' (Younghusband, Capt. G. T. *The Queen's Commission: How to prepare for it, How to obtain it and How to use it*, 1891, 52.)

irregular units, considerable numbers of non-'gentlemen' were commissioned.

'Some of the most reliable officers I had [in the Scottish Horse],' Lord Tullibardine (see p. 228) told the Royal Commission, 'were appointed through the ranks. They were of all classes, and were promoted purely on their merits. Many of them were not what is termed gentlemen by birth, but I never kept a man who did not behave himself. Perhaps almost the best officer I had in the corps had been a farm hand and was the son of a small farmer in Perthshire, while another had been a footman in civilian life. This last fact was, of course, only known to me . . . .

'A man known as a gentleman at home makes the best officer, as if you give him an order you can be tolerably certain that it will be carried out, his only fault being that he is too much inclined to luxury, having independent means. By this I do not mean that I do not approve of "messes" – as I do – considering that officers require to a certain extent the food they have been accustomed to, and also that they require better feeding than the men, owing to their having to use their head more, and being put to a greater nervous strain.'[14]

The extreme seriousness of the persistence of the officer shortage almost up to 1914 can only be appreciated when it is realized that it constituted a grave threat to the very viability of Haldane's scheme for an expeditionary force. The steps which he and his successor took to try to fill the commissioned ranks, and with what measure of success they met, will be considered in the next and final volume of this work.

20

'Q. Do the men in the ranks [of the cavalry]
represent the average intelligence of the
country?

'A. No. (Major Allenby dissents).' [So did
French.]

> The Report of the Dickson Committee,
> 1900

'A large percentage of those who are brought to
the recruiting depots are deficient in elementary
knowledge, and have to be turned over to the
schoolmaster to receive instruction of a kind
which at their age ought not to be necessary.'

> SIR GEORGE ARTHUR in 1907

'Some [cavalry] regiments have smarter uniforms
than others, and always can get more recruits.'

> HAIG in 1903[1]

*Rank and file: types – reasons for enlisting – shortage of recruits
– terms of service – cost – training time – civilian contempt – pay –
pensions – Army Pay Corps – health – crime – education – good
conduct badges – canteens – wives – in India – Luck's scheme*

'The business of an army,' wrote Amery in 1902, 'especially of a
voluntary army, is to be an efficient fighting machine and not a
nursery, however beneficial, for the wastrels of lower-class society.'
Six years later Haldane was writing to his mother that there was 'an
anxious business before us over the unemployed. The Army at all
events makes a good opening for them; we shall provide over
20,000 places this winter, with £375,000 in food and pay for the
men. That is something quite new and I am pleased.'[2]* The following year, 1909, 'well over 90%' of men inspected prior to enlistment
were unemployed.[3] This statistic is a very rare one, for as a rule
prospective recruits were required to state their previous trade but
not whether they were actually employed in it.[4]

Towards the end of the 19th century there were never less than

---

* A minor reform of Haldane's was to recruit men for the Special Reserve
only in the autumn. He hoped thereby that they would emerge six months later
as 'well fed' and 'physically looked after . . . with the sense that they were men.'
(Spiers: *Haldane*, 148).

750,000 paupers in Britain, yet the number of recruits always fell short of 40,000. How many of the paupers were too old or unfit is not known, but there must have been a large reservoir of eligible unemployed which the army failed to attract. It is difficult to discover what the correlation between pauperism and unemployment and recruiting actually was. It is safe to say, though, that recruiting tended to become more difficult when the country was prosperous and employment rates were high.* For instance, recruiting definitely slumped in 1911 at a time when trade began a noticeable revival. In that year labour exchanges were opened and emigration was speeded up, particularly to Canada.[5]

It is interesting to note that Irishmen constituted 27.9% of the army's other ranks in 1870, but that by 1912 the figure was only 9.1%. This drop was due to the continual emigration from Ireland of the period. In 1899 the Irish agricultural labourer was providing 12.4% (of which number incidentally only 17.7% were Roman Catholics).† In 1903 Amery was 'certain that our best cavalry soldiers come from Ireland now', largely because so many of them could ride before they enlisted.[6]

For obvious reasons the vast majority of men kept no record of their motives for enlisting. It is therefore impossible ever to know what they were. A man of a better class who joined up during the war gave his reasons for doing so: 'Here I was cooped up in a city warehouse a strong active fellow full of high spirits and a desire to see the world. What more to the taste could be than a few months in a different land, . . . to see life and to escape for a time the monotony of existence, and if other volunteers were to speak the truth they would tell you the same thing.'[7] Whether this man remained in the army after the war or not is not known. He would not, probably, have enjoyed the 'monotony of existence' inseparable from peacetime soldiering.

From 1903 to 1914 the annual intake of recruits for the whole army varied between just under 29,000 and just over 35,000.‡ Of the twenty-six years ending in 1912 the annual intake only brought

---

* Nevertheless between 1859 and 1888, pauperism was lowest in 1877–8, yet recruitment, instead of falling too, remained relatively high. (*Report of Committee on Questions with Respect to the Militia*, 1890, Appx 2.)

† One recruiting sergeant told a recruit 'no fancy religions in the Army. If you're not C. of E. or R.C., you'll have to be Wesleyan.' (Wyndham: *Drum*, 14.)

‡ Of which about 12,000 were furnished by the Militia. (Spiers: *Haldane*, 92.)

the numbers up to establishment in eight of them. From 1908 to 1914 there was always a shortfall in recruiting. In both 1908 and 1912 for instance the effective strength was more than 3,000 short of establishment. The Special Reserve was about 16% short which was proportionately considerably greater than in the army as a whole.[8]* By May, 1914, the regular army was 10,900, or 6%, below establishment.[9]

To obtain sufficient recruits to compensate for the wastage caused by death, discharge and desertion remained right up to 1914 a major problem for an army based on voluntary service. It is only in very recent times that the army has been able to dispense with its reliance upon the destitute unemployed, in short much of the scum of the population, for its recruits.†

In the ten years before the Boer War as many as 50,000 men of what was known as the 'special' class were accepted as recruits, that is men who were either below the age limit or who lacked the physique necessary for service abroad or even hard work anywhere. When the Boer War came, therefore, a very large proportion of the men in the 1st Class Reserve, instead of completing the army to war strength as they were meant to do, were in practice required to supersede that part of it which was unfit for service. As Amery put it, 'the inefficient half of the active army thus became the real reserve, and was gradually sent to the front as it matured to efficiency during the war.' Further, between 1881 and 1902 not less than 48% of men were lost to the army from one cause or another before they qualified for the Reserve.[10] Over the same period the short service terms of enlistment for all arms were seven years with the Colours and five with the Reserve. In 1902 this was drastically altered by Brodrick to three with the Colours and nine with the Reserve, with higher pay for service abroad.[11] It was hoped that under this scheme 75% would re-enlist. In the event less than 20% had done so by the end of 1903. His claim, therefore, that 'even with European complications we could afford to stoke up India' fell rather flat.[12] In one draft for India ninety-seven out of its 100 men were on the three-

---

* Including men in the Reserve the effective strength of other ranks between 1895 and 1910 was between 1.5 % and 1.8 % of the total male population of the United Kingdom, much the same as it had been ever since Waterloo. (Spiers: *A & S*, 35, 36.)

† Unskilled labourers (agricultural and, increasingly, from the class of 'town casuals'), formed between 45 % and 48 % of all recruits between 1907 and 1913. (Spiers: *A & S*, 61.)

year engagement. This meant that they would only serve there for a few months![13] In an effort to solve what had always been insoluble Arnold-Forster in 1904 and 1905 changed the terms of service again. For the cavalry of the line they became, first, eight with the Colours and four with the Reserve (nine and three for the infantry) and, second, seven and five, and there they remained till 1914.[14] In fact both Brodrick and Arnold-Forster achieved more than they are usually credited with. Brodrick had 'exploited the war and post-war booms in recruiting by introducing his nine-year period of Reserve service for those who enlisted between 1902 and 1904', thereby bloating the Reserve and bequeathing to Haldane a large surplus. Arnold-Forster, on the other hand, by enlisting some 38,000 recruits in the period 1904 to 1905 under his eight- and nine-year Colour service scheme made sure that there would be an unusually low wastage from the Colours in the last years of Haldane's term of office.[15] As has been shown the recruiting problem became much more acute after that.*

One way and another, whether the army was short of establishment or not, the cost of shipping men back and forward from India, Egypt and South Africa at frequent intervals was always very considerable and the larger the numbers who were serving only a short time overseas, the more expensive a business it became. In 1908 the difference between the cost of a fully trained private soldier of the cavalry of the line at home was nearly £20 less than for one in India.†

* There was a sudden boost in recruiting early in 1909. This was due to the impact made by Major Guy du Maurier's only play, *An Englishman's Home*, a dramatized account of an invasion. 'It is extraordinary how the play,' wrote Haig, 'draws crowded houses every night and how impressed the audience seem to be with the gravity of the scenes. I trust that good may result and "universal training" may become the law of the land.' (Diary, 3 Feb. 1909, *Haig*, 393.) In London, especially, hitherto the least successful of the recruiting areas for the Territorials, recruits poured in. On one day, Haldane recorded with amazement, 300 men applied to join. (Haldane to his mother, 6 Feb., 1909, Haldane MSS NLS MS 5,981 f. 47.) Du Maurier, an infantryman, elder son of George, brother of Sir Gerald and uncle of Daphne, was killed in 1915 aged fifty.

† Average annual cost of a trained private:

	At home	In India
Cavalry	£62 11s 4d	£82 5s 5d
Horse Artillery	£64 7s 4d	£86 14s 0d
Infantry	£57 8s 9d	£75 6s 2d

'The figures for at home include charges for barracks, arms, ammunition, &c. The figures for India include, in addition, charges for the capitation rate, passage, &c.' ([Official] 'The Annual Cost of the Soldier', *Cav. Jnl*, I, 1096, 373.)

As it always had it took much longer to train a cavalryman than it did an infantryman. Haig thought 'for a mounted man you must train him for three years, taking the average intelligence of the recruit.' He added that it should be possible 'to train a good average cavalry soldier in four months to take his place in the ranks; he is then able to charge, but I do not think he will have the intellectual knowledge to fit him to go on service'. He believed that in those initial four months a man could be taught 'to start his horse, to stop his horse, to back, to turn to the right and left, to circle to the right and left, and passage'. In a year's time after that 'he ought to be quite fit to take the field' but he would need the full three years before he could be 'a good scout able to go out on his own responsibility'.[16]

*   *   *

'There was in the minds of the ordinary God-fearing citizen no such thing as a good soldier; to have a member who had gone for a soldier,' wrote Wavell in 1953, 'was for many families a crowning disgrace.'[17] This was the everlasting basis of the recruiting dilemma. Brodrick, in 1903, introduced for the first time character references to confirm the sobriety, honesty and respectability of intending recruits. At the same time every recruit's educational attainments had to be tested and recorded on joining his regiment.[18] More importantly, while the war was still on he had radically improved army pay. For the first time no man over nineteen was to actually receive less than 1s a day. Both Arnold-Forster and Haldane had continued Brodrick's process of raising medical standards and attempting to make the ex-soldier's employment prospects better.* Haldane's

---

It was assessed in 1585 that the cost of putting a military horseman in the field was £25. (Cruickshank, C. G. *The Elizabethan Army*, 2nd ed., 1966, 30.)

* In this they largely failed. Throughout the period about one in four men joined the ranks of the unemployed on discharge, many of them unemployable vagrants. (Spiers: *A & S*, 67.)

Roberts was greatly distressed to learn at a dinner celebrating the fiftieth anniversary of the Indian Mutiny that large numbers of the veterans were in the workhouse in bitterest poverty. He at once launched under the King's patronage an appeal which in twelve months raised over £38,000. This was enough to remove 800 men who had fought in India during the Mutiny from the workhouses and enable them to live in modest comfort. (James, 432.)

Before labour exchanges were instituted, there were fourteen charitable societies which helped to provide jobs for, amongst others, ex-servicemen. There were also employment registers kept by the War Office and by regimental

efforts to make 'more of the civilian's life, in the way of telegraphy, shorthand, the keeping of accounts, engineering and so forth fit with the soldier's life' and thus adapt him better for employment on discharge came to little because of trade union obstruction.[19]

Evelyn Wood and Smith-Dorrien both instituted measures to ameliorate restrictions on the movements of men during their off-duty hours. The obnoxious picquet system by which they were rounded up after evenings on the town was abolished. Efforts were also made to stop the riotous scenes of drunkenness which outraged respectable opinion on the days when ex-servicemen received their pensions and reservists their pay. The War Office paid these at quarterly intervals, in advance, involving the receipt of a large lump sum on payment days, which was 'a direct cause of thriftlessness and an indirect cause of pauperism'. The Board of Guardians found that their workhouse inmates discharged themselves on pension days only to return a few days later suffering from the after-effects of drink, while employers lamented the absenteeism which occurred for days after the quarterly payments to reservists. Nothing was done to alter this system because the War Office said that the cost of more frequent payments would be too great.[20]

Recruiting for the ranks of the cavalry was not helped by the system whereby a man who wished to enlist in a particular regiment was told that he could not do so, that he must enlist in 'corps of Hussars' or 'corps of Dragoons'. Haig gave the Royal Commission an example of what was then likely to happen to him:

> 'He is posted to a regiment, say at home; possibly a Hussar regiment in India wants a draft, and they draft him from his regiment at home; next, possibly, his new regiment may be sent home and he is transferred to another Hussar regiment out there to finish his term of enlistment, so that there are three regiments he has been in. Lastly he goes to the Reserve, and on mobilization is probably called up for a fourth.'

This last arrangement he thought 'most pernicious. In the cavalry small parties are often isolated and in difficult situations. It is most essential that all the men must have been brought up in the same regiment and be animated by the same traditions and *esprit de corps*.

---

districts; but only 5 % of men found jobs through these. A certain amount of preferential consideration was also given by the Post Office and some government departments. (Spiers: *Haldane*, 145–6.)

... Regiments at home ought to have enough of their own reservists to make them up to war strength. Continental states do this because cavalry cannot be improvised.'[21] The system was never, in fact, altered.

None of the great efforts made in these post-war years by successive Secretaries of State resulted in attracting a better class of men by banishing the ingrained contempt with which enlistment was viewed. Throughout the period about half of all recruits, as has been shown, were unskilled labourers and about the same proportion failed to meet the amended medical criteria. In 1910, for example, of the 63,751 men who presented themselves for enlistment, 35,165 – 55.2% – were rejected.[22]

Another short-lived experimental reform designed to make enlistment more attractive to a higher class was the voluntary replacement of deferred pay (which had been introduced in 1876 so that a man on completing his Colour service received a lump sum on discharge (see Vol III, p. 36)), by a messing allowance and a gratuity of £1 for every year of his service. Lord Lansdowne thought that, though deferred pay may have acted as a check on desertion, it was also a 'strong inducement to men to leave the Colours'.[23] The prospects of effecting better living conditions were limited by the fact that the costly business of improving old barracks and building new ones failed to keep up with the increasing social expectations of the time.

But the over-riding difficulty was the question of pay. Brodrick had 'the gravest reservations whether any increase of pay we could give, unless we give something like double, would really bring in a different stamp of recruit.'[24] The trouble here was that the rates of pay were becoming more and more uncompetitive with civilian wages. The poorest agricultural labourer was paid 2s more than the weekly net pay of 11s 4½d which, after two years' service, was received by the infantry private.[25] As late as 1914 the private was getting less pay than anyone in civilian life, except girls under eighteen. The actual rates of pay did not alter between the 1870s and 1913. A trooper and a bandsman still received before deductions 1s 2d (1s 9d in the Household Cavalry), which was 2d above an infantry private's pay. A sergeant-major received pay of 5s 4d (corporal-major, Household Cavalry, 5s 10d). The highest paid warrant officer in the cavalry was the armourer-sergeant-major who got 7s a day which was the same as the maximum which an army schoolmaster or a sergeant-major-instructor at Sandhurst could

61. Taylor Equipment, 1911 (see p. 399)

62. Equipment, 1913

attain to. The highest paid warrant officer in the army was the band-master of the Duke of York's Military School, who obtained 7s 6d. There were certain ways in which clever and industrious men could earn more. For instance Sergeant Seed of the 3rd Hussars became 'acting schoolmaster' to his regiment whilst in India, and received a 'Government Reward' of £12 for passing tests in Pushtu: 'not bad pay,' he reckoned, 'for three months spare time'. Pensions of all sorts remained virtually unaltered between 1900 and 1913. 'Per-manent' pensions on discharge ranged, for a trooper, from 8d after twenty-one years with an additional penny a year after that to a maximum of 9d. A sergeant, after twelve years, received 2s 9d a day.[26]

In 1888 the Army Pay Corps had been created. Till then all pay had been in the hands of regimental paymasters. These were replaced in that year by station paymasters under the Quartermaster-General's department. But the soldier's pay account was still com-piled by his own regiment's officers. The system broke down under the stresses of the Boer War. This was not only because it entailed the squadron commander paying the men as 'sub-accountant' to the paymaster while his mind was, or ought to have been, on other more vital matters. It was also because the Army Pay Corps in South Africa, serving what eventually became the equivalent of six or seven Army Corps, employed never more than sixty-five officers and 268 clerks, when 130 officers and 440 clerks would have been the proper, efficient establishment. It was not until 1913 that a new system was evolved by which a fixed pay centre determined what was due to each man, the regimental officer merely handing out that sum once a week.[27]

*   *   *

In some respects standards showed marked improvements. For example, in the cavalry of the line mortality per 1,000 men declined from 4.5 in 1903 to 2.7 in 1909* and admissions to hospital per 100 declined throughout the army at home from 58.7 in 1903 to 37.8 in 1909.[28]

The decrease in all forms of crime, especially drunkenness, which had been taking place in the last decades of the 19th century, con-tinued in the first thirteen years of the 20th. Fines for drunkenness

* In the Household Cavalry and the Foot Guards the figure in 1909 was 3.1, due, no doubt, to the notoriously insanitary barracks in London.

in 1872 totalled 51,501. By 1912–13, they had sunk to 9,230. This was a tribute to the increased speed at which improvements had been made to the amenities of barracks. 'The reason why soldiers drink,' wrote an infantry private in about 1903 'is because they have such uncomfortable barrack-rooms. Half the men would never go near the canteen if this weren't the case. Make the troops comfortable, and you'll make them sober.'[29] The temperance movement in the army, which had spread from India where Roberts had been the prime mover (see Vol III, p. 134), grew apace from 1893 onwards. In that year the Army Temperance Association (Home Organization) was organized under the authority of the Chaplain-General. Soon there was a branch in every regiment. The prefix 'Royal' was added in 1902 and the Association lasted until, with the higher standard of recruit, it died a natural death in 1958. Numerous medals, such as the Havelock Cross and the Roberts Badge, were awarded to men after varying periods of abstinence. These were only to be worn on appropriate occasions and had to be pinned on the right breast.

Educational standards, on the other hand, showed only a modest advance. Between 1907 and 1913, the illiteracy rate remained steady at 11%. During the same period the number of those who possessed a 3rd-class Certificate fluctuated between 69% and 72%. This matched the standard set for nine-year olds in civilian elementary schools.[30] Until they had obtained this certificate all soldiers were required from 1906 onwards[31] to attend army schools. The most marked indication of progress was the fact that the number of men gaining *any* class of certificate rose from 41.8% in 1904 to 75.8% nine years later.[32] There was a considerable decline in the number of men who were discharged soon after enlistment as being unlikely to make efficient soldiers. Even more encouraging was the decrease in the number of desertions between attestation and final approval. In 1898 there had been 593, in 1906, 406, but in 1910 there were only 107.[33]

There were four degrees of good conduct badge available for men to sew on to the left arm of their jackets. Two years with an un-sullied defaulter sheet entitled a man under the rank of corporal to the first badge. Unless he was getting service pay, he drew an extra penny a day. He had to wait five years for a second and twelve for a third badge. After eighteen years without a 'regimental entry', he could earn a fourth. 'This,' remarked one man in 1912, 'is a lot for 4d [a day extra], especially when it is remembered that good-conduct badges are much easier lost than won.'[34] In 1903 'the great majority of soldiers of over two years' service' were receiving good conduct pay, which was costing £130,000 a year.[35]

*　　*　　*

In spite of a determination by both Treasury and War Office not to increase spending on the ordinary education of other ranks and their children, considerable scrutiny of the question took place after the Boer War. There were inter-departmental and War Office committees on Army Schools and on the conditions of service for members of the Corps of Army Schoolmasters and the Corps of Army Schoolmistresses (see Vol III, p. 73). These committees had produced by 1914 a few useful reforms. A sufficiency of civilian candidates for teaching posts, which entailed long hours, especially in the evenings, as well as liability for service overseas, was hard to achieve. In 1901 almost the same number of schoolmasters as were recruited from civil life came as pupil-teachers from the Duke of York's School and the Royal Hibernian Military School (see Vol II, pp. 293, 294). By 1914 a much greater proportion was recruited from these sources and from the Queen Victoria School at Dunblane. This had been opened in 1908 as a memorial to Scottish soldiers and sailors who had fallen in the war. It accommodated about three hundred boys.

All Army Schoolmasters wore smart uniforms of blue frock coat and peaked cap. By 1912 the initial pay was 4s a day. This could increase to 16s 6d a day. A pension of £200 was provided on retirement. Private Horace Cowley Wyndham believed that as schoolmasters had free quarters, food and clothing, their job was 'among the "plums" to which the well-educated soldier can legitimately aspire'.[36] In 1905 a considerably improved, less mechanical curriculum for adult soldiers and their children was introduced in Army schools and methods of teaching were brought more into line with civilian ones. In 1907 the gradual extinction of infant schools within the army was begun, reflecting both economy and, possibly, the general advance in educational standards. A little later it was decided that, as a general principle, army schools were to be maintained only for adult soldiers and no schoolteachers were to be retained for teaching children alone. Wherever practicable, soldiers' children were increasingly sent to the local civilian schools. In 1907 there took place a thorough enquiry into the whole system of army education. It was carried out by Board of Education inspectors and resulted in the introduction of training methods more or less the same as those in civilian teaching colleges. In 1909 the Board recognized army schoolmasters as 'certificated teachers'. This meant that when they took up civilian posts after leaving the army they could count their 'army service for increments on the recognized scale of salaries'.[37]

*   *   *

'Many efficient soldiers are driven out of the [cavalry] Service by overwork, and especially during the first six months of a man's service.' Thus the report of Major-General Dickson's Committee, set up by French in South Africa in 1900.[38] 'I suppose,' said one typical recruiting corporal to three recruits who expressed a wish to join the Dragoons, 'I suppose you think yourselves too smart for the infantry. Perhaps you're fond of riding though. Well, I hope you're fond of grooming dirty horses. That's what you'll do most of.' An ex-trooper of the 12th Lancers, Mr J. Espiner, wrote: '[In 1906] life for a recruit was one long continual grind, and we never had a forty-hour week!' Reveille was at 5.30, after which beds were made up and the barrack room swept. At 5.45 came 'the most miserable call in the Army, the warning for Stables. What "Stables" sounded for, fifteen minutes after, I never found out as we were always in stables by then: perhaps it was to give the Trumpeter something to do.' When the stables had been cleaned, the recruit groomed his own horse. After this all except the guard went off to collect forage, some, 'the lucky ones', for corn, the rest for hay which was stuffed into a vast net under which eight men staggered back. Watering and feeding over, breakfast in the barrack room followed, during which, while eating, the man was usually dressing for Riding School. The squadron commander's inspection was followed by riding training which lasted till 10.00 or 10.30 'according to what instructor we had and what kind of mood he was in. Often it wasn't a very good one and we would be kept in to the last minute and what we called him would be a lot worse than what he called us, the only difference being that he said his out loud!' On his temper depended the chance of beer and a hunk of bread with cheese costing 1½d for each at the canteen, because at 10.45 'Warning for Stables' sounded: 'Same old dodge; off to Stables: trumpeter again wasting his time at 11 a.m.' This time the recruit had only his own horse to deal with. When it was passed as clean he generally turned his attention to his saddlery until 12.45 and 'that lovely call – Feed the Bs, Feed the Bs and File Away'. The afternoon began with foot-drill from 2 to 3 p.m. and continued with gymnastics from 3.45 to 4, followed by further work on the polishing of saddles. The third 'Stables' of the day filled three-quarters of an hour from 4.45 and was succeeded by tea. Kit cleaning followed. Jack-boots for Riding School and Wellingtons for foot-drill had to be cleaned, the jack-boots alone requiring half-an-hour. There were also the sword, belt, lance, rifle and spurs to get spotless. Very often the man shaved at this point in the day, not having had time to do so in the morning. By 9 p.m if he was lucky he could at last go off duty. The cleaning of saddlery was one of the most exacting and time-consuming chores. The leather had to be kept soft with saddle-soap and parts of the saddle had to be polished. The girths had to be constantly greased to retain their suppleness. All the parts which were affected by sweat – and in India this generally meant all of them – had to be sponged off before being soaped. Bits and curb-chains had to be burnished and brass buckles and bosses polished. For parades, especially those in full-dress review order, special attention had to be paid to the cleaning of swords and scabbards, rifles and bandoliers, and the leather knee-grips of khaki breeches had to be treated with coloured powder of the correct tinge. Sword slings and sword knots, boots and spurs had also to be constantly attended to.

Trooper Espinei found that the help of the old soldiers in his troop was both forthcoming and vital. 'Muck in – we all wear spurs' was their motto. Recruits were excused the Main Guard until they had been dismissed the Riding School, but had to go on Night Guard. Often all the men of a troop were seen getting a man ready for this exacting duty. The food lacked variety, as it always had done: 'the same old diet week after week. If we knew the day it was we knew what dinner was on; and if we did forget what day it was we knew directly the dinner came up.'[39]

*   *   *

'Dear Mother,

'You will probably be surprised to hear,' wrote eighteen-year old 'Bertie' Seed in 1900, 'that I have enlisted and I hope you will not be alarmed. . . . My regiment is the 3rd Hussars. . . . I have had some dinner in the canteen for 2½d. . . .

'I shall not get my arms tattooed, don't be afraid of that. A lot of the soldiers here get it done.'

In January, 1901, Seed was sent to the 'Musketry Camp' at Lydd. 'Here I am,' he told his mother, 'at the seaside, having a holiday and never paying a penny for it. Free board and lodging, all found and paid 25/6 per month. That's cheap if you like.'[40]

* * *

For recreation, both cricket and football held their own, and in India pig-sticking was becoming as much a sport for other ranks as it was for officers. There were also occasional interruptions to the pure tenor of regimental life in barracks. In 1912, for instance, 'C' Squadron of the 12th Lancers found itself detailed to take part in a film of the battle of Waterloo. All expenses were paid and £100 was handed to the regimental welfare fund. 'An accommodating American,' says the regimental historian, 'made the rounds of all the pubs at night to pay for drinks. The fact that Napoleon could not ride and that a sergeant in the regiment appropriated Wellington's boots nearly prevented the film being made and 'C' Sqn from taking part in the most exciting, best paid and least painful battle of the regiment's long history.'[41]*

* * *

The canteen system which in the last decades of the 19th century had ensured considerable improvements in the quality and price of the food and drink supplied (see Vol III, pp. 53–4) underwent at the outbreak of the war some modifications which continued that

---

* This film, 'The Battle of Waterloo', which was released in July, 1913, was the first expensive British spectacle employing thousands of extras. It was produced by the British and Colonial Kinematograph Company and was advertised as containing '2,000 Soldiers, 116 Scenes, 1,000 horses, 50 Cannons'. It was a great financial if not critical success, the brain-child of J. B. Macdowell, later one of the official cinematographers in the First World War, whose director was Charles Weston. The squadron was the 'nucleus' of the film. It was loaned to Macdowell from Weedon Barracks and supplemented by some 1000 local men. A special train brought down over 100 horses from Tilling's of London. Napoleon in exile at St Helena was filmed at Rottingdean! The film took only five days to shoot and cost £1,800. (Information kindly supplied by the British Film Institute; Humfrey, R. *Careers in the Films*, 1938, 31–3; Low, Rachael *History of the British Film*, 1949, I, 98; ' "The Battle of Waterloo": British History Reconstructed by Britons', *Bioscope*, 3 July 1913, 51; 'Our Poster Gallery: "The Battle of Waterloo" ', *Bioscope*, 14 Aug. 1913, 24.)

improvement.* But more important for the future of regimental canteens was the founding in 1894 of the Canteen and Mess Co-Operative Society by three officers, one of whom was Captain Lionel Fortescue of the 17th Lancers, who were unhappy about the quality of too many of the contractors and the goods they supplied. This Society soon began to compete with the private firms to their considerable chagrin. Though the war upset the progress of the enterprise, an Interdepartmental War Office Committee which sat in 1902 recommended the establishment of a Soldiers' Central Co-Operative Society for the whole army. Unfortunately a minority of its members – two out of eight – disagreed, as also did a number of the older commanding officers. 'They knew little or nothing of the co-operative movement,' as Fortescue's brother wrote in his *Canteens in the British Army*, 'and especially scouted the suggestion that any commanding officer should invest the profits of his canteen in any co-operative society.' In consequence the existing 'Tenant System' under which canteens were let out to contractors was con-tinued, and so, too, was a certain degree of bribery and corruption, in spite of a War Office approved list of firms.† In the winter of 1913–14 what came to be known as 'the Canteen Scandal' revealed, as the result of a prosecution, the offering of bribes by employees of one of the approved firms and their acceptance by some of its military customers. These last, both officers and non-commissioned officers, were dismissed the Army.[42] The reforms which followed will be discussed in the final volume of this work.

Trooper J. Hanlon who joined the 12th Lancers in 1909 found the 'wet canteen' full of 'dangerous temptations'. One of these was 'purchasing cheap popularity with the old boozing sweats'. This, however, got him 'nowhere, as the old-timers took [his] money and gave [him] a pint of beer to last all night.' The Garrison Institute Coffee Shop had 'capital attractions' for him. These were 'light and heat, commodities only too rare in the barrack-room'. On the other hand the Garrison Recreation Room 'was only too often a dismal failure'. So was the library. 'I don't think it was supposed to be used,' he complained, 'except to find the post corporal for the

---

* There is no evidence to show that either the quality or quantity of the food provided free as rations improved over the period covered by this volume.

† The advantage of the 'tenant' system was that no officers or men were employed in its operation. Further the risk of perishable stock being left on hand when regiments moved station was avoided, as contractors would sell it to the incoming unit. (Wyndham: *Drum*, 45.)

purpose of buying stamps. The books were locked up and could be had only by appointment, and the other literature was usually periodicals like the *Cavalry Journal* [see p. 402] in which old-time warriors used to blow off steam about the "Arme Blanche", etc. It was impossible, in any case, to see to read at night as the only light was an oil lamp suspended above the table to illuminate the room, but which cast the shadow of its base upon the table.'[43]

Trooper 'Bertie' Seed of the 3rd Hussars was sent during the war to a holding regiment at Aldershot because at just nineteen he was too young to go out to South Africa. He spent his evenings in the 'splendid' Soldiers' Home there, where a sergeant-major cared for the men's 'spiritual comfort', as he told his mother, and 'two ladies provided refreshments'.[44]

The fashion for founding regimental Old Comrades' Associations within regiments had started in the 1890s. Now they were beginning to proliferate. For instance the 11th Hussars' Cavalry Benefit Association was designed to 'promote *esprit de corps*, find employment for old 11th Hussars, give relief to deserving cases, care for old comrades in their old age and to run the Annual Regimental Dinner'. The 12th Lancers' Regimental Association was started in 1911 with the help of the Regimental Homes and Benefits Agency. Its aims were much the same as those of the 11th's association, to which was specifically added: 'To assist wives and families of members who are in distressed circumstances.'[45]

The situation of other ranks' wives remained much the same as it always had been. The Standing Orders of the 21st Lancers in Dublin in 1902 stated: 'It cannot be too often impressed on non-commissioned officers and men that they are on no account to marry without leave, and their marrying at all is an act of folly; inconvenience to the service and poverty and loss of independence to the individual being the too frequent result.' The 9th Lancers' Order Book laid it down that men married without leave were 'to be treated in every respect as single men, and under no circumstances to be permitted to participate in any of the advantages to which those married with leave are entitled'. The increasing provision, slow though the process was, of married quarters for officially married men led to the numbers of them being slightly increased. When the 3rd Dragoon Guards went to Ireland in 1904 only six wives accompanied them, but in 1912 when they were sent to Egypt, there were forty-three.[46] By 1912 it could be said that a wife 'on the strength' enjoyed some solid advantages. She had free quarters of two or more rooms, one being fitted with a cooking range. Basic furniture, bedding, fuel, coal and gas were provided. She also received free education for her children, as well as medical attendance. By doing laundry work for her squadron she could earn a little extra. For this purpose most barracks found for her a 'drying green', hot water and even mangles. The wife of a sergeant was said to be well enough off to employ a charwoman.[47]

* * *

For the other ranks even more than for the officers, life in India was, as it ever had been, a comparatively luxurious business. When Trooper Seed arrived with the 3rd Hussars in 1903, one of his first letters home declared:

> 'From what I can see of it at present, Indian soldiering appears to be a sort of gentleman's life. . . . I was about to make my bed up when a native walked up to me and told me he was the polish boy. In quick time he had my boots off, grabbed my jacket and was off like a shot. He was back directly with them cleaned and then made my bed up. He made my bed down again at dinner time and in the afternoon cleaned my things again, folded my cloak, water bottle, etc., in regimental fashion. In fact he cleans everything in the way of personal equipment – all for the magnificent sum of eight pence per week.'[48]

Trooper Hanlon of the 12th Lancers also appreciated the unwonted luxury: 'It was good to send for the bearer and say "I'm for guard tonight, I want a good turn-out", the result being that lance, sword, boots, brasses, buttons and spurs would all be at your bedside ready to put on at the appointed time. All that you had to do personally was to attend to your rifle.' For a few annas extra a man's saddlery could be cleaned to the very highest standards. 'All this,' wrote Hanlon, 'went to make life fairly tolerable during the great heat of the summer when, after early morning parades and stables, and possibly a lecture, all one had to do during the long afternoons was to lie and sweat under the punkahs.'[49]

One of the less pleasing aspects of the hot season was the double duty which fell upon those who had to remain with the skeleton regiment in the plains, about half their comrades having gone on leave to the hills. All the regiment's horses had to be looked after by only half the usual number of men.

'As a matter of barrack routine,' records the historian of the 7th Hussars, 'the horses required to be watered at least four times a day – more in hot weather – and had to be led out to the water troughs (where they either refused to drink or else gulped the water down and then splashed everyone near them). After watering they had to be fed – four times a day with grain and chaff and twice with hay, to say nothing of feeds of bran, linseed and boiled stuff for certain animals – before they were finally bedded down at night. . . . [Much time was taken up with] grooming, clipping, tail-pulling and hoof-picking. . . . Throughout the night stable guards were on duty to guard against the innumerable forms of mischief which a stableful of troop horses could get up to – there was always a horse or two in every troop which knew how to slip its head-collar, get out and go careering over the barrack square, with the stable guard cursing in full pursuit.'[50]

The incidence of disease in certain stations in India underwent a dramatic decline in the first years of the century. When the 12th Lancers arrived in India in 1902, Trooper Hanlon found that precautions against fever were primitive. After evening stables 'a basin of quinine was dished out to all hands, and each troop took a whisky-bottleful to be placed in the bungalow for the night. If any man felt feverish he got up and had a go at the bottle.' Inoculation against enteric fever had been practised in South Africa with disappointing results. It soon, however, emerged from its inefficient infancy and the results in India were highly encouraging. The number of men who accepted inoculation rose each year as the admissions for, and deaths from, the disease declined. The 17th Lancers were fortunate in having attached to them a doctor, Captain E. J. Luxmore, who had been sent out specially to study the problem. On arrival in 1905 only 130 men received inoculations. In that year 108 were admitted with the disease and twenty-two died of it. In 1906, with 332 inoculated, there were only fifty admissions and nine deaths. In 1907 eighteen admissions resulted in four deaths. The War Office ordered Luxmore to extend his activities beyond the regiment, and he soon persuaded many hundreds of men to accept inoculation with splendid results.[51] The other chief cause of mortality was heat stroke.

* * *

Messing in India was carried out under troop arrangements. The basic ration of 1 lb of meat, 1 lb of bread, 2½ ozs of sugar, ¾ oz of tea and 4 ozs of rice was issued daily to each man and cooked as required by the troop cook. Often the men would exchange some of the rice for such commodities as salt and luxuries like curry. There was always around the bungalows a host of the various 'wallahs' touting all kinds of meat, butter, cheese, eggs and numerous other items of food and drink.[52]

The earlier efforts made by Roberts and others to control the consumption of alcohol, not only amongst the European but also among the native troops, were strenuously pursued. General Sir O'Moore Creagh, who became Commander-in-Chief in 1909, established at Simla during the hot weather of 1912

> 'an Indian Army Temperance Association on the lines of the British one, but it was to include the abstention from intoxicating drugs. Drink was doing much harm not only among the native troops but also in the villages from which soldiers were enlisted. An able retired Indian Army officer accepted the post of secretary, and he went round the villages to secure the services of other pensioned officers for local work and to form temperance associations all over the country.'[53]

It is difficult to assess what advantage was taken of the various temperance associations which catered for European troops (see Vol III, pp. 133–4), but, as at home, the incidence of crime committed under the influence of drink declined considerably up to 1914. Trooper Seed of the 3rd Hussars was probably not typical, but he chose his friends among what were known variously as the 'bun wallahs', 'wad punchers' and 'tea busters'. He frequented the Soldiers' Home, the 'Prayer Room' and the branch of the Army Temperance Association at Sialkot.[54]

* * *

Colonel Valentine Baker, in 1868, had made an abortive effort to introduce into the cavalry the squadron system (see Vol II, p. 442). A quarter of a century later, in 1892, this organizational reform was officially promulgated. In the following year an equally important change took place. Up to 1893 recruits were enlisted for a particular regiment and had the right in peacetime to remain in it for the whole of their service. Now, by special Army Order of March, 1893,

recruits were to be enlisted instead for four 'corps': the Household Cavalry, Dragoons, Lancers and Hussars. (See also p. 479.) This reform, which was designed to simplify recruiting, organizational and mobilization arrangements, led to the trial of a scheme put forward by, and known by the name of, Lieutenant-General George Luck (see Vol III, p. 136) when he was Inspector-General of Cavalry, in 1897.* Luck's system grouped all regiments in threes within the classifications of 'regiments abroad', 'regiments at home on the higher establishment' and 'regiments at home on the lower establishment'. The eight higher establishment regiments were exempted from providing drafts for overseas so that they could be ready to take the field at the shortest notice. The eight lower establishment regiments were, on mobilization, to be made up to the higher establishment, in men and horses, from the reserve.†
One of the hoped-for advantages of the system was to be the abolition of the depot system. This would have effected a considerable economy and, more important, ensured the higher standards of training which could be given in regiments than at the depots.

The chief flaw which prevented the system's success was its absolute dependance upon two of the three regiments in each group always being stationed at home. This 'normal' situation, in fact, never existed. Right from the start it proved necessary to retain depots for the provision of drafts for the one regiment which was in Egypt and the two that were in South Africa. After the war, and because of it, the disorganization of the three-group system was glaringly demonstrated. In 1903 only eleven regiments, instead of the 'normal' sixteen, were at home, seven being kept in South Africa, over and above the nine in India and those elsewhere overseas. In fact, though only four were then considered necessary at the Cape, the large number of depots at home which the dislocation of Luck's system necessitated, meant that there was no accommodation at home for the three which ought to have been brought back to Britain. In fact, only three of the nine three-regiment groups were in 1903 'correctly situated'.[55]

After endless discussion and many attempts to reconcile divergent

---

* Army Order 41, 1897. For war, the scheme provided for two three-regiment brigades and a Divisional Cavalry.

† The higher establishment service squadrons – (each regiment consisted of three service squadrons and one reserve squadron) – were to be mounted on 'thoroughly serviceable' horses, the less efficient horses being assigned to lower establishment regiments. (WO 120/Gen. No./6302, 10 Nov. 1903, 13.)

views, a new system was devised and promulgated by Army Order 168 of 1905. How this worked between that year and the First World War will be discussed in the final volume of this work.

*   *   *

Until 1909 the word 'trooper' applied to a cavalryman had always been an unofficial colloquialism. In that year a first step was taken at the King's instance to regularize it. An Army Order decreed that 'the word "trooper" will in future be employed instead of the word "private", to describe a private soldier of the Household Cavalry'.[56] The designation was not made official in the cavalry of the line until after the First World War.

21

'Kitchener is the man to drive through a campaign with relentless energy. [But] you have only to go to Lord Cromer or to the Foreign Office to ascertain what is the effect he produces, when let loose in administration.'

CURZON to Lord George Hamilton, Secretary of State for India, 6 September, 1899

'[Kitchener] thinks that when I go, he will get rid of the Military Member, and with a new Viceroy, ignorant of India, and probably less strong-willed than himself, that he will be the ruler of the country in everything but name.'

CURZON to Lord George Hamilton, 14 May, 1903

'I found [when Commander-in-Chief] I had plenty to do without having control of what I called the "spending departments", and my fear is that future Commanders-in-Chief, who may not have had your unique experience, might be unable to cope with the amount of office work they would have to deal with, and, at the same time, carry on their inspections in the thorough manner that is so essential for the efficiency of the Army in India.'

ROBERTS to Kitchener, 19 May, 1904[1]

(i)

India: Curzon–Kitchener dispute – Curzon's resignation – army reforms

In India between 1899 and 1914, with very few exceptions (the Boxer Rebellion in China of 1900–1901 and the Tibetan expedition of 1904 being the least unimportant), the army saw no active service. The whole period was remarkable, too, for the almost total lack of internal disturbances, which was fortunate especially during the Boer War since Lord Curzon at that time took the risk of virtually denuding the sub-continent of white troops.* Until 1907 the threat from the

---

* By early 1901 nearly half of the 70,000 British troops in India were away or on the point of leaving. Beside those sent to South Africa, 1,300 had been sent

Russians was taken more seriously than ever before, largely because of their speedy completion of the Orenburg-Tashkent railway. Though this menace never came to anything, it had its effect upon the celebrated conflict between the Viceroy and the Commander-in-Chief, which ended in Kitchener forcing Curzon's resignation in 1905. Kitchener was undoubtedly wrong in this unseemly squabble between two strong-willed men. It was marked, especially on the Commander-in-Chief's part, by much intentional misrepresentation and behind the scenes chicanery. Kitchener wished to do away with the post of Military Member of the Governor-General's Council, of which he, too, was a member. He alleged that the holder of that position, a mere major-general, was responsible for putting a brake on the Commander-in-Chief's actions and reforms.* In fact, this form of dual control was, in the Indian context, a particularly efficient system, which had worked very well for the last seventy years or so.

The almost complete emasculation of the Military Member's job which Kitchener engineered meant that the Commander-in-Chief became both the initiator and the sole judge of all military policy. It also placed far too great a burden of work on one man's shoulders. It was almost as if the duties of Commander-in-Chief and War Minister were combined in one man. It meant, as Curzon put it, the demise of that 'hitherto uncontested, essential and in the long run indestructible subordination of military to civil authority' which was essential to the proper 'administration of all well-conducted states'.[2] The old system, with its division of duties between the two posts, was not unlike that between the General Staff and the War Office in European countries. It rested upon a sensible segregation of training and planning for war, and supply. Though there were, as in all systems, flaws in it, Curzon conceded to Kitchener certain extra powers which certainly ameliorated most of them.† But Kitchener

---

to China at the time of the Boxer Rebellion in 1900. Some 20,000 native troops also went on that expedition.

India also supplied for both theatres of war twenty-one million rounds of ammuntion, 114,000 shells and over a million items of clothing, as well as huge quantities of saddlery and miscellaneous items such as blankets.

* Some of Kitchener's reforms were offensive to native units' susceptibility; others were wildly unrealistic and based on totally incorrect facts.

† An example of friction within the system was given by Smith-Dorrien when he was Adjutant-General in India. The Commander-in-Chief, General Sir Arthur Power Palmer (see p. 500) recommended that the establishment of eight camels for each Indian cavalry regiment should be doubled and the number of

was determined to attain, chiefly by foul means, including clandestine correspondence with Balfour and Esher, as complete a dictatorship over all military matters as he had enjoyed in Egypt and South Africa. This he achieved – and exercised – till he left India in 1909. The result, even before he returned home, was a great degree of the chaos for which he was becoming famous. By 1911 the machine had broken down. Even Kitchener admitted that he had 'miscalculated the possible harm that incapacity might achieve' under Commanders-in-Chief of 'ordinary ability'![3] When the arrangement came to be put to a real test, as it was in Mesopotamia during the First World War, it was acknowledged to be the overriding cause of the appalling disasters of that campaign.*[4] The details of the controversy do not directly concern the mounted arm and need not therefore be rehearsed here.[5]

*　　*　　*

Two years before Kitchener arrived in India, Curzon wrote to him that he saw 'absurd and uncontrolled expenditure; I observe a lack of method and system; I detect slackness and jobbery; and in some respects I lament a want of fibre and tone. . . . On the other hand, in point of organization, equipment, rapidity of mobilization and fighting capacity, I believe that our army would take a high place, even among continental forces.'[6] It was these good points of the army in India which Kitchener's autocratic determination to control it single-handed did much to impair. In the first three years of Curzon's administration – he became Viceroy in 1899 – there were effected or put in train considerable reforms. The reduction of provincial garrisons so as to increase the field force, for instance, which

---

horses reduced by eight, since he and the colonels of every regiment (all of whom had been consulted) believed that camels were more efficient for certain routine tasks such as orderly duties. According to Smith-Dorrien, although the measure would actually have saved money, it was referred to the Military Department. It came back 'with a brief minute signed by a captain, saying that the Government of India did not agree – and that was the end of that.' Smith-Dorrien's stories should not always be taken at face value. (Smith-Dorrien, 297–8.)

* The Report of the Mesopotamia Commission stated that 'the combination of the duties of the Commander-in-Chief and Military Member of Council cannot adequately be performed by any one man in time of war. [It] is at once over-centralized at its head and cumbrous in its duality below.' (Quoted in Cadell, Sir P. *History of the Bombay Army*, 1938, 255.)

Kitchener later continued, had already been put forward by Curzon. The most important of the others were the doubling of the reserves of the native army, the start of a programme for self-sufficiency in armaments and ammunition, the rearming of all three arms, the reorganization of the transport system, the building of railways in the troublesome frontier areas and extensive measures of decentralization. Later he gave Kitchener every support with such reforms as a fairer system of disablement pensions, increases in kit allowance, improved police efficiency and the creation of the first Indian Staff College at Quetta (see p. 464).

'Lord Curzon was suffering from a severe attack of "poor black man". That is, protecting the poor Indian from the assaults of the brutal British soldiery.'

LIEUTENANT COLONEL GEORGE YOUNGHUSBAND,
commanding the Guides Cavalry

'A very improper order was in force in India to the effect that a telegram was to be sent to the HQ of Government direct when any serious occurrence took place between a white and a black man.'

GENERAL SIR BINDON BLOOD, G.O.C.,
Punjab, 1902

'The English may be in danger of losing their command of India because they have not learned how to command themselves.'

LORD CURZON in 1902[1]

(ii)

India: case of Atu, the cook, and 9th Lancers

'I will not be a party to any of the scandalous hushing-up of bad cases,' wrote Curzon to Kitchener in 1902, 'or to the theory that a white man may kick or batter a black man to death with impunity because he is only a "damned nigger".'[2] To Brodrick, who became Secretary of State for India in 1903, Curzon wrote: 'Nobody ever dares to tell the inner side of things in India. . . . You can scarcely credit the sympathy with wrongdoing that there is here – even among the highest – provided that the malefactor is an Englishman.' In this matter Curzon had the full-hearted support of Kitchener. In one week alone four instances of unprovoked assault came to the notice of the Commander-in-Chief, who in July, 1903, took 'the task,' as Curzon put it, 'off my shoulders and the generals and colonels who used to snap their fingers at me are dancing timorously to the new tune.'[3] There had been far too many cases in recent years.* In 1899 an old Burmese woman had been raped in broad daylight by men of the West Kent Regiment in Rangoon. The regiment was punished and banished to the horrors of the Aden station. Early the next year a private of the Royal Scots Fusiliers smashed in a punkah-wallah's head with a dumb-bell. He was given a stiff punishment to which Curzon insisted wide publicity should be given: 'Punishment,' he said, 'is not a sufficient deterrent, unless known; publicity given to punishment is.'[4] Cases where white juries acquitted soldiers of causing deaths, particularly some which took place on 'shooting parties', were brought to his notice. He set up an investigatory committee. In writing the minutes for it, he was not blind to the fact that natives were sometimes insolent and that trumped-up cases were not unknown, but he asserted that the feeling had been largely created by the British. 'The conduct of a small number of British soldiers may,' he wrote, 'sensibly affect the position of all Englishmen, and the attitude of all natives. . . . The natural position of a British soldier should be that of a source of protection and not of alarm to the people.'[5]

The best known case of 'nigger-bashing' concerned the 9th Lancers, one of the very smartest and most aristocratic of all the regiments of cavalry of the line. In brief what happened is that the headquarters of the regiment arrived at its new station in mid-afternoon. That evening much drinking took place. 'There was a great quantity of beer which the soldiers themselves could not get through: so,' according to the Inspector of Police, 'they kept giving it to the

* In the twenty years before Curzon arrived in India eighty-four natives had been killed in recorded cases of violence between British soldiers and natives, and fifty-seven seriously injured. During the whole of the last half of the nineteenth century only on two occasions had Europeans been hanged for the murder of natives. (Curzon, 11.)

cooks.' One of these was a man called Atu. 'At 9 p.m.,' he told the Cantonment Magistrate the following day, 'I was returning to my home when two soldiers of the [headquarters squadron of the] regiment called me saying "Come here – which is our Bungalow?" I pointed it out to them. They then said they wanted a woman.' When he failed to respond, they attacked him, breaking two of his ribs and punching him about the face. Curzon's voluminous notes on the case state that

'he was left lying out all night. On the next morning he was found in such an enfeebled condition that he had to be carried into camp on a stretcher, and was at once sent to hospital. The case was so bad that the Cantonment Magistrate was sent for to take his dying deposition. The District Superintendent, Police and Inspector visited the scene of the outrage and found the ground still covered with big patches of blood. On the day after he seemed so much better that they thought he might pull through. Thereupon everyone, civil and military combined, conspired to hush up the whole affair. No enquiry was instituted, no evidence taken and until the man died a week or more later, nothing was done.

'A Court of Enquiry is [then] held by order of the Officer Commanding [Major Spencer Walpole Follett, who had served with the regiment in South Africa]. It consists of two captains and a subaltern, not one of whom understood a word of Hindustani.'

They examined no one except four native witnesses: no doctor, no police inspector, no soldier! Nevertheless Follett's report stated that the matter had been 'investigated in every possible way; but owing to the evidence being entirely native [!] it appears to be impossible to bring the guilty man to justice.' The evidence was commented upon by the officer commanding the District as 'meagre'. Consequently a fresh enquiry was ordered, nearly a month after the outrage. The new court was headed by a colonel and composed of officers from regiments other than the 9th Lancers. The regimental surgeon, sergeant-major, sergeants and the station police inspector gave evidence. Naturally enough, so long after the event, little new light was thrown upon the case.[6]

Soon afterwards a second outrage occurred: a punkah-wallah was killed by Private Munton of the regiment. The Commander-in-

Chief, Sir Arthur Power Palmer,* Kitchener's predecessor, at once sent Major-General Boyce Albert Combe to conduct a local enquiry into the circumstances of the two cases. This, again, not surprisingly, shed little further light upon the first one. (The second was comparatively straightforward.†)

The most amazing part of the whole sorry story is the comments made by Lieutenant-General Sir Bindon Blood (see p. 219) commanding in the Punjab, in forwarding Combe's report. Among other things he accused Atu of being 'probably very drunk' for which there was hardly a shred of evidence; yet he found it hard to 'understand how Atu could have walked so far [nearly two miles] in his injured state', thus contradicting his previous accusation. He assumed that the poor man had 'something discreditable to conceal' because some of his statements were confused which, in the circumstances, was not surprising. He asserted that Atu's brother-in-law, who said that he could not identify the assailants in the dark, was 'with him at the time of his assault', although in fact he of course ran away when the troopers started to menace Atu. Blood went on to insinuate, against all the evidence, and 'almost in the same breath, that the guilty parties were (1) drunken natives, (2) men of the Gordon Highlanders, (3) men of the Depot of the 9th Lancers, not of the Head Quarters – anybody in fact', as Curzon scathingly put it, 'but the parties to whom all the evidence points'. Blood's most astonishing statement is that it was 'evident that the assailants could hardly have belonged to the Head Quarters of the 9th, which only arrived at Sialkot about five hours before the outrage occurred.' 'What,' commented Curzon, 'there is to prevent a soldier who arrives at a place at 4.30 p.m. from wanting a native woman at 9.30 p.m., or from assaulting a native who fails to provide him with one, is not explained. Prior residence in a locality is not essential either to the promptings of lust, or to the perpetration of crime.' Blood's conclusion was that 'disciplinary action is quite out of the question.'[7]

Curzon's castigation of Blood, running to many pages in his own

---

* Palmer had served in Hodson's Horse during the Mutiny and had seen much active service in, amongst other campaigns, the 1867–8 Abyssinian War, the 2nd Afghan War and in the Sudan in 1885. He became Commander-in-Chief in 1900. He died aged sixty-four in 1904.

† Munton kicked the man more than once and with violence, but Lieutenant-General Blood (see below) 'found' that there was only one kick and that 'a slight one with the bare foot'! (Curzon, 8.)

hand, must surely be unprecedented in the annals of civil/military relations. 'Really,' he says at one point, 'can ineptitude further go?' He described the report as 'a purely *ex-parte* statement, couched in the style of an advocate and animated by the spirit of a partisan. . . . A striking illustration of the mental and moral obsession which is one of the main difficulties that I experience in dealing with these cases.' When Smith-Dorrien, then Adjutant-General in India, read Blood's report, he remarked to his personal assistant, 'General [Blood] has fallen into the jaws of the lion.' When within two days Curzon's blistering minute came back to him, he commented, 'Little did I think how headlong he had done so.'[8] Typical of Blood's attitude and inefficiency was his remark that as the 9th Lancers had recently been in South Africa none of its men would be likely to assault a native, for 'the excellent reason that the natives there are usually well able and ready to defend themselves'. Combe, on the other hand, advised that regiments fresh from South Africa should be given a special warning, coming from 'rough service in a country where the lives of black men are not held of much account', while the Commander-in-Chief summed up the case thus: 'It is not perhaps surprising that the officers of a regiment coming from a country where blacks are knocked about somewhat indiscriminately did not at first take much notice of the occurrence.'[9]

Both the Commander-in-Chief and the Military Member of the Council recommended that officers and men of the 9th on leave should be recalled, that all leave should be cancelled for six months and that the regiment should be given a private dressing-down in the most forceful terms. With these punishments Curzon was in full agreement. It was also suggested that the regiment should be excluded from the forthcoming Coronation Durbar (called by the troops the 'Curzonation' Durbar). From this further chastisement, however, Curzon decided to save them. Of all this nothing was at first made public, but grossly ill-informed gossip at home became so intense that it was decided to issue a statement to the press (mentioning no officers by name). Even this failed to suppress the spate of angry rumours. One of these was that officers and men who were at home at the time of the assault were also to be punished. This came to the ears of the King who at first protested at the severity of the penalties imposed, but who, when given the accurate picture, said that he thought the regiment had got off lightly.[10]

By now Kitchener had succeeded Palmer and was as behind Curzon as was Lord George Hamilton, Brodrick's predecessor as

Secretary of State for India. Both agreed with the Viceroy that 'a most salutory lesson' would be taught to the military when it was known that he was standing up 'even against the crack regiment of the British Army – packed though it be with Duke's sons, Earl's sons, and so on. . . . If we yield to military and aristocratic clamour,' as he wrote to Hamilton, 'no Viceroy will dare go on with the work that I have begun.' Roberts, often inclined to snobbery, wrote from London to suggest that Curzon should announce the remission of the punishments at the Durbar. When, however, Curzon replied that he had set his face 'like a flint' against the argument that 'a native's life does not count', Roberts withdrew the idea. He no doubt found it easier to do so in view of the trouble he had had with the case of bullying in the Life Guards with which he had just had to deal (see p. 456).[11]

The strength of the ill-feeling with which Curzon had to contend from the British upper classes in India was cruelly demonstrated when the great Durbar of 1903 was staged. As the 9th passed the saluting base they were greeted with 'a loud continuous roar of applause',[12] the mass of European spectators rising to their feet as a man. The Viceroy's determination and courage were thus ill rewarded.

The regimental historian, writing as late as 1939, regretted the 'unfortunate clash between men of the regiment and some truculent natives', but deplored even more the measures taken to prevent such things happening in the future. These, he believed, would disappoint 'some of the natives themselves, whose amiable habit it was to annoy soldiers with the intention of making them commit themselves in some way to give them an excuse for reporting them, or with the alternative resource, it may be presumed, of exacting some form of mild blackmail.' It is not, perhaps, irrelevant to note that 'towards the end of the regiment's stay in India strict military habits appear to have become somewhat relaxed, to the disquiet of Colonel Willoughby who felt called upon to issue an order forbidding men to wear their hair long over the forehead or to walk about barracks with cigarettes, cigars, etc., behind the ears.'[13]

APPENDIX

1. Goldman says that the division's strength was 2,754 of all ranks with 2,871 horses. This probably excludes the RHA batteries and the mounted infantry brigades. Amery gives what is probably the *establishment*, as opposed to the *actual numbers present*, as 3,907 regular cavalry, 1,293 RHA and 315 in the ammunition columns. He gives 4,912 mounted infantry in the two MI brigades, as well as a further 1,020 of miscellaneous mounted units. (Goldman, 73; Amery, III, 376.)

The five brigades were made up as follows: (All figures are very approximate. They probably represent more the numbers that ought to have existed rather than those actually present.)

1st Cavalry Brigade (Porter, who did not join till 15 February, having succeeded Babington who had been removed from command on Roberts's orders (see p. 50)):

1,917
- 6th Dragoon Guards (Carabiniers) (464)
- 2nd Dragoons (Scots Greys) (438)
- one squadron, 6th (Inniskilling) Dragoons, which, commanded by Allenby, was attached to the Scots Greys (Yardley, 37)   (464)
- one squadron, 14th Hussars
- one squadron, N.S.W. Lancers
- 'Q', 'T' and 'U' Batteries, RHA (551)

2nd Cavalry Brigade (Brigadier-General Robert George Broadwood) (see p. 140):

1,954
- Composite Regiment, Household Cavalry (625)
- 10th Hussars (458)
- 12th Lancers (500)
- 'G' and 'P' Batteries, RHA (371)

3rd Cavalry Brigade (Brigadier-General James Redmond Patrick Gordon (see p. 134), who came straight from India and did not take over till 11 February):

1,329
- 9th Lancers (418 and 422 horses (Colvin, 62))
- 16th Lancers (540)
- 'O' and 'R' Batteries, RHA (371)

Each cavalry brigade had an ammunition column, a detachment of the Army Service Corps, a field hospital, a bearer company, a field troop of Royal Engineers and six transport companies. Some 150 Rimington's Guides were distributed among the brigades.

The 16th Lancers had only been in the country twelve days when the operation started. Coming from India their horses refused maize, which is the staple South African grain. (Smith, 30.)

The mounted infantry brigades seem to have varied so much over the next few weeks both as to composition and commanders that it is best to give all the units without allocating them:

5,782
- 1 to 8 Battalions, MI (3,533)
- New South Wales Mounted Rifles (120)
- Queensland MI (275)
- Two companies, New Zealand Mounted Rifles (204)
- Roberts's Horse (550)
- Kitchener's Horse (400)
- Nesbitt's Horse (250)
- Grahamstown Volunteer Mounted Infantry MI (200)
- City Imperial Volunteer MI (known as 'the Lord Mayor's Own') (250)

Lieutenant-Colonels Edwin Alfred Hervey, Alderson, Ormelie Hannay and Charles Parker Ridley were MI brigade commanders. (Amery, III 376–7; Maurice, I, 436–7.)

---

2. *Note on the various enquiring bodies set up in 1901 and 1902 with respect to the remount question, and their Reports.* (See p. 288.)

(1) *The Committee on Horse Purchase in Austro-Hungary* [Cd. 882], 1902. (The Welby Committee.)

Early in 1901 a Conservative Member of Parliament, Sir John Blundell Maple, Bt,* made certain allegations against the Remount Department, 'as to bribes given to certain British officers in relation to the purchase of horses in Austro-Hungary'. (Welby, 2.) As a result of these a Parliamentary Committee was set up under Sir Charles Welby, Bt, the Assistant Under-Secretary at the War Office. Though its Report was signed in August, 1901, it was not presented to Parliament till just before the Supplementary Army Estimates debate in the Commons on 31 January,

* Maple was MP for Dulwich and head of the upholstery firm in Tottenham Court Road. He was also a wealthy race-horse breeder and owner. During his career on the turf he won 544 races including the Cesarewitch and the Two Thousand Guineas. He died, aged fifty-eight, in 1903.

1902. This delay was due to litigation in which one of the officers referred to was involved and which had only just been completed. The fact that Members had so little time to digest the report and its supporting evidence did not inhibit them from making the wildest charges. Truman was bitterly attacked although the Report made it quite clear that all the important indictments should have been directed against the Imperial Yeomanry Committee. On the day following the debate Truman was sent for by Mr Brodrick, the Secretary of State for War. Lord Roberts, by then Commander-in-Chief, and the Quartermaster-General were present at the interview.

> 'I was asked certain questions,' said Truman in evidence to the Court of Enquiry which was later instituted [see (2) below], 'and the Quartermaster-General explained that I had nothing to do with the transactions of the Yeomanry Committee. In the afternoon I was again sent for by Lord Roberts, who, in the presence of the Quarter-master-General, pointed to "The Times", containing a report of the debate, and told me that Mr Brodrick considered the feeling in the Commons was so strong against me that I had better resign.'

Truman was given forty hours in which to consider this suggestion. After that period had expired he had two further interviews. At the second he was again requested to resign.

> 'Mr Brodrick and Lord Roberts informed me that they had formed the opinion that I was not competent for my post, and I may mention that about this date the Secretary of State informed the House that he had been aware since the previous August that I was not conducting my work to his satisfaction. . . . It should be noted that he had never warned me, nor sent me any message to this effect, neither had any of my superiors found fault with me or given me any opportunity to alter my system if considered necessary. On the other hand, in the previous autumn (in 1900), when Lord Lansdowne was retiring, he had sent for me and thanked me personally for my work. At the conclusion of this last interview, Lord Roberts offered me an inquiry.'

(2) *Court of Enquiry on the Administration of the Army Remount Department* [Cd. 994], 1902. (President, General Sir Robert Biddulph.)

This Truman accepted, asking that he might have the assistance of counsel and a grant towards paying his fees. After the first sitting of the Court, at which his counsel* appeared, his grant was 'so cut down' that Truman could not afford to retain him.

* Mr (later Sir) Henry Dickens, KC, sixth son of Charles Dickens, the novelist.

'I then asked for the assistance of a General Officer who was willing to help me, but his services were denied to me. Though the Court has been held with closed doors, I have been forbidden the use of the Report made in November last by a Committee [see (3) below] under Lord Stanley [then Financial Secretary to the War Office, and later, as Earl of Derby, Secretary of State for War during the last two years of the First World War], . . . a document which I considered material to my defence.'

The Court's Report stated that instances of fraud had been alleged and widely published. The Court was informed by the War Office that there was only known one instance of fraud on the part of officers or civilians serving under Truman. This was the case of Veterinary-Captain Smith, who was attached to the Purchasing Commission in New Orleans. The horse dealer in Texas who accused Smith of soliciting and receiving large sums of money on commission, on being pressed for proofs, eventually declined to prove his charge. Smith was advised to take legal steps to clear his character. These, which would have 'rendered him liable to heavy costs', he failed to do. Instead he left New Orleans for home and was tried by court-martial for being absent from duty without leave.

Allusion had been made in Parliament to the fact that Truman had a personal interest in Messrs Houlder Bros. The interest, it turned out, amounted to a capital sum of £35. The Quartermaster-General as well as the Court rightly decided that so small a holding had in no way influenced Truman. 'This appears to illustrate,' states the Report of the Court, 'the ease with which, in an excited state of public feeling, the most innocent and insignificant act on the part of an official may become the basis of grave and unfounded accusations.' (Biddulph, 30–1, 284.)

(3) *Committee appointed by the Secretary of State for War to consider the Supply of Remounts for the Army* [A.726], 1902. (The Stanley Committee.)

This Committee, which was appointed with a view to the *future* supply of remounts, held thirteen meetings between June and November. Its Report was signed on 28 November, 1901. The report and the evidence were confidential and therefore almost certainly not available to Parliament when the Commons discussed the Remount question on 31 January, 1902. Much of the evidence was favourable to Truman.

(4) *Reports by Officers appointed by the Commander-in-Chief to inquire into the Working of the Remount Department Abroad* [Cd 995], 1902.

These reports were presented to Parliament. The officers who reported on operations in the United States and Canada were General Sir Robert Macgregor Stewart and Lieutenant-Colonel E. Holland; in Austro-

Hungary, Lieutenant-General Sir Montagu Gilbert Gerard; in South Africa and Australia, Major-General Viscount Downe.

(5) *Army (Remounts): Reports, Statistical Tables and Telegrams received from South Africa, June, 1899 to 22 January, 1902* [Cd 963], 1902.

The most important of these were: (1) the Report by Lieutenant-Colonel W. H. Birkbeck, who was sent out as Assistant Inspector of Remounts, which he rendered to the Commander-in-Chief in South Africa; (2) the Veterinary Report from the Principal Veterinary Officer in Pretoria; (3) the Report of the GOC, Lines of Communication, Natal.

3. *South African War, 1899–1902 – casualties: regular cavalry regiments: variations, official and* Times *histories.*

	Maurice, IV, 692–3 (1910)		Amery, VII, 18, 19, 20, 21 (1909)	
	Offrs	ORs	Offrs	ORs
Household Cavalry (composite regiment)	8	137	8	88
1st Dragoon Guards	14	71	14	71
2nd ,, ...	9	91	9	92
3rd ,, ...	3	88	3	88
4th ,, ...	1	2	—	—
5th ,, ...	7	91	7	91
6th ,, ...	10	140	8	156
7th ,, ...	11	162	11	173
1st Dragoons	7	135	7	135
2nd ,, ...	12	246	13	256
3rd Hussars	1	31	1	31
4th ,, ...	2	12	—	—
5th Lancers	11	164	11	166
6th Dragoons	17	172	18	175
7th Hussars	3	11	3	11
8th ,, ...	11	90	11	90
9th Lancers	16	21	21	211
10th Hussars	15	199	15	199
11th ,, ...	4	12	—	—
12th Lancers	13	131	11	137
13th Hussars	5	155	5	161
14th ,, ...	3	77	4	111

16th Lancers	..	..	..	20	146	20	146
17th ,,	..	..	..	14	151	13	186
18th Hussars	..	..	..	17	282	17	282
19th ,,	..	..	..	5	260	5	260
20th ,,	..	..	..	2	8	2	8
21st Lancers	..	..	..	1	3	—	—
				242	3088	237	3324

4. Of the engagements in which the regular cavalry took some part during the guerrilla period of the South African War, the following are a few of the more interesting. Lack of space accounts for the fact that none of these is discussed in the chapters dealing with the period. (See, chiefly, Chapter XIII (iv).)

(1) 6 February, 1901. Lake Chrissie, E. Transvaal. *5th Lancers.* (Stampede induced by Boer dawn charge.) (Maurice, IV, 114; Willcox, 278.)

(2) 24 March, 1901. Wildfontein or Hartebeestefontein, W. Transvaal. *6th Inniskilling Dragoons.* ('. . . model of pursuing tactics', Maurice, IV, 135.) (Maurice, IV, 135; Yardley, 240; Doyle, 612.)

(3) 16 October, 1901. Halfmanshof, Twenty-Four River, Cape Colony. *16th Lancers.* (Charge by one squadron.) (Maurice, IV, 359; Graham, 196.)

(4) 21 October, 1901. Roi Kraal, Slangappiesberg, E. Transvaal. *18th and 19th Hussars.* (Marling, 288–9.)

(5) 16 December, 1901. Beschuitfontein, Cape Colony. *5th Lancers* and *10th Hussars.* (Kritzinger chased, wounded and made prisoner.) (Maurice, IV, 367; Amery, V, 543: Willcox, 280.)

(6) 23 December, 1901. Kordemoersfontein, near Calvinia, Cape Colony. *16th Lancers.* (Graham, 197; Maurice, IV, 365.)

(7) 3 February, 1902. Nooitgedachte, near Springs, E. Transvaal. *5th Dragoon Guards, 18th and 19th Hussars.* (Marling, 295; Maurice, IV, 513.)

(8) 18 February, 1902. Klippan, E. Transvaal. *5th Dragoon Guards* and *2nd Dragoons (Royal Scots Greys).* (One squadron of the Greys decimated.) (Pomeroy, 260; Kruger, 465; Maurice, IV, 513; Amery, V, 461–2.)

5. *List of War Office Committees on cavalry and yeomanry matters, 1900 to 1913.*

(1) *Organization, Arms and Equipment of the Yeomanry Force,* 1900
(Chairman, Lord Harris) Cd 466

(2) *Revise of Yeomanry Regulations,* 1902
(Chairman, Viscount Ebrington) 0070/3050

(3) *Provision of Horses for the Imperial Yeomanry at Home,* 1902
(Chairman, Viscount Ebrington) A 756

(4) *Yeomanry Reserve,* 1903
(Chairman, F. T. Marzials, Esq., Accountant-General) 0070/3150

(5) *Cavalry Re-organization,* 1904
(Chairman, Colonel J. R. P. Gordon) A 889

(6) *Deficiency of Officers in the Cavalry,* 1905
(Chairman, Major-General H. D. Hutchinson) A 986

(7) *Cavalry Sword,* 1908
(Chairman, Major-General H. J. Scobell) 54/Cavalry/861

(8) *Cavalry – Peace Organization and Mobilization Arrangements,* 1909
(Chairman, Major-General D. Haig) A 1308

(9) *Cyclists for the Cavalry Division,* 1913
(Chairman, Major-General E. H. H. Allenby) A 1648

(10) *Cavalry Reservists,* 1913
(Chairman, Major-General E. H. H. Allenby) A 1666

6. *Some variations in actual numbers of all ranks in certain regiments of cavalry of the line at different dates.*

(1)	2 DG	1908	760 (Home)
		1911	696 (Home)
(2)	3 DG	1904	673 (Home)
(3)	6 DG	1908	515 (South Africa)
(4)	1 RD	1902	1134 (of which 569 dismounted. For Kaiser's inspection)
		1904	641 (First time ever in India)
		1911	583 (South Africa)
(5)	4 H	1909	592 (Home)
(6)	7 H	1905	715 (Home)
		1911	537 (India)
(7)	8 H	1906	740 (Home)
		1909	498 (India)
(8)	9 L	1902	405 (India)

		1903	626 (India)
		1906	516 (South Africa)
		1910	579 (Home)
(9)	13 H	1904	617 (India)
(10)	15 H	1909	490 (South Africa)
		1913	477 (Home)

(Sources: regimental histories.)

7. *Some miscellaneous facts.*

(1) In 1903 the Household Cavalry furnished a Sovereign's Escort for the State visit of President Loubet of France. This was the first time the head of a republic had been thus honoured. (Arthur, III, 2.)

(2) It was usual to grant twenty-eight days' leave to all ranks after a lengthy period of foreign service. (Stewart, 238.)

(3) It was calculated that a squadron of cavalry, moving complete at war strength, ought to be able to entrain in not more than fifty minutes. (Morrison, Maj. Royal Dragoons *Notes on Military Law* . . ., 1898.)

(4) The average daily march time of a cavalry division in 1909 was twenty-five miles 'which is all that horsed wagons' could accomplish. (Mayhew, Lt-Col M. J. & Skeffington Smyth, Maj. G. 'Motor Cars with the Cavalry Division', *Cav. Jnl*, IV, 442.)

(5) The battle honours of Blenheim, Ramillies, Oudenarde and Malplaquet were not added to the standards of the regiments present at those battles until 1882. The distinctions for Warburg (1760), Beaumont and Willems (1794) were not given to the regiments present at those battles until 1906. The greatest number of battle honours awarded to any cavalry regiment was eighteen for the 16th Lancers. Next came the 9th Lancers with sixteen (Pomeroy, vi; Barrett: *7H*, 203; Graham, 236.)

Household Cavalry and Line Cavalry

	1899	1900	1901	1902	1903
Household Cavalry (1660)	H/A	H/A	H	H	H
1st D.G. (1685)	H	H	A	A	A/H
2nd D.G. (1685)	H	H	H/A	A	A
3rd D.G. (1685)	H	H	H/A	A	A
4th D.G. (1685)	I	I	I	I	I
5th D.G. (1685)	I/A	A	A	A/I	I
6th D.G. (1685)	H/A	A	A	A	A/I
7th D.G. (1688)	H	H/A	A	A	A
1st D. (1661)	H/A	A	A	A/H	H
2nd D. (1678)	H/A	A	A	A	A
6th D. (1689)	H/A	A	A	A/H	H
3rd H. (1685)	I	I	I/A	A/I	I
4th H. (1685)	I	I	I	I	I
5th L. (1858)	A	A	A	A/H	H
7th H. (1690)	H/A	A	A	A	A
8th H. (1693)	H	H/A	A	A	A/H
9th L. (1715)	I/A	A	A	A/I	I
10th H. (1715)	H/A	A	A	A/I	I
11th H. (1715)	I/E/A	E/A	E/A	E/A	E/H
12th L. (1715)	H/A	A	A	A/I	I
13th H. (1715)	H/A	A	A	A/H	H
14th H. (1715)	H/A	A	A	A	A/H
15th H. (1759)	H/I	I	I	I	I
16th L. (1759)	I	I/A	A	A	A
17th L. (1759)	H	H/A	A	A/H	H
18th H. (1759)	A	A	A	A/H	H
19th H. (1759)	A	A	A	A	A/H
20th H. (1759)	I	I	I/A	A	A/E
21st H. (1759)	E/H	H	H	H	H

Key: A: South Africa   I: India
      E: Egypt and the Sudan   H: Home (i.e. U.K.)

Regiments: Stations from 1899-1931

1904	1905	1906	1907	1908	1909	1910	1911	1912	1913
H	H	H	H	H	H	H	H	H	H
H	H	H	H/I	I	I	I	I	I	I
A	A	A	A	H	H	H	H	H	H
A/H	H	H	H	H	H	H	H	H	H
A	A	A	A	A/H	H	H	II	H	H
I/A	A	A	A	A/H	H	H	H	H	H
I	I	I	I	A	A	A	A	A	H
A/H	H	H	H	H/E	E	E/I	I	I	I
H/I	I	I	I	I	I	I	I/A	A	A
A	A/H	H	H	H	H	H	H	H	H
H	H	E	E	I	I	I	I	I	I
I	I	I	I/A	A	A	A	A/H	H	H
I	I/A	A	A	A	A/H	H	H	II	H
H	H	H	H	H	H	H	H	H	H
A	A/H	H	H	H	II	II	II/I	I	I
H	H	H	H	H	H/I	I	I	I	I
I	I	I/A	A	A	A	A/H	H	H	H
I	I	I	I	I	I	I	I	I/A	A
H	H	II	H	H	H	H	H	H	H
I	I	I	I	I	I	I/A	A	A	A
H/I	I	I	I	I	I	I	I	I	I
H	H	H/I	I	I	I	I	I	I	I
I	I	I	I	I	I/A	A	A	A	A/H
A/H	H	H	H	H	H	II	H	H	H
H	H/I	I	I	I	I	I	I	I	I
H	H	H	H	H	H	H	H	H	H
H	H	H	H	H	H	H	H	H	H
E/H	H	H	H	H	H	H	H	H	H
H	H	H	H	H	H	H	H	H/I	I

ABBREVIATIONS USED IN THE
FOOTNOTES AND SOURCE NOTES

Only those sources which occur more than once in the footnotes or source notes are included in this list.

Airlie	[Anon.] *The Happy Warrior: A Short Account of the Life of Lord Airlie,* 1901
Akers-Douglas	[Akers-Douglas Report] *Report of the Committee appointed to consider the Education and Training of the Officers of the Army* (Cd 982), 1902
Almack	Almack, Edward *The History of the Second Dragoons, 'Royal Scots Greys',* 1908
Amery	(ed.) Amery, L. S. *The Times History of the War in South Africa 1899–1902,* 7 vols (I, 1900; II, 1902; III, 1905; IV, (ed.) Williams, B., 1906; V, (ed.) Childers, Erskine, 1907; VI, 1909; VII, Appendices and Index, 1909)
Amery: *Army*	Amery, L. S. *The Problem of the Army,* 1903
Andrew	Andrew, Bt-Maj. A. W. *Cavalry Tactics of To-day,* 1903
Arthur	Arthur, Capt. Sir George *The Story of the Household Cavalry,* II, 1909 and III, 1926
Arthur: *K*	Arthur, Sir George *Life of Lord Kitchener,* 3 vols, 1920
Atkinson	Atkinson, C. T. *History of the Royal Dragoons, 1661–1934,* 1934
Baden-Powell	Baden-Powell, Lt-Gen. Sir Robert *Memories of India: Recollections of Soldiering and Sport* [1915]
Baden-Powell: *Training*	[Baden-Powell] The Inspector of Cavalry 'Recent Steps in Cavalry Training in England', *Cav. Jnl,* I, 1906
Barrett	Barrett, C. R. B. *The 7th (Q.O.) Hussars,* 2 vols, 1914
Barrett: *XIII H*	Barrett, C. R. B. *History of the XIII Hussars,* 2 vols, 1911
Barrow	Barrow, Gen. Sir George de S. *The Fire of Life* [1942]
Bernhardi	Bernhardi, Gen. von *Cavalry in Future Wars,* trans. Goldman, C. S., 1906
Bernhardi: *W & P*	Bernhardi, Gen. von *Cavalry in War and Peace,* trans. Bridges, Maj. G. T. M., 1910
Biddulph	*Court of Enquiry on the Administration of the Army Remount Department since January 1899,* 1902 (Pres.: Biddulph, Gen. Sir R.)
Birdwood	Birdwood, F-M Lord *Khaki and Gown: An Autobiography,* 1941
Birkbeck	*Army (Remounts) Reports, Statistical Tables and Telegrams Received from South Africa, June, 1899 to 22 January, 1902,* 1902
Blood	Blood, Gen. Sir Bindon *Four Score Years and Ten,* 1933

Bolitho   Bolitho, H. *The Galloping Third*, 1963

Bond   Bond, Brian 'Doctrine and Training in the British Cavalry, 1870–1914', (ed.) Howard, Michael *The Theory and Practice of War: Essays Presented to Captain B. H. Liddell Hart on his 70th Birthday*, 1967

Brereton   Brereton, J. M. *A History of the 4th/7th Royal Dragoon Guards and Their Predecessors, 1685–1980*, 1982

Broadwood   Broadwood, Brig.-Gen. R. G. 'The Place of Fire Tactics in the Training of the British Cavalry', *Cav. Jnl*, I, 1906

Browne   Browne, Brig. J. G. and Bridges, Lt-Col E. J. ((ed.) Miller, Maj. J. A. T.) *Historical Record of the 14th (King's) Hussars, 1900–1922*, 1932

Burnett   Burnett, Maj. C. *The 18th Hussars in South Africa . . . 1899–1902*, 1905

Burnett: *18H, 06-22*   Burnett, Brig.-Gen. C. *The Memoirs of the 18th (Queen Mary's Own) Royal Hussars, 1906–1922*, 1922

Cav. Jnl   *The Cavalry Journal*

Cav. Trng   [Official] *Cavalry Training*

Childers: *German*   Childers, Erskine *German Influence on British Cavalry*, 1911

Childers: *War*   Childers, Erskine *War and the Arme Blanche*, 1910

Churchill   Churchill, W. S. *My Early Life: A Roving Commission*, 1930

Churchill: *Companion*   Churchill, Randolph S. *Winston S. Churchill, Companion Volume I, Pt 2, 1896–1900*, 1967

Churchill: *Hamilton* Churchill, W. S. *Ian Hamilton's March*, 1900

Clowes   Clowes, Lt-Col P. L. Papers (Diary), NAM 5712–59

Colvile   Colvile, Maj.-Gen. Sir H. E. *The Work of the Ninth Division*, 1901

Colvin   Colvin, Bt Lt-Col F. F. and Gordon, Capt. E. R. *Diary of the 9th (Queen's Royal) Lancers during the South African Campaign, 1899 to 1902*, 1904

Cooke   (ed.) Cooke, J. H. *5,000 Miles with the Cheshire Yeomanry in South Africa*, 1914

Cooper   Cooper, Duff *Haig*, I, 1935

Crum   Crum, Maj. F. M. *With The Mounted Infantry in South Africa . . . 1899–1902*, 1903

Curzon   *Notes by H.E. the Viceroy . . .: Assaults committed on a native cook . . .*, MSS Eur. F111/402, India Office Library

Davies-Cooke   Davies-Cooke, 2nd-Lt A. G. K., 10th Hussars, Papers, NAM 7104-25

Despatches   *South African Despatches*, I, Feb. 1901

De Wet   De Wet, C. R. *Three Years War*, 1902

Digby   (ed.) Digby 'An Imperial Yeoman's Service Memories of South Africa', *Indian Ink, being Splashes from Various Pens in aid of the Imperial Indian War Fund*, 1914

Dilks   Dilks, David *Curzon in India*, 2 vols, 1968

Doyle   Conan Doyle, A. *The Great Boer War*, Complete Edition, 1902

Du Cane   (trans.) Du Cane, Col H. *The War in South Africa, the Advance to Pretoria after Paardeberg, the Upper Tugela Campaign, etc., March, 1900 to September, 1900: Prepared in the Historical Section of the Great General Staff, Berlin,* 1906

Duncalf   Duncalf, Tpr J., 21 Coy, Cheshire Imperial Yeomanry, Papers, NAM 8104-56

Dundonald   Dundonald, Lt-Gen. The Earl of *My Army Life,* 1926

Esher   Brett, M. V. *Journals and Letters of Reginald, Viscount Esher,* 2 vols, 1934

Evans   Evans, Maj.-Gen. Roger *The Years Between: The Story of the 7th Queen's Own Hussars, 1911–1937,* 1965

Farrar-Hockley   Farrar-Hockley, Maj.-Gen. A. *Goughie: The Life of General Sir Hubert Gough . . .,* 1975

Farwell   Farwell, Byron *The Great Boer War,* 1977

Fitzgibbon   Fitzgibbon, Maurice *Arts Under Arms: An University Man in Khaki,* 1901

Fitzpatrick   Fitzpatrick, J. P. *South African Memories,* 1932

Forbes   Forbes, Maj.-Gen. A. *A History of the Army Ordnance Services,* II, 1929

French   French, Maj. Hon. G. *The Life of Field-Marshal Sir John French . . .,* [1931]

French: *Role*   French, Lt-Gen. Sir J. D. P. *Report to the Army Council on the Role of the Cavalry by the Commander of the 1st Army Corps,* 7 Mar., 1904, 20/Cav/112, WO32/6782 5220 (Copy in the Royal Archives, RA XI/65b)

Fuller   Fuller, Maj.-Gen. J. F. C. *The Last of the Gentlemen's Wars: A Subaltern's Journal of the War in South Africa, 1899–1902,* 1937

Gardner   Gardner, Brian *Allenby,* 1965

Gilbert   Gilbert, Sharrad H. *Rhodesia – and After, being the Story of the 17th and 18th Battalions of Imperial Yeomanry in South Africa,* 1901

Gilmour   Gilmour, Capt. J. (MS) *A Record of the 20th Company, Imperial Yeomanry.* (The property of Sir John Gilmour Bt, DSO, TD)

Godley   Godley, Col A. J. 'The Development of Mounted Infantry Training at Home', *Cav. Jnl,* I, 1906

Godley: M.I.   Godley, Col A. J. 'Mounted Infantry', *Cav. Jnl,* IV, 1909

Godwin-Austen   Godwin-Austen, Bt-Maj. A. R. *The Staff and the Staff College,* 1927

Goldman   Goldman, C. S. *With General French and the Cavalry in South Africa,* 1902

Gore   (ed.) Gore, Lt-Col St John *The Green Horse in Ladysmith,* 1901

Gough   Gough, Gen. Sir H. *Soldiering On,* 1954

Graham   Graham, Col H. *History of the Sixteenth, the Queen's, Light Dragoons (Lancers), 1759 to 1912,* 1912

Abbreviations

Griffith	Griffith, K. *Thank God We Kept the Flag Flying: The Siege and Relief of Ladysmith 1899–1900*, 1974
Haig	(ed.) Haig, Countess *Douglas Haig: His Letters and Diaries*, I ('Advance Proof Copy' of a work which was never published. The property of the 2nd Earl Haig of Bemersyde)
Haig: *Cav.*	Haig, Maj.-Gen. D. *Cavalry Studies: Strategical and Tactical*, 1907
Haig: diary	Haig's various Boer War military diaries and orders, NLS
Haig: 'Notrefe'	'Notrefe' [D. Haig] *Cavalry Taught by Experience: A Forecast of Cavalry under Modern War Conditions*, 1910
Hamilton	Hamilton, Col H. B. *Historical Record of the 14th (King's) Hussars*, 1901
Hancock	(ed.) Hancock, W. K. and Van der Poel *Selections from the Smuts Papers*, I, 1966
Hansard: (C)	*Hansard's Parliamentary Debates*, House of Commons
Hansard: (L)	*Hansard's Parliamentary Debates*, House of Lords
Harvey	Harvey, Col J. R. and Cape, Lt-Col H. A. *The History of the 5th Lancers, 1689–1921*, 1921
Headlam	Headlam, Maj.-Gen. Sir John *The History of the Royal Artillery from the Indian Mutiny to the Great War*, III, 1940
Head	Head, Lt S. S. 'The Wear and Tear of Horses During the South African War', *Journal of Comparative Pathology and Therapeutics*, 31 Dec., 1903
Henderson	Henderson, Col G. F. R. *The Science of War – A Collection of Essays and Lectures, 1891–1903*, 1933
Hillegas	Hillegas, Howard C. *With the Boer Forces*, 1900
Hobson	Hobson, Lt-Col G. W. *Some XII Royal Lancers*, 1936
Holmes	Holmes, Richard *The Little Field-Marshal: Sir John French*, 1981
HRAVC	Smith, Maj.-Gen. Sir Frederick *A History of the Royal Army Veterinary Corps 1796–1919*, 1927
Hutchinson: *Deficiency*	[Hutchinson Report] *Report of Committee on the Deficiency of Officers in the Cavalry*, WO A.986, 1905
Jackson	Jackson, Murray Cosby *A Soldier's Diary: South Africa, 1899–1901*, 1913
JAHR	*Journal of the Society for Army Historical Research*
James	James, David *Lord Roberts*, 1954
JRUSI	*Journal of the Royal United Service Institution*
Kipling	Kipling, Rudyard *The Five Nations*, 1904
Kruger	Kruger, Rayne *Good-bye Dolly Gray: The Story of the Boer War*, 5th edn, 1964
Lane	Lane, Lt A. H. 'Horses for War Purposes', *United Service Magazine*, Apr., 1912
Lumley	Lumley, Capt. L. R., MP *History of the Eleventh Hussars (Prince Albert's Own), 1908–1934*, 1936
Luvaas	Luvaas, Jay *The Education of an Army: British Military Thought, 1815–1940*, 1965

Macready	Macready, Gen. Sir Nevil *Annals of an Active Life*, 1928
McElligott	McElligott, QMS James *Royal Scots Greys: South Africa, 1899–1901*, [1901]
Maguire	Maguire, T. Miller *Guerrilla or Partisan War*, 1904
Makins	(ed.) Makins, Lt-Col E. *The Royals in South Africa, 1899–1902*, 1914
Manoeuvres, 1903	[Official] *Report on Combined Manoeuvres, Sept. 1903*
Marling	Marling, Col Sir Percival, Bt, VC *Rifleman and Hussar*, 1931
Maude	Maude, Lt-Col F. N. *Cavalry: Its Past and Future*, 1903
Maurice	Maurice, Maj.-Gen. Sir Frederick *History of the War in South Africa 1899–1902* (the Official History), 4 vols (I, 1906; II, 1907; III, 1908 (not by Maurice: author not specified); IV, 1910 (by Grant, Capt. M. H.))
Maydon	Maydon, J. G. *French's Cavalry Campaign*, 1902
Meintjes	Meintjes, J. *De la Rey – Lion of the West*, 1966
Micholls	Micholls, Maj. G. A. *History of the 17th Lancers, 1895–1924*, 1931
Millin	Millin, Sarah G. *General Smuts*, I, 1936
Morton	Morton, Sqn Sgt-Maj. J. W. *8th (King's Royal Irish) Hussars: Diary of the South African War, 1900–1902*, 1905
Mosley	Mosley, Nicholas *Julian Grenfell: His Life and the Times of His Death, 1888–1915*, 1976
Mussenden	MS *Letters of Captain F. Mussenden, 8th Hussars, October, 1899–October, 1901*. (Property of the late Robert Poore-Saurin-Watts Esq.)
NAM	National Army Museum
NLS	National Library of Scotland
Oatts: *3DG/6DG*	Oatts, Lt-Col L. B. *I Serve: Regimental History of the 3rd Carabiniers*, 1966
Oatts: *14H/20H*	Oatts, Lt-Col L. B. *Emperor's Chambermaids: The Story of the 14th/20th King's Hussars*, 1973
Otley	Otley, C. B. 'The Social Origins of British Army Officers', *Sociological Review*, XVIII, No. 2 (New Series), July 1970
Pakenham	Pakenham, Thomas *The Boer War*, 1979
Pay	*Royal Warrant for the Pay . . . of the Army*, 1900 and 1913
Pearce	Pearce, H. H. S. *The History of Lumsden's Horse*, 1903
Peel	Peel, Hon. S. *Trooper 8008, I.Y.*, 1902
Phillipps	Phillipps, L. March *With Rimington*, 1901
Pomeroy	Pomeroy, Maj. Hon. R. L. *The Story of the 5th Princess Charlotte of Wales's Dragoon Guards*, 2 vols, 1924
PPW	[Anon.] *Pen Pictures of the War by Men at the Front*, n.d.
Rankin	[Rankin, J. R. J.] *A Subaltern's Letters to His Wife*, 1901
Rawlinson	Rawlinson Papers, Diary, NAM 5201-33
R.C.	*Report of His Majesty's Commissioners appointed to Inquire into the Military Preparations and Other Matters connected with the War in South Africa* (the Elgin Report), 1903, 4 vols (I: Report; II and III: evidence; IV: appendices)

Abbreviations

R.D.A.	*Reports by Officers Appointed by the Commander-Chief to Inquire into the Working of the Remount Department Abroad,* 1902
Reckitt	Reckitt, B. N. *The Lindley Affair: A Diary of the Boer War,* Hull, 1972
Reitz	Reitz, Deneys *Commando: A Boer Journal of the Boer War,* 1929
Repington	Repington, Lt-Col Charles à Court *Vestigia,* 1919
Rimington	Rimington, Maj.-Gen. M. F. *Our Cavalry,* 1912
Roberts	Roberts, F-M Earl 'Circular Memorandum', 1 Mar., 1903, 54/Cav/430, WO32/6782 5220
Robertson	Robertson, F-M Sir William, Bt *From Private to Field-Marshal,* 1921
Rose-Innes	Rose-Innes, C. *With Paget's Horse to the Front,* 1901
Russell	Russell, Tpr Alfred, 6th (Inniskilling) Dragoons, MS Diary. (Property of Sqn-Ldr J. A. H. Russell, RAF (retd))
Sampson	Sampson, V. and Hamilton, I. *Anti-Commando,* 1931
Schikkerling	Schikkerling, R. W. *Commando Courageous,* 1964
Sessions	Sessions, Harold *Two Years with Remount Commissions,* 1903
Seton-Karr	Seton-Karr, Henry, MP *The Call to Arms 1900–1901 or A Review of the Imperial Yeomanry Movement,* 1902
Sheppard	Sheppard, Maj. E. W. *The Ninth Queen's Royal Lancers, 1715–1936,* 1939
Smith	Smith, Maj.-Gen. Frederick *A Veterinary History of the War in South Africa, 1899–1902, 1919 (completed, 1914)*
Smith-Dorrien	Smith-Dorrien, Gen. Sir Horace *Memories of Forty-eight Years' Service,* 1925
Spiers: *A & S*	Spiers, E. M. *The Army and Society, 1815–1914,* 1980
Spiers: *Cav.*	Spiers, E. M. 'The British Cavalry, 1902–1914', *JAHR,* LVII, 1979
Spiers: *Haldane*	Spiers, E. M. *Haldane: An Army Reformer,* 1980
Spurgin	Spurgin, Karl B. *On Active Service with the Northumberland and Durham Yeomen under Lord Methuen: South Africa, 1900–1901,* 1902
Stanley	*Report of the Committee Appointed by the Secretary of State for War to Consider the Supply of Remounts for the Army . . .,* (the Stanley Report), 1902
Stanley: *Expenses*	*Report of the Committee on Expenses Incurred by Officers of the Army* (the Stanley Report), 1903
Steele	Steele, Col S. B. *Forty Years in Canada,* 1915
Steevens	Steevens, G. W. *From Capetown to Ladysmith: An Unfinished Record of the South African War,* 1900
Stewart	Stewart, P. F. *The History of the XII Royal Lancers,* 1950
Stirling	Stirling, John *Our Regiments in South Africa, 1899–1902: Their Record, Based on the Despatches,* 1903
Stirling: *C*	Stirling, John *The Colonials in South Africa,* 1907

Taylor   Taylor, William L. 'The Debate over Changing Cavalry Tactics and Weapons, 1900–1914', *Military Affairs* (USA), Winter 1964–5

Thomas   Thomas, Hugh *The Story of Sandhurst*, 1961

Thompson   Thompson, Col C. W. *Seventh (Princess Royal's) Dragoon Guards: The Story of the Regiment (1688–1882)* and *With the Regiment in South Africa* (Campbell, Maj. N. D. H.; Whetherly, Capt. W. S.; Holland, Capt. J. E. D.), 1913

Tullibardine   Tullibardine, The Marchioness of *A Military History of Perthshire, 1899–1902*, 1908 (article by Oppenheim, Capt. L.)

Tylden   Tylden, Maj. G. *Horses and Saddlery . . .*, 1965

Tylden: *AFSA*   Tylden, Maj. G. *The Armed Forces in South Africa*, 1954

Viljoen   Viljoen, Gen. Ben *My Reminiscences of the Anglo-Boer War*, 1903

Wallace   Wallace, R. L. *The Australians at the Boer War*, 1976

Ward   Ward, Col E. W. D. *Précis for the Army Council: Role of Cavalry and its Armament*, Jan., 1905, 20/Cav/112, WO32/6782 5220

Ward: *Officers*   Ward, Col E. W. D. *Interim Report of the Committee on the Provision of Officers*, 1907

Waters   (trans.) Waters, Col W. H. H. *The War in South Africa, Oct. 1899 to Feb., 1900: Prepared in the Historical Section of the Great General Staff*, Berlin, 2nd edn, 1905

Welby   *Report of the Committee on Horse Purchase in Austro-Hungary . . .* (the Welby Report), 1902

Whyte & Atteridge Whyte, F. and Atteridge, A. H. *A History of the Queen's Bays (the 2nd Dragoon Guards) 1685–1929*, 1930

Willcox   Willcox, W. T. *The Historical Records of the Fifth (Royal Irish) Lancers . . .*, 1908

Williams   Williams, Capt. G. T. *The Historical Records of the Eleventh Hussars Prince Albert's Own*, 1908

WO   War Office

Wylly   Wylly, Col H. C. *XVth (The King's) Hussars, 1759 to 1913*, 1914

Wyndham   Mackail, J. W. and Wyndham, G. *Life and Letters of George Wyndham*, I, n.d.

Wyndham: *Drum*   Wyndham, Horace *Following the Drum*, 1912

XIII H   [Anon.] *XIII Hussars: South African War, October 1899–October 1902*, n.d.

Yardley   Yardley, Lt-Col J. Watkins *With the Inniskilling Dragoons: The Record of a Cavalry Regiment during the Boer War, 1899–1902*, 1904

Young   (ed.) Young, Lt-Col F. W. *The Story of the Staff College, 1858–1958*, 1958

Younghusband   Younghusband, Sir G. *A Soldier's Memories*, 1917

SOURCE NOTES

CHAPTER I (pp. 31–37)

(i)

1 Wyndham, G. to his mother, *Wyndham*, I, 361. *Report*, R.C., I, 273; quoted in Longford, Elizabeth *Jameson's Raid* . . ., 1982, 132; Minute, 21 May, 1900, *R.C.*, I, 28; *Wyndham*, I, 356; Waters, I, 33
2 Report, *R.C.*, I, 40, 41

(ii)

1 May, Lt-Col E. S. *A Retrospect on the South African War*, 1901, 5; Waters, I, 12; Maurice, I, 86
2 Pakenham, 41; Waters, I, 20; *Haig*, 193
3 Hillegas, 112
4 Hillegas, 70, 91
5 Hillegas, 61, 81–92
6 Hillegas, 93
7 Amery, II, 84
8 Amery, II, 75; Hillegas, 76; Gilbert, 279–80; Maurice, I, 80
9 Maurice, I, 69; Amery, II, 54

CHAPTER II (pp. 38–46)

1 Marling, 243; Settle, J. H. (ed.) *Anecdotes of Soldiers in Peace and War*, 1905, 445
2 *Hart's Annual Army List*, 1889, 160
3 Crum, 90; Burnett, 1
4 Amery, II, 149
5 Crum, 32; Burnett, 10; Marling, 245
6 *R.C.*, III, 402
7 Amery, II, 170
8 Marling, 245, 247–8, 279
9 Reitz, 29
10 Burnett, 16–18
11 Burnett, 19
12 Reitz, 29–30
13 Quoted in Griffith, 38
14 Burnett, 21
15 Reitz, 30

16 Maurice, I, 462
17 *R.C.*, III, 402
18 Quoted in Griffith, 38
19 Burnett, 12
20 Amery, II, 173
21 *R.C.*, III, 402
22 Maurice, I, 462
23 Hillegas, 71–2

CHAPTER III (pp. 47–60)

1 Gore, 22; *PPW*, I, 65; Farwell, 72; Rawlinson, 21 Nov., 1899
2 11 Dec., 1901, Rawlinson; Gore, 9
3 Gibson, 15, 18, 19, 20, 21, 22; Atkins, J. B. *The Relief of Ladysmith*, 1900, 131; Cooper, 378
4 Maurice, IV, 85; Amery, V, 144; Smith-Dorrien, 278
5 Maurice, IV, 134–5, 484; Amery, V, 224–5; Smith, 162a; Gibson, 271–87
6 Waters, 35; Haig, 152
7 Maurice, I, 160
8 Headlam, 317
9 Haig, 150–1
10 Pomeroy, I, 236
11 Rawlinson, 29 Sep., 1899; Cooper, I, 377
12 Haig, 151
13 Gibson, 31
14 Sampson, 113, 115
15 Gibson, 35
16 Maurice, I, 167; Haig: diary, 3155 33/8
17 Pomeroy, 239
18 Gore, 26–27
19 Gore, 17–18
20 Gore, 13
21 *PPW*, I, 64, 65
22 Viljoen, 34
23 Farwell, 73
24 Willcox, 219
25 Burnett, 35
26 Gore, 11
27 Gore, 13, 14
28 Gore, 19
29 Gore, 28–9
30 Gore, 21–2
31 Waters, 37
32 *Haig*, 158
33 Farwell, 73
34 Waters, 37; Maurice, I, 464
35 Willcox, 219

CHAPTER IV (pp. 61–68)

1 Repington, 196
2 Amery, II, 212
3 Buller to Lansdowne, 9 Sep., 1899, *Lansdowne Papers*, quoted in Pakenham, 97
4 Marling, 253
5 Gore, 42
6 Amery, II, 235; Capt. C. J. Steavenson, 30 Oct., 1899, Liverpool Museum, quoted in Pakenham, 607
7 Conan Doyle, 113
8 Amery, II, 255
9 *Haig*, 168–9, 170
10 Pakenham, 168–9; Amery, II, 291
11 Smith, 43, 44; Amery, III, 175
12 Willcox, 256
13 Burnett, 71
14 Pomeroy, I, 248–9
15 Willcox, 256

CHAPTER V (pp. 69–77)

1 Maurice, I, 201; Dundonald, 89; *Wyndham*, 396; Airlie, 81
2 Atkinson, 349, 351–3; Makins, 15
3 *XIII H*, 1–3
4 *R.C.*, II, 17–26, 580–2, IV, 343–55; Gilbert, 157
5 Dundonald, 117; Tylden: *AFSA*, 169
6 Churchill, 321; Repington, 199; Farwell, 255
7 Maurice, IV, 164, 401; Gilbert, 161
8 Amery, II, 296; 28 Jul., 1901, *Haig*, 243; Gilbert, 161; Fitzgibbon, 167; 16 Dec., 1899, *Mussenden*; De Wet, 104; Amery, V, 38
9 Dundonald, 99
10 Birdwood, 100
11 Dundonald, 78, 80, 84–5, 85–6; description of Dundonald military water cart, 27 Feb., 1901 *Birmingham Post*; *R.C.*, IV, 346
12 Gough, 70; Farrar-Hockley, 46, 57
13 Fitzpatrick, 153–4
14 Stirling: *C*, 10, 39, 51, 68; Maurice, I, 332–73; Amery, II, 422–57; Pemberton, W. B. *Battles of the Boer War*, 1964, 120–45; Dundonald, 89–112

CHAPTER VI (pp. 78–86)

1 Phillipps, 15; PRO 30/67, WO 132/15; Amery, II, 324; *Wyndham*, 378
2 Colvin, 5
3 Lord F. Blackwood to his father, the Marquess of Dufferin and Ava, 12 Oct., 1899, Colvin, 6–9
4 Methuen's evidence, *R.C.*, II, 120
5 Smith, 18; Colvin, 17

6   Methuen's evidence, *R.C.*, II, 120

7   *R.C.*, III, 26–7, 583; Colvile, 23–4; Rankin, 32; Phillipps, 3, 6

8   Phillipps, 8

9   *R.C.*, II, 129

10 Maurice, I, 216–17

11 *R.C.*, II, 120

12 Maurice, I, 308

13 Maurice, I, 321; Colvin, 39; Amery, II, 406. See also Sheppard, 193–5 and Stewart, 188–91

14 Maurice, I, 240–1; Amery, II, 339. See also Colvin, 28–32

15 Amery, I, 360

16 Maurice, I, 285–301; Amery, II, 382

17 Farwell, 374; Wallace, 33–6; Birdwood, 123–4

CHAPTER VII (pp. 87–103)

1   Pakenham, 253; Peel, 2, 167; *R.C.*, III, 290; Glover, Lady (ed.) *Lest We Forget Them: Our Sailors and Soldiers, 1899–1900*, [1900], 23; Wilkinson, F. *Australia at the Front: A Colonial View of the Boer War*, 1901, 286

2   Buller to Lansdowne, 16 Dec., 1899 (Cypher telegram No. 56)

3   *Wyndham*, 382

4   Wyndham papers; Wolseley to Lansdowne, Lansdowne to Wolseley, 28 and 30 Dec., 1899, WO 32/7866, quoted in Pakenham, 252–3

5   Amery, III, 15, VI, 269; Maurice, I, 414; *R.C.*, II, 517, III, 274, 275, 282, 293, 310; Churchill: *Hamilton*, 51

6   *R.C.*, II, 517, III, 294, 299, 520, 521; Cooke, 99, 103, 107; Gilbert, 288, 289

7   Fitzgibbon, 42, 90

8   *R.C.*, III, 275, 291, IV, 474; Amery, III, 15–18

9   *R.C.*, II, 517, III, 274, 284, 287; Rose-Innes, 3, 23, 31

10 See, especially, *R.C.*, III, 287; Peel, 7; Lord Kitchener's *Despatches*, 8 Jul., 1901, Cd 695, p. 471

11 Maurice, I, 414; Seton-Karr, 18; *R.C.*, II, 524–8, III, 276, 277, 280, 309

12 *R.C.*, II, 520, 526–7, III, 288, 305–6

13 Smith, 54, 147, 305, 308; Gilbert, 264

14 *R.C.*, II, 518, III, 288, 309, 312

15 *R.C.*, II, 519

16 Wetton, T. C. *Reminiscences of the 34th Battalion, Imperial Yeomanry*, [1907], 1; *R.C.*, 281

17 *R.C.*, 290, 299; Smith, 54

18 *R.C.*, III, 290, 293, 312; Smith, 147; 27 Oct., 1901, Gardner, 50; *Haig*, 30 Mar., 1902; Wallace, 322; 8 Jan., 1901, Gilmour, 5

19 Maurice, III, 110; Amery, IV, 217

20 Maurice, IV, 73, 345; Smith, 162a; Amery, V, 244; Doyle, 652–3

21 Amery, V, 327; Smith, 168; Doyle, 631

22 Amery, V, 438

23 Maurice, IV, 393–5; Amery, V, 431–44; Pakenham, 542–4; De Wet, 341–5; Smith, 176; Doyle, 693–6

24   *R.C.*, II, 132
25   Doyle, 716

CHAPTER VIII (pp. 104–110)

1   Amery, II, 292–3; French, 65; *Haig*, 185; *Haig*, 197
2   Maurice, I, 277; Amery, III, 123
3   21, 23 Nov., letter, 26 Nov., 1899, *Haig*, diary, 180, 185
4   *R.C.*, III, 411, 412
5   23 Dec., 1899, 4 Jan., 1900, *Haig*, letters, 192, 195
6   Maurice, I, 277–8
7   *Airlie*, 71, 106
8   12 July, 1900, Clowes; *Haig*, 187
9   Stirling: *C*, 337; *Haig*, 188
10   *Haig*, 191
11   Smith, 19, 20
12   Barry, Maj. S. L., 10th Hussars 'Signalling in the Cavalry during the Late South African War', *Cav. Jnl*, I (1906), 170
13   Maurice, II, 250–2
14   Sir Joseph Laycock to Lady Haig, [1934?], *Haig*, 201

CHAPTER IX (pp. 111–114)

1   Quoted in James, 262; Kitchener to 'an intimate friend', Arthur: *K*, I, 267
2   Roberts to Lansdowne, 16 Dec., 1899, Roberts 110–11, I, I, Min. of Defence Library, quoted in Pakenham, 244–5
3   Kitchener to Ralli, 30 Jan., 1900, Arthur: *K*, I, 270–1
4   *Haig*, 204; Buller to USS for War, 20 Dec., 1899, Maurice, I, 381
5   Maurice, I, 415; Amery, III, 347, 350
6   Wallace, 79
7   Amery, III, 95
8   Amery, IV, 506

CHAPTER X (pp. 115–123)

(i)

1   Maurice, II, 344
2   Dundonald, 133
3   Maurice, II, 341
4   Dundonald, 116
5   Dundonald, 120–22
6   Dundonald, 123; Maurice, II, 631
7   Amery, III, 222; Maurice, II, 360–1; Dundonald, 124–5
8   Maurice, II, 632; Dundonald, 127–8
9   Maurice, II, 633; Amery, III, 221; *R.C.*, II, 178
10   Dundonald, 133
11   Dundonald, 135

(ii)

1 Birdwood, 106
2 Pakenham, 345–6
3 Davis, Richard Harding *Adventures and Letters*, (ed.) Davis, C. B., 1917, 273273
4 Reitz, 88, 90; Maj. Freiherr von Reitzenstein, quoted in Du Cane, 284
5 Farrar-Hockley, 52; Gough, 74
6 Lyttelton, Gen. Sir Neville *Eighty Years, Soldiering, Politics, Games*, [1927], 230; 2 Mar., 1900, Rawlinson
7 Du Cane, 285–6

CHAPTER XI (pp. 124–193)

(i)

1 Goldman, 77; Amery, III, 388; *Haig*, 205; Stewart, 195
2 *Haig*, 199; *R.C.*, III, 402
3 Maurice, I, 416, II, 1
4 Yardley, 36; Amery, III, 357
5 Amery, III, 359
6 Haig: diary, 3155/33/36, NLS; *Haig*, 204; Headlam, 529; Smith, 31
7 Home and Overseas Correspondence of Lord Roberts, Ministry of Defence Library, 24–5; Arthur, II, 703; Amery, III, 364, 367
8 Amery, III, 371; Goldman, 73; Smith, 30; *Airlie*, 85; *Haig*, 203
9 Yardley, 38; Maurice, II, 18; Amery, III, 381; Haig: diaries, 3155/33/150, NLS; Goldman, 74; *Haig*, 203
10 *Haig*, 204; Goldman, 78; Yardley, 39; Smith, 32
11 *Haig*, 204; Smith, 32; Stewart, 193; Lt Hon. A. Meade's Journal in Arthur, II, 713; Colvin, 65; Yardley, 41
12 Maydon, 134; Stewart, 194
13 *Haig*, 204; Smith, 32; Colvin, 65; Stewart, 194
14 Stewart, 202; Maurice, II, 33; Haig: diary, 3155/33/176, NLS; Goldman, 81
15 Smith, 33
16 Goldman, 85; *Haig*, 204–5; Yardley, 42
17 *Haig*, 205; Graham, 172
18 Smith, 34; Colvin, 68; Goldman, 83–4
19 Pakenham, 327
20 Amery, III, 395; Roberts's Introduction to Childers, x
21 Maurice, II, 36; *Haig*, 205
22 Smith, 34; Head, 300; Yardley, 43

(ii)

1 Childers, 93; Maurice, III, 29; Phillipps, 73
2 Colvin, 69, 70; Waters, 159; Goldman, 91; Smith, 34; Graham, 173; Yardley, 46; Maurice, II, 87

3   Graham, 173; Kitchener to French, 16 Feb., 1900, French Papers, quoted in Holmes, 94–5; Goldman, 102; Haig: diaries, 3155/33/188, NLS
4   Smith, 36; Headlam, 361; Amery, III, 415–16; Stewart, 197; Arthur, II, 714
5   Haig: diaries, 3155/33/196, NLS; Pakenham, 334
6   De Wet, 57
7   Haig: diary, 3155/33/197, NLS
8   Haig: diaries, 3155/33/202, NLS; Goldman, 115–16; Stewart, 202–3
9   Headlam, 491, 501; Longstaff, Maj. F. V. and Atteridge, A. Hilliard *The Book of the Machine Gun*, 1917, 42

(iii)

1   Maydon, 174; 16 Mar., 1900, Home and Overseas Corres., Ministry of Defence Library; De Wet, 69; Airlie, 91; Phillipps, 87
2   Haig: diary, 3155/33/224–6, NLS, 232; Colvin, 79; Hobson, 221
3   Roberts's notes for Lansdowne enclosed by N. Chamberlain, 28 Aug., 1900, NAM/7101/23/IV
4   Amery, L. S. *My Political Life*, 1954, I, 299
5   Holmes, 98
6   *R.C.*, I, 464–5
7   Childers, 135
8   Amery, III, 560
9   Maurice, 197; Yardley, 49; Goldman, 130
10   Maurice, II, 196–7
11   *Haig*, 207
12   Holmes, 100–1
13   Hobson, 220
14   Maurice, II, 203; Smith, 213; Maydon, 180; Airlie, quoted in Stewart, 205
15   *R.C.*, I, 465
16   *Haig*, 207
17   Goldman, 138
18   Smith, 42

(iv)

1   Phillipps, 94; quoted in Farwell, 240; Churchill: *Hamilton*, 40; Childers, 239; Smith-Dorrien, 179
2   Stewart, 205
3   Wallace, 183, 184
4   Maurice, II, 259–60
5   Smith, 51
6   Broadwood's Despatch, 20 Apr., 1900, *Despatches*, 95
7   Maurice, II, 275–6
8   De Wet, 89
9   Headlam, 410–11
10   Narrative of Maj. Hornby, commanding 'Q' Battery, quoted in Pakenham, 393
11   Headlam, 410

12 Maurice, II, 283
13 Goldman, 184
14 *Despatches*, 96
15 Lt-Col Sir H. Rawlinson's Diary, NAM/5201/33, 7/2, quoted in Pakenham, 392
16 Goldman, 186
17 *Despatches*, 96
18 Conan Doyle, 380
19 *Despatches*, 96
20 Goldman, 186
21 Maurice, II, 286, 288
22 Childers, 182; Goldman, 186
23 De Wet, 91
24 Pakenham, 393
25 *Despatches*, 96
26 *Despatches*, 96
27 Smith-Dorrien, 175
28 Smith-Dorrien, 177
29 Roberts's Despatch 19 June, 1900, *Despatches*, 94
30 Farwell, 261
31 Smith-Dorrien, 178–9
32 Maurice, II, 596
33 Kipling, R. 'The Parting of the Columns', *The Five Nations*, 161
34 Haig: diaries, 3155/33/36, NLS
35 Amery, III, 14–15

(v)

1   Maurice, III, 27; quoted in Holmes, 102; quoted in Brereton, 279; Morton, 26; Amery, IV, 160
2   Maurice, II, 214–15; De Wet, 104; Amery, IV, 56–63
3   Goldman, 198–200; Smith, 53; *Haig*, 210
4   *Mussenden*, 29 Mar., 1900; Haig: diary, 3155/35/72, NLS
5   Stewart, 206
6   *Haig*, 211
7   5 Apr., 1900, quoted in Holmes, 102
8   *Haig*, 210
9   14 Apr., 1900, quoted in Holmes, 102
10 Yardley, 56
11 Maurice, III, 27; Smith, 68, 69
12 *Haig*, 212
13 Smith, 77
14 Smith, 70
15 President Steyn's memoirs, trans. for Farwell by Adv. G. E. Steyn, Farwell, 252
16 Smith, 71; compare Maurice, III, 62: 'Cavalry Division ... loss of nearly half their mobility from wastage in horseflesh'. Maurice, III, 536 contradicts this estimate. Amery, IV, 112 gives yet another set of figures

17 Smith, 72, 73
18 Maurice, III, 103
19 Arthur, II, 734–5; Maurice, III, 45; Churchill: *Hamilton*, 148
20 Morton, 24, 25
21 Hamilton to E. Childers, 30 Oct., 1910, Hamilton Papers, Liddell Hart Centre for Military Archives, King's College, London, 7/3/15
22 Goldman, 228; Bernhardi: *W&P*, xi–xiii; Childers: *German*, 28–32
23 Yardley, 61
24 Yardley, 75
25 Maurice, III, 63; Amery, IV, 149
26 Peel, 55, 110
27 Pakenham, 436–7; Reckitt, 15; Younghusband, 164; *Morning Post*, 6 June, 1900; Farwell, 269
28 Fitzgibbon, 86, 93
29 *R.C.*, IV, 416–17
30 Maurice, III, 115
31 Fitzgibbon, 120–1
32 Maurice, III, 117
33 Maurice, III, 121; Reckitt, 39
34 *R.C.*, IV, 416–17
35 Fitzgibbon, 163
36 *R.C.*, IV, 417
37 Fitzgibbon, 166, 167
38 *R.C.*, IV, 417
39 *R.C.*, IV, 416; Amery, IV, 257; there is some conflict of evidence as to the exact casualty figures on both sides
40 Maurice, III, 125; Younghusband, 164
41 Kruger, 312
42 *R.C.*, IV, 417; Amery, IV, 258; Colvile, 188–9; Maurice, III, 116
43 Letter from Conan Doyle, *Pall Mall Gazette*, 9 Jan., 1901
44 Almack, 97
45 Maurice, III, 205
46 Conan Doyle, 452
47 Hobson, 228–9; Stewart, 212; Maurice, III, 214
48 Hobson, 230
49 *Airlie*, 103
50 Arthur, II, 750; Churchill: *Hamilton*, 388
51 Conan Doyle, 452
52 Smith, 82
53 Hamilton, Ian *Listening for the Drums*, 1944, 240; Smuts Papers (I, 547 61), quoted in Pakenham, 434
54 *Reports on Military Operations in South Africa and China*, US War Dept, quoted in Farwell, 264
55 Pakenham, 453; Marling, 295
56 Amery, IV, 195
57 Farrar-Hockley, 56
58 Buller to Lady Buller, 15 May, 1900, quoted in Pakenham, 453
59 Dundonald, 165

60 Smith, 85
61 Birdwood, 112
62 Dundonald, 164; *R.C.*, I, 351–2; IV, 172; Steele, 340; Dundonald, 167; Maurice, III, 234
63 Dundonald, 166
64 Gore to Lt-Gen. Calthorpe, 2 Sep., 1900, Gore, 141, 144, 145, 147
65 Stirling, 448; Kipling, 109–10
66 *XIII H*, 30, 31, 41
67 Burnett, 96, 99, 102
68 Stirling: *C*, 271–6; *Who Was Who*, II, 992; Tylden: *AFSA*, 187
69 Cutlack, F. M. *Breaker Morant: A Horseman Who Made History*, 1962, 43–74; Renar, F. *Bushman and Buccaneer*, 1902, 3–47; Amery, V, 200; Pakenham, 538–9; Stirling: *C*, 280, 281; Tylden: *AFSA*, 41, 49, 137

CHAPTER XII (pp. 194–211)

(i)

1 Quoted in Pakenham, 435; *Black and White Budget*, 26 Sep., 1900; Farrar-Hockley, 59
2 Smith, 82, 83
3 *Haig*, 3 July, 1900, 215
4 *Despatches*, 52–3
5 Farwell, 307
6 Maurice, III, 237–8
7 Maurice, III, 238–40; Amery, IV, 350–2; Goldman, 301–5; McElligot, 7–9
8 Home and Overseas Corres. of Roberts, WO Lib., II, 34–5, 37; Pakenham, 448
9 *Haig*, 215
10 Maurice, III, 321
11 French's diary, 20, 25 July, 1900, Holmes, 107
12 Smith, 84, 97
13 Maurice, III, 322
14 Smith, 97
15 Maurice, III, 392, 540
16 Maurice, III, 393; Macready, I, 101
17 25 Sep., 1900, Rawlinson

(ii)

1 Kipling, R. 'Chant-Pagan-English Irregular: '99–'02', *The Five Nations*, 1904, 148; Gardner, 36; Roberts to Brodrick, 2 Sep., 1901, quoted in James, 380
2 13 Sep., 1900, Clowes; 17 Sep., 1900, *Haig*, 217
3 Goldman, 354–83; Smith, 102; Holmes, 109–10
4 Macready, I, 93
5 19 Sep., 1900, *Haig*, 218
6 26 Oct., 1900, Morton, 67

7 Goldman, 389, 394, 395–6, 398, 401; Maurice, III, 428–35; Amery, V, 47–9; Russell, 37
8 Smith, 90
9 De Wet, 162, 186; Kruger, 336; Gilbert, 171; Amery, IV, 418
10 16 Aug., 1900, Rawlinson
11 Amery, IV, 432; Smith, 91
12 *Haig*, 221
13 Smith-Dorrien, 255–60; Morrison, Lt E. W. B., R. Canadian Artillery, *With the Guns in South Africa*, 1901, quoted in Smith, 112; Maurice, III, 441–3; Amery, V, 51–2
14 Maurice, III, 448–54; Amery, V, 61–2; Wallace, 294–7

CHAPTER XIII (pp. 212–278)

(i)

1 Quoted in Pakenham, 535; 29 Oct., 1900, *Haig*, 219; Gardner, 41; (ed.) Miller, Mrs M. and Helen R. *A Captain in the Gordons*, n.d., 114; 8 Jul., 1901, *Haig*, 242; Howland, F. H. *The Chase of De Wet*, 1901, 110; 16 Apr., 1901, Gilmour, 156; De Wet, 243
2 Worsfold, W. Basil *Lord Milner's Work in South Africa*, 1906, 459
3 Kruger, 380
4 Younghusband, Sir George *A Soldier's Memories*, 1917, 184; Cooper, 86
5 Birdwood, 125; Kitchener to Brodrick, Feb., 1901, Kitchener to Milner, Mar., 1901, quoted in Pakenham, 490; 23 Mar., 21 Apr., 1901, Gilmour, 128, 165
6 Cmd 605, 1901, 17
7 Brereton, 291; 28 Jul., 1901, 242, 7 Sep., 1901, *Haig*, 248
8 *Haig*, 219
9 Amery, V, 5
10 Doyle, 652
11 Maurice, III, 498
12 *Haig*, 234
13 Farwell, 353, 383
14 Phillipps, 188
15 9 June, 6, 14 July, 1901, Marling, 277, 278; Brereton, 288; Oatts *14H/20H*, 308
16 Headlam, 481; Farwell, 351
17 Oatts *14H/20H*, 311–12; Morton, 119–20, 122, 123; 18 Feb., 1902, Duncalf; Cooke, 367
18 Headlam, 469, 491
19 Kipling, 178; *Haig*, 236; Allenby, 4 Oct., 1901, Gardner, 50
20 Hubert Gough's letters, Jul.–Sep., 1901, quoted in Pakenham, 530
21 Marling, 295

(ii)

1 Gardner, 45; Smuts to Stead, W. T., 4 Jan., 1902, Hancock, I, 467; H & S

Gough's letters, Jul.–Sep., 1901, quoted in Pakenham, 530; Kipling, 'M.I.', 1904, 152; Kitchener, MS Y/30, 33

2 *Haig*, 271; Stirling: *C*, 252–3; Tylden: *AFSA*, 208; Gilbert, 214

3 Stirling: *C*, 253–4; Tylden: *AFSA*, 118

4 Stirling: *C*, 238–9, 277, 279; Tylden: *AFSA*, 50–1, 92, 113, 115, 206

5 *R.C.*, II, 446–62; Tullibardine, 30–59: Stirling, 282–97; Tylden: *AFSA*, 156–7

6 Reitz, 196

7 Kruger, 478; Millin, I, 160, 161

8 Amery, V, 389

9 Hancock, I, 433

10 Maurice, IV, 274–7; *Haig*, 249–50; Reitz, 225–33; Micholls, 50–2

11 Willcox, 280

12 Pomeroy, 252; Oatts, *14H/20H*, 310; Smith, 112; Crum, 169

13 Morrison, Lt E. W. B., Royal Canadian Artillery *With the Guns in South Africa*, 1901, quoted in Smith, 111

14 Pakenham, 568. Amery (V, 408) says only 1,960

15 Brereton, 289; Doyle, 640, 701; Farwell, 364; Kruger, 420; Amery, V, 406–10

16 Oatts *14H/20H*, 307, 309; Yardley, 201; De Wet, 274; Farwell, 380; Millin, 145

17 Haig's evidence, *R.C.*, III, 411

18 Graham, 190

19 Micholls, 39; Colvin, 159; Brereton, 287; Oatts, *14H/20H*, 302; Thompson, 117; Harvey, 206, 208; Smith-Dorrien, 260, 263; Willcox, 275–6

20 Crum, 90; Wallace, 79

21 Haig's evidence, *R.C.*, III, 411

(iii)

1 Andrew, 90

2 *Haig*, 240; Brereton, 286

3 Yardley, 221; Marling, 274, 276

4 22 Mar., 1901, Davies-Cooke; Digby, 33

5 Russell, 96; 7 Jan., 1901, Clowes; Russell, 105

6 Fuller, 44; 17 Feb., 1901, Gilmour, 64

7 Burridge, Sgt-Maj. G. MS *'Autobiography'* (Property of Mrs Robins), 21; *R.C.*, I, 116

8 Marling, 292; Russell, 54

9 *Airlie*, 82

10 *Haig*, 254; 13 Mar., 1901, Clowes; Morton, 43; Stewart, 245; Colvin, 129

11 Bolitho, 195; Barrett, II, 3; Fuller, 23, 24

12 An anon. letter, 3 May, 1900, Clowes

13 Andrew, 90

(iv)

1 Kipling, 'M.I.', 'The Lesson (1899–1902)', 1904, 112, 152; Doyle, 651; Peel, 140; Farwell, 293

2 De Wet, 214–16

3 10 Nov., 1900, *Army and Navy Gazette*, 1089

4 De Wet, 214–16; Maurice, III, 486–8; Amery, V, 16; Headlam, 456; Jackson, 152–4

5 Marquis, T. G. *Canada's Sons on Kopje and Veldt*, 1900, 467

6 Maurice, III, 493

7 Graham, 191; Maurice, IV, 52; Amery, V, 41–2

8 Schikkerling, 207

9 Maurice, IV, 137; Smith, 162; Amery, V, 227–8

10 Smith, 151a; Maurice, IV, 31; Doyle, 562; Amery, V, 117

11 Brereton, 289; Thompson, 143–4; Maurice, IV, 247; Amery, V, 301; Doyle, 637; Kruger, 437; Pakenham, 513; Farwell, 384

12 Fraser, Harry to Mrs Steyn, 24 July., 1901 (coll. of Adv. G. E. Steyn), quoted in Farwell, 423

13 Tpr S. Edinborough, CMR, MS, 26 Jul., 1901, quoted in Pakenham, 527; Colvin, 238–43; Scobell-McCalmont, 9 Sep., 1901, Mortimer-McCalmont, 9 Sep., 1901, NAM 6807/492/4; Maurice, IV, 240–2; Amery, V, 319–20; Smith, 170a; Doyle, 649

14 Smith, 167a; Crum, 177, 203; Spurgin, 119

15 Gardner, 51

16 Rawlinson, 10 Dec., 1901; Oatts: *3DG/6DG*, 190

17 Maurice, IV, 407–9; *R.C.*, II, 451

18 Makins, 172–3; Atkinson, 376; Maurice, IV, 505

19 Commandant-General L. Botha to General C. Botha, 23 Oct., 1901, quoted in Maurice, IV, 305

20 Maurice, IV, 306–15; Smith, 177–3; Headlam, 462; Amery, V, 361–76; Farwell, 358–61; Kruger, 449–50; Doyle, 670–6; Pakenham, 536; Childers: *War*, 245

21 Smith, 164–5, 174–5; Maurice, IV, 352–4, 359–60; Stewart, 221; Reitz, 278; Brereton, 290; Atkinson, 375

22 Maurice, IV, 398–9; Smith, 209b

23 Gibson, 251–9; Doyle, 592; Maurice, IV, 129; Amery, V, 111

24 Gibson, 312–16, 320; Kruger, 468; Maurice, IV, 386; Amery, V, 427–31; Doyle, 689–90

25 Schikkerling, 283–5; Marling, 284–5; Burnett, 180–3; Maurice, IV, 214; Amery, V, 328; Smith, 184a

26 Yardley, 233–5

27 Yardley, 296–8; see also Maurice, IV, 336; Amery, V, 419–21

28 Thompson, 152, 153; Brereton, 290, 291; see also Amery, V, 422, 445

29 L. Botha to B. Viljoen, 12 Sep., 1901, Maurice, IV, 216

30 Farrar-Hockley, 56, 57

31 Smith, 171a

32 4 Oct., 1901, Gardner, 49

33 Farrar-Hockley, 65–6

34 Gough, 84

35 Maurice, IV, 217–18; Amery, V, 339–40; Doyle, 613; Kruger, 446; Farwell, 357–8; Childers: *War*, 244

36 Maurice, IV, 379–80; Amery, V, 456–8; Childers: *War*, 247

37 Maurice, IV, 185–9; Amery, V, 281–4; Kruger, 433; Pakenham, 513–14; Headlam, 464; Childers: *War*, 241
38 Maurice, IV, 299–301; Amery, V, 383–5; Doyle, 683; Headlam, 464–5; Childers: *War*, 248
39 Maurice, IV, 411–15; Kruger, 480–1; Doyle, 720–2; Amery, V, 498–9; Smith, 212b; Pakenham, 549; Childers: *War*, 248
40 Doyle, 724
41 Maurice, IV, 417–21; Amery, V, 502–8; Smith, 213a; *Standard*, 14 Apr., 1902; Kruger, 481–3; Doyle, 722–6; Farwell, 388–9
42 Maurice, IV, 494–7; Smith, 221; Kruger, 486–7; Amery, V, 520–4; Headlam, 479; Doyle, 730–33; Childers: *War*, 249
43 White and Atteridge, 178; Barrett, II, 188; Maurice, IV, 518–19; Smith, 219; Doyle, 706–8; Childers: *War*, 247
44 Kemp in conversation with Lt Fleming Gibson, Gibson, 345
45 Pakenham, 559
46 Account of Lt Carlos Hickie, Grenfell's signals officer, quoted in Pakenham, 559
47 Tullibardine, 59
48 Maurice, IV, 601
49 Pakenham, 559
50 Hamilton to Lord Roberts, 18 Apr., 1902, Sampson, 176
51 Hamilton to Lord Roberts, 18 May, 1902, enclosed in letter to Churchill, Hamilton Papers, King's College, London, quoted in Pakenham, 559
52 Hamilton to Roberts, 18 Apr., 1902, Sampson, 176
53 Gibson, 341. Maurice, IV, 499–504; Amery, V, 531–7; Smith, 221–2; Childers, 239; Pakenham, 558–60; Kruger, 489–90; Headlam, 479; Sampson, 169–80; Doyle, 733–5
54 Millin, I, 163
55 Atkinson, 377 *et al.*
56 Amery, VI, 440, 444
57 Head, 310
58 Goldman, viii; *R.C.*, II, 430; Childers: *War*, 112; 8 Jan., 1901, Gilmour, 4–5
59 8 Sep., 1902, *Haig*, 289
60 Marling, 309

CHAPTER XIV (pp. 279–354)

(i)

1 Maurice, I, 443; Stanley, vii, 20, 21; Biddulph, 33; Amery, VI, 421, *Hansard: (C)*, 1902, 140
2 Stanley, 1; *R.C.*, IV, 232
3 Biddulph, 2
4 Stanley, 5
5 Stanley, 3–4; Biddulph, 94
6 Stanley, 49

7   Biddulph, 5, 39–42; Stanley, 3
8   Biddulph, 2, 29, 30
9   Biddulph, 7
10 Stanley, 1, 3–4; Biddulph, 28, 75, 84, 86
11 Biddulph, 33, 80
12 Amery, VI, 420; Biddulph, 2, 32; Stanley, 59
13 Biddulph, 22
14 Stanley, xi, 4, 10, 27
15 Birkbeck, 39
16 Smith, V, 226; *R.C.*, I, 97, III, 44, IV, 258
17 *Hansard:* (*C*), 1902, 244; Biddulph, 34, 125; Smith, 139
18 Biddulph, 28, 31, 363, 364, 368; Smith, 132–3, 120, 175, 201–2, 205, 226;
    Lane; Amery, VI, 435, 437; Micholls, 47
19 French, Maj. Hon. Gerald (ed.) *Some War Diaries, Addresses and Cor-
    respondence of F-M The Earl of Ypres*, 1937, 21; *R.C.*, II, 44
20 *R.C.*, IV, 232
21 Welby, 65; Biddulph, 2
22 Smith, 121–2; Biddulph, 28; Lane
23 *R.D.A.*, 3
24 *R.C.*, IV, 231
25 Biddulph, 87, 88; Smith, 123, 132, 133
26 *R.C.*, IV, 231; Biddulph, 280
27 Biddulph, 250
28 *R.C.*, IV, 232; Sessions, 8; *R.D.A.*, 52
29 Biddulph, 54; Maurice, I, 109
30 Smith, 253; Biddulph, 90; Oatts, *14H/20H*, 266
31 Biddulph, 183
32 Biddulph, 76–9, 130, 142, 144, 210, 212, 329; Maurice, I, 107; *R.C.*, I, 97
33 Stanley, xii; Capt. Hon. R. H. Marsham, Biddulph, 44; G. Lambert, MP,
    27 Jun., 1901 *Hansard:* (*C*), 1901, 140
34 Sessions, 232
35 Biddulph, 80, 159, 160, 292, 293
36 Stanley, 65; *R.D.A.*, 11, 51
37 Sessions, 233; Biddulph, 83
38 Biddulph, 179, 141; Macready, I, 119; 21 Nov., 1899, *Mussenden*; Birkbeck
    24
39 *R.D.A.*, 5, 12, 14, 17, 18, 30
40 Sessions, 135, 145, 178
41 Sessions, 144; *R.D.A.*, 29, 31, 32
42 Sessions, 137, 171, 174–5; Biddulph, 43, 44
43 *R.D.A.*, 6; Sessions, 134, 162–4; Biddulph, 24, 43
44 Sessions, 221; Biddulph, 187
45 Welby, 60
46 Vet.-Col Queripel's and Lt-Gen. Gerard's Reports, Biddulph, 12–13, 186,
    187, 189, 214; *R.D.A.*, 49, 50, 51, 57
47 Welby, 28
48 Welby, 60
49 *R.D.A.*, 49

50 *R.D.A.*, 50
51 *R.D.A.*, 66
52 *R.D.A.*, 51
53 *R.D.A.*, 50
54 Welby, 53
55 Welby, 60
56 Welby, 34, 52
57 Biddulph, 10, 77, 195–7, 271; *R.D.A.*, 83; Sessions, 197, 200, 201, 202; Stanley, 69; *R.C.*, III, 43
58 Biddulph, 6; Sessions, 116
59 Maj.-Gen. Sir Edwin Collen's evidence, *R.C.*, III, 496

(ii)

1   Biddulph, 20, 233; Smith, vi, 240; Yardley, 218
2   Biddulph, 20, 44, 231, 255; Sessions, 222–3; Stanley, 29; Smith, 239
3   Biddulph, 17; Smith, 51
4   Sessions, 29; *R.C.*, II, 466; Biddulph, 97, 174; Stanley, 29; Smith, 239
5   *R.C.*, II, 404; Smith, 239
6   Col T. Deane's evidence, *R.C.*, II, 43
7   *R.D.A.*, 77–81; Birdwood, 119 (refers to footnote)
8   Birkbeck, 52, 53; Biddulph, 176; *R.D.A.*, 81; Head, 300–1, 310–11; Papers of a senior sergeant in the Royal Dragoons, NAM 7203-42; Smith, 227
9   Biddulph, 15, 36, 202
10 Smith, 267; Birkbeck, 11
11 Smith, 87, 267–8; Hobson, 211; *R.D.A.*, 81; Birkbeck, 25; *R.C.*, III, 43; Biddulph, 37, 95, 96, 164; Thompson, 77–8; Pearce, 112; Amery, VI, 430
12 Biddulph, 11, 12, 37, 88, 164; Birkbeck, 19; Smith, 126, 269; Stanley, 65
13 Biddulph, 64, 126
14 Biddulph, 95, 124, 176, 218; *R.D.A.*, 77, 80; *R.C.*, III, 43; Peel, 160; Roberts to Lansdowne, tel. 29 Mar., 1900, letter, 1 Apr., 1900, *Home and Overseas Correspondence by F-M Lord Roberts, 12 Dec., 1899 to 4 June, 1900*, 85, 87–8; Hamilton, 506–8
15 Birkbeck, 4, 21, 28
16 Biddulph, 36, 127, 218, 230, 232, 255; *R.C.*, II, 450
17 Biddulph, 88, 244; Smith, 240, 241, 242, 243; Amery, VI, 442–3; *R.C.*, I, 279
18 Smith, 244, 277; Schikkerling, 209; Fleming, G. to Wolseley *Reports on African Horse-Sickness*, 27 Oct., 1888, forwarding reports by Nunn, J. A., 14 Sep., 1887, 13 Jun, 16 Oct., 1888, WO 116/Cape/35; Brereton, 281
19 *HRAVC*, 202; Smith, 205
20 *HRAVC*, 203–4; paper by Francis Duck, *Veterinary Journal*, Vol. XXIV, 1887; Smith, vii; *R.C.*, IV, 100; Biddulph, 161–2
21 *HRAVC*, 204; Smith, 9, 19, 29, 120, 199, 223, 224
22 Smith, 49, 97, 137–9, 189, 202–6
23 Smith, 194
24 17 May, 1900, Clowes

(iii)

1   Sessions, 25; Birkbeck, 21; 'The London Bushorse', *This England,* winter, 1983; Gilbey, Sir W., Bt, *Small Horses in War,* 1900, 3; *R.C.,* III, 311; Peel, 31; Meintjes, 150
2   The chief references to horse types and qualities occur in: *R.C.,* II, 450, 466, III, 412, IV, 432–42; Biddulph, 196–7, 358–61; Smith, 8, 229–31; *R.D.A.,* 78; *Airlie,* 91; Oatts *14H/20H,* 301, 302; Oatts *3DG/6DG,* 188, 190, 191; Thompson, 128, 131, 132; Atkinson, 377; *Haig,* 5 Aug., 1902, 285; Phillipps, 174; Steele, 340, 352; Mills, Col G. A. *Report on the Causes which led to the ill-feeling between the Boers and the Zulus . . .,* 1902, quoted in Warwick, Peter *Black People and the South African War . . .,* 1983; Head, 302, 306; 13 Apr., 1900, *Mussenden;* Cooke, 162, 305; Maguire, 73–8; Tylden, 29
3   Wallace, 288; Brereton, 280
4   Head, 301

(iv)

1   S. S. M. Cobb, 7DG, to his wife, 25 Feb., 1901, Cobb Papers, NAM 7802-4; *R.C.,* I, 117; Thompson, 115; *R.C.,* I, 533; *R.C.,* II, 466
2   Smith, 230; Asst Inspector, Remounts, SA to IGR, WO, 27 Nov., 1901; Smith, 41–2; Goldman, 440; *R.C.,* II, 304–5; Marling, 276
3   Smith, VI, 14, 15, 16, 29–30, 187, 198, 236; Biddulph, 131, 218; *R.C.,* I, 29; II, 531, IV, 101; Cochrane, Maj. R. C. 'Veterinary Hospitals during the War', *United Service Mag.,* Nov., 1913, 164
4   Smith, 29
5   Gilbert, 264; Smith, 187–8, 195
6   Rankin, 47

CHAPTER XV (pp. 355–375)

1   Baden-Powell, R. S. S. 'What Lies Before Us', *Cavalry Journal,* I, 10, 1906; *R.C.,* IV, 170; Baden-Powell, 233; Smith, 35; *R.C.,* III, 305; Fuller, 267; Biddulph, 12
2   *R.C.,* III, 31
3   *R.C.,* II, 110; Stewart, 201; *R.C.,* I, 8; Smith, iv; Rose-Innes, 32
4   Smith, IV; Brereton, 280; Biddulph, 228; Spurgin, 211
5   Amery, VI, 445; Burgoyne, F-M Sir J. *Military Opinions,* 1895, 447; Mercer, Gen. C. *Journal of the Waterloo Campaign,* 1927 edn, 42
6   *R.C.,* III, 613, 27–8; *R.C.,* II, 28
7   *R.C.,* III, 404
8   *R.C.,* I, 45–6, II, 440
9   *R.C.,* II, 301
10 *R.C.,* III, 404

11   *R.C.*, I, 533, II, 331, III, 27, 28
12   *R.C.*, II, 585
13   Smith, 236; *R.C.*, II, 305
14   Amery, VI, 439; *R.C.*, I, 296
15   Maurice, II, 13; 'M.I.', *Rudyard Kipling's Verse*, 538; Smith, 35; *R.C.*, II, 451
16   Smith, 59, 245–51
17   Tylden, 149: *R.C.*, I, 180; Smith, 248; *R.C.*, II, 453; Stewart, 201
18   Forbes, II, 56; Amery, VI, 452; Smith, 247; Haig: diary, 3155(35)/74/84/ (36), NLS; Micholls, 36–7; Tylden, 153
19   Tylden, 153; *R.C.*, III, 425, IV, 354; Biddulph, 12, 126; Smith, 248, 84
20   Shepphard, 190–1; Smith, 18; *R.C.*, II, 463
21   Tylden, 151–3; Head, 302; Biddulph, 228
22   Smith, vi; Biddulph, 12; Head, 300
23   *R.C.*, III, 402, 405, 410; Andrew, 114
24   *R.C.*, III, 403, 405
25   *R.C.*, II, 531; Smith, 250; *Haig*, 205
26   Fitzgibbon, 87–8; 10 July, 1901, Duncalf
27   Yardley, 138
28   21 July, 1900, Yardley, 133
29   Crum, 214

CHAPTER XVI (pp. 376–423)

(i)

1   Quoted in Dilks, I, 121; *The Chester Chronicle*, 2 Dec., 1905, 7, quoted in Spiers: *A & S*, 264; Haldane, *Hansard: (C)*, 8 Mar., 1906; *Esher*, II, 186; Haig to Esher, Esher MSS, 5/32; Barnett, C. *Britain and Her Army, 1509–1970*, 1970, 367
2   Cooper, I, 104–5
3   *Haig*: diary, 9 and 10 June, 1906, 347
4   *Haig*: diary, 18 Feb., 1909, 395
5   Spiers: *Haldane*, 71, 80
6   Spiers: *Haldane*, 73
7   Haldane to Esher, 8 Sep., 1906, Esher MS, 10/27
8   Haig's diary, 8 Nov., 1907, Haig MSS, Vol. 2g, NLS
9   Haig to Esher, 9 Sep., 1906, Esher MS, 10/27
10   Spiers: *Haldane*, 88
11   'A Preliminary Memorandum on the present situation. Being a rough note for consideration by the Members of the Army Council', 1 Jan., 1906, Haldane MSS, 5918, f. 44, NLS
12   Esher to Sir A. Bigge (Private Sec. to the Prince of Wales), 27 Mar., 1908, Esher MSS, 16/12
13   Spiers: *Haldane*, 172, 181, 182, 184, 186
14   Spiers: *Haldane*, 152
15   Haig: diary, 23 Dec., 1908, 391

1   Quoting Hamilton's official report, Hamilton, I. B. M. *The Happy Warrior*, 1966; Broadwood, 92; French's Preface to 'P.S.' *Cavalry in Action in the Wars of the Future* (trans. from the French by Formby, J.), 1905, v; Roberts's Introduction to Childers: *War*, xii; Bernhardi: *W & P*, 19; Rimington, 17

2   25 Sep., 1903, Haig: diary; Roberts to Kitchener, 28 Jan., 1904, NAM R/122/7/608

3   Haig: *Cav.*, 8–9

4   Haig: *Cav.*, 15

5   Haig: *Cav.*, 17–18

6   Cooper, I, 378, 379

7   Haig MSS, Vol. 61, Box 4, NLS

8   Kitchener to Roberts, 12 May, 1904, NAM R/33/131

9   Churchill, Army Estimates debate, 14 Apr., 1904, *Hansard:* (*C*), CXXXIII, 230

10 Memo. 'The Future Role of Cavalry', Dundonald, 181

11 Roberts, 6; see also Roberts, FM Earl 'Cavalry Armament', 1 Mar., 1903, *JRUSI*, XLVII, 1903, 580, 581; Ward, 2

12 Maude, vii–viii

13 Rimington, 29, 51

14 Childers: *War*, XII

15 Cooper, I, 379

16 Haig to Herbert Jessel, MP, late of 17th Lancers and later 1st Baron Jessel, 7 Apr., 1903, *Haig*, 298–9

17 Bond, 112; Spiers: *Cav.*, 77; Roberts to Hamilton, 28 Feb., 1904, Roberts to Arnold-Forster, 5 Jan., 1905, Arnold-Forster to Roberts, 30 Jan., 1905 in James, 440, 441; Ward, 2

18 Preface, 1 Feb., 1904, to [Official] *Cavalry Training (Provisional)*, 1904, iii–viii; Spiers: *Cav.*, 74

19 Childers: *War*, vi, xi–xii; *Cav. Trng*, 1907, Sec. 142

20 Ffrench-Blake, R. L. V. *The 17th/21st Lancers*, 1968, 102; French: *Role*, 2–3

21 Roberts to Wood, 29 Sep., 1901, NAM R/122/2/140

22 Hamilton's evidence, *R.C.*, II, 110, 111

23 Arnold-Forster's diary, 29 Feb., 1904, Arnold-Forster MSS, BM, Add. MSS, 50, 336, f. 189

24 French's evidence, *R.C.*, II, 306

25 Henderson, Lt-Col C. F. R., 'Introduction', Sternberg, Count *My Experiences of the Boer War*, 1901, xxxii

26 *Cav. Trng*, 1907, 187; *Cav. Trng*, 1912, 268; Dasent, A. I. *Piccadilly in Three Centuries*, 1920, 146–7

27 French to Roberts, 10 Nov., 1901, NAM 7101/23/30

28 Andrew, 69

29 Goldman, C. S., Preface to Bernhardi, x

30 Maude, 273

31 Maude, viii

32 Childers: *German*, 9, 23; French: *Role*, 2
33 Barnett, Correlli *Britain and Her Army, 1509–1970*, 1970, 368
34 See Bond, 114
35 Hamilton, Sir I. *A Staff Officer's Scrap Book*, I, 1905, 131–2; see also one vol. ed., 1912, 340, 356, 426; Bond, 112–14; Taylor, 174–5
36 Lt-Gen. J. Keith Fraser in discussion after lecture by Benson, Capt. G. E. 'Smokeless Powder and its Probable Effect upon the Tactics of the Future', *Aldershot Military Society*, 23 Mar., 1893, 16; Bond, 107
37 Broadwood, 92; Roberts, 6
38 May, Lt-Col E. S. *A Retrospect on the South African War*, 1901, 206, 207
39 Baden-Powell, Lt-Gen. Sir R. *Memories of India*, [1915], 82; Henderson, 61; French: *Role*, 1, 2
40 Haig to Hutton, 29 Dec., 1903, Hutton MSS, BM Add. MSS, 50, 086
41 Roberts's Introduction to Childers: *War*, xv
42 French's Preface to Bernhardi: *W & P*, vii
43 Wood to Lyttelton, 29 Mar., 1904, WO 32/6782; Baden-Powell Memorandum, 10 Mar., 1904, WO 32/6782
44 See Bond, 114 and Holmes, 160
45 Roberts to Kitchener, 28 Apr., 1904, Kitchener to Roberts, 5 May, 1904, James, 440
46 Army Order 158, June, 1909
47 Nicholson to Roberts, 14 June, 1909 NAM R/52/134
48 Gough, 94
49 Hutton, Lt-Col E. T. H. *Five Lectures on Mounted Infantry*, 1891, V, 2
50 French to Seely, 20 Sep., 1913, Mottistone Papers, quoted in Holmes, 162
51 Spiers: *Cav.*, 78
52 Godley: M.I., 54
53 Taylor, 176
54 See Spiers: *Cav.*, 78
55 Godley: M.I., 143–4; *Annual Reports, Inspector of Cavalry*, 1905, quoted in Bond, 110
56 Henderson, 59; 2 Apr., 1903, *Haig*
57 Godley: M.I., 143–4
58 Spiers: *Cav.*, 78–9; de Lisle to Roberts, 7 June, 1910, NAM R/223; Childers to Roberts, 8 Mar., 1910, NAM R/222
59 Repington, C. a C. *Essays & Criticism*, 1911, 81–8; 'Parliament and the Army', *Times*, 24 Mar., 1911; 'The Mounted Troops of the Expeditionary Force', *Times*, 15 Feb., 1912; 'The Army Exercises', *Times*, 30 Sep., 1912; see also Luvaas, 316–17
60 'P.S.', *Cavalry in Action in the Wars of the Future: Studies in Applied Tactics*, trans. Formby, J., 1905, v, vi
61 Bernhardi, xxiv; Bernhardi: *W & P*, xi
62 Childers: *War*, ix, xii, xiii
63 Childers: *German*, iv, 66; Bernhardi: *W & P*, 111, 325
64 Childers: *German*, 159, 214–15
65 Roberts to Brodrick, 16 Sep., 1902, quoted in James, 387
66 Koch, Col Ludwich 'Cavalry Training in Summer', trans. Bell, H. *Journal of the United States Cavalry Association*, XX, 1909, 147

67 de Négrier, Gen. F. *Lessons of the Russo-Japanese War*, trans. Spiers, E. Louis, 1906, 73–4, 77

68 Taylor, 176

69 de Pardieu, Maj. M. F. *A Critical Study of German Tactics and of the New German Regulations*, trans. Martin, C. F., 1912; Loir, Capt. M. *Cavalry*, trans. British General Staff, 1916, 89

70 'Cavalry Instruction', *Journal of the United States Cavalry Association*, XXIV, 1914, 877

71 Wrangel, Count G. *The Cavalry in the Russo-Japanese War*, trans. Montgomery, J., 1907, 56

72 Rolleston, Lt-Col Lancelot, *Yeomanry Cavalry: or Mounted Infantry*, 1901, 26

73 Rimington, 56; see Balck, Col Wm *Tactics*, trans. Krueger, Walter (2 vols), 1914, II, 108–10

74 Smith-Dorrien, 359

75 Robertson, 165

76 French to Roberts, 6 Mar., 1904, James, 440

77 11 Sep., 1908 Haig: diary; Holmes, 162

78 *Annual Report of the Inspector General of the Forces*, 1909; 'Report on a Cavalry Staff Ride held by the Director of Staff Duties, 1–6 Mar., 1909', Haig MSS, vol. 82, p. 30, NLS; Haig: 'Notrefe' 62

79 *Annual Reports of the Inspector General of Forces*, 1912, 4–21, 1913, 4–20, quoted in Bond, 117

80 Edmonds, Brig.-Gen. Sir James E., Unpublished Autobiography, XXII, 12, Edmonds papers, Liddell Hart Centre for Military Archives, King's College, London, quoted in Holmes, 149

81 Wilson diary, 25 Sep., 1913, Wilson Papers, Imperial War Museum, quoted in Holmes, 149

82 Holmes, 149

83 Bond, 119

84 Childers: *German*, 209

85 Terraine, 34

CHAPTER XVII (pp. 424–449)

(i)

1 Saadi (Muslih-ud-Din), (1184–1291), in *Gulistan (Rose Garden)*, 273; WO32/6781 5220/3; *R.C.*, II, 404; Browne, 253

2 Bolitho, 192

3 Goodenough, Lt-Gen. W. H. and Dalton, Lt-Col J. C. *The Army Book for the British Empire*, 1893, 202; Army Order 237, 1902

4 Wylly, 336, 339

5 Barrett: *XIII H*, 231–2, 235, 247; Browne, 244, 246, 252; see also Lumley, 10, for improvements in 11th Hussars' musketry between 1910 and 1913

6 Browne, 241, 247

7 Williams, 293, 295

8 Micholls, 68

9   Evans, 9; Spiers: *A & S*, 55
10 *Annual Report of the Inspector-General of the Forces*, 1904
11 See Barratt: *XIII H*, 221
12 Pomeroy, 262
13 Williams, 294
14 Barry, Maj. S. L., 10th Hussars, 'Signalling in the Cavalry during the late South African War', *Cav. Jnl*, I, 168–9
15 *R.C.*, III, 402
16 Nalder, Maj.-Gen. R. F. H. *The Royal Corps of Signals: A History of its Antecedents and Development (circa 1800–1955)*, 1958, 51, 52
17 Pomeroy, 268
18 Lindley, Col the Hon. J. E. 'The Cavalry School at Netheravon', *Cav. Jnl*, I, 1906, 49–51; see also Army Order 288, 1907; *King's Regulations*, 1912, 172–4
19 Brereton, 303
20 Harris, R. G. 'Personalities . . . at the Saugor Cavalry School, India, 1910', *JAHR*, LVIII, No. 235, Autumn, 1980

(ii)

1   Lumley, 6; *R.C.*, II, 404; *R.C.*, I, 46; Churchill, 78; Roberts, 6
2   Baden-Powell, Maj.-Gen. R. S. S. 'What Lies Before Us', *Cav. Jnl*, I, 4, 8–9
3   Henderson, 77
4   Haig: *Cav.*, 3
5   Haig: 'Notrefe', 40, 41, 42
6   Sheppard, 186–7
7   Lumley, 11
8   Bond, 117
9   Micholls, 57
10 Baden-Powell: *Training*, 129, 130, 131; Amery: *Army*, 208; Rimington, 18
11 Barnett, Correlli *Britain & Her Army*, 1970, 328
12 *R.C.*, I, 45
13 *R.C.*, IV, 170–1
14 8 Nov., 1900, 'Report on the Organization and Equipment of Cavalry by Gen. Officer commanding Cavalry Division . . .' (Maj.-Gen. J. B. B. Dickson's Committee), 4
15 *R.C.*, III, 404
16 Baden-Powell, 28
17 Baden-Powell: *Training*, 133
18 *R.C.*, II, 404
19 Spurgin, 158–9
20 Baden-Powell: *Training*, 134
21 *Manoeuvres, 1903*, 4
22 *Manoeuvres, 1903*, 52
23 *Manoeuvres, 1903*, 55
24 *Manoeuvres, 1903*, 80

25 Micholls, 72
26 Evans, 109–10
27 Burnett: *18H*, 7
28 *Manoeuvres, 1903,* 53, 55
29 Bond, 110, 117
30 Pomeroy, 118
31 Williams, J. E., Staff-Sgt-Maj., Instructor of Fencing, 6D, 'Cavalry Swordsmanship', *Cav. Jnl,* I, 472
32 Churchill, 78
33 Rolleston, Lt-Col L. *Yeomanry Cavalry: or Mounted Infantry,* 1901, 18–19
34 *R.C.,* II, 425
35 Andrew, 10
36 Amery: *Army,* 196, 197
37 Gardner, 62

(iii)

1 Esher to M. V. Brett, 1 Jan., 1910, Esher, II, 432
2 *R.C.,* I, 12
3 Evidence of Maj.-Gen. Sir Elliott Wood, *R.C.,* I, 101
4 *London Gazette,* 3 Mar., 1903; Army Order 185, 1906; Guthkelch, Capt. C. N. 'The Motor Volunteers Corps', *The Waggoner,* Mar., 1981, 23–4
5 Mayhew, Lt-Col M. J. (administering Army Motor Reserve) & Skeffington Smyth, Maj. G. (late 9L, Permanent Staff Officer, Army Motor Reserve), 'Motor Cars with the Cavalry Division', *Cav. Jnl,* IV (1909), 438–42; Army Order 368, 1913
6 Brereton, 303

(iv)

1 *R.C.,* II, 114
2 Pomeroy, 231; Williams, 290; Oatts: *3DG/6DG,* 194; Barrett: *XIII H,* 217; Brereton, 304–5; Harvey, 210
3 *Airlie,* 82; Gordon Committee, 1900, WO32/6781 5220/12
4 Brereton, 304
5 Robson (see note 7), 47
6 Robson (see note 7), 56
7 Robson, 81. Brian Robson's *Swords of the British Army,* 1975, is the only totally reliable work on the subject. Norman J. Crook's 'The British Pattern 1908 Cavalry Sword', *Canadian Journal of Arms Collecting,* May, 1973, gives the fullest technical description of that weapon.
8 Quoted in Tylden, 156. See also Horton, Maj. J. 'The Evolution of the Cavalry Saddle', *Cav. Jnl,* IV, 1909

CHAPTER XVIII (pp. 450–452)

1 Taillefer, Nugent *The British Cavalry Songs,* 1866, 129

2 'Memo. upon the Military Forces in the United Kingdom', *Parl. Papers*, Cd 3297, Feb., 1907
3 *R.C.*, II, 290, 291
4 *Parl. Papers*, Cd 2993, July, 1906, Appx
5 Arnold-Forster, H. O. *The Army in 1906*, 1906, 126
6 *Imperial Yeomanry Training Return*, 1905; Ward: *Officers*, 5
7 *R.C.*, II, 477
8 *R.C.*, II, 310
9 Teagarden, E. M. 'The Last Days of the British Cavalry', *Army Journal* (USA), 3/20

CHAPTER XIX (pp. 453–473)

(i)

1 *R.C.*, II, 308–9; Akers-Douglas, 32; Curzon to Brodrick, 8 Jan., 1900, quoted in Dilks, I, 197; Esher to Duchess of Sutherland, 7 Sep., 1906, Esher, II, 184; Rimington, 156
2 Maguire, T. Miller 'The Military Education of Officers', *National Review*, XXXVI, Dec., 1900, 508, 514
3 Pollock, Lt-Col A. W. A. 'Military Education', *Fortnightly Review*, LXXXI, 1907, 344; 19 Nov., 1907, Journal, *Esher*, 261; 8 Mar., 1906, *Hansard: (C)*
4 Rankin, 57
5 *The Times*
6 Ismay, Lord *The Memoirs of General the Lord Ismay*, 1960, 4
7 Mosley, 190; Barrow, 16; [Cairnes (Capt. W. E.)] *Social Life in the British Army by a British Officer*, 1900, 38
8 Otley, 224, 225
9 Roberts to Adjt-Gen., 2 Aug., 1902, Roberts to Brodrick, 3, 10, 13 Aug., 1902, NAM 7101-23-122-4 (70–3, 76–7, 82–4, 89–90); information kindly provided by the Household Cavalry Museum (Lt-Col A. D. Meakin)
10 Sitwell, Osbert *Pound Wise*, 1963, 72; Hackett, Gen. Sir John *The Profession of Arms*, 1983, 133
11 *Airlie*, 65; Corbett, A. F. *Service through Six Reigns*, 1953, 47; Bolitho, 190; Amery: *Army*, 197
12 MacLean A. H. H. *Public Schools and the War in South Africa*, 1902, 12; Otley, C. B. 'Public School and Army', *New Society*, VIII, No. 216, 756
13 Akers-Douglas, 2, 20, 29, 32
14 Thomas, 163
15 Akers-Douglas, 11, 19, 21, 22, 23, 24, 27; Amery: *Army*, 197
16 An anonymous officer's account, Thomas, 170
17 Smyth, Sir J. *Sandhurst*, 1961, 142, 143
18 Thomas, 167
19 Akers-Douglas, 2
20 Army Orders 133 and 220, 1904
21 Staff Coll. Regs issued with Army Order 38, 1904
22 Special Army Order, 9 Apr., 1903

23 Akers-Douglas, 32
24 Army Order 812, 1904; Roberts, 7
25 WO/A.816, 1903; Thomas, 166
26 Maude, Col F. N. *War and the World's Life*, 1907, 171
27 Young, 20
28 Young, 3
29 Young, 22
30 Godwin-Austen, 248–54
31 Yardley, 250–1
32 *Cav. Jnl*, VIII, 241
33 Gregory, Maj. S. in Stewart, 233
34 Evans, 12–13
35 Mosley, 189, 191, 195

(ii)

1 Barnett, C. *Britain and Her Army*, 1970, 314; *R.C.*, IV, 170; Appx, Hutchinson: *Deficiency*, 3, 7
2 *R.C.*, I, 388; Rimington, 155
3 Ward: *Officers*, 3–4
4 Stanley: *Expenses*, 7, 8, 9
5 Army Orders 1, 3, 63, 170, 1903, and 4, 46, 1904
6 Hayter, Sir A., *Hansard:* (C), 23 Feb., 1905, 1116
7 Hutchinson: *Deficiency*, 3, 7
8 Spiers: *Haldane*, 135
9 Appx, Hutchinson: *Deficiency*, 8
10 Akers-Douglas, 35–6
11 Akers-Douglas, 10
12 Evidence of Grove, Maj.-Gen. Sir Coleridge, *R.C.*, I, 61, 63–4
13 Spiers: *Haldane*, 142
14 *R.C.*, II, 450

CHAPTER XX (pp. 474–493)

1 *Report on the Organization and Equipment of Cavalry* (Maj.-Gen. J. B. B. Dickson), WO32/678 5220, 1900; Arthur, G. 'The Soldier as Student', *Fornightly Review*, LXXXII (New Series), 1907, 622; *R.C.*, II, 410
2 Amery, II, 18; 21 Oct., 1908, Haldane MSS, NLS MS 5,980, ff. 138
3 *Report of the Health of the Army, 1909*, Cd. 5,477, XLVII, 2, 1911, quoted in Spiers: *Haldane*, 149
4 Spiers: *A & S*, 44
5 Spiers: *Haldane*, 149, 182
6 Spiers: *A & S*, 48; Dunlop, Col J. K. *The Development of the British Army, 1899–1914 . . .*, 1938, 31; Amery: *Army*, 208
7 Anon. 'A South African Trip', *Club Life*, 4 May, 1901, quoted in Price, R. *An Imperial War and the British Working Class*, 1972, quoted in Farwell, 377
8 Spiers: *A & S*, 37, 38; Spiers: *Haldane*, 149
9 Spiers, *Haldane*, 143

10   Amery, II, 19, 20
11   General Order 80, 1881; Army Order 73, 1902; *Recruiting Regulations*, 1903
12   Brodrick to J. Chamberlain, 10 Sep., 1901, quoted in Dilks, I, 210
13   Dilks, I, 210
14   Special Army Order, 27 Dec., 1904; Army Orders 7 and 168, 1905
15   Spiers: *Haldane*, 143
16   *R.C.*, II, 411
17   Wavell, F-M Earl *Soldiers and Soldiering*, 1953, 125
18   Barrett: *XIII H*, 215
19   Spiers: *Haldane*, 145, 216, 217
20   Spiers: *Haldane*, 146
21   *R.C.*, II, 402, 410
22   Spiers: *A & S*, 43
23   *R.C.*, I, 254; *Pay*
24   *Hansard:* (*C*), 8 Mar., 1901
25   Clapham, J. H. *An Economic History of Modern Britain*, 1926, III, 98–9
26   Grenfell, Capt. R. *Service Pay*, 1944, 16; Bolitho, 191; *Pay*
27   *R.C.*, I, 122, 123; Carver, F-M Lord *The Seven Ages of the British Army*, 1984, 157
28   Spiers: *A & S*, 47
29   Wyndham: *Drum*, 33; 'S.C.W.', 'Temperance and its Rewards in the British Army', *Annual Report*, NAM, 1976–7, 15, 16
30   Spiers: *A & S*, 64–6
31   *W.O. Committee on Service Pay* (the Franklyn Committee), A.1077, 1906
32   Spiers: *Haldane*, 148
33   Spiers: *A & S*, 43
34   Wyndham: *Drum*, 127
35   *R.C.*, I, 254
36   Wyndham: *Drum*, 42
37   Dasant Committee (50/Gen.No./4218), 1901; Bowles Committee (W.O. A.927), 1904; Portsmouth Committee (50/Gen.No./4687), 1906; Hawkins, Maj. T. H. & Brimble, L. J. F. *Adult Education: The Record of the British Army*, 1947, 38, 39
38   WO32/6781 5220, 4
39   Wyndham: *Drum*, 10; Stewart, 227–30; Evans, 5
40   Bolitho, 190
41   Stewart, 238–9
42   Fortescue, John *A Short Account of Canteens in the British Army*, 1928, 33–45; *Report of the Canteen and Regimental Institutes Committee* (Earl Grey Report), 1902 (Cd 1424)
43   Stewart, 229
44   Bolitho, 190
45   Lumley, 16; Stewart, 235–6
46   21 Lancers' *Standing Orders*, 1902, No. 14; Sheppard, 183; Oatts: *3DG/6DG*, 196
47   Wyndham: *Drum*, 50–1
48   Bolitho, 191
49   Stewart, 233

50   Evans, 5
51   Stewart, 233; Micholls, 80, 81
52   Stewart, 230
53   Creagh, Gen. Sir O'Moore *The Autobiography of* [n.d., 1925?], 284
54   Bolitho, 191
55   *W.O. Selected Papers: Cavalry Organization*, 1907, WO20/Cav./72, WO120/Gen.No./6302, etc.
56   Army Order 160, 1909

CHAPTER XXI (pp. 494–502)

(i)

1   Hamilton Papers, India Office Library; quoted in James, 420
2   Speech by Curzon at Byculla Club, Bombay, 16 Nov., 1905, Raleigh, Sir T. (ed.) *Lord Curzon in India*, II, 312–32
3   Kitchener to Birdwood, 24 Jan., 1912, Birdwood Papers, India Office Library
4   See Dilks, II, 253–4; for a defence of Kitchener, see Terraine, 32–3
5   By far the fullest account is to be found in Dilks, I and II, on which most of the present narrative is based. If it is inevitably biased in Curzon's favour, the present author, after extensive research, believes that the evidence supports such a bias
6   Curzon to Kitchener, 21 Aug., 1900

(ii)

1   Younghusband, Maj.-Gen. Sir George, *Forty Years a Soldier*, 1923, 233; Blood, 346; Curzon, 12
2   Curzon to Kitchener, 14 Dec., 1902, quoted in Dilks, I, 213
3   Curzon to Brodrick, 2 July, 1903, quoted in Dilks, II, 31
4   Minute by Curzon, 8 Jan., 1900, quoted in Dilks, I, 199
5   Quoted in Dilks, I, 200
6   Curzon, 1, 2, 4, 6
7   Curzon, 4–7
8   Smith-Dorrien, 317
9   Curzon, 6, 7, 8
10   Knollys to Curzon, 8 Jan., 1903, quoted in Dilks, I, 213
11   Curzon to Hamilton, 27 Nov., 1902; Curzon to Roberts, 28 Dec., 1902; Roberts to Curzon, 23 Jan., 1903
12   Barrow, 88
13   Sheppard, 227

INDEX

Index

Index

Index

Index

cavalry, 214; his guerrilla war policy, 217; institutes 'drives', 219; pourparlers with De la Rey, 272; his indifference to and ignorance of remount question, 321, 327, 337; issues orders re shoeing, 322; his views on Australian horses, 347; his policy of centralization, 364; becomes national hero, 377; proposes Indian Staff College, 464; C-i-C, India, 495–7, 501; conflict with Curzon, 495–6

Knight, Maj.-Gen. Sir Wyndham Charles (1863–1942), 91, 92, 97, 100

Knox, Maj. Eustace Chaloner, at Talana Hill, 41–5

Knox, Maj.-Gen. Sir William George (1847–1916), 345, 346

Koch, Col Ludwich, 418

Kock, Gen. J. H. M., 50

Kritzinger, Commandant Pieter Henrick, 230, 248

Kroonstad *Krijgsraad*, 17 Mar., 1900, 154

Kruger, Stephanus Johannes Paulus (Oom Paul) (1825–1904), 32, 195, 206; re-equips Transvaal forces, 34; leaves for Europe, 210

Labell and Weissman of Koslow (horse dealers), 314

Ladysmith Relief Force, 70, 76

Lamlng, Maj. Henry Thornton (1863–1934), at Talana Hill, 41–2

laminitis, 347, 358, 362

lance, 392, 393, 448; abolished, 1903, 391; reinstated, 1909, 410

Lane, Acting-Vet.-Maj. Arthur Henry, 195, 290

Lansdowne, Henry Charles Keith Petty-Fitzmaurice, 5th Marquess of (1845–1927), 89, 112, 127, 329, 480, 505

Lathom, Edward George Bootle-Wilbraham, 2nd Earl of (1864–1910), 93

Lawrence, Gen. Hon. Sir Herbert Alexander (1861–1943), 105

Lawrence, Sir John Laird Mair, 1st Baron (1811–1879), 105

Lawrence, Brig.-Gen. Richard Charles Bernard (1857–   ), 284–5, 304

Leader, Maj.-Gen. Henry Peregrine (1865–1934), 253

Leary, Pte J., 6D, 261

Le Gallais, Lt-Col P. W. J., killed at Bothaville, 244–5

Leitrim, Maj. Charles Clements, 5th Earl of (1879–1952), 177

Lemmer, Gen. (–1902), 268

Lewison (horse contractor), 314

Leigh, L/Cpl Trumpeter, 14H, 205

Liebenberg, Gen. P. J., 267

Lindley, Maj.-Gen. Hon. John Edward (1860–1925), 428

Listowel, Lt Richard Granville Hare, 4th Earl of (1866–1931), 177; at Lindley, 180

Little, Brig.-Gen. Malcolm Orme (1857–1931), 208

Live Stock Recovery Department, 292

Loch, Henry Brougham, 1st Baron (1827–1900), 94

Long, Brig.-Gen. Sir Arthur (1866–1941), 337–8

Long, Col Charles James, 76

Longford, Temp. Brig.-Gen. Thomas Pakenham, 5th Earl of (1864–1915), at Lindley, 177, 180

Lonsdale, Col Hugh Cecil Lowther, 5th Earl of (1857–1944), 89

Lötter, Commandant Johannes, 248–50

Loubet, Emile, President of France (1838–1929), 510

Lovat, Maj.-Gen. Simon Joseph Fraser, 14th Baron (1871–1933), 94, 451

Love, Pte H., 6D, 261

Lowe, Maj.-Gen. William Henry Muir (1861–1944), 169, 438

Lucas, Col Alfred George (1854–1941), 88, 90, 94, 96, 97

Luck, Gen. Sir George (1840–1916), 492

Lumley, Col Hon. Osbert Victor George Atheling (1862–1923), 402

Lumsden, Col Dugald M'Tavish (1851–1915), 202–3

Luxmore, Capt. E. J., 490

Lyttelton, Gen. Sir Neville Gerald (1845–1931), 122, 327, 396, 409, 410

McCrea, Tpr Thomas, 13th Bn, I.Y., at Lindley, 180

Macdowell, J. B., film producer, 486

Mackenzie, Maj. Donald, 74

Mackenzie, Brig.-Gen. Sir Duncan (1859–1932), 259

MacKinnon, Gen. Sir William Henry (1852–1929), 450

M'Kormick, Sgt, 5DG, 59

Maguire, Dr Thomas Miller, 454

Mahon, Gen. Sir Bryan Thomas (1862–1930), in relief of Kimberley, 173–4; in march to Barberton, 203; at Van Wyksvlei, 205

Malan, Commandant W., 231

Maple, Sir John Blundell, 1st bt (1845–1903), 504

Maritz, Commandant Salomon Gerhardus ('Mannie'), 257

Index

Index

Index

Index

RAILWAY DISTANCES	miles
Cape Town to:	
De Aar	501
Kimberley	647
Mafeking	870
Naauwpoort	570
Norval's Pont	628
Bloemfontein	750
Johannesburg	1014
Pretoria	1040
Durban to:	
Pietermaritzburg	70
Ladysmith	189
Glencoe	231
Johannesburg	483
Pretoria	511
Port Elizabeth to:	
Naauwpoort	270
Bloemfontein	450
Johannesburg	714
Pretoria	740